FUNDAMENTALS OF PATTERN RECOGNITION

PRENTICE-HALL INFORMATION AND SYSTEM SCIENCE SERIES
Thomas Kailath, editor

BERGER
Rate Distortion Theory: A Mathematical Basis for Data Compression

DI FRANCO AND RUBIN
Radar Detection

DOWNING
Modulation Systems and Noise

DUBES
The Theory of Applied Probability

FRANKS
Signal Theory

GOLOMB, BAUMERT, EASTERLING, STIFFLER, AND VITERBI
Digital Communications with Space Applications

LINDSEY
Synchronous Phase Control Systems

LINDSEY AND SIMON
Telecommunication Theory

PATRICK
Fundamentals of Pattern Recognition

RAEMER
Statistical Communication Theory and Applications

VAN DER ZIEL
Noise: Sources, Characterization, Measurement

FUNDAMENTALS OF PATTERN RECOGNITION

EDWARD A. PATRICK

Department of Electrical Engineering
Purdue University

PRENTICE-HALL, INC., Englewood Cliffs, N.J.

ISBN: 0-13-342014-0

Library of Congress Catalog Card Number: 76-172281

Printed in the United States of America

10 9 8 7 6 5 4 3 2 1

PRENTICE-HALL INTERNATIONAL, INC., *London*
PRENTICE-HALL OF AUSTRALIA, PTY. LTD., *Sydney*
PRENTICE-HALL OF CANADA, LTD., *Toronto*
PRENTICE-HALL OF INDIA PRIVATE LIMITED, *New Delhi*
PRENTICE-HALL OF JAPAN, INC., *Tokyo*

Acknowledgments

Many individuals have influenced the author during the six years that this book was in preparation. It is impossible to express gratitude to all of them. A few of these people are: Dr. Lou Liporace, Dr. F. P. Fischer, Dr. Friend Bechtel, Dr. Pete Costello, Leon Shen, George Carayannopoulos, Bob Agnew, and Frank Stelmack. Others whose friendship and discussion have been appreciated include Dr. Tom Kailath, Dr. J. C. Hancock, Dr. Laveen Kanal, Dr. John Sammon, Dr. Sidney Yakowitz, Dr. Norm Abramanson, Dr. Michael Watanabe, Dr. Tom Cover, Mr. George Miller, Dr. William Gregg, Dr. D. Lainiotis, Dr. Henry Teicher, Dr. William Studden, Larry Hostetler, George Molnar, Dr. Ken Fukunaga, Dr. Ray Jarvis, Dr. John Spragins, Dr. Paul Cooper, Dr. Dave Cooper, Dr. K. S. Fu, Dr. G. Ball, Dr. Nils Nilsson, Dr. Fabian Monds, Dr. Paul Wintz, and Dr. John Luh. Special thanks are due Leon Shen for proofreading the manuscript.

Table of Contents

1-8.1 Definition for Finite Mixtures · 1-8.2 Conditions for Identifiability · 1-8.3 Identifiable Families

2-11.1 Binomial · 2-11.2 Multinomial · 2-11.3 Gaussian–Unknown $\mathbf{m}$ · 2-11.4 Gaussian–Unknown Σ^{-1} · 2-11.5 Gaussian–Unknown $\mathbf{m}$ and Σ^{-1} · 2-11.6 Poisson–Unknown α · 2-11.7 Rayleigh–$\rho = 1/\sigma$ Unknown · 2–11.8 Exponential–Unknown λ · 2-11.9 Density–Finitely Discretized Parameter Space

2-21.1 Beta and Dirichlet Distributions · 2-21.2 Order Statistics · 2-21.3 Ordering Functions for Multidimensions · 2-21.4 Examples of Distribution-Free Tolerance Regions

Preface

This text explores the theoretical and practical procedures for classifying patterns from their measurements. A pattern can, for example, be a disease complex with measurements consisting of symptoms, signs, case history, and test results for a patient. As another example, a pattern can be a submarine or non-submarine target with measurements corresponding to properties of a sequence of sonar echos. Other examples of patterns include brain cells, blood cells, cancer cells, chromosomes, crops, clouds, angiograms and ultrasonic echo-grams of organ scans, x-rays, etc.

Chapter 1 is introductory, presenting basic material on sets, vectors, vector spaces, and notation for estimating parameters characterizing a density function of pattern measurements. Because such a density function can have multiple modes or otherwise be non-Gaussian, provision is made for the density function to be a mixture of density functions. The discussion of vector spaces provides for treating waveforms, sets of measurements, and pictures; however, throughout the first five chapters only sets of measurements (finite size vectors) are considered. Procedures for reducing dimensionality are considered in Chapter 6. These include statistical approaches and a new approach where a priori problem knowledge reflecting correlations among measurements is inserted. In Section 1-2 of Chapter 1, some fundamentals of approximation theory are presented; the material there shows that a waveform or picture is in an infinite dimensional space. Knowledge about the kinds of patterns provides relationships among the dimensions in the measurement space to produce a finite dimensional vector. For waveforms, conventional basis functions are one of the ways (but not necessarily the best way) for introducing this problem knowledge to reduce dimensionality. In Section 1-3 the notation used for estimation and decision making in subsequent chapters is presented. In Section 1-4 it is shown how to approach estimation and decision making when given a sequence of patterns (their measurement vectors) which are not statistically independent. Section 1-5 emphasizes the importance of unsupervised estimation (including clustering) when the pattern observations are supervised. Section 1-6 presents a brief discussion of identifiability, a necessary and sufficient condition for unsupervised estimation to be possible. Then, in retrospect, Section 1-7 reminds the reader that the difference between supervised and unsupervised estimation is one of a priori knowledge and complexity.

Chapter 2 presents properties of estimation frequently used throughout the book. A guiding framework for the book is the Bayes estimation and decision making procedure. It is shown in Chapter 5, for example, that a Bayes estimator essentially is an average of the effects of many stochastic approximation estimators; consequently the Bayes estimator is not starting point dependent in many problems for which a stochastic approximation estimator would be. Sections 2-2, 2-3, and 2-4 present estimator properties of convergence, consistency, bias, efficiency, and sufficient statistics. Then Bayes, maximum likelihood, stochastic approximation estimation, and decision directed estimation procedures are presented. Of these techniques, Bayes is the most general partly because a theoretical estimator with mean square error lower than that for a Bayes estimator using quadratic loss function has never been found and partly because it generates other estimation procedures. Whereas, in the Bayes approach the a posteriori density of the fixed but unknown parameter vector is computed for each possible parameter vector in the parameter space, the maximum likelihood estimator selects as the estimator the parameter vector which a posteriori has largest probability. Stochastic approximation is a method of searching for a parameter vector which maximizes a prescribed criteria.

Pseudo-deterministic hillclimb, discussed in Section 5-3.7 is a form of estimation where an estimate of a criterion (for example, a regression function) is made at each of an acceptable set of points in the parameter space; then the parameter point maximizing the estimated criterion is chosen as the estimator. Decision-directed estimators are introduced in Section 2-20 in a natural way by using estimates of auxiliary parameters in calculating the a posteriori density used by Bayes. In Section 2-9 the basic problem of estimating the mean of a distribution using both current and a priori data is presented; Section 2-11 provides an extension to include both the mean vector and covariance matrix. In Section 2-17 an example of eliminating nuisance parameters to improve parameter estimate performance is presented. *The presence of nuisance parameters in raw data is the basic problem plaguing the practitioner of pattern recognition.* The dimensionality reduction process of converting a waveform or picture to feature vector (pattern), or a data vector to a feature vector eliminates nuisance parameters when "correctly" accomplished. Section 2-21 presents an introduction to tolerance regions, coverages, and their distributions; these concepts are used in discussing the k-nearest-neighbor decision rules in Chapter 4. The information function is considered in Section 2-24 because it arises naturally in Bayes estimation and the Bayes decision rule.

Chapter 3 presents decision rules, again with emphasis on the Bayes approach and practical results useful to the practitioner. Two kinds of rules, parametric decision rules and nonparametric decision rules, are considered. An underlying Bayes framework again prevails throughout. Sections 3-2 and 3-4 present well known results concerning the Bayes minimum risk decision rule so often discussed in books on communications theory. Almost without exception, these books do not provide the techniques for estimating the parameters characterizing these decision rules such as mean vectors, covariance matrices, and a priori class probabilities.† The *minimum conditional risk* decision rule introduced in Section 3-2.4 does provide all this facility. The subsections in Section 3-3 deal with decision rules, based on local density estimation, and remain within the Bayes framework even though underlying densities may be nonparametric. Local density estimation is based on the tolerance regions concept used late in Chapter 4.

Section 3-4 deals with the all important Gaussian decision rules: Bayes minimum risk decision rules for use when the categories have Gaussian distributions. In Section 3-4.4, provision is made for each class density to be a mixture of Gaussian densities. This provides a parametric approximation to nonparametric densities where practical clustering techniques (Chapter 5) can be used to estimate parameters.‡ Such suggests what is likely to be one of the most practical approaches to decision making (pattern recognition).

There are decision rules which may not appear to involve density estimation, such as the nearest neighbor rule. It can be shown, however, that these rules do fit within the framework of decision rules utilizing local density estimation. When a decision rule is designed for M categories and samples from the respective categories are unsupervised, and in addition each category can have multiple modes, estimating each category density can be difficult. Chapter 4 is concerned with estimating the density function for a category where supervised samples are available from that category. Section 4-2 provides an introduction to nonparametric density estimation calling upon work by Abramanson, Braverman, Keehn, Aizerman, Rozo-

---

†Estimation of a priori class probabilities is an *unsupervised estimation problem;* this is the reason it has not been adequately treated previously.

‡This is an unsupervised estimation problem. The approach may be one of the most important and practical approaches to general decision making.

noer, Kashap, Blaydon, Fix† and Hodges†, Whittle†, Rosenblatt†, Watson, Leadbetter, Cacoullos, Van Ryzin, Sebestyen†, Ball†, Hall†, Loftsgaarden†, Quesenberry†, Cover†, Hart†, Patrick†, Fischer†, and others. Section 4-3.1 presents (what will be called) the kNN_1 rule (first k-nearest neighbor decision rule) attributed to Fix and Hodges. Section 4-3.2 presents the kNN_2 (second k-nearest neighbor decision rule) attributed to Cover and Hart. Section 4-3.3 presents the kNN_3 (third k-nearest neighbor decision rule) attributed to Patrick and Fischer. A comparison of these decision rules is provided in Section 4-3.4; rules related to these kNN rules, such as a rule with reject option by Hellman, a rule by Specht based on a polynomial approximation, and a rule using potential functions are compared. Section 4-4 presents Cover-Hart bounds for the $1NN_2$ rule. A kNN_2 rule with a reject option is presented in Section 4-5 where it also is shown how the reject option can be applied to a kNN_3 rule. In Section 4-6, an upper bound for risk of a kNN_3 rule is presented. Section 4-7 provides a computer simulated example of estimating metrics for kNN_3 rules. The consistency of kNN_3 rules is demonstrated in Section 4-8. Moments of kNN_3 rule risk are derived in Section 4-9; asymptotic point risk of kNN_3 rules is presented in Section 4-10; results for small sample convergence rates of kNN_3 rules are presented in Sections 4-7 and 4-12.

Chapter 5 presents fundamental results for unsupervised estimation including clustering, again all discussed within the Bayes framework. Although the clustering techniques are naturally developed using the Bayes framework, they can be considered as an individual area of research. An introduction to the Bayes solution is presented in Section 5-2 showing how the information function naturally arises. Section 5-3 presents convergence rates for Bayes a posteriori density and estimators showing that a rate faster than $1/n$ is possible when there is a finite number of points in the parameter space. In Section 5-3.5 a criterion different from the information function is used to provide an a posteriori type approach somewhat different from Bayes. In Section 5-3.6 an estimator called the Quasi-Bayes Estimator is presented; this method involves computing several stochastic approximation estimates, all using the same observables, but having different starting points, and then forming a weighted average in which the weighting coefficients of all the estimates except the one closest (according to a criterion) to the true parameter point diminish to 0 rapidly. Unsupervised estimation techniques utilizing Robbins functions are presented in Section 5-3.8.

Section 5-4 presents clustering techniques: the first technique presented in Section 5-4.2 naturally arises from the information function in the Bayes solution; using this approach as a vantage point, it is possible to visualize how all other clustering techniques relate to the Bayes solution. The cluster-

---

†These authors provide material which comprises the bulk of the Chapter.

xvi

ing techniques presented in subsequent subsections are Cluster Map (a gravity technique), Chain Map, Maximin, Continuity Map, a clustering technique with interactive use of problem knowledge, growing clusters from cluster centers, and clustering using a priori supplied similarity function.

Chapter 6 concerns the very important problem of reducing dimensionality. The first eleven sections present conventional methods of reducing dimensionality through statistical procedures; but beginning in Section 6-12, it is stressed that these approaches are far from sufficient. Rather, it is shown why an approach is needed where problem knowledge can be inserted in the decision rule and how the use of problem knowledge enhances performance and probably is the most important topic in pattern recognition.

In Chapter 7 a new approach is presented where training samples in the measurement space is only one of two important ways to facilitate the decision-making process. The other is to use relationships supplied by man where he uses his field of knowledge about the problem. This approach essentially is the *scientific method* and Chapter 7 is appropriately called, *Pattern Recognition Through Statistical Verification of A Priori Problem Knowledge.*

E.A.P.

List of Notation

I Notation for Measurement Vectors

Symbol	*Interpretation*
x	scalar (complex number when there is no confusion)
x_i	subscripted scalar
$\mathbf{x}$	vector (if $\mathbf{x}$ is an L-tuple, $\mathbf{x} = [x_1, x_2, \ldots, x_L]$
$\mathbf{x}_j$	subscripted vector ($\mathbf{x}_j = [x_{j1}, x_{j2}, \ldots, x_{jL}]$)
$\dot{\mathbf{x}}_n$	sequence of n vectors $\dot{\mathbf{x}}_n = [\mathbf{x}_1, \mathbf{x}_2, \ldots, \mathbf{x}_n]$
$\mathbf{X}$	matrix, $\mathbf{X} = [x_{ij}]_{LL}$ is an $L \times L$ square matrix
$\mathscr{A}, \mathscr{B}, \mathscr{C}, \mathscr{D}, \mathscr{E} \ldots \mathscr{V}$	spaces
$\mathscr{X}$	measurement space, $\mathbf{x} \in \mathscr{X}$. Usually $\mathscr{X} = \mathscr{V}_L$ defined below. Also called observation space or sample space
Ω	class or category space
ω_i	ith class or category
i	ith class or category
P_i	a priori probability of ith category. Also $P(\omega_i)$
$\mathbf{x}_j^i$	jth vector sample from category i. It sometimes is convenient to denote this $(\mathbf{x}_j, \omega_i)$ or $(\mathbf{x}_j, i)$
$\dot{\mathbf{x}}_{n_i}^i$	sequence of n_i vector samples from class i.

Symbol	Interpretation
Ω'	decision space, $\Omega' \geq \Omega$
$\mathscr{V}_L$	L dimensional vector space. Also $\mathscr{X} = \mathscr{V}_L$.
$\mathscr{E}_L$	class (or space) of L-tuples of complex numbers
$C_{(0,1)}$	class of continuous functions defined on the portion of the real line between 0 and 1, $(0, 1)$
$\mathscr{E}_\infty$	infinite dimensional Euclidean space (Hilbert space); i.e., space of L-tuples when $L = \infty$.
$\mathscr{P}_L$	class of polynomials of dimension $L + 1$. That is, a function can be represented by a linear combination of $l, x, x^2, \ldots . x^L$.
$\mathscr{T}_L$	class of complex trigonometric polynomials of degree L.
$\|\mathbf{x}\|$	norm
$(\mathbf{x}, \mathbf{y})$	inner product
$\|\mathbf{x}\| = \left[\sum_{i=1}^{L} \mathbf{x}_i^2 \right]^{1/2}$	Euclidean norm
$d^2(\mathbf{x}, \mathbf{y}) = \|\mathbf{x} - \mathbf{y}\|^2 = \|\mathbf{x}\|^2 + \|\mathbf{y}\|^2 - 2\,\mathrm{Re}(\mathbf{x}, \mathbf{y})$	normed vector space distance for inner product vector space
$\mathscr{T}$	class of linear transformations
$A, B, C, D, \ldots$	sets or, sometimes scalars; for example, R is global risk, L_{ij} is a loss.
A^c	complimentary set
$\mathbf{X}^t, \mathbf{X}^{-1}$	transposed and inverse matrices
$\triangleq$	means "is equal to by definition"
iff	if and only if
$\Rightarrow$	implies
$(0, 1)$	part of real line, $0 < x < 1$
$E_\mathbf{y}[R(\mathbf{y})]$	the subscript $\mathbf{y}$ on E indicates the random vector for taking the expectation
$\exists$	there exists
$\in, \subset$	is in
$\notin$	is not in
$\forall$	for all
δ_{ij}	delta function. $\delta_{ij} = 1$, $i = j$, $\delta_{ij} = 0$, $i \neq j$.
$a \mid b$	a conditioned on given b
a/b	a divided by b
$\binom{a}{b}$	$\dfrac{a!}{b!(a - b)!}$, binomial coefficients

Symbol	*Interpretation*
$f(\mathbf{x})$	density function at $\mathbf{x}$
$f(\mathbf{x}\,\vert\,\omega_i)$	density at $\mathbf{x}$ when $\mathbf{x}$ is classified from category i. Also called ith class-conditional probability density. Also denoted $f(\mathbf{x}\,\vert\,i)$, and $f_i(\mathbf{x})$.
$f(\mathbf{x}\,\vert\,\omega_i,\,\mathbf{b}_i)$	ith class-conditional density which is characterized by the vector set of parameters $\mathbf{b}_i$. That is, given $\mathbf{b}_i$, this density function is completely known and could be stored in a computer.
$\mathbf{m}_i \triangleq$	$E[\mathbf{x}\,\vert\,\omega_i]$. Sometimes one of the vectors in $\mathbf{b}_i$.
$\boldsymbol{\Sigma}_i \triangleq$	$E[(\mathbf{x} - \mathbf{m}_i)(\mathbf{x} - \mathbf{m}_i)^t\,\vert\,\omega_i]$
$N(\mathbf{x}\,\vert\,\mathbf{m}_i,\,\boldsymbol{\Sigma}_i)$	Gaussian density at $\mathbf{x}$.
n_i	number of training samples from ith class.
n	$n = n_1 + n_2 + \cdots + n_M$: total number of measurement vectors from all M classes.
$\mathbf{n}$	$\mathbf{n} = [n_1, n_2, \ldots n_M]$
M	number of classes.
$d(\mathbf{x})$	a decision rule assigns $\mathbf{x}$ to class $d(\mathbf{x})$.
$L(j, i)$ or L_{ji}	loss incurred when the decision rule $d(\mathbf{x}) = j$ but $\mathbf{x}$ is from class i.
$r(d(\mathbf{x}))$	risk when using decision rule $d(\mathbf{x})$ at the observation (measurement) point $\mathbf{x}$.
R	average risk (averaged over the observation space) for the decision rule. Also $r(d)$.
$\dot{\mathbf{x}}_\mathbf{n}$	vector of M sets of supervised training vectors: n_1 vector from class 1, n_2 vectors from class 2, $\ldots$
$R(\dot{\mathbf{x}}_n)$	average risk of a decision rule which is "trained" using samples $\dot{\mathbf{x}}_n$.
r^*	optimum risk at $\mathbf{x}$ (i.e., the minimum possible risk at $\mathbf{x}$ using a Bayes decision rule).
R^*	optimum average risk.

Symbol	*Interpretation*
$\eta_i(\mathbf{x})$	probability $\mathbf{x}$ belongs to category i. Using previous definitions,

$$\eta_i(\mathbf{x}) = \frac{P_i f_i(\mathbf{x})}{\sum_{i=1}^{M} P_i f_i(\mathbf{x})}$$

Symbol	Interpretation
parameter conditional independence	$\mathbf{x}_1, \mathbf{x}_2, \ldots, \mathbf{x}_n$ can be statistically independent when $f(\mathbf{x}\mid\mathbf{b})$ is known; i.e., $\mathbf{b}$ is known. This sometimes is more precisely called parameter conditional independence. If $\mathbf{b}$ is unknown, $\mathbf{x}_1, \mathbf{x}_2, \ldots, \mathbf{x}_n$ are not in general statistically independent.
$(\mathbf{b})_n$	estimator, depending on samples $\mathbf{x}_1, \mathbf{x}_2, \ldots, \mathbf{x}_n$, for $\mathbf{b}^*$. Sometimes $\hat{\mathbf{b}}$ for convenience.
$g_n(x)$	empirical density function using n samples (one dimensional)
$g_n(\mathbf{x})$	empirical density function utilizing tolerance regions.
$\dfrac{1}{n}\sum_{s=1}^{n} h(\mathbf{x}_s\mid\mathbf{b})$	an empirical estimate of $\int h(\mathbf{x}\mid\mathbf{b})h(\mathbf{x}\mid\mathbf{b}^*)dx$ where $\mathbf{x}_1, \mathbf{x}_2, \ldots, \mathbf{x}_n$ come from $h(\mathbf{x}\mid\mathbf{b}^*)$.

IV Notation for Sample Based Decision Rules (in particular the $k\mathrm{NN}_3$ decision rule)

Symbol	Interpretation
$\mathscr{I}_i(\mathbf{x}; \dot{\mathbf{x}}_n)$	tolerance region formed at $\mathbf{x}$ for the ith class using training samples $\dot{\mathbf{x}}_n$
$\Phi_i(\mathbf{x}; \dot{\mathbf{x}}_n)$	volume of region $\mathscr{I}_i(\mathbf{x}; \dot{\mathbf{x}}_n)$
$k_i(\mathbf{x})$	number of samples from ith class in $\mathscr{I}_i(\mathbf{x}; \dot{\mathbf{x}}_n)$
$\mathscr{D}_j(\dot{\mathbf{x}}_n)$	the decision rule $d(\mathbf{x}; \dot{\mathbf{x}})$ induces M sets $\{\mathscr{D}_1(\dot{\mathbf{x}}), \mathscr{D}_2(\dot{\mathbf{x}}), \ldots, \mathscr{D}_M(\dot{\mathbf{x}})\}$ where $\mathbf{x} \in \mathscr{D}_j(\dot{\mathbf{x}})$ if and only if $d(\mathbf{x}; \dot{\mathbf{x}}_n) = \omega_j$.
μ_n^δ	$E_{\dot{\mathbf{x}}_n}[R^\delta(\dot{\mathbf{x}}_n)]$, the δth moment of risk.
$q^n_{j_1,\ldots,j_\delta}(\mathbf{x}^{(1)}, \mathbf{x}^{(2)}, \ldots, \mathbf{x}^{(\delta)})$	$P_r[d(\mathbf{x}^{(v)}; \dot{\mathbf{x}}_n) = \omega_{j_v}, v = 1, 2, \ldots \delta]$. That is, the probability the decision rule simultaneously classifies δ points in the observation space as above.

V Notation for Clustering and Unsupervised Estimation

A. Basic Notation

$\mathscr{F}$	family or class of density functions $f_1(\mathbf{x}), f_2(\mathbf{x}), \ldots, f_N(\mathbf{x})$
$\boldsymbol{\alpha}^i$	$\boldsymbol{\alpha}^1, \boldsymbol{\alpha}^2, \ldots, \boldsymbol{\alpha}^N$ are the parameters characterizing $f_1(\mathbf{x}), f_2(\mathbf{x}), \ldots, f_N(\mathbf{x})$ respectively.
$h(\mathbf{x})$	$\displaystyle\sum_{i=1}^{N} f(\mathbf{x}\,|\,\boldsymbol{\alpha}^i)P_i$ is a mixture of the N functions in the class $\mathscr{F}$.
$P_i \ \triangleq$	ith mixing parameter; $P_i = P(\boldsymbol{\alpha}^i)$
$\mathbf{b}$	$[\boldsymbol{\alpha}^1, \boldsymbol{\alpha}^2, \ldots, \boldsymbol{\alpha}^N, P_1, P_2, \ldots, P_N]$ is the solution vector. Note that $\boldsymbol{\alpha}^1, \boldsymbol{\alpha}^2, \ldots, \boldsymbol{\alpha}^N$ all are known. The mixing parameters $P_1, P_2, \ldots, P_N$ are determined to obtain a "fit" for $h(\mathbf{x})$.

B. Notation when it is Known there are M Classes

M	the known number of classes, $M \leq N$
$\mathbf{b}_i$	parameters characterizing ith class. This $\mathbf{b}_i$ is one of the parameters $\boldsymbol{\alpha}^1, \boldsymbol{\alpha}^2, \ldots, \boldsymbol{\alpha}^N$.
$f(\mathbf{x}\,|\,i)$	density of $\mathbf{x}$ when $\mathbf{x}$ is from class i.
$f(\mathbf{x}\,|\,\mathbf{b}_i, i)$	density of $\mathbf{x}$ when $\mathbf{x}$ is from class i with parameters $\mathbf{b}_i$ characterizing the density.
P_i	a priori probability of ith class.
$\mathbf{b}$	$[\mathbf{b}_1, \mathbf{b}_2, \ldots, \mathbf{b}_M, P_1, P_2, \ldots, P_M]$; all these entries can be unknown, including M.

C Notation when each class can be sorted individually (certain Clustering Techniques)

M	unknown number of classes; M is determined by counting the numbers of classes found.
$\mathbf{b}_i$	parameters characterizing ith class or cluster found.
P_i	probability mass in ith class or cluster.

D General Problem

$\boldsymbol{\alpha}^1, \boldsymbol{\alpha}^2, \ldots, \boldsymbol{\alpha}^N$	N known parameter points
$\mathscr{A}$	parameter space, $\boldsymbol{\alpha}^i \in \mathscr{A}$
$\mathscr{P}$	parameter space, $P(\boldsymbol{\alpha}^i) \in \mathscr{P}$

M' an upper bound on the number of classes, known to the experimenter, $M \leq M' \leq N$.

$\mathbf{b}^k$ denotes the kth solution vector

M_k number of classes in kth solution vector. That is, the number of the mixing parameters $P_1, P_2, \ldots, P_N$ which are non-zero.

$\mathbf{b}_1^k, \mathbf{b}_2^k, \ldots, \mathbf{b}_{M_k}^k$ the actual M_k parameter points corresponding to the kth solution which has M_k classes.

p_i^k probability attached to $\mathbf{b}_i^k$

$\mathbf{b}^k$ $[\mathbf{b}_1^k, \mathbf{b}_2^k, \ldots \mathbf{b}_{M_k}^k, P_1^k, P_2^k, \ldots, P_{M_k}^k]$

Comment: one way of resolving samples $\mathbf{x}_1, \mathbf{x}_2, \ldots, \mathbf{x}_n$ into clusters is the kth way. For the kth way there are M_k clusters. For example, cluster i is characterized by location parameters and shape parameters in $\mathbf{b}_i^k$. The mass in cluster i is P_i^k

VI   Notation for Dimensionality Reduction

It is difficult to precisely isolate procedures usually called feature extraction, feature selection, and classification. Dimensionality reduction, therefore, is a broad term used in this book describing converting a vector of measurements $\mathbf{x}$ to the one dimensional decision function $d(\mathbf{x})$. The following definitions will help to describe several "steps" in the dimensionality reduction process.

Observation Space
    or
Measurement Space: Space for a finite number of measurements $x_1, x_2, \ldots, x_L$ (or infinite number) with no apriori problem knowledge relating these measurements.

Feature Space: Space with points $\mathbf{y} = [y_1, y_2, \ldots, y_l]$ where y_i is the ith feature obtained as a function of the measurements utilizing apriori problem knowledge. Known or suspected relationships among $x_1, x_2, \ldots, x_L$ are utilized.

Decision Space: Set of real numbers indexing the classes which can be decided.

Class Space: Set of real numbers indexing the actual
                                classes. The number of points in the class
                                space is $\leq$ the number of points in the
                                decision space. The dual concepts of class
                                space and decision space are important
                                when the number of classes M is unknown.

A block diagram utilizing the above definitions is shown in the figure below:

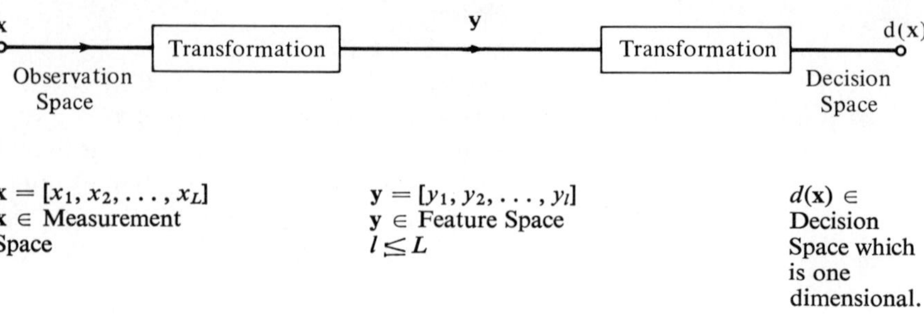

$\mathbf{x} = [x_1, x_2, \ldots, x_L]$
$\mathbf{x} \in$ Measurement
Space

$\mathbf{y} = [y_1, y_2, \ldots, y_l]$
$\mathbf{y} \in$ Feature Space
$l \leq L$

$d(\mathbf{x}) \in$
Decision
Space which
is one
dimensional.

CHAPTER 1

Introduction

1-1 Medical, Social, and Military Applications

Pattern recognition has application in computer assisted medical diagnosis and treatment, drug interaction studies, multiphasic screening and analysis, neurobiological signal processing, sonar detection and classification, information management systems, image processing, process control, etc. For example, automatic analysis and classification of photomicrographs of tissue cells can be used in blood tests, cancer tests, brain-tissue studies, and recognition of chromosome properties for genetic studies. Clinical data such as electrocardiograms and electroencephalograms can be analyzed and classified using pattern-recognition techniques [11, 14]. Analysis of signals in the brain's cortex which are in response to visual and auditory stimulation is another application. Besides medical problems, many applications are found in the military area which involve aerial photography. Also, there are problems arising from satellite weather, earth-resource photography, and sensing for life on remote planets [13, 21, 22, 23]. In the communications area, pattern recognition is fundamental for such problems as detecting and classifying targets using sonar or radar and equalizing intersymbol interference. The reading list at the end of the chapter includes some recent published books in the area of pattern recognition [10, 12, 21, 22, 23].

Although estimation is a very important part of pattern-recognition and communications problems [2, 3, 4, 6, 7, 15], other operations are usually necessary to provide a complete solution. Feature extraction, for example, is a very important operation very specialized to the pictures, vectors, or waveforms being processed. Essentially, feature extraction incorporates the problem model and converts the picture or waveform to a vector which is then processed by techniques discussed in this book. On the other hand, there are computer-aided display techniques which assist an operator in interpreting the results of pattern analysis and classification. This gets us into the problem of determining what the computer does best and what man does best; clearly there is an economic tradeoff. Sometimes there is a technological barrier such as represented by the fact that the eye's retina or the ear's cochlea are much better at parallel processing than the most complex computer configuration, or that man's field of knowledge about a problem may not be available to the computer.

In pattern recognition and communications, raw data usually is in the form of waveforms or pictures.† It is generally accepted that the first operation applied to such data should convert the data to vector format, utilizing a priori knowledge about the problem. It is further generally accepted that classification performance depends on the accuracy of the supplied knowledge. The first operation, invariably called preprocessing or feature extraction, is highly problem dependent and usually has not been conveniently described mathematically; it has been an art. Because of the artistic nature of preprocessing or feature extraction, there is a tendency for practitioners of pattern recognition in, say, medicine to communicate only slightly with practitioners in sonar or neurobiological signal processing or remote sensing. In addition to considering feature extraction, this book presents operations (which can be implemented by computer hardware or software) for analysis and classification of both supervised and unsupervised vectors. The unsupervised techniques presented also have very important application for when the data is supervised.

The difference between supervised and unsupervised classification is the amount of a priori knowledge available. To discuss this difference, suppose that a set of n vectors is available prior to the $(n + 1)$st vector, whose classification or category is to be determined. These first n vectors are called *training vectors* and the $(n + 1)$st vector is called the *candidate vector* or *test vector* or just the vector to be classified. If the classifications of the n vectors are known, the training is said to be supervised; otherwise the training is unsupervised. A theoretical development in this book is based on the mathematical fact that both supervised and unsupervised training may be formulated as a classical estimation problem (see Chapter 2). Unsupervised training, however, causes the problem solution to generally be much more complex than when there is supervised training. Because of this, we try to simplify the unsupervised problem by developing estimation procedures that are as prac-

---

†This includes the more convenient form, vectors. Data also can be tabular as in medical case histories which, after some work, may be put in vector format.

                                              Introduction   Chap. 1

tical as possible (for example, clustering techniques in Chapter 5). To accomplish this may well require leaving the framework of robust statistics and applying engineering intuition.

To illustrate the difference between supervised and unsupervised training, consider this simple example. Let $\mathbf{x} = [x_1, x_2]$ be a vector typical of the training vectors. Suppose there are n training vectors $\mathbf{x}_1, \mathbf{x}_2, \ldots, \mathbf{x}_n$ which group into three categories or clusters as shown in Figure 1.1. If the classifi-

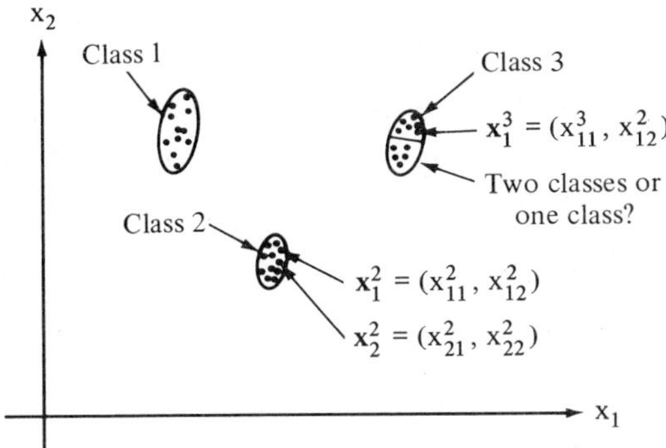

Fig. 1.1 Illustration of three clusters of unsupervised samples

cations of these samples are known, it is easy to calculate properties of each of the three categories. For example, the mean and second-order moments of the probability density function of each category can be simply estimated by a sample mean and a sample covariance matrix, respectively. If the classifications of these samples are unknown, one of the first unsupervised problems is to determine the number of categories. For example, should the samples labeled class 3 be placed into the classes as suggested by the solid line? This question may be answered if a priori knowledge is available such as "there is a category whose variance in a given dimension is approximately half the variance in the same dimension of another category." The utilization of such a priori knowledge by man is obvious; our problem is how to make it available in a computer operation that is automatically to sort the samples into categories. The problem is more complicated as dimensionality increases.

This problem of sorting samples into categories is basic to many problems in pattern recognition and communications. The following examples are typical of those for which the techniques in this book are developed:

1. Even if vectors $\mathbf{x}_1, \mathbf{x}_2, \ldots, \mathbf{x}_n$ are all from the same category (thus they are supervised), they may still occur in groups. The groups envisioned may correspond to modes in the density function of each sample $\mathbf{x}$. In order to store this density in memory (knowledge of the density is basic to classification) it may be most practical to

locate and store the locations and shape of the modes; this requires unsupervised estimation procedures (usually involving "clustering").

2. When the vectors $\mathbf{x}_1, \mathbf{x}_2, \ldots, \mathbf{x}_n$ are not from the same category, the objective is to sort them into categories. This is accomplished using unsupervised estimation procedures (including clustering). It is possible that $\mathbf{x}_1, \mathbf{x}_2, \ldots, \mathbf{x}_n$ are supervised samples from a category having a density with multiple modes; in this case subcategories of the category are determined using unsupervised estimation techniques applied to the supervised samples from this category. Locating these subcategories makes it possible to store the densities of each category with sufficient accuracy and small storage.

3. After locating categories and subcategories, it is then necessary to estimate properties of the subcategories. Properties selected could include a mean vector, covariance matrix,† and a distance measure.‡ These are not independent operations; for example, estimates of properties of subcategories are used to help define the subcategories into which a category is partitioned. Then the refined definition of the subcategories should provide for better estimation of the properties of the subcategories.

1-2 Mathematical Notation and Operations

1-2.1 Introduction

Throughout this book certain notation will be used repeatedly and it is advantageous to discuss it in a single section. Of fundamental importance is the vector space which is defined in a natural way in Section 1-2.2 after first discussing sets, metrics, fields, normed spaces, and inner-product spaces.§ In Section 1-2.3 properties of vector spaces are discussed and examples of vector spaces presented in Section 1-2.4. In Section 1-2.5, the natural isomorphism giving rise to matrix notation from vector spaces is presented. Basic notation for defining probability densities used in studying supervised estimation and mixing parameters fundamental to the study of unsupervised estimation are introduced in this section.‖

†For example, as used in the Gaussian decision rule in Section 3-4.

‡For example, as used in the kNN$_3$ decision rule in Section 4-3.3.

§A light, introduction to vectors and their applications may be found, for example, in Churchill [1, 5].

‖Notation for unsupervised estimation can get quite complicated. For this reason, four sets of notation are listed in the "LIST OF NOTATION". All of these sets of notation are consistent with each other. The simplest notation is that in Set B or Set C; these sets are used most often when discussing clustering. Set A is basic notation for introducing unsupervised estimation within the framework of finite mixtures; set D provides for using a priori knowledge in the finite mixture approach.

Boldface lower case letters, $\mathbf{a}, \mathbf{b}, \ldots, \mathbf{x}, \mathbf{y}, \mathbf{z}, \boldsymbol{\alpha}, \boldsymbol{\beta}, \boldsymbol{\gamma}, \boldsymbol{\delta}, \ldots$ are used to denote vectors and lower case letters $a, b, \ldots, x, y, z$ used to denote scalars.† A subscripted scalar is denoted x_i and a subscripted vector $\mathbf{x}_i$. A sequence of n vectors is denoted $\dot{\mathbf{x}}_n$ and classes or spaces are denoted by English script upper case letters $\mathscr{A}, \mathscr{B}, \mathscr{C}, \mathscr{D}, \ldots \ldots \mathscr{F}, \mathscr{G}, \mathscr{H}, \ldots$. A general L-dimensional vector space is denoted $\mathscr{V}_L$ with, for example, the space of L-tuples denoted $\mathscr{E}_L$. Sets are denoted‡ $A, B, \ldots, Z$ and matrices $\mathbf{A}, \mathbf{B}, \ldots,$ $\mathbf{Z}$. The symbol t is used to indicate transpose as in the vector transpose $\mathbf{x}^t$ and matrix transpose $\mathbf{X}^t$. The inverse, if it exists, of the matrix $\mathbf{X}$ is denoted $\mathbf{X}^{-1}$. That $\mathbf{x}$ is a vector point in a space $\mathscr{V}$ is denoted $\mathbf{x} \in \mathscr{V}$. The conjugate of a complex number a is denoted $\bar{a}$.

1-2.2 Sets, Metric, Topology, Field, and Spaces

Set, Subset, and Class of Sets

A collection of elements is a *set*; an element a of A is denoted $a \in A$. Sets are denoted $A, B, C, \ldots, Z$. An *empty set*, denoted $\varnothing$, contains no elements. A is said to be a *subset* of B if every element of A is an element of B, written $A \subset B$. Two sets A and B are said to be equal, denoted§ $A = B$, iff $A \subset B$ and $A \supset B$. Unless otherwise stated, all sets are considered subsets of a larger nonempty set called the "*universe*" U. A set of sets is called a *class* of sets and denoted by a script uppercase letter $\mathscr{A}, \mathscr{B}, \mathscr{C}, \ldots$.

Set Operations

The *difference* of two sets A and B is a set denoted $A - B$ and is the set of elements of A which do not belong to B. In particular, the difference of any set A from the "universe" is called the *complement* of A and denoted A^c.

The *intersection* of two sets A and B, denoted $A \cap B$, is the set of points common to A and B. If $A \cap B = \varnothing$, the sets are called *disjoint*.

The *union* of two sets A and B, $A \cup B$, is the set of points that belong to at least one of the sets A or B.

The *Cartesian product* of two sets A and B, denoted $A \times B$, of an ordered pair is the set whose elements are those ordered pairs (a, b) for which $a \in A$, $b \in B$. This also is called a *cross-product* space.

A *function f* on X to Y or $f: X \longrightarrow Y$ is a rule of correspondence between the elements of a set X (called the *domain*) and the elements of a set Y (called

---

†More generally, $a, b, c, \ldots$ are used for complex numbers in a space C; the space of scalars is denoted $\mathscr{G}$.

‡An upper case letter occasionally is used for other purposes.

§iff means if and only if. See list of notation when you do not recognize a symbol.

the *range*) such that for all $x \in X$ there exists a unique element $y \in Y$ such that $y = f(x); f(x)$ is called the value of f at x.† If $f(X) = Y$, we say that f maps X *onto* Y. A function f is called *one to one* if for every $y \in Y$ there exists a unique element $x \in X$ such that $f(x) = y$.

An *inverse* f^{-1} of f is a function on Y to X such that $f^{-1}(y)$ is a unique element $x \in X$, where $f(f^{-1}(y)) = y$. For all $y \in Y$, the inverse exists and is unique if f is one to one.

Metric

A *metric* on a set A is a function d on $A \times A \longrightarrow R$, where R is the set of real numbers, which satisfies the following conditions for all‡ $(x, y) \in A \times A$ and $z \in A$:

1. $d(x, y) \geq 0$ and $d(x, y) = 0$ iff $x = y$
2. $d(x, y) = d(y, x)$
3. $d(x, y) \leq d(x, z) + d(z, y)$

A *metric space* is a collection of sets with a metric defined on it. Throughout this book the discussion usually will concern metric spaces.

Neighborhood, Open and Closed Sets, and Dense Set

A *neighborhood* of an element x, denoted $N_\rho(x)$, is a set of elements y such that $d(x, y) < \rho$, where ρ is a positive real number.

A set A is *open* if for all $a \in A$ there exists a neighborhood $N_\rho(a)$ such that $N_\rho(a) \subset A$. A set A is *closed* if A^c is open.

A set A is said to *be dense* in B if for every $b \in B$ and $\epsilon > 0$, there exists an $a \in A$ such that $d(a, b) < \epsilon$.

Example: Every continuous function can be approximated by a polynomial; thus the set of polynomials is dense in the set of continuous functions.

An element $a \in A$ is an accumulation point of the set A if every $N_\rho(a)$ contains infinitely many elements of A.

Proposition: A is a closed set if and only if it contains all its accumulation points.

Example: Every set with a finite number of elements is closed.

---

† $f(X) \triangleq \{f(x) : x \in X\}$.
‡ $A \times A$ is a cross product space.

Topology and Topological Space

A *topology* in a space is a class of sets closed under certain set operations. The space where a topology is defined is called a *topological space*. An example of a topological space is the class of all open sets closed under arbitrary unions and finite intersections. Obviously this is a brief introduction to a topological space; it is included to call the reader's attention to a mathematical facility for describing complex structures.

Field

A *field* is a set F and functions $+$ and $\cdot$ on $F \times F$ to F such that the following requirements are satisfied:

1. For all $x, y,$ and z in F, $x + (y + z) = (x + y) + z$.
2. For all x and y in F, $x + y = y + x$.
3. There exists a unique element 0 (zero) such that for all $x \in F$, $x + 0 = 0 + x = x$.
4. For each $x \in F$ there corresponds a unique inverse $(-x)$ (called the *additive inverse*) such that $x + (-x) = (-x) + x = 0$. A consequence of (4) is that the equation $a + x = b$ has a unique solution $x \in F$—that is, $x = (-a) + b$ for all a and b in F.
5. For all x, y and z in F, $x \cdot (y \cdot z) = (x \cdot y) \cdot z$.
6. For all x and y in F, $x \cdot y = y \cdot x$.
7. There exists an element in 1 (called the *neutral element* or *unity*) in the set of nonzero elements of F denoted $F - 0$, such that for all $x \in F$, $x \cdot 1 = 1 \cdot x = x$.
8. For every $x \in F - 0$ there exists a unique element x^{-1} (called the *multiplicative inverse*) such that $x \cdot x^{-1} = x^{-1} \cdot x = 1$. It then follows that for all $a, b \in F$ and $a \neq 0$, the equation $a \cdot x = b$ has a unique solution—$x = a^{-1}b$.
9. For all $x, y,$ and z in F, $x \cdot (y + z) = x \cdot y + x \cdot z$.

Norm, Inner Product, and Vector Spaces

A *normed space* over a field F is a space $\mathscr{X}$ with elements x and operations $+$ and $\cdot$, and for $a \in F$, $a \cdot x \in \mathscr{X}$, and furthermore if for all $x_1, x_2 \in \mathscr{X}$, then $x_1 + x_2 \in \mathscr{X}$ and there is a real-valued function† $\|\cdot\|$ such that

1. $\|x\| \geq 0$, $\|x\| = 0$ if and only if $x = 0$.
2. $\|a \cdot x\| = |a| \|x\|$.
3. $\|x_1 + x_2\| \leq \|x_1\| + \|x_2\|$.

†$\|\cdot\|$ is generic for $\|x\|, \|y\|$ etc.

An *inner-product space* over a field F is a space $\mathscr{X}$ with elements x, operations $+$ and $\cdot$, and a complex-valued function defined on $\mathscr{X} \times \mathscr{X}$, denoted $(,)$; for $a \in F$, then $a \cdot x \in \mathscr{X}$. Furthermore, if $x_1, x_2 \in \mathscr{X}$, then $(x_1 + x_2) \in \mathscr{X}$ and

1. $(x, y) = \overline{(y, x)}$.
2. $(a \cdot x, y) = a \cdot (x, y)$.
3. $(x_1 + x_2, y) = (x_1, y) + (x_2, y)$.
4. $(x, x) \geq 0$ with $(x, x) = 0$ if and only if $x = 0$.

A *vector space* over a field F is a set $\mathscr{X}$ with elements x denoted $\mathbf{x}$ and operations $+$ and $\cdot$ such that if $\mathbf{x}_1$ and $\mathbf{x}_2$ are in $\mathscr{X}$, then $\mathbf{x}_1 + \mathbf{x}_2 \in \mathscr{X}$; and if $a \in F, \mathbf{x} \in \mathscr{X}$, then $a \cdot \mathbf{x} \in \mathscr{X}$. Furthermore, the following properties hold:

1. $\mathbf{x}_1 + \mathbf{x}_2 = \mathbf{x}_2 + \mathbf{x}_1$ *commutative.*
2. $(\mathbf{x}_1 + \mathbf{x}_2) + \mathbf{x}_3 = \mathbf{x}_1 + (\mathbf{x}_2 + \mathbf{x}_3)$, $(ab) \cdot \mathbf{x} = a(b \cdot \mathbf{x})$ *associative.*
3. $a \cdot (\mathbf{x}_1 + \mathbf{x}_2) = a \cdot \mathbf{x}_1 + a \cdot \mathbf{x}_2$, $(a + b) \cdot \mathbf{x} = a \cdot \mathbf{x} + b \cdot \mathbf{x}$ *distributive.*
4. There exists an element of $\mathscr{X}$ called the zero element $\mathbf{0}$ such that for all $\mathbf{x} \in \mathscr{X}, \mathbf{x} + \mathbf{0} = \mathbf{x}$.
5. $1 \cdot \mathbf{x} = \mathbf{x}$.

For convenience the operation denoted $\cdot$ above will be implied. The elements of $\mathscr{X}$ are called *vectors* and the elements of F are called *scalars*.

Vector spaces with a metric, norm, or inner product defined on them are called *metric vector space*, *norm vector space*, and *inner-product vector space*, respectively. It follows that from the definition of inner-product vector space,

$$(\mathbf{x}, a\mathbf{y}) = \overline{(a\mathbf{y}, \mathbf{x})} = \overline{(a(\mathbf{y}, \mathbf{x}))} = \bar{a}(\mathbf{x}, \mathbf{y}).$$

An inner product defines a norm:

$$\|\mathbf{x}\| = {_+}\sqrt{(\mathbf{x}, \mathbf{x})}.$$

A norm defines a metric:

$$d(\mathbf{x}, \mathbf{y}) \triangleq \|\mathbf{x} - \mathbf{y}\|.$$

An inner product defines a metric:

$$d(\mathbf{x}, \mathbf{y}) = \sqrt{(\mathbf{x} - \mathbf{y}, \mathbf{x} - \mathbf{y})}.$$

From the above it follows that, for an inner-product space,

$$d(\mathbf{x}, \mathbf{y}) = (\mathbf{x} - \mathbf{y}, \mathbf{x} - \mathbf{y}) = \|\mathbf{x}\|^2 + \|\mathbf{y}\|^2 - 2 \text{ real } [(\mathbf{x}, \mathbf{y})].$$

1-2.3 Properties of Vector Spaces

Linear Independence

A set of vectors $\mathbf{x}_1, \mathbf{x}_2, \ldots, \mathbf{x}_n \in \mathscr{X}$ is *linearly independent* if $a_1\mathbf{x}_1 + a_2\mathbf{x}_2 + \cdots + a_n\mathbf{x}_n = \mathbf{0} \Rightarrow a_1 = a_2 = \cdots = a_n = 0$. The vectors are *linearly dependent* if they are not linearly independent.

Spanning Set

It is convenient to let $\mathrm{span}(\mathbf{x}_1, \mathbf{x}_2, \ldots, \mathbf{x}_n)$ be the set of all *linear combinations* of the vectors $\mathbf{x}_1, \mathbf{x}_2, \ldots, \mathbf{x}_n$.

Finite-Dimensional Vector Spaces and Basis

A vector space $\mathscr{X}$ is said to be *finite-dimensional* if there exists a finite set of vectors $\mathbf{x}_1, \mathbf{x}_2, \ldots, \mathbf{x}_n$ in $\mathscr{X}$ such that

$$\mathscr{X} = \mathrm{span}(\mathbf{x}_1, \mathbf{x}_2, \ldots, \mathbf{x}_n).$$

If these n vectors are linearly independent, they constitute a *basis* for $\mathscr{X}$.

Orthogonality and Orthonormality

Two vectors $\mathbf{x}$ and $\mathbf{y}$ (in an inner-product space) are *orthogonal* denoted $\mathbf{x} \perp \mathbf{y}$ if

$$(\mathbf{x}, \mathbf{y}) = 0.$$

If, in addition, $(\mathbf{x}, \mathbf{x}) = (\mathbf{y}, \mathbf{y}) = 1$, the vectors are *orthonormal*. We denote by $\mathbf{x} \perp \mathscr{Y}$ that a vector $\mathbf{x}$ is orthogonal to a space $\mathscr{Y}$; this means $\mathbf{x} \perp \mathbf{y} \ \forall \mathbf{y} \in \mathscr{Y}$.

Linear Manifold

A space $\mathscr{W} \subset \mathscr{V}$ is a *linear manifold* if $\mathbf{x}, \mathbf{y} \in \mathscr{W}$ implies that $a\mathbf{x} + b\mathbf{y} \in \mathscr{W}$, where $a, b \in F$.

Gramm–Schmidt Process

Suppose that $\mathscr{W}$ is spanned by $\boldsymbol{\alpha}_1, \ldots, \boldsymbol{\alpha}_k$. Then $\mathscr{W}$ has an orthonormal basis $\mathbf{b}_1, \ldots, \mathbf{b}_L$, where $L \leq k$. One way to obtain this orthonormal basis is the Gram–Schmidt process described below. Let

$$\mathbf{b}_1 = \frac{\boldsymbol{\alpha}_1}{\|\boldsymbol{\alpha}_1\|}$$

Then a vector $\mathbf{b}_2$ orthonormal to $\mathbf{b}_1$ is constructed as follows.† Let $\mathbf{b}_2' = \boldsymbol{\alpha}_2 - c\mathbf{b}_1$, where c is determined by:

$$(\mathbf{b}_2', \mathbf{b}_1) = (\boldsymbol{\alpha}_2, \mathbf{b}_1) - c = 0.$$

Thus,

$$c = (\boldsymbol{\alpha}_2, \mathbf{b}_1).$$

and

$$\mathbf{b}_2 = \frac{\boldsymbol{\alpha}_2 - (\boldsymbol{\alpha}_2, \mathbf{b}_1)\mathbf{b}_1}{\|\boldsymbol{\alpha}_2 - (\boldsymbol{\alpha}_2, \mathbf{b}_1)\mathbf{b}_1\|}$$

$$\vdots$$

$$\mathbf{b}_L = \frac{\boldsymbol{\alpha}_L - \sum_{j=1}^{L-1} (\boldsymbol{\alpha}_L, \mathbf{b}_j)\mathbf{b}_j}{\left\|\boldsymbol{\alpha}_L - \sum_{j=1}^{L-1} (\boldsymbol{\alpha}_L, \mathbf{b}_j)\mathbf{b}_j\right\|}.$$

The set A is *linearly dense* in the set B if the linear manifold spanned by the elements of A is dense in B.

Example: The sequence or set $\{1, x, x^2, \ldots\}$ is linearly dense in the space of continuous functions defined on the interval $0 < x < 1$.

Proposition: If $\mathbf{x}_1, \mathbf{x}_2, \ldots, \mathbf{x}_n$ are orthogonal vectors (not the zero vector) in an inner-product space, then $\mathbf{x}_1, \mathbf{x}_2, \ldots, \mathbf{x}_n$ are linearly independent.

Complete Vector Spaces

A sequence of vectors $\mathbf{a}_1, \mathbf{a}_2, \ldots, \mathbf{a}_n$, denoted $\{\mathbf{a}_s\}_{s=1}^n$, is said to converge to a vector $\mathbf{a}$ if for every $\epsilon > 0$ there exists an integer n_ϵ such that for $n > n_\epsilon$,

$$d(\mathbf{a}, \mathbf{a}_n) < \epsilon,$$

which is sometimes written $\lim_{n\to\infty} \mathbf{a}_n = \mathbf{a}$ or just $\mathbf{a}_n \longrightarrow \mathbf{a}$.

A sequence is a *Cauchy sequence* if for every $\epsilon > 0 \; \exists \; n_\epsilon \ni$ for all $m, n > n_\epsilon$,

$$d(\mathbf{a}_m, \mathbf{a}_n) < \epsilon.$$

Proposition: Every convergent sequence is a Cauchy sequence.

---

†An interactive computer aid is to observe $\|\boldsymbol{\alpha}_L - \sum_{j=1}^{L-1} (\boldsymbol{\alpha}_L, \mathbf{b}_j)\mathbf{b}_j\|$ as L increases toward K; this displays the "amount" that $\boldsymbol{\alpha}_L$ contributes beyond what $\mathbf{b}_1, \mathbf{b}_2, \ldots, \mathbf{b}_{L-1}$ already contribute.

A complete vector space is a metric vector space such that every Cauchy sequence in the space is a convergent sequence and the limit is in the space. *A complete, inner-product vector space is called a* Hilbert space. A schematic of the relationships among the various spaces is shown in Figure 1.2.

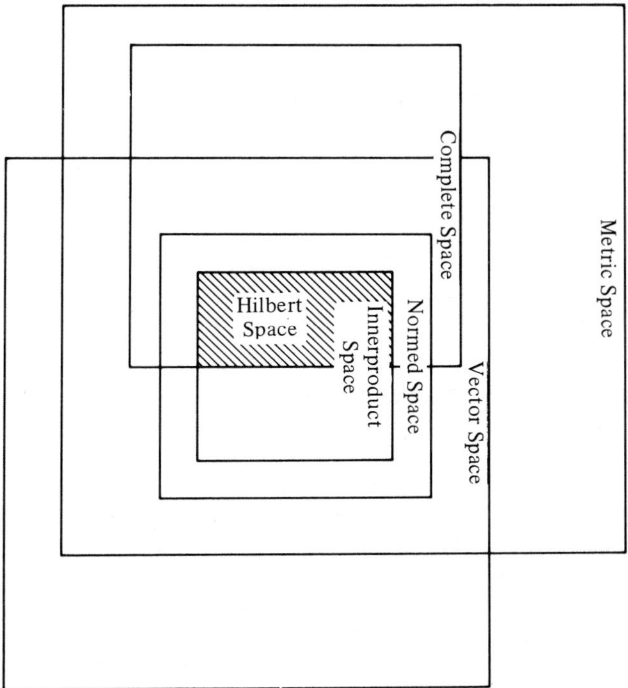

Fig. 1.2 Comparison of spaces

Projection

Let $\mathcal{W} \subset \mathcal{V}$ be a finite-dimensional linear manifold spanned by orthonormal vectors $\boldsymbol{\alpha}_1, \ldots, \boldsymbol{\alpha}_L$ and assume that $\mathbf{b} \in \mathcal{V}$. The projection of $\mathbf{b}$ on the linear manifold is denoted $\mathbf{b}_1$.

Projection Theorem: For any vector $\mathbf{b} \in \mathcal{V}$ and $\mathcal{W}$ a linear manifold contained in $\mathcal{V}$, there exist vectors $\mathbf{b}_1$ and $\mathbf{b}_2$ such that

1. $\mathbf{b} = \mathbf{b}_1 + \mathbf{b}_2$,
2. $\mathbf{b}_1 \in \mathcal{W}, \mathbf{b}_2 \perp \mathcal{W}$,

and this decomposition is unique. A three-dimensional illustration $L = 3$

is shown in Figure 1.3. The quantity $\|\mathbf{b}_2\| = \|\mathbf{b} - \mathbf{b}_1\|$ is defined as the "distance of $\mathbf{b}$ from $\mathscr{W}$."

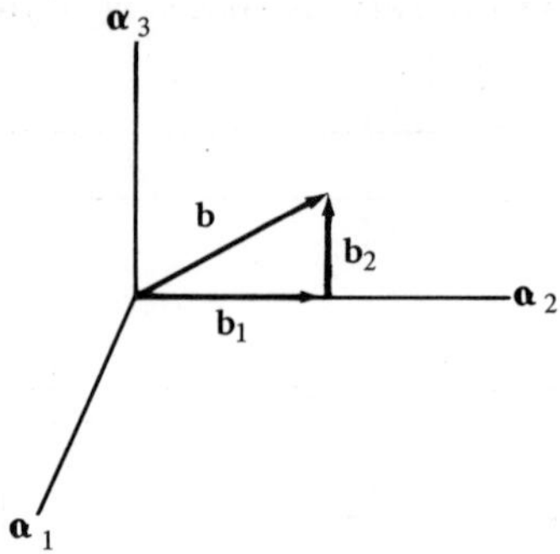

Fig. 1.3 Illustration of projection

Proposition: For any vector $\mathbf{b} \in \mathscr{V}$ and $\mathscr{W}$ a linear manifold contained in $\mathscr{V}$ it follows from the projection theorem that for every $\boldsymbol{\gamma} \in \mathscr{W}$, $\|\mathbf{b} - \mathbf{b}_1\| \leq \|\mathbf{b} - \boldsymbol{\gamma}\|$ and $=$ holds for $\boldsymbol{\gamma} = \mathbf{b}_1$ (that is, the projection of $\mathbf{b}$ on $\mathscr{W}$).

Example: Suppose that $f(x)$ is a continuous function defined on the interval $0 < x < 1 : f(x) \in C(0, 1)$. Then find a function $\mathbf{p}_* \in \mathscr{P}_L$ where $\mathscr{P}_L$ is the space of polynomials of degree less than L such that

$$\|\mathbf{f} - \mathbf{p}_*\| \leq \|\mathbf{f} - \mathbf{p}\|, \qquad \text{for all } \mathbf{p} \in \mathscr{P}_L.$$

Solution: According to the projection theorem, $\mathbf{p}_*$ should be the projection of f onto $\mathscr{P}_L$. To find this projection, proceed as follows:

1. Find an orthonormal basis for $\mathscr{P}_L$ [for example, apply the Gram–Schmidt process, using the spanning set $1, x, x^2, \ldots, x^{L-1}$, and denote the basis $\boldsymbol{\alpha}_0(x), \boldsymbol{\alpha}_1(x), \ldots, \boldsymbol{\alpha}_{L-1}(x)$].
2. Then the projection onto $\mathscr{P}_L$ is

$$\mathbf{p}_* = \sum_{k=0}^{L-1} (\mathbf{f}, \boldsymbol{\alpha}_k)\boldsymbol{\alpha}_k(x) = \sum_{k=0}^{L-1} \left[\int_0^1 \mathbf{f}(\xi)\boldsymbol{\alpha}_k(\xi)\, d\xi \right] \boldsymbol{\alpha}_k(x) \triangleq \sum_{k=0}^{L-1} c_k \boldsymbol{\alpha}_k(x).$$

Bessel's Inequality

For any $\mathbf{b} \in \mathscr{V}$ where $\mathscr{V}$ is an inner-product vector space with an orthonormal basis $\{\boldsymbol{\alpha}_1, \boldsymbol{\alpha}_2, \ldots\}$, then

$$\sum_{k=1}^{\infty} |(\mathbf{b}, \boldsymbol{\alpha}_k)|^2 \leq \|\mathbf{b}\|^2.$$

Schwarz–Cauchy Inequality

For any $\boldsymbol{\alpha}, \mathbf{b} \in \mathcal{V}$ where $\mathcal{V}$ is an inner-product vector space,

$$|(\boldsymbol{\alpha}, \mathbf{b})| \leq \|\boldsymbol{\alpha}\| \, \|\mathbf{b}\|.$$

Triangle Inequality

For any $\boldsymbol{\alpha}, \mathbf{b} \in \mathcal{V}$ where $\mathcal{V}$ is a normed vector space,

$$\|\boldsymbol{\alpha} + \mathbf{b}\| \leq \|\boldsymbol{\alpha}\| + \|\mathbf{b}\|.$$

Transformation

A transformation of a vector $\boldsymbol{\alpha} \in \mathcal{V}$ to a vector $\mathbf{b} \in \mathcal{W}$ is denoted $\mathcal{T}\boldsymbol{\alpha} : \mathcal{V} \rightarrow \mathcal{W}$. Let the domain and range of this transformation be defined as follows:

domain of $\mathcal{T} \triangleq \mathcal{D}_\mathcal{T}$: set of elements $\boldsymbol{\alpha} \in \mathcal{V}$ for which $\mathcal{T}\boldsymbol{\alpha}$ is defined;
range of $\mathcal{T} \triangleq \mathcal{R}_\mathcal{T}$: set of images $\mathbf{b} = \mathcal{T}\boldsymbol{\alpha}$ for each $\boldsymbol{\alpha} \in \mathcal{D}_\mathcal{T}$.

The transformation $\mathcal{T}$ is a *linear transformation* if and only if

$$\mathcal{T}(a\boldsymbol{\alpha}_1 + b\boldsymbol{\alpha}_2) = a\mathcal{T}\boldsymbol{\alpha}_1 + b\mathcal{T}\boldsymbol{\alpha}_2.$$

The *inverse*, $\mathcal{T}^{-1}$, where $\mathcal{T}^{-1}(\mathcal{T}\boldsymbol{\alpha}) = \boldsymbol{\alpha}$, of a transformation $\mathcal{T}$ exists if and only if

$$\mathcal{T}\boldsymbol{\alpha}_1 = \mathcal{T}\boldsymbol{\alpha}_2 \Rightarrow \boldsymbol{\alpha}_1 = \boldsymbol{\alpha}_2 \qquad \text{for all } \boldsymbol{\alpha}_1, \boldsymbol{\alpha}_2 \in \mathcal{D}_\mathcal{T}.$$

Thus the inverse $\mathcal{T}^{-1}$ is defined on the range of the transformation $\mathcal{T}$.

Theorem: If $\mathcal{T}$ is a linear transformation, then $\mathcal{T}^{-1}$ exists if and only if $\mathcal{T}\boldsymbol{\alpha} = \mathbf{0} \Rightarrow \boldsymbol{\alpha} = \mathbf{0}$, where $\mathbf{0}$ is the zero vector.

Concerning continuity, a transformation $\mathcal{T}$ is *continuous* at a point $\boldsymbol{\alpha} \in \mathcal{V}$ if $\boldsymbol{\alpha}_n \rightarrow \boldsymbol{\alpha}$ implies that $\mathcal{T}\boldsymbol{\alpha}_n \rightarrow \mathcal{T}\boldsymbol{\alpha}$.

Example: Suppose that $\boldsymbol{\alpha}$ is in a special space of linear functions $ax + b$ with $\boldsymbol{\alpha} \in \mathcal{V}$ and $\mathcal{T}$ is the operation of differentiation with respect x. Then for $\boldsymbol{\alpha} \in \mathcal{D}_\mathcal{T}$, $\mathcal{T}\boldsymbol{\alpha}$ is the constant a.

Example: Suppose that $\boldsymbol{\alpha}$ is in the space of continuous functions and $\mathcal{T}$ is the operation of differentiation. Then the range of $\mathcal{T}$ is the space of functions which are derivatives of differentiable functions. The domain is the space of differentiable functions.

1-2.4 Examples of Vector Spaces†

In this section several examples of vector spaces are discussed along with some properties, such as an appropriate inner product.

$\mathscr{P}_L$: Vector Space of Polynomials

A basis for the vector space of polynomials is $\{1, x, \ldots, x^{L-1}\}$. A vector in $\mathscr{P}_L$ is the linear combination

$$\mathbf{x} = a_0 + a_1 x + \cdots + a_{L-1} x^{L-1}.$$

$\mathscr{E}_L$: Vector Space of L-tuples

A basis for the vector space of L-tuples is $\{\mathbf{e}_1, \mathbf{e}_2, \ldots, \mathbf{e}_L\}$, where $\mathbf{e}_1 = [1, 0, \ldots, 0]$, etc. An inner product, for two points $\mathbf{x}$ and $\mathbf{y} \in \mathscr{E}_L$, is

$$(\mathbf{x}, \mathbf{y}) = x_1 \bar{y}_1 + x_2 \bar{y}_2 + \cdots + x_L \bar{y}_L,$$

$$(\mathbf{x}, \mathbf{x}) = \sum_{i=1}^{L} |x_i|^2.$$

The norm is taken as the positive square root $\|\mathbf{x}\| = \sqrt{(\mathbf{x}, \mathbf{x})}$. This vector space is the *Euclidean* vector space.

$\mathscr{E}_\infty$: Infinite-Dimensional Euclidean Space (called l_2)

Any vectors $\boldsymbol{\alpha}$ and $\mathbf{b}$ in $\mathscr{E}_\infty$ contain an unlimited number of components, $\boldsymbol{\alpha} = [\alpha_1, \alpha_2, \ldots]$, $\mathbf{b} = [b_1, b_2, \ldots]$. The inner product is defined

$$(\boldsymbol{\alpha}, \mathbf{b}) = \sum_{k=1}^{\infty} \alpha_k \bar{b}_k.$$

All vectors in $\mathscr{E}_\infty$ must have finite norm:

$$\|\boldsymbol{\alpha}\|^2 = \sum_{k=1}^{\infty} |\alpha_k|^2 < \infty.$$

The finite norm is sufficient to give a finite inner product,

$$\|(\boldsymbol{\alpha}, \mathbf{b})\| \le \sum_{k=1}^{\infty} |\alpha_k \bar{b}_k| \le \|\boldsymbol{\alpha}\| \|\mathbf{b}\| < \infty.$$

It also follows that $\boldsymbol{\alpha} + \mathbf{b} \in \mathscr{E}_\infty$ as a result of the finite norm; this follows

†Notation R_1 denotes the real line.

because by the triangle inequality for scalars, $|a_i + b_i| \leq |a_i| + |b_i|$. Therefore

$$|a_i + b_i|^2 \leq (|a_i| + |b_i|)^2 = |a_i|^2 + |b_i|^2 + 2|a_i||b_i|.$$

But

$$2|a_i||b_i| \leq |a_i|^2 + |b_i|^2$$

since $(|a_i| - |b_i|)^2 \geq 0$; thus

$$\sqrt{\sum_{k=1}^{L} |a_k + b_k|^2} \leq \sqrt{2} \sqrt{\sum_{k=1}^{L} |a_k|^2} + \sqrt{2} \sqrt{\sum_{k=1}^{L} |b_k|^2} \leq \sqrt{2} \, (\|\boldsymbol{\alpha}\| + \|\mathbf{b}\|),$$

and thus

$$\lim_{L \to \infty} \sqrt{\sum_{k=1}^{L} |a_k + b_k|^2} \leq \sqrt{2} (\|\boldsymbol{\alpha}\| + \|\mathbf{b}\|) < \infty.$$

Because the components of the vectors in $\mathscr{E}_\infty$ are indexed by the integers, the space $\mathscr{E}_\infty$ is called a *countably infinite vector space*.

$C_{(0,1)}$: *Vector Space of Continuous Functions*

Definite two vectors $\mathbf{x}, \mathbf{y} \in C_{(0,1)}$ as

$$\mathbf{x} = f(z), \qquad 0 < z < 1,$$

$$\mathbf{y} = g(z), \qquad 0 < z < 1.$$

Then $\mathbf{x} + \mathbf{y}$ and $a\mathbf{x}$ are $f(z) + g(z)$ and $af(z)$, respectively. An inner product is

$$(\mathbf{x}, \mathbf{y}) = \int_0^1 f(z) \overline{g(z)} \, dz$$

and the (norm)² is

$$\|\mathbf{x}\|^2 = \int_0^1 |f(z)|^2 \, dz.$$

Vector Space $\mathscr{T}_L$ of Complex Trigonometric Polynomials

Define two vectors $\mathbf{x}, \mathbf{y} \in \mathscr{T}_L$ as

$$\mathbf{x} = f(z) = \sum_{s=-L}^{L} \frac{c_s e^{isz}}{\sqrt{2\pi}}, \qquad 0 < z < 2\pi,$$

$$\mathbf{y} = g(z) = \sum_{s=-L}^{L} \frac{d_s e^{isz}}{\sqrt{2\pi}}, \qquad 0 < z < 2\pi.$$

where $i = \sqrt{-1}$.

Then $\mathbf{x} + \mathbf{y}$ and $a\mathbf{x}$ are $f(z) + g(z)$ and $af(z)$, respectively. An inner product is

$$(\mathbf{x}, \mathbf{y}) = \int_0^{2\pi} f(z)\overline{g(z)}\, dz,$$

$$\|\mathbf{x}\|^2 = \int_0^{2\pi} |f(z)|^2\, dz \geq 0.$$

Because

$$\frac{1}{2\pi} \int_0^{2\pi} e^{isz}\,\overline{e^{ilz}}\, dz = \frac{1}{2\pi} \int_0^{2\pi} e^{i(s-l)z}\, dz = \begin{cases} 1, & s = l, \\ 0, & s \neq l, \end{cases}$$

it follows that

$$(\mathbf{x}, \mathbf{y}) = \sum_{k=-L}^{L} c_k \overline{d_k}, \qquad \|\mathbf{x}\|^2 = \sum_{k=-L}^{L} |c_k|^2.$$

Intervalized Basis Functions

An important method of feature extraction from waveforms utilizes intervalized polynomials defined by *partitioning* the domain $a \leq t \leq b$ using P nonoverlapping intervals. On the pth interval, let

$$\varphi_{p,d}(t) = \begin{cases} 0, & t \notin p\text{th region}, \\ \text{basis function}, & \text{otherwise}. \end{cases}$$

Then the set

$$\{\varphi_{p,d}(t)\}_{d=1}^{D_p}$$

is a set of D_p orthonormal basis functions for representing a vector defined on this pth interval. If the objective is to represent a function $f(t)$ for $a \leq t \leq b$, the expansion

$$f(t) = \sum_{p=1}^{P} \sum_{d=0}^{D_p} x_{p,d}\varphi_{p,d}(t)$$

is used. This approach may be used in an interactive system where P, D_p, and the regions are selected interactively. Selecting the intervals automatically is a relatively complex problem, whereas the human operator can select them relatively easily. One problem, however, is that intervals selected for the function from an ensemble of functions may not be the best intervals for another function in the ensemble.

A *mathematical* difficulty with the above intervalized basis functions is satisfying continuity conditions at the interval boundaries. Spline functions† were developed in an attempt to help solve these problems; but this is not to imply that they will provide better ultimate performance in practice. Let

$$f(t) = a_0 + a_1 t + a_2 t^2 + a_3 t^3$$
$$+ b_1(x - z_1)_+^3 + b_2(x - z_2)_+^3 + \cdots + b_m(x - z_m)_+^3,$$

where

$$(x - z_i)_+^3 = \begin{cases} (x - z_i)^3, & \text{for } x \geq z_i, \\ 0, & \text{for } x < z_i. \end{cases}$$

This is called a "cubic" spline-function expansion.

One-Dimensional Discrete Fourier Transform

Let $f(z)$ exist for $0 < z \leq L$ and

$$\mathbf{x} = f(z), \qquad 0 < z \leq L.$$

Choose basis functions $\boldsymbol{\gamma}_0, \boldsymbol{\gamma}_1, \ldots, \boldsymbol{\gamma}_{L-1}$, where

$$\boldsymbol{\gamma}_r = \frac{e^{i2\pi r z/L}}{\sqrt{L}}, \qquad 0 < z \leq L, \ i = \sqrt{-1}, \ r = 1, 2, \ldots, L.$$

It is convenient, for digital-computer programming, to let L be an integer and discretize z such that

$$\frac{z}{L} = \frac{1}{L}, \frac{2}{L}, \ldots, \frac{k}{L}, \ldots, \frac{L-1}{L}, 1.$$

Then

$$\boldsymbol{\gamma}_r = \frac{1}{\sqrt{L}}[e^{i2\pi r 1/L}, e^{i2\pi r 2/L}, \ldots, e^{i2\pi r (L-1)/L}, 1].$$

Thus, the representation of $\mathbf{x}$, denoted $\hat{\mathbf{x}}$, is

$$\hat{\mathbf{x}} = \sum_{r=1}^{L} c_r \boldsymbol{\gamma}_r$$

---

†Spline functions get their name from the fact that approximations in two adjoining intervals are adjusted so as to be continuous at the boundary between the intervals, similar to the draftsman's spline. Spline functions are discussed in approximation theory literature.

with

$$c_r = (\mathbf{x}, \mathbf{y}) = \sum_{k=1}^{L} x_k e^{-i2\pi rk/L}, \qquad r = 1, 2, \ldots, L,$$

because

$$\mathbf{x} = [f(1), f(2), \ldots, f(L)] \triangleq [x_0, x_1, \ldots, x_L].$$

Note that

$$(\boldsymbol{\gamma}_r, \boldsymbol{\gamma}_l) = \frac{1}{L} \sum_{k=1}^{L} e^{i2\pi rk/L} e^{i2\pi lk/L} = \frac{1}{L} \sum_{k=1}^{L} e^{i2\pi(r-l)k/L} = \begin{cases} 1, & r = l, \\ 0, & r \neq l, \end{cases}$$

and thus for two vectors,

$$\mathbf{x} = \sum_{r=1}^{L} c_r \boldsymbol{\gamma}_r$$

$$\mathbf{y} = \sum_{r=1}^{L} d_r \boldsymbol{\gamma}_r,$$

it follows that

$$(\mathbf{x}, \mathbf{y}) = \left(\sum_{r=1}^{L} c_r \boldsymbol{\gamma}_r \right)^t \left(\sum_{l=1}^{L} \bar{d}_l \boldsymbol{\gamma}_l \right) = \sum_{r=1}^{L} c_r \bar{d}_r,$$

$$(\mathbf{x}, \mathbf{x}) = \sum_{r=1}^{L} |c_r|^2.$$

Two-Dimensional Discrete Fourier Transform

Let $f(z, u)$ exist for $0 < z \leq L$, $0 < u \leq L$, and choose basis functions

$$\boldsymbol{\gamma}_{rl} = \frac{1}{L} e^{j2\pi rz/L} e^{j2\pi ru/L}, \qquad 0 < z \leq L, 0 < u \leq L.$$

Let L be an integer and discretize both z and u and interpret $\boldsymbol{\gamma}_{rl}$ as a partitioned vector or a matrix. As always, denote $\mathbf{x}$ as

$$\mathbf{x} = f(z, u), \qquad 0 < z \leq L, 0 < u \leq L,$$

which may be a picture. Then

$$\hat{\mathbf{x}} = \sum_{r=1}^{L} \sum_{l=1}^{L} c_{rl} \boldsymbol{\gamma}_{rl} = \sum_{r=1}^{L} \sum_{l=1}^{L} c_{rl} e^{i2\pi(rz+lu)/L}, \qquad 0 < z \leq L, 0 < u \leq L,$$

$$c_{rl} = (\mathbf{x}, \boldsymbol{\gamma}_{rl}) = \sum_{k=1}^{L} \sum_{s=1}^{L} x_{ks} e^{-i2\pi(rk+ls)/L},$$

because

$$\mathbf{x} = [f(1, 1), f(1, 2), \ldots, f(k, s), \ldots, f(L, L)].$$

It is not difficult to show that, for two discretized pictures,

$$\mathbf{x} = \sum_{r=1}^{L} \sum_{l=1}^{L} c_{rl} \mathbf{\gamma}_{rl}$$

$$\mathbf{y} = \sum_{r=1}^{L} \sum_{l=1}^{L} d_{rl} \mathbf{\gamma}_{rl},$$

it follows that

$$(\mathbf{x}, \mathbf{y}) = \sum_{r=1}^{L} \sum_{l=1}^{L} c_{rl} \bar{d}_{rl},$$

$$(\mathbf{x}, \mathbf{x}) = \sum_{r=1}^{L} \sum_{l=1}^{L} |c_{rl}|^2.$$

Space of Square-Integrable Functions

The space of square-integrable functions, sometimes denoted $L_2(0, 1)$, is defined on the interval $(0, 1)$. If $\mathbf{x} = x(t)$, $0 < t < 1$, then

$$\mathbf{x} \in L_2(0, 1) \text{ iff } \int_0^1 |x(t)|^2 \, dt < \infty.$$

As usual,

$$\mathbf{x} + \mathbf{y} = x(t) + y(t),$$

$$a\mathbf{x} = ax(t).$$

To show that $L_2(0, 1)$ is a vector space, it is sufficient that if

1. $\mathbf{x} \in L_2(0, 1)$, then $a\mathbf{x} \in L_2(0, 1)$, $a < \infty$.

and

2. $\mathbf{x}, \mathbf{y} \in L_2(0, 1)$, then $\mathbf{x} + \mathbf{y} \in L_2(0, 1)$.

Statement 1 is true because if $\mathbf{x} \in L_2(0, 1)$, then $\int_0^1 |x(t)|^2 \, dt \triangleq m < \infty$. But

$$\int_0^1 |ax(t)|^2 \, dt = |a|^2 \int_0^1 |x(t)|^2 \, dt = |a|^2 m < \infty.$$

Statement 2 is true because if $\mathbf{x} \in L_2(0, 1)$, $\mathbf{y} \in L_2(0, 1)$, then, by the triangle inequality,

$$|x(t) + y(t)| \leq |x(t)| + |y(t)|, \qquad\qquad \forall t,$$

$$|x(t) + y(t)|^2 \leq |x(t)|^2 + |y(t)|^2 + 2|x(t)||y(t)| \qquad \forall t.$$

and thus

$$\int_0^1 |x(t) + y(t)|^2\, dt \leq \int_0^1 |x(t)|^2\, dt + \int_0^1 |y(t)|^2\, dt + 2\int_0^1 |x(t)||y(t)|\, dt$$

$$= m_1 + m_2 + 2\int_0^1 |x(t)||y(t)|\, dt.$$

But

$$2|x(t)||y(t)| \leq |x(t)|^2 + |y(t)|^2 \qquad \forall t$$

Since

$$(|x(t)| - |y(t)|)^2 \geq 0$$

so,

$$\int_0^1 |x(t) + y(t)|^2 \leq 2(m_1 + m_2) < \infty.$$

O_L: Space of Objects

Properties such as the number of peaks, length l, energy E, power E/l, etc. can constitute a basis for the vector space of waveforms for a particular problem. One member of such a basis set could be an object defined as a major peak with a minor peak to either side. Such a basis set description has application in medicine in describing chest sounds due to respiration or heart electrocardiograms. Objects in the basis set can be associated with the biophysics of the organism or organisms giving rise to the waveforms. Man is exceptionally good at discovering these pragmatic kinds of basis sets. After he has discovered them, there appear no theoretical reasons which prevent automatic use.

1-2.5 Isomorphism† Between $\mathscr{E}_L$ and Matrices

An important relationship can be constructed between operations in $\mathscr{E}_L$ and operations with matrices. Formally, let $\mathscr{E}_L$ be an L-dimensional

†Speaking informally, two algebraic systems of the same nature are said to be isomorphic if there is a one-to-one mapping of one onto the other which preserves all relevant properties (from Rudin [9], p. 86).

vector space spanned by linear independent vectors $\gamma_1, \gamma_2, \ldots, \gamma_L$. If $\alpha \in \mathscr{E}_L$, then $\alpha = \sum_{s=1}^{L} x_s \gamma_s$, where x_s is real or complex. Denote this representation

$$\alpha \xrightarrow{\gamma} \begin{bmatrix} x_1 \\ x_2 \\ \cdot \\ \cdot \\ \cdot \\ x_L \end{bmatrix} \triangleq [x_i]_L.$$

Suppose that there are two such relationships,

$$\alpha \xrightarrow{\gamma} [x_1, x_2, \ldots, x_L] \triangleq [x_i]_L,$$

$$b \xrightarrow{\gamma} [y_1, y_2, \ldots, y_L] \triangleq [y_i]_L,$$

where $\alpha \xrightarrow{\gamma} x$ means that α is transformed to an L-tuple x via knowledge of the basis vectors $\gamma_1, \gamma_2, \ldots, \gamma_L$. Then the following hold:

$$c\alpha \xrightarrow{\gamma} \begin{bmatrix} cx_1 \\ cx_2 \\ \cdot \\ \cdot \\ \cdot \\ cx_L \end{bmatrix}, \qquad \alpha + b \xrightarrow{\gamma} \begin{bmatrix} x_1 + y_1 \\ x_2 + y_2 \\ \cdot \\ \cdot \\ \cdot \\ x_L + y_L \end{bmatrix}.$$

Let $\mathscr{T}$ be a linear transformation such that

$$\mathscr{T}\gamma_i = \sum_{j=1}^{L} t_{ji} \gamma_j, \qquad i = 1, 2, \ldots, L,$$

which results since $\mathscr{T}$ transforms $\mathscr{E}_L \longleftrightarrow \mathscr{E}_L$.

If $b = \mathscr{T}\alpha$,

$$b = \sum_{i=1}^{L} y_i \gamma_i = \mathscr{T} \sum_{i=1}^{L} x_i \gamma_i = \sum_{i=1}^{L} x_i \mathscr{T}\gamma_i = \sum_{j=1}^{L} \left(\sum_{i=1}^{L} t_{ji} x_i \right) \gamma_j$$

since $\mathscr{T}$ is a linear transformation. Thus

$$y_i = \sum_{j=1}^{L} t_{ij} x_j, \qquad i = 1, 2, \ldots, L,$$

or we can denote this last equation as

$$[y_i]_L \triangleq [t_{ij}]_{L,L} [x_j]_L$$

and we write

$$\mathscr{T} \xrightarrow{\ \gamma\ } \begin{bmatrix} t_{11} & t_{12} & \cdots & t_{1L} \\ t_{21} & t_{22} & \cdots & t_{2L} \\ \cdot & & & \\ \cdot & & & \\ \cdot & & & \\ t_{L1} & \cdot & \cdots & t_{LL} \end{bmatrix} = [t_{ij}]_{LL}.$$

It is now appropriate to define

$$[a..]_{L,l}[b..]_{l,r} = \left[\sum_{k=1}^{l} a_{ik} b_{kj} \right]_{L,r},$$

$$[t..]_{l,l}[x.]_{l,1} = \left[\sum_{k=1}^{l} t_{ik} x_k \right]_{l,1}.$$

The interpretation is that $\mathbf{b} = \mathscr{T}\boldsymbol{\alpha}$ is represented in $\mathscr{E}_L$ by $[y.] = [t..][x.]$.

Now that an isomorphism has been exhibited, operations can be described in terms of matrix operations. Indeed, this is not necessary and from the mathematical analysis point of view is not general. It is convenient, however, since much of the work in subsequent chapters is in terms of matrix operations.

1-2.6 Some Properties of Orthonormal Sequences

Proposition: If $\{\boldsymbol{\alpha}_i\}$ is an orthonormal (o.n.) sequence in $\mathscr{E}_\infty$ and $\boldsymbol{\alpha} = \sum_{i=1}^{\infty} c_i \boldsymbol{\alpha}_i$, then $c_i = (\boldsymbol{\alpha}, \boldsymbol{\alpha}_i)$ (generalized Fourier series).

Proof: By hypothesis, $\boldsymbol{\alpha} = \lim_{n \to \infty} \sum_{i=1}^{n} c_i \boldsymbol{\alpha}_i$. Therefore,

$$(\boldsymbol{\alpha}, \boldsymbol{\alpha}_j) = \left(\lim_{n \to \infty} \sum_{i=1}^{n} c_i \boldsymbol{\alpha}_i, \boldsymbol{\alpha}_j \right)$$

$$= \lim_{n \to \infty} \left(\sum_{i=1}^{n} c_i \boldsymbol{\alpha}_i, \boldsymbol{\alpha}_j \right) = c_j.$$

Theorem: Let $\{\boldsymbol{\alpha}_i\}$ be an o.n. sequence in $\mathscr{V}$. The following statements are equivalent:

1. $\boldsymbol{\alpha} = \sum_{i=1}^{\infty} (\boldsymbol{\alpha}, \boldsymbol{\alpha}_i)\boldsymbol{\alpha}_i$, for all $\boldsymbol{\alpha} \in \mathscr{V}$.
2. $(\boldsymbol{\alpha}, \mathbf{b}) = \sum_{i=1}^{\infty} (\boldsymbol{\alpha}, \boldsymbol{\alpha}_i)(\boldsymbol{\alpha}_i, \mathbf{b})$, $\forall \boldsymbol{\alpha}, \mathbf{b} \in \mathscr{V}$.
3. $\|\boldsymbol{\alpha}\|^2 = \sum_{i=1}^{\infty} |(\boldsymbol{\alpha}, \boldsymbol{\alpha}_i)|^2$, Parseval identity, $\forall \boldsymbol{\alpha} \in \mathscr{V}$.
4. $(\boldsymbol{\alpha}, \boldsymbol{\alpha}_i) = 0$, $i = 1, 2, \ldots$; then $\boldsymbol{\alpha} = \mathbf{0}$.
5. The $\{\boldsymbol{\alpha}_i\}$ is a complete orthonormal sequence.

Proposition: Let $\{\alpha_i\}$ be an o.n. sequence in $\mathscr{V}$, with $\{c_i\}$ any numbers. Then

$$\left\| \alpha - \sum_{i=1}^{\infty} (\alpha, \alpha_i)\alpha_i \right\| \leq \left\| \alpha - \sum_{i=1}^{\infty} c_i \alpha_i \right\| \text{ and equality holds iff } c_i = (\alpha, \alpha_i).$$

Proposition: Let $\{\alpha_i\}$ be an o.n. sequence in $\mathscr{V}$. Then, for every

$$\alpha \in \mathscr{E}, \ \alpha = \sum_{i=1}^{\infty} (\alpha, \alpha_i)\alpha_i \text{ iff } \{\alpha_i\} \text{ linearly dense in } \mathscr{V}.$$

So we must make sure that the o.n. system is dense in $\mathscr{V}$ if α is to be expanded without error in terms of the o.n. system.

1-2.7 Characteristic Value Problems

Consider the matrix equation

$$\mathbf{Ax} = \lambda\mathbf{x}, \tag{1}$$

which can be rewritten

$$(\mathbf{A} - \lambda\mathbf{I})\mathbf{x} = \mathbf{0}. \tag{2}$$

There is a solution $\mathbf{x} \neq \mathbf{0}$ to (2) if and only if

$$|\mathbf{A} - \lambda\mathbf{I}| = 0. \tag{3}$$

That is,

$$\begin{vmatrix} a_{11} - \lambda & a_{12} & \cdots & a_{1L} \\ a_{21} & a_{22} - \lambda & \cdots & a_{2L} \\ \vdots & & & \\ a_{L1} & & & a_{LL} - \lambda \end{vmatrix} = 0.$$

Important eigenvalue–eigenvector properties are the following:

1. *Similarity:* If there exists a nonsingular matrix $\mathbf{P}$ such that $\mathbf{B} = \mathbf{PAP}^{-1}$, the square matrices $\mathbf{A}$ and $\mathbf{B}$ are said to be similar. Any eigenvalue of $\mathbf{A}$ also is an eigenvalue of $\mathbf{B}$.
2. If $\mathbf{A}$ is a *conjugate symmetric* matrix, eigenvalues of $\mathbf{A}$ are real.
3. If $\mathbf{A}$ is *conjugate symmetric*, eigenvectors corresponding to different eigenvalues are orthogonal.
4. Further properties of a *conjugate symmetric* matrix are:

i. The eigenvectors of an Lth-order symmetric matrix $\mathbf{A}$ span $\mathscr{E}_L$.

ii. If an eigenvalue λ_j has multiplicity k, there will be exactly k eigenvectors with eigenvalue λ_j in any set of L orthonormal eigenvectors of $\mathbf{A}$.

iii. If an eigenvalue λ_j has multiplicity k, the eigenvectors corresponding to λ_j span a subspace of $\mathscr{E}_L$, of dimension k.

iv. If one or more eigenvalues have multiplicity $k \geq 2$, there will be an infinite number of different sets of orthonormal eigenvectors of $\mathbf{A}$ which span $\mathscr{E}_L$, corresponding to the different ways of selecting orthonormal sets to span the subspaces with dimension $k \geq 2$.

Diagonalization of Symmetric Matrices

Let $\mathbf{u}_1, \ldots, \mathbf{u}_L$ be orthonormal eigenvectors of $\mathbf{A}$ spanning $\mathscr{E}_L$ and form the matrix $\mathbf{Q} = (\mathbf{u}_1, \ldots, \mathbf{u}_L)$. Then $\mathbf{Q}^t = [\mathbf{u}_1^t, \mathbf{u}_2^t, \ldots, \mathbf{u}_L^t]$,

$$\mathbf{Q}^t\mathbf{Q} = [\mathbf{u}_i^t\mathbf{u}_j]_{LL} = [\delta_{ij}]_{LL} = \mathbf{I}, \tag{4}$$

and thus

$$\mathbf{Q}^t = \mathbf{Q}^{-1};$$

$\mathbf{Q}$ is called an *orthogonal matrix*.

The matrix $\mathbf{Q}$ can be used to diagonalize the matrix $\mathbf{A}$ such that the resulting diagonal matrix has diagonal terms equal to the eigenvalues of $\mathbf{A}$. This is easily obtained as follows:

$$\mathbf{Q}^t\mathbf{A}\mathbf{Q} = [\mathbf{u}_i^t\mathbf{A}\mathbf{u}_j]_{LL} = [\lambda_j\mathbf{u}_i^t\mathbf{u}_j]_{LL} = [\lambda_j\delta_{ij}]_{LL}$$
$$\triangleq \mathbf{D}. \tag{5}$$

1-2.8 Quadratic Forms

A quadratic form is

$$f = \sum_{i=1}^{L}\sum_{j=1}^{L} x_i a_{ij} x_j = \mathbf{x}^t\mathbf{A}\mathbf{x} = \sum_{i=1}^{L} x_i(\mathbf{A}\mathbf{x})_i \tag{6}$$

where $(\mathbf{A}\mathbf{x})_i$ is defined the ith component of the column vector $\mathbf{A}\mathbf{x}$. The value of a quadratic form is unchanged if $\mathbf{A}$ is replaced by a symmetric matrix $\mathbf{B} = [b_{ij}]_{LL}$ where

$$b_{ij} = \frac{a_{ij} + a_{ji}}{2} \tag{7}$$

Thus we may assume that the matrix $\mathbf{A}$ associated with a quadratic form is symmetric.

1-2.9 Change of Variables

It may be possible to simplify a quadratic form $\mathbf{x}^t\mathbf{A}\mathbf{x}$ by the change of variables

$$\mathbf{x} = \mathbf{Ry}, \qquad \mathbf{R} \text{ non-singular,} \tag{8}$$

giving

$$f = (\mathbf{Ry})^t\mathbf{A}\mathbf{Ry} = \mathbf{y}^t\mathbf{R}^t\mathbf{A}\mathbf{Ry} \triangleq \mathbf{y}^t\mathbf{By} \tag{9}$$

with

$$\mathbf{B} \triangleq \mathbf{R}^t\mathbf{A}\mathbf{R} \tag{10}$$

If $\mathbf{R} = \mathbf{Q}$, the matrix whose columns are orthonormal eigevectors of $\mathbf{A}$, then

$$\mathbf{f} = \mathbf{y}^t\mathbf{Q}^t\mathbf{A}\mathbf{Q}\mathbf{y} = \mathbf{y}^t\mathbf{Dy} = \sum_{j=1}^{L} \lambda_j y_j^2 \tag{11}$$

1-2.10 Maximizing Quadratic Form

Suppose that $\|\mathbf{A}\mathbf{x}\| \leq \mu\|\mathbf{x}\|$ and $\|\mathbf{x}\| \leq c$. Then the quadratic form

$$F = \sum_{i=1}^{L}\sum_{j=1}^{L} x_i a_{ij} x_j^t$$

has a bound on $|F|$,

$$|F| \leq c\mu \tag{12}$$

For $L = 3$, $F(\mathbf{x}) = \text{constant}$ might appear as shown in Figure 1.4. The vector

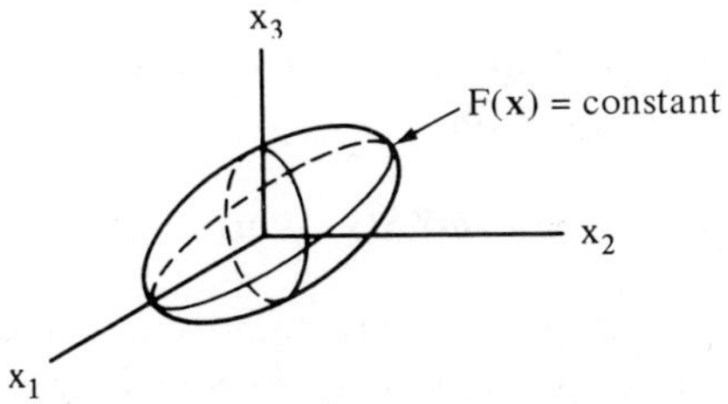

Fig. 1.4 Illustration of $F(\mathbf{x}) = \text{constant}$

$\mathbf{v}_1$ is an eigenvector corresponding to eigenvalue λ_1, $\mathbf{v}_2$ to λ_2, and $\mathbf{v}_3$ to λ_3 as indicated below:

$$\lambda_1 = \max_{\mathbf{x}} \left[\frac{F(\mathbf{x})}{\mathbf{x}^t \mathbf{x}} \right] = F(\mathbf{v}_1)$$

$$\lambda_2 = \max_{\mathbf{x}} \left[\frac{F(\mathbf{x})}{\mathbf{x}^t \mathbf{x}} \bigg| (\mathbf{x}, \mathbf{v}_1) = 0 \right] = F(\mathbf{v}_2)$$

$$\lambda_3 = \max_{\mathbf{x}} \left[\frac{F(\mathbf{x})}{\mathbf{x}^t \mathbf{x}} \bigg| (\mathbf{x}, \mathbf{v}_1) = (\mathbf{x}, \mathbf{v}_2) = 0 \right] = F(\mathbf{v}_3)$$

For $\|\mathbf{x}\| = c$, an example is shown in Figure 1.5 exhibiting $\mathbf{v}_1$ and $\mathbf{v}_2$.

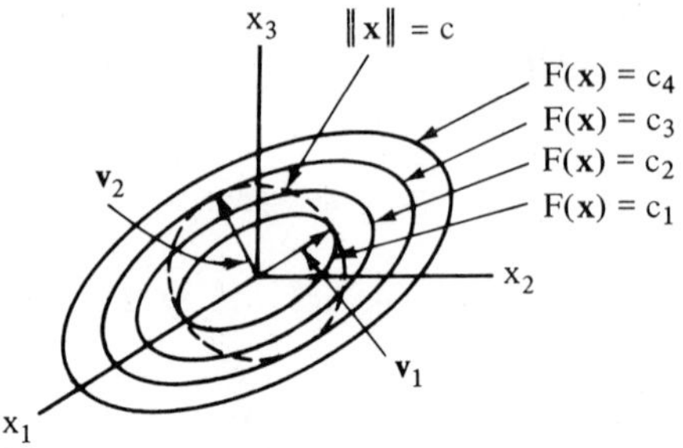

Fig. 1.5 Equipotentials for a quadratic form

In general,

$$\lambda_1 = \max_{\mathbf{x}} \frac{\mathbf{x}^t \mathbf{A} \mathbf{x}}{\|\mathbf{x}^t \mathbf{x}\|} = \frac{\mathbf{v}_1^t \mathbf{A} \mathbf{v}_1}{\|\mathbf{v}_1^t \mathbf{v}_1\|}$$

$$\vdots$$

$$\lambda_L = \max_{\mathbf{x}} \frac{\mathbf{x}^t \mathbf{A} \mathbf{x}}{\|\mathbf{x}^t \mathbf{x}\|}, \qquad (\mathbf{x}, \mathbf{v}_{L-1}) = 0, \ldots, (\mathbf{x}, \mathbf{v}_1) = 0. \tag{13}$$

1-2.11 Equipotentials Derived Using Quadratic Form

Replacing $\mathbf{x}$ by $(\mathbf{x} - \mathbf{m})$ in (6) results in a quadratic form $q = (\mathbf{x} - \mathbf{m})^t \mathbf{A} (\mathbf{x} - \mathbf{m})$. The equation

$$q(\mathbf{x}) = (\mathbf{x} - \mathbf{m})^t \mathbf{A} (\mathbf{x} - \mathbf{m}) = \text{constant} \tag{14}$$

defines a surface on which points $\mathbf{x}$ are equidistant (non Euclidean distance $q(\mathbf{x})$) from the mean point $\mathbf{m}$. This suggests attaching mass to points in $\mathcal{V}_L$ by defining a measure

$$\exp\left(-\frac{1}{2} q(\mathbf{x})\right).$$

It can be shown that

$$\int_{\mathscr{V}_L} \exp\left(-\frac{1}{2}q(\mathbf{x})\right) d\mathbf{x} = |\mathbf{A}^{-1}|^{1/2}(2\pi)^{L/2}. \tag{15}$$

Letting $\boldsymbol{\Sigma} = \mathbf{A}^{-1}$, we see that the function

$$f(\mathbf{x}) = \frac{1}{|\boldsymbol{\Sigma}|^{1/2}(2\pi)^{L/2}} \exp\left(-\frac{1}{2}(\mathbf{x} - \mathbf{m})^t \boldsymbol{\Sigma}^{-1}(\mathbf{x} - \mathbf{m})\right) \tag{16}$$

is a probability density function. This is, of course, the multivariate Gaussian probability density function.

1-2.12 Derivatives of Determinants and Scalar Vector Products

Occasionally there is need to differentiate vectors or quadratic forms. The following are a few elementary results.

Let $\mathbf{x} \triangleq [x_1, x_2, \ldots, x_L]$ and the grediant with respect to $\mathbf{x}$ denoted

$$\nabla_{\mathbf{x}} \triangleq \left[\frac{\partial}{\partial x_1}, \frac{\partial}{\partial x_2}, \ldots, \frac{\partial}{\partial x_L}\right],$$

then

$$\nabla_{\mathbf{x}}\mathbf{x}^t\mathbf{x} = 2\mathbf{x} \tag{17}$$

$$\nabla_{\mathbf{x}}\mathbf{x}^t\mathbf{y} = \mathbf{y}. \tag{18}$$

Let

$$\boldsymbol{\Sigma} = \begin{bmatrix} \alpha_{11}, \alpha_{12}, \ldots, \alpha_{1L} \\ \vdots \qquad\qquad \vdots \\ \alpha_{L1} \quad \cdots \quad \alpha_{LL} \end{bmatrix}, \; \ni \alpha_{ij} = \alpha_{ij}$$

and let

$$\boldsymbol{\alpha}_j = [\alpha_{1j}, \alpha_{2j}, \ldots, \alpha_{Lj}],$$

then

$$\boldsymbol{\Sigma} = (\boldsymbol{\alpha}_1, \boldsymbol{\alpha}_2, \ldots, \boldsymbol{\alpha}_L).$$

Let

$$\boldsymbol{\Delta} = (\nabla_{\boldsymbol{\alpha}_1}, \nabla_{\boldsymbol{\alpha}_2}, \ldots, \nabla_{\boldsymbol{\alpha}_L})$$

then

$$\Delta \| \Sigma \| = \begin{bmatrix} \delta_{11}, \delta_{12}, \ldots, \delta_{1L} \\ \cdot & & \cdot \\ \cdot & & \cdot \\ \delta_{L1} & \ldots & \delta_{LL} \end{bmatrix} = \Delta^{+} \tag{19}$$

where δ_{ij} is the determinant of the ijth co-factor matrix.

Finally

$$\nabla_{\mathbf{x}}(\mathbf{x}^t \Sigma \mathbf{y}) = \Sigma \mathbf{y} \tag{20}$$

Result (20) has application if one is differentiating to obtain maximum likelihood estimators when the samples have multivariate Gaussian statistics.

1-3 Unsupervised Estimation Notation

A picture, waveform, data, or pattern to be classified is denoted by an L dimensional column vector $\mathbf{x}$,

$$\mathbf{x} = \begin{bmatrix} x_1 \\ x_2 \\ \cdot \\ \cdot \\ \cdot \\ x_L \end{bmatrix}$$

presuming that a feature extraction operation has made the conversion to an L-tuple. Henceforth unless otherwise stated, a vector $\mathbf{x}$ is understood to be an L-tuple and in the observation space (also called measurement space) $\mathscr{X}$. A sequence of n vectors is denoted $\dot{\mathbf{x}}_n = [\mathbf{x}_1, \mathbf{x}_2, \ldots, \mathbf{x}_n]$ where [ ] is understood to mean a column vector†. When the n vectors are identically distributed any one of them is referred to generically as $\mathbf{x}$. When the n vectors are not identically distributed because of nonstationary statistics it is generally necessary to consider the density of $\dot{\mathbf{x}}_n$.

Let $\mathbf{x} \in \mathscr{V}_L$ and have a probability distribution $F(\mathbf{x})$ and probability density $f(\mathbf{x})$. To solve engineering problems arising in pattern recognition and communications, families of parametric distributions such as the Gaussian and multinomial are frequently used. Another family frequently used is the family whose members are linear combinations of Gaussian distributions. These families are called parametric because their members can be characterized by a finite number of parameters. In comparison, an example of a non-

---

†Note that $\dot{\mathbf{x}}_n \in \mathscr{X}^n$, the cross-product space.

parametric family is the family of distributions symmetric about a point
in $\mathscr{V}_L$.

Parameter Space and Family of Distributions

In this book the symbol $\mathscr{A}$ will be used to denote the *vector space of
parameters* where a parameter point $\boldsymbol{\alpha}$ in the space characterizes a probability
distribution. A family of distributions is defined $\mathscr{F}$,

$$\mathscr{F} = \{F(\mathbf{x}\,|\,\boldsymbol{\alpha}); \ \boldsymbol{\alpha} \in \mathscr{A}, \ \mathbf{x} \in \mathscr{V}_L\}. \tag{1}$$

Suppose a sequence of random vector observation's $\mathbf{x}_1, \mathbf{x}_2, \ldots, \mathbf{x}_n$ are
identically distributed from $F(\mathbf{x}\,|\,\boldsymbol{\alpha}^*)$ where $\boldsymbol{\alpha}^*$ is unknown to the observer.
An estimator for $\boldsymbol{\alpha}^*$ can be obtained as a function of the observations using
any of several approaches discussed in Chapter 2 and Chapter 5. Denote
this estimator $\boldsymbol{\alpha}(\mathbf{x}_1, \mathbf{x}_2, \ldots, \mathbf{x}_n)$ or for brevity $(\boldsymbol{\alpha})_n$.

Unsupervised Estimation

Suppose that associated with each of the samples $\mathbf{x}_1, \mathbf{x}_2, \ldots, \mathbf{x}_n$ is a
probability distribution with the possibility of some of the samples being
from, say, $F(\mathbf{x}\,|\,\boldsymbol{\alpha}^1)$, some from $F(\mathbf{x}\,|\,\boldsymbol{\alpha}^2)$, etc. where $\boldsymbol{\alpha}^1$ and $\boldsymbol{\alpha}^2$ are in $\mathscr{A}$. In
other words, any sample $\mathbf{x}$ could be from any one of the member distri-
butions in the family $\mathscr{F}$. It is appropriate to define a *mixing distribution*
$G(\boldsymbol{\alpha})$ in a space $\mathscr{G}$ which describes the probability that point $\boldsymbol{\alpha}$ characterizes
the mixture (defined below). Formally, the sample $\mathbf{x}$ has a distribution

$$H(\mathbf{x}) = \int F(\mathbf{x}\,|\,\boldsymbol{\alpha})\,dG(\boldsymbol{\alpha}) \tag{2}$$

which is called a *mixture* (see [24, 25, 26, 20, 19, 18, 17, 16]). The most interesting case for engineering is where there are a finite number of points $\boldsymbol{\alpha}^1$,
$\boldsymbol{\alpha}^2, \ldots, \boldsymbol{\alpha}^N$ in the parameter space $\mathscr{A}$. Then the mixing distribution is

$$G(\boldsymbol{\alpha}) = \sum_{i=1}^{N} P(\boldsymbol{\alpha}^i)\delta(\boldsymbol{\alpha} - \boldsymbol{\alpha}^i) \tag{3}$$

where

$$\delta(\boldsymbol{\alpha} - \boldsymbol{\alpha}^i) = \begin{cases} 1, & \boldsymbol{\alpha} = \boldsymbol{\alpha}^i \\ 0, & \boldsymbol{\alpha} \neq \boldsymbol{\alpha}^i. \end{cases}$$

Substituting (3) into (2) gives the *finite mixture*

$$H(\mathbf{x}) = \sum_{i=1}^{N} F(\mathbf{x}\,|\,\boldsymbol{\alpha}^i)P(\boldsymbol{\alpha}^i). \tag{4a}$$

It is important to stress that the parameter points $\boldsymbol{\alpha}^1, \boldsymbol{\alpha}^2, \ldots, \boldsymbol{\alpha}^N$ in (4a) are *all known* because they constitute the parameter space which is specified a priori; the unknowns in (4a) are the mixing parameters $P(\boldsymbol{\alpha}^1), P(\boldsymbol{\alpha}^2), \ldots, P(\boldsymbol{\alpha}^N)$ which are in a space $\mathscr{P}$ of mixing parameters. Note that there is a cross product space $\mathscr{A} \times \mathscr{P}$ containing the pairs $(\boldsymbol{\alpha}^i, P(\boldsymbol{\alpha}^i))$. To stress that the mixing parameters are unknown, it is appropriate to write (4a) as

$$H(\mathbf{x} \mid P(\boldsymbol{\alpha}^1), P(\boldsymbol{\alpha}^2), \ldots, P(\boldsymbol{\alpha}^N)) = \sum_{i=1}^{N} F(\mathbf{x} \mid \boldsymbol{\alpha}^i) P(\boldsymbol{\alpha}^i) \tag{4b}$$

which is a mixture distribution conditioned on being given the mixing parameters.

Classes are defined as the superscripts or indexes of those parameter vectors among $\boldsymbol{\alpha}^1, \boldsymbol{\alpha}^2, \ldots, \boldsymbol{\alpha}^N$ which have non-zero mixing parameters. Let the number of classes be M with corresponding parameter points $\mathbf{b}_1, \mathbf{b}_2, \ldots, \mathbf{b}_M$ and associated *class probabilities* $P_1, P_2, \ldots, P_M$. Note that $M \leq N$; and in practice M may be unknown but an upper bound $M' \geq M$ is known. We will say that $\mathbf{b}_i$ is the parameter point characterizing the ith class conditional distribution $F(\mathbf{x} \mid i)$. It also is appropriate to define $F(\mathbf{x} \mid i, \mathbf{b}_i)$.

Let

$$\mathbf{b} = [\mathbf{b}_1, \mathbf{b}_2, \ldots, \mathbf{b}_M, P_1, P_2, \ldots, P_M] \tag{5}$$

where $\mathbf{b} \in \mathscr{A}^M \times \mathscr{P}^M \triangleq \mathscr{B}^M$ and M is a variable, $1 \leq M \leq M'$. Then the mixture distribution conditioned on $\mathbf{b}$ is

$$H(\mathbf{x} \mid \mathbf{b}) = \sum_{i=1}^{M} F(\mathbf{x} \mid i, \mathbf{b}_i) P_i \tag{6}$$

where

$$\sum_{i=1}^{M} P_i = 1, \qquad P_i > 0, \, i = 1, 2, \ldots, M$$

$$\mathbf{b}_i \neq \mathbf{b}_j, \, i \neq j.$$

If the space $\mathscr{B}^{M'}$ is discrete containing parameter points $\mathbf{b}^k$, $k = 1, 2, \ldots, V$ with the superscript on $\mathbf{b}^k$ indexing the particular value, then

$$\mathbf{b}^k = [\mathbf{b}_1^k, \mathbf{b}_2^k, \ldots, \mathbf{b}_{M_k}^k, P_1^k, P_2^k, \ldots, P_{M_k}^k] \tag{7}$$

is the kth parameter vector with M_k classes. The mixture when $\mathscr{B}^{M'}$ is discrete is

$$H(\mathbf{x} \mid \mathbf{b}^k) = \sum_{i=1}^{M_k} F(\mathbf{x} \mid i, \mathbf{b}_i^k) P_i^k, \qquad k = 1, 2, \ldots, V \tag{8}$$

It is convenient to summarize the constraints placed on points in $\mathscr{B}^{M'}$ to obtain the set of admissible solutions:

1. $\mathbf{b}^k \in \mathscr{A}^{M_k} \times \mathscr{P}^{M_k}$
2. $\sum_{i=1}^{M_k} P_i^k = 1.$
3. $\mathbf{b}_i^k \neq \mathbf{b}_j^k, \qquad i \neq j,$ for $1 \leq i, j \leq M_k,$ for each k.
4. if a reordering of the $\mathbf{b}_i^k$ entries in $\mathbf{b}^k$ produces $\mathbf{b}^t$, then $\mathbf{b}^k$ is defined not different from $\mathbf{b}^t$. This simply states that *naming categories* is not accomplished in unsupervised estimation.
5. additional restrictions† on the points $\mathbf{b}_i^k$ and P_i^k can be introduced to further reduce the number of points in $\mathscr{B}^{M'}$.

†This reduction of the number of points in $\mathscr{B}$ can improve performance as shown in Chapter 5. This is basic to dimensionality reduction or feature extraction discussed in Chapter 6 and Chapter 7.

Examples of $\mathbf{b}^k \in \mathscr{B}^{M'}$

Consider an example where we arbitrarily set the upper bound on the number of categories at $M' = 10$. Let $\mathbf{x}_1, \mathbf{x}_2, \ldots, \mathbf{x}_n$ be 2-dimensional vectors as illustrated in Figure 1.6a. One possible partition corresponding to the first possible mixture point, $\mathbf{b}^1$, is shown in Figure 1.6b with $M^1 = 3$. Another possible partition is shown in Figure 1.6c with $M^2 = 6$, correspond-

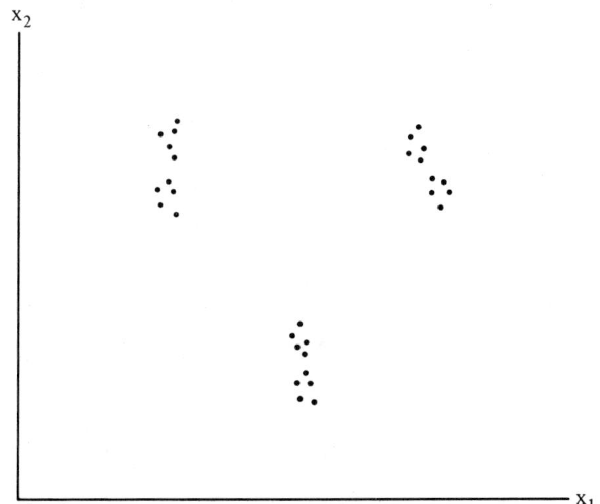

Fig. 1.6a Samples in observation space

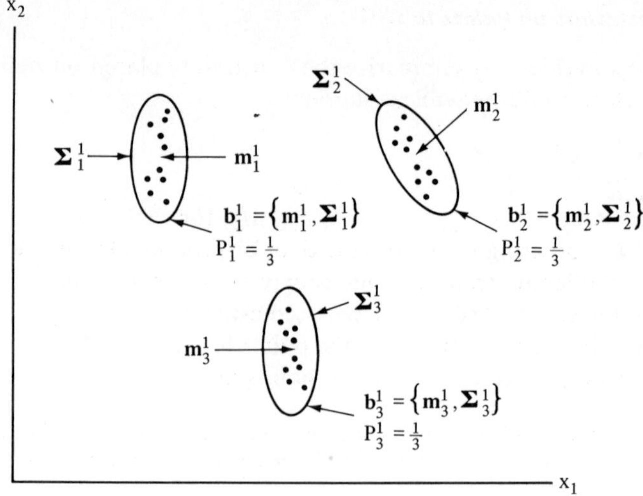

Fig. 1.6b Possible subset with $M = 3$ ($k = 1$ indicates first possible solution)

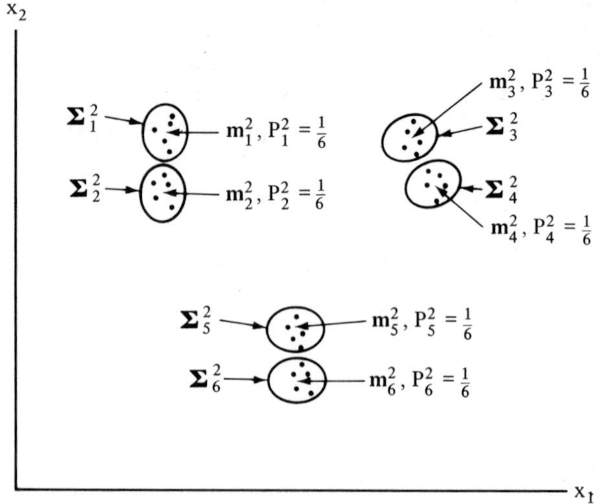

Fig. 1.6c Possible subset with $M = 6$ (e.g., $k = 2$ which indicates the second possible solution)

ing to the second possible mixture point, $\mathbf{b}^2$. In these illustrations $\mathbf{b}_i^k$ contains a mean vector or cluster center and a covariance matrix and P_i^k is proportional to the number of samples in the ith cluster of the kth solution. The clusters in this example can easily be located by eye; but whether the $M =$

3 partition or the $M = 6$ partition is correct depends upon a prior knowledge.† Without appropriate a priori knowledge it is impossible to determine the number of clusters (i.e. the value of M).

As suggested above, unsupervised estimation may be viewed as clustering; however, the reader is warned that results from clustering may not make sense although it may be expedient when dimensionality (L) is large and the number of samples n is small. The mathematics of unsupervised estimation will show precisely which problems can be solved. *These results show that clustering makes sense only in terms of a priori knowledge used.* For example, the results of clustering may not make sense when interpreted by man who is using a field of knowledge not incorporated in the clustering procedure. Careful study of unsupervised estimation shows that highly overlapping categories can be separated using theoretical techniques. These techniques require a priori knowledge that may not, in practice, be available. When limited *a priori* knowledge is available, clustering techniques may offer practical solutions if the categories are not highly overlapping (this being sufficient a priori knowledge).

Two Approaches to a Solution

Mixture (4b) suggests one approach to resolving a mixture while mixture (8) suggests another approach.

Approach 1 Mixture (4b) suggests constructing N filters corresponding to the N parameter points $\alpha^1, \alpha^2, \ldots, \alpha^N$ with the outputs of these filters, P_1, $P_2, \ldots, P_N$. Because the parameter points $\alpha^1, \alpha^2, \ldots, \alpha^N$ all are known, the filters can be designed a priori. A disadvantage of this approach occurs when N is very large or when there is difficulty in designing the N filters.

Approach 2 Mixture (8) suggests searching for a solution vector $\mathbf{b}^k$. Constraints placed on $\mathscr{B}^{M'}$, such as $M \leq M'$, restrict the number V of parameter points involved in the search.

Example: The following example of a mixture is related to a 2 dimensional histogram with 10×10 bins.

$$\text{Let } f(\mathbf{x}\,|\,\boldsymbol{\alpha}^t) \triangleq \begin{cases} 1 & \text{if } \begin{cases} \alpha_1^t \leq x_1 < \alpha_1^t + 1 \\ \alpha_2^t \leq x_2 < \alpha_2^t + 1 \end{cases} \\ 0 & \text{otherwise} \end{cases}$$

where $\boldsymbol{\alpha}^t = [\alpha_1^t, \alpha_2^t]$ with α_1^t equal to the greatest integer less than or equal

†See Section 5-4.

to $t/10$ and α_2^t equal to the remainder of $t/10$, for $t = 0, 1, 2, \ldots, 99$. Thus $N = 100$.

Thus $f(\mathbf{x} \mid \boldsymbol{\alpha}^0)$ looks like

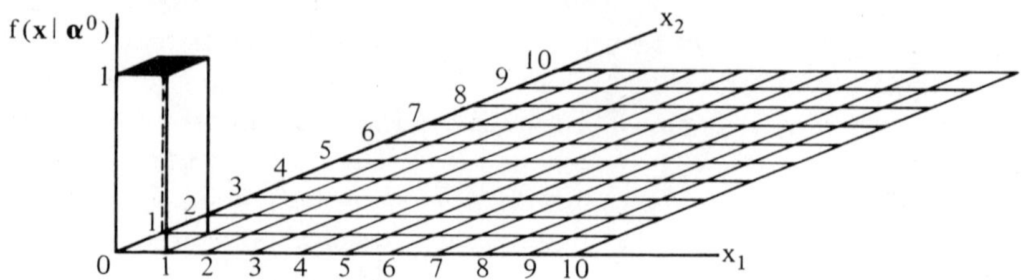

while $f(\mathbf{x} \mid \boldsymbol{\alpha}^{24})$ looks like

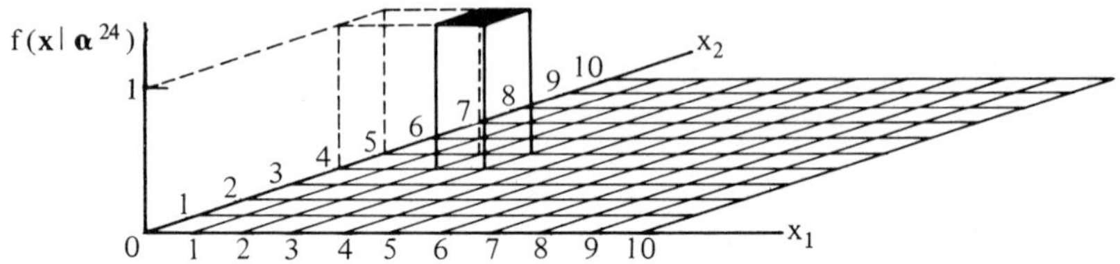

Let

$$h(\mathbf{x} \mid \{P(\boldsymbol{\alpha}^t)\}_{t=0}^{99}) = \sum_{t=0}^{99} f(\mathbf{x} \mid \boldsymbol{\alpha}^t) P(\boldsymbol{\alpha}^t).$$

The mixture corresponds to the density of a histogram with $P(\boldsymbol{\alpha}^t)$ of the mass falling in bin $\boldsymbol{\alpha}^t$. If M is known then the mixture can be written by specifying only those $\boldsymbol{\alpha}^t$ such that $P(\boldsymbol{\alpha}^t) > 0$.

Letting b_i be the ith such $\boldsymbol{\alpha}^t$ and P_i be the corresponding $P(\boldsymbol{\alpha}^t)$,

$$h(\mathbf{x} \mid \{\mathbf{b}_i, P_i\}_{i=1}^M) = \sum_{i=1}^M f(\mathbf{x} \mid \mathbf{b}_i) P_i$$

Thus for a situation shown below

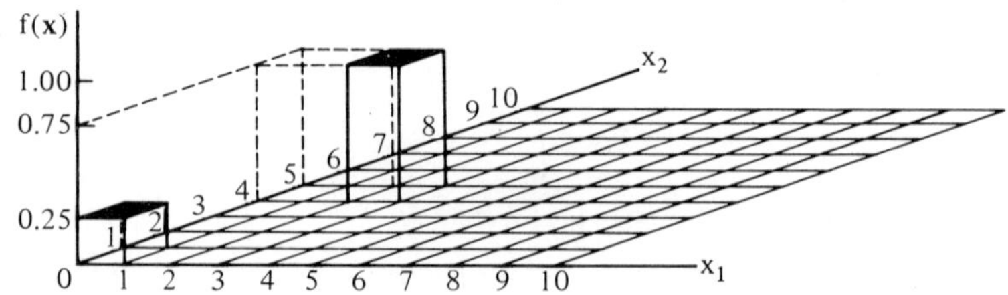

Introduction   *Chap. 1*

where

$$M = 2, \mathbf{b}_1 = [0, 0], P_1 = .25, \mathbf{b}_2 = [2, 4], P_2 = .75,$$

then

$$h(\mathbf{x} \mid \mathbf{b}_1, P_1, \mathbf{b}_2, P_2) = \sum_{i=1}^{2} f(\mathbf{x} \mid \mathbf{b}_i) P_i$$

$$= f(\mathbf{x} \mid [0, 0]) \cdot .25 + f(\mathbf{x} \mid [2, 4]) \cdot .75.$$

If M is unknown but an upper bound M' is known then

$$h(\mathbf{x} \mid \{\mathbf{b}_i, P_i\}_{i=1}^{M'}) = \sum_{i=1}^{M'} f(\mathbf{x} \mid \mathbf{b}_i) P_i$$

where the P_i, $i = M + 1, M + 2, \ldots, M'$, are 0. The number of scalars required to specify a mixture $h(\mathbf{x})$ using $\{\mathbf{b}_i, P_i\}_{i=1}^{M'}$ is $3M'$ (2 for each $\mathbf{b}_i$ and 1 for each P_i). For small M' this approach requires less complexity than

$$h(\mathbf{x} \mid \{P(\boldsymbol{\alpha}^t)\}_{t=0}^{99}) = \sum_{t=0}^{99} f(\mathbf{x} \mid \boldsymbol{\alpha}^t) P(\boldsymbol{\alpha}^t),$$

a representation requiring $N = 100$ scalars $P(\boldsymbol{\alpha}^t)$, $t = 1, 2, \ldots, 100$; the specific values are:

$$P(\boldsymbol{\alpha}^t) = \begin{cases} .25 & t = 0 \\ .75 & t = 24 \\ 0 & \text{otherwise.} \end{cases}$$

On the basis of comparison using storage as the only criterion, the approach using $\{\mathbf{b}_i, P_i\}_{i=1}^{M'}$ is advantageous if $M' \leq 33$. However, there is usually some cost associated with determining $\{\mathbf{b}_i\}_{i=1}^{M'}$ from $\{\boldsymbol{\alpha}^t\}_{t=1}^{N}$ which involves locating the $\boldsymbol{\alpha}^t$ such that $P(\boldsymbol{\alpha}^t) > 0$. Therefore, in reality M' must be sufficiently smaller than that calculated only on the basis of storage to compensate for this extra cost.

1-4 Dependent Samples, Nonstationary Class Probabilities, and Sequence Probabilities

Considerable attention has been given to problems for which samples $\mathbf{x}_1, \mathbf{x}_2, \ldots, \mathbf{x}_n$ are not statistically independent. In this respect the theory of Markoff random processes have been studied in detail. The purpose of this section is not to present material on Markoff processes which can be found elsewhere. Rather we construct the mixture for when the samples are statistically dependent.

It is appropriate to denote M classes by $\omega_1, \omega_2, \ldots, \omega_M$; any one of these classes can be "active to produce" $\mathbf{x}$. For a sequence $\dot{\mathbf{x}}_n$ of n samples, there are $W = M^n$ possible events corresponding to the different ways classes can be active to cause $\dot{\mathbf{x}}_n$.

Let ω_{si} denote the event $\mathbf{x}_s$ is from category i and define the rth possible sequence

$$\pi_r = (\omega^r_{1i}, \omega^r_{2i}, \ldots, \omega^r_{ni}), \qquad r = 1, 2, \ldots, M^n, \tag{1}$$

where $\mathbf{x}_s$ is assumed to be from the category i corresponding to ω^r_{si} in the rth sequence. The events

$$(\dot{\mathbf{x}}_n, \pi_r), \qquad r = 1, 2, \ldots, M^n = W \tag{2}$$

constitute a mutually exclusive and exhaustive partition of the event $\dot{\mathbf{x}}_n$. Thus,

$$H(\dot{\mathbf{x}}_n) = \sum_{r=1}^{W} F(\dot{\mathbf{x}}_n, \pi_r) = \sum_{r=1}^{W} F(\dot{\mathbf{x}}_n \mid \pi_r) P(\pi_r) \tag{3}$$

where $P(\pi_r)$ will be called a *sequence probability*. Let $F(\dot{\mathbf{x}}_n \mid \pi_r)$ be characterized by a vector point $\mathbf{c}^k_r$ and denote the parameter vector point characterizing the mixture (3) by $\mathbf{c}^k$,

$$\mathbf{c}^k = \{\mathbf{c}^k_r, P^k(\pi_r)\}_{r=1}^{W_k}; \tag{4}$$

then

$$H(\dot{\mathbf{x}}_n \mid \mathbf{c}^k) = \sum_{r=1}^{W_k} F(\dot{\mathbf{x}}_n \mid \pi_r, \mathbf{c}^k_r) P^k(\pi_r) \tag{5}$$

is in the class of mixtures for this problem. Similar to the constraints presented in Section 1-3, constraints on $\mathbf{c}^k$ are needed to define an admissible set of parameter points.

For the above formulation it is not assumed that $\mathbf{x}_1, \mathbf{x}_2, \ldots, \mathbf{x}_n$ are parameter conditionally independent or that $P(\omega_i)$ is independent of the samples. The following exercise will prove helpful in understanding the dependencies.

Calculating $P(\omega_{ni})$ in terms of Sequence Probabilities

Denote by $\mathcal{R}$ a subset of the sequences π_r which contains the event ω_{ni}. Thus

$$p(\omega_{ni}) = \sum_{\pi_r \in \mathcal{R}} p(\omega_{ni}, \pi_r) = \sum_{\omega_{ni} \text{ is last entry in } \pi_r} P(\pi_r)$$

which shows that $p(\omega_{ni})$ can be computed in terms of sequence probabilities.

In Section 3-2.5 it is shown that a posteriori density of the fixed but unknown parameters naturally involves the sequence probabilities. Thus the Bayes solution requires that the sequence probabilities be estimated.

As an example, consider the probability of the event ω_{ni} (the event $\mathbf{x}_n$ is from category i) given $\mathbf{x}_1, \mathbf{x}_2, \ldots, \mathbf{x}_n$. If a priori $P(\omega_i) = P_i$ is fixed, then

$$P(\omega_{ni} | \dot{\mathbf{x}}_{n-1}, P_i) = P_i.$$

This assumption that $P(\omega_i) = P_i$ is fixed may not be acceptable; for example suppose that the probability of a rare disease† or an enemy submarine† is $P_i = .0001$ with respect to the relative frequency of occurrence of such a category in "day-to-day life". If samples $\mathbf{x}_n$ currently "favor" the rare disease or an epidemic or enemy submarine, then it may be that $P(\omega_{ni} | \dot{\mathbf{x}}_{n-1}) \gg .0001$.

A difficulty is that in this world of a limited number of n samples, estimation of $F(\dot{\mathbf{x}}_n | \pi_r)$, $P(\pi_r)$, $r = 1, 2, \ldots, W$ may be impractical. Then problem knowledge becomes helpful. A more detailed discussion of sequence probabilities is found in Patrick [17] and in Section 3-2.5.

1-5 Importance of Unsupervised Estimation Even When Category Samples Are Supervised

Suppose there is only one category in the sense that samples from only one pattern category are presented. Then it is still possible that the density function of the category concerned has multiple modes and should be represented by a mixture density. In fact this is one of the most important applications for unsupervised estimation.

If a density function has local regions where the density is high, then it often is important to know the covariance of the density just in each local region. The local covariance is used in this local region for the purpose of measuring distance with a non-Euclidean distance measure.

1-6 Resolving the Mixture

Suppose that $\mathbf{x}$ has density $h(\mathbf{x} | \mathbf{b}^*)$ where

$$h(\mathbf{x} | \mathbf{b}^*) = \sum_{i=1}^{M} f_i(\mathbf{x} | \mathbf{b}_i^*) P_i^*$$

†Computer medical diagnosis involving a sequence of symptoms in the treatment—diagnosis cycle and automatic detection and classification of a sequence of sonar echos are good examples of problems involving sequences.

and the * is used to denote that the parameters are the true parameters. Then, when can we take a function

$$h(\mathbf{x}\,|\,\mathbf{b}) = \sum_{i=1}^{M} f_i(\mathbf{x}\,|\,\mathbf{b}_i)P_i$$

and estimate $\mathbf{b}$ such that the estimate converges to $\mathbf{b}^*$? The technical answer is that this can be done when the family $\mathscr{F}$ is identifiable (see the basic definition of Identifiability by Teicher [18], and subsequent papers by Yakowitz and Spragins [19], and Patrick and Hancock [20]; see Section 1-8).

For example, if $h(\mathbf{x}\,|\,\mathbf{b}^*)$ is a mixture of Gaussian density functions then it can be decomposed into the component Gaussian density functions $f_i(\mathbf{x}\,|\,\mathbf{b}_i^*)$ in only one way. However, suppose we are given $h(\mathbf{x})$ as shown below. In this example, $h(\mathbf{x})$ is a mixture of component densities $f_i(\mathbf{x})$ where each is characterized by a location parameter, amplitude parameter, and duration parameter. It is not in general possible to resolve this mixture.

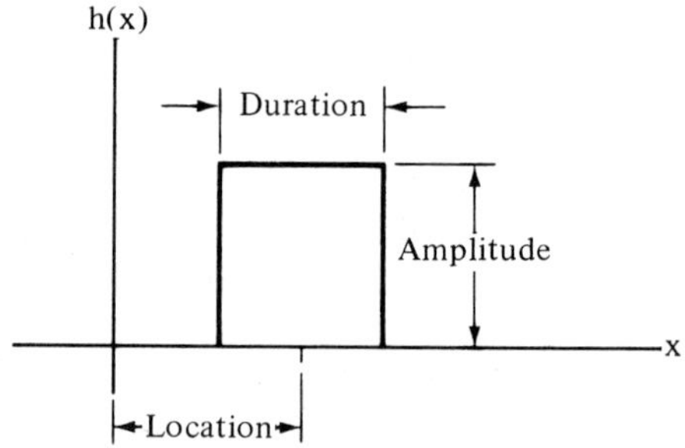

Another problem frequently encountered in practice results because of small sample size. Suppose that the samples shown in Figure 1.6a are actually from a mixture of six Gaussian density functions. Given an infinite number of samples, it would be possible to learn that there are exactly six of these Gaussian members along with their exact locations and the corresponding a priori category probabilities. However, for the small sample size shown, determining that there are six categories without further a priori knowledge is impossible.

1-7 Definition of Unsupervised Estimation

We have illustrated that in order for there to be unsupervised estimation, the distribution of $\mathbf{x}$, $F(\mathbf{x})$, must be a mixture. Furthermore, given n samples $\mathbf{x}_1, \mathbf{x}_2, \ldots, \mathbf{x}_n$, some are from $F(\mathbf{x}\,|\,\boldsymbol{\alpha}^1)$, some from $F(\mathbf{x}\,|\,\boldsymbol{\alpha}^2)$, etc. This implies that in unsupervised estimation we try to decide which samples are from which category, for the purpose of estimating the parameters characterizing that category.

On the other hand, if we are given the form

$$h(\mathbf{x}\,|\,\mathbf{b}) = \sum_{i=1}^{M} f(\mathbf{x}\,|\,\mathbf{b}_i)P_i$$

and asked to estimate $\mathbf{b}$, then some of the same estimation approaches (maximum-likelihood, Bayes's) apply just as when there is no mixture. This would imply that there is no conceptual difference between supervised and unsupervised estimation; however, there is a real and practical difference—complexity. For this reason, clustering techniques that tend to reduce operating complexity constitute a popular unsupervised estimating approach.

Because there can be less a priori knowledge in problems requiring unsupervised estimation, unique estimation procedures may not exist.

1-8 Identifiable Mixtures

1-8.1 Definition for Finite Mixtures

In the context of finite mixtures previously introduced, identifiability means that there is the following uniqueness of representation:

$$\sum_{i=1}^{M} c_i F(\mathbf{x}\,|\,\boldsymbol{\alpha}^i) = \sum_{j=1}^{M'} c'_j F'(\mathbf{x}\,|\,\boldsymbol{\alpha}^j)$$

implies

1. $M = M'$
2. for each i, $1 \leq i \leq M$, there exists uniquely j, $1 \leq j \leq M'$ such that

$$c_i = c'_j \text{ and } F(\mathbf{x}\,|\,\boldsymbol{\alpha}^i) = F'(\mathbf{x}\,|\,\boldsymbol{\alpha}^j).$$

Hereafter, F_i will mean $F(\mathbf{x}\,|\,\boldsymbol{\alpha}^i)$ unless we need to specify the argument, in which case we will write $F_i(\mathbf{x})$.

1-8.2 Conditions for Identifiability

Theorem 1: A necessary and sufficient condition that the class $\mathscr{H}$ of all finite mixtures of the family $\mathscr{F}$ be identifiable is that $\mathscr{F}$ be a linearly independent set over the field of real numbers (Yakowitz and Spragins [19],Teicher [26]).

Proof: Necessity—Let

$$\sum_{i=1}^{N} a_i F_i = 0 \quad \forall \mathbf{x} \in \mathscr{V}_L, \; a_i \text{ real number}$$

be a linear relation in $\mathscr{F}$. Assume that the a_i's are subscripted so that $a_i < 0$ iff $i < M$.

We then have

$$\sum_{i=1}^{M} a_i F_i + \sum_{i=M+1}^{N} a_i F_i = 0 \longrightarrow \sum_{i=1}^{M} |a_i| F_i = \sum_{i=M+1}^{N} |a_i| F_i.$$

Since the F_i are distribution functions (d.f. or c.d.f.), $F_i(\infty) = 1$ so that

$$\sum_{i=1}^{M} |a_i| = \sum_{i=M+1}^{N} |a_i| \triangleq b > 0.$$

Thus if we define $c_i = |a_i|/b$ we have $\sum_{i=1}^{M} c_i' F_i = \sum_{i=M+1}^{N} c_i F_i$. Since $c_i > 0$, $1 \le i \le N$ and since $\sum_{i=1}^{M} c_i = \sum_{i=M+1}^{N} c_i = 1$ the coefficients c_i satisfy the requirements for mixing parameters. The relation $\sum_{i=1}^{M} c_i F_i = \sum_{i=M+1}^{N} c_i F_i$ asserts that there exist two distinct representations of the finite mixture so that $\mathscr{H}$ cannot be identifiable. Since the proof of necessity requires that $\mathscr{H}$ is identifiable, we are led to a contradiction which followed from assuming that the members of the family $\mathscr{F}$ are linearly dependent. Consequently, the conclusion follows that $\mathscr{F}$ is a linearly independent set over the field of real numbers.

Sufficiency.   If $\mathscr{F}$ is a linearly independent set then it is a basis for span $\mathscr{F}$. If there were two distinct representations of the same mixture, implied by the nonidentifiability of $\mathscr{H} \subset \text{span } \mathscr{F}$, this would contradict the unique representation property of a basis. This does not mean that there exists only one representation of the mixture but rather, that given a basis for span $\mathscr{F}$ consisting of $\{F_i\}_{i=1}^{N}$, the relation $H = \sum_{i=1}^{N} c_i F_i = \sum_{i=1}^{N} d_i F_i$ implies $c_i = d_i$, $1 \le i \le N$. This unique representation property of a basis allows the conclusion that $\mathscr{F}$ is a linearly independent set is sufficient for identifiability.

Theorem 2:   A necessary and sufficient condition that the class $\mathscr{H} = \{\sum_{i=1}^{K} c_i F_i(x) : c_i \ge 0, \sum_{i=1}^{K} c_i = 1\}$ of all finite mixtures of the family $\mathscr{F} = \{F_1(\mathbf{x}), \ldots, F_K(\mathbf{x})\}$ be identifiable is that there exist K vectors $\mathbf{x}_1, \mathbf{x}_2, \ldots, \mathbf{x}_K$ for which the determinant of $F_i(\mathbf{x}_j) \; i, j = 1, \ldots, K$ does not vanish.

Although a proof of this theorem is given in Teicher [26] the proof here is based upon results familiar from a study of simultaneous linear equations.

Consider the relation

$$\sum_{i=1}^{K} c_i F_i(\mathbf{x}) \equiv \sum_{i=1}^{K} \hat{c}_i F_i(\mathbf{x})$$

where $\sum_{i=1}^{K} c_i = \sum_{i=1}^{K} \hat{c}_i = 1$. Letting $d_i = c_i - \hat{c}_i$ $i = 1, \ldots, K$ we have $\sum_{i=1}^{K} d_i F_i(\mathbf{x}) \equiv 0$. Since this is true for all $\mathbf{x}$ we surely have $\sum_{i=1}^{K} d_i F_i(\mathbf{x}_j) = 0$ $j = 1, \ldots, K$. In matrix notation this becomes

$$\begin{bmatrix} F_1(\mathbf{x}_1) & \cdots & F_K(\mathbf{x}_1) \\ F_1(\mathbf{x}_2) & \cdots & \\ \cdot & & \cdot \\ \cdot & & \cdot \\ \cdot & & \cdot \\ F_1(\mathbf{x}_K) & \cdots & F_K(\mathbf{x}_K) \end{bmatrix} \cdot \begin{bmatrix} d_1 \\ \cdot \\ \cdot \\ \cdot \\ d_K \end{bmatrix} = \mathbf{0}$$

or $\mathbf{F}\mathbf{d} = \mathbf{0}$.

By hypothesis det $\mathbf{F} \neq 0$ so that the only solution is $\mathbf{d} = \mathbf{0}$, i.e. $c_i = \hat{c}_i$, $i = 1, \ldots, K$. From this we conclude that $\mathscr{H}$ is identifiable.

Proof of Necessity

Similarly, the hypothesis of identifiability requires that

$$\sum_{i=1}^{K} c_i F_i(\mathbf{x}) \equiv \sum_{i=1}^{K} \hat{c}_i F_i(\mathbf{x})$$

imply that $c_i = \hat{c}_i$ $i = 1, \ldots, K$. Thus the matrix equation becomes

$$\begin{bmatrix} F_1(x_1) & \cdots & F_K(x_1) \\ \cdot & \cdot & \\ \cdot & \cdot & \\ \cdot & & \\ F_1(x_K) & & F_K(x_K) \end{bmatrix} \cdot \begin{bmatrix} c_1 - \hat{c}_1 \\ \cdot \\ \cdot \\ \cdot \\ c_K - \hat{c}_K \end{bmatrix} = \mathbf{0}$$

To assure a unique solution, namely $c_i = \hat{c}_i$ $i = 1, \ldots, K$ we must have det $\mathbf{F} \neq 0$.

The following Theorem is useful for determining whether a particular family is identifiable (Teicher [26]).

Theorem 3: Let $\mathscr{F} = \{F_i\}$ be a family of cdf's with transforms $\varphi_i(t)$ defined for $t \in S_{\varphi_i}$ (the domain of φ_i) such that the map $M : F_i \longrightarrow \varphi_i$ is linear and one-to-one. Suppose that there exists a total ordering of the F_i's such that $F_i < F_j$ implies

1. $S_{\varphi_i} \subseteq S_{\varphi_j}$
2. the existence of some $t_1 \in \bar{S}_{\varphi_i}$ ($\bar{A}$ denotes the closure of A), t_1 independent of φ_j, such that

$$\lim_{t \to t_1} \frac{\varphi_j(t)}{\varphi_i(t)} = 0.$$

Then the class $\mathcal{H}$ of all finite mixtures of $\mathcal{F}$ is identifiable.

Proof: Suppose that there are two finite sets of elements of $\mathcal{F}$, for example, $\mathcal{F}_1 = \{F_i, 1 \le i \le K\}$ and $\mathcal{F}_2 = \{\hat{F}_j, 1 \le j \le \hat{K}\}$ such that

$$\sum_{i=1}^{K} c_i F_i \equiv \sum_{j=1}^{\hat{K}} \hat{c}_j \hat{F}_j, \quad 0 < c_i, \hat{c}_j \le 1,$$

and

$$\sum_{i=1}^{K} c_i = \sum_{j=1}^{\hat{K}} \hat{c}_j = 1.$$

Without loss of generality index the cdf's so that $F_i < F_j$, $\hat{F}_i < \hat{F}_j$ for $i < j$. If $F_1 \neq \hat{F}_1$ suppose that $F_1 \le \hat{F}_1$. Then $F_1 < \hat{F}_j$, $1 \le j \le \hat{K}$. Transforming both sides of

$$\sum_{i=1}^{K} c_i F_i \equiv \sum_{j=1}^{\hat{K}} \hat{c}_j \hat{F}_j$$

we have

$$\sum_{i=1}^{K} c_i \varphi_i(t) \equiv \sum_{j=1}^{\hat{K}} \hat{c}_j \hat{\varphi}_j(t)$$

which may be written as

$$c_1 + \sum_{i=2}^{K} c_i \frac{\varphi_i(t)}{\varphi_1(t)} \equiv \sum_{j=1}^{\hat{K}} \hat{c}_j \frac{\hat{\varphi}_j(t)}{\varphi_1(t)}.$$

Let $T_1 = S_{\varphi_1} \cap \{t \mid \varphi_1(t) \neq 0\}$ and note that as $t \to t_1$ we have $c_1 = 0$ which contradicts the assumption that $c_i > 0$ so that we must have $F_1 = \hat{F}_1$. Thus we may write

$$(c_1 - \hat{c}_1) + \sum_{i=2}^{K} c_i \frac{\varphi_i(t)}{\varphi_1(t)} \equiv \sum_{j=2}^{\hat{K}} \hat{c}_j \frac{\hat{\varphi}_j(t)}{\varphi_1(t)}.$$

Again, letting $t \to t_1$ in T_1 we have $c_1 = \hat{c}_1$ so that

$$\sum_{i=2}^{K} c_i F_i \equiv \sum_{j=2}^{\hat{K}} \hat{c}_j \hat{F}_i.$$

Continuing this procedure a finite number of times we conclude that $F_i = \hat{F}_i$ and $c_i = \hat{c}_i$ for $i = 1, 2, \ldots, \min\{K, \hat{K}\}$.

Now if $K \neq \hat{K}$ we assume $\hat{K} < K$ so that

$$\sum_{i=\hat{K}+1}^{K} c_i F_i \equiv 0$$

from which we have $c_i = 0$ for $\hat{K} + 1 \leq i \leq K$ again contradicting the assumptions so that we must have $K = \hat{K}$. Thus $c_i = \hat{c}_i$, $F_i = \hat{F}_i$ and $K = \hat{K}$, $1 \leq i \leq K$ so that $\mathscr{F}_1 = \mathscr{F}_2$ and identifiability ensues.

1-8.3 Identifiable Families

Using Theorem 3 we can easily investigate the identifiability of several common families.

Proposition 1 The class of all finite mixtures of Gamma distributions is identifiable.

Proof: The cdf is given by $F(x\,|\,\theta, \alpha) = \theta^{\alpha}[\Gamma(\alpha)]^{-1} \int_0^x y^{\alpha-1} e^{-\theta y}\,dy$, $\quad \alpha, \theta > 0$. The Laplace transform is

$$\varphi(t;\theta, \alpha) = \left(1 + \frac{t}{\theta}\right)^{-\alpha} \quad \text{for } t > -\theta.$$

In accordance with the Theorem we will order these by

$$F_1(x\,|\,\theta_1, \alpha_1) < F_2(x\,|\,\theta_2, \alpha_2)$$

if

1. $\theta_1 < \theta_2$ or
2. $\theta_1 = \theta_2$ but $\alpha_1 > \alpha_2$.

Then $S_{\varphi_1} = (-\theta_1, \infty) \leq (-\theta_2, \infty) = S_{\varphi_2}$ and

$$\lim_{t \to -\theta_1} \frac{\varphi_2(t;\theta_2, \alpha_2)}{\varphi_1(t;\theta_1, \alpha_1)} = \lim_{t \to -\theta_1} \frac{(1 + t/\theta_2)^{-\alpha_2}}{(1 + t/\theta_1)^{-\alpha_1}} = 0.$$

Thus theorem 3 is applicable.

Proposition 2 The class of all finite mixtures of one dimension normal distributions is identifiable.

Proof: Let $N = N(x\,|\,\theta, \sigma^2)$ denote the normal cdf with mean θ and variance σ^2. The Laplace transform of N is $\varphi(t\,|\,\theta, \sigma^2) = \exp\left[(\sigma^2 t^2)/2 - \theta t\right]$. Again, according to the Theorem we will order the family by $N_1 = N(x|\theta_1, \sigma_1^2) < N(x|\theta_2, \sigma_2^2) = N_2$ if

1. $\sigma_1 > \sigma_2$ or
2. $\theta_1 < \theta_2$ if $\sigma_1 = \sigma_2$.

If we let $S_\varphi = (-\infty, \infty)$ and $t_1 = +\infty$ we see that

$$\lim_{t \to +\infty} \frac{\varphi_2(t)}{\varphi_1(t)} = \lim_{t \to \infty} \frac{\exp\left[(\sigma_2^2 t^2)/2 - \theta_2 t\right]}{\exp\left[(\sigma_1^2 t^2)/2 - \theta_1 t\right]}$$

$$= \lim_{t \to \infty} \exp\left[\frac{t^2}{2}(\sigma_2^2 - \sigma_1^2) + t(\theta_1 - \theta_2)\right]$$

$$= 0 \quad \text{if } \sigma_1 > \sigma_2 \text{ or if } \sigma_1 = \sigma_2 \text{ and } \theta_2 > \theta_1.$$

Thus Theorem 3 is applicable.

Using this result we will now show that the L-dimensional Gaussian family is identifiable.

Proposition 3   The family $\mathscr{F}$ of L-dimensional Gaussian cdf's generates identifiable finite mixtures.

Proof: Suppose $\mathscr{F}$ is not identifiable. Let $\mathbf{m}_i$ denote the mean vector and let $\boldsymbol{\Sigma}_i$ denote the covariance matrix. The nonidentifiability of $\mathscr{F}$, in terms of moment generating functions (the mgf of the multivariate Gaussian is $\varphi(\mathbf{t}) = \exp\left[\mathbf{t'm} + \frac{1}{2}\mathbf{t'\Sigma t}\right]$ where $\mathbf{t'}$ denotes the transpose of the L-dimensional column vector $\mathbf{t}$ for purposes of this proof) means that for some $K \geq 1$,

$$\sum_{j=1}^{K} d_j \exp\left[\mathbf{t'm}_j + \frac{1}{2}\mathbf{t'\Sigma}_j\mathbf{t}\right] \equiv 0$$

where the pairs $(\boldsymbol{\Sigma}_j, \mathbf{m}_j)$ are all distinct. Letting $\mathbf{t} = c\mathbf{u}$ with c a scalar we have

$$\sum_{j=1}^{K} d_j \exp\left[\left(\frac{c^2}{2}\right)\mathbf{u'\Sigma}_j\mathbf{u} + c\mathbf{u'm}_j\right] \equiv 0.$$

If all the $\boldsymbol{\Sigma}_j$, $1 \leq j \leq K$ are identical, all $\mathbf{m}_j$ $1 \leq j \leq K$ are distinct. Thus, for all $\mathbf{u}$ outside of those on a finite number of hyperplanes, the pairs of real numbers $(\mathbf{u'\Sigma}_j\mathbf{u}, \mathbf{u'm}_j)$ $1 \leq j \leq K$ are distinct. Now, if all the $\boldsymbol{\Sigma}_j$ are not identical then without loss of generality assume that $\boldsymbol{\Sigma}_1, \ldots, \boldsymbol{\Sigma}_j$ are the only distinct matrices among $\boldsymbol{\Sigma}_1, \ldots, \boldsymbol{\Sigma}_K$. Then for $\mathbf{u}$ not lying on a finite number of conics, the real numbers $\mathbf{u'\Sigma}_i\mathbf{u}$ $1 \leq i \leq j$ are all distinct. By assumption all of the pairs $(\boldsymbol{\Sigma}_i, \mathbf{m}_i)$ are distinct so that the $\mathbf{m}_i$ associated with the $\boldsymbol{\Sigma}_i$ $1 \leq i \leq j$ are distinct. Thus, outside a finite number of hyperplanes the corresponding numbers $\mathbf{u'm}_i$ are all distinct. Thus for $\mathbf{u}$ not lying on a certain finite number of conics or hyperplanes the pairs of real numbers $(\mathbf{u'\Sigma}_i\mathbf{u}, \mathbf{u'm}_i)$ $1 \le i \le K$ are distinct. But for such a choice of $\mathbf{u}$, the condition

$$\sum_{i=1}^{K} d_i \exp\left[\left(\frac{c^2}{2}\right)\mathbf{u'\Sigma}_i\mathbf{u} + c\mathbf{u'm}_i\right] \equiv 0$$

implies the nonidentifiability of the class of finite mixtures of one dimensional normal distributions, contrary to proposition 2.

The following is a list of some additional known results concerning identifiability:

1. The set of all finite mixtures of the family of Cauchy densities is identifiable. The proof is found in the literature [18, 19, 26].

2. The family of all non-degenerate negative binomial distributions induces an identifiable set of finite mixtures.

Proof: The negative binomial density is

$$f(x; p, r) = \binom{r + x - 1}{r - 1} p^r q^x$$

where $q = 1 - p, r > 0, \ 0 \le p < 1$. The generating function is $[p/(1 - qt)]^r$. If we order the functions as $f_1 < f_2$ if

1) $p_2 > p_1$ or
2) $p_2 = p_1$ and $r_2 < r_1$

then

$$S_{\varphi_1} = \{t : (1 - p_1)^{-1} > |t|\} \subset \{t : (1 - p_2)^{-1} > |t|\} = S_{\varphi_2}.$$

If $t_1 \triangleq (1 - p_1)^{-1} = q_1^{-1}$ then

$$\lim_{t \to t_1} \frac{\varphi_2(t)}{\varphi_1(t)} = \lim_{t \to t_1} \frac{p_2^{r_2}(1 - q_1 t)^{r_1}}{p_1^{r_1}(1 - q_2 t)^{r_2}} = 0$$

so that Theorem 3 is applicable.

3. Let $\mathscr{F} = \{F(\mathbf{x}\,|\,\boldsymbol{\alpha}^i)\}$ be a finite family of L-dimensional normal cdf's with $\boldsymbol{\alpha}^i = (\mathbf{m}_i, \boldsymbol{\Sigma}_i)$ where $\mathbf{m}_i = (m_{i1}, m_{i2}, \ldots, m_{in})$ is the mean vector and $\boldsymbol{\Sigma}_i = [\sigma^i_{jK}]$ is the covariance matrix. If the family is ordered as $N_1 < N_2 < \cdots < N_m$ if
   1) $\sigma^1_{11} > \sigma^2_{11}, \ldots, \sigma^K_{KK} > \sigma^{K+1}_{KK}, \ldots$ or

$\qquad$ 2) $\quad \sigma_{KK}^{K} = \sigma_{KK}^{K+1}$ but $m_{K+1,K} > m_{KK}$

then the family is identifiable, since Theorem 3 applies with $S_{\varphi_i} = (-\infty, \infty)$ $i = 1, \ldots, M$ and $\mathbf{t} = (\infty, t_2, \ldots, t_l)$ $t_2, \ldots, t_l$ finite.

4. Let $\mathscr{F} = \{\mathbf{x}; v_i, \{p_j^i\}_{j=1}^{R}, 0 < p_j^i < 1, i = 1, 2, \ldots, M\}$ be a family of multinomial cdf's for v_i fixed and where R is the number of probabilities characterizing the cdf. Here v_i is the number of samples from the same class i in sequence. That is, it is known that when a sample $\mathbf{x}_1$ comes from class i, a sequence $\mathbf{x}_1, \mathbf{x}_2, \ldots, \mathbf{x}_v$ will come from class i. A sufficient condition that the class of all finite mixtures of at most M elements of $\mathscr{F}$ be identifiable is that $v_i \geq 2M - 1$ (Patrick and Hancock [20]).

The above condition is not necessary. Although no analytical results are available, it is expected that the requirement $v \geq 2M - 1$ will be relaxed with increasing a priori knowledge concerning relationships among the $p_j^i, j = 1, 2, \ldots, R$, for each class i. For example, when $R \longrightarrow \infty$ and the p_j^i are related Gaussian, we know that $v = 1$ is sufficient. As another example, suppose p_j^i is the probability in the jth bin of an L-dimensional histogram for class i; then there are many examples for which the respective classes are separable (do not have common bins with positive mass) where the mixture is identifiable with $v = 1$.

Comment: At this time, many of the practical problems in pattern recognition are made identifiable through the existence of sufficient a priori knowledge to make the component distributions separated.

In disease definition, however, there is considerable doubt that many diseases are correctly defined in terms of symptoms. For example, is the family of liver diseases consisting of so called hepatitis, cirrhosis, and chronic obstruction identifiable? If not, what should be the definitions of component diseases?

Suggested Reading for Chapter 1

[1] R. V. Churchill, *Fourier Series and Boundary Value Problems*, McGraw-Hill Book Company, Inc., New York, 1963.

[2] J. M. Wozencraft and I. M. Jacobs, *Principles of Communication Engineering*, John Wiley & Sons, Inc., New York, 1965, Chap. V.

[3] A. Papoulis, *Probability, Random Variables, and Stochastic Processes*, McGraw-Hill Book Company, Inc., New York, 1965, Chap. 10.

[4] G. R. Cooper, and C. D. McGillem, *Methods of Signal and System Analysis*, Holt Rheinhart & Winston HRW Series in EE, Electronics & Systems, 1967, Chap. 3.

[5] R. V. Churchill, *Complex Variables and Applications*, 2nd ed., McGraw-Hill Book Company, Inc., New York, 1960.

[6] W. B. Davenport, and W. L. Root, *An Introduction to the Theory of Random Signals and Noise*, McGraw-Hill Book Company, Inc., New York, 1958.

[7] M. Schwartz, *Information Transmission, Modulation, and Noise*, McGraw-Hill Book Company, Inc., New York, 1959.

[8] R. V. Hogg and A. T. Craig, *Introduction to Mathematical Statistics*, The Macmillian Company, New York, 1965.

[9] W. Rudin, *Real and Complex Analysis*, McGraw-Hill Book Company, Inc., New York, 1966.

[10] N. J. Nilsson, *Learning Machines*, McGraw-Hill Book Company, Inc., New York, 1965.

[11] G. Nagy, State of the Art in Pattern Recognition, *Proc. IEEE*, Vol. 56, No. 5, pp. 836–862, May 1968.

[12] G. S. Sebestyen, *Decision Making Process in Pattern Recognition*, The Macmillan Company, New York, 1962.

[13] Y.-C. Ho and A. K. Agrawala, On Pattern Classification Algorithms— Introduction and Survey, *Proc. IEEE*, Vol. 56, No. 12, pp. 2101–2114, Dec. 1968.

[14] Special Issue on Technology and Health Services, *Proc. IEEE*, Vol. 57, No. 11, 1969.

[15] H. L. Van Trees, *Detection, Estimation, and Modulation Theory*, John Wiley & Sons, Inc., New York, 1968.

[16] E. A. Patrick, and J. P. Costello, On Unsupervised Estimation Problems, *IEEE Trans. Information Theory*, Vol. IT-16, No. 5, pp. 556–569, Sept. 1970.

[17] E. A. Patrick, On a Class of Unsupervised Estimation Systems, *IEEE Trans. Information Theory*, Vol. IT-14, pp. 407–415, May 1968.

[18] H. Teicher, Identifiability of Product Measures, *Ann. Math. Statistics*, Vol. 38, No. 4, pp. 1300–1302, Aug. 1967.

[19] S. Yakowitz, and J. Spragins, On the Identifiability of Finite Mixtures, *Ann. Math. Statistics*, Vol. 39, No. 1, pp. 209–214, 1968.

[20] E. A. Patrick and J. C. Hancock, Non-Supervised Sequential Classification and Recognition of Patterns, *IEEE Trans. Information Theory*, Vol. IT-12, No. 3, pp. 362–372, July 1966.

[21] L. Kanal, ed., *Pattern Recognition*, Thompson Book Co., Washington, D.C., 1968.

[22] L. M. Uhr, *Pattern Recognition Theory:* theory, simulations, and dynamic models of form perception and discovery, N. Y., Wiley, 1966.

[23] G. C. Cheng, J. Y. Pollock, R. S. Ledley and A. Rosenfeld, eds., Symposium on Automatic Photo Interpretation, Wash. D.C., 1967. *Pictorial Pattern Recog. Proc.*, Thompson Book Co., Washington, D.C., 1968.

[24] H. Teicher, On the Mixture of Distributions, *Ann. Math. Statistics*, Vol. 31, pp 55–73, 1960.

[25] H. Teicher, Identifiability of Mixtures, *Ann. Math. Statistics*, Vol. 32, pp 244–248, 1961.

[26] H. Teicher, Identifiability of Finite Mixtures, *Ann. Math. Statistics*, Vol. 34, pp 1265–1269, Dec. 1963.

Problems

[1] (a) Show that the vectors $\boldsymbol{\varphi}_n = e^{i2\pi n t}$, $-\infty < n < +\infty$, form an orthonormal set in $L_2(0, 1)$ using the inner product $(\mathbf{f}, \mathbf{g}) = \int_0^1 f(t)\overline{g(t)}\, dt$, where $\mathbf{f} = f(t)$, $0 < t < 1$, $\mathbf{g} = g(t)$, $0 < t < 1$.

(b) Expand the vector $\mathbf{a} = a(t) = a_1 \sin 2\pi k_1 t + a_2 \cos 2\pi k_2 t$, $0 < t < 1$, in terms of the vectors $\{\boldsymbol{\varphi}_n\}_{n=-\infty}^{\infty}$ from part (a).

[2] Prove the projection proposition.

[3] Show that the denominators in the Gram–Schmidt process are never zero if the original vectors are linearly independent.

[4] Find the two-dimensional Fourier transform of the rectangular picture defined as

$$f(x, y) = \begin{cases} 1, & -w \le x \le w, \ -h \le y \le h, \\ 0, & \text{elsewhere.} \end{cases}$$

The two-dimensional Fourier transform is defined as

$$F(jw, ju) = \int_{-\infty}^{\infty} \int_{-\infty}^{\infty} f(x, y) e^{-(jwx + juy)}\, dx\, dy.$$

Sketch your result.

[5] Find the two-dimensional Fourier transform of the picture defined by

$$f(x, y) = \begin{cases} 1, & 0 < x^2 + y^2 \le R^2, \\ 0, & \text{elsewhere.} \end{cases}$$

Sketch your results.

[6] Span $(\mathbf{x}_1, \mathbf{x}_2, \ldots, \mathbf{x}_L) = \{\mathbf{v} \in \mathcal{V} : \mathbf{v} = a_1\mathbf{x}_1 + a_2\mathbf{x}_2 + \cdots + a_L\mathbf{x}_L\}$ is a linear manifold spanned by $\mathbf{x}_1, \mathbf{x}_2, \ldots, \mathbf{x}_L$.

(a) Show that this linear manifold can be spanned by L other vectors.
(b) Can this linear manifold be spanned by more than L other vectors?
(c) Can this linear manifold be spanned by less than L other vectors?

[7] Show that the zero vector and $\mathcal{V}$ are linear manifolds in $\mathcal{V}$.

[8] Show that $\mathcal{P}_l$ is a linear manifold in $\mathcal{P}_L$ for $l \le L$.

[9] Show that span $(\mathbf{x}_1, \mathbf{x}_2, \ldots, \mathbf{x}_L)$ can be spanned by less than L vectors if $\mathbf{x}_1, \mathbf{x}_2, \ldots, \mathbf{x}_L$ are linearly dependent.

[10] (a) Is $[1, 1, 1, \ldots] \in \mathscr{E}_\infty$?
(b) Is $[1, 1/\sqrt{2}, 1/\sqrt{3}, \ldots] \in \mathscr{E}_\infty$?
(c) Is $[1, \frac{1}{2}, \frac{1}{3}, \ldots] \in \mathscr{E}_\infty$?

[11] The observation vector $\mathbf{x}$ is one-dimensional and is from a mixture of five density functions, where the ith member density function has the Gaussian

form

$$f(x \mid m_i, \sigma_i) = \frac{1}{\sqrt{2\pi}\sigma_i} \exp\left[-\frac{(x - m_i)^2}{2\sigma_i^2}\right].$$

(a) What is L, M, and the family $\mathscr{F}$?

(b) Show, in general, that if $(\mathbf{x}, i)$, $i = 1, 2, \ldots, M$, are mutually exclusive and exhaustive events, then

$$f(\mathbf{x}) = \sum_{i=1}^{M} f(\mathbf{x}, i) P(i).$$

(c) For the family $\mathscr{F}$ under consideration, with reference to the form

$$f(\mathbf{x} \mid \mathbf{b}) = \sum_{i=1}^{M} f(\mathbf{x} \mid i, \mathbf{b}_i) P_i,$$

what is $\mathbf{b}_i$ and what is $\mathbf{b}$?

(d) What are the constraints on the parameters in $\mathbf{b}$?

[12] Suppose that for part (a) in Problem 11 we are given n statistically independent and identically distributed samples $\mathbf{x}_1, \mathbf{x}_2, \ldots, \mathbf{x}_n$ with density $f(\mathbf{x})$.

(a) What parameters could we try to estimate using these samples?

(b) Are the samples supervised or unsupervised? How many categories are there?

[13] Suppose that there are M categories having respective densities $f_i(\mathbf{x})$, $i = 1, 2, \ldots, M$. If each category density is itself a mixture of multivariate Gaussian densities, then

$$f_i(\mathbf{x}) = \sum_{j=1}^{M_i} f(\mathbf{x} \mid \mathbf{m}_{ij}, \Sigma_{ij}) p(j \mid i), \qquad i = 1, 2, \ldots, M.$$

(a) What is the form of the density of $\mathbf{x}$, denoted $h(\mathbf{x})$?

(b) Suppose that we are given n statistically independent and identically distributed samples $\mathbf{x}_1, \mathbf{x}_2, \ldots, \mathbf{x}_n$ from $h(\mathbf{x})$. Are they supervised or unsupervised?

(c) Suppose that we have n_i samples from $f_i(\mathbf{x})$; in what sense are they unsupervised?

[14] Suppose that there are M categories having respective densities $f_i(\mathbf{x})$, $i = 1, 2, \ldots, M$, and prior probabilities P_i, $i = 1, 2, \ldots, M$. Let $f_i(\mathbf{x})$ be characterized by the parameter point $\mathbf{b}_i$. The vector of fixed but unknown parameters is $\mathbf{b} = \{\mathbf{b}_i, P_i\}_{i=1}^{M}$.

(a) Discuss the difference between the parameter point [Eq. (7) of Section 1-3]

$$\mathbf{b}^k = \{\mathbf{b}_i^k, P_i^k\}_{i=1}^{M_k},$$

and the parameter point $\mathbf{b}_i$, which characterizes the ith class.

(b) Suppose that

$$\mathbf{b} = [\mathbf{b}_1, \mathbf{b}_2, \ldots, \mathbf{b}_M, P_1, P_2, \ldots, P_M]$$

and a criterion

$$\eta(\mathbf{b}) = E[\ln h(\mathbf{x}\,|\,\mathbf{b})] = \int \ln h(\mathbf{x}\,|\,\mathbf{b})h(\mathbf{x}\,|\,\mathbf{b}^*)\,d\mathbf{x}$$

has a unique maximum $\eta(\mathbf{b}^*)$ when $\mathbf{b} = \mathbf{b}^*$ (including $M = M^*$). Briefly suggest how $\eta(\mathbf{b})$ might be used to produce an estimator for $\mathbf{b}^*$.

(c) If we are given n samples $\mathbf{x}_1, \mathbf{x}_2, \ldots, \mathbf{x}_n$, then

$$\hat{\eta}(\mathbf{b}) = \frac{1}{n} \sum_{s=1}^{n} \ln h(\mathbf{x}_s\,|\,\mathbf{b})$$

may be a good estimate of $\eta(\mathbf{b})$. Why?

(d) Suppose that $h(\mathbf{x})$ is the density of $\mathbf{x}$, but we also say that the density is characterized by the true parameter point $\mathbf{b}^*$ and denote the density $h(\mathbf{x}\,|\,\mathbf{b}^*)$. Then, presumably, $h(\mathbf{x}) = h(\mathbf{x}\,|\,\mathbf{b}^*)$. Discuss the meanings of $h(\mathbf{x})$ and $h(\mathbf{x}\,|\,\mathbf{b}^*)$ and the above equality. Is one representation parametric and the other representation nonparametric?

[15] The notation $p(\mathbf{x}\,|\,\boldsymbol{\alpha})$ means the probability of $\mathbf{x}$ given $\boldsymbol{\alpha}$. The notation $p(\mathbf{x};\boldsymbol{\alpha})$ means the probability of $\mathbf{x}$ that is a function of the parameter vector $\boldsymbol{\alpha}$.

(a) Suppose we are given $p(\mathbf{x}\,|\,\boldsymbol{\alpha})$ and $p(\boldsymbol{\alpha})$. Compute, using, Bayes's theorem, $p(\boldsymbol{\alpha}\,|\,\mathbf{x})$.

(b) The computation of $p(\boldsymbol{\alpha}\,|\,\mathbf{x})$ above required $p(\mathbf{x}\,|\,\boldsymbol{\alpha})$. Discuss, at this point, why $p(\mathbf{x};\boldsymbol{\alpha})$ may or may not be better notation than $p(\mathbf{x}\,|\,\boldsymbol{\alpha})$.

[16] Discuss the application of Bayes's theorem,

$$f(\mathbf{b}\,|\,\dot{\mathbf{x}}_n) = \frac{f(\dot{\mathbf{x}}_n\,|\,\mathbf{b})f(\mathbf{b})}{f(\dot{\mathbf{x}}_n)},$$

and the fact that a value for $\mathbf{b}$ *is being tried* in $f(\dot{\mathbf{x}}_n\,|\,\mathbf{b})$, even though $\mathbf{b}$ is unknown.

[17] Suppose that $h(\mathbf{x})$ is a mixture of one-dimensional Gaussian functions with known variances,

$$f(x\,|\,\boldsymbol{\alpha}_i) = \frac{1}{\sqrt{2\pi\sigma}} \exp\left[-\frac{1}{2}(x - m_i)^2/\sigma^2\right],$$

where $\boldsymbol{\alpha}_i = m_i$ because σ is known. Then

$$h(x\,|\,P_1, P_2, \ldots, P_N) = \sum_{j=1}^{N} \frac{P_i}{\sqrt{2\pi\sigma}} \exp\left[-\frac{1}{2}(x - m_i)^2/\sigma^2\right].$$

(a) Suppose that functions $\varphi_i(\mathbf{x})$ derived from $\{f(\mathbf{x}\,|\,\boldsymbol{\alpha}^i)\}_{i=1}^{N}$ are available such that $P_i = \int \varphi_i(\mathbf{x})h(\mathbf{x})\,d\mathbf{x}$ (see Problem 19†). Suggest estimators for P_i using $\varphi_i(\mathbf{x})$, $i = 1, 2, \ldots, N$.

†The reader may also refer to Section 5-3.8, where the functions $\varphi_i(\mathbf{x})$ are derived and called Robbin's functions.

(b) Why is the approach suggested in (a) impractical for large N?

(c) Suppose that we know that m_i is one of the integers $1, 2, 3, \ldots, 1000$. What is N?

(d) If we know $M = 2$, $\sigma = 1$, $P_1 = P_2 = \frac{1}{2}$, and $|m_2 - m_1| = 50$, suggest estimators for m_1 and m_2.

(e) Suppose that we know $M = 2$ and, with complete generality, $m_1 < m_2$. Specify all the constraints on Eq. (5) of Section 1-3.

[18] Let $\mathbf{x}_1, \mathbf{x}_2, \ldots, \mathbf{x}_n$ be samples from $h(\mathbf{x})$,

$$h(\mathbf{x} \mid P_1, P_2, \ldots, P_N) = \sum_{i=1}^{N} f(\mathbf{x} \mid \boldsymbol{\alpha}^i) P_i,$$

but $P_1, P_2, \ldots, P_N$ are unknown. At most there are M' nonzero mixing parameters, $P_1, P_2, \ldots, P_N$, and the true number is M.

(a) Convince yourself that the functions $f(\mathbf{x} \mid \boldsymbol{\alpha}^i)$ are known and, even so, that this is an unsupervised estimation problem.

(b) Suppose that with sample $\mathbf{x}_s$ you are given a parameter vector $\boldsymbol{\alpha}^i$ with the knowledge that $\mathbf{x}_s$ is from $f(\mathbf{x} \mid \boldsymbol{\alpha}^i)$. Is this a supervised estimation problem? Does $P_i =$ the relative number of samples from $f(\mathbf{x} \mid \boldsymbol{\alpha}^i)$?

(c) If functions $\varphi_i(\mathbf{x})$ derived from $\{f(\mathbf{x} \mid \boldsymbol{\alpha}^i)\}_{i=1}^{N}$ are available (see Problem 19) considering the relationship $P_i = \int \varphi_i(\mathbf{x}) h(\mathbf{x}) \, d\mathbf{x}$, we could form the estimators

$$\hat{P}_i = \frac{1}{n} \sum_{s=1}^{n} \varphi_i(\mathbf{x}_s)$$

and a decision rule: Decide $\mathbf{x}$ from $f(\mathbf{x} \mid \boldsymbol{\alpha}^a)$ if

$$\hat{P}_a f(\mathbf{x} \mid \boldsymbol{\alpha}^a) = \max_i \{\hat{P}_i f(\mathbf{x} \mid \boldsymbol{\alpha}^i)\}_{i=1}^{N}.$$

Are we concluding that unsupervised estimation basically is a decision-making problem?

[19] Given $f(\mathbf{x} \mid \boldsymbol{\alpha}^1), f(\mathbf{x} \mid \boldsymbol{\alpha}^2), \ldots, f(\mathbf{x} \mid \boldsymbol{\alpha}^N)$, define

$$\varphi_i(\mathbf{x}) = \frac{f^{\perp}(\mathbf{x} \mid \boldsymbol{\alpha}^i)}{\|f^{\perp}(\mathbf{x} \mid \boldsymbol{\alpha}^i)\|^2}, \qquad i = 1, 2, \ldots, N,$$

where $f^{\perp}(\mathbf{x} \mid \boldsymbol{\alpha}^i)$ is the component of $f(\mathbf{x} \mid \boldsymbol{\alpha}^i)$ in the subspace orthogonal to the subspace spanned by $\{f(\mathbf{x}) \mid \boldsymbol{\alpha}^j)\}_{\substack{j=1 \\ j \neq i}}^{N}$.

(a) Show that

$$\int \varphi_j(\mathbf{x}) f^{\perp}(\mathbf{x} \mid \boldsymbol{\alpha}^i) \, d\mathbf{x} = \delta_{ji},$$

where

$$\delta_{ji} = \begin{cases} 1, & j = i, \\ 0, & j \neq i. \end{cases}$$

(b) Using the result from (a) show that

$$P_i = \int \varphi_i(\mathbf{x}) h(\mathbf{x}) \, d\mathbf{x}.$$

[20] It has been conjectured that the only difference between supervised estimation and unsupervised estimation is a degree of a priori knowledge and a degree of complexity.
(a) Elaborate.
(b) Suppose M, $\mathbf{b}_1, \mathbf{b}_2, \ldots, \mathbf{b}_{M-1}$, $P_1, P_2, \ldots, P_M$ and $\mathscr{F}$ are all known, where

$$h(\mathbf{x}\,|\,\mathbf{b}) = \sum_{i=1}^{M} f(\mathbf{x}\,|\,\mathbf{b}_i) P_i,$$

but we do not care about associating $f(\mathbf{x}\,|\,\mathbf{b}_i)$ with the concept of a category. All we wish to accomplish is to estimate $\mathbf{b}$. Is this an unsupervised estimation problem?

[21] (a) Show that if the functions $f(\mathbf{x}\,|\,\boldsymbol{\alpha}^1), f(\mathbf{x}\,|\,\boldsymbol{\alpha}^2), \ldots, f(\mathbf{x}\,|\,\boldsymbol{\alpha}^N)$ are linearly independent, then all functions $\varphi_1(\mathbf{x}), \varphi_2(\mathbf{x}), \ldots, \varphi_N(\mathbf{x})$ defined in Problem 19 are nonzero. Otherwise, one or more of the $\varphi_i(\mathbf{x})$ functions is identically zero for all $\mathbf{x} \in \mathscr{X}$.
(b) Show that if the functions $f(\mathbf{x}\,|\,\boldsymbol{\alpha}^i) \subset \mathscr{F}$, $i = 1, 2, \ldots, N$, are linearly independent, then an $h(\mathbf{x})$, which is a mixture of M of the functions, can be uniquely decomposed.

[22] Show that Gaussian functions $f(\mathbf{x}\,|\,\boldsymbol{\alpha}^i)$, $i = 1, 2, \ldots, N$, are linearly independent under reasonable conditions.

[23] Suppose that $h(\mathbf{x})$ is a mixture of functions $f(\mathbf{x}\,|\,\boldsymbol{\alpha}^i) \subset \mathscr{F}$, $i = 1, 2, \ldots, N$, where $\mathscr{F}$ is the Gaussian family. Create a new family of functions $\mathscr{F}'$ consisting of functions (assume N is an even integer)

$$g(\mathbf{x}\,|\,\boldsymbol{\gamma}^1) = \frac{f(\mathbf{x}\,|\,\boldsymbol{\alpha}^1) + f(\mathbf{x}\,|\,\boldsymbol{\alpha}^2)}{2},$$

$$g(\mathbf{x}\,|\,\boldsymbol{\gamma}^2) = \frac{f(\mathbf{x}\,|\,\boldsymbol{\alpha}^3) + f(\mathbf{x}\,|\,\boldsymbol{\alpha}^4)}{2},$$

$$\vdots$$

$$g(\mathbf{x}\,|\,\boldsymbol{\gamma}^{N/2}) = \frac{f(\mathbf{x}\,|\,\boldsymbol{\alpha}^{N-1}) + f(\mathbf{x}\,|\,\boldsymbol{\alpha}^N)}{2}.$$

Are these new functions linearly independent?

[24] In this problem it is shown in several steps that $\eta(\mathbf{b}^*) = \max_{\mathbf{b}} \{\eta(\mathbf{b})\}$, where $h(\mathbf{x}\,|\,\mathbf{b}^*)$ is the true density.
(a) Show that $\ln x \leq x - 1$. (*Hint:* Take the derivative of $\ln x$ at $x = 1$ and the resulting slope is a line $y = x - 1$ which bounds $\ln x$.)
(b) Using (a), show that

$$\int \ln \left[\frac{h(\mathbf{x}\,|\,\mathbf{b}')}{h(\mathbf{x}\,|\,\mathbf{b}^*)}\right] h(\mathbf{x}\,|\,\mathbf{b}^*)\,dx \leq \int \left[\frac{h(\mathbf{x}\,|\,\mathbf{b}')}{h(\mathbf{x}\,|\,\mathbf{b}^*)} - 1\right] \ln h(\mathbf{x}\,|\,\mathbf{b}^*)\,d\mathbf{x} = 0,$$

and thus proves that $\eta(\mathbf{b}')$ cannot be greater than $\eta(\mathbf{b}^*)$.

(c) Show that $\eta(\mathbf{b}') \neq \eta(\mathbf{b}^*)$ except if $h(\mathbf{x}\,|\,\mathbf{b}') = h(\mathbf{x}\,|\,\mathbf{b}^*)$ for all $\mathbf{x}$.

(d) Show that the statement $h(\mathbf{x}\,|\,\mathbf{b}') = h(\mathbf{x}\,|\,\mathbf{b}^*)$ for all $\mathbf{x}$ is not the definition of identifiability.

(e) Show that the above integrals exist if $h(\mathbf{x}\,|\,\mathbf{b})$ are square integrable.

[25] Suppose that it is known a priori that $\mathscr{F}$ is Gaussian, $M = 2$, $L = 1$, $\sigma_1 = \sigma_2 = \sigma$ is known, and both means m_1 and m_2 are unknown ($m_1 \neq m_2$).

(a) Does it make any difference whether m_1 is associated with class 1 or class 2?

(b) Do we known a priori that $m_1 < m_2$? If we do, can we eliminate all points in the two-dimensional parameter space $\mathscr{A}$ shown in Figure 1.7 where $m_1 > m_2$?

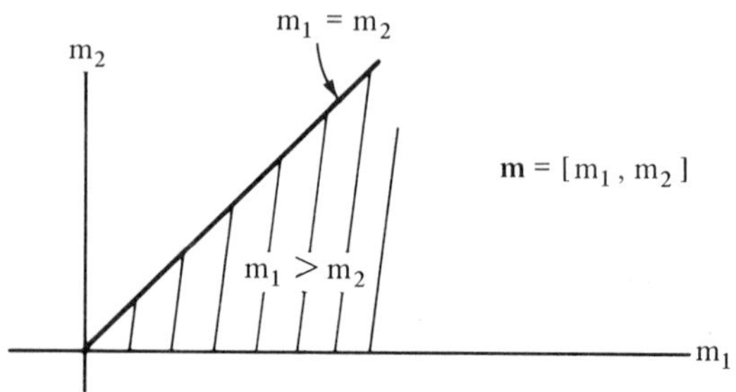

Fig. 1.7

(c) Show that if you calculate $p(m_1, m_2, |\,\mathbf{x}_1, \mathbf{x}_2, \ldots, \mathbf{x}_n)$ without the constraint $m_1 < m_2$, this a posteriori density $p(m_1, m_2\,|\,\mathbf{x}_1, \mathbf{x}_2, \ldots, \mathbf{x}_n)$ will not converge to a Dirac delta function at the true parameter point $[m_1^*, m_2^*]$. (The author has a movie available demonstrating this result.)

[26] Discuss why the class of polynomials is dense in the class of continuous functions and also why the class of polynomials is contained in the class of continuous functions.

CHAPTER 2

Elementary Properties of Estimators

2-1 Introduction

Classical statistics provides the foundations for supervised and unsupervised estimation. First, there are properties of estimators that can be defined essentially independent of the estimation technique; these properties concern convergence of random variables, convergence of functions of random variables, asymptotic distribution of a random variable, estimator bias, estimator consistency, estimator efficiency, the Cramèr–Rao lower bound on variance, and sufficient statistics. Second, there are techniques for obtaining estimators that can be analyzed and compared using the above properties. These techniques are Bayes maximum likelihood, maximum a posteriori, decision directed, minimum distance, stochastic approximation, and the method of moments. Of these techniques, Bayes is the most general, partially because a theoretical estimator with mean-square error lower than that for a Bayes estimator using quadratic loss function has never been found. Whereas in the Bayes approach the a posteriori density of the fixed but unknown parameter vector is computed for each possible parameter vector in the parameter space, the maximum-likelihood estimator selects as the estimator the parameter vector which a posteriori has largest probability.† Stochastic approxima-

---

†This also is a Bayes estimator where a loss of zero is assigned to the parameter vector which a posteriori has largest probability. However, Bayes, unlike maximum likelihood, allows for multiple starting points as well as many other flexibilities.

tion is a method of searching for a parameter vector that maximizes a prespecified criterion. One important criterion which naturally arises in the Bayes solution is the information function. For example, an appropriate criterion can be used in either a stochastic-approximation estimator or a maximum-likelihood estimator. Bayes, being the most general approach, can be used as a framework under which to evaluate and visualize the other techniques.

In the following section convergence almost everywhere, convergence with probability 1, and convergence in mean square are discussed and related to the weak law and strong law of large numbers. The laws of large numbers play a fundamental role in the convergence of all the estimation techniques, including Bayes.

2-2 Convergence†

Convergence Almost Everywhere or with Probability 1

Suppose an experiment is performed to produce n random vectors. Let the experiment be one of an infinite number of experiments that could have been performed, and index or label any particular experiment by a real number η. Let the random vectors resulting from experiment η be

$$\gamma_1(\eta), \gamma_2(\eta), \ldots, \gamma_n(\eta). \tag{1}$$

If for some real number $\epsilon > 0$ there exists an integer n_0 such that

$$\|\gamma_n(\eta) - \gamma\| < \epsilon \qquad \text{for every } n > n_0, \tag{2}$$

then we say that $\gamma_n(\eta)$ tends to a limit γ for the specific experiment η. If (2) is true for every experiment η, then the sequence (1) is said to *converge everywhere*. Convergence everywhere is a restrictive experimental requirement; it is less restrictive to require that (1) converge in the sense of (2) for almost all experiments. Or, put in terms of the relative frequency concept of probability, the latter requirement is that the relative frequency of experiments producing a converging sequence is close to 1. This motivates the definition of *convergence with probability* 1 (*w.p.* 1) *or convergence almost everywhere*

---

†Discussions of convergence may also be found in Fisz [5], Wilks [3], Loève [8], and others; a discussion of convergence from an engineering vantage point is found in Papoulis [7]. An introduction to probability theory is found in Cramer [1] with a more advanced treatment in Cramer [2]. Another reference book for probability theory is Parzen [6], and another introduction is found in Hogg and Craig [40]. A very light use of probability theory with applications to digital communications is found in Schwartz [47].

(*a.e.*). Convergence w.p. 1 will be denoted,† for any $\epsilon > 0$ and $\delta > 0$,

$$p\{\eta : \|\boldsymbol{\gamma}_n - \boldsymbol{\gamma}\| < \epsilon\} > 1 - \delta, \qquad n > n_0,$$

or

$$p\{\eta : \lim_{n \to \infty} \boldsymbol{\gamma}_n = \boldsymbol{\gamma}\} = 1$$

or

$$p\{\boldsymbol{\gamma}_n \longrightarrow \boldsymbol{\gamma}\} = 1 \tag{3}$$

or

$$\boldsymbol{\gamma}_n \xrightarrow{\text{w.p. } 1} \boldsymbol{\gamma},$$

where the probability distribution is understood to be over the possible experiments or sequences η, i.e., the number of experiments for which $\|\boldsymbol{\gamma}_n - \boldsymbol{\gamma}\| > \epsilon$ can be made small.

Convergence in Mean Square

The average of the square distance $\|\boldsymbol{\gamma}_n(\eta) - \boldsymbol{\gamma}\|^2$ with respect to the probability distribution on the possible experiments η is denoted $E\{\|\boldsymbol{\gamma}_n - \boldsymbol{\gamma}\|^2\}$. Then $\boldsymbol{\gamma}_n$ converges in mean square (*m.s.*) to $\boldsymbol{\gamma}$ if

$$\lim_{n \to \infty} E[\|\boldsymbol{\gamma}_n - \boldsymbol{\gamma}\|^2] = 0, \tag{4}$$

which is also written

$$\boldsymbol{\gamma}_n \xrightarrow{\text{m.s.}} \boldsymbol{\gamma}.$$

Convergence in Probability

For convergence almost everywhere it is required that for $n > n_0$ almost all experiments η produce sequences (1) such that (2) is true. This requirement can be relaxed further by allowing *any* experiment η to violate (2) with low probability. There still will be convergence with high probability, but *any* experiment η might violate (2) for some value of $n > n_0$. Therefore, convergence of $\boldsymbol{\gamma}_n$ to $\boldsymbol{\gamma}$ in probability is expressed

$$p\{\|\boldsymbol{\gamma}_n(\eta) - \boldsymbol{\gamma}(\eta)\| < \epsilon\} > 1 - \delta \qquad \text{for } n > n_0$$

†Other notations for w.p. 1 are almost certainly (a.c.) and almost always (a.a.).

or

$$p\{\|\boldsymbol{\gamma}_n(\boldsymbol{\eta}) - \boldsymbol{\gamma}(\boldsymbol{\eta})\| > \epsilon\} \leq \delta \qquad \text{for } n > n_0$$

or

$$\lim_{n\to\infty} p\{\|\boldsymbol{\gamma}_n - \boldsymbol{\gamma}\| > \epsilon\} = 0 \tag{5}$$

or

$$p \lim_{n\to\infty} \boldsymbol{\gamma}_n = \boldsymbol{\gamma}$$

or

$$\boldsymbol{\gamma}_n \xrightarrow{\ p\ } \boldsymbol{\gamma}.$$

Convergence in Mean Square Implies Convergence in Probability

If

$$\boldsymbol{\gamma}_n \xrightarrow{\ \text{m.s.}\ } \boldsymbol{\gamma},$$

then

$$\boldsymbol{\gamma}_n \xrightarrow{\ p\ } \boldsymbol{\gamma},$$

because (from probability theory: Tchebycheff's theorem),

$$p[\|\boldsymbol{\gamma}_n - \boldsymbol{\gamma}\| > \epsilon] \leq \frac{E[\|\boldsymbol{\gamma}_n - \boldsymbol{\gamma}\|^2]}{\epsilon^2},$$

assuming

$$E[\|\boldsymbol{\gamma}_n - \boldsymbol{\gamma}\|^2] < \infty.$$

Weak Law and Strong Law of Large Numbers

When does a sequence $\boldsymbol{\gamma}_n$ converge w.p. 1 to $\boldsymbol{\gamma}$ or in probability to $\boldsymbol{\gamma}$? Are there ways of determining when a sequence $\boldsymbol{\gamma}_n$ arising in a practical problem converges? The weak law and strong law of large numbers apply to convergence in probability and convergence almost certainly, respectively. Both apply to a sequence $\boldsymbol{\gamma}_n$ of the form

$$\boldsymbol{\gamma}_n = \frac{1}{n} \sum_{s=1}^{n} \mathbf{v}_s - E[\mathbf{v}] \tag{6}$$

where $\mathbf{v}_1, \mathbf{v}_2, \ldots, \mathbf{v}_n$ are random vectors with mean $E[\mathbf{v}]$ and variance appropriately constrained for convergence.

This type of sequence arises often in practice. For example, compute the a posteriori density of $\mathbf{b}$ using Bayes theorem:

$$f(\mathbf{b} \mid \mathbf{x}_1, \mathbf{x}_2, \ldots, \mathbf{x}_n) = \frac{\prod_{s=1}^{n} h(\mathbf{x}_s \mid \mathbf{b}) p(\mathbf{b})}{f(\mathbf{x}_1, \ldots, \mathbf{x}_n)}$$

$$= \exp \left[\frac{1}{n} \sum_{s=1}^{n} \ln h(\mathbf{x}_s \mid \mathbf{b}) \right] c,$$

where c is appropriately defined and $\mathbf{x}_1, \ldots, \mathbf{x}_n$ are assumed statistically independent. The convergence properties of $h(\mathbf{b} \mid \mathbf{x}_1, \mathbf{x}_2, \ldots, \mathbf{x}_n)$ involve the sequence

$$\gamma_n = \frac{1}{n} \sum_{s=1}^{n} \ln h(\mathbf{x}_s \mid \mathbf{b}) - E[\ln h(\mathbf{x} \mid \mathbf{b})].$$

Weak Law

Various cases of the weak law are as follows:

1. $\gamma_n \xrightarrow{p} 0$ if $\mathrm{Var}(\mathbf{v}_s) \leq$ constant, for all s, and $\mathbf{v}_1, \mathbf{v}_2, \ldots, \mathbf{v}_n$ are statistically independent and identically distributed.
2. $\gamma_n \xrightarrow{p} 0$ if

$$\lim_{n \to \infty} \left(\frac{1}{n^2} \right) \mathrm{Var} \left(\sum_{s=1}^{n} \mathbf{v}_s \right) = 0.$$

3. $\gamma_n \xrightarrow{p} 0$ if
   (a) the random vectors $\mathbf{v}_1, \mathbf{v}_2, \ldots, \mathbf{v}_n$ are statistically independent, identically distributed;
   (b) $E[\mathbf{v}_s] =$ constant, for all s.
4. $\gamma_n \xrightarrow{p} 0$ if

$$\lim_{n \to \infty} \left(\frac{1}{n^2} \right) \sum_{s=1}^{n} \mathrm{Var}(\mathbf{v}_s) = 0.$$

Strong Law

Various cases of the strong law are as follows:

1. $\gamma_n \xrightarrow{w.p.1} 0$ if
   (a) $\mathbf{v}_1, \ldots, \mathbf{v}_n$ are statistically independent;

(b) $\sum_{s=1}^{\infty} \text{Var}(\mathbf{v}_s)/s^2 < \infty$.

2. $\boldsymbol{\gamma}_n \xrightarrow{\text{w.p.1}} \mathbf{0}$ if

    (a) $\mathbf{v}_1, \ldots, \mathbf{v}_n$ are statistically independent and identically distributed;

    (b) $E[\mathbf{v}_s] < \infty$.

Properties of Functions of Converging Sequences

There are several properties of functions of converging sequences important for the study of estimators. Since proofs for these properties are found in several books on statistics, they will not be given here. For convenience, the properties will be numbered.

Property 1 Suppose there are two sequences $\{\mathbf{x}_1, \mathbf{x}_2, \ldots, \mathbf{x}_n\}$ and $\{\mathbf{w}_1, \mathbf{w}_2, \ldots, \mathbf{w}_n\}$, and $\|\mathbf{x}_n - \mathbf{w}_n\| \xrightarrow{p} 0$ and $\mathbf{x}_n \xrightarrow{p} \mathbf{x}$; then $\mathbf{w}_n \xrightarrow{p} \mathbf{x}$.

Property 2 Suppose there is a sequence $\{\mathbf{x}_1, \mathbf{x}_2, \ldots, \mathbf{x}_n\}$; then if $\mathbf{x}_n \xrightarrow{p} \mathbf{x}$ and $g(\mathbf{x})$ is continuous, $g(\mathbf{x}_n) \xrightarrow{p} g(\mathbf{x})$.

The definition of convergence in distribution is as follows: If $\mathbf{x}_n$ is distributed as $F_n(\mathbf{x})$, then $\mathbf{x}_n$ converges in distribution to $\mathbf{x}$ if $\lim_{n \to \infty} F_n(\mathbf{x}) = F(\mathbf{x})$ at continuity points of $F(\mathbf{x})$.

Property 3 If $\mathbf{x}_n \xrightarrow{p} \mathbf{x}$, then $\lim_{n \to \infty} F_n(\mathbf{x}) = F(\mathbf{x})$ at continuity points of $F(\mathbf{x})$. This follows because $\lim_{n \to \infty} p_n[\mathbf{x}_n \leq a] = p[\mathbf{x} \leq a]$ if $\mathbf{x}_n \xrightarrow{p} \mathbf{x}$, where $\mathbf{x}_n$ and $\mathbf{x}$ are random variables.

Two random variables have the same distribution if they have the same moments. In Chapter 4 moments of risk of a class of decision rules are calculated which depend upon a set of samples. The risk is a random variable because the set of samples is random. Usually decision rules are designed using only the first moment of risk, but they could be designed using the distribution of risk (all the moments of risk).

Property 4 If $\mathbf{x}_n$ has a characteristic function $\varphi_n(\mathbf{t})$, then $\mathbf{x}_n$ converges in distribution to a random vector $\mathbf{x}$ if and only if (iff) $\varphi_n(\mathbf{t})$ converges to a function $\varphi(\mathbf{t})$ continuous at $\mathbf{t} = \mathbf{0}$, where $\varphi(\mathbf{t})$ is the characteristic function of $\mathbf{x}$.

Other properties are listed in the following sections.

2-3 Consistency, Bias, and Efficiency

Consistency deals with whether an estimator $(\tilde{\mathbf{b}})_n$ converges in some sense to its true value $\mathbf{b}^*$. The importance of an estimator being consistent is obvious.

Consistency. The sequence $(\mathbf{b})_n$ is called a consistent estimate (simple consistency) for $\mathbf{b}^*$ if $(\mathbf{b})_n \xrightarrow{p} \mathbf{b}^*$.

Squared-error consistency. The estimator $\mathbf{b}_n$ is called a squared-error consistent estimator of $\mathbf{b}^*$ if $\lim_{n\to\infty} E[\|(\mathbf{b})_n - \mathbf{b}^*\|^2] = 0$.

Property 5 If $(\mathbf{b})_n$ is a squared-error consistent estimate of $\mathbf{b}^*$, then

$$\lim_{n\to\infty} \mathrm{Var}[(\mathbf{b})_n] = \lim_{n\to\infty} E[\|(\mathbf{b})_n - E[(\mathbf{b})_n]\|^2] = 0,$$

$$\lim_{n\to\infty} E[(\mathbf{b})_n] = \mathbf{b}^*,$$

because

$$
\begin{aligned}
E[\|(\mathbf{b})_n - \mathbf{b}^*\|^2] &= E[\|(\mathbf{b})_n - E[(\mathbf{b})_n] + E[(\mathbf{b})_n] - \mathbf{b}^*\|^2] \\
&= E[\|(\mathbf{b})_n - E[(\mathbf{b})_n]\|^2] + \|E[(\mathbf{b})_n] - \mathbf{b}^*\|^2 \\
&= \mathrm{Var}((\mathbf{b})_n) + \|E[(\mathbf{b})_n] - \mathbf{b}^*\|^2
\end{aligned}
$$

and in the limit

$$0 = \lim_{n\to\infty} \mathrm{Var}((\mathbf{b})_n) + \lim_{n\to\infty} \|E[(\mathbf{b})_n] - \mathbf{b}^*\|^2.$$

Property 6 Squared-error consistency implies simple consistency. This is, of course, analogous to convergence in mean square, implying convergence in probability.

Property 7 Simple consistency does not imply square-error consistency.

Unbiased estimate. $(\mathbf{b})_n$ is called an unbiased estimate of $\mathbf{b}^*$ if $E[(\mathbf{b})_n] = \mathbf{b}^*$. The difference $E[(\mathbf{b})_n] - \mathbf{b}^*$ is called the *bias*, or $\|E[(\mathbf{b})_n - \mathbf{b}^*]\|^2$ can be called a *bias distance*. It follows that

$$E[\|(\tilde{\mathbf{b}})_n - \mathbf{b}^*\|^2] = \mathrm{Var}(\mathbf{b})_n + \text{bias distance.} \tag{1}$$

Efficient Estimate

If $(\hat{\mathbf{b}})_n$ is an unbiased estimate of $\mathbf{b}^*$ and no other unbiased estimate of $\mathbf{b}^*$ has smaller variance than $(\hat{\mathbf{b}})_n$, then $(\hat{\mathbf{b}})_n$ is called an *efficient*, or *minimum-variance unbiased*, *estimate*.

Efficiency. If $(\tilde{\mathbf{b}})_n$ is an unbiased estimate of $\mathbf{b}^*$ and an efficient estimate, $(\hat{\mathbf{b}})_n$, exists, then the efficiency of $(\tilde{\mathbf{b}})_n$ in estimating $\mathbf{b}^*$ is

$$\mathrm{eff}((\tilde{\mathbf{b}})_n \mid \mathbf{b}^*) = \frac{\mathrm{Var}((\hat{\mathbf{b}})_n \mid \mathbf{b}^*)}{\mathrm{Var}((\tilde{\mathbf{b}})_n \mid \mathbf{b}^*)} \le 1. \tag{2}$$

2-4 Sufficient Statistics

It is desirable to replace samples $\mathbf{x}_1, \mathbf{x}_2, \ldots, \mathbf{x}_n$ by a statistic or estimator such that the statistic does not grow in complexity as n increases. If the variance of parameter estimation does not increase, the replacement seems justified. For example, in estimating $\mathbf{b}^* = E[\mathbf{x}]$ when $\mathbf{x}$ is a Gaussian ra .dom vector, the sample mean $1/n \sum_{s=1}^{n} \mathbf{x}_s$ is a sufficient statistic. For most unsupervised estimation problems, a practical sufficient statistic (as defined above) does not exist.

The author believes that the concept of sufficiency should be defined as *what is sufficient to represent the a posteriori density* $f(\mathbf{b} \,|\, \dot{\mathbf{x}}_n)$ *of the parameter vector* $\mathbf{b}$ *characterizing the sample probability density* $h(\mathbf{x})$. If $h(\mathbf{x})$ is a single Gaussian density function and $\mathbf{b} = \mathbf{m}$, the mean, then the sample mean $(\mathbf{m})_n = 1/n \sum_{s=1}^{n} \mathbf{x}_s$ is a sufficient statistic for characterizing the a posteriori density $f(\mathbf{m} \,|\, \dot{\mathbf{x}}_n)$. In general, when $h(\mathbf{x})$ is a mixture, it is necessary to evaluate $f(\dot{\mathbf{x}}_n \,|\, \mathbf{b})$ for each value of $\mathbf{b}$ in the parameter space $\mathscr{B}^{M'}$ and there is no way to reduce this complexity. One approach at simplification is to discretize the parameter space $\mathscr{B}^{M'}$ to contain V points. Then, it is reasonable to refer to $f(\dot{\mathbf{x}}_n \,|\, \mathbf{b}^r)$, $r = 1, 2, \ldots, V$, as sufficient statistics.†

The following definition of a sufficient statistic is the statistician's definition, formulated before mixture densities were studied.

Sufficient Statistic (Statistician's Definition)

Let $\mathbf{x}_1, \mathbf{x}_2, \ldots, \mathbf{x}_n$ be parameter conditionally independent and identically distributed random vectors from density $h(\mathbf{x} \,|\, \mathbf{b}^*)$. A statistic $\mathbf{s}_1$ is called *sufficient for estimating* $\mathbf{b}^*$ if given any other $n - 1$ statistics $\mathbf{s}_2, \mathbf{s}_3, \ldots, \mathbf{s}_n$, the conditional density of $f(\mathbf{s}_2, \mathbf{s}_3, \ldots, \mathbf{s}_n \,|\, \mathbf{s}_1)$ is independent of $\mathbf{b}^*$.

Remarks

1. Independent of $\mathbf{b}^*$: note that $h(x) = \frac{1}{2}$, $b^* - 1 < x < b^* + 1$, depends on $\mathbf{b}^*$.
2. If $f(\mathbf{s}_2, \mathbf{s}_3, \ldots, \mathbf{s}_n \,|\, \mathbf{s}_1)$ is independent of $\mathbf{b}^*$, then there is no information about $\mathbf{s}_1$ in the vectors $\mathbf{s}_2, \mathbf{s}_3, \ldots, \mathbf{s}_n$.

Property 8   Neyman–Fischer Theorem: $\tilde{\mathbf{b}}$ is sufficient for estimating $\mathbf{b}^*$ if and only if ($\tilde{\mathbf{b}}$ a function of samples $\mathbf{x}_1, \mathbf{x}_2, \ldots, \mathbf{x}_n$)

$$\prod_{s=1}^{n} h(\mathbf{x}_s \,|\, \mathbf{b}^*) = v(\tilde{\mathbf{b}} \,|\, \mathbf{b}^*) w(\mathbf{x}_1, \mathbf{x}_2, \ldots, \mathbf{x}_n \,|\, \tilde{\mathbf{b}})$$

†It is shown in Chapter 5 that $1/n \sum_{s=1}^{n} \ln h(\mathbf{x}_s|\mathbf{b}^r)$, $r = 1, 2, \ldots, V$, are equivalently sufficient.

or, equivalently,

$$\prod_{s=1}^{n} h(\mathbf{x}_s \,|\, \mathbf{b}^*) = v(\tilde{\mathbf{b}} \,|\, \mathbf{b}^*) w(\mathbf{x}_1, \mathbf{x}_2, \ldots, \mathbf{x}_n), \tag{1}$$

where $v(\tilde{\mathbf{b}} \,|\, \mathbf{b}^*)$ is the density of $\tilde{\mathbf{b}}$ and $w(\mathbf{x}_1, \ldots, \mathbf{x}_n)$ is independent of $\mathbf{b}^*$.

Property 9 Rao–Blackwell Theorem: Let $\mathbf{x}_1, \mathbf{x}_2, \ldots, \mathbf{x}_n$ be samples from $h(\mathbf{x} \,|\, \mathbf{b}^*)$. If $\tilde{\mathbf{b}}$ is a sufficient statistic for $\mathbf{b}^*$ and $\hat{\mathbf{b}}$ is an unbiased estimate of $\mathbf{b}^*$, then $g(\tilde{\mathbf{b}}) = E[\hat{\mathbf{b}} \,|\, \tilde{\mathbf{b}}]$ is an unbiased estimate of $\mathbf{b}^*$ and

$$\mathrm{Var}(g(\tilde{\mathbf{b}}) \,|\, \mathbf{b}^*) \leq \mathrm{Var}(\hat{\mathbf{b}} \,|\, \mathbf{b}^*). \tag{2}$$

2-5 Regularity Conditions for a Density

Let $\mathbf{b} = (\theta_1, \theta_2, \ldots, \theta_n)$ characterize the density $h(\mathbf{x})$. The density $h(\mathbf{x} \,|\, \mathbf{b})$ is said to be *regular with respect to its first θ_i derivative* if

$$\int \frac{\partial}{\partial \theta_i} [h(\mathbf{x} \,|\, \mathbf{b})] \, d\mathbf{x} = \frac{\partial}{\partial \theta_i} \int h(\mathbf{x} \,|\, \mathbf{b}) \, d\mathbf{x}.$$

It then follows that

$$E\left\{ \frac{\partial}{\partial \theta_i} [\ln h(\mathbf{x} \,|\, \mathbf{b})] \right\} = \int \frac{\partial}{\partial \theta_i} [\ln h(\mathbf{x} \,|\, \mathbf{b})] h(\mathbf{x} \,|\, \mathbf{b}) \, d\mathbf{x}$$

$$= \int \frac{\partial}{\partial \theta_i} [h(\mathbf{x} \,|\, \mathbf{b})] \, d\mathbf{x} = \frac{\partial}{\partial \theta_i} \int h(\mathbf{x} \,|\, \mathbf{b}) \, d\mathbf{x} = \frac{\partial}{\partial \theta_i} [1] = 0, \tag{1}$$

which says the expected value of the statistic $\partial[\ln h(\mathbf{x}_s \,|\, \mathbf{b})]/\partial \theta_i$ is zero for all s.

The density $h(\mathbf{x} \,|\, \mathbf{b})$ is said to be *regular with respect to its second θ_i derivative* if

$$\int \frac{\partial^2}{\partial \theta_i^2} [h(\mathbf{x} \,|\, \mathbf{b})] \, d\mathbf{x} = \frac{\partial^2}{\partial \theta_i^2} \int [h(\mathbf{x} \,|\, \mathbf{b})] \, d\mathbf{x}.$$

It then follows that

$$E\left\{ \frac{\partial^2}{\partial \theta_i^2} [\ln h(\mathbf{x} \,|\, \mathbf{b})] \right\} < 0, \tag{2}$$

because

$$\frac{\partial^2}{\partial \theta_i^2} \int h(\mathbf{x} \,|\, \mathbf{b}) \, d\mathbf{x} = \int \left[\frac{\partial^2}{\partial \theta_i^2} \ln h(\mathbf{x} \,|\, \mathbf{b}) \right] h(\mathbf{x} \,|\, \mathbf{b}) \, d\mathbf{x}$$

$$+ \int \left[\frac{\partial}{\partial \theta_i} \ln h(\mathbf{x} \,|\, \mathbf{b}) \right]^2 h(\mathbf{x} \,|\, \mathbf{b}) \, d\mathbf{x} = 0;$$

and since

$$\int \left[\frac{\partial}{\partial \theta_i} \ln h(\mathbf{x} \mid \mathbf{b}) \right]^2 h(\mathbf{x} \mid \mathbf{b}) \, d\mathbf{x} > 0,$$

it follows that

$$\int \left[\frac{\partial^2}{\partial \theta_i^2} \ln h(\mathbf{x} \mid \mathbf{b}) \right] h(\mathbf{x} \mid \mathbf{b}) \, d\mathbf{x} < 0.$$

Note that the information function $\eta(\mathbf{b}, \mathbf{b}^*) = \int \ln h(\mathbf{x} \mid \mathbf{b}) h(\mathbf{x} \mid \mathbf{b}^*) \, d\mathbf{x}$ will be an extremum at $\mathbf{b} = \mathbf{b}^*$ *if the first regularity condition is satisfied. If, in addition, the second regularity condition is satisfied, then this extremum is a maximum. Furthermore, $\mathbf{b}^*$ is unique if the family $\mathscr{F}$ of densities $f_i(\mathbf{x})$ in the mixture $h(\mathbf{x})$ is identifiable.*

2-6 Cramèr–Rao Lower Bound

If the density $h(\mathbf{x} \mid \mathbf{b})$ is regular with respect to its first and second derivatives, then a lower bound on the variance of unbiased estimators for $\mathbf{b}$ can be determined.

Cramèr–Rao Lower Bound (One Parameter)

If $(b)_n$ is any unbiased estimator for b, for any b in the cross-product parameter space, then

$$\text{(a)} \qquad E[((b)_n - b)^2] \geq \frac{1}{E\left\{ \left[\dfrac{\partial \ln h(\dot{\mathbf{x}}_n \mid b)}{\partial b} \right]^2 \right\}} \qquad (1)$$

or

$$\text{(b)} \qquad \text{Var}[(b)_n] \geq \frac{1}{nE\left\{ \left[\dfrac{\partial \ln h(\mathbf{x} \mid b)}{\partial b} \right]^2 \right\}} = \frac{1}{-nE\left[\dfrac{\partial^2}{\partial b^2} \ln h(\mathbf{x} \mid b) \right]}, \qquad (2)$$

where $\mathbf{x}$ is generic notation for any of the parameter conditionally independent samples $\mathbf{x}_1, \mathbf{x}_2, \ldots, \mathbf{x}_n$ and the first and second regularity conditions are satisfied.

Proof: Because $(b)_n$ is unbiased,

$$E[(b)_n - b] \triangleq \int h(\dot{\mathbf{x}}_n \mid b)[(b)_n - b] \, d\dot{\mathbf{x}}_n = 0,$$

Elementary Properties of Estimators *Chap. 2*

$$\frac{\partial}{\partial b} \int h(\dot{\mathbf{x}}_n \,|\, b)[(b)_n - b] \, d\dot{\mathbf{x}}_n = \int \frac{\partial}{\partial b} \{h(\dot{\mathbf{x}}_n \,|\, b)[(b)_n - b]\} \, d\dot{\mathbf{x}}_n = 0;$$

then

$$\underbrace{- \int h(\dot{\mathbf{x}}_n \,|\, b) \, d\dot{\mathbf{x}}_n}_{-1} + \int \frac{\partial}{\partial b}[h(\dot{\mathbf{x}}_n \,|\, b)][(b)_n - b] \, d\dot{\mathbf{x}}_n = 0.$$

Observe that

$$\frac{\partial h(\dot{\mathbf{x}}_n \,|\, b)}{\partial b} = \frac{\partial \ln h(\dot{\mathbf{x}}_n \,|\, b)}{\partial b} h(\dot{\mathbf{x}}_n \,|\, b).$$

Thus

$$\int \left[\frac{\partial \ln h(\dot{\mathbf{x}}_n \,|\, b)}{\partial b} \right] h(\dot{\mathbf{x}}_n \,|\, b)[(b)_n - b] \, d\dot{\mathbf{x}}_n = 1$$

or

$$\int \left[\frac{\partial \ln h(\dot{\mathbf{x}}_n \,|\, b)}{\partial b} \sqrt{h(\dot{\mathbf{x}}_n \,|\, b)} \right] \left\{ \sqrt{h(\dot{\mathbf{x}}_n \,|\, b)}[(b)_n - b] \right\} \, d\dot{\mathbf{x}}_n = 1.$$

The Schwarz inequality for vector spaces (see Chapter 1) is

$$(\mathbf{a}, \mathbf{b}) \leq \sqrt{\|\mathbf{a}\|^2 \|\mathbf{b}\|^2}.$$

For the function space under consideration,

$$(\mathbf{a}, \mathbf{b}) = \int a(\dot{\mathbf{x}}_n) b(\dot{\mathbf{x}}_n) \, d\dot{\mathbf{x}}_n.$$

Applying the Schwarz inequality,

$$\left\{ \int \left[\frac{\partial \ln h(\dot{\mathbf{x}}_n \,|\, b)}{\partial b} \right]^2 h(\dot{\mathbf{x}}_n \,|\, b) \, d\dot{\mathbf{x}}_n \right\} \left\{ \int [(b)_n - b]^2 h(\dot{\mathbf{x}}_n \,|\, b) \, d\dot{\mathbf{x}}_n \right\} \geq 1.$$

Equality holds if there is a match $\mathbf{a} = k\mathbf{b}$:

$$\frac{\partial \ln h(\dot{\mathbf{x}}_n \,|\, b)}{\partial b} \sqrt{h(\dot{\mathbf{x}}_n \,|\, b)} = k \sqrt{h(\dot{\mathbf{x}}_n \,|\, b)}[(\hat{b})_n - b],$$

where k is a constant (not dependent on $(\mathbf{b})_n$), i.e.,

$$\frac{\partial \ln h(\dot{\mathbf{x}}_n \,|\, b)}{\partial b} = k[(b)_n - b].$$

Thus part (a) of the Cramèr–Rao lower bound is proved. To prove part (b), note that

$$E\left\{\left[\frac{\partial \ln h(\dot{\mathbf{x}}_n \,|\, b)}{\partial b}\right]^2\right\} = E\left\{\left[\frac{\partial \ln \prod_{s=1}^{n} h(\mathbf{x}_s \,|\, b)}{\partial b}\right]^2\right\}$$

$$= E\left\{\left[\frac{\partial}{\partial b} \sum_{s=1}^{n} \ln h(\mathbf{x}_s \,|\, b)\right]^2\right\}$$

$$= nE\left\{\left[\frac{\partial}{\partial b} \ln h(\mathbf{x} \,|\, b)\right]^2\right\},$$

because

$$E\left\{\frac{\partial}{\partial b}[\ln h(\mathbf{x}_s \,|\, b)] \frac{\partial}{\partial b}[\ln (\mathbf{x}_j \,|\, b)]\right\}\bigg|_{j \neq s} = \left(E\left\{\frac{\partial}{\partial b} \ln h(\mathbf{x} \,|\, b)\right\}\right)^2$$

since $\mathbf{x}_s$ and $\mathbf{x}_j$ are parameter conditionally independent and because

$$E\left[\frac{\partial}{\partial b} \ln h(\mathbf{x} \,|\, b)\right] = \int \frac{\partial}{\partial b}[\ln h(\mathbf{x} \,|\, b)]h(\mathbf{x} \,|\, b) \, d\mathbf{x}$$

$$= \int \frac{\partial h(\mathbf{x} \,|\, b)}{\partial b} \, d\mathbf{x} = \frac{\partial}{\partial b} \int h(\mathbf{x} \,|\, b) \, d\mathbf{x} = 0$$

if the first regularity condition holds.

Cramèr–Rao Lower Bound (Multidimensional)

If $\hat{\mathbf{b}} = [\hat{\theta}_1, \hat{\theta}_2, \ldots, \hat{\theta}_q]$ is any unbiased estimator for $\mathbf{b}$, where $\mathbf{b} = [\theta_1, \theta_2, \ldots, \theta_q]$ is any parameter vector in the cross-product parameter space, then for any two sets of constants $c_1, \ldots, c_q$ and $c'_1, \ldots, c'_q$, not all constants in either set being zero,

(a)
$$\mathrm{Var}\left(\sum_{p=1}^{q} c'_p \hat{\theta}_p\right) = E\left[\left(\sum_{p=1}^{q} c'_p \hat{\theta}_p - \sum_{p=1}^{q} c'_p \theta_p\right)^2\right]$$

$$\geq \frac{\left(\sum_{k=1}^{q} c'_k c_k\right)^2}{\int \left[\sum_{k=1}^{q} c_k \frac{\partial}{\partial \theta_k} \ln h(\dot{\mathbf{x}}_n \,|\, \mathbf{b})\right]^2 h(\dot{\mathbf{x}}_n \,|\, \mathbf{b}) \, d\dot{\mathbf{x}}_n}.$$

(b)
$$\mathrm{Var}\left(\sum_{p=1}^{q} c'_p \hat{\theta}_p\right) = E\left[\left(\sum_{p=1}^{q} c'_p \hat{\theta}_p - \sum_{p=1}^{q} c'_p \theta_p\right)^2\right] \tag{3}$$

$$\geq \underset{(c_1, \ldots, c_q)}{\mathrm{l.u.b.}} \frac{\left(\sum_{p=1}^{q} c_p c'_p\right)^2}{nE\left\{\left[\sum_{p=1}^{q} c_p \frac{\partial}{\partial \theta_p} \ln h(\mathbf{x} \,|\, \theta_p)\right]^2\right\}}, \tag{4}$$

where the first and second regularity conditions are satisfied.

Proof: Because $(\hat{\mathbf{b}})_n$ is unbiased,

$$E\left[\sum_{p=1}^{q}(\hat{\theta}_p - \theta_p)c'_p\right] = 0,$$

$$\frac{\partial}{\partial\theta_k}\int h(\dot{\mathbf{x}}_n\,|\,\mathbf{b})\left[\sum_{p=1}^{q}c'_p(\hat{\theta}_p - \theta_p)\right]d\dot{\mathbf{x}}_n$$

$$= \int \frac{\partial}{\partial\theta_k}\left\{h(\dot{\mathbf{x}}_n\,|\,b)\left[\sum_{p=1}^{q}c'_p(\hat{\theta}_p - \theta_p)\right]\right\}d\dot{\mathbf{x}}_n = 0;$$

then

$$-c'_k\int h(\dot{\mathbf{x}}_n\,|\,\mathbf{b})\,d\dot{\mathbf{x}}_n + \int\left[\frac{\partial}{\partial\theta_k}h(\dot{\mathbf{x}}_n\,|\,\mathbf{b})\right]\left[\sum_{p=1}^{q}c'_p(\hat{\theta}_p - \theta_p)\right]d\dot{\mathbf{x}}_n = 0.$$

Thus

$$\int\left[\frac{\partial}{\partial\theta_k}h(\dot{\mathbf{x}}_n\,|\,\mathbf{b})\right]\left[\sum_{p=1}^{q}c'_p(\hat{\theta}_p - \theta_p)\right]d\dot{\mathbf{x}}_n = c'_k.$$

Multiplying both sides by c_k, summing over k, and squaring gives

$$\left\{\int\left[\sum_{k=1}^{q}\frac{\partial}{\partial\theta_k}h(\dot{\mathbf{x}}_n\,|\,\mathbf{b})c_k\right]\left[\sum_{p=1}^{q}c'_p(\hat{\theta}_p - \theta_p)\right]d\dot{\mathbf{x}}_n\right\}^2 = \left(\sum_{k=1}^{q}c'_kc_k\right)^2.$$

Observe that

$$\frac{\partial}{\partial\theta_k}h(\dot{\mathbf{x}}_n\,|\,\mathbf{b}) = \frac{\partial\ln h(\dot{\mathbf{x}}_n\,|\,\mathbf{b})}{\partial\theta_k}h(\dot{\mathbf{x}}_n\,|\,\mathbf{b}).$$

Thus

$$\left(\int\left[\sum_{k=1}^{q}c_k\frac{\partial\ln h(\dot{\mathbf{x}}_n\,|\,\mathbf{b})}{\partial\theta_k}\sqrt{h(\dot{\mathbf{x}}_n\,|\,\mathbf{b})}\right]\left\{\sqrt{h(\dot{\mathbf{x}}_n\,|\,\mathbf{b})}\left[\sum_{p=1}^{q}c'_p(\hat{\theta}_p - \theta_p)\right]\right\}d\dot{\mathbf{x}}_n\right)^2$$

$$= \left(\sum_{k=1}^{q}c'_kc_k\right)^2.$$

The Schwarz inequality for the function space under consideration is

$$(\mathbf{a}, \mathbf{b}) \le \sqrt{\|\mathbf{a}\|^2\|\mathbf{b}\|^2}$$

$$= \int a(\dot{\mathbf{x}}_n)b(\dot{\mathbf{x}}_n)\,d\dot{\mathbf{x}}_n.$$

Applying the Schwarz inequality,

$$\left\{\int \left[\sum_{k=1}^{q} c_k \frac{\partial}{\partial \theta_k} \ln h(\dot{\mathbf{x}}_n | \mathbf{b})\right]^2 h(\dot{\mathbf{x}}_n | \mathbf{b}) \, d\dot{\mathbf{x}}_n\right\}\left\{\int \left[\sum_{p=1}^{q} c'_p(\hat{\theta}_p - \theta_p)\right]^2 h(\dot{\mathbf{x}}_n | \mathbf{b}) \, d\dot{\mathbf{x}}_n\right\}$$

$$\geq \left(\sum_{k=1}^{q} c'_k c_k\right)^2$$

or

$$\int \left[\sum_{p=1}^{q} c'_p(\hat{\theta}_p - \theta_p)\right]^2 h(\dot{\mathbf{x}}_n | \mathbf{b}) \, d\dot{\mathbf{x}}_n \geq \frac{\left(\sum_{k=1}^{q} c'_k c_k\right)^2}{\int \left[\sum_{k=1}^{q} c_k \frac{\partial}{\partial \theta_k} \ln h(\dot{\mathbf{x}}_n | \mathbf{b})\right]^2 h(\dot{\mathbf{x}}_n | \mathbf{b}) \, d\dot{\mathbf{x}}_n},$$

which proves (a). The proof of (b) follows by expanding the denominator on the right-hand side of the above equation and observing that $\mathbf{x}_1, \ldots, \mathbf{x}_n$ are statistically independent and that the expected value of $\partial h(\dot{\mathbf{x}}_n | \mathbf{b})/\partial \theta_k$ is zero.

Information

$E\{[\partial \ln h(\mathbf{x} | \mathbf{b})/\partial \theta_i]^2\}$ has been called *information* in statistical literature.† Note that for the one-parameter problem, a larger "information" corresponds to a smaller Cramèr–Rao lower bound.‡

2-7 Maximum-Likelihood Estimation

The function $L(\mathbf{x}_1, \mathbf{x}_2, \ldots, \mathbf{x}_n | \mathbf{b}) = \ln \prod_{s=1}^{n} h(\mathbf{x}_s | \mathbf{b})$ is called the likelihood function of parameter conditionally independent samples $\mathbf{x}_1, \mathbf{x}_2, \ldots, \mathbf{x}_n$, where $\mathbf{x}$ has density $h(\mathbf{x} | \mathbf{b})$. If $(\mathbf{b})_n$ satisfies

$$L(\dot{\mathbf{x}}_n | (\mathbf{b})_n) \geq L(\dot{\mathbf{x}}_n | \mathbf{b}) \tag{1}$$

for all $\mathbf{b}$, $(\mathbf{b})_n$, $\mathbf{b}^*$ in the product parameter space, then $(\mathbf{b})_n$ is the maximum-likelihood estimate (M.L.E.) of $\mathbf{b}^*$. In many cases $(\mathbf{b})_n$ may be obtained as a solution to the equations§

$$\frac{\partial}{\partial \theta_i} \ln h(\dot{\mathbf{x}}_n | \mathbf{b}) = 0 \qquad i = 1, 2, \ldots, q, \tag{2a}$$

---

†This function should not be confused with the information function $\int \ln h(\mathbf{x} | \mathbf{b}) \, h(\mathbf{x} | \mathbf{b}) \, d\mathbf{x}$ used frequently in engineering.

‡See also Section 2-24.

§It also may be necessary to consider mixed partial derivatives.

$$\frac{\partial^2}{\partial \theta_i^2} \ln h(\dot{\mathbf{x}}_n \,|\, \mathbf{b}) < 0 \qquad i = 1, 2, \ldots, q, \tag{2b}$$

where $\mathbf{b} = [\theta_1, \theta_2, \ldots, \theta_q]$. Using the gradient $\nabla_\mathbf{b}$ with respect to $\mathbf{b}$, (2a) is equivalent to

$$\nabla_\mathbf{b} \ln L(\dot{\mathbf{x}}_n \,|\, \mathbf{b}) = \left[\frac{\partial \ln h(\dot{\mathbf{x}}_n \,|\, \mathbf{b})}{\partial \theta_1}, \ldots, \frac{\partial \ln h(\dot{\mathbf{x}}_n \,|\, \mathbf{b})}{\partial \theta_q} \right] = \mathbf{0}.$$

Property 10 Let $\mathbf{x}_1, \mathbf{x}_2, \ldots, \mathbf{x}_n$ be n parameter conditionally independent samples from $h(\mathbf{x} \,|\, \mathbf{b}^*)$. If a sufficient statistic $\tilde{\mathbf{b}}$ of $\mathbf{b}^*$ exists and the M.L.E. $\hat{\mathbf{b}}$ exists, then $\hat{\mathbf{b}} = g(\tilde{\mathbf{b}})$; that is, the M.L.E. is a function of the sufficient statistic.

Proof: If $\mathbf{b}$ is sufficient, then $L(\mathbf{x}_1, \mathbf{x}_2, \ldots, \mathbf{x}_n \,|\, \mathbf{b}) = v(\tilde{\mathbf{b}}, \mathbf{b}) w(\mathbf{x}_1, \ldots, \mathbf{x}_n)$, so that the maximum of $L(\mathbf{x}_1, \mathbf{x}_2, \ldots, \mathbf{x}_n \,|\, \mathbf{b})$ occurs for $\mathbf{b}$ maximizing $v(\tilde{\mathbf{b}}, \mathbf{b})$.

The conditions for convergence and the asymptotic distribution of a M.L.E. are presented in the following theorems. The theorems are similar to those in Wilks ([3], p. 360). Unfortunately, Wilks's theorems are weak because they were not derived with mixtures $h(\mathbf{x} \,|\, \mathbf{b})$ in mind; therefore, we add somewhat to the theorems to make them stronger.

M.L.E. Convergence Theorem

Let $\mathbf{x}_1, \mathbf{x}_2, \ldots, \mathbf{x}_n$ be independent and identically distributed vectors from $h(\mathbf{x} \,|\, \mathbf{b}^*)$, where $\mathbf{b}^* = [\theta_1^*, \theta_2^*, \ldots, \theta_q^*]$ and assume that $h(\mathbf{x} \,|\, \mathbf{b})$ is regular with respect to its first θ_j derivatives.† Let $\partial h(\mathbf{x} \,|\, \mathbf{b})/\partial \theta_j$ be a continuous function of $\mathbf{b}$ for all $\mathbf{x}$, except possibly a set of zero probability. Then there exists a sequence of vectors with the form $\tilde{\mathbf{b}}_n = [\tilde{\theta}_{n1}, \ldots, \tilde{\theta}_{nq}]$, which converge with probability 1. If the solution maximizing the likelihood function is unique for $n \geq$ some n_0, the sequence converges with probability 1. The convergence will be to the true parameter and will be *unique* given the second regularity condition and identifiability. *This is a local solution.*

If $h(\mathbf{x} \,|\, \mathbf{b})$ is regular with respect to its second θ_j derivatives,† then $\tilde{\mathbf{b}}$, the maximum-likelihood solution, is asymptotically normal as follows:

M.L.E. Asymptotic Distribution Theorem

If $h(\mathbf{x} \,|\, \mathbf{b})$ is regular with respect to its first and second θ_j derivatives and if $\tilde{\mathbf{b}}$ is a unique solution of the likelihood function for $n \geq$ some n_0 and measurable with respect to $h(\mathbf{x}_1, \mathbf{x}_2, \ldots, \mathbf{x}_n \,|\, \mathbf{b}^*)$, then $\tilde{\mathbf{b}}$ is asymptotically dis-

†For definitions of first- and second-order regularity conditions, see Section 2-5.

tributed for large n according to the q-variate normal density with mean vector $[\theta_1^*, \theta_2^*, \ldots, \theta_q^*]$ and covariance matrix $[nc_{jk}(\mathbf{b}^*)]_{LL}^{-1}$, where

$$c_{jk}(\mathbf{b}^*) = -\int \left[\frac{\partial^2}{\partial\theta_j\,\partial\theta_k} \ln h(\mathbf{x}\,|\,\mathbf{b})\right] \bigg| h(\mathbf{x}\,|\,\mathbf{b}^*)\,d\mathbf{x} \qquad \begin{aligned} &\\ &\theta_j = \theta_j^*, \\ &\theta_k = \theta_k^*. \end{aligned} \tag{3}$$

The previous results for M.L.E. convergence properties based on the two regularity conditions on $h(\mathbf{x}\,|\,\mathbf{b})$ are less general than results by LeCam [18].

LeCam's Convergence Lemma for M.L.E.

Suppose

1. $\mathbf{b}$ is a vector point in an open subset of $\mathscr{V}_q$, the product parameter space.
2. $\int_{\mathscr{V}_q} \|\mathbf{b}\| \prod_{s=1}^{n} h(\mathbf{x}_s\,|\,\mathbf{b})f_0(\mathbf{b})\,d\mathbf{b} < \infty$, w.p. 1 for all $\mathbf{b}$, where $f_0(\mathbf{b})$ is an a priori density on $\mathbf{b}$.
3. $\partial \ln h(\mathbf{x}\,|\,\mathbf{b})/\partial\theta_i$ and $\partial^2 \ln h(\mathbf{x}\,|\,\mathbf{b})/\partial\theta_i\,\partial\theta_j$ exist and are continuous in $\mathbf{b}$ for almost all $\mathbf{x}$.
4. $E_{\mathbf{b}}^*\left(\text{Sup}\left|\dfrac{\partial^2 \ln h(\mathbf{x}\,|\,\mathbf{s})}{\partial\theta_i\,\partial\theta_j}\right| : \|\mathbf{s} - \mathbf{b}^*\| < e(\mathbf{b}^*),\ \mathbf{s} \in \mathscr{V}_q\right) < \infty$ for some

$e(\mathbf{b}^*)$ and all i and j, $\mathbf{b}^*$ [$E_{\mathbf{b}}^*$ indicates expectation with respect to $h(\mathbf{x}\,|\,\mathbf{b}^*)$].

Define U as a compact neighborhood of $\mathbf{b}^*$, where $(\mathbf{b})_n$ is the value of $\mathbf{b}$ such that

$$\sum_{s=1}^{n} \ln h(\mathbf{x}_s\,|\,(\mathbf{b})_n) = \max\left[\sum_{s=1}^{n} \ln h(\mathbf{x}_s\,|\,\mathbf{b}) : \mathbf{b} \in U\right]$$

and $(\mathbf{b})_n$ is unique for $n > n_0$; then there exists a $U(\mathbf{b}^*)$ such that, for $n \geq n_0$

$$(\mathbf{b})_n \xrightarrow{\text{w.p.1}} \mathbf{b}^*$$

and there exists $n_0(\mathbf{x}_1, \mathbf{x}_2, \ldots, \mathbf{x}_n, \ldots)$ such that

$$\sum_{s=1}^{n} \nabla[\ln h(\mathbf{x}_s\,|\,(\mathbf{b})_n)] = \mathbf{0}.$$

In both the M.L.E. convergence theorem and LeCam's convergence lemma for M.L.E., an assumption is made that the solution $(\mathbf{b})_n$ is unique for $n \geq n_0$. Such a uniqueness condition is required for proving convergence of all estimation procedures based on an estimated gradient.

Because the maximum-likelihood estimator $(\mathbf{b})_n$ is a solution to

$$\nabla_{\mathbf{b}} \sum_{s=1}^{n} \ln h(\mathbf{x}_s \mid \mathbf{b}) = \sum_{s=1}^{n} \nabla_{\mathbf{b}} \ln h(\mathbf{x}_s \mid \mathbf{b}) = \mathbf{0},$$

it is natural to define a vector of functions $\mathbf{l}'(\mathbf{b}, \mathbf{b}^*)$ as

$$\mathbf{l}'(\mathbf{b}, \mathbf{b}^*) = \int \nabla_{\mathbf{b}} \ln h(\mathbf{x} \mid \mathbf{b}) h(\mathbf{x} \mid \mathbf{b}^*)\, d\mathbf{x}$$

and observe that

$$\frac{1}{n} \sum_{s=1}^{n} \nabla_{\mathbf{b}} \ln h(\mathbf{x}_s \mid \mathbf{b}) \xrightarrow{\text{w.p.}1} \mathbf{l}'(\mathbf{b}, \mathbf{b}^*).$$

For the Robbins–Monroe stochastic-approximation procedure discussed in Section 2-12, the vector $\mathbf{l}'((\mathbf{b}), \mathbf{b}^*)$ is used as a "regression function." Thus, maximum-likelihood estimation is related to stochastic approximation.

2-8 Bayes Estimation†

Just as in M.L.E., $\mathbf{b}$ is considered a fixed but unknown parameter vector in Bayes estimation. However, an important difference is that for Bayes the a posteriori density $f(\mathbf{b} \mid \dot{\mathbf{x}}_n)$ is computed for *all* points $\mathbf{b}$ in the parameter space. Accordingly, Bayes provides for weighting a parameter point $\mathbf{b}$ by its a posteriori probability. Also, Bayes provides for associating a loss with any particular $\mathbf{b}$ selected as the true parameter vector.

Let $f(\mathbf{b})$ be an a priori density on $\mathbf{b}$ to account for uncertainty. Denote the Bayes estimate $(\mathbf{b})_n$ and assign a loss function $L((\mathbf{b})_n, \mathbf{b})$ for selecting $(\mathbf{b})_n$ when $\mathbf{b}$ is the true parameter vector. Then for a given $f(\mathbf{b})$,

$$\text{average loss} = \int L((\mathbf{b})_n, \mathbf{b}) f(\mathbf{b})\, d\mathbf{b}. \tag{1}$$

Bayes Estimator

For a given $f(\mathbf{b})$ the estimate minimizing $\int L((\mathbf{b})_n, \mathbf{b}) f(\mathbf{b})\, d\mathbf{b}$ is called the Bayes estimate (B.E.), corresponding to (or against) the a priori density $f(\mathbf{b})$. When the a posteriori density $f(\mathbf{b} \mid \dot{\mathbf{x}}_n)$ is available rather than $f(\mathbf{b})$, the *average*

†Estimation is uninteresting to the engineer unless a problem model is involved to enhance parameter estimation or the estimation leads to a decision rule.

conditional loss is

$$\text{average conditional loss} = \int L((\mathbf{b})_n, \mathbf{b}) f(\mathbf{b} \mid \dot{\mathbf{x}}_n) \, d\mathbf{b}. \tag{2}$$

If we further average with respect to the sample set $\dot{\mathbf{x}}_n$, the average loss is

$$\text{risk} = \int\!\!\int L((\mathbf{b})_n, \mathbf{b}) f(\mathbf{b} \mid \dot{\mathbf{x}}_n) \, d\mathbf{b} \, h(\dot{\mathbf{x}}_n) \, d\dot{\mathbf{x}}_n$$

$$= \int d\mathbf{b} \int L((\mathbf{b}_n), \mathbf{b}) f(\mathbf{b}, \dot{\mathbf{x}}_n) \, d\dot{\mathbf{x}}_n \triangleq R. \tag{3}$$

Property 11 Let $\mathbf{x}_1, \mathbf{x}_2, \ldots, \mathbf{x}_n$ be statistically independent and identically distributed as $h(\mathbf{x} \mid \mathbf{b}^*)$. The Bayes estimator $(\mathbf{b})_n$ against a priori density $f(\mathbf{b})$ and *square law loss* function $L((\mathbf{b})_n, \mathbf{b}) = c(\mathbf{b}) \|(\mathbf{b})_n - \mathbf{b}\|^2$, where $c(\mathbf{b})$ is a function of $\mathbf{b}$, is given by

$$(\mathbf{b})_n = \frac{\displaystyle\int \mathbf{b} c(\mathbf{b}) \prod_{s=1}^{n} h(\mathbf{x}_s \mid \mathbf{b}) f(\mathbf{b}) \, d\mathbf{b}}{\displaystyle\int c(\mathbf{b}) \prod_{s=1}^{n} h(\mathbf{x}_s \mid \mathbf{b}) f(\mathbf{b}) \, d\mathbf{b}} \tag{4}$$

and, if $c(\mathbf{b}) = 1$,

$$(\mathbf{b})_n = \int \mathbf{b} f(\mathbf{b} \mid \dot{\mathbf{x}}_n) \, d\mathbf{b}, \tag{5}$$

where†

$$f(\mathbf{b} \mid \dot{\mathbf{x}}_n) = \frac{\displaystyle\prod_{s=1}^{n} h(\mathbf{x}_s \mid \mathbf{b}) f(\mathbf{b})}{\displaystyle\int [\text{numerator}] \, d\mathbf{b}}. \tag{6}$$

This result is proved below for $c(\mathbf{b}) = 1$ and $\mathbf{b} = b$, a real parameter. The extension of the result to $\mathbf{b}$, a vector set of parameters, is left as a problem.

Proof of Property 11

$$R = \int_{-\infty}^{\infty} db \int_{-\infty}^{\infty} [(b)_n - b]^2 f(b, \dot{\mathbf{x}}_n) \, d\dot{\mathbf{x}}_n,$$

$$f(b, \dot{\mathbf{x}}_n) = f(b \mid \dot{\mathbf{x}}_n) h(\dot{\mathbf{x}}_n),$$

so that

$$R = \int_{-\infty}^{\infty} h(\dot{\mathbf{x}}_n) \, d\dot{\mathbf{x}}_n \int_{-\infty}^{\infty} [(b)_n - b]^2 f(b \mid \dot{\mathbf{x}}_n) \, db.$$

---

†It should be emphasized that b^* is a *fixed* but unknown parameter vector. Our a priori knowledge concerning b^* is described by $f(\mathbf{b})$, an a priori density function.

Observe that $h(\dot{\mathbf{x}}_n)$ is nonnegative; therefore, R can be minimized by the solution $(b)_n$, which minimizes the inner integral for every $\dot{\mathbf{x}}_n$. Solving,

$$\frac{\partial}{\partial (b)_n} \int [(b)_n - b]^2 f(b \,|\, \dot{\mathbf{x}}_n)\, db = -2 \int_{-\infty}^{\infty} bf(b \,|\, \dot{\mathbf{x}}_n)\, db + 2(b)_n \int_{-\infty}^{\infty} f(b \,|\, \dot{\mathbf{x}}_n)\, db$$

$$= 0.$$

But because $\displaystyle\int_{-\infty}^{\infty} f(b \,|\, \dot{\mathbf{x}}_n)\, db = 1$,

$$(b)_n = \int bf(b \,|\, \dot{\mathbf{x}}_n)\, db$$

is the solution. To verify that this solution is a minimum, we compute the second derivative,

$$\frac{\partial^2}{\partial^2 (b)_n} \int [(b)_n - b]^2 f(b \,|\, \dot{\mathbf{x}}_n)\, db = 2,$$

which is positive, as it should be for a minimum.

Under the conditions of this section, the a posteriori density $f(\mathbf{b} \,|\, \dot{\mathbf{x}}_n)$ is computed as follows:

$$f(\mathbf{b} \,|\, \dot{\mathbf{x}}_n) = \frac{h(\mathbf{x}_1, \mathbf{x}_2, \ldots, \mathbf{x}_n \,|\, \mathbf{b}) f(\mathbf{b})}{h(\mathbf{x}_1, \mathbf{x}_2, \ldots, \mathbf{x}_n)}$$

or

$$f(\mathbf{b} \,|\, \dot{\mathbf{x}}_n) = \frac{f(\mathbf{x}_n \,|\, \mathbf{x}_1, \mathbf{x}_2, \ldots, \mathbf{x}_{n-1}, \mathbf{b}) f(\mathbf{b} \,|\, \dot{\mathbf{x}}_{n-1})}{f(\mathbf{x}_n \,|\, \dot{\mathbf{x}}_{n-1})}.$$

If $\mathbf{x}_1, \mathbf{x}_2, \ldots, \mathbf{x}_n$ are statistically independent and identically distributed as $h(\mathbf{x} \,|\, \mathbf{b}^*)$, then

$$f(\mathbf{b} \,|\, \dot{\mathbf{x}}_n) = \frac{\displaystyle\prod_{s=1}^{n} h(\mathbf{x}_s \,|\, \mathbf{b}) f(\mathbf{b})}{h(\dot{\mathbf{x}}_n)} = \frac{\left[\exp \frac{1}{n} \sum_{s=1}^{n} \ln h(\mathbf{x}_s \,|\, \mathbf{b}) \right]^{n} f(\mathbf{b})}{f(\dot{\mathbf{x}}_n)}.$$

It will be of interest for subsequent work to note that under relatively unrestrictive conditions, either by the weak law or strong law of large numbers,

$$\lim_{n \to \infty} \frac{1}{n} \sum_{s=1}^{n} \ln h(\mathbf{x}_s \,|\, \mathbf{b}) \longrightarrow \int \ln h(\mathbf{x} \,|\, \mathbf{b}) h(\mathbf{x} \,|\, \mathbf{b}^*)\, d\mathbf{x} \triangleq \eta(\mathbf{b})$$

in probability or with probability 1.

A theme throughout this book is that the Bayes concept is basic because it provides the a posteriori density $f(\mathbf{b}|\dot{\mathbf{x}}_n)$ for all points $\mathbf{b}$ in the parameter space. With this a posteriori density it is possible to define many kinds of estimators. For example, the point $(\mathbf{b})_n$ for which $f(\mathbf{b}|\dot{\mathbf{x}}_n)$ is maximum (assuming uniqueness) is called the *maximum a posteriori estimator*. The maximum a posteriori estimator may be considered a Bayes estimator because it requires the a posteriori density $f(\mathbf{b}|\dot{\mathbf{x}}_n)$. A difference between the Bayes estimator given by (2) for a square law loss function and the maximum a posteriori estimator is due to different loss functions. To obtain the maximum a posteriori estimator, a loss of zero is assigned to the a posteriori most probable parameter point while a loss of one is assigned to all other parameter points. Thus Eq. (2) and the maximum a posteriori estimator are both Bayes estimators but they use different loss functions. The advantages and disadvantages of several different loss functions are summarized below:

Square Law Loss Function

The square law loss function $L((\mathbf{b})_n, \mathbf{b}) = \|(\mathbf{b})_n - \mathbf{b}\|^2$ leads to the familiar form of the Bayes estimator (5),

$$(\mathbf{b})_n = \int \mathbf{b} f(\mathbf{b}|\dot{\mathbf{x}}_n)\, d\mathbf{b}.$$

This loss function suppresses values of $\mathbf{b}$ which have highest a posteriori probability of error from $\mathbf{b}^*$, while enhancing values of $\mathbf{b}$ having highest a posteriori probability of being $\mathbf{b}^*$. *Thus an advantage of the square law loss function is that it suppresses large errors.* For problems where large parameter estimation errors lead to wrong decisions, the square law loss function is desirable because it suppresses large errors.

An obvious example of where the square law loss function is undesirable is where $f(\mathbf{b}|\dot{\mathbf{x}}_n)$ has maxima at two points $\mathbf{b}^1$, $\mathbf{b}^2$ and the estimator $(\mathbf{b})_n$ approximately would be $(\mathbf{b}^1 + \mathbf{b}^2)/2$, but $\mathbf{b}^*$ actually is close to either $\mathbf{b}^1$ or $\mathbf{b}^2$. Such a situation can be created if identifiability constraints are not imposed which would eliminate one of these solutions.

Zero–One Loss Function

A loss function assigning zero loss to the point $\mathbf{b}$ at which $f(\mathbf{b}|\dot{\mathbf{x}}_n)$ is maximum has the disadvantage that maximum, for small sample sizes, could be because of noise or bad samples; then a large error could result. A possible advantage of this loss function is that an integral such as in (5) need not be computed; however, this usually is a small advantage for unsupervised estimation problems where $\mathbf{x}$ has a mixture density $h(\mathbf{x})$ and $f(\mathbf{b}|\dot{\mathbf{x}}_n)$ must be computed at each point $\mathbf{b}$ in the parameter space anyway.

2-9 Bayes Estimator for Mean Vector (Covariance Matrix Known)

Let $\mathbf{x}$ be an L-dimensional Gaussian observation vector with mean $\mathbf{m}$ and covariance matrix $\mathbf{\Phi}$:

$$f(\mathbf{x}|\mathbf{m}) = c_1 \exp\{-\tfrac{1}{2}[(\mathbf{x} - \mathbf{m})^t\mathbf{\Phi}^{-1}(\mathbf{x} - \mathbf{m})]\}, \tag{1}$$

where c_1 is a constant and *it is understood that $\mathbf{\Phi}$ is known.*

A frequently used model views $\mathbf{x}$ as the vector sum of a fixed vector $\mathbf{m}$ and a random vector $\mathbf{n}$, the latter corresponding to noise. Letting vector addition $\mathbf{m} + \mathbf{n}$ be represented by $\oplus$, a model of $\mathbf{x} = \mathbf{n} + \mathbf{m}$ is shown as follows:

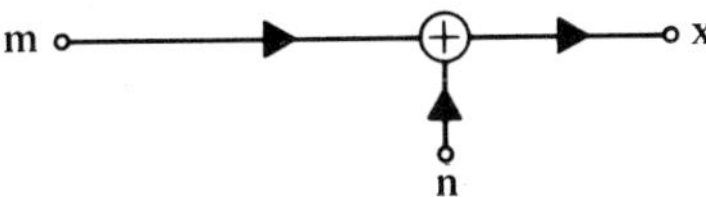

In this model,

$$\mathbf{\Phi} = E[\mathbf{nn}^t],$$

$$\mathbf{m} = E[\mathbf{x}].$$

Denote (as always) the true value of $\mathbf{m}$ by $\mathbf{m}^*$, unknown to the statistician, diagnostician, or classifier. An a priori guess is that the true value of $\mathbf{m}$ is $\mathbf{m}_a$; let the uncertainty in this guess be described by a density function,

$$f(\mathbf{m}) = c_2 \exp\{-\tfrac{1}{2}[(\mathbf{m} - \mathbf{m}_a)^t\mathbf{\Sigma}_a^{-1}(\mathbf{m} - \mathbf{m}_a)]\}. \tag{2}$$

The objective is to find the a posteriori density $f(\mathbf{m}|\mathbf{x}_1, \mathbf{x}_2, \ldots, \mathbf{x}_n)$ and thus the Bayes estimator of $\mathbf{m}^*$ given n statistically independent, identically distributed samples $\mathbf{x}_1, \mathbf{x}_2, \ldots, \mathbf{x}_n$. Hopefully, $f(\mathbf{m}|\mathbf{x}_1, \mathbf{x}_2, \ldots, \mathbf{x}_n)$ will, for large n, become a delta function† at $\mathbf{m}^*$.

†A delta function at $\mathbf{m}^*$ concentrates a probability of 1 at $\mathbf{m}^*$, thus giving all points not at $\mathbf{m}^*$ zero probability.

Using Bayes theorem† and one sample $\mathbf{x}_1$,

$$
\begin{aligned}
f(\mathbf{m}\,|\,\mathbf{x}_1) &= \frac{f(\mathbf{x}_1\,|\,\mathbf{m})f(\mathbf{m})}{f(\mathbf{x}_1)} \\
&= \frac{c_1 c_2 \exp\{-\tfrac{1}{2}[(\mathbf{x}_1 - \mathbf{m})^t \boldsymbol{\Phi}^{-1}(\mathbf{x}_1 - \mathbf{m})]\}}{f(\mathbf{x}_1)} \\
&\qquad\qquad\qquad \times \exp\{-\tfrac{1}{2}[(\mathbf{m} - \mathbf{m}_a)^t \boldsymbol{\Sigma}_a^{-1}(\mathbf{m} - \mathbf{m}_a)]\}/f(\mathbf{x}_1) \\
&= c_3 \exp\{-\tfrac{1}{2}[\mathbf{m}^t(\boldsymbol{\Phi}^{-1} + \boldsymbol{\Sigma}_a^{-1})\mathbf{m} - 2\mathbf{m}^t(\boldsymbol{\Phi}^{-1}\mathbf{x}_1 + \boldsymbol{\Sigma}_a^{-1}\mathbf{m}_a)]\}, \qquad (3)
\end{aligned}
$$

where

$$
c_3 = \frac{c_1 c_2 \exp\{-\tfrac{1}{2}[\mathbf{x}_1^t \boldsymbol{\Phi}^{-1}\mathbf{x}_1 + \mathbf{m}_a^t \boldsymbol{\Sigma}_a^{-1}\mathbf{m}_a]\}}{f(\mathbf{x}_1)}.
$$

It can be shown‡ that $f(\mathbf{m}\,|\,\mathbf{x}_1)$ is multivariate Gaussian if $f(\mathbf{x}_1\,|\,\mathbf{m})$ and $f(\mathbf{m})$ are multivariate Gaussian. Hence $f(\mathbf{m}\,|\,\mathbf{x}_1)$ has the multivariate Gaussian form

$$
\begin{aligned}
f(\mathbf{m}\,|\,\mathbf{x}_1) &= k_1 \exp\{-\tfrac{1}{2}[(\mathbf{m} - (\boldsymbol{\mu})_1)^t (\boldsymbol{\Sigma})_1^{-1}(\mathbf{m} - (\boldsymbol{\mu})_1)]\} \\
&= k_1 \exp\{-\tfrac{1}{2}[\mathbf{m}^t(\boldsymbol{\Sigma})_1^{-1}\mathbf{m} + (\boldsymbol{\mu})_1^t(\boldsymbol{\Sigma})_1^{-1}(\boldsymbol{\mu})_1 - 2\mathbf{m}^t(\boldsymbol{\Sigma})_1^{-1}(\boldsymbol{\mu})_1]\} \\
&= k_2 \exp\{-\tfrac{1}{2}[\mathbf{m}^t(\boldsymbol{\Sigma})_1^{-1}\mathbf{m} - 2\mathbf{m}^t(\boldsymbol{\Sigma})_1^{-1}(\boldsymbol{\mu})_1]\}, \qquad (4)
\end{aligned}
$$

where

$$
k_2 = k_1 \exp\{-\tfrac{1}{2}[(\boldsymbol{\mu})_1^t(\boldsymbol{\Sigma})_1^{-1}(\boldsymbol{\mu})_1]\}
$$

is a normalization constant.

Comparing (4) with (3), we obtain

$$
(\boldsymbol{\Sigma})_1^{-1}(\boldsymbol{\mu}_1) = \boldsymbol{\Phi}^{-1}\mathbf{x}_1 + \boldsymbol{\Sigma}_a^{-1}\mathbf{m}_a
$$

or

$$
(\boldsymbol{\mu})_1 = (\boldsymbol{\Sigma})_1 \boldsymbol{\Phi}^{-1}\mathbf{x}_1 + (\boldsymbol{\Sigma})_1 \boldsymbol{\Sigma}_a^{-1}\mathbf{m}_a \qquad (5)
$$

Also,

$$
(\boldsymbol{\Sigma})_1^{-1} = (\boldsymbol{\Phi}^{-1} + \boldsymbol{\Sigma}_a^{-1})
$$

---

†It cannot be emphasized enough that $\mathbf{m}$ is not a random vector! Our lack of knowledge causes $\mathbf{m}$ to appear to us as a random vector; under Bayes iteration, our knowledge increases.

‡Problem 9; i.e., Gaussian reproduces itself under Bayes iteration.

or

$$(\mathbf{\Sigma})_1 = (\mathbf{\Phi}^{-1} + \mathbf{\Sigma}_a^{-1})^{-1}$$
$$= [\mathbf{\Sigma}_a^{-1}(I + \mathbf{\Sigma}_a\mathbf{\Phi}^{-1})]^{-1}$$
$$= [\mathbf{\Sigma}_a^{-1}(\mathbf{\Phi} + \mathbf{\Sigma}_a)\mathbf{\Phi}^{-1}]^{-1}$$
$$= \mathbf{\Phi}(\mathbf{\Phi} + \mathbf{\Sigma}_a)^{-1}\mathbf{\Sigma}_a. \tag{6}$$

Using Bayes theorem and n samples $\mathbf{x}_1, \mathbf{x}_2, \ldots, \mathbf{x}_n$,

$$f(\mathbf{m} \,|\, \mathbf{x}_1, \mathbf{x}_2, \ldots, \mathbf{x}_n) = \frac{\prod_{s=1}^{n} f(\mathbf{x}_s \,|\, \mathbf{m}) f(\mathbf{m})}{f(\mathbf{x}_1, \mathbf{x}_2, \ldots, \mathbf{x}_n)}$$
$$= \frac{f(\mathbf{x}_n \,|\, \mathbf{m}) f(\mathbf{m} \,|\, \mathbf{x}_1, \mathbf{x}_2, \ldots, \mathbf{x}_{n-1})}{f(\mathbf{x}_1, \mathbf{x}_2, \ldots, \mathbf{x}_n)}. \tag{7}$$

It can be shown by induction that $f(\mathbf{m} \,|\, \mathbf{x}_1, \mathbf{x}_2, \ldots, \mathbf{x}_n)$ is multivariate Gaussian for any n. The mean and covariance of $\mathbf{m}$ given $\dot{\mathbf{x}}_n$ will be denoted $(\mathbf{\mu})_n$ and $(\mathbf{\Sigma})_n$, respectively. It is not difficult to show† using induction that the equivalent of (6) for $(\mathbf{\Sigma})_n$ when n samples are processed is

$$(\mathbf{\Sigma})_n = \mathbf{\Phi}[\mathbf{\Phi} + (\mathbf{\Sigma})_{n-1}]^{-1}(\mathbf{\Sigma})_{n-1}$$
$$= \frac{\mathbf{\Phi}}{n}\left(\mathbf{\Sigma}_a + \frac{\mathbf{\Phi}}{n}\right)^{-1}\mathbf{\Sigma}_a. \tag{8}$$

The extension of (5) for n samples will be clearer after rewriting (5) as

$$(\mathbf{\mu})_1 = \mathbf{\Phi}(\mathbf{\Phi} + \mathbf{\Sigma}_a)^{-1}\mathbf{\Sigma}_a\mathbf{\Phi}^{-1}\mathbf{x}_1 + \mathbf{\Phi}(\mathbf{\Phi} + \mathbf{\Sigma}_a)^{-1}\mathbf{m}_a$$
$$= \mathbf{\Phi}[(\mathbf{\Phi}\mathbf{\Sigma}_a^{-1})(\mathbf{\Phi} + \mathbf{\Sigma}_a)]^{-1}\mathbf{x}_1 + \mathbf{\Phi}(\mathbf{\Phi} + \mathbf{\Sigma}_a)^{-1}\mathbf{m}_a$$
$$= \mathbf{\Phi}[\mathbf{\Phi}\mathbf{\Sigma}_a^{-1}(I + \mathbf{\Sigma}_a\mathbf{\Phi}^{-1})\mathbf{\Phi}]^{-1}\mathbf{x}_1 + \mathbf{\Phi}(\mathbf{\Phi} + \mathbf{\Sigma}_a)^{-1}\mathbf{m}_a$$
$$= \mathbf{\Phi}[(\mathbf{\Phi}\mathbf{\Sigma}_a^{-1} + I)\mathbf{\Phi}]^{-1}\mathbf{x}_1 + \mathbf{\Phi}(\mathbf{\Phi} + \mathbf{\Sigma}_a)^{-1}\mathbf{m}_a$$
$$= (\mathbf{\Phi}\mathbf{\Sigma}_a^{-1} + I)^{-1}\mathbf{x}_1 + \mathbf{\Phi}(\mathbf{\Phi} + \mathbf{\Sigma}_a)^{-1}\mathbf{m}_a$$
$$= \mathbf{\Sigma}_a(\mathbf{\Phi} + \mathbf{\Sigma}_a)^{-1}\mathbf{x}_1 + \mathbf{\Phi}(\mathbf{\Phi} + \mathbf{\Sigma}_a)^{-1}\mathbf{m}_a. \tag{9}$$

It can be shown using an induction proof‡ that for n samples (9) extends to

$$(\mathbf{\mu})_n = \mathbf{\Sigma}_a\left(\mathbf{\Sigma}_a + \frac{1}{n}\mathbf{\Phi}\right)^{-1}\frac{1}{n}\sum_{s=1}^{n}\mathbf{x}_s + \frac{1}{n}\mathbf{\Phi}\left(\mathbf{\Sigma}_a + \frac{1}{n}\mathbf{\Phi}\right)^{-1}\mathbf{m}_a. \tag{10}$$

†Do Problem 10.
‡Do Problem 11.

Since $(\boldsymbol{\mu})_n$ is the mean of $\mathbf{m}$ with respect to $f(\mathbf{m}\,|\,\mathbf{x}_1, \mathbf{x}_2, \ldots, \mathbf{x}_n)$, it follows that

$$(\boldsymbol{\mu})_n = E[\mathbf{m}\,|\,\mathbf{x}_1, \mathbf{x}_2, \ldots, \mathbf{x}_n],$$

which is the Bayes estimator of $\mathbf{m}^*$ using quadratic loss function.†

In summary, the Bayes estimator $(\boldsymbol{\mu})_n$ (with quadratic loss function) of the mean vector $\mathbf{m}^*$ is given by (10) with $\mathbf{m}_a$ an a priori guess with uncertainty prescribed by a covariance $\boldsymbol{\Sigma}_a$. The covariance of $(\boldsymbol{\mu})_n$ after n samples is given by (8).

The above result is under the assumption that $\mathbf{x}$ has a Gaussian distribution with unknown mean $\mathbf{m}^*$ and known covariance $\boldsymbol{\Phi}$.

Diagonal Covariance Matrices

When

$$\boldsymbol{\Phi} = \sigma^2 \mathbf{I}, \qquad \boldsymbol{\Sigma}_a = \sigma_a^2 \mathbf{I}, \tag{11}$$

then $(\boldsymbol{\Sigma})_n$ and $(\boldsymbol{\mu})_n$ simplify. Inserting (11) in (8),

$$(\boldsymbol{\Sigma})_n = \sigma_a^2 \left[\left(\sigma_a^2 + \frac{1}{n}\sigma^2 \right) \mathbf{I} \right]^{-1} \frac{1}{n}\sigma^2 \mathbf{I}$$

$$= \frac{\sigma_a^2 \sigma^2}{n(\sigma_a^2 + (1/n)\sigma^2)}\mathbf{I} = \frac{\sigma^2}{n}\frac{1}{(1 + \sigma^2/n\sigma_a^2)}\mathbf{I}. \tag{12}$$

If in addition to assumption (11), $\sigma^2 \ll \sigma_a^2$, then

$$(\boldsymbol{\Sigma})_n \cong \frac{1}{n}\sigma^2 \mathbf{I}$$

and, if $\sigma^2 \gg n\sigma_a^2$,

$$(\boldsymbol{\Sigma})_n \cong \sigma_a^2 I.$$

For large n,

$$(\boldsymbol{\Sigma})_n \cong \frac{1}{n}\sigma^2 \mathbf{I}.$$

Assuming (11), $\boldsymbol{\mu}_n$ simplifies to

$$(\boldsymbol{\mu})_n = \frac{1}{n}\sigma_a^2 \left(\sigma_a^2 + \frac{1}{n}\sigma^2 \right)^{-1} \sum_{s=1}^{n} \mathbf{x}_s + \frac{1}{n}\sigma^2 \left(\sigma_a^2 + \frac{1}{n}\sigma^2 \right)^{-1} \mathbf{m}_a$$

$$= \frac{\sigma_a^2}{\sigma_a^2 + (1/n)\sigma^2} \frac{1}{n}\sum_{s=1}^{n} \mathbf{x}_s + \left(\frac{(1/n)\sigma^2}{\sigma_a^2 + (1/n)\sigma^2} \right)\mathbf{m}_a. \tag{13}$$

†Do Problem 12.

For large n, it is easy to see from the above that

$$(\boldsymbol{\mu})_n \xrightarrow{p} E[\mathbf{x}] = \mathbf{m}^*, \tag{14}$$

$$\lim_{n \to \infty} (\boldsymbol{\Sigma})_n = \mathbf{0}. \tag{15}$$

Using the strong law of large numbers,

$$(\boldsymbol{\mu})_n \xrightarrow{\text{w.p.1}} E[\mathbf{x}] = \mathbf{m}^*. \tag{16}$$

Convergence rates of Bayes estimators are discussed in Chapter 5 for the general case of mixture densities. The results there also apply to the current problem of estimating the mean vector of a normal distribution.

Signal-Design Comment

The uncertainty $(\boldsymbol{\Sigma})_n$ in the estimator $(\boldsymbol{\mu})_n$ does not depend on the true mean vector $\mathbf{m}^*$. Thus, increasing signal energy will not reduce uncertainty in the Bayes estimate of $\mathbf{m}^*$.

Effective Noise

Because the a posteriori density of $\mathbf{x}$, $f(\mathbf{x} \mid \mathbf{x}_1, \mathbf{x}_2, \ldots, \mathbf{x}_n)$, is

$$f(\mathbf{x} \mid \mathbf{x}_1, \mathbf{x}_2, \ldots, \mathbf{x}_n) = \int f(\mathbf{x} \mid \mathbf{m}) f(\mathbf{m} \mid \mathbf{x}_1, \mathbf{x}_2, \ldots, \mathbf{x}_n)\, d\mathbf{m}, \tag{17}$$

it can be shown† that $f(\mathbf{x} \mid \mathbf{x}_1, \mathbf{x}_2, \ldots, \mathbf{x}_n)$ is Gaussian with mean $(\boldsymbol{\mu})_n$ and covariance $(\boldsymbol{\Sigma})_n + \boldsymbol{\Phi}$. Thus, applying the strong law of large numbers,

$$f(\mathbf{x} \mid \mathbf{x}_1, \mathbf{x}_2, \ldots, \mathbf{x}_n) \xrightarrow{\text{w.p.1}} N(\mathbf{x} \mid \mathbf{m}^*, \boldsymbol{\Phi}),$$

where we also have applied (16) and (17). It follows, therefore, that the effective noise is $(\boldsymbol{\Sigma})_n + \boldsymbol{\Phi}$ after n samples. The effective noise converges to the actual noise $\boldsymbol{\Phi}$ with probability 1.

The above interpretation is very useful in practice because it shows that *the effect of estimating a probability density at* $\mathbf{x}$ *is to increase the covariance of* $\mathbf{x}$ *over the case of known distribution.*

†Do Problem 14; we have used $h(\mathbf{x} \mid \mathbf{m}, \mathbf{x}_1, \ldots, \mathbf{x}_n) = h(\mathbf{x} \mid \mathbf{m})$ or that the samples are parameter conditionally independent.

2-10 Bayes Estimate for Mean Vector and Covariance Matrix

Just as in Section 2-9, let $\mathbf{x}$ be an L-dimensional Gaussian observation vector with mean $\mathbf{m}$ and covariance matrix $\boldsymbol{\Phi}$. Now let both $\mathbf{m}$ and $\boldsymbol{\Phi}$ be unknown and

$$f(\mathbf{x}\,|\,\mathbf{m}, \boldsymbol{\Phi}) = c \, \exp\{-\tfrac{1}{2}[(\mathbf{x} - \mathbf{m})'\boldsymbol{\Phi}^{-1}(\mathbf{x} - \mathbf{m})]\}. \tag{1}$$

It will be convenient to use the inverse covariance matrix $\mathbf{A} \triangleq \boldsymbol{\Phi}^{-1}$.

In the previous section the Gaussian distribution was used to prescribe an a priori guess with a priori prescribed uncertainty for the fixed but unknown mean vector. A distribution that has, in various research papers, been prescribed a priori for the fixed but unknown covariance matrix is the Wishart distribution.

Wishart Distribution

1. If $(\mathbf{x}_1, \mathbf{x}_2, \ldots, \mathbf{x}_n)$ are L-dimensional vector samples $(L < n)$ from the normal distribution $N(\mathbf{x}\,|\,\mathbf{m}, \boldsymbol{\Phi})$ and if $\{v_{ij}\}$ are elements of the scatter matrix of the sample about the population mean $\mathbf{m}$, i.e.,

$$v_{ij} = v_{ji} = \sum_{s=1}^{n} (x_{si} - m_i)(x_{sj} - m_j),$$

then the elements of $[v_{ij}]_{LL}$ have the probability density function,

$$f(\{v_{ij}\}) = \frac{|\varphi_{ij}|^{(1/2)n}\,|v_{ij}|^{(1/2)(n-L-1)} \exp(-\tfrac{1}{2}\sum\limits_{i,\,j=1}^{L} \varphi_{ij}v_{ij})}{2^{(1/2)Ln}\,\pi^{(1/4)L(L-1)}\Gamma\left(\dfrac{n}{2}\right)\Gamma\left(\dfrac{n-1}{2}\right)\cdots\Gamma\left(\dfrac{n-L+1}{2}\right)}, \tag{2}$$

where

$$\boldsymbol{\Phi} = [\varphi_{ij}]_{LL}$$

and $f(\{v_{ij}\}) = 0$ in the region for which $\{v_{ij}\}$ is not positive definite. For convenience, denote this distribution by $W(\{v_{ij}\}\,|\,L, n, \boldsymbol{\Phi})$.

2. It can be shown that

$$E[|v_{ij}|] = L!\binom{n}{L}|\varphi_{ij}|$$

and therefore that

$$\lim_{n\to\infty} E[v_{ij}] = \varphi_{ij}.$$

Other properties of the scatter matrix $[v_{ij}]$ and the Wishart distribution are as follows.

3. If $\{v_{ij}^1\}$ and $\{v_{ij}^2\}$ are independent sets having respective Wishart distributions with parameters L, n_1, $\boldsymbol{\Phi}$ and L, n_2, $\boldsymbol{\Phi}$, the set $\{v_{ij}^1 + v_{ij}^2\}$ has the Wishart distribution with parameters L, $n_1 + n_2$, and $\boldsymbol{\Phi}$.

4. Let $\{u_{ij}\}$ be the scatter matrix about the sample mean; i.e.,

$$u_{ij} = \sum_{s=1}^{n} (x_{si} - \bar{x}_i)(x_{sj} - \bar{x}_j),$$

where

$$\bar{x}_i = \frac{1}{n} \sum_{s=1}^{n} x_{si};$$

then

if $\mathbf{x}_1, \mathbf{x}_2, \ldots, \mathbf{x}_n$ are from $N(\mathbf{x}|\mathbf{m}, \boldsymbol{\Phi})$, then the elements of $\{u_{ij}\}$ and the sample means $\bar{\mathbf{x}} = [\bar{x}_1, \bar{x}_2, \ldots, \bar{x}_L]$ are independent sets of random variables having the distributions $W(\{u_{ij}\}|L, n-1, \boldsymbol{\Phi})$ and $N(\bar{\mathbf{x}}|\mathbf{m}, (1/n)\boldsymbol{\Phi})$, respectively. Thus,

$$f(\{u_{ij}\}, \bar{\mathbf{x}}|\mathbf{m}, \boldsymbol{\Phi}) = W(\{u_{ij}\}|L, n-1, \boldsymbol{\Phi})N\left(\bar{\mathbf{x}}|\mathbf{m}, \frac{1}{n}\boldsymbol{\Phi}\right).$$

It is now possible to conclude the following[†] from properties 3 and 4:

5. If $\mathbf{x}_1, \mathbf{x}_2, \ldots, \mathbf{x}_{n_1}$ and $\mathbf{x}_{n_1+1}, \ldots, \mathbf{x}_{n_1+n_2}$ are samples from $N(\mathbf{x}|\mathbf{m}, \boldsymbol{\Phi})$ with corresponding independent scatters $\{u_{ij}^1\}$ and $\{u_{ij}^2\}$, then the elements $\{u_{ij}^1 + u_{ij}^2\}$ and

$$\bar{\mathbf{x}} = \frac{n_1}{n_1 + n_2} \frac{1}{n_1} \sum_{s=1}^{n_1} \mathbf{x}_s + \frac{n_2}{n_1 + n_2} \frac{1}{n_2} \sum_{s=n_1+1}^{n_1+n_2} \mathbf{x}_s$$

are independent sets of random variables having the distributions

$$W(\{u_{ij}^1 + u_{ij}^2\}|L, n_1 + n_2 - 1, \boldsymbol{\Phi}) \text{ and } N\left(\bar{\mathbf{x}}|\mathbf{m}, \frac{1}{n_1 + n_2}\boldsymbol{\Phi}\right).$$

Application

Suppose we are given samples from a Gaussian distribution $N(\bar{\mathbf{x}}|\mathbf{m}, \boldsymbol{\Phi})$ and $\mathbf{m}$ and $\boldsymbol{\Phi}$ are fixed, but unknown, parameters. It usually is important and

†See reference [3].

sometimes necessary to use an a priori "guess" for $\mathbf{m}$ and $\boldsymbol{\Phi}$. Let this "guess" be expressed in terms of a sample mean and scatter matrix as follows:

A Priori Guess

n_1: effective number of a priori samples,

$$\boldsymbol{\mu}^1 = \frac{1}{n_1} \sum_{s=1}^{n_1} \mathbf{x}_s,$$

$$[u_{ij}^1] = \left[\frac{1}{n_1 - 1} \sum_{s=1}^{n_1} (x_{si} - \mu_i^1)(x_{sj} - \mu_j^1) \right] \triangleq \boldsymbol{\Phi}^1.$$

Current Estimate

n_2: number of current samples,

$$\boldsymbol{\mu}^2 = \frac{1}{n_2} \sum_{s=n_1+1}^{n_1+n_2} \mathbf{x}_s, \qquad \text{current mean estimate,}$$

$$[u_{ij}^2] = \left[\frac{1}{n_2 - 1} \sum_{s=n_1+1}^{n_1+n_2} (x_{si} - \mu_i^2)(x_{sj} - \mu_j^2) \right] = \boldsymbol{\Phi}^2.$$

The new estimate of the mean vector and covariance matrix using both a priori and current samples is

$$n = n_1 + n_2,$$

$$(\boldsymbol{\mu})_n = \frac{n_1}{n_1 + n_2} \boldsymbol{\mu}^1 + \frac{n_2}{n_1 + n_2} \boldsymbol{\mu}^2, \tag{3}$$

$$(\boldsymbol{\Phi})_n = \frac{n_1}{n_1 + n_2} \boldsymbol{\Phi}^1 + \frac{n^2}{n_1 + n_2} \boldsymbol{\Phi}^2. \tag{4}$$

Since n_1 is fixed, as n_2 increases,

$$(\boldsymbol{\mu})_n \xrightarrow{\text{w.p.1}} E[\mathbf{x}] = \mathbf{m}^*,$$

$$(\boldsymbol{\Phi})_n \xrightarrow{\text{w.p.1}} \boldsymbol{\Phi}^*,$$

where $\mathbf{m}^*$ and $\boldsymbol{\Phi}^*$ are the true mean and covariance matrix, respectively.

Successive Updating

There are applications, such as in clustering, where it is appropriate to update r times. The previous results can be generalized to this application by defining n_i, $\boldsymbol{\Phi}^i$, $\boldsymbol{\mu}^i$, $i = 1, 2, \ldots, r$. Then, with

$$n = \sum_{i=1}^{r} n_i, \tag{5}$$

the new estimates of mean vector and covariance matrix are

$$(\boldsymbol{\mu})_n = \sum_{i=1}^{r} \frac{n_i}{n} \boldsymbol{\mu}^i, \tag{6}$$

$$(\boldsymbol{\Phi})_n = \sum_{i=1}^{r} \frac{n_i}{n} \boldsymbol{\Phi}^i. \tag{7}$$

This procedure has application where, at each stage, there is uncertainty and, say, the actual mean vector $\mathbf{m}^*$ is changing. This occurs in a tracking situation. Of course, the uncertainty will never be removed unless confidence can be eventually established by n_r becoming large.

Modification for Growing Clusters

One approach to clustering is to *grow* clusters (see Section 5-4.8). It is appropriate in this section, where mean and covariance updating is introduced, to discuss a few rules for updating having application in growing clusters. One objective is to show that the statistical approach based on estimation has limitations; another approach is to discuss how procedures based on rules (devised for the problem concerned) can be developed.

Suppose that there is a cluster of samples $\mathbf{x}_1, \mathbf{x}_2, \ldots, \mathbf{x}_n$, as shown:

Define $\boldsymbol{\mu}^i$ as before but let

$$(\boldsymbol{\Phi})_n = \sum_{i=1}^{r} \frac{n_i}{n} \boldsymbol{\Phi}^i + \sum_{i=2}^{r} (\boldsymbol{\mu}^i - \boldsymbol{\mu}^{i-1})(\boldsymbol{\mu}^i - \boldsymbol{\mu}^{i-1})^t. \tag{8}$$

Then suppose that $\boldsymbol{\mu}^1, \boldsymbol{\mu}^2, \boldsymbol{\mu}^3$, and $\boldsymbol{\mu}^4$ for $r = 4$ are as shown:

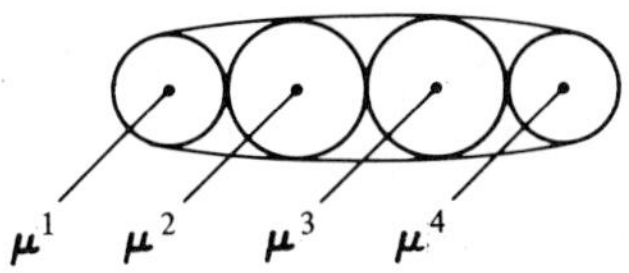

We see that $(\boldsymbol{\mu})_n$ defined according to (6) will tend to be near the average value of the cluster and $(\boldsymbol{\Phi})_n$ *given by (8) will have grown to fit the cluster.*

There are numerous other considerations when growing clusters. The following are problems that require special consideration.

Problem 1

Suppose there are two clusters, as shown,

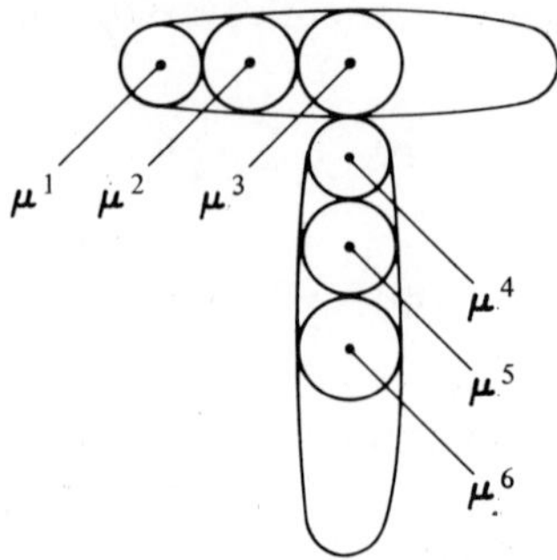

where it is possible that the successive means will be as shown because of the method used to select selective sets of samples. Clearly, a covariance matrix given by (7) is incorrect. A possible remedy is to compute

$$\sum_{i=1}^{2} \frac{n_i}{n} \Phi^i + (\mu^2 - \mu^1)(\mu^2 - \mu^1)',$$

$$\sum_{i=5}^{6} \frac{n_i}{n} \Phi^i + (\mu^6 - \mu^5)(\mu^6 - \mu^5)',$$

and observe that they are significantly different. This suggests that there are two significant directions; the procedure could be begun again, growing clusters only in these two directions.

Problem 2

Suppose there is one boomerang-shaped cluster, as shown:

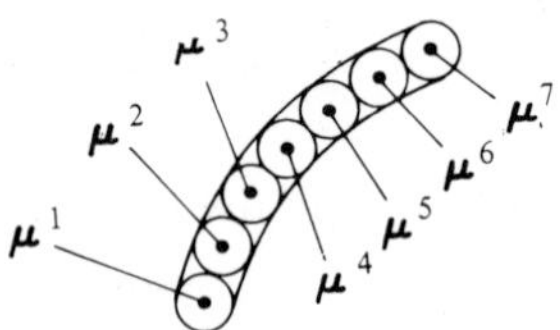

Then

$$(\mu^i - \mu^{i-1})(\mu^i - \mu^{i-1})', \qquad i = 1, 2, 3, 4, 5, 6, 7,$$

would be consistently changing in significant direction and could be used to indicate the presence of such a boomerang-shaped cluster.

     Elementary Properties of Estimators   Chap. 2

There are many possible configurations in which clusters can present themselves in a particular problem. For example, they can appear as shown:

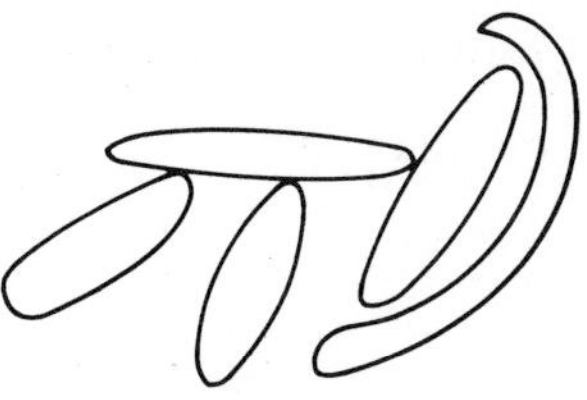

A reasonable approach to separating clusters such as these is to use a "context"-table approach. In this approach, a spherical cluster could be used as a basic element. Then clusters of various shapes could be listed in the table and the problem under consideration built up using basic clusters. *This demonstrates the limitation of an approach limited only to statistical considerations.* As these examples have shown, rules can be developed to handle specific problems. Estimation procedures are very important, but once estimation is understood, the student or practitioner of pattern recognition should realize that he is just beginning: *He must study the "problem knowledge" associated with his particular problem and discover how this knowledge can be used to enhance estimation of parameters. Chapter 6 provides an introduction to the viable frontier of using problem knowledge in the pattern-recognition process.*

2-11 Reproducing Densities and Bayes Estimates

The probability density function $f(\mathbf{b})$ is said to reproduce itself with respect to the conditional density $h(\mathbf{x}\,|\,\mathbf{b})$ if $f(\mathbf{b}\,|\,\mathbf{x})$ is in the same family of functions as $f(\mathbf{b})$, differing only in the values of the parameters characterizing members in the family. For example, if $f(\mathbf{b})$ is Gaussian and

$$f(\mathbf{b}\,|\,\mathbf{x}) = \frac{h(\mathbf{x}\,|\,\mathbf{b})f(\mathbf{b})}{f(\mathbf{x})}$$

also is Gaussian, then $f(\mathbf{b})$ is reproducing in the above sense.

Now two theorems and a corollary are presented concerning reproducing densities. Also, a table is presented listing probability densities which are reproducing along with the Bayes estimators for parameters involved.

Reproducing Density Existence Theorem 1

If the samples $\mathbf{x}_1, \ldots, \mathbf{x}_n$ are parameter conditionally independent and identically distributed, then a reproducing a priori density $f(\mathbf{b})$ exists if and only if the samples $\mathbf{x}_1, \ldots, \mathbf{x}_n$ admit a sufficient statistic of fixed finite dimension for estimating $\mathbf{b}^*$.

Proof

Suff. Assume a sufficient statistic of fixed finite dimension r exists,

$$\mathbf{s}_n = [s_{n1}, s_{n2}, \ldots, s_{nr}]. \tag{1}$$

Since

$$f(\mathbf{b} \mid \dot{\mathbf{x}}_n) = \frac{f(\dot{\mathbf{x}}_n \mid \mathbf{b}) f(\mathbf{b})}{\int [\text{num}] \, d\mathbf{b}}$$

and by the Neyman–Fischer theorem

$$f(\dot{\mathbf{x}}_n \mid \mathbf{b}) = v(\mathbf{s}_n \mid \mathbf{b}) w(\dot{\mathbf{x}}_n), \tag{2}$$

it follows that

$$f(\mathbf{b} \mid \dot{\mathbf{x}}_n) = \frac{v(\mathbf{s}_n \mid \mathbf{b}) w(\dot{\mathbf{x}}_n) f(\mathbf{b})}{\int [\text{num}] \, d\mathbf{b}}. \tag{3}$$

Since $w(\dot{\mathbf{x}}_n)$ is independent of $\mathbf{b}$, it factors out of the integral; therefore,

$$f(\mathbf{b} \mid \dot{\mathbf{x}}_n) = \frac{v(s_{n1}, s_{n2}, \ldots, s_{nr} \mid \mathbf{b}) f(\mathbf{b})}{\int [\text{num}] \, d\mathbf{b}}. \tag{4}$$

This is a fixed function of the parameters $s_{n1}, s_{n2}, \ldots, s_{nr}$ for all n. Hence, the a posteriori densities differ only in the values assigned to these parameters and they all have the same functional form. Thus they are reproducing with respect to one another. Therefore, if $f(\mathbf{b})$ has a factor of the form $v(s_0 \mid \mathbf{b})$ where s_0 is the sufficient statistic for an "a priori set" of (fictitious) vectors $\mathbf{x}_1, \mathbf{x}_2, \ldots, \mathbf{x}_m$, then it has the same form as $f(\mathbf{b} \mid \dot{\mathbf{x}}_n)$ for all n and thus a reproducing a priori density exists.

Necc. If a reproducing a priori density $f(\mathbf{b})$ exists, then $f(\mathbf{b} \mid \dot{\mathbf{x}}_n)$ is of fixed functional form expressible in terms of a fixed set of r parameters regardless of n:

$$f(\mathbf{b} \mid \dot{\mathbf{x}}_n) = v(s_{n1}, \ldots, s_{nr}, \mathbf{b}).$$

Thus,

$$f(\dot{\mathbf{x}}_n \mid \mathbf{b}) = \frac{f(\mathbf{b} \mid \dot{\mathbf{x}}_n) f(\dot{\mathbf{x}}_n)}{f(\mathbf{b})}$$

$$= v(s_{n1}, \ldots, s_{nr}) f(\dot{\mathbf{x}}_n),$$

where v depends on $\dot{\mathbf{x}}_n$ only through $\mathbf{s}_n$ and $f(\dot{\mathbf{x}}_n)$ does not depend on $\mathbf{b}$.

Elementary Properties of Estimators   Chap. 2

Therefore, by the Neyman–Fischer theorem a sufficient statistic of fixed finite dimension exists.

Theorem

If a reproducing a priori density exists, then $f(\mathbf{b})$ is a reproducing density if and only if it is of the form

$$f(\mathbf{b}) = \frac{v(\mathbf{s}_0 \mid \mathbf{b}) r(\mathbf{b})}{\int [\text{num}] \, d\mathbf{b}}, \tag{5}$$

where $r(\mathbf{b})$ is any nonnegative function of $\mathbf{b}$ such that the integral in the denominator exists and $r(\mathbf{b})$ contains no factor of the form $[v(\mathbf{s}_0 \mid \mathbf{b})]^{-1}$.

Proof

Suff.   This was shown in suff. proof of the previous theorem.

Necc.   Assume a reproducing density exists. Then $f(\mathbf{b} \mid \dot{\mathbf{x}}_n)$ and $f(\mathbf{b})$ are of the same form. But in the proof of the previous theorem it was shown the a posteriori density is of the form

$$\frac{v(\mathbf{s}_n \mid \mathbf{b}) f(\mathbf{b})}{\int [\text{num}] \, d\mathbf{b}}.$$

Thus $f(\mathbf{b})$ must be of the same form, i.e., contain a factor of the form $f(\mathbf{s}_0 \mid \mathbf{b})$ if it is to reproduce.

Corollary

If a reproducing a priori density exists, then the sequence of a posteriori densities computed by Bayes iteration becomes reproducing after a few observations, regardless of whether $f(\mathbf{b})$ is reproducing or not.

Proof: After n observations,

$$f(\mathbf{b} \mid \dot{\mathbf{x}}_n) = \frac{f(\dot{\mathbf{x}}_n \mid \mathbf{b}) f(\mathbf{b})}{\int [\text{num}] \, d\mathbf{b}} = \frac{v(\mathbf{s}_n \mid \mathbf{b}) f(\mathbf{b})}{\int [\text{num}] \, d\mathbf{b}}$$

and by the second theorem, this form is reproducing.

This corollary indicates that the existence of a sufficient statistic of fixed finite dimension is really the fundamental property in obtaining reproducing a posteriori densities.

In cases where reproducing densities exist, it is often easiest to generate them by choosing an "a priori set" of m_0 (fictitious) observations to generate $\mathbf{s}_0$ and a nonnegative function $r(\mathbf{b})$ and setting

$$f(\mathbf{b}) = \frac{f(\dot{\mathbf{x}}_{m_0} \mid \mathbf{b})r(\mathbf{b})}{\int [\text{num}] \, d\mathbf{b}}$$

or equivalently if only the sufficient statistic is chosen,

$$f(\mathbf{b}) = \frac{v(\mathbf{s}_0 \mid \mathbf{b})r(\mathbf{b})}{\int [\text{num}] \, d\mathbf{b}}.$$

The "a priori set" of observations and $r(\mathbf{b})$ can be chosen to represent various forms and amounts of a priori knowledge.

Reproducing densities cannot always exist. In particular, if $f(\dot{\mathbf{x}}_n \mid \mathbf{b})$ is a mixture, then since generally no sufficient statistic of fixed finite dimension exists, no reproducing a priori density exists. As an example, suppose $M = 2$, $L = 1$, and the family is Gaussian:

$$h(x \mid m_1, m_2, \sigma_1^2, \sigma_2^2, p)$$

$$= \frac{p}{\sqrt{2\pi}\sigma_1} \exp\left[-\frac{(x - m_1)^2}{2\sigma_1^2}\right] + \frac{(1 - p)}{\sqrt{2\pi}\sigma_2} \exp\left[-\frac{(x - m_2)^2}{2\sigma_2^2}\right]. \tag{6}$$

Dynkin [52] has shown that no nontrivial sufficient statistic exists for the above density if at least one of the parameters m_1, m_2, σ_1^2, σ_2^2, or p is unknown. The trivial sufficient statistics are the samples themselves. Therefore, no sufficient statistic of fixed finite dimensions exists, and by the first theorem no reproducing a priori density can exist for the mixture.

In the following table a list of familiar densities which have been shown to be reproducing are presented. These densities are discussed in detail in Section 2-11. The reader should note that any density has a finitely discretized density characterized by "bin probabilities" $p^1, p^2, \ldots, p^V$ (see density 9 in the table).

In general, data generally represented $\mathbf{x}$ will not have a distribution which is reproducing. There are, however, several important, well-known distributions which are reproducing. These reproducing distributions, especially the Gaussian, can be used as building blocks for constructing reproducing representations of nonreproducing distributions.

No.	Prob. Distribution of Samples	Fixed but Unknown Parameters	Reproducing Density	Bayes Estimate for Quadratic Loss
1	Binomial	p	Beta; r_0, n_0	$(p)_n = (r + r_0 + 1)/(n + n_0 + 2)$
2	Multinomial (V bins)	$1, \ldots, p_V$	Dirichlet; $r_{01}, r_{02}, \ldots, r_{0V}, n_0 = \sum_{v=1}^{V} r_{0v}$	$(p_v)_n = (r_v + r_{0v} + 1)/(n + n_0 + V)$
3	Gaussian	$\mathbf{m}$	Gaussian; $\mathbf{m}_0, \boldsymbol{\Sigma}_0$	$(\mathbf{m})_n = \frac{1}{n}\boldsymbol{\Sigma}\left[\frac{1}{n}\boldsymbol{\Sigma} + \boldsymbol{\Sigma}_0\right]^{-1}\mathbf{m}_0 + \boldsymbol{\Sigma}_0\left[\frac{1}{n}\boldsymbol{\Sigma} + \boldsymbol{\Sigma}_0\right]^{-1}\left(\frac{1}{n}\sum_{j=1}^{n}\mathbf{x}_j\right)$
4	Gaussian	$\boldsymbol{\Sigma}^{-1}$	Wishart; $v_0, \boldsymbol{\Sigma}_0$	$(\boldsymbol{\Sigma})_n = \frac{v_0}{n + r_0}\boldsymbol{\Sigma}_0 + \frac{n}{n + r_0}\left(\frac{1}{n}\sum_{j=1}^{n}(\mathbf{x}_j - \mathbf{m})(\mathbf{x}_j - \mathbf{m})^t\right)$
5	Gaussian	$\mathbf{m}, \boldsymbol{\Sigma}^{-1}$	Gaussian–Wishart; $n_0, \mathbf{m}_0, v_0, \boldsymbol{\Sigma}_0$	$(\mathbf{m})_n = \frac{n_0}{n + n_0}\mathbf{m}_0 + \frac{n}{n + n_0}\left(\frac{1}{n}\sum_{j=1}^{n}\mathbf{x}_j\right)$ $(\boldsymbol{\Sigma})_n = \frac{1}{n + v_0}\{[(n-1)\mathbf{S} + n\bar{\mathbf{x}}_n\bar{\mathbf{x}}_n^t] + [v_0\boldsymbol{\Sigma}_0 + n_0\mathbf{m}_0, \mathbf{m}_0^t] - (n + n_0)(\mathbf{m})_n(\mathbf{m})_n^t\}$ where $\mathbf{S}_n = \frac{1}{n-1}\sum_{j=1}^{n}(\mathbf{x}_j - \bar{\mathbf{x}}_n)(\mathbf{x}_j - \bar{\mathbf{x}}_n)^t$ $\bar{\mathbf{x}}_n = \frac{1}{n}\sum_{j=1}^{n}\mathbf{x}_j$
6	Poisson	α	Gamma; τ_0, m_0	$(a)_n = \left(1 + m_0 + \sum_{j=1}^{n} m_j\right)\Big/\left(\tau_0 + \sum_{j=1}^{n} \tau_j\right)$
7	Rayleigh	$\rho = 1/\sigma 2$	Gamma; b_0, c_0	$(\rho)_n = (b_0 + n + 1)/\left(c_0 + \sum_{j=1}^{n} x_j^2/2\right)$
8	Exponential	λ	Gamma; b_0, c_0	$(\lambda)_n = (b_0 + n + 1)/\left(c_0 + \sum_{j=1}^{n} x_j\right)$
9	Density with finitely discretized parameter space	p^v	Discrete $\{(p^v)_0\}_{v=1}^{V}$ at $\{\mathbf{b}^v\}_{v=1}^{V}$	$(\mathbf{b})_n = \sum_{v=1}^{V} \mathbf{b}^v(p^v)_n$ $(p^v)_n = \dfrac{h(\mathbf{x}_n \mid \mathbf{b}^v)(p^v)_{n-1}}{\sum_{v=1}^{V} h(\mathbf{x}_n \mid \mathbf{b}^v)(p^v)_{n-1}}$

2-11.1 Binomial

Let **x** be one-dimensional and

$$x_s = \begin{cases} 1, & \text{with probability } p, \\ 0, & \text{with probability } 1 - p. \end{cases} \tag{7}$$

To find a simple reproducing density (simple meaning $r(\mathbf{b}) = $ constant) a specific a priori sequence $\dot{\mathbf{x}}_{n_0}$ consisting of r_0 ones and $n_0 - r_0$ zeros is assumed. By the second theorem of the previous section,

$$f(p) = \frac{f(\dot{\mathbf{x}}_{n_0}|p)}{\int f(\dot{\mathbf{x}}_{n_0}|p)\,dp} = \begin{cases} \dfrac{p^{r_0}(1 - p)^{n_0 - r_0}}{\int_0^1 p^{r_0}(1 - p)^{n_0 - r_0}\,dp}, & 0 < p < 1, \\[6pt] 0, & \text{otherwise,} \end{cases}$$

But

$$\int_0^1 p^{r_0}(1 - p)^{n_0 - r_0}\,dp = \frac{\Gamma(r_0 + 1)\Gamma(n_0 - r_0 + 1)}{\Gamma(n_0 + 2)}.$$

Thus a reproducing a priori density is

$$f(p) = \begin{cases} \dfrac{\Gamma(n_0 + 2)}{\Gamma(r_0 + 1)\Gamma(n_0 - r_0 + 1)} p^{r_0}(1 - p)^{n_0 - r_0}, & 0 < p < 1, \\[6pt] 0, & \text{otherwise,} \end{cases} \tag{8}$$

which is the beta density with parameters r_0 and n_0.

Now if $\dot{\mathbf{x}}_n$ has r ones and $n - r$ zeros,

$$f(p|\dot{\mathbf{x}}_n) = \frac{f(\dot{\mathbf{x}}_n|p)f(p)}{\int (\text{num})\,dp} = \frac{p^r(1 - p)^{n-r}[c(r_0, n_0 - r_0)p^{r_0}(1 - p)^{n_0 - r_0}]}{\int [\text{num}]\,dp}$$

$$= \frac{p^{r+r_0}(1 - p)^{n+n_0-(r+r_0)}}{\int_0^1 p^{r+r_0}(1 - p)^{n+n_0-(r+r_0)}\,dp} \qquad \text{where } c(r_0, n_0 - r_0) \text{ is constant}$$

and therefore,

$$f(p|\dot{\mathbf{x}}_n)$$

$$= \begin{cases} \dfrac{\Gamma(n + n_0 + 2)}{\Gamma(r + r_0 + 1)\Gamma[n + n_0 - (r + r_0) + 1]} p^{r+r_0}(1 - p)^{n+n_0-(r+r_0)}, & 0 < p < 1, \\[6pt] 0, & \text{otherwise,} \end{cases}$$
$$\tag{9}$$

which is also the beta density with parameters $r + r_0$ and $n + n_0$.

Bayes Estimate

The Bayes estimate of p for quadratic loss is $(p)_n = E[(p \mid \dot{\mathbf{x}}_n)]$. Since $f(p \mid \dot{\mathbf{x}}_n)$ has the beta density with parameters $r + r_0$ and $n + n_0$ its mean is therefore $(r + r_0 + 1)/(n + n_0 + 2)$. Thus,

$$(p)_n = \frac{r + r_0 + 1}{n + n_0 + 2}, \tag{10a}$$

where there are r ones in $\dot{\mathbf{x}}_n$. Or in recursive form,

$$(p)_n = \frac{x_n}{n + n_0 + 2} + \frac{n + n_0 + 1}{n + n_0 + 2}(p)_{n-1}, \tag{10b}$$

where

$$(p)_0 = \frac{r_0 + 1}{n_0 + 2}. \tag{10c}$$

2-11.2 Multinomial

Let $\mathbf{x}$ be multidimensional or one-dimensional with

$$\mathbf{x}_s \in \begin{cases} \mathscr{I}_1 \text{ with probability } p_1 \\ \mathscr{I}_2 \text{ with probability } p_2 \\ \vdots \\ \mathscr{I}_V \text{ with probability } p_V, \, p_V = 1 - \sum_{v=1}^{V-1} p_v, \end{cases} \tag{11}$$

where $\mathscr{I}_1, \mathscr{I}_2, \ldots, \mathscr{I}_V$ are a set of nonoverlapping regions which cover the observation space. It can be convenient to write (11) as

$$\mathbf{x}_s = \begin{cases} 1 \text{ with probability } p_1 \\ 2 \text{ with probability } p_2 \\ \vdots \\ V \text{ with probability } p_V. \end{cases} \tag{12}$$

Define

$$\mathbf{p} = [p_1, p_2, \ldots, p_V]. \tag{13}$$

To find a simple reproducing density, a specific a priori sequence $\dot{\mathbf{x}}_{n_0}$

consisting of r_{01} ones, r_{02} twos, $\ldots$, and $r_{0V} = n_0 - \sum_{j=1}^{R-1} r_{0j}$ V's is assumed. By the second theorem,

$$f(\mathbf{p}) = \frac{f(\dot{\mathbf{x}}_{n_0} \mid \mathbf{p})}{\int f(\dot{\mathbf{x}}_{n_0} \mid \mathbf{p}) \, d\mathbf{p}}$$

$$= \begin{cases} \dfrac{p_1^{r_{01}} p_2^{r_{02}} \cdots p_V^{r_{0V}}}{\int_0^1 \int_0^{1-p_1} \cdots \int_0^{1-\sum_{v=1}^{V-1} p_v} p_1^{r_{01}} p_2^{r_{02}} \cdots p_V^{r_{0V}} \, dp_V \, dp_{V-1} \cdots dp_1} \\ \qquad\qquad\qquad\qquad\qquad\qquad\qquad p_v \geq 0, \quad \sum_{v=1}^{V} p_v = 1, \\[2mm] 0, \qquad\qquad\qquad\qquad\qquad\qquad\qquad \text{otherwise,} \end{cases}$$

The denominator is

$$\frac{\Gamma(r_{01} + 1)\Gamma(r_{02} - 1) \cdots \Gamma(r_{0V} + 1)}{\Gamma(n_0 + V)}$$

Thus a reproducing a priori density is

$$f(\mathbf{p}) = \begin{cases} \dfrac{\Gamma(n_0 + V)}{\Gamma(r_{01} + 1) \cdots \Gamma(r_{0V} + 1)} \, p_1^{r_{01}} p_2^{r_{02}} \cdots p_V^{r_{0V}}, & p_v \geq 0, \ \sum_{v=1}^{V} p_v = 1, \\[2mm] 0, & \text{otherwise,} \end{cases}$$

$$(14)$$

which is the Dirichlet density with parameters r_{0v}, $v = 1, \ldots, V$, where $n_0 = \sum_{v=1}^{V} r_{0v}$.

Now if $\dot{\mathbf{x}}_n$ has r_1 ones, r_2 twos, $\ldots$, and $r_V = n - \sum_{v=1}^{V-1} r_v$ V's, then

$$f(\mathbf{p} \mid \dot{\mathbf{x}}_n) = \frac{p_1^{r_1} p_2^{r_2}, \ldots, \, p_V^{r_V} [c(r_{01}, \ldots, r_{0V}) p_1^{r_{01}} p_2^{r_{02}} \cdots p_V^{r_{0V}}}{\int [\text{num}] \, d\mathbf{p}}$$

$$= \frac{p_1^{(r_1 + r_{01})} p_2^{(r_2 + r_{02})} \cdots p_V^{(r_V + r_{0V})}}{\int [\text{num}] \, d\mathbf{p}}$$

and therefore,

$$f(\mathbf{p} \mid \dot{\mathbf{x}}_n) = \begin{cases} \dfrac{\Gamma(n + n_0 + V)}{\Gamma(r_1 + r_{01} + 1) \cdots \Gamma(r_V + r_{0V} + 1)} p_1^{(r_1 + r_{01})} p_2^{(r_2 + r_{02})} \cdots p_V^{(r_V + r_{0V})}, \\ \qquad\qquad\qquad\qquad\qquad\qquad\qquad p_v \geq 0, \ \sum_{v=1}^{V} p_v = 1, \\[2mm] 0, \qquad\qquad\qquad\qquad\qquad\qquad\qquad \text{otherwise,} \end{cases}$$

$$(15)$$

which is also the Dirichlet density as expected.

The Bayes estimate of $\mathbf{p}$ for quadratic loss is

$$(\mathbf{p})_n = E[\mathbf{p} \mid \dot{\mathbf{x}}_n].$$

Since $f(\mathbf{p} \mid \dot{\mathbf{x}}_n)$ has the Dirichlet density with parameters $r_j + r_{0j}, j = 1, \ldots,$ V, the mean of $\mathbf{p}$, is

$$\left[\frac{r_1 + r_{01} + 1}{n + n_0 + V}, \frac{r_2 + r_{02} + 1}{n + n_0 + V}, \ldots, \frac{r_V + r_{0V} + 1}{n + n_0 + V} \right].$$

Thus,

$$(p_v)_n = \frac{r_v + r_{0v} + 1}{n + n_0 + V}, \tag{16}$$

where there are r_v v's in $\dot{\mathbf{x}}_n$. Or in recursive form,

$$(p_v)_n = \frac{\delta_v(\mathbf{x}_n)}{n + n_0 + V} + \frac{n + n_0 + V - 1}{n + n_0 + V}(p_v)_{n-1}, \tag{17}$$

where $(p_v)_0 = (r_{0v} + 1)/(n_0 + V)$ and

$$\delta_v(\mathbf{x}_n) = \begin{cases} 1, & \text{if } \mathbf{x}_n = v, \\ 0, & \text{if } \mathbf{x}_n \neq v. \end{cases}$$

2-11.3 Gaussian—Unknown m

Assume $\mathbf{x}$ is L-dimensional, $\mathbf{\Sigma}$ known, and

$$f(\mathbf{x} \mid \mathbf{m}) = \frac{1}{(2\pi)^{L/2} |\mathbf{\Sigma}|^{1/2}} \exp[-\tfrac{1}{2}(\mathbf{x} - \mathbf{m})'\mathbf{\Sigma}^{-1}(\mathbf{x} - \mathbf{m})].$$

To find a simple reproducing density, a specific a priori sequence $\dot{\mathbf{x}}_{n_0}$ is assumed. By the second theorem,

$$f(\mathbf{m}) = \frac{f(\dot{\mathbf{x}}_{n_0} \mid \mathbf{m})}{\int f(\dot{\mathbf{x}}_{n_0} \mid \mathbf{m}) \, d\mathbf{m}} = \frac{\prod\limits_{j=1}^{n_0} f(\mathbf{x}_j \mid \mathbf{m})}{\int [\text{num}] \, d\mathbf{m}}$$

$$= \frac{\exp[-\tfrac{1}{2} \sum\limits_{j=1}^{n_0} (\mathbf{x}_j - \mathbf{m})'\mathbf{\Sigma}^{-1}(\mathbf{x}_j - \mathbf{m})]}{\int [\text{num}] \, d\mathbf{m}}.$$

Now,

$$\sum_{j=1}^{n_0} (\mathbf{x}_j - \mathbf{m})^t \, \Sigma^{-1} \, (\mathbf{x}_j - \mathbf{m}) = (\mathbf{m} - \bar{\mathbf{x}}_{n_0})^t \left(\frac{1}{n_0}\Sigma\right)^{-1} (\mathbf{m} - \bar{\mathbf{x}}_{n_0})$$

$$+ \sum_{j=1}^{n_0} (\mathbf{x}_j - \bar{\mathbf{x}}_{n_0})^t \Sigma^{-1} (\mathbf{x}_j - \bar{\mathbf{x}}_{n_0}),$$

where

$$\bar{\mathbf{x}}_{n_0} \triangleq \frac{1}{n_0} \sum_{j=1}^{n_0} \mathbf{x}_j.$$

Thus,

$$f(\mathbf{m}) = \frac{k(\Sigma, \dot{\mathbf{x}}_{n_0}) \exp\left[-\tfrac{1}{2}(\mathbf{m} - \bar{\mathbf{x}}_{n_0})^t \left(\frac{1}{n_0}\Sigma\right)^{-1} (\mathbf{m} - \bar{\mathbf{x}}_{n_0})\right]}{\int [\text{num}] \, d\mathbf{m}}.$$

Now this is the Gaussian form with respect to $\mathbf{m}$. Thus, the normalizing constant is

$$\frac{1}{(2\pi)^{L/2} \left|\dfrac{1}{n_0}\Sigma\right|^{1/2}}.$$

Let $\Sigma_0 = \dfrac{1}{n}\Sigma$ and $\mathbf{m}_0 = \bar{\mathbf{x}}_{n_0}$.

Then a reproducing a priori density is

$$f(\mathbf{m}) = \frac{1}{(2\pi)^{L/2} |\Sigma_0|^{1/2}} \exp[-\tfrac{1}{2}(\mathbf{m} - \mathbf{m}_0)^t \Sigma_0^{-1}(\mathbf{m} - \mathbf{m}_0)], \qquad (18)$$

which is Gaussian with parameters Σ_0 and $\mathbf{m}_0$. Now,

$$f(\mathbf{m} \,|\, \dot{\mathbf{x}}_n) = \frac{f(\dot{\mathbf{x}}_n \,|\, \mathbf{m}) f(\mathbf{m})}{\int [\text{num}] \, d\mathbf{m}}.$$

But, as before, $f(\dot{\mathbf{x}}_n \,|\, \mathbf{m})$ can be written

$$f(\dot{\mathbf{x}}_n \,|\, \mathbf{m}) = k(\Sigma, \dot{\mathbf{x}}_n) \exp\left[-\tfrac{1}{2}(\mathbf{m} - \bar{\mathbf{x}}_n)^t \left(\frac{1}{n}\Sigma\right)^{-1} (\mathbf{m} - \bar{\mathbf{x}}_n)\right],$$

where

$$\bar{\mathbf{x}}_n = \frac{1}{n} \sum_{j=1}^{n} \mathbf{x}_j.$$

Thus,

$$f(\mathbf{m} \mid \dot{\mathbf{x}}_n) = \frac{c(\boldsymbol{\Sigma}, \boldsymbol{\Sigma}_0, \dot{\mathbf{x}}_n) \exp[-\frac{1}{2}(\mathbf{m} - \bar{\mathbf{x}}_n)^t\left(\frac{1}{n}\boldsymbol{\Sigma}\right)^{-1}(\mathbf{m} - \bar{\mathbf{x}}_n) - \frac{1}{2}(\mathbf{m} - \mathbf{m}_0)^t\boldsymbol{\Sigma}^{-1}(\mathbf{m} - \mathbf{m}_0)]}{\int [\text{num}] \, d\mathbf{m}}.$$

But

$$(\mathbf{m} - \bar{\mathbf{x}}_n)^t\left(\frac{1}{n}\boldsymbol{\Sigma}\right)^{-1}(\mathbf{m} - \bar{\mathbf{x}}_n) + (\mathbf{m} - \mathbf{m}_0)^t\boldsymbol{\Sigma}_0^{-1}(\mathbf{m} - \mathbf{m}_0)$$

$$= \mathbf{m}^t\left(\frac{1}{n}\boldsymbol{\Sigma}\right)^{-1}\mathbf{m} - 2\mathbf{m}^t\left(\frac{1}{n}\boldsymbol{\Sigma}\right)^{-1}\bar{\mathbf{x}}_n + \bar{\mathbf{x}}_n^t\left(\frac{1}{n}\boldsymbol{\Sigma}\right)^{-1}\bar{\mathbf{x}}_n$$

$$+ \mathbf{m}(\boldsymbol{\Sigma}_0)^{-1}\mathbf{m} - 2\mathbf{m}^t(\boldsymbol{\Sigma}_0)^{-1}\mathbf{m}_0 + \mathbf{m}_0^t\boldsymbol{\Sigma}_0^{-1}\mathbf{m}_0.$$

Collecting terms,

$$= \mathbf{m}^t\boldsymbol{\Sigma}_n^{-1}\mathbf{m} - 2\mathbf{m}^t\boldsymbol{\Sigma}_n^{-1}\mathbf{m}_n + d(\dot{\mathbf{x}}_n, \boldsymbol{\Sigma}, \mathbf{m}_0, \boldsymbol{\Sigma}_0),$$

where

$$\boldsymbol{\Sigma}_n^{-1} = (\boldsymbol{\Sigma}_0)^{-1} + \left(\frac{1}{n}\boldsymbol{\Sigma}\right)^{-1};$$

$$\mathbf{m}_n = \boldsymbol{\Sigma}_n\left[(\boldsymbol{\Sigma}_0)^{-1}\mathbf{m}_0 + \left(\frac{1}{n}\boldsymbol{\Sigma}\right)^{-1}\bar{\mathbf{x}}_n\right].$$

Completing the square by adding and subtracting $\mathbf{m}_n^t\boldsymbol{\Sigma}_n^{-1}\mathbf{m}_n$ we have

$$= (\mathbf{m} - \mathbf{m}_n)^t\boldsymbol{\Sigma}_n^{-1}(\mathbf{m} - \mathbf{m}_n) + d_0(\dot{\mathbf{x}}_n, \boldsymbol{\Sigma}, \mathbf{n}_0, \boldsymbol{\Sigma}_0).$$

Therefore,

$$f(\mathbf{m} \mid \dot{\mathbf{x}}_n) = \frac{\exp[-\frac{1}{2}(\mathbf{m} - \mathbf{m}_n)^t\boldsymbol{\Sigma}_n^{-1}(\mathbf{m} - \mathbf{m}_n)]}{\int [\text{num}] \, d\mathbf{m}},$$

which, as expected, has the Gaussian form w.r.t., $\mathbf{m}$. Normalizing gives

$$f(\mathbf{m} \mid \dot{\mathbf{x}}_n) = \frac{1}{(2\pi)^{L/2} |\boldsymbol{\Sigma}_n|^{1/2}} \exp[-\frac{1}{2}(\mathbf{m} - \mathbf{m}_n)^t\boldsymbol{\Sigma}_n^{-1}(\mathbf{m} - \mathbf{m}_n)], \qquad (19\text{a})$$

where

$$\boldsymbol{\Sigma}_n = \boldsymbol{\Sigma}_0\left[\frac{1}{n}\boldsymbol{\Sigma} + \boldsymbol{\Sigma}_0\right]^{-1}\frac{1}{n}\boldsymbol{\Sigma} \qquad (19\text{b})$$

and

$$\mathbf{m}_n = \frac{1}{n}\mathbf{\Sigma}\left[\frac{1}{n}\mathbf{\Sigma} + \mathbf{\Sigma}_0\right]^{-1}\mathbf{m}_0 + \mathbf{\Sigma}_0\left[\frac{1}{n}\mathbf{\Sigma} + \mathbf{\Sigma}_0\right]^{-1}\frac{1}{n}\sum_{j=1}^{n}\mathbf{x}_j. \qquad (19c)$$

Bayes Estimate

The Bayes estimate of $\mathbf{m}$ for quadratic loss is $(\mathbf{m})_n = E[\mathbf{m}\,|\,\dot{\mathbf{x}}_n]$. Since $f(\mathbf{m}\,|\,\dot{\mathbf{x}}_n)$ is Gaussian with mean $\mathbf{m}_n$,

$$(\mathbf{m})_n = \frac{1}{n}\mathbf{\Sigma}\left[\frac{1}{n}\mathbf{\Sigma} + \mathbf{\Sigma}_0\right]^{-1}\mathbf{m}_0 + \mathbf{\Sigma}_0\left[\frac{1}{n}\mathbf{\Sigma} + \mathbf{\Sigma}_0\right]^{-1}\left(\frac{1}{n}\sum_{j=1}^{n}\mathbf{x}_j\right). \qquad (20a)$$

Or in recursive form,

$$(\mathbf{m})_n = \mathbf{\Sigma}(\mathbf{\Sigma} + \mathbf{\Sigma}_{n-1})^{-1}(\mathbf{m})_{n-1} + \mathbf{\Sigma}_{n-1}[\mathbf{\Sigma} + \mathbf{\Sigma}_{n-1}]^{-1}\mathbf{x}_n, \qquad (20b)$$

where

$$\mathbf{\Sigma}_n = \mathbf{\Sigma}(\mathbf{\Sigma} + \mathbf{\Sigma}_{n-1})^{-1}\mathbf{\Sigma}_{n-1}. \qquad (20c)$$

2-11.4 Gaussian—Unknown $\mathbf{\Sigma}^{-1}$

If $\mathbf{x}$ is L-dimensional with $\mathbf{m}$ known,

$$f(\mathbf{x}\,|\,\mathbf{\Sigma}^{-1}) = \frac{|\mathbf{\Sigma}^{-1}|^{1/2}}{(2\pi)^{L/2}}\exp[-\tfrac{1}{2}(\mathbf{x} - \mathbf{m})'\mathbf{\Sigma}^{-1}(\mathbf{x} - \mathbf{m})].$$

To find a simple reproducing density a specific a priori sequence $\dot{\mathbf{x}}_{n_0}$ is assumed. By the second theorem,

$$f(\mathbf{\Sigma}^{-1}) = \frac{f(\dot{\mathbf{x}}_{n_0}\,|\,\mathbf{\Sigma}^{-1})}{\displaystyle\int f(\dot{\mathbf{x}}_{n_0}\,|\,\mathbf{\Sigma}^{-1})\,d\mathbf{\Sigma}^{-1}}$$

$$= \frac{\dfrac{|\mathbf{\Sigma}^{-1}|^{n_0/2}}{(2\pi)^{n_0 L/2}}\exp[-\tfrac{1}{2}\sum_{j=1}^{n_0}(\mathbf{x}_j - \mathbf{m})'\mathbf{\Sigma}^{-1}(\mathbf{x} - \mathbf{m})]}{\displaystyle\int [\text{num}]\,d\mathbf{\Sigma}^{-1}}.$$

Define $\mathbf{V}_{n_0} = \sum_{j=1}^{n_0}(\mathbf{x}_j - \mathbf{m})(\mathbf{x}_j - \mathbf{m})'$; then from the identity

$$\operatorname{tr}\mathbf{V}_{n_0}\mathbf{\Sigma}^{-1} = \sum_{j=1}^{n_0}(\mathbf{x}_j - \mathbf{m})'\mathbf{\Sigma}^{-1}(\mathbf{x}_j - \mathbf{m}), \qquad (21)$$

the form becomes

$$f(\mathbf{\Sigma}^{-1}) = c(n_0, \dot{\mathbf{x}}_{n_0})|\mathbf{\Sigma}^{-1}|^{n_0/2} \exp[-\tfrac{1}{2}\operatorname{tr} \mathbf{V}_{n_0}\mathbf{\Sigma}^{-1}]$$
$$= c(n_0, \dot{\mathbf{x}}_{n_0})|\mathbf{\Sigma}^{-1}|^{(v_0-L-2)/2} \exp[-\tfrac{1}{2}\operatorname{tr} v_0\mathbf{\Sigma}_0\mathbf{\Sigma}^{-1}], \qquad (22)$$

where

$$v_0 = n_0 + L + 2, \qquad \mathbf{\Sigma}_0 = \frac{1}{v_0}\mathbf{V}_{n_0}.$$

This is the Wishart form with respect to $\mathbf{\Sigma}^{-1}$. The normalizing constant is

$$\left|\frac{v_0}{2}\mathbf{\Sigma}_0\right|^{(v_0-1)/2} \Bigg/ \left[\pi^{L(L-1)/4} \prod_{j=1}^{L} \Gamma\left(\frac{v_0-j}{2}\right)\right].$$

Thus a reproducing a priori density is

$$f(\mathbf{\Sigma}^{-1}) = \begin{cases} \dfrac{\left|\dfrac{v_0}{2}\mathbf{\Sigma}_0\right|^{(v_0-1)/2}}{\left[\pi^{L(L-1)/4} \prod\limits_{j=1}^{L} \Gamma\left(\dfrac{v_0-j}{2}\right)\right]} |\mathbf{\Sigma}^{-1}|^{(v_0-L-2)/2} \exp[-\tfrac{1}{2}\operatorname{tr} v_0\mathbf{\Sigma}_0\mathbf{\Sigma}^{-1}]; \\[6pt] \qquad\qquad\qquad\qquad \mathbf{\Sigma}^{-1} \text{ positive definite, symmetric,} \\ 0, \qquad\qquad\qquad\qquad \text{otherwise,} \end{cases}$$

$$(23)$$

which is Wishart [11, 53, 54] with parameters $\mathbf{\Sigma}_0$ and v_0. Now,

$$f(\mathbf{\Sigma}^{-1} \mid \dot{\mathbf{x}}_n) = \frac{f(\dot{\mathbf{x}}_n \mid \mathbf{\Sigma}^{-1})f(\mathbf{\Sigma}^{-1})}{\int [\text{num}]\, d\mathbf{\Sigma}^{-1}}.$$

But, as above, $f(\dot{\mathbf{x}}_n \mid \mathbf{\Sigma}^{-1})$ can be written

$$f(\dot{\mathbf{x}}_n \mid \mathbf{\Sigma}^{-1}) = \frac{|\mathbf{\Sigma}^{-1}|^{n/2}}{(2\pi)^{nL/2}} \exp[-\tfrac{1}{2}\operatorname{tr} \mathbf{V}_n\mathbf{\Sigma}^{-1}],$$

where

$$\mathbf{V}_n = \sum_{j=1}^{n} (\mathbf{x}_j - \mathbf{m})(\mathbf{x}_j - \mathbf{m})^t.$$

So

$$f(\mathbf{\Sigma}^{-1} \mid \dot{\mathbf{x}}_n) = c|\mathbf{\Sigma}^{-1}|^{(n+v_0-L-2)/2} \exp[-\tfrac{1}{2}[\operatorname{tr} v_0\mathbf{\Sigma}_0\mathbf{\Sigma}^{-1} + \operatorname{tr} \mathbf{V}_n\mathbf{\Sigma}^{-1}]].$$

But $\mathrm{tr}\ v_0\boldsymbol{\Sigma}_0\boldsymbol{\Sigma}^{-1} + \mathrm{tr}\ \mathbf{V}_n\boldsymbol{\Sigma}^{-1} = \mathrm{tr}\ (v_0\boldsymbol{\Sigma}_0 + \mathbf{V}_n)\boldsymbol{\Sigma}^{-1}$, so

$$f(\boldsymbol{\Sigma}^{-1}\,|\,\dot{\mathbf{x}}_n) = \begin{cases} \dfrac{\left|\dfrac{v_n}{2}\boldsymbol{\Sigma}_n\right|^{(v_n-1)/2}}{\left[\pi^{L(L-1)/4}\displaystyle\prod_{j=1}^{L}\Gamma\left(\dfrac{v_n-j}{2}\right)\right]}\,|\boldsymbol{\Sigma}^{-1}|^{(v_n-L-2)/2}\exp[-\tfrac{1}{2}\,\mathrm{tr}\ v_n\boldsymbol{\Sigma}_n\boldsymbol{\Sigma}^{-1}]; \\[4pt] \qquad\qquad\qquad\qquad\boldsymbol{\Sigma}^{-1}\ \text{positive definite, symmetric,} \\ 0, \qquad\qquad\qquad\qquad\text{otherwise,} \end{cases}$$

$$(24)$$

which, as expected, has the Wishart form with parameters

$$v_n = v_0 + n, \qquad \boldsymbol{\Sigma}_n = \frac{v_0\boldsymbol{\Sigma}_0 + n\left(\dfrac{1}{n}\displaystyle\sum_{j=1}^{n}(\mathbf{x}_j - \mathbf{m})(\mathbf{x}_j - \mathbf{m})^t\right)}{v_0 + n}.$$

Bayes Estimate

The Bayes estimate of $\boldsymbol{\Sigma}^{-1}$ for quadratic loss is $(\boldsymbol{\Sigma}^{-1})_n = E[\boldsymbol{\Sigma}^{-1}\,|\,\dot{\mathbf{x}}_n]$. Since $f(\boldsymbol{\Sigma}^{-1}\,|\,\dot{\mathbf{x}}_n)$ is Wishart with mean $(\boldsymbol{\Sigma}_n)^{-1}$,

$$(\boldsymbol{\Sigma}^{-1})_n = (\boldsymbol{\Sigma}_n)^{-1}.$$

And since $\boldsymbol{\Sigma} = (\boldsymbol{\Sigma}^{-1})^{-1}$, the corresponding estimate of $\boldsymbol{\Sigma}$ is

$$(\boldsymbol{\Sigma})_n = \boldsymbol{\Sigma}_n = \frac{v_0}{n + v_0}\boldsymbol{\Sigma}_0 + \frac{n}{n + v_0}\left[\frac{1}{n}\sum_{j=1}^{n}(\mathbf{x}_j - \mathbf{m})(\mathbf{x}_j - \mathbf{m})^t\right]. \qquad (25a)$$

In recursive form,

$$(\boldsymbol{\Sigma})_n = \frac{n + v_0 - 1}{n + v_0}(\boldsymbol{\Sigma})_{n-1} + \frac{(\mathbf{x}_n - \mathbf{m})(\mathbf{x}_n - \mathbf{m})^t}{n + v_0}. \qquad (25b)$$

Letting $v_n = n + v_0 = v_{n-1} + 1$,

$$(\boldsymbol{\Sigma})_n = \frac{v_{n-1}}{v_n}(\boldsymbol{\Sigma})_{n-1} + \frac{(\mathbf{x}_n - \mathbf{m})(\mathbf{x}_n - \mathbf{m})^t}{v_n}. \qquad (25c)$$

2-11.5 Gaussian—Unknown m and $\boldsymbol{\Sigma}^{-1}$

If $\mathbf{x}$ is L-dimensional,

$$f(\mathbf{x}\,|\,\mathbf{m}, \boldsymbol{\Sigma}^{-1}) = \frac{|\boldsymbol{\Sigma}^{-1}|^{1/2}}{(2\pi)^{L/2}}\exp[-\tfrac{1}{2}(\mathbf{x} - \mathbf{m})^t\boldsymbol{\Sigma}^{-1}(\mathbf{x} - \mathbf{m})].$$

To find a simple reproducing density a specific a priori sequence $\dot{\mathbf{x}}_{n_0}$ is

Elementary Properties of Estimators   *Chap. 2*

assumed. By the second theorem,

$$f(\mathbf{m}, \boldsymbol{\Sigma}^{-1}) = \frac{f(\dot{\mathbf{x}}_{n_0} \mid \mathbf{m}, \boldsymbol{\Sigma}^{-1})}{\int\!\int [\text{num}]\, d\mathbf{m}\, d\boldsymbol{\Sigma}^{-1}}$$

$$= \frac{\dfrac{|\boldsymbol{\Sigma}^{-1}|^{n_0/2}}{(2\pi)^{n_0 L/2}} \exp[-\tfrac{1}{2} \sum_{j=1}^{n_0} (\mathbf{x}_j - \mathbf{m})^t \boldsymbol{\Sigma}^{-1}(\mathbf{x}_j - \mathbf{m})]}{\int\!\int [\text{num}]\, d\mathbf{m}\, d\boldsymbol{\Sigma}^{-1}}.$$

Now,

$$\sum_{i=1}^{n_0} \left[\left(\frac{1}{n_0} \sum_{j=1}^{n_0} \mathbf{x}_j\right)^t \boldsymbol{\Sigma}^{-1}\mathbf{x}_i \right] = n_0 \left[\left(\frac{1}{n_0} \sum_{j=1}^{n_0} \mathbf{x}_j\right)^t \boldsymbol{\Sigma}^{-1} \left(\frac{1}{n_0} \sum_{i=1}^{n_0} \mathbf{x}_i\right) \right].$$

Therefore,

$$\sum_{j=1}^{n_0} (\mathbf{x}_j - \mathbf{m})^t \boldsymbol{\Sigma}^{-1}(\mathbf{x}_j - \mathbf{m}) = \sum_{j=1}^{n_0} (\mathbf{x}_j - \mathbf{m})^t \boldsymbol{\Sigma}^{-1}(\mathbf{x}_j - \mathbf{m}) + 2 \sum_{i=1}^{n_0} [\bar{\mathbf{x}}_{n_0}^t \boldsymbol{\Sigma}^{-1}\mathbf{x}_i]$$
$$- 2n_0 [\bar{\mathbf{x}}_{n_0}^t \boldsymbol{\Sigma}^{-1}\bar{\mathbf{x}}_{n_0}],$$

where

$$\bar{\mathbf{x}}_{n_0} = \frac{1}{n_0} \sum_{j=1}^{n_0} \mathbf{x}_j.$$

Expanding and recollecting terms gives

$$\sum_{j=1}^{n_0} (\mathbf{x}_j - \mathbf{m})^t \boldsymbol{\Sigma}^{-1}(\mathbf{x}_j - \mathbf{m}) = (\mathbf{m} - \bar{\mathbf{x}}_{n_0})^t \left(\frac{1}{n_0}\boldsymbol{\Sigma}\right)^{-1}(\mathbf{m} - \bar{\mathbf{x}}_{n_0}) + \operatorname{tr} \mathbf{V}_{n_0}\boldsymbol{\Sigma}^{-1},$$

where,

$$\mathbf{V}_{n_0} = \sum_{j=1}^{n_0} (\mathbf{x}_j - \bar{\mathbf{x}}_{n_0})(\mathbf{x}_j - \bar{\mathbf{x}}_{n_0})^t.$$

Thus

$$f(\mathbf{m}, \boldsymbol{\Sigma}^{-1}) = \frac{\left|\left(\dfrac{1}{n_0}\boldsymbol{\Sigma}\right)^{-1}\right|^{1/2}}{(2\pi)^{L/2}} \exp\left[-\tfrac{1}{2}(\mathbf{m} - \bar{\mathbf{x}}_{n_0})^t \left(\frac{1}{n_0}\boldsymbol{\Sigma}\right)^{-1}(\mathbf{m} - \bar{\mathbf{x}}_{n_0})\right] \cdot$$

$$\frac{|\boldsymbol{\Sigma}^{-1}|^{(n_0-1)/2}}{n_0^{L/2}(2\pi)^{((n_0-1)L)/2}} \exp\left[-\tfrac{1}{2} \operatorname{tr} \mathbf{V}_{n_0}\boldsymbol{\Sigma}^{-1}\right] \Big/ \int\!\int [\text{num}]\, d\mathbf{m}\, d\boldsymbol{\Sigma}^{-1}. \quad (26)$$

Now the first factor in $f(\mathbf{m}, \boldsymbol{\Sigma}^{-1})$ depends on $\mathbf{m}$ in the same manner as a Gaussian density depends on its argument, while the second factor depends on $\boldsymbol{\Sigma}^{-1}$ in the same manner as a Wishart density depends on its argument. Letting

$$v_0 = n_0 + L + 1, \qquad \boldsymbol{\Sigma}_0 = \frac{1}{v_0}\,\mathbf{V}_{n_0}, \qquad \mathbf{m}_0 = \bar{\mathbf{x}}_{n_0}$$

and normalizing gives

$f(\mathbf{m}_0, \boldsymbol{\Sigma}^{-1})$

$$= \begin{cases} \dfrac{\left|\left(\dfrac{1}{n_0}\boldsymbol{\Sigma}\right)^{-1}\right|^{1/2}}{(2\pi)^{L/2}}\,\exp\left[-\tfrac{1}{2}(\mathbf{m}-\mathbf{m}_0)^t\left(\dfrac{1}{n_0}\boldsymbol{\Sigma}\right)^{-1}(\mathbf{m}-\mathbf{m}_0)\right]\cdot \\[2ex] \dfrac{\left|\dfrac{v_0}{2}\boldsymbol{\Sigma}_0\right|^{(v_0-1)/2}}{\left[\pi^{L(L-1)/4}\displaystyle\prod_{j=1}^{L}\Gamma\left(\dfrac{v_0-j}{2}\right)\right]}\,|\boldsymbol{\Sigma}^{-1}|^{(v_0-L-2)/2}\exp[-\tfrac{1}{2}\operatorname{tr} v_0\boldsymbol{\Sigma}_0\boldsymbol{\Sigma}^{-1}], \\[3ex] \qquad\qquad\qquad\qquad\qquad \boldsymbol{\Sigma}^{-1} \text{ positive definite, symmetric,} \\[1ex] 0, \qquad\qquad\qquad\qquad\qquad\quad\ \text{otherwise.} \end{cases} \qquad (27)$$

By integrating first with respect to $\mathbf{m}$ and then noting $f(\mathbf{m}, \boldsymbol{\Sigma}^{-1}) = f(\mathbf{m}\,|\,\boldsymbol{\Sigma}^{-1})f(\boldsymbol{\Sigma}^{-1})$ one can interpret the above density. This density implies that $\boldsymbol{\Sigma}^{-1}$ is chosen from a Wishart density with parameters v_0 and $\boldsymbol{\Sigma}_0$. The mean then comes from a Gaussian density with mean $\mathbf{m}_0$ and covariance matrix $1/n_0\,\boldsymbol{\Sigma}$, the parameter n_0 reflecting the confidence in $\mathbf{m}_0$ as the value of the true mean.

Thus a reproducing a priori density is composite Gaussian–Wishart form [11], with parameters n_0, $\mathbf{m}_0$, v_0, and $\boldsymbol{\Sigma}_0$. Now,

$$f(\mathbf{m}, \boldsymbol{\Sigma}^{-1}\,|\,\dot{\mathbf{x}}_n) = \frac{f(\dot{\mathbf{x}}_n\,|\,\mathbf{m}, \boldsymbol{\Sigma}^{-1})f(\mathbf{m}, \boldsymbol{\Sigma}^{-1})}{\displaystyle\iint [\text{num}]\,d\mathbf{m}\,d\boldsymbol{\Sigma}^{-1}}.$$

Expanding and collecting terms as before,

$$f(\dot{\mathbf{x}}_n\,|\,\mathbf{m}, \boldsymbol{\Sigma}^{-1}) = \frac{1}{(2\pi)^{nL/2}}\,|\boldsymbol{\Sigma}^{-1}|^{n/2}\exp[-\tfrac{1}{2}\operatorname{tr}\mathbf{V}_n\boldsymbol{\Sigma}^{-1}]\cdot$$

$$c\exp\left[-\tfrac{1}{2}(\mathbf{m}-\bar{\mathbf{x}}_n)^t\left(\frac{1}{n}\boldsymbol{\Sigma}\right)^{-1}(\mathbf{m}-\bar{\mathbf{x}}_n)\right].$$

Thus,

$$f(\mathbf{m}, \boldsymbol{\Sigma}^{-1}\,|\,\dot{\mathbf{x}}_n) = c\,|\boldsymbol{\Sigma}^{-1}|^{(n+v_0-L-1)/2}\exp[-\tfrac{1}{2}\operatorname{tr}\mathbf{V}_n\boldsymbol{\Sigma}^{-1} + \operatorname{tr} v_0\boldsymbol{\Sigma}_0\boldsymbol{\Sigma}^{-1}]\cdot$$

$$\exp\left[-\tfrac{1}{2}(\mathbf{m}-\mathbf{m}_0)^t\left(\frac{1}{n_0}\boldsymbol{\Sigma}\right)^{-1}(\mathbf{m}-\mathbf{m}_0) - \tfrac{1}{2}(\mathbf{m}-\bar{\mathbf{x}}_n)^t\left(\frac{1}{n}\boldsymbol{\Sigma}\right)^{-1}(\mathbf{m}-\bar{\mathbf{x}}_n)\right]$$

where

$$\mathbf{V}_n = \sum_{j=1}^{n}(\mathbf{x}_j - \bar{\mathbf{x}}_n)(\mathbf{x}_j - \bar{\mathbf{x}}_n)^t$$

and

$$\bar{\mathbf{x}}_n = \frac{1}{n} \sum_{j=1}^{n} \mathbf{x}_j.$$

Expanding the terms in the second exponent gives

$$-\frac{1}{2}\left\{\mathbf{m}^t\left[\left(\frac{1}{n_0}\boldsymbol{\Sigma}\right)^{-1} + \left(\frac{1}{n}\boldsymbol{\Sigma}\right)^{-1}\right]\mathbf{m} - 2\mathbf{m}^t\left[\left(\frac{1}{n_0}\boldsymbol{\Sigma}\right)^{-1}\mathbf{m}_0 + \left(\frac{1}{n}\boldsymbol{\Sigma}\right)^{-1}\bar{\mathbf{x}}_n\right]\right.$$

$$\left. + \mathbf{m}_0^t\left(\frac{1}{n_0}\boldsymbol{\Sigma}\right)^{-1}\mathbf{m}_0 + \bar{\mathbf{x}}_n^t\left(\frac{1}{n}\boldsymbol{\Sigma}\right)^{-1}\bar{\mathbf{x}}_n\right\}$$

$$= -\frac{1}{2}\left\{\mathbf{m}^t\left(\frac{1}{n+n_0}\boldsymbol{\Sigma}\right)^{-1}\mathbf{m} - 2\mathbf{m}^t\left(\frac{1}{n+n_0}\boldsymbol{\Sigma}\right)^{-1}\left(\frac{n_0}{n+n_0}\mathbf{m} + \frac{n}{n+n_0}\bar{\mathbf{x}}_n\right)\right.$$

$$\left. + \mathbf{m}_0^t\left(\frac{1}{n_0}\boldsymbol{\Sigma}\right)^{-1}\mathbf{m}_0 + \bar{\mathbf{x}}_n^t\left(\frac{1}{n}\boldsymbol{\Sigma}\right)^{-1}\bar{\mathbf{x}}_n\right\}.$$

Completing the square by adding and subtracting

$$\left(\frac{n_0}{n+n_0}\mathbf{m}_0 + \frac{n}{n+n_0}\bar{\mathbf{x}}_n\right)^t\left(\frac{1}{n+n_0}\boldsymbol{\Sigma}\right)^{-1}\left(\frac{n_0}{n+n_0}\mathbf{m}_0 + \frac{n}{n+n_0}\bar{\mathbf{x}}_n\right)$$

gives

$$= -\frac{1}{2}\left\{(\mathbf{m} - \mathbf{m}_n)^t\left(\frac{1}{n+n_0}\boldsymbol{\Sigma}\right)^{-1}(\mathbf{m} - \mathbf{m}_n) + n_0\mathbf{m}_0^t\boldsymbol{\Sigma}^{-1}\mathbf{m}_0\right.$$

$$\left. + n\bar{\mathbf{x}}_n^t\boldsymbol{\Sigma}^{-1}\bar{\mathbf{x}}_n - (n + n_0)\mathbf{m}_n^t\boldsymbol{\Sigma}^{-1}\mathbf{m}_n\right\},$$

where $\mathbf{m}_n = n_0/(n + n_0)\,\mathbf{m}_0 + n/(n + n_0)\,\bar{\mathbf{x}}_n$.

Since $\mathbf{x}^t\boldsymbol{\Sigma}^{-1}\mathbf{x} = \mathrm{tr}\,\boldsymbol{\Sigma}^{-1}\mathbf{x}\mathbf{x}^t$, substituting this back into $f(\mathbf{m}, \boldsymbol{\Sigma}^{-1}\,|\,\dot{\mathbf{x}}_n)$ gives

$$f(\mathbf{m}, \boldsymbol{\Sigma}^{-1}\,|\,\dot{\mathbf{x}}_n) = c\,|\boldsymbol{\Sigma}^{-1}|^{(n+n_0-L-1)/2}\exp\left\{-\tfrac{1}{2}(\mathbf{m} - \mathbf{m}_n)^t\left(\frac{1}{n+n_0}\boldsymbol{\Sigma}\right)^{-1}(\mathbf{m} - \mathbf{m}_n)\right\} \cdot$$

$$\exp\{-\tfrac{1}{2}[\mathrm{tr}\,([\mathbf{V}_n + v_0\boldsymbol{\Sigma}_0 + n_0\mathbf{m}_0\mathbf{m}_0^t + n_0\bar{\mathbf{x}}_n\bar{\mathbf{x}}_n^t + (n + n_0)\mathbf{m}_n\mathbf{m}_n^t]\boldsymbol{\Sigma}^{-1})]\}.$$

Thus, letting

$$\mathbf{S}_n = \frac{1}{n-1}\mathbf{V}_n = \frac{1}{n-1}\sum_{j=1}^{n}(\mathbf{x}_j - \bar{\mathbf{x}}_n)(\mathbf{x}_j - \bar{\mathbf{x}}_n)^t$$

$$n_n = n + n_0$$

$$v_n = n + v_0$$

$$\mathbf{m}_n = \frac{n_0}{n+n_0}\mathbf{m}_0 + \frac{n}{n+n_0}\left(\frac{1}{n}\sum_{j=1}^{n}\mathbf{x}_j\right)$$

and

$$\boldsymbol{\Sigma}_n = \frac{1}{n + v_0}([(n-1)\mathbf{S}_n + n\bar{\mathbf{x}}_n\bar{\mathbf{x}}_n^t] + (v_0\boldsymbol{\Sigma}_0 + n_0\mathbf{m}_0\mathbf{m}_0^t) - n_n\mathbf{m}_n\mathbf{m}_n^t)$$

gives

$$f(\mathbf{m}, \boldsymbol{\Sigma}^{-1} \,|\, \dot{\mathbf{x}}_n) = k \left| \left(\frac{1}{n_n}\boldsymbol{\Sigma}\right)^{-1} \right|^{1/2} \exp\left\{-\tfrac{1}{2}(\mathbf{m}-\mathbf{m}_n)^t\left(\frac{1}{n_n}\boldsymbol{\Sigma}\right)^{-1}(\mathbf{m}-\mathbf{m}_n)\right\} \cdot$$

$$|\boldsymbol{\Sigma}^{-1}|^{(v_n-L-2)/2} \exp\{-\tfrac{1}{2}\operatorname{tr} v_n\boldsymbol{\Sigma}_n\boldsymbol{\Sigma}^{-1}\}.$$

which, as expected, has the composite Gaussian–Wishart form with parameters n_n, $\mathbf{m}_n$, v_n, and $\boldsymbol{\Sigma}_n$. Thus normalizing,

$f(\mathbf{m}, \boldsymbol{\Sigma}^{-1} \,|\, \dot{\mathbf{x}}_n)$

$$= \begin{cases} \dfrac{\left|\left(\dfrac{1}{n_n}\boldsymbol{\Sigma}\right)^{-1}\right|^{-/2}}{(2\pi)^{L/2}} \exp\left\{-\tfrac{1}{2}(\mathbf{m}-\mathbf{m}_n)^t\left(\dfrac{1}{n_n}\boldsymbol{\Sigma}\right)^{-1}(\mathbf{m}-\mathbf{m}_n)\right\} \cdot \\[2em] \dfrac{\left|\dfrac{v_n}{2}\boldsymbol{\Sigma}_n\right|^{(v_n-1)/2}}{\left[\pi^{L(L-1)/4}\displaystyle\prod_{j=1}^{L}\Gamma\left(\dfrac{v_n-j}{2}\right)\right]} |\boldsymbol{\Sigma}^{-1}|^{(v_n-L-2)/2} \exp\{-\tfrac{1}{2}\operatorname{tr} v_n\boldsymbol{\Sigma}_n\boldsymbol{\Sigma}^{-1}\}; \\[2em] \qquad\qquad\qquad \boldsymbol{\Sigma}^{-1} \text{ positive definite, symmetric,} \\ 0, \qquad\qquad\qquad\qquad \text{otherwise.} \end{cases} \qquad (28)$$

Bayes Estimate

The Bayes estimates of $\mathbf{m}$ and $\boldsymbol{\Sigma}^{-1}$ for quadratic loss are

$$(\mathbf{m})_n = E[\mathbf{m}\,|\,\dot{\mathbf{x}}_n], \quad (\boldsymbol{\Sigma}^{-1})_n = E[\boldsymbol{\Sigma}^{-1}\,|\,\dot{\mathbf{x}}_n].$$

But

$$E[\mathbf{m}\,|\,\dot{\mathbf{x}}_n] = \int E(\mathbf{m}\,|\,\boldsymbol{\Sigma}^{-1}, \dot{\mathbf{x}}_n)f(\boldsymbol{\Sigma}^{-1}\,|\,\dot{\mathbf{x}}_n)\,d\boldsymbol{\Sigma}^{-1}$$

and

$$E[\mathbf{m}\,|\,\boldsymbol{\Sigma}^{-1}, \dot{\mathbf{x}}_n] = \mathbf{m}_n \text{ independent of } \boldsymbol{\Sigma}^{-1}.$$

Thus,

$$(\mathbf{m})_n = \mathbf{m}_n = \frac{n_0}{n + n_0}\mathbf{m}_0 + \frac{n}{n + n_0}\left(\frac{1}{n}\sum_{j=1}^{n}\mathbf{x}_j\right) \qquad (29a)$$

and

$$(\Sigma^{-1})_n = (\Sigma_n)^{-1}.$$

Since $\Sigma = (\Sigma^{-1})^{-1}$, the corresponding estimate of Σ is

$$(\Sigma)_n = \Sigma_n = \frac{1}{n + v_0}\{[(n-1)S_n + n\bar{\mathbf{x}}_n\bar{\mathbf{x}}_n^t] + [v_0\Sigma_0 + n_0\mathbf{m}_0\mathbf{m}_0^t] - n_n\mathbf{m}_n\mathbf{m}_n^t\}.$$

$$(29b)$$

2-11.6 Poisson—Unknown α

Let $\mathbf{x} = [m, \tau]$ denote the number of events m in time τ.

To find a simple reproducing density a specific a priori sample of m_0 events in time τ_0 is assumed.

By the second theorem,

$$f(\alpha) = \frac{f(\mathbf{x}_0\,|\,\alpha)}{\int f(\mathbf{x}_0\,|\,\alpha)\,d\alpha} = \begin{cases} \dfrac{\dfrac{(\alpha\tau_0)^{m_0}e^{-\alpha\tau_0}}{m_0!}}{\displaystyle\int_0^\infty \dfrac{(\alpha\tau_0)^{m_0}}{m_0!}e^{-\alpha\tau_0}\,d\alpha}, & \alpha \geq 0, \\[6pt] 0, & \text{otherwise.} \end{cases}$$

But

$$\int_0^\infty (\alpha\tau_0)^{m_0}e^{-\alpha\tau_0}\,d\alpha = \frac{1}{\tau_0}\int_0^\infty \theta^{m_0}e^{-\theta}\,d\theta = \frac{1}{\tau_0}\Gamma(m_0 + 1).$$

So a reproducing density is

$$f(\alpha) = \begin{cases} \dfrac{\tau_0^{m_0+1}}{\Gamma(m_0 + 1)}\alpha^{m_0}e^{-\alpha\tau_0}, & \alpha \geq 0, \\[6pt] 0, & \text{otherwise,} \end{cases}$$

$$(30)$$

the gamma density with parameters τ_0, m_0.

Now if $\mathbf{x}_i$ has m_i events in time τ_i,

$$f(\alpha\,|\,\dot{\mathbf{x}}_n) = \frac{f(\dot{\mathbf{x}}_n\,|\,\alpha)f(\alpha)}{\int [\text{num}]\,d\alpha}.$$

So

$$f(\alpha\,|\,\dot{\mathbf{x}}_n) = \begin{cases} c\alpha^{(m^0 + \sum_{j=1}^n m_j)}e^{-\alpha(\tau_0 + \sum_{j=1}^n \tau_j)}, & \alpha \geq 0, \\[6pt] 0, & \text{otherwise,} \end{cases}$$

$$(31)$$

which is also the gamma density, as expected, with parameters

$$n_n = m_0 + \sum_{j=1}^{n} m_j, \qquad \tau_n = \tau_0 + \sum_{j=1}^{n} \tau_j$$

and normalizing constant

$$c = \frac{\tau_n^{n_n+1}}{\Gamma(n_n + 1)}.$$

Bayes Estimate

The Bayes estimate of α for quadratic loss is

$$(\alpha)_n = E(\alpha \mid \dot{\mathbf{x}}_n) = \frac{n_n + 1}{\tau_n} = \frac{1 + m_0 + \sum_{j=1}^{n} m_j}{\tau_0 + \sum_{j=1}^{n} \tau_j}. \tag{32}$$

2-11.7 Rayleigh—$\rho = 1/\sigma^2$ Unknown

$$f(x \mid \rho) = \rho x e^{-(x^2 \rho)/2} u(x), \qquad \rho > 0.$$

To find a simple reproducing density a specific a priori $\dot{\mathbf{x}}_{n_0}$ is assumed. By the second theorem,

$$f(\rho) = \frac{f(\dot{\mathbf{x}}_{n_0} \mid \rho)}{\int f(\dot{\mathbf{x}}_{n_0} \mid \rho)\, d\rho} = \begin{cases} \dfrac{\rho^{n_0}\left(\prod\limits_{j=1}^{n_0} x_j\right) e^{-\rho(\sum_{j=1}^{n_0} x_j^2/2)}}{\int [\text{num}]\, d\rho}, & \rho \geq 0, \\[4mm] 0, & \text{otherwise.} \end{cases}$$

But this has the gamma density form with respect to ρ with parameters $b_0 = n_0$ and $c_0 = \sum_{j=1}^{n_0} x_j^2/2$; thus a reproducing a priori density is, after normalizing,

$$f(\rho) = \begin{cases} \dfrac{c_0^{b_0+1}}{\Gamma(b_0 + 1)} \rho^{b_0} e^{-\rho c_0}, & \rho \geq 0, \\[4mm] 0, & \text{otherwise.} \end{cases} \tag{33}$$

Now,

$$f(\rho \mid \dot{x}_n) = \frac{f(\dot{\mathbf{x}}_n \mid \rho) f(\rho)}{\int [\text{num}]\, d\rho} = \frac{k\left(\prod\limits_{j=1}^{n} x_j\right) \rho^{n+b_0} e^{-\rho\left(c_0 + \sum_{j=1}^{n} x_j^2/2\right)}}{\int [\text{num}]\, d\rho},$$

which also has the gamma form, as expected, with respect to p. Thus normalizing,

$$f(p \mid \dot{x}_n) = \begin{cases} \dfrac{c_n^{b_n+1}}{\Gamma(b_n+1)} p^{b_n} e^{-pc_n}, & p \geq 0, \\ 0, & \text{otherwise,} \end{cases} \tag{34}$$

where

$$b_n = b_0 + n$$

$$c_n = c_0 + \sum_{j=1}^{n} x_j^2/2.$$

Bayes Estimate

The Bayes estimate of p for quadratic loss is

$$(p)_n = E(p \mid \dot{x}_n) = \frac{b_n + 1}{c_n} = \frac{b_0 + n}{c_0 + \sum_{j=1}^{n} x_j^2/2}. \tag{35}$$

2-11.8 Exponential—Unknown λ

$$f(x \mid \lambda) = \lambda e^{-\lambda x} u(x), \qquad \lambda > 0.$$

To find a simple reproducing density a specific a priori sequence $\dot{x}_{n_0}$ is assumed.

By the second theorem,

$$f(\lambda) = \frac{f(\dot{x}_{n_0} \mid \lambda)}{\int f(\dot{x}_{n_0} \mid \lambda)\, d\lambda} = \begin{cases} \dfrac{\lambda^{n_0} e^{-\lambda(\sum_{j=1}^{n_0} x_j)}}{\int [\text{num}]\, d\lambda}, & \lambda \geq 0, \\ 0, & \text{otherwise.} \end{cases}$$

But this has the gamma density form with respect to λ with parameters $b_0 = n_0, c_0 = \sum_{j=1}^{n_0} x_j$. Thus a reproducing a priori density is, after normalizing,

$$f(\lambda) = \begin{cases} \dfrac{c_0^{b_0+1}}{\Gamma(b_0+1)} \lambda^{b_0} e^{-\lambda c_0}, & \lambda \geq 0, \\ 0, & \text{otherwise.} \end{cases} \tag{36}$$

Now,

$$f(\lambda\,|\,\dot{\mathbf{x}}_n) = \frac{f(\dot{\mathbf{x}}_n\,|\,\lambda)f(\lambda)}{\int [\text{num}]\,d\lambda} = \frac{K\lambda^{n+b_0}e^{-\lambda}\left(c_0 + \sum\limits_{j=1}^{n} x_j\right)}{\int [\text{num}]\,d\lambda},$$

which also has the gamma form, as expected, with respect to λ. Thus, normalizing,

$$f(\lambda\,|\,\dot{x}_n) = \begin{cases} \dfrac{c_n^{b_n+1}}{\Gamma(b_n+1)}\lambda^{b_n}e^{-\lambda c_n}, & \lambda \geq 0, \\ 0, & \text{otherwise,} \end{cases} \tag{37}$$

where

$$b_n = b_0 + n$$

$$c_n = c_0 + \sum_{j=1}^{n} x_j.$$

Bayes Estimate

The Bayes estimate of λ for quadratic loss is

$$(\lambda)_n = E[\lambda\,|\,\dot{x}_n] = \frac{b_n+1}{c_n} = \frac{b_0+n+1}{c_0 + \sum\limits_{j=1}^{n} x_j}, \tag{38}$$

2-11.9 Density—Finitely Discretized Parameter Space

Suppose that $h(\mathbf{x}\,|\,\mathbf{b})$ is any density function, possibly a mixture.

If $\mathscr{B}$ is discrete with V possible values of $\mathbf{b}^v$, then any a priori density $f(\mathbf{b})$ is simply a set of V values of p^v, such that $p^v \geq 0$, $\sum_{v=1}^{V} p^v = 1$, each p^v being the a priori probability that $\mathbf{b}^v$ is the true parameter.

Obviously after receiving samples $\mathbf{x}_1, \ldots, \mathbf{x}_n$, the a posteriori probability density on $\mathscr{B}$ will be discrete, with mass only at the set $\{\mathbf{b}^v\}_{v=1}^{V}$. Only the p^v's will have changed.

The a posteriori density will be, after $\mathbf{x}_1$,

$$(p^v)_1 = p(\mathbf{b} = \mathbf{b}^v\,|\,\mathbf{x}_1) = \frac{h(\mathbf{x}_1\,|\,\mathbf{b}^v)(p^v)_0}{\text{NORM}_1}.$$

Since it must be true that $\sum_{v=1}^{V}(p^v)_1 = 1$,

$$\text{NORM}_1 = \sum_{v=1}^{V} h(\mathbf{x}_1\,|\,\mathbf{b}^v)(p^v)_0,$$

where $\{(p^v)_0\}^V$ are the a priori probabilities on $\mathscr{B}$. Thus,

$$(p^v)_1 = \frac{h(\mathbf{x}_1 \mid \mathbf{b}^v)(p^v)_0}{\sum\limits_{v=1}^{V} h(\mathbf{x}_1 \mid \mathbf{b}^v)(p^v)_0}, \qquad v = 1, 2, \ldots, V.$$

Therefore, after n observations, assuming parameter conditional independence and identically distributed $\mathbf{x}_i$, the recursive formula is

$$(p^v)_n = \frac{h(\mathbf{x}_n \mid \mathbf{b}^v)(p^v)_{n-1}}{\sum\limits_{v=1}^{V} h(\mathbf{x}_n \mid \mathbf{b}^v)(p^v)_{n-1}}, \qquad v = 1, 2, \ldots, V. \tag{39}$$

Thus the density is reproducing regardless of the form of $h(\mathbf{x} \mid \mathbf{b})$.

Bayes Estimate

The Bayes estimate of $\mathbf{b}$ for quadratic loss is

$$(\mathbf{b})_n = E[\mathbf{b} \mid \dot{\mathbf{x}}_n] = \sum_{v=1}^{V} \mathbf{b}^v (p^v)_n. \tag{40}$$

2-12 Stochastic Approximation

It is straightforward to show (see Section 2-8, for example) that the information function

$$\eta(\mathbf{b}, \mathbf{b}^*) = \int \ln h(\mathbf{x} \mid \mathbf{b}) h(\mathbf{x} \mid \mathbf{b}^*) \, d\mathbf{x} \tag{1}$$

naturally arises when using the Bayes approach to compute the a posteriori density $f(\mathbf{b} \mid \dot{\mathbf{x}}_n)$. Also, in Section 2-7† it is shown that the vector of functions

$$\mathbf{l}'(\mathbf{b}, \mathbf{b}^*) = \int \nabla_\mathbf{b}[\ln h(\mathbf{x} \mid \mathbf{b})] h(\mathbf{x} \mid \mathbf{b}^*) \, d\mathbf{x} \tag{2}$$

naturally arises from maximum-likelihood estimation. In the current section the stochastic-approximation procedure for studying an estimator $(\mathbf{b})_n$ is developed based on the concept of a "regression function," $\boldsymbol{\rho}(\mathbf{b}, \mathbf{b}^*)$. One of these procedures, called the *Kiefer–Wolfowitz procedure*, can use $\boldsymbol{\rho}(\mathbf{b}, \mathbf{b}^*) = \eta(\mathbf{b}, \mathbf{b}^*)$. Another procedure, called the *Robbins–Monro procedure*, can use $\mathbf{l}'(\mathbf{b}, \mathbf{b}^*)$ as a vector of regression functions. Both the Kiefer–Wolfowitz pro-

†See also Section 2-14.

cedure and the Robbins–Monro procedure can be shown as special cases of the *Dvoretzky procedure.*

In Chapter 5 it is shown in detail how in the Bayes minimum-conditioned-risk solution, the function $\eta(\mathbf{b}, \mathbf{b}^*)$, is computed for all points $\mathbf{b}$ in the parameter space. Essentially an application of the Keifer–Wolfowitz stochastic approximation procedure seeks the solution maximizing $\eta(\mathbf{b})$. We shall see that Bayes involves a multitude of stochastic-approximation estimators.

Regression Function

To introduce the idea behind stochastic approximation, suppose that $\mathbf{x}_1, \mathbf{x}_2, \ldots, \mathbf{x}_n$ each have density $h(\mathbf{x}|\mathbf{b}^*)$, where $\mathbf{b}^*$ is fixed but unknown. Let $\boldsymbol{\xi}(\mathbf{x}, \mathbf{b})$ be a vector random variable which depends upon a random vector $\mathbf{x}$ and a fixed parameter vector $\mathbf{b}$. The regression of the random vector $\boldsymbol{\xi}(\mathbf{x}, \mathbf{b})$ on (or in terms of) a density $h(\mathbf{x}|\mathbf{b}^*)$ is defined as

$$\boldsymbol{\rho}(\mathbf{b}, \mathbf{b}^*) \triangleq \int \boldsymbol{\xi}(\mathbf{x}, \mathbf{b})h(\mathbf{x}|\mathbf{b}^*)\,d\mathbf{x}, \tag{3a}$$

and an estimate of this regression function is

$$(\boldsymbol{\rho}(\mathbf{b}))_n = \frac{1}{n}\sum_{s=1}^{n}\boldsymbol{\xi}(\mathbf{x}_s, \mathbf{b}). \tag{3b}$$

If $\boldsymbol{\rho}(\mathbf{b}, \mathbf{b}^*)$ has certain desirable properties at and near $\mathbf{b} = \mathbf{b}^*$, it may be possible to utilize $(\boldsymbol{\rho}(\mathbf{b}))_n$ in estimating $\mathbf{b}^*$.

When $\rho(\mathbf{b}, \mathbf{b}^*) = \eta(\mathbf{b}, \mathbf{b}^*)$, then

$$\xi(\mathbf{x}, \mathbf{b}) = \ln h(\mathbf{x}|\mathbf{b}). \tag{4}$$

If

$$\boldsymbol{\xi}(\mathbf{x}, \mathbf{b}) = \nabla_{\mathbf{b}} \ln h(\mathbf{x}|\mathbf{b}), \tag{5}$$

then

$$\boldsymbol{\rho}(\mathbf{b}, \mathbf{b}^*) = \mathbf{l}'(\mathbf{b}, \mathbf{b}^*). \tag{6}$$

It is stressed that in practice $\boldsymbol{\rho}(\mathbf{b}, \mathbf{b}^*)$ is not known for a particular problem because $\mathbf{b}^*$ is unknown. The problem should, however, specify the functional form of $\rho(\mathbf{b}, \mathbf{b}^*)$ by specifying the form of $\boldsymbol{\xi}(\mathbf{x}, \mathbf{b})$ and the form of $h(\mathbf{x}|\mathbf{b})$. Using samples $\boldsymbol{\xi}(\mathbf{x}_1, \mathbf{b}), \boldsymbol{\xi}(\mathbf{x}_2, \mathbf{b}), \ldots, \boldsymbol{\xi}(\mathbf{x}_n, \mathbf{b})$, an estimator $(\boldsymbol{\rho}(\mathbf{b}))_n$ can be constructed.

Before proceeding to fundamental theoretical results, an example relating stochastic approximation to Bayes estimation is helpful.

Example: Bayes Related

Let $\mathbf{x}_1, \mathbf{x}_2, \ldots, \mathbf{x}_n$ be n parameter conditionally independent and identically distributed observation vectors with distribution $h(\mathbf{x}\,|\,\mathbf{b}^*)$, where $\mathbf{b}^*$ is fixed but unknown. For any vector $\mathbf{b}$ in the cross-product parameter space $\mathscr{B}^{M'}$, define

$$
\begin{aligned}
\xi_1 &\triangleq \ln h(\mathbf{x}_1\,|\,\mathbf{b}) = \xi(\mathbf{x}_1, \mathbf{b}), \\
\xi_2 &\triangleq \ln h(\mathbf{x}_2\,|\,\mathbf{b}) = \xi(\mathbf{x}_2, \mathbf{b}), \\
&\quad\ \vdots \\
\xi_n &\triangleq \ln h(\mathbf{x}_n\,|\,\mathbf{b}) = \xi(\mathbf{x}_n, \mathbf{b}),
\end{aligned}
\tag{7a}
$$

and estimate $\rho(\mathbf{b}, \mathbf{b}^*)$ using

$$
(\rho(\mathbf{b}))_n = \frac{1}{n}\sum_{s=1}^{n}\xi_s = \frac{1}{n}\sum_{s=1}^{n}\ln h(\mathbf{x}_s\,|\,\mathbf{b}),
\tag{8a}
$$

which is an estimate of the function

$$
\rho(\mathbf{b}, \mathbf{b}^*) = \int \ln h(\mathbf{x}\,|\,\mathbf{b})h(\mathbf{x}\,|\,\mathbf{b}^*)\,d\mathbf{x} = \eta(\mathbf{b}, \mathbf{b}^*).
\tag{9a}
$$

The Bayes procedure requires that an estimator of the form (8a) be obtained at *each point* $\mathbf{b}$ *in the product parameter space*. This shows one of the generalities of Bayes and limitations of stochastic approximation.

Example: Maximum-Likelihood Related

Let all be the same as in the previous example except that

$$
\begin{aligned}
\xi_1 &= \nabla_\mathbf{b}\ln h(\mathbf{x}_1\,|\,\mathbf{b}), \\
\xi_2 &= \nabla_\mathbf{b}\ln h(\mathbf{x}_2\,|\,\mathbf{b}), \\
&\quad\ \vdots \\
\xi_n &= \nabla_\mathbf{b}\ln h(\mathbf{x}_n\,|\,\mathbf{b}),
\end{aligned}
\tag{7b}
$$

and estimate $\boldsymbol{\rho}(\mathbf{b}, \mathbf{b}^*)$ using

$$
(\boldsymbol{\rho}(\mathbf{b}))_n = \frac{1}{n}\sum_{s=1}^{n}\nabla_\mathbf{b}\ln h(\mathbf{x}_s\,|\,\mathbf{b}),
\tag{8b}
$$

which is an estimate of the vector function

$$
\boldsymbol{\rho}(\mathbf{b}, \mathbf{b}^*) = \int \nabla_\mathbf{b}[\ln h(\mathbf{x}\,|\,\mathbf{b})]h(\mathbf{x}\,|\,\mathbf{b}^*)\,d\mathbf{x}.
\tag{9b}
$$

Kiefer–Wolfowitz Procedure (b = b, a Scalar)

Suppose the functional $\xi(\mathbf{x}, b)$ is known and samples $\mathbf{x}_1, \mathbf{x}_2, \ldots, \mathbf{x}_n$ are available. One of the requirements of the Kiefer–Wolfowitz procedure is that the variance of the random variable $\xi(\mathbf{x}, b)$ be finite:

$$\int_{-\infty}^{\infty} [\xi(\mathbf{x}, b) - \rho(b, b^*)]^2 h(\mathbf{x} \mid b^*) \, d\mathbf{x} \le \text{constant}. \tag{10}$$

Another requirement concerns the behavior of $\rho(b, b^*)$ near $b = b^*$:

$$\rho(b, b^*) \text{ is strictly increasing for } b < b^*,$$
$$\rho(b, b^*) \text{ is strictly decreasing for } b > b^*. \tag{11}$$

Then two infinite sequences of positive numbers, $a_1, a_2, \ldots$ and $c_1, c_2, \ldots$, are selected with the following properties:

$$\text{(a)} \quad \lim_{s \to \infty} c_s = 0;$$

$$\text{(b)} \quad \sum_{s=1}^{\infty} a_s = \infty; \tag{12}$$

$$\text{(c)} \quad \sum_{s=1}^{\infty} a_s c_s < \infty;$$

$$\text{(d)} \quad \sum_{s=1}^{\infty} a_s^2 c_s^{-2} < \infty.$$

For example, acceptable sequences would be

$$a_s = s^{-1}, \qquad s = 1, 2, \ldots.$$
$$c_s = s^{-1/3}, \qquad s = 1, 2, \ldots.$$

A recursive estimator for b^*, given observation vectors $\mathbf{x}_1, \mathbf{x}_2, \ldots,$ $\mathbf{x}_n, \mathbf{x}_{n+1}$ and the functional $\xi(\mathbf{x}, b)$ (used in the Kiefer–Wolfowitz procedure) is

$$(b)_{n+1} = (b)_n + a_n \frac{\xi(\mathbf{x}_{n+1}, (b)_n + c_n) - \xi(\mathbf{x}_{n+1}, (b)_n - c_n)}{c_n}. \tag{13}$$

If the regression function

$$\rho(b, b^*) = \int \xi(\mathbf{x}, b) h(\mathbf{x} \mid b^*) \, d\mathbf{x} \tag{14}$$

also satisfies the regularity conditions stated below, then $(b)_n$ converges in mean square (and thus also in probability) to b^*. Note that the term

$$\frac{\xi(\mathbf{x}_{n+1}, (b)_n + c_n) - \xi(\mathbf{x}_{n+1}, (b)_n - c_n)}{c_n} \tag{15}$$

is a differential of $\xi(\mathbf{x}_{n+1}, b)$ at $b = (b)_n$. If this differential is positive, the estimate $(b)_n$ is increased to approach b^*; if negative, $(b)_n$ is decreased to approach b^*.

Regularity Conditions on $\rho(b, b^*)$ for Kiefer–Wolfowitz (One-Parameter) Procedure

Expression (15) is an estimate of the slope of the regression function (14) at $b = (b)_n$. If $(b)_{n+1}$ is to be closer to b^* than $(b)_n$, the expected value of this slope should be either negative or positive, depending on whether $(b)_n > b^*$ or $(b)_n < b^*$. Such a requirement is imposed by the following regularity conditions:

1. There exist positive numbers d and e such that for any b', b'',

$$|b' - b^*| + |b'' - b^*| < d \text{ implies that} \, |\rho(b', b^*) - \rho(b'', b^*)|$$
$$< e|b' - b''|.$$

2. There exist positive numbers q and r such that

$$|b' - b''| < q \text{ implies that} \, |\rho(b', b^*) - \rho(b'', b^*)| < r.$$

3. For every $\delta > 0$, there exists a positive number $\pi(\delta)$ such that $|b - b^*| > \delta$ implies that†

$$\inf \frac{|\rho(b + c, b^*) - \rho(b - c, b^*)|}{c} > \pi(\delta), \qquad 0 < c < \tfrac{1}{2}\delta.$$

Practical Considerations

Condition 1 prevents the derivative of $\rho(b, b^*)$ from being too large in a neighborhood of $b = b^*$, because

$$|b' - b''| = |b' - b'' + b^* - b^*| = |b' - b^* + b^* - b''| \leq |b' - b^*|$$
$$+ |b^* - b''|$$

or, practically speaking, the derivative of $\rho(b, b^*)$ at $b = b^*$ is zero. Condition 2 prevents $\rho(b, b^*)$ from rising too steeply at any point b and producing unacceptable estimates. Condition 3 prevents $\rho(b, b^*)$ from being too flat at points b distant from b^* by bounding the absolute value of the derivative of $\rho(b, b^*)$ from below.

†inf denotes infimum.

An example of a regression function satisfying regularity conditions 1, 2, and 3 is

$$\rho(b, b^*) = \exp[-(b - b^*)^2], \qquad b_1 \leq b \leq b_2,$$

which is as shown:

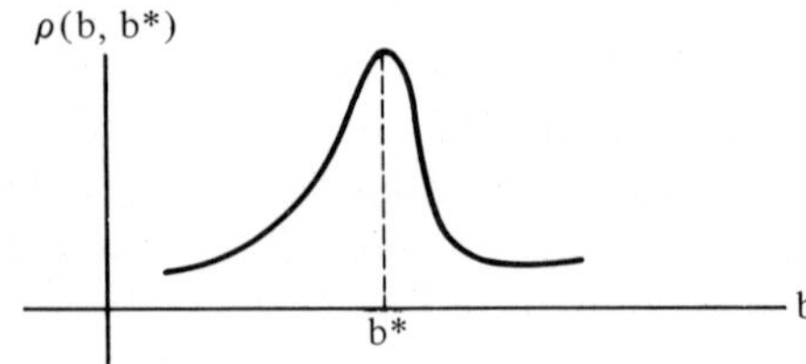

Kiefer and Wolfowitz's original paper presenting this procedure was published in 1952 [13].

Dvoretzky Procedure (One Parameter)

A generalization of the Kiefer–Wolfowitz procedure [13] and procedures or modifications due to other researchers, including the Robbins and Monro procedure [15] discussed in the next subsection, has been provided by Dvoretzky [17]. Dvoretzky's procedure can be motivated by the Kiefer–Wolfowitz scheme [13]: To the terms in the numerator on the right-hand side of (13) add and subtract $\rho((b)_n + c_n, b^*) - \rho((b)_n - c_n, b^*)$, to obtain

$$(b)_{n+1} = (b)_n + \frac{a_n}{c_n}[\rho((b)_n + c_n, b^*) - \rho((b)_n - c_n, b^*)] + y_n$$

$$\triangleq T_n + y_n, \tag{16}$$

with

$$y_n \triangleq \frac{a_n}{c_n}\{[\xi(\mathbf{x}_{n+1}, (b)_n + c_n) - \rho(b)_n + c_n, b^*)]$$
$$- [\xi(\mathbf{x}_{n+1}, (b)_n - c_n) - \rho(b)_n - c_n, b^*)]\}. \tag{17}$$

The sequence T_n is a deterministic sequence converging to b^* provided that a_n, c_n, and T_n satisfy certain conditions determined by Dvoretzky and found in his paper; y_n is interpreted as a noise term converging at least in probability to zero. The reader interested in Dvoretzky's formulation is referred to the literature [17, 14]. For practical engineering purposes, the previously discussed Kiefer–Wolfowitz formulation and the following Robbins–Monro formulation illustrate the essentials of stochastic approximation.

In the estimator portrayed by Eq. (13) (the Kiefer–Wolfowitz procedure), the estimate $(b)_n$ is updated to $(b)_{n+1}$ by estimating the derivative of $\xi(\mathbf{x}_n, b)$ at $b = (b)_n$. Since a requirement is that $E[\xi(\mathbf{x}, b)]$ be maximum at $b = b^*$, the expected value of the derivative of $\xi(\mathbf{x}, b)$ is zero at $b = b^*$. (Note that for the Kiefer–Wolfowitz procedure, $\rho(b, b^*) = E[\xi(\mathbf{x}, b)]$.)

For the Robbins–Monro procedure [15] a regression function is used such that $\rho(b, b^*) = 0$ for $b = b^*$. Such a regression function is consistent with the maximum-likelihood-estimation approach.

Let $\rho(b, b^*)$ be defined as in (3a) with the following properties:

1. $\rho(b, b^*) < d|b| + e < \infty$ for all b and suitable constants d and e and

2. $\inf \ \rho(b, b^*) > 0, \qquad \dfrac{1}{k} < b^* - b < k,$

   $\sup \ \rho(b, b^*) < 0, \qquad \dfrac{1}{k} < b - b^* < k,$

   for all integers k.

3. $\sum_{s=1}^{\infty} a_s = \infty$, $\sum_{s=1}^{\infty} a_s^2 < \infty$; for example, $a_s = 1/s$, $s = 1, 2, \ldots.$

Then starting with an arbitrary b_0, the recursive sequence $\{b_n\}$ defined by

$$(b)_{n+1} = (b)_n - a_n \xi(\mathbf{x}_{n+1}, (b)_n) \tag{18}$$

converges to b^* both in mean square and in probability.

The Robbins–Monro recursive relationship (18) can be converted to the Dvoretzky form by adding and subtracting $\rho((b)_n, b^*)$ to obtain

$$(b)_{n+1} = (b)_n - a_n \rho((b)_n, b^*) + y_n, \tag{19}$$

with

$$y_n = a_n[\xi(\mathbf{x}_n, (b)_n) - \rho((b)_n, b^*)]. \tag{20}$$

An example of a regression function $\rho(b, b^*)$ satisfying conditions 1 and 2 is as shown, where $b_1 \leq b \leq b_2$:

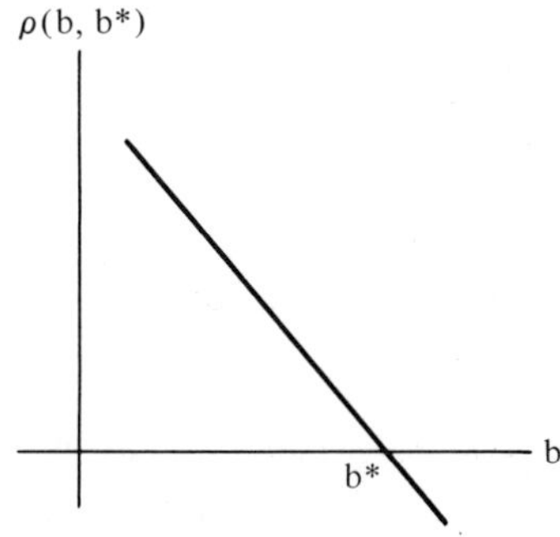

Example: $L = 1$. Suppose that

$$h(x \mid b^*) \neq 0, \qquad b_1 \leq x \leq b_2,$$

$$E[x \mid b^*] = \int xh(x \mid b^*)\, dx = b^*,$$

$$\xi(x, b) = x - b, \qquad a_n = \frac{1}{n}.$$

Then

$$\rho(b, b^*) = \int_{b_1}^{b_2} (x - b)h(x \mid b^*)\, dx = b^* - b$$

and, according to (18),

$$(b)_{n+1} = (b)_n + \frac{1}{n}[x_{n+1} - (b)_n].\tag{21}$$

Suppose that $(b)_n > b^*$; then $E[x_{n+1} - (b)_n] = E[x_{n+1}] - (b)_n = b^* - (b)_n < 0$, so that $(b)_{n+1} < (b)_n$, which is in the direction from $(b)_n$ toward b^*, as it should be.

Extension of Kiefer–Wolfowitz Procedure to Multiparameters

Assume that $\rho(\mathbf{b}, \mathbf{b}^*) = \int \xi(\mathbf{x}, \mathbf{b})h(\mathbf{x} \mid \mathbf{b}^*)\, d\mathbf{x}$ has a unique maximum at $\mathbf{b} = \mathbf{b}^*$. Let there be constants satisfying

$$
\begin{aligned}
&\text{(a)} \quad \lim_{s \to \infty} c_s = 0; \\[2mm]
&\text{(b)} \quad \sum_{s=1}^{\infty} a_s = \infty; \\[2mm]
&\text{(c)} \quad \sum_{s=1}^{\infty} a_s c_s < \infty; \\[2mm]
&\text{(d)} \quad \sum_{s=1}^{n} \left(\frac{a_s}{c_s}\right)^2 < \infty.
\end{aligned}
\tag{22}
$$

Let $\mathbf{b}$ be a vector point in a space spanned by an orthonormal spanning set $\mathbf{e}_1, \mathbf{e}_2, \ldots, \mathbf{e}_q$. Construct a random vector $\boldsymbol{\xi}$ by taking $q + 1$ independent observations

$$\xi(\mathbf{x}, \mathbf{b}),\ \xi(\mathbf{x}, \mathbf{b} + c\mathbf{e}_1),\ \ldots,\ \xi(\mathbf{x}, \mathbf{b} + c\mathbf{e}_q),$$

and define

$$\delta_{\mathbf{x}, \mathbf{b}, c_n} \triangleq [(\xi(\mathbf{x}, \mathbf{b} + c_n\mathbf{e}_1) - \xi(\mathbf{x}, \mathbf{b})), (\xi(\mathbf{x}, \mathbf{b} + c_n\mathbf{e}_2) - \xi(\mathbf{x}, \mathbf{b})),$$
$$\ldots, (\xi(\mathbf{x}, \mathbf{b} + c_n\mathbf{e}_q) - \xi(\mathbf{x}, \mathbf{b}))]. \tag{23}$$

Then a recursive estimator for $\mathbf{b}^*$ is

$$(\mathbf{b})_{n+1} = (\mathbf{b})_n + a_n \frac{\delta_{\mathbf{x}_{n+1}, (\mathbf{b})_n, c_n}}{c_n}. \tag{24}$$

Note that

$$\frac{\delta_{\mathbf{x}_{n+1}, (\mathbf{b})_n, c_n}}{c_n}$$

is the vector in the direction of the maximum slope of the plane determined by the $q + 1$ vectors

$$\xi(\mathbf{x}_{n+1}, (\mathbf{b})_n), \xi(\mathbf{x}_{n+1}, (\mathbf{b})_n + c_n\mathbf{e}_1), \cdots, \xi(\mathbf{x}_{n+1}, (\mathbf{b})_n + c_n\mathbf{e}_q).$$

A theorem due to Blum [37, 38] states that $(\mathbf{b})_{n+1}$ given by (24) converges with probability 1 to $\mathbf{b}^*$ if, in addition to (22), the following regularity conditions on the regression function

$$\rho(\mathbf{b}, \mathbf{b}^*) = \int \xi(\mathbf{x}, \mathbf{b})h(\mathbf{x} \mid \mathbf{b}^*) \, d\mathbf{x}$$

are satisfied:

1. $\rho(\mathbf{b}, \mathbf{b}^*)$ is continuous in $\mathbf{b}$ with continuous first and second derivatives.

2. $\int (\xi(\mathbf{x}, \mathbf{b}) - \rho(\mathbf{b}, \mathbf{b}^*))^2 h(\mathbf{x} \mid \mathbf{b}^*) \, d\mathbf{x} \leq$ constant.

3. For every positive number ϵ there exists a positive number $\rho(\epsilon)$ such that

$$\|\mathbf{b} - \mathbf{b}^*\| \geq \epsilon \text{ implies } \rho(\mathbf{b}, \mathbf{b}^*) \leq \rho(\mathbf{b}^*, \mathbf{b}^*),$$

$$\|\mathbf{d}(\mathbf{b}, \mathbf{b}^*)\| \geq \rho(\epsilon),$$

   where the vector of first partial derivatives of $\rho(b, b^*)$ with respect to the components of $\mathbf{b}$ is denoted $\mathbf{d}(\mathbf{b}, \mathbf{b}^*)$.

4. The second partial derivatives $\partial^2 \rho(\mathbf{b}, \mathbf{b}^*)/\partial\theta_i\,\partial\theta_j$ are bounded for $i, j = 1, 2, \ldots, q$, where θ_i is the ith component of $\mathbf{b}$.

For completeness we can define $\boldsymbol{\rho}(\mathbf{b}, \mathbf{b}^*)$:

$$\boldsymbol{\rho}(\mathbf{b}, \mathbf{b}^*) \triangleq \int \frac{\boldsymbol{\delta}_{\mathbf{x}, \mathbf{b}, c}}{c} h(\mathbf{x} \,|\, \mathbf{b}^*) \, d\mathbf{x},$$

although the procedure just presented does not directly involve this vector of regression functions. It is possible, however, to form an estimator

$$(\boldsymbol{\rho}(\mathbf{b}))_n = \frac{1}{n} \sum_{s=1}^{n} \frac{\boldsymbol{\delta}_{\mathbf{x}_s, \mathbf{b}, c}}{c} = \mathbf{0}$$

and seek a solution $(\mathbf{b})_n$ to this equation; note the similarity between this and the maximum-likelihood solution given by (8b).

The literature abounds with papers on stochastic approximation, including, in addition to the references already given, Venter [14]; Saridis and Stein [20]; Sakrison [22]; Saridis, Nikolic, and Fu [23]; Tsypkin [25]; Fu [43]; Dubins and Savage [21]; Wolfowitz [39]; and Kesten [42].

A book by Henrici [16] also is useful when considering stochastic approximation precedures.

In Section 2-13 the difficult application of stochastic approximation to a mixture of Gaussian density functions is discussed. One reason for the difficulty arises from the necessity of imposing constraints relevant to the mixing parameters.†

In Section 2-14 the relationship between maximum-likelihood estimation and stochastic approximation is discussed further. Then in Section 2-15 it is shown how a regression function denoted $\gamma(\mathbf{b})$, which is a Bayes-related function, can be used to construct either a Kiefer–Wolfowitz type of estimator or a Robbins–Monro type of estimator for the parameters characterizing a Gaussian mixture. In Section 2-16 the information function $\eta(\mathbf{b})$ is used for stochastic approximation.

2-13 Application of Stochastic Approximation to Gaussian Mixtures

Let $f_i(\mathbf{x}) \in \mathscr{F}$, where $\mathscr{F}$ is the family of L-dimensional Gaussian p.d.f.'s with mean vector $\mathbf{m}_i$ and covariance matrix $\boldsymbol{\Sigma}_i = \sigma_i^2 \mathbf{I}$. That is,

$$\mathbf{b}_i = [\mathbf{m}_i, \boldsymbol{\Sigma}_i],$$

$$f(\mathbf{x} \,|\, \mathbf{b}_i, i) = \frac{\tau_i^L}{(2\pi)^{L/2}} \exp\left[\frac{-\tau_i^2 (\mathbf{x} - \mathbf{m}_i)'(\mathbf{x} - \mathbf{m}_i)}{2}\right],$$

---

†Essentially the same problems arise if the approach is maximum-likelihood estimation.

where $\tau_i = 1/\sigma_i$. Select as the regression function

$$\eta(\mathbf{b}) = \int [\ln h(\mathbf{x}\,|\,\mathbf{b})]h(\mathbf{x})\,d\mathbf{x}, \tag{1}$$

where

$$h(\mathbf{x}\,|\,\mathbf{b}) = \sum_{i=1}^{M'} f(\mathbf{x}\,|\,\mathbf{b}_i, i)P_i$$

and (as always)

$$\mathbf{b} = [\mathbf{b}_1, \mathbf{b}_2, \ldots, \mathbf{b}_{M'}, P_1, P_2, \ldots, P_{M'}]. \tag{2}$$

The constraints on the mixing parameters $P_1, P_2, \ldots, P_{M'}$ are

$$\sum_{i=1}^{M'} P_i = 1, \qquad P_i \geq 0. \tag{3}$$

Or, by letting

$$d_i = \sum_{j=1}^{i-1} P_j, \qquad d_1 = 0,$$

(3) is equivalent to

$$0 \leq P_i \leq 1 - d_i, \qquad i = 1, 2, \ldots, M' - 1,$$
$$P_{M'} = 1 - d_{M'}. \tag{4}$$

We wish to take the derivative of $\eta(\mathbf{b})$ with respect to all the parameters in $\mathbf{b}$. Assuming that $\eta(\mathbf{b})$ is regular with respect to these partial derivatives, the respective derivatives can be taken inside the integral sign. The derivatives are as follows:

$$\nabla_{\mathbf{m}_i}[\ln \sum_{i=1}^{M'} f(\mathbf{x}\,|\,\mathbf{b}_i, i)P_i] = \frac{P_i \tau_i^2 (\mathbf{x} - \mathbf{m}_i) f(\mathbf{x}\,|\,\mathbf{b}_i, i)}{h(\mathbf{x}\,|\,\mathbf{b})}, \tag{5}$$

$$\frac{\partial}{\partial \tau_i}[\ln \sum_{i=1}^{M'} f(\mathbf{x}\,|\,\mathbf{b}_i, i)P_i] = \frac{P_i f(\mathbf{x}\,|\,\mathbf{b}_i, i)}{h(\mathbf{x}\,|\,\mathbf{b})}\left[\frac{L}{\tau_i} - \tau_i(\mathbf{x} - \mathbf{m}_i)'(\mathbf{x} - \mathbf{m}_i)\right], \tag{6}$$

$$\frac{\partial}{\partial P_i}[\ln \sum_{i=1}^{M'} f(\mathbf{x}\,|\,\mathbf{b}_i, i)P_i] = \frac{1}{h(\mathbf{x}\,|\,\mathbf{b})}[f(\mathbf{x}\,|\,\mathbf{b}_i, i) - f(\mathbf{x}\,|\,\mathbf{b}_{M'}, M')], \quad i \neq M', \tag{7}$$

where in the last expression we have used

$$P_{M'} = 1 - \sum_{i \neq M'} P_i. \tag{8}$$

Observe a difficulty: When $\tau_i \rightarrow 0$, $\partial \ln h(\mathbf{x}\,|\,\mathbf{b})/\partial\tau_i$ approaches infinity and when $P_i \rightarrow 0$, $\partial \ln h(\mathbf{x}\,|\,\mathbf{b})/\partial P_i$ may become very large. To avoid this difficulty and satisfy the constraints (6), Young and Coraluppi [44] suggested introducing two new variables, w_i and γ_i:

$$w_i = \tau_i - \frac{1}{\tau_i} = \frac{1}{\sigma_i} - \sigma_i, \qquad 0 < \tau_i < \infty, \tag{9a}$$

i.e.,

$$\tau_i = \frac{1}{\sigma_i} = \frac{1}{2}(w_i + \sqrt{w_i^2 + 4}), \tag{9b}$$

and

$$\gamma_i = \frac{2P_i - (1 - d_i)}{P_i(1 - d_i - P_i)}, \qquad 0 \le P_i \le 1 - d_i, \tag{10a}$$

i.e.,

$$P_i = \frac{1}{2\gamma_i}[(1 - d_i)\gamma_i - 2 + \sqrt{(1 - d_i)^2\gamma_i^2 + 4}]. \tag{10b}$$

Equation (9a) is a one-to-one map of the open interval $(0, \infty)$ into the interval $(-\infty, \infty)$; (10a) is a one-to-one map, for each P_i, of the closed interval $[0, 1 - d_i]$ into the interval $[-\infty, \infty]$. Therefore, we can estimate w_i and γ_i with the constraints on τ_i and P_i being automatically satisfied.

Based on the Robbins–Monro approach,

$$(\mathbf{m}_i)_{n+1} = (\mathbf{m}_i)_n + a_n \frac{\partial}{\partial\mathbf{m}_i} \ln h(\mathbf{x}\,|\,\mathbf{b})\Big|_{\substack{\mathbf{x}=\mathbf{x}_n \\ \mathbf{b}=(\mathbf{b})_n}}, \tag{11}$$

$$(w_i)_{n+1} = (w_i)_n + a_n \left[\frac{\partial\tau_i}{\partial w_i}\bigg|_{\tau_i=(\tau_i)_n} \frac{\partial}{\partial\tau_i} \ln h(\mathbf{x}\,|\,\mathbf{b}_i, i)\bigg|_{\substack{\mathbf{x}=\mathbf{x}_n \\ \mathbf{b}=(\mathbf{b})_n}}\right], \tag{12}$$

$$(\gamma_i)_{n+1} = (\gamma_i)_n + a_n \left[\sum_{r=i}^{M'-1} \frac{\partial P_r}{\partial\gamma_i}\bigg|_{P_r=(P_r)_n} \frac{\partial}{\partial P_r} \ln h(\mathbf{x}\,|\,\mathbf{b}_i, i)\bigg|_{\substack{\mathbf{x}=\mathbf{x}_n \\ \mathbf{b}=(\mathbf{b})_n}}\right], \tag{13}$$

where $\{a_n\}$ satisfies the usual constraints

$$\sum_{s=1}^{\infty} a_s = \infty, \qquad \sum_{s=1}^{\infty} a_s^2 < \infty.$$

Algorithms (11), (12), and (13) are evaluated by means of (5), (6), (7), (9b), (10b), and the relationships

$$\frac{\partial\tau_i}{\partial w_i} = \frac{1}{2}\left[1 + \frac{w_i}{\sqrt{w_i^2 + 4}}\right],$$

$$\frac{\partial P_i}{\partial \gamma_i} = \frac{1}{\gamma_i^2}\left[1 - \frac{2}{\sqrt{(1-d_i)^2\gamma_i^2 + 4}}\right],$$

$$\frac{\partial P_r}{\partial \gamma_i} = -\frac{1}{2}\sum_{j=i}^{r-1}\frac{\partial P_j}{\partial \gamma_i}\left[1 + \frac{(1-d_r)\gamma_r}{\sqrt{(1-d_r)^2\gamma_r^2 + 4}}\right], \qquad i < r < M'.$$

This approach of hill climbing using an estimated regression function has the disadvantage† that large sample sizes may be required because of poor starting points. In practice there are usually a limited number of samples.

An alternative approach is to use rules based, perhaps, on the moments of a cluster (when the cluster is suspected to be composed of two or more clusters) for splitting a cluster. Then $\eta(\mathbf{b})$ can be used to evaluate the quality of the split.

Approaches related to the one presented in this section are Wolfe [46] and Patrick [45]. The formal method [Eqs. (9) and (10)] of introducing constraints may not be as practical as simply introducing the constraints during computer solution by disallowing solution points violating the constraints (as in Section 2-15).

2-14 Example: Maximum-Likelihood-Related Regression Function

As defined in Section 2-7, the maximum-likelihood estimator for $\mathbf{b}^*$ when $\mathbf{x}$ has density $h(\mathbf{x}|\mathbf{b}^*)$ is the solution of the equation

$$\sum_{s=1}^{n}\nabla_{\mathbf{b}}[\ln h(\mathbf{x}_s|\mathbf{b})] = \mathbf{0} \tag{1a}$$

and the equations

$$\frac{1}{n}\sum_{s=1}^{n}\frac{\partial^2}{\partial\theta_i^2}\ln(\mathbf{x}_s|\mathbf{b}) < 0, \qquad i = 1, 2, \ldots, q,$$

where

$$\mathbf{b} = [\theta_1, \theta_2, \ldots, \theta_q]. \tag{1b}$$

Then,

1. if $h(\mathbf{x}|\mathbf{b})$ is regular with respects to its first derivatives,

$$\int \nabla_{\mathbf{b}}[\ln h(\mathbf{x}|\mathbf{b})]h(\mathbf{x}|\mathbf{b})\,d\mathbf{x} = \nabla_{\mathbf{b}}\int h(\mathbf{x}|\mathbf{b})\,d\mathbf{x} = \mathbf{0}; \tag{2a}$$

†Bayes would not have this disadvantage.

2. if $h(\mathbf{x}\,|\,\mathbf{b})$ is regular with respect to its second derivatives,

$$\lim_{\theta_i \to \theta^*_i} \frac{\partial}{\partial \theta_i} \int \frac{\partial}{\partial \theta_i} [\ln h(\mathbf{x}\,|\,\mathbf{b})] h(\mathbf{x}\,|\,\mathbf{b}^*)\,d\mathbf{x} < 0, \qquad i = 1, 2, \ldots, q. \tag{2b}$$

Proof: Condition 1 follows because the first regularity condition is $\int \nabla_\mathbf{b} h(\mathbf{x}\,|\,\mathbf{b})\,d\mathbf{x} = \nabla_\mathbf{b} \int h(\mathbf{x}\,|\,\mathbf{b})\,d\mathbf{x}$. Condition 2 follows because

$$\frac{\partial}{\partial \theta_i} \int \frac{\partial}{\partial \theta_i} [\ln h(\mathbf{x}\,|\,\mathbf{b})] h(\mathbf{x}\,|\,\mathbf{b}^*)\,d\mathbf{x} = \frac{\partial}{\partial \theta_i} \int \frac{1}{h(\mathbf{x}\,|\,\mathbf{b})} \frac{\partial h(\mathbf{x}\,|\,\mathbf{b})}{\partial \theta_i} h(\mathbf{x}\,|\,\mathbf{b}^*)\,d\mathbf{x}$$

$$= -\int \frac{1}{h^2(\mathbf{x}\,|\,\mathbf{b})} \left[\frac{\partial h(\mathbf{x}\,|\,\mathbf{b})}{\partial \theta_i}\right]^2 h(\mathbf{x}\,|\,\mathbf{b}^*)\,d\mathbf{x}$$

$$+ \int \frac{1}{h(\mathbf{x}\,|\,\mathbf{b})} \frac{\partial^2 h(\mathbf{x}\,|\,\mathbf{b})}{\partial \theta_i^2} h(\mathbf{x}\,|\,\mathbf{b}^*)\,d\mathbf{x} \triangleq a(\mathbf{b}, \mathbf{b}^*).$$

Then

$$\lim_{\mathbf{b} \to \mathbf{b}^*} a(\mathbf{b}, \mathbf{b}^*) = -(\text{positive number}) + 0 < 0.$$

We conclude that the function

$$l'_b = \int \nabla_\mathbf{b} [\ln h(\mathbf{x}\,|\,\mathbf{b})] h(\mathbf{x}\,|\,\mathbf{b}^*)\,d\mathbf{x} \tag{3}$$

is the zero vector when $\mathbf{b} = \mathbf{b}^*$ and each component has negative slope at $\mathbf{b} = \mathbf{b}^*$. For example, if $\mathbf{b}$ is a one-dimensional real variable, l'_b may be as shown:

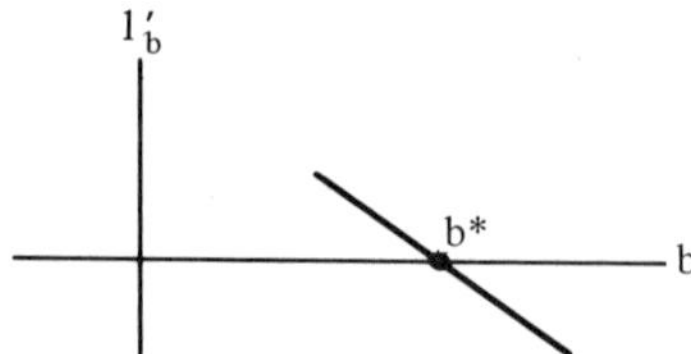

In the language of stochastic approximation, l'_b is a "regression function" of the Robbins–Monro form. Note that

$$\begin{aligned} l'_b > 0, & \qquad b < b^*, \\ l'_b < 0, & \qquad b > b^*. \end{aligned} \tag{4}$$

This suggests the following procedure for estimating $\mathbf{b}^*$: Let the estimate of $\mathbf{b}^*$, denoted $(\mathbf{b})_n$, be given in terms of $(\mathbf{b})_{n-1}$ and $\mathbf{x}_n$ as follows:

$$(\mathbf{b})_r = a_n (\mathbf{b})_{n-1} + c_n \nabla_\mathbf{b} \ln h(\mathbf{x}_n\,|\,\mathbf{b})\,|_{\mathbf{b}=(\mathbf{b})_{n-1}}. \tag{5}$$

Elementary Properties of Estimators   Chap. 2

To illustrate this, suppose that

Example 1 $L = 1$, $b = E[x]$, and

$$h(x \mid b) = \frac{1}{\sqrt{2\pi}\,\sigma} \exp\left[-\frac{1}{2} \frac{(x - b)^2}{\sigma^2} \right].$$

Then

$$\frac{\partial}{\partial b} \ln h(x \mid b) = \frac{x - b}{\sigma^2}$$

such that

$$(b)_n = a_n(b)_{n-1} + c_n[x_n - (b)_{n-1}]. \tag{6}$$

Example 2 In the above example, $h(\mathbf{x} \mid \mathbf{b})$ was chosen a Gaussian p.d.f. If the samples $\mathbf{x}_1, \ldots, \mathbf{x}_n$ are unsupervised, then $h(\mathbf{x} \mid \mathbf{b})$ is a much more complicated function and

$$\frac{\partial}{\partial b}[\ln h(\mathbf{x}_n \mid b)]\big|_{b=(b)_{n-1}} = \frac{\partial}{\partial b}\Big[\ln \sum_{i=1}^{M'} f(\mathbf{x}_n \mid b_i)P_i\Big]\big|_{b=(b)_{n-1}}$$

is not as easy to evaluate. We still require that $\partial h(\mathbf{x} \mid \mathbf{b})/\partial b$ and $\partial^2 h(\mathbf{x} \mid \mathbf{b})/\partial b^2$ both be integrable in order for the estimates to converge.

2-15 Stochastic Approximation Using a Projection Function

When samples $\mathbf{x}_1, \mathbf{x}_2, \ldots, \mathbf{x}_n$ are samples from a mixture density $h(\mathbf{x} \mid \mathbf{b}^*)$, a suitable regression function to be used in stochastic approximation for estimating $\mathbf{b}^*$ is one having either a unimodal maximum at $\mathbf{b}^*$ (Kiefer–Wolfowitz procedure) or one having a unique zero at $\mathbf{b}^*$ (Robbins–Monro procedure).

A function having a unique maximum at $\mathbf{b}^*$ is $\gamma(\mathbf{b})$,

$$\gamma(\mathbf{b}) = 2E[h(\mathbf{x} \mid \mathbf{b})] - \| h(\mathbf{x} \mid \mathbf{b}) \|^2, \tag{1}$$

discussed in detail in Section 5-3.5. To utilize the Robbins–Monro method, the derivative of $\gamma(\mathbf{b})$ with respect to $\mathbf{b}$ can be used as a regression function.

Kiefer–Wolfowitz Example Using $\gamma(\mathbf{b})$

In general, the unknown parameters in $\mathbf{b}$ to be estimated include the parameters indexing the M class-conditional density functions as well as the M mixing parameters P_i, $i = 1, 2, \ldots, M$. The mixing parameters are naturally constrained to be nonnegative and to sum to 1. Although the constraint that the estimates of the P_i sum to 1 may be imposed by means of the Lagrange-multiplier method, the constraint of nonnegatives is analytically unwieldy. Both constraints can be imposed simply as follows: As each P_i, $1 \leq i \leq M - 1$, is estimated in order, if the estimate falls outside the interval $[0, 1 - \sum_{j=1}^{i-1} P_j]$, the estimate is moved to the nearer end point. Finally, P_M is estimated by $1 - \sum_{j=1}^{M-1} P_j$. The estimation problem, then, amounts to seeking the stationary point of $\gamma(\mathbf{b})$, the constraints on the mixing parameters being handled as indicated.

Let $(\mathbf{b})_n$ denote the estimator for $\mathbf{b}^*$ at stage n, where the n observations $\mathbf{x}_1, \mathbf{x}_2, \ldots, \mathbf{x}_n$ have been processed; let $(b^k)_n$ denote the kth parameter (component) in $(\mathbf{b})_n$. With $(b^k)_0$ chosen arbitrarily,† $(b^k)_{n+1}$ is computed recursively according to the expression

$$(b^k)_{n+1} = (b^k)_n + \frac{a_n(y_{2n}^k - y_{2n-1}^k)}{2c_n}. \tag{2}$$

The quantity $(y_{2n}^k - y_{2n-1}^k)/2c_n$ is an estimate of the slope of the regression function $\gamma(\mathbf{b})$ in the kth direction; i.e.,

$$
\begin{aligned}
y_{2n}^k &= 2h(\mathbf{x}_n \,|\, (\mathbf{b})_n + c_n\mathbf{e}_k) - \|h(\mathbf{x} \,|\, (\mathbf{b})_n + c_n\mathbf{e}_k)\|^2, \\
y_{2n-1}^i &= 2h(\mathbf{x}_n \,|\, (\mathbf{b})_n - c_n\mathbf{e}_k) - \|h(\mathbf{x} \,|\, (\mathbf{b})_n - c_n\mathbf{e}_k)\|^2.
\end{aligned}
\tag{3}
$$

Thus the estimator $(\mathbf{b})_n$ climbs the surface $\gamma(\mathbf{b})$ in the direction of the estimated gradient. The nonnegative numbers $\{a_s\}_{s=1}^n$ and $\{c_s\}_{s=1}^n$ are infinite sequences satisfying

$$\lim_{s \to \infty} c_s = 0,$$

$$\sum_{s=1}^{\infty} a_s = \infty,$$

$$\sum_{s=1}^{\infty} a_s c_s < \infty, \tag{4}$$

$$\sum_{s=1}^{\infty} a_s^2 c_s^{-2} < \infty.$$

The vector $\mathbf{e}_k$ has a kth component of 1 and zeros elsewhere.

$\mathcal{F}$: Gaussian Family

If $\mathcal{F}$ is the family of multivariate Gaussian d.f.'s, then $h(\mathbf{x}\,|\,\mathbf{b})$ is

$$h(\mathbf{x}\,|\,\mathbf{b}) = \sum_{i=1}^{M} P_i N(\mathbf{x}\,|\,\mathbf{m}_i, \mathbf{\Sigma}_i), \tag{5}$$

†Performance at stage n can be greatly affected by the choice of starting point.

with

$$\mathbf{b} = \{P_i, \mathbf{m}_i, \mathbf{\Sigma}_i\}_{i=1}^{M}. \tag{6}$$

The norm of $h(\mathbf{x}\,|\,\mathbf{b})$ is defined by

$$\| h(\mathbf{x}\,|\,\mathbf{b}) \|^2 \triangleq \int h^2(\mathbf{x}\,|\,\mathbf{b})\, d\mathbf{x} = \sum_{i=1}^{M} \sum_{j=1}^{M} P_i P_j c_{ij}, \tag{7}$$

where

$$c_{ij} = \int N(\mathbf{x}\,|\,\mathbf{m}_i, \mathbf{\Sigma}_i) N(\mathbf{x}\,|\,\mathbf{m}_j, \mathbf{\Sigma}_j)\, d\mathbf{x}. \tag{8}$$

By completing the square, the integral in (8) may be carried out to yield

$$\begin{aligned}
c_{ij} = (2\pi)^{-L/2} (|\mathbf{\Sigma}_i| \cdot |\mathbf{\Sigma}_j|)^{-1/2} \cdot |\mathbf{\Sigma}_i^{-1} + \mathbf{\Sigma}_j^{-1}|^{-1/2} \\
\times \exp\left[-\tfrac{1}{2}(\mathbf{m}_i - \mathbf{m}_{ij})^t \mathbf{\Sigma}_i^{-1}(\mathbf{m}_i - \mathbf{m}_{ij})\right. \\
\left. - \tfrac{1}{2}(\mathbf{m}_j - \mathbf{m}_{ij})^t \mathbf{\Sigma}_j^{-1}(\mathbf{m}_j - \mathbf{m}_{ij})\right],
\end{aligned} \tag{9}$$

where

$$\mathbf{m}_{ij} = (\mathbf{\Sigma}_i^{-1} + \mathbf{\Sigma}_j^{-1})^{-1}(\mathbf{\Sigma}_i^{-1}\mathbf{m}_i + \mathbf{\Sigma}_j^{-1}\mathbf{m}_j). \tag{10}$$

Thus the noisy measurements of $\gamma(\mathbf{b})$ based on $\dot{\mathbf{x}}_n$ are computed as

$$\begin{aligned}
y_{2n}^k = 2 \sum_{i=1}^{M} P_i N(\mathbf{x}_n\,|\,((\mathbf{m}_i)_n, (\mathbf{\Sigma}_i)_n) + c_n \mathbf{e}_k) \\
- \sum_{i=1}^{M} \sum_{j=1}^{M} P_i P_j c_{ij},
\end{aligned} \tag{11a}$$

$$\begin{aligned}
y_{2n-1}^k = 2 \sum_{i=1}^{M} P_i N(\mathbf{x}_n\,|\,((\mathbf{m}_i)_n, (\mathbf{\Sigma}_i)_n) - c_n \mathbf{e}_k) \\
- \sum_{i=1}^{M} \sum_{j=1}^{M} P_i P_j c_{ij}.
\end{aligned} \tag{11b}$$

Robbins–Monro Example Using $\gamma(\mathbf{b})$

Estimators of the Robbins–Monro type based on $\gamma(\mathbf{b})$ may be derived by using the derivative of $\gamma(\mathbf{b})$ with respect to the various parameters in $\mathbf{b}$ as the regression functions. These estimators will be formulated for an assumption of "high signal-to-noise ratio" with $\mathscr{F}$ Gaussian:

$$(\mathbf{m}_i - \mathbf{m}_j)^t \mathbf{\Sigma}_i^{-1}(\mathbf{m}_i - \mathbf{m}_j) + (\mathbf{m}_j - \mathbf{m}_i)^t \mathbf{\Sigma}_j^{-1}(\mathbf{m}_j - \mathbf{m}_i) > d,$$
$$i, j = 1, 2, \ldots, M, \, i \neq j, \tag{12}$$

where $d \gg 1$. Note that $c_{ij} \cong 0$ under assumption (12).

Since $\gamma(\mathbf{b})$ is maximized at $\mathbf{b}^*$ (see Section 5-3.5), the first-order derivatives of $\gamma(\mathbf{b})$ are zero at $\mathbf{b} = \mathbf{b}^*$. To obtain the Robbins–Monro estimators, then, set to zero the derivatives of the expected value of

$$t(\mathbf{x}\,|\,\mathbf{b}) \triangleq 2h(\mathbf{x}\,|\,\mathbf{b}) - \|\,h(\mathbf{x}\,|\,\mathbf{b})\,\|^2. \tag{13}$$

Because of assumption (12),

$$t(\mathbf{x}\,|\,\mathbf{b}) \cong 2h(\mathbf{x}\,|\,\mathbf{b}) - \sum_{i=1}^{M} P_i^2 c_{ii} = (2\pi)^{-L/2} \sum_{i=1}^{M} P_i\,|\,\mathbf{\Sigma}_i\,|^{-1/2}$$

$$\times\, \{2\exp[-\tfrac{1}{2}(\mathbf{x} - \mathbf{m}_i)^t\mathbf{\Sigma}_i^{-1}(\mathbf{x} - \mathbf{m}_i)] - 2^{-1/2}P_i\}. \tag{14}$$

To define the estimators for P_i, $\mathbf{m}_i$, and $\mathbf{\Sigma}_i$, the derivatives of $t(\mathbf{x}\,|\,\mathbf{b})$ with respect to these quantities are required. The derivative with respect to P_i is

$$\frac{\partial t(\mathbf{x}\,|\,\mathbf{b})}{\partial P_i} = 2N(\mathbf{x}\,|\,\mathbf{m}_i,\,\mathbf{\Sigma}_i) - 2^{1/2}(2\pi)^{-L/2}\,|\,\mathbf{\Sigma}_i\,|^{-1/2}P_i, \tag{15}$$

and the derivatives with respect to $\mathbf{m}_i$ and $\mathbf{\Sigma}_i$ are

$$\frac{\partial t(\mathbf{x}\,|\,\mathbf{b})}{\partial \mathbf{m}_i} = 2P_i N(\mathbf{x}\,|\,\mathbf{m}_i,\,\mathbf{\Sigma}_i)\mathbf{\Sigma}_i^{-1}(\mathbf{x} - \mathbf{m}_i), \tag{16}$$

$$\frac{\partial t(\mathbf{x}\,|\,\mathbf{b})}{\partial \mathbf{\Sigma}_i} = P_i N(\mathbf{x}\,|\,\mathbf{m}_i,\,\mathbf{\Sigma}_i) \cdot (\mathbf{\Sigma}_i - (\mathbf{x} - \mathbf{m}_i)(\mathbf{x} - \mathbf{m}_i)^t). \tag{17}$$

Denote by $(P_i)_n$, $(\mathbf{m}_i)_n$, and $(\mathbf{\Sigma}_i)_n$ the Robbins–Monro estimators for P_i, $\mathbf{m}_i$, and $\mathbf{\Sigma}_i$, respectively, with the starting points $(P_i)_0$, $(\mathbf{m}_i)_0$, and $(\mathbf{\Sigma}_i)_0$ arbitrary; the estimators are defined recursively as follows:

$$(P_i)_{n+1} = (P_i)_n + a_n\{2N(\mathbf{x}_n\,|\,(\mathbf{m}_i)_n,\,(\mathbf{\Sigma}_i)_n)$$
$$- 2^{1/2}(2\pi)^{-L/2}\,|\,(\mathbf{\Sigma}_i)_n\,|^{-1/2}(P_i)_n\}, \tag{18}$$

$$(\mathbf{m}_i)_{n+1} = (\mathbf{m}_i)_n - a_n\{2(P_i)_{n+1}N(\mathbf{x}_n\,|\,(\mathbf{m}_i)_n,\,(\mathbf{\Sigma}_i)_n)$$
$$(\mathbf{\Sigma}_i)_n^{-1} \cdot (\mathbf{x}_n - (\mathbf{m}_i)_n)\}, \tag{19}$$

$$(\mathbf{\Sigma}_i)_{n+1} = (\mathbf{\Sigma}_i)_n - a_n(P_i)_{n+1}N(\mathbf{x}_n\,|\,(\mathbf{m}_i)_{n+1},\,(\mathbf{\Sigma}_i)_n)$$
$$\times\, [(\mathbf{\Sigma}_i)_n - (\mathbf{x}_n - (\mathbf{m}_i)_{n+1})(\mathbf{x}_n - (\mathbf{m}_i)_{n+1})^t]. \tag{20}$$

The positive numbers $\{a_s\}_{s=1}^{\infty}$ satisfy

$$\sum_{s=1}^{\infty} a_s = \infty,$$

$$\sum_{s=1}^{\infty} a_s^2 < \infty.$$

Notice that the estimator for $\mathbf{m}_i$ incorporates the updated estimate $(P_i)_{n+1}$ for P_i and the estimator for $\boldsymbol{\Sigma}_i$ incorporates the updated estimate for both P_i and $\mathbf{m}_i$. The constraints that the mixing parameters be nonnegative and sum to 1 are imposed in the same manner as with the Kiefer–Wolfowitz estimators.

2-16 Stochastic Approximation Using the Information Function

In this section stochastic-approximation procedures will be used to estimate $\mathbf{b}^*$ using $\eta(\mathbf{b}, \mathbf{b}^*) = \int \ln h(\mathbf{x}\,|\,\mathbf{b}) h(\mathbf{x}\,|\,\mathbf{b}^*)\,d\mathbf{x}$ as the regression function. Constraints to be imposed on parameters in $\mathbf{b}$ are as follows:

1. $P_i \geq 0.$
2. $\sum_{i=1}^{M'} P_i = 1.$
3. Constraints sufficient for identifiability are imposed; for example, if $\mathscr{F}$ is the family of one-dimensional Gaussian functions, then $m_1 < m_2 < \cdots < m_{M'}$ is the constraint.

Constraint 3 has to be imposed for unique convergence and to eliminate points from the parameter space which would reduce convergence rate. Of course, this constraint is consistent with conditions required by stochastic approximation—a unique local extremum or zero in the regression function.

Robbins–Monro

The Robbins–Monro procedure with constraint 2 can utilize

$$\nabla_{\mathbf{b}} \int \left\{ \ln\left(h(\mathbf{x}\,|\,\mathbf{b})\right) - \lambda\left[\left(\sum_{i=1}^{M'} P_i\right) - 1\right]\right\} h(\mathbf{x}\,|\,\mathbf{b}^*)\,d\mathbf{x}\,\bigg|_{\mathbf{b}=\mathbf{b}^*} = \mathbf{0}. \tag{1}$$

Assuming that the gradient and integral can be interchanged and letting $P_i = Q_i^2$ to satisfy constraint 1, then from Eq. (1) it follows that

$$\int [2Q_i f(\mathbf{x}\,|\,\mathbf{b}_i^*) - 2Q_i \lambda h(\mathbf{x}\,|\,\mathbf{b}^*)]\,d\mathbf{x} = 0, \qquad i = 1, 2, \ldots, M'. \tag{2}$$

Performing the integration in Eq. (2) results in $\lambda = 1$. Hence the estimator is

$$(Q_i)_{n+1} = (Q_i)_n + a_n \xi_{Q_i}(\mathbf{x}_n, (\mathbf{b})_n), \tag{3}$$

where

$$\xi_{Q_i}(\mathbf{x}_n, (\mathbf{b})_n) = 2(Q_i)_n L_i(\mathbf{x}_{n+1}, (\mathbf{b})_n) - 2(Q_i)_n, \tag{4}$$

with

$$L_i(\mathbf{x}_{n+1}, (\mathbf{b})_n) \triangleq \frac{f(\mathbf{x}_{n+1}|(\mathbf{b}_i)_n)}{h(\mathbf{x}_{n+1}|(\mathbf{b})_n)}.$$

It is interesting that

$$\sum_{i=1}^{M'} (Q_i)_{n+1}(Q_i)_n = 1 \tag{5a}$$

or

$$\sum_{i=1}^{M'} [(Q_i)_{n+1}]^2 = 1 + O\left(\frac{1}{n^2}\right). \tag{5b}$$

Equations (5a) and (3) suggest the final form:

$$(P_i)_{n+1} = [(Q_i)_n]^2 + 2a_n[(Q_i)_n]^2[(L_i\mathbf{x}_{n+1}, (\mathbf{b})_n) - 1]. \tag{6}$$

If the family $\mathscr{F}$ is assumed Gaussian, then (6) still applies, with the following estimators for the mean vectors $\mathbf{m}_i$ and covariance matrices $\mathbf{\Sigma}_i$:

$$(\mathbf{m}_i)_{n+1} = (\mathbf{m}_i)_n + a_n(\mathbf{\Sigma}^{-1})_n[\mathbf{x}_{n+1} - (\mathbf{m}_i)_n][(Q_i)_n]^2 L_i(\mathbf{x}_{n+1}(\mathbf{b})_n), \tag{7}$$

$$(\mathbf{\Sigma}_i)_{n+1} = (\mathbf{\Sigma}_i)_n + a_n[(\mathbf{x}_{n+1} - (\mathbf{m}_i)_n)(\mathbf{x}_{n+1} - (\mathbf{m}_i)_n)^t - (\mathbf{\Sigma}_i)_n][(Q_i)_n]^2 L_i(\mathbf{x}_{n+1}, (\mathbf{b})_n). \tag{8}$$

2-17 Eliminating Nuisance Parameters

To introduce nuisance parameters, consider the maximum-likelihood estimator $(\mathbf{\Sigma})_n$ for a covariance matrix $\mathbf{\Sigma}^*$, given parameter conditionally independent samples $\mathbf{x}_1, \mathbf{x}_2, \ldots, \mathbf{x}_n$, when the mean vector $\mathbf{m}^* = E[\mathbf{x}]$ is unknown,

$$(\mathbf{\Sigma})_n = \frac{1}{n-1} \sum_{s=1}^{n} (\mathbf{x}_s - (\mathbf{m})_n)(\mathbf{x}_s - (\mathbf{m})_n)^t,$$

where $(\mathbf{m})_n = 1/n \sum_{s=1}^{n} \mathbf{x}_s$. Because $\mathbf{m}^*$ is unknown, the estimator $(\mathbf{m})_n$ for $\mathbf{m}^*$ is a nuisance when estimating $(\mathbf{\Sigma})_n$. The estimator $(\mathbf{\Sigma})_n$ above will have a larger variance than if $\mathbf{m}^*$ were known. Ferguson [49] is a reference containing examples of nuisance parameters that correspond to translation parameters and scale parameters.

An example arising in classifying waveforms is as follows: Suppose that a waveform $f(t)$ is time-sampled at times $t_1, t_2, \ldots, t_k$ producing samples $x_1, x_2, \ldots, x_k$. The waveform can, according to the sampling theorem of communications theory, be reconstructed from these samples as

$$f(t) = \sum_{k=1}^{K} x_k \varphi_k(t),$$

where $\varphi_k(t)$ are basis functions of $(\sin t)/t$ type. Suppose, however, that it were also known a priori that, say, $f(t_2) = af(t_1)$. Then one could define a basis function

$$\psi_1(t) = \begin{cases} a, & t = t_2, \\ 1, & t = t_1, \end{cases}$$

$$f(t) = c_k \psi_k(t), \qquad t_1 \leq t \leq t_2,$$

with

$$c_1 = \frac{f(t_1) + af(t_2)}{a^2 + 1}.$$

In other words, rather than two measurements x_1 and x_2, there is a single feature c_1; *this is dimensionality reduction using a priori knowledge*. Extending this procedure, one could expect to obtain a representation

$$f(t) = \sum_{k=1}^{K'} c_k \psi_k(t), \qquad K' < K.$$

In this section it will be shown that for pattern recognition, dimensionality reduction by eliminating nuisance parameters can improve performance!

Suppose a pattern-recognition solution is formulated as follows: There are n_i L-dimensional samples from each of M classes, $i = 1, 2, \ldots, M$, where measurements have been "appropriately chosen"; then estimate $f_i(\mathbf{x})$, $i = 1, 2, \ldots, M$, and make decisions using these estimated densities in the Bayes decision rule.† *If there are an unlimited number of training samples, this procedure can produce a good performance; if there are a limited number of training samples, this procedure can produce a poor performance.*

A problem model may be useful in reducing the number of parameters characterizing each category's statistics. Parameters eliminated might be referred to as nuisance parameters because the necessity of estimating them can increase overall decision-rule uncertainty. It is possible for a carefully chosen problem model to reduce the number of training samples required to achieve a specified performance. *Although this probably is the most important problem in pattern recognition*, it is only beginning to receive attention

†The Bayes decision rule is discussed in Chapter 3.

by researchers in pattern recognition who have avoided particular applications in their theoretical developments; of course, the application produces the model.

The philosophy behind an approach showing how the problem model can be used to eliminate nuisance parameters and enhance performance is provided through the Bayes updating procedures (presented in Sections 2-9 and 2-11). *The Bayes philosophy provides for using a "fuzzy guess" in parameter estimation; thus, it may be possible to use an estimate of one parameter as a "fuzzy guess" for estimating another parameter.*

To illustrate how a problem model can enhance performance, suppose that there is a waveform $x(t)$,

$$x(t) = [s(t) + n(t)] \sin \omega t, \tag{1}$$

where $s(t)$ is deterministic and $n(t)$ is from a white-noise random process.

In the absence of problem knowledge, the conventional procedure† of time sampling can be used to convert $x(t)$ to a vector of measurements. Accordingly, $x(t)$ is converted to a vector

$$\begin{aligned} \mathbf{x} &= [x(t_1), x(t_2), \ldots, x(t_k)] \\ &\triangleq [x_1, x_2, \ldots, x_k]. \end{aligned} \tag{2}$$

If $\mathbf{x}$ is, say, from one of two categories, it is important to know the densities of $\mathbf{x}$ for the two categories. Suppose these densities are Gaussian with the means and covariances unknown. Then estimation of these means and covariances is very important for providing distance measures for use in the Bayes decision rule. It has often been conjectured by researchers in pattern recognition that uncertainties resulting from estimating a covariance matrix (using fixed sample size) increase as dimensionality increases; what occurs is an increase in uncertainty in the distance measure [perhaps a distance measure of the form $(\mathbf{x} - \mathbf{m})^t \mathbf{\Sigma}^{-1}(\mathbf{x} - \mathbf{m})$].

It is not "good design" for uncertainty to increase as dimensionality increases; rather, uncertainty should decrease if the dimensionality is properly used. We shall illustrate with $k = 2$.

Suppose problem knowledge is available providing relationships between the statistics of x_1 and x_2,

$$\mathbf{x} = [x_1, x_2],$$

where the relationships are

$$m_2 = am_1 \tag{3}$$

†This elementary procedure is mentioned in Chapter 1.

and

$$\text{Var}[x_2] = a^2 \, \text{Var}[x_1]. \tag{4}$$

Let n samples $\mathbf{x}_s = [x_{s1}, x_{s2}]$, $s = 1, 2, \ldots, n$, be available and assume that $\mathbf{x}$ has a Gaussian distribution with x_1 and x_2 having respective variances σ^2 and $a\sigma^2$.

Bayes estimators† for m_1 and m_2 are

$$(m_1)_n = \frac{1}{n} \sum_{s=1}^{n} x_{s1},$$

$$(m_2)_n = \frac{1}{n} \sum_{s=1}^{n} x_{s2}, \tag{5}$$

without using specific a priori guesses. The a posteriori uncertainties in these estimators are σ^2/n and $a^2\sigma^2/n$, respectively.

Now, in the spirit of Bayes, suppose that we treat $a(m_1)_n$ as an a priori guess‡ for m_2 with uncertainty $a^2\sigma^2/n$. Then the a posteriori estimator for m^2 is

$$(m_2)_n = \frac{(a^2\sigma^2)/n}{(a^2\sigma^2)/n + (1/n)\sigma^2} \frac{1}{n} \sum_{s=1}^{n} x_{s2} + \frac{\sigma^2/n}{(a^2\sigma^2)/n + \sigma^2/n} a(m_1)_n$$

$$= \frac{a^2}{a^2 + 1} \frac{1}{n} \sum_{s=1}^{n} x_{s2} + \frac{1}{a^2 + 1} a(m_1)_n, \tag{6}$$

with variance

$$(\sigma^2)_n = \frac{\sigma^2}{n} \frac{a^2}{a^2 + 1} \tag{7}$$

in the estimate $(m_2)_n$ as an estimator for m_2^*.

Case a = 0

If $a = 0$ is the model, then

$$(m_2)_n = a(m_1)_n = 0$$

with uncertainty

$$(\sigma^2)_n = 0.$$

---

†Strictly speaking, they are maximum-likelihood estimators and ϵ Bayes estimators.

‡We have used all a priori knowledge, because there is no correlation between $(m_1)_n$ and $x_{11}, x_{12}, \ldots, x_{n2}$, since the noise was assumed to be white.

Case a = ∞

If $a = \infty$, then

$$(m_2)_n = \frac{1}{n} \sum_{s=1}^{n} x_{s2}$$

with uncertainty

$$(\sigma^2)_n = \frac{\sigma^2}{n}.$$

As would be expected, the case where $a = 1$ effectively corresponds to doubling the number of training samples by using the model, as opposed to not using the model.

A General Solution

Where there are k samples according to (2), and a relationship exists between the jth and the kth sample,

$$x_j = a_{jk} x_k, \qquad \forall \, j, k, \tag{8}$$

and it follows that the uncertainty in any m_j estimate is reduced by the relationships (8).

This procedure of reducing uncertainty using a linear model is equivalent to that obtained in matched filtering. An interpretation of the relationships (8) is that they constitute an a priori signal or basis function which correlates high with the waveform $x(t)$.

The a priori signal or basis function is only one way to introduce a priori knowledge. Another way is through nonlinear functions. The nonlinear function can be much more powerful, because it allows a relationship such as (8) to depend upon the arguments. This appears especially important in pattern recognition, where the objective is discrimination between patterns and a priori knowledge is likely to be in the form of relationships.

Applications

There are numerous applications where the problem model might be useful in enhancing performance. One frequently encounters problems in estimating the autocorrelation function of stationary or nonstationary reverberation or noise: What basis functions should be used in generating the feature space $\mathcal{V}_L$? Is anything known about relationships among the components or vectors in $\mathcal{V}_L$, possibly leading to a new space $\mathcal{V}_l$, $l < L$? This topic is treated in Chapter 6.

2-18 Marginal a posteriori Density of a Parameter in b

Sometimes it is desirable to obtain the a posteriori probability density of a single parameter θ in $\mathbf{b}$. The Bayes estimator of one parameter, for example, is calculated from the marginal a posteriori density of that parameter. Therefore, let θ_{kj} be some parameter in $\mathbf{b}_k$ which in turn is, of course, in $\mathbf{b}$. The a posteriori density of θ_{kj} is obtained by integrating $f(\mathbf{b}\,|\,\dot{\mathbf{x}}_n)$ with respect to all parameters in $\mathbf{b}$ except θ_{kj}. Integrating,

$$
f(\theta_{kj}\,|\,\dot{\mathbf{x}}_n) = \frac{\sum_{i \neq k} \int P_i f(\mathbf{x}_n\,|\,\mathbf{b}_i,\,i) f(\mathbf{b}\,|\,\dot{\mathbf{x}}_{n-1})\,d\bar{\mathbf{b}}}{f(\mathbf{x}_n\,|\,\dot{\mathbf{x}}_{n-1})}
$$
$$
+ \frac{\int P_k f(\mathbf{x}_n\,|\,\mathbf{b}_k,\,k) f(\mathbf{b}\,|\,\dot{\mathbf{x}}_{n-1})\,d\bar{\mathbf{b}}}{f(\mathbf{x}_n\,|\,\dot{\mathbf{x}}_{n-1})}, \tag{1}
$$

where $\bar{\mathbf{b}}$ for the above equation is defined as the vector not containing parameter θ_{kj} but containing all other parameters in $\mathbf{b}$.

Define "weighting coefficients"

$$
(w_i)_n = \frac{f(\mathbf{x}_n,\,i\,|\,\dot{\mathbf{x}}_{n-1},\,\theta_{kj})}{f(\mathbf{x}_n\,|\,\dot{\mathbf{x}}_{n-1})}, \tag{2a}
$$

with the result that (1) can be rewritten in terms of these weighting coefficients as

$$
f(\theta_{kj}\,|\,\dot{\mathbf{x}}_n) = \left\{ \sum_{i \neq k} (w_i)_n + (w_k)_n \frac{E_{\bar{\mathbf{b}}}[f(\mathbf{x}_n,\,k\,|\,\theta_{kj},\,\bar{\mathbf{b}}_k,\,\dot{\mathbf{x}}_{n-1})]}{f(\mathbf{x}_n,\,k\,|\,\mathbf{x}_{n-1})} \right\} f(\theta_{kj}\,|\,\dot{\mathbf{x}}_{n-1}), \tag{2b}
$$

where

$$
E_{\bar{\mathbf{b}}}[f(\mathbf{x}_n,\,k\,|\,\theta_{kj},\,\bar{\mathbf{b}}_k,\,\dot{\mathbf{x}}_{n-1})] \triangleq \int f(\mathbf{x}_n,\,k\,|\,\bar{\mathbf{b}}_k,\,\theta_{kj}) f(\mathbf{b}\,|\,\theta_{kj},\,\dot{\mathbf{x}}_{n-1})\,d\bar{\mathbf{b}} \tag{2c}
$$

and $\bar{\mathbf{b}}_k$ is defined as the vector not containing parameter θ_{kj} but containing all other parameters in $\mathbf{b}_k$.

The interpretation of (2) is as follows:

1. $\sum_{i \neq k} (w_i)_n$ is the probability, given $\dot{\mathbf{x}}_{n-1}$, that pattern class k did not cause $\mathbf{x}_n$. With probability $\sum_{i \neq k} (w_i)_n$, $f(\theta_{kj}\,|\,\dot{\mathbf{x}}_{n-1})$ is retained at the nth stage as the a posteriori density of θ_{kj}.
2. $(w_k)_n$ is the probability, given $\dot{\mathbf{x}}_{n-1}$, that $\mathbf{x}_n$ is from class k. Thus, with probability $(w_k)_n$, the density $f(\theta_{kj}\,|\,\dot{\mathbf{x}}_{n-1})$ is updated using $\mathbf{x}_n$ as if it were known from class k.

3. The expectation $E_{\bar{\mathbf{b}}}[f(\mathbf{x}_n, k \,|\, \theta_{kj}, \bar{\mathbf{b}}_k, \dot{\mathbf{x}}_{n-1})]$ is involved in (2) because $f(\mathbf{x}_n, k \,|\, \bar{\mathbf{b}}_k)$ is, in general, a function of fixed but unknown parameters other than θ_{kj}.

The Bayes estimator for θ_{kj} assuming a quadratic loss function is

$$(\theta_{kj})_n = \int \theta_{kj} f(\theta_{kj} \,|\, \dot{\mathbf{x}}_n) \, d\theta_{kj} \tag{3}$$

for a continuous-product parameter space and

$$(\theta_{kj})_n = \sum_{r=1}^{v} \theta_{kj}^r p(\theta_{kj}^r \,|\, \dot{\mathbf{x}}_n) \tag{4}$$

for a discrete product parameter space.

It is important to stress that the $(\theta_{kj})_n$ cannot be evaluated in general without the joint a posteriori density $f(\mathbf{b} \,|\, \dot{\mathbf{x}}_n)$ on the other parameters.

The previous result is general in that θ_{kj} is any scalar parameter in $\mathbf{b}_k$. It shows that, although an iterative form exists for $f(\theta_{kj} \,|\, \dot{\mathbf{x}}_n)$, this form depends on $f(\mathbf{b} \,|\, \dot{\mathbf{x}}_{n-1})$ through $(w_i)_n$ and the reduced joint density $f(\mathbf{b}_k \,|\, \dot{\mathbf{x}}_{n-1})$ through (2c).

To continue further, it follows that the a posteriori density $f(\mathbf{b}_k \,|\, \dot{\mathbf{x}}_n)$ in iterative form, in terms of

$$(w_i)_n = \frac{f(\mathbf{x}_n, i \,|\, \dot{\mathbf{x}}_{n-1}, \mathbf{b}_k)}{f(\mathbf{x}_n \,|\, \dot{\mathbf{x}}_{n-1})}, \tag{5a}$$

is

$$f(\mathbf{b}_k \,|\, \dot{\mathbf{x}}_n) = \left[\sum_{i \neq k} (w_i)_n + (w_k)_n \frac{E_{\bar{\mathbf{b}}}[f(\mathbf{x}_n, k \,|\, \mathbf{b}_k, \dot{\mathbf{x}}_{n-1})]}{f(\mathbf{x}_n, k \,|\, \dot{\mathbf{x}}_{n-1})} \right] f(\mathbf{x}_k \,|\, \dot{\mathbf{x}}_{n-1}), \tag{5b}$$

where

$$E_{\bar{\mathbf{b}}}[f(\mathbf{x}_n, k \,|\, \mathbf{b}_k, \dot{\mathbf{x}}_{n-1})] = \int f(\mathbf{x}_n \,|\, k, \mathbf{b}_k) P_k f(\mathbf{b} \,|\, \dot{\mathbf{x}}_{n-1}) \, d\bar{\mathbf{b}} \tag{5c}$$

and $\bar{\mathbf{b}}$ contains all parameters in $\mathbf{b}$ except $\mathbf{b}_k$. Thus the iterative calculation of $f(\mathbf{b}_k \,|\, \dot{\mathbf{x}}_n)$ in (5b) depends on the joint density $f(\mathbf{b} \,|\, \dot{\mathbf{x}}_{n-1})$ through $(w_i)_n$ [this is given by (5a) and the marginal density $f(P_k \,|\, \dot{\mathbf{x}}_{n-1})$ through (5c)]. Obviously if the a priori class probabilities P_k are known, then the only dependency on joint a posteriori density is through the weighting coefficients (5a).

Likewise, the a posteriori density for the kth mixing parameter P_k in iterative form, in terms of

$$(w_i)_n = \frac{f(\mathbf{x}_n, i \,|\, \dot{\mathbf{x}}_{n-1}, P_k)}{f(\mathbf{x}_n \,|\, \dot{\mathbf{x}}_{n-1})}, \tag{6a}$$

is

$$f(P_k | \dot{\mathbf{x}}_n) = \left[\sum_{i \neq k} (w_i)_n + (w_k)_n \frac{E_{\bar{\mathbf{b}}}[f(\mathbf{x}_n, k | P_k, \mathbf{b}, \dot{\mathbf{x}}_{n-1})]}{f(\mathbf{x}_n, k | \dot{\mathbf{x}}_{n-1})} \right] f(P_k | \dot{\mathbf{x}}_{n-1}), \quad (6b)$$

where

$$E_{\bar{\mathbf{b}}}[f(\mathbf{x}_n, k | P_k, \mathbf{b}, \dot{\mathbf{x}}_{n-1})] = P_k \int f(\mathbf{x}_n | k, \bar{\mathbf{b}}) f(\bar{\mathbf{b}} | \dot{\mathbf{x}}_{n-1}) \, d\bar{\mathbf{b}} \qquad (6c)$$

and $\bar{\mathbf{b}}$ in this case is defined as the vector not containing P_k but containing all other entries in $\mathbf{b}$. Thus the iterative calculation of $f(P_k | \dot{x}_n)$ in (6b) depends on the joint density $f(\mathbf{b} | \dot{\mathbf{x}}_{n-1})$ through $(w_i)_n$ and the reduced density $f(\mathbf{b}_k | \dot{\mathbf{x}}_{n-1})$ through (6c).

The vector $\bar{\mathbf{b}}$ will be called an auxiliary parameter vector and is seen to be a "nuisance."

From these results we draw the important conclusion that a marginal, a posteriori probability density must be calculated from the joint, a posteriori probability density.

A great deal of simplification results by approximating (5b) by using estimators $(P_k)_{n-1}$ and $(\mathbf{b}_k)_{n-1}$ rather than $f(\bar{\mathbf{b}} | \dot{\mathbf{x}}_{n-1})$. This is because the fundamental difficulty of unsupervised estimation is how to store the joint a posteriori density $f(\mathbf{b} | \mathbf{x}_{n-1})$; there is relatively little difficulty in storing estimators $(P_k)_{n-1}$ and $(\mathbf{b}_k)_{n-1}$. With the approximations,

$$E_{\bar{\mathbf{b}}}[f(\mathbf{x}_n, k | \mathbf{b}_k, \dot{\mathbf{x}}_{n-1})] = (P_k)_{n-1} f(\mathbf{x}_n | k, \mathbf{b}_k), \qquad (7a)$$

$$f(\mathbf{x}_n, k | \dot{\mathbf{x}}_{n-1}) = (P_k)_{n-1} f(\mathbf{x}_n | \dot{\mathbf{x}}_{n-1}), \qquad (7b)$$

(5b) greatly simplifies and

$$(w_i)_n = \frac{(P_i)_{n-1} f(\mathbf{x}_n | i, (\mathbf{b}_i)_{n-1})}{\sum_{j=1}^{M} (P_j)_{n-1} f(\mathbf{x}_n | j, (\mathbf{b}_{ij})_{n-1})}. \qquad (7c)$$

The parameters $(P_i)_{n-1}$ and $(\mathbf{b}_i)_{n-1}$ are estimates of *auxiliary parameters* that we must put up with. With assumptions (7), the Bayes estimate $(\mathbf{b}_k)_n$ is

$$(\mathbf{b}_k)_n = \int \mathbf{b}_k f(\mathbf{b}_k | \dot{\mathbf{x}}_n) \, d\mathbf{b}_k = \left[\sum_{i \neq k} (w_i)_n \right] (\mathbf{b}_k)_{n-1}$$

$$+ [(w_k)_n] \int \mathbf{b}_k \frac{f(\mathbf{x}_n | k, \mathbf{b}_k)}{f(\mathbf{x}_n | \dot{\mathbf{x}}_{n-1})} f(\mathbf{b}_k | \dot{\mathbf{x}}_{n-1}) \, d\mathbf{b}_k, \qquad (8a)$$

where the integral on the right is the Bayes estimator for $\mathbf{b}_k^*$, because now there are supervised samples from class k.

In like manner,

$$(P_k)_n = \int P_k f(P_k \,|\, \dot{\mathbf{x}}_n)\, dP_k = \left[\sum_{i \neq k} (w_i)_n\right](P_k)_{n-1}$$

$$+ \, [(w_k)_n] \int \frac{P_k}{\int P_k f(P_k \,|\, (\mathbf{b}_k)_{n-1},\, \dot{\mathbf{x}}_{n-1})\, dP_k} f(P_k \,|\, \dot{\mathbf{x}}_{n-1})\, dP_k. \qquad (8b)$$

Now $(w_i)_n$ defined by (2a) is correct—no approximations—but to evaluate $(w_i)_n$ requires that the joint density $f(\mathbf{b} \,|\, \dot{\mathbf{x}}_n)$ be available. Using the approximation (7c) can lead to difficulty if estimates of auxiliary parameters $(\mathbf{b}_i)_{n-1}$ and $(P_i)_{n-1}$ are not "sufficiently" close to $\mathbf{b}_i^*$ and P_i^*. A possible difficulty is illustrated in the following example.

Example. Suppose $h(\mathbf{x})$ is a mixture of Gaussian densities and $\mathbf{b}_k = \mathbf{m}_k$, the mean vector. Assume that $f(\mathbf{m}_k \,|\, \mathbf{x}_{n-1})$ has a Gaussian density at stage $n - 1$. Then it is not difficult to show that (8a) becomes

$$(\mathbf{m}_k)_n = \left[\sum_{i \neq k} (w_i)_n\right](\mathbf{m}_k)_{n-1} + [(w_k)_n]\left[\frac{\mathbf{x}_n}{n} + \frac{n-1}{n}(\mathbf{m}_k)_{n-1}\right], \qquad (9a)$$

which is equivalent to

$$(\mathbf{m}_k)_n = (\mathbf{m}_k)_{n-1} + \frac{1}{n}[(w_k)_n][\mathbf{x}_n - (\mathbf{m}_k)_{n-1}];$$

but it is possible that $(w_k)_n$ will become arbitrarily close to zero and incorrectly prevent further updating of this kth class mean.

If we assume that $f(P_k \,|\, \dot{\mathbf{x}}_{n-1})$ has the beta density, then (8b) becomes

$$(P_k)_n = \left[\sum_{i \neq k} (w_i)_n\right](P_k)_{n-1} + [(w_k)_n]\left[\frac{1}{n} + \frac{n-1}{n}(P_k)_{n-1}\right] \qquad (9b)$$

or

$$(P_k)_n = (\mathbf{P}_k)_{n-1} + \frac{1}{n}[(w_k)_n][1 - (P_k)_{n-1}].$$

2-19 Bayes Suggestion for Stochastic Approximation

In Section 2-12 the Kiefer–Wolfowitz type of estimator for $\mathbf{b}^*$,

$$(\mathbf{b})_{n+1} = (\mathbf{b})_n + a_n \frac{\delta_{\mathbf{x}_{n+1},\, (\mathbf{b})_n,\, c_n}}{c_n},$$

where

$$\delta_{\mathbf{x}, \mathbf{b}, c_n} = [(\xi(\mathbf{x}, \mathbf{b} + c_n\mathbf{e}_1) - \xi(\mathbf{x}, \mathbf{b})), \ldots, (\xi(\mathbf{x}, \mathbf{b} + c_n\mathbf{e}_q) - \xi(\mathbf{x}, \mathbf{b}))],$$

is discussed. Results from the previous section, where estimators for auxiliary parameters are used, provide the estimator

$$(\mathbf{b}_k)_{n+1} = (\mathbf{b}_k)_n + [(w_k)_{n+1}]\left\{\left[\int \mathbf{b}_k \frac{f(\mathbf{x}_{n+1} \mid k, \mathbf{b}_k)}{f(\mathbf{x}_{n+1} \mid \dot{\mathbf{x}}_{n-1})} f(\mathbf{b}_k \mid \dot{\mathbf{x}}_n)\, d\mathbf{b}_k\right] - (\mathbf{b}_k)_n\right\},$$

which is similar in form to the Kiefer–Wolfowitz procedure except for the presence of the probabilistic weighting factor $[(w_k)_{n+1}]$ in the Bayes suggested procedure. Comparing these two procedures, one might modify the Kiefer–Wolfowitz procedure to become

$$(\mathbf{b})_{n+1} = (\mathbf{b}_n) + a_n \frac{\delta'_{\mathbf{x}_{n+1}, (\mathbf{b})_n, c_n}}{c_n}, \tag{1a}$$

where

$$\delta'_{\mathbf{x}_{n+1}, (\mathbf{b}_n), c_n} = \{(w_1)_n[\xi(\mathbf{x}_{n+1}, \mathbf{b}_n + c_n\mathbf{e}_1) - \xi(\mathbf{x}_{n+1}, (\mathbf{b})_n)], \ldots,$$

$$(w_M)_n[\xi(\mathbf{x}_{n+1}(\mathbf{b})_n + c_n\mathbf{e}_q) - \xi(\mathbf{x}_{n+1}, (\mathbf{b})_n)]\}, \tag{1b}$$

and $(w_1)_n$ is the weighting coefficient for class 1 and $(w_M)_n$ the weighting coefficient† for class M. The effect of using (1b) is to cause *strong local jumps* in parameter values for the class from which $\mathbf{x}_{n+1}$ came with high probability. Conditions when (1a) [using (1b)] will converge to $\mathbf{b}^*$ are not generally known, but such convergence would seem to be a very good idea based on Bayes when sequentially processing samples $\mathbf{x}_1, \mathbf{x}_2, \ldots, \mathbf{x}_n$.

2-20 Decision-Directed Estimators Suggested by Bayes

The results in Eq. (2) of Section 2-18 suggest the "decision-directed estimator," for θ_{kj} any parameter for the kth class,

$$f(\theta_{kj} \mid \dot{\mathbf{x}}_n) = \begin{cases} f(\theta_{kj} \mid \dot{\mathbf{x}}_{n+1}), & \text{if } \sum_{i \neq 1} (w_i)_n > (w_k)_n, \\[2ex] \dfrac{E_{\mathbf{b}}[f(\mathbf{x}_{n,k} \mid \theta_{kj}, \dot{\mathbf{x}}_{n-1})]}{f(\mathbf{x}_{n.k} \mid \dot{\mathbf{x}}_{n-1})} f(\theta_{kj} \mid \dot{\mathbf{x}}_{n-1}), & \text{otherwise.} \end{cases} \tag{1}$$

†It is assumed in (1b) that θ_1 is one of the parameters which characterizes class 1 and so forth on to θ_q being the last parameter which characterizes class M.

Assuming (7a), (7b), and (7c) of Section 2-18,

$$
f(\theta_{kj}\,|\,\dot{\mathbf{x}}_n) =
\begin{cases}
f(\theta_{kj}\,|\,\dot{\mathbf{x}}_{n-1}), & \text{if } \sum_{i\neq k} (w_i)_n > (w_k)_n, \\[2ex]
\dfrac{f(\mathbf{x}_n\,|\,(\bar{\mathbf{b}}_k)_{n-1},\,\theta_{kj},\,k)}{f(\mathbf{x}_n\,|\,(\bar{\mathbf{b}}_k)_{n-1},\,k)}\,f(\theta_{kj}\,|\,\dot{\mathbf{x}}_{n-1}), & \text{otherwise.}
\end{cases}
\tag{2}
$$

Under these decision-directed assumptions, Eq. (5a) of Section 2-18 becomes

$$
f(\mathbf{b}_k\,|\,\dot{\mathbf{x}}_n) =
\begin{cases}
f(\mathbf{b}_k\,|\,\dot{\mathbf{x}}_{n-1}), & \text{if } \sum_{i\neq k} (w_i)_n > (w_k)_n, \\[2ex]
\dfrac{f(\mathbf{x}_n\,|\,\mathbf{b}_k,\,k)f(\mathbf{b}_k\,|\,\dot{\mathbf{x}}_{n-1})}{f(\mathbf{x}_n\,|\,k)}, & \text{otherwise.}
\end{cases}
\tag{3a}
$$

The simple conclusion is: Do not update class k parameters if $\sum_{i\neq k} (w_i)_n > (w_k)_n$ which defines the region of the measurement space where, at stage n, a sample $\mathbf{x}$ is decided not from class k. Utilizing estimates of auxiliary parameters, a simple way to obtain the weighting coefficients is

$$
(w_i)_n = \frac{(P_i)_{n-1}f(\mathbf{x}_n\,|\,i,\,(\mathbf{b}_i)_{n-1})}{\sum_{j=1}^{M} (P_j)_{n-1}f(\mathbf{x}_n\,|\,j,\,(\mathbf{b}_j)_{n-1})}.
\tag{3b}
$$

Example.   Suppose that $\mathbf{b}_k = \mathbf{m}_k$, a mean vector, and that $\mathscr{F}$ is the family of multivariate Gaussian densities. Then

$$
(\mathbf{m}_k)_n =
\begin{cases}
(\mathbf{m}_k)_{n-1}, & \sum_{i\neq k} (w_i)_n > (w_k)_n \\[2ex]
\left[\dfrac{\mathbf{x}_n}{n} + \dfrac{n-1}{n}(\mathbf{m}_k)_{n-1}\right], & \text{otherwise.}
\end{cases}
\tag{4}
$$

One should certainly be aware of results such as from the examples resulting in Eq. (9) of Section 2-18 and Eq. (4) above.

Discussion.   Stochastic-approximation procedures are in many ways a bad approach. For example, why not store samples $\mathbf{x}_1, \mathbf{x}_2, \ldots, \mathbf{x}_n$, estimate $\eta(\mathbf{b})$ as $(\eta(\mathbf{b}))_n = 1/n \sum_{s=1}^{n} \ln(\mathbf{x}_s\,|\,\mathbf{b})$ for a reasonable number of points $\mathbf{b}$, and search for the $\mathbf{b}$ maximizing $(\eta(\mathbf{b}))_n$? This fairly good idea, called *stochastic hill climb*, is discussed in Chapter 5. When in doubt, go to Bayes, which says to form $(\eta(\mathbf{b}))_n$ at all points $\mathbf{b}$ in the parameter space—you cannot go wrong theoretically.

Stochastic-approximation procedures have merit in a tracking situation, but then the Bayes suggested estimators [(8a) and (8b) of Section 2-18] should be very good because their use of estimators of auxiliary parameters,† $(P_i)_{n-1}$ and $(\mathbf{b}_i)_{n-1}$, should be good in such a tracking situation.

---

†An auxiliary parameter is a parameter estimate for a fixed but unknown parameter, recalling that Bayes generally requires utilization of a posteriori density of that parameter.

To complete the picture at this time, mention should be made of the quasi-Bayes estimator discussed in Chapter 5. The quasi-Bayes estimator retains the desirable simplicity of stochastic approximation while utilizing the average or parallel processing property of Bayes.

Because a regression function can have multiple modes, stochastic approximation can fail; Bayes cannot fail if used properly.

One last comment: Clustering techniques discussed in Chapter 5 provide very nicely for using such a priori knowledge as the fact that the mean vectors of the classes are near the respective modes of $h(\mathbf{x})$; because it is relatively easy to find such modes, clustering techniques have great appeal. As another example, suppose it is known that the classes do not have overlapping densities; then it is possible to grow clusters sequentially, another relatively simple procedure.

2-21 Tolerance Regions and Their Construction

2-21.1 Beta and Dirichlet Distributions

In Chapter 4 considerable attention is given to local density estimation. In particular, a decision rule called the $k\mathrm{NN}_3$ decision rule is developed utilizing the tolerance region concept. A tolerance region is important because the expected probability in the region is equal to the number of samples in the region divided by $n + 1$, where n is the number of samples. Furthermore, the uncertainty about the probability in a tolerance region is described by the Dirichlet distribution defined as follows:

Suppose n samples $\mathbf{x}_1, \mathbf{x}_2, \ldots, \mathbf{x}_n$ are used to construct δ tolerance regions, these regions utilizing $k_1, k_2, \ldots, k_\delta$ samples, respectively, in their construction, $k = k_1 + k_2 + \cdots + k_\delta$. Now, the coverage of a tolerance region is the measure of the region with respect to the measure generating the observations; loosely speaking, it is the probability mass in the region. Denote the coverages of the respective regions $u_1, u_2, \ldots, u_\delta$. Then the joint probability density of these coverages is Dirichlet,

$$
f(u_1, u_2, \ldots, u_\delta \,|\, k_1, k_2, \ldots, k_\delta; n - k + 1)
$$

$$
= \frac{n!}{\prod_{v=1}^{\delta} [(k_v - 1)!](n - k)!} u_1^{k_1 - 1} - \cdots u_\delta^{k_\delta - 1}(1 - u_1 - \cdots - u_\delta)^{n-k},
$$
$$
0 \le u_i \le 1
$$
$$
\sum_{i=1}^{\delta} u_i \le 1, \qquad (1)
$$

sometimes denoted $D(k_1, k_2, \ldots, k_\delta; k_{\delta+1})$, where $k_{\delta+1} = n - k$.

With the introduction, the essentials of tolerance region construction will now be presented.

Gamma Function and Distribution

The *gamma function* $\Gamma(g)$,

$$\Gamma(g) = \int_0^\infty x^{g-1} e^{-x}\, dx, \tag{2}$$

is used in the definition of the *gamma density*,

$$f(x) = \frac{x^{\mu-1} e^{-x}}{\Gamma(\mu)}, \qquad \mu > 0. \tag{3}$$

The rth moment μ_r of the *gamma density* is

$$\mu_r = \frac{\Gamma(\mu + r)}{\Gamma(\mu)} \tag{4}$$

from which it follows that

$$E[x] = \mu, \qquad \sigma^2(x) = \mu. \tag{5}$$

The definition of the gamma density (3) arises naturally from the gamma function (2), which itself naturally arises in the definition of factorials.

Beta Distribution

The beta density is defined

$$f(u) = \frac{\Gamma(k_1 + k_2)}{\Gamma(k_1)\Gamma(k_2)} u^{k_1-1}(1 - u)^{k_2-1} \tag{6}$$

for $0 < u < 1$, and $f(u) = 0$ elsewhere. Associated with the beta distribution is the relationship

$$\frac{\Gamma(k_1)\Gamma(k_2)}{\Gamma(k_1 + k_2)} = \int_0^1 x^{k_1-1}(1 - x)^{k_2-1}\, dx; \tag{7}$$

The rth moment of (6) is

$$\mu_r = \frac{\Gamma(k_1 + k_2)\Gamma(k_1 + r)}{\Gamma(k_1 + k_2 + r)\Gamma(k_1)}, \tag{8}$$

from which it follows that

$$E[u] = \frac{k_1}{k_1 + k_2}, \qquad \sigma^2(u) = \frac{k_1 k_2}{(k_1 + k_2)^2(k_1 + k_2 + 1)}. \qquad (9)$$

The beta density frequently is denoted $B_e(k_1, k_2)$ and the beta distribution function is denoted $I(v_1, v_2)$ and called the *incomplete beta function*.

Dirichlet Distribution

A natural extension of the beta density to δ degrees of freedom gives the Dirichlet density,

$$f(u_1, u_2, \ldots, u_\delta)$$

$$= \frac{\Gamma(k_1 + \cdots + k_{\delta+1})}{\Gamma(k_1) \cdots \Gamma(k_{\delta+1})} u_1^{k_1 - 1} \cdots u_\delta^{k_\delta - 1}(1 - u_1 - \cdots - u_\delta)^{k_{\delta+1} - 1}, \qquad (10)$$

at any point in the region: $\{(u_1, u_2, \ldots, u_\delta): u_i \geq 0, i = 1, 2, \ldots, \delta, \sum_{i=1}^{\delta} u_i \leq 1\}$. Obviously for $\delta = 1$, $D(k_1; k_2)$ is identical with $B_e(k_1, k_2)$.

Several useful properties of the Dirichlet density are as follows:

Property 1 If $\mathbf{u} = [u_1, u_2, \ldots, u_\delta]$ has the δ-variate Dirichlet distribution $D(k_1, \ldots, k_\delta; k_{\delta+1})$, then the marginal distribution of $[u_1, u_2, \ldots, u_{\delta_1}]$, $\delta_1 < \delta$, is the δ_1-variate Dirichlet distribution $D(k_1, \ldots, k_{\delta_1}; k_{\delta_1+1} + \cdots + k_{\delta+1})$.

Property 2 If $\mathbf{u} = [u_1, u_2, \ldots, u_\delta]$ has the δ-variate Dirichlet distribution $D(k_1, k_2, \ldots, k_\delta; k_{\delta+1})$, the sum $u_1 + u_2 + \cdots + u_\delta$ has the beta distribution $B_e(k_1 + \cdots + k_\delta, k_{\delta+1})$.

Next suppose that the following transformation is introduced:

$$\begin{aligned}
y_1 &= u_1 \\
y_2 &= u_1 + u_2 \\
&\;\;\vdots \\
y_\delta &= u_1 + u_2 + \cdots + u_\delta.
\end{aligned} \qquad (11)$$

Then

$$f(y_1, y_2, \ldots, y_\delta)$$

$$= \frac{\Gamma(k_1 + \cdots + k_{\delta+1})}{\Gamma(k_1) \cdots \Gamma(k_{\delta+1})} y_1^{k_1 - 1}(y_2 - y_1)^{k_2 - 1} \cdots (y_\delta - y_{\delta-1})^{k_\delta - 1}(1 - y_\delta)^{k_{\delta+1} - 1}$$

$$(12)$$

and sometimes is called the *ordered k-variate Dirichlet distribution* denoted $D^*(k_1, k_2, \ldots, k_\delta; k_{\delta+1})$.

2-21.2 Order Statistics

For $L = 1$, let $\mathbf{x}_n = [x_1, x_2, \ldots, x_n]$ be from a population having a continuous distribution function $F(x)$. Rearrange $x_1, x_2, \ldots, x_n$ in order from least to greatest obtaining reordered values $x_{(1)}, x_{(2)}, \ldots, x_{(n)}$, where $x_{(1)} \leq x_{(2)} \leq \cdots \leq x_{(n)}$, which are called the *order statistics*. The intervals $(-\infty, x_{(1)}], (x_{(1)}, x_{(2)}], \ldots, (x_{(n)}, +\infty]$ are called sample blocks $\mathscr{I}_1, \mathscr{I}_2, \ldots, \mathscr{I}_{n+1}$, respectively, and the functions $F(x_{(1)}), F(x_{(2)}) - F(x_{(1)}), \ldots, 1 - F(x_{(n)})$ of these blocks are called coverages $u_1, u_2, \ldots, u_{n+1}$.

A basic computation leads to the following fundamental property:

Property (*distribution of order statistics*).   If $x_{(1)}, x_{(2)}, \ldots, x_{(n)}$ are the order statistics of samples from a continuous distribution function $F(x)$, the random variables $F(x_{(1)}), F(x_{(2)}), \ldots, F(x_{(n)})$ have the ordered n-variable Dirichlet distribution $D^*(1, 1, \ldots, 1; 1)$.

From the above basic property concerning distribution of order statistics, the following properties are derived:

Property.   Any $\delta(\delta < n)$ of the coverages $u_1, u_2, \ldots, u_{n+1}$ have the δ-variate Dirichlet distribution $D(1, 1, \ldots, 1; n - \delta + 1)$.

Property.   The sum of any δ of the coverages $u_1, u_2, \ldots, u_{n+1}$ has the beta distribution $B_e(\delta, n - \delta + 1)$.

2-21.3 Ordering Functions for Multidimensions

To extend the concept of order statistics, coverages, and their distribution to multidimensions $(L > 1)$ requires introducing ordering functions. An *ordering function* $g(x_1, x_2, \ldots, x_L)$ is introduced such that $w = g(x_1, x_2, \ldots, x_L)$ is a random variable which has a continuous distribution function $H(w)$. Then the random variables

$$
\begin{aligned}
w_1 &= g(\mathbf{x}_1) \\
w_2 &= g(\mathbf{x}_2) \\
&\;\; \vdots \\
w_n &= g(\mathbf{x}_n)
\end{aligned}
\tag{13}
$$

are samples from $H(w)$ and these samples can be ordered. Coverages

$$u_1 = H(w_{(1)})$$
$$u_2 = H(w_{(2)}) - H(w_{(1)})$$
$$\vdots \qquad \vdots$$
$$u_n = H(w_{(n)}) - H(w_{(n+1)})$$

are defined to correspond to regions $\mathscr{I}_1, \mathscr{I}_2, \ldots, \mathscr{I}_n$ obtained using the "ordering curves" $w = g(\mathbf{x}_\xi)$

Property (*L-Dimensional Extension*). The coverages obtained using the ordering function $g(\mathbf{x})$ for L-dimensional samples $\mathbf{x}$ have the same properties possessed by coverages for one-dimensional samples $x_1, x_2, \ldots, x_n$.

Discussion

The ordering function $g(\mathbf{x})$ discussed above makes no provision for dependence on the samples or the stage the procedure is at in producing ordered numbers $w_{(1)}, w_{(2)}, \ldots, w_{(n)}$. Next, consideration should be given to whether such generalized ordering functions are possible. Before proceeding to consider "generalized ordering functions," consider how a priori knowledge affects things. First, it appears that the ordering function $g(\mathbf{x})$ is immaterial because the underlying distribution could be any continuous distribution. The order statistics resulting from use of the order function produce coverages which remain distribution-free irrespective of the ordering function.

If something about the underlying statistics is known that suggests a particular ordering function $g(\mathbf{x})$, then it appears that coverages corresponding to resulting order statistics no longer are distribution-free because the resulting tolerance regions "favor the underlying density." However, a particular ordering function $g(\mathbf{x})$ can be chosen of any form with the order statistics remaining distribution-free with respect to all possible underlying continuous distributions.

The reader is warned that distribution-free statistics or nonparametric studies may not be useful to him because man can possess knowledge of relationships which would require an infinite number of samples to learn using distribution-free procedures. Man knows these relationships by studying the problem using a fantastic visual sensor, auditory sensor, and then using inductive and deductive powers to make the conclusions resulting in relationships.

A more nearly generalized procedure for constructing tolerance regions was suggested by Kemperman [35] in 1956. In the construction, two persons† are involved: a statistician (S) and his assistant (A). A has the n samples $\mathbf{x}_1$, $\mathbf{x}_2$, ..., $\mathbf{x}_n$ while at the outset S does not. S has at his disposal a class of orderings ϕ in the observation space $\mathscr{X}$.

In the first step of the construction, S selects an ordering ϕ_1 and a positive integer m_0, $m_0 \leq n$, and asks A to give him the m_0th smallest observation $\mathbf{x}^*(1)$ with respect to ϕ_1, together with the two sets of indices corresponding to the $m_0 - 1$ and $m_1 - 1 = n - m_0$ observations which are smaller or larger than $\mathbf{x}^*(1)$. Now, S can draw the (m_0, m_1) − partition $\chi = \mathscr{I}_0 \cup \mathscr{I}^* \cup \mathscr{I}_1$ of $\mathscr{X}$ with respect to ϕ_1 and the sets of the n observations, where

$$\mathscr{I}_0 = \{\mathbf{x} \in \mathscr{X} : \phi_1(\mathbf{x}) < \mathbf{x}^*(1)\},$$

$$\mathscr{I}^* = \{\mathbf{x} \in \mathscr{X} : \phi_1(\mathbf{x}) = \mathbf{x}^*(1)\},$$

and

$$\mathscr{I}_1 = \{\mathbf{x} \in \mathscr{X} : \phi_1(\mathbf{x}) > \mathbf{x}^*(1)\}.$$

Let $D^0(0) = \mathscr{X}$, $D^1(j) = \mathscr{I}_j$ $(j = 0, 1)$, and $D_1^* = \mathscr{I}^*$.

After k steps, $0 \leq k \leq n - 1$, S has obtained a partition of $\mathscr{X}$ into $k + 1$ disjoint regions $D^k(j)$ $(j = 0, 1, \ldots, k)$ and k boundary sets $D_i^*(i = 1, 2, \ldots, k)$. Further, for each of these $2k + 1$ sets, S knows precisely the set of indices corresponding to the observations $\mathbf{x}_i$ within the set. For each boundary set $D_i^*(i = 1, 2, \ldots, k)$, S knows the actual value of the boundary observation $\mathbf{x}^*(i)$ in D_i^*.

Forming Subregions Within Regions Already Formed

Continuing, the $(k + 1)$th step of the construction proceeds as follows: His choice depending, *in any way whatsoever*, on the knowledge acquired, S chooses (i) a distinguished region $D = D^k(j^*)$ among those of the $k + 1$ regions $D^k(j)$ $(j = 0, 1, \ldots, k)$ which contain at least one observation; (ii) a positive integer m_0 not larger than the number $m - 1$ of observations in D; (iii) an ordering function ϕ_{k+1}.

S then asks A for the m_0th smallest observation $\mathbf{x}^*(k + 1)$ in D with respect to ϕ_{k+1}, together with the two sets of indices corresponding to the $m_0 - 1$ or $m_1 = m - m_0 - 1$ observations in D which are smaller or larger than $\mathbf{x}^*(k + 1)$, respectively.

---

†Two persons are used because the person cannot let his construction depend at will on the samples.

Using the acquired value $\mathbf{x}^*(k + 1)$, S is now able to draw the (m_0, m_1)-partition $D = D_0 \cup D^* \cup D_1$ of D with respect to ϕ_{k+1} and the $m - 1$ observations in D. Afterwards, he renumbers the regions $D^k(0), \ldots, D^k(j^* - 1), D_0, D_1, D^k(j^* + 1), \ldots, D^k(k)$ as $D^{k+1}(j)$ $(j = 0, 1, \ldots, k + 1)$, in this order. Finally, let $D^*_{k+1} = D^*$.

After exactly n steps the construction stops. Then S has obtained a partition of $\mathscr{X}$ into $n + 1$ disjoint regions $D^n(j)$ $(j = 0, 1, \ldots, n)$, and n boundary sets D^*_k $(k = 1, 2, \ldots, n)$.

Property. The coverages $u_1, u_2, \ldots, u_n$ corresponding to $D^n(1)$, $D^n(2)$, $\ldots, D^n(n)$ have the Dirichlet distribution $D(1, 1, \ldots, 1; 1)$.

Fraser's Construction Procedure

Fraser [4] presents a construction procedure using n ordering functions $\phi_1(\mathbf{x})$, $\phi_2(\mathbf{x}), \ldots, \phi_n(\mathbf{x})$, $j - 1$ real variables $r_1, r_2, \ldots, r_{j-1}$, and functions $p_1, p_2, \ldots, p_n$. When the function ϕ_j is used, the real values $r_1, r_2, \ldots, r_{j-1}$ are values, respectively, of the function $\phi_1, \phi_2, \ldots, \phi_{j-1}$. $P_j = p_j(r_1, r_2, \ldots, r_{j-1})$ is an integer in $1, 2, \ldots, n$, and which integer it is may depend on $j - 1$ real variables $r_1, \ldots, r_{j-1}$.

First the n values $\phi_1(\mathbf{x}_1), \ldots, \phi_1(\mathbf{x}_n)$ are examined and the p_1th largest value chosen,

$$\max_{i=1}^{n}(p_1)\phi_1(\mathbf{x}_i).$$

The $\mathscr{X}$ is divided into two regions,

$$\mathscr{I}_1 = \{\mathbf{x}: \phi_1(\mathbf{x}) > \max_{i=1}^{n}(p_1)\phi_1(\mathbf{x}_i)\},$$

$$\mathscr{I}_1^c = \{\mathbf{x}: \phi_1(\mathbf{x}) < \max_{i=1}^{n}(p_1)\phi_1(\mathbf{x}_i)\}.$$

Next, to show possible dependence upon $\max_{i=1}^{n}(p_1)\phi_1(\mathbf{x}_i)$ let

$$\phi_2(\mathbf{x}) = \phi_2(\mathbf{x}; \max_{i=1}^{n}(p_1)\phi_1(\mathbf{x}_i)),$$

$$p_2 = p_2(\max_{i=1}^{n}(p_1)\phi_1(\mathbf{x}_i)).$$

For p_2 one of the integers $1, 2, \ldots, p_1 - 1$, the region $\mathscr{I}_1$ is divided into $\mathscr{I}_2$ and $\mathscr{I}_2^c$:

$$\mathscr{I}_2 = \mathscr{I}_1^c \cap \{\mathbf{x}: \phi_2(\mathbf{x}) > \max_{\mathbf{x}_i \in \mathscr{I}_1^c}(p_2)\phi_2(\mathbf{x}_i)\},$$

$$\mathscr{I}_2^c = \mathscr{I}_1^c \cap \{\mathbf{x}: \phi_2(\mathbf{x}) < \max_{\mathbf{x}_i \in \mathscr{I}_1^c}(p_2)\phi_2(\mathbf{x}_i)\}.$$

This procedure is continued using at the jth stage $\phi_j(\mathbf{x})$ and p_j. Finally, $n + 1$ regions $\mathscr{I}_1, \mathscr{I}_2, \ldots, \mathscr{I}_{n+1}$ are obtained.

Property. Using the rules prescribed by Fraser, coverages $u_1, u_2, \ldots,$ u_{n+1} corresponding to the regions $\mathscr{I}_1, \mathscr{I}_2, \ldots, \mathscr{I}_{n+1}$ as outlined above have the Dirichlet distribution $D(1, 1, \ldots, 1; 0)$.

Basic Theory for Tolerance Region

A question frequently asked is whether a tolerance region can be any function of the samples. For example, can the family of ellipsoids centered at the sample mean be used to order the samples? To answer this question, begin with how the property concerning the distribution of order statistics on the real line is derived:

If $F(x)$ is any continuous distribution, then any *arbitrary point* x has a corresponding value $y = F(x)$ such that

$$p[Y \leq y] = p[X \leq F^{-1}(y)] = y.$$

That is, the distribution of $F(x)$ at any arbitrary point x is uniform on $[0, 1]$.

For n samples $x_1, x_2, \ldots, x_n$, the joint probability density of $y_\xi = F(x_\xi)$, $\xi = 1, 2, \ldots, n$, is

$$f(y_1, y_2, \ldots, y_n) = 1, \qquad 0 \leq y_\xi \leq 1, \xi = 1, 2, \ldots, n.$$

Next, form the order statistics $y_{(1)}, y_{(2)}, \ldots, y_{(n)}$ of the samples $y_1, y_2, \ldots, y_n$. There are $n!$ points $[y_1, y_2, \ldots, y_n]$ corresponding to $[y_{(1)}, y_{(2)}, \ldots, y_{(n)}]$. Thus,

$$f(y_{(1)}, y_{(2)}, \ldots, y_{(n)}) = n!, \qquad 0 \leq y_{(1)} \leq y_{(2)} \leq \cdots \leq y_{(n)} \leq 1,$$

which is the ordered n-variate Dirichlet distribution $D^*(1, 1, \ldots, 1; 1)$. We can refer to $y_{(1)}, y_{(2)} - y_{(1)}, \ldots, y_{(n)} - y_{(n-1)}, 1 - y_{(n)}$ as basic coverages.

Property Concerning Sums of Basic Coverages

If $u_1, u_2, \ldots, u_s$ are sums of $k_1, k_2, \ldots, k_s$, respectively, of the basic coverages $y_{(1)}, y_{(2)} - y_{(1)}, \ldots, y_{(n)} - y_{(n-1)}, 1 - y_{(n)}$, then the distribution of $u_1, u_2, \ldots, u_s$ is the s-variate Dirichlet distribution $D(k_1, k_2, \ldots, k_s; n - k_1 - \cdots - k_s + 1)$.

Now, a basic requirement from the above is that any sample x_ξ have a distribution $y_\xi = F(x_\xi)$ which is uniform. If the ordering procedure in any way causes $y_{(\xi)} = F(x_{(\xi)})$ not to have a uniform distribution, then the order statistics are not distribution-free. For example, a family of ellipses with center at an arbitrary point $\mathbf{x}$ tells nothing about the distribution $y_{(1)} = F(\mathbf{x}_{(1)})$ of the first-order sample. But a family of ellipses with center at the sample mean of $\mathbf{x}_1, \mathbf{x}_2, \ldots, \mathbf{x}_n$ suggests something about the distribution of $y_{(1)} = F(x_{(1)})$. Furthermore, modifying the shape of the ellipses based on the samples influences the distribution of $y_{(1)} = F(x_{(1)})$.

Can a priori Knowledge Be Introduced in Tolerance Region Construction?

A priori knowledge cannot be introduced in tolerance region construction. Certainly, the shape of the ellipses mentioned above can be selected arbitrarily, but they must not reflect knowledge of the probability distribution. Once tolerance regions are formed, it is possible, say, to analyze the distributions of $r = (u_1 + u_2)/2$ because the average of the first two coverages contributes to problem analysis. However, one cannot use problem knowledge that two regions of $\mathscr{X}$ have the same probability mass when constructing the tolerance regions.

All this suggests that structures in the probability distribution cannot be learned with a finite number of samples. Rather, a set of structures should be postulated a priori and then analyzed for how well the n samples match each respective structure. This is precisely what is accomplished using the a posteriori density $f(\mathbf{b}\,|\,\dot{\mathbf{x}}_n)$ in the Bayes parametric approach.

2-21.4 Examples of Distribution-Free Tolerance Regions

Example 1 The interval formed between the largest and smallest of n, one-dimensional samples.

Example 2 The set of all points $\mathbf{x}$ closer to $\mathbf{m}$ using arbitrary metric $d(\mathbf{x}, \mathbf{m})$ than the rth closest to $\mathbf{x}$ of n samples, $r < n$.

Example 3 Let the ordering function be $g(\mathbf{x}) = \sqrt{x_1^2 + x_2^2}$, $L = 2$. Then the tolerance region boundaries are concentric circles as shown in Figure 2.1.

Example 4 An example for $L = 2$ suggested by Tukey [36] is shown in Figure 2.2, where multiple order functions are used. This type of tolerance region construction is especially suitable for implementation on a digital computer or using special-purpose digital computer hardware.

Example 5 If it is known that $f(\mathbf{x})$ is $N(\mathbf{m}, \mathbf{\Sigma})$, the function

$$g(\mathbf{x}\,|\,\mathbf{m}, \mathbf{\Sigma}) = (\mathbf{x} - \mathbf{m})\mathbf{\Sigma}^{-1}(\mathbf{x} - \mathbf{m})$$

can be used to form distribution free tolerance regions.

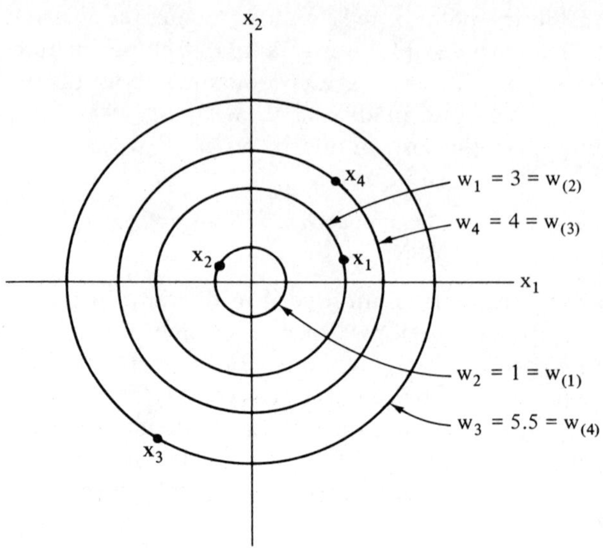

Fig. 2.1 Circular Tolerance Regions

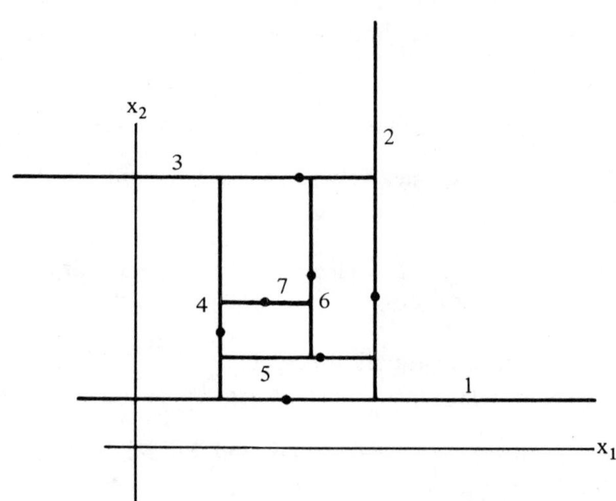

Fig. 2.2 Tolerance Regions Utilizing Straight Line Ordering Functions

Example 6 Given $\mathbf{x}_1, \mathbf{x}_2, \ldots, \mathbf{x}_n$ and $\hat{\boldsymbol{\Sigma}} = (1/n) \sum_{s=1}^{n} (\mathbf{x}_s - \hat{\mathbf{m}})'(\mathbf{x}_s - \hat{\mathbf{m}})$, the function

$$g(\mathbf{x} \,|\, \mathbf{y}, \boldsymbol{\Sigma}) = (\mathbf{x} - \mathbf{y})\boldsymbol{\Sigma}^{-1}(\mathbf{x} - y)$$

can be used to form distribution-free tolerance regions for samples $\mathbf{x}_{n+1}$, $\mathbf{x}_{n+2}, \ldots$.

Example 7 For the ordering function in Example 6, distribution-free tolerance regions do not result for samples $\mathbf{x}_1, \mathbf{x}_2, \ldots, \mathbf{x}_n$.

Tolerance regions for one class can be determined using training samples from that class which are a function of another set of variables. In particular, Anderson and Benning [51] used properties of clusters in training samples from another class as these variables. With this approach, regions in the measurement space can be determined within which there is such probability of error as to "reserve judgment" as to the class of subsequent unclassified samples in that region.

2-22 Density Representation Using Orthonormal Basis Functions

In Chapter 3 it is shown that a minimum-probability-of-error decision rule decides that $\mathbf{x}$ is from category $d(\mathbf{x})$ if

$$d(\mathbf{x}) = \mathrm{Index}[\max_i \{P_i f_i(\mathbf{x})\}_{i=1}^{M}]. \tag{1}$$

In pattern recognition and communications, densities $f_i(\mathbf{x})$ may be unknown and must be estimated. A problem is how to estimate $f_i(\mathbf{x})$ for finite sample size n and limited storage.

Density estimation for a parametric family $\mathscr{F}$ is considered in Sections 2-1 through 2-12. In Section 2-9 results provided by Abramson and Braverman [10] and Keehn [11] for estimating the mean vector and covariance matrix of a Gaussian density were presented. For the case where the Gaussian assumption is not valid, Aizerman, Braverman, and Rozonoer [24], using a set of complete orthonormal basis functions $\{\psi_{ji}(\mathbf{x})\}$, represent $f(\mathbf{x}|\omega_j)$ as

$$\hat{f}(\mathbf{x}|\omega_j) = \sum_{i=1}^{R} c_{ji}\psi_{ji}(\mathbf{x}), \tag{2}$$

where $\{\psi_{ji}(\mathbf{x})\}$ are *assumed known a priori* and $\{c_{ji}\}$ are estimated. They show that for c_{ji} appropriately estimated,

$$f(\mathbf{x}|\hat{\boldsymbol{\alpha}}_j) = \sum_{i=1}^{R} \hat{c}_{ji}\psi_{ji}(\mathbf{x}) \xrightarrow[\forall \mathbf{x}]{P} f(\mathbf{x}|\boldsymbol{\alpha}_j). \tag{3}$$

Tsypkin [25] also uses an orthonormal set $\{\psi_{ji}\}_{i=1}^{R}$ and (2) but does not assume the set complete. He shows that for c_{ji} appropriately estimated, the integral square error (ISE)

$$\text{ISE} = \int (f(\mathbf{x}|\omega_j) - \hat{f}(\mathbf{x}|\omega_j))^2 \, d\mathbf{x} \tag{4}$$

is minimized. Kaskyap and Blaydon [26] assume only that $\{\psi_{ji}\}_{i=1}^{R}$ is a set of linearly independent functions. Using (2) and an appropriate $\hat{c}_{ji}$, they show that mean square error (MSE)

$$\text{MSE} = \int_{D} (f(\mathbf{x}|\omega_j) - \hat{f}(\mathbf{x}|\omega_j))^2 f(\mathbf{x}|\omega_j) \, d\mathbf{x}$$

is minimized.

Rosenblatt [27] uses an estimate of the form (2), where the set $\{\psi_{ji}(\mathbf{x})\}$ is a known function of the n_j samples and $c_{ji} = 1/n_j$.

An approach where storage complexity grows linearly with n_j is to let $\psi_{ji}(\mathbf{x})$ be placed at the ith sample from class j; specifically, let

$$\psi_{ji}(\mathbf{x}) = \frac{1}{\sigma_{n_j}} K\left(\frac{|\mathbf{x} - \mathbf{x}_i^j|^2}{\sigma_{n_j}}\right),$$

where σ_{n_j} and K satisfy conditions discussed in Chapter 4. This approach can be shown to utilize a local density-measuring philosophy with a distance measure specified by the function $K(\cdot)$. This philosophy is used in Chapter 4, which deals with supervised estimation and decision making. Much of the early work on local density function estimation is by Parzen [28]. The reader will also find of interest Whittle [30], Watson and Leadbetter [31], Murthy [29], Loftsgaarden and Quesenberry [33], and Cooper and Tabczynski [32].

Another well-known approach is the histogram technique, where $\{\psi_{ji}\}_{i=1}^{R}$ is the set of indicator functions on the regions of a partition of the observation space; especially,

$$\psi_{ji}(\mathbf{x}) = \begin{cases} 1, & \mathbf{x} \text{ in the } i\text{th region,} \\ 0, & \text{otherwise,} \end{cases}$$

$$\hat{c}_{ji} = \frac{1}{W(i)} \frac{n_j(i)}{n_j},$$

where $n_j(i)$ is the number of training observations from class ω_j that are in the ith region and $W(i)$ is the volume of that region.

All these approaches, which essentially attempt to represent $f(\mathbf{x}|\omega_j)$ with a form (2), can also be interpreted as trying to find functional components in the density. Note that (2) has a form that is a special case of a mixture; thus unsupervised estimation techniques also can be used to represent $f(\mathbf{x}|\omega_j)$. It must be emphasized, however, that Eq. (2) is not a very general

Elementary Properties of Estimators   *Chap. 2*

form of mixture because the component functions $\psi_{ji}(\mathbf{x})$ are assumed known. In general, the structure and locations of the components $\psi_{ji}(\mathbf{x})$ are unknown and must be estimated; this is one of the most general and important problems in unsupervised pattern recognition.

2-23 Weighting Functions versus Condensing Functions

In order to represent the density $f(\mathbf{x})$ at $\mathbf{x}$ given samples $\mathbf{x}_1, \mathbf{x}_2, \ldots, \mathbf{x}_n$, one approach is to use weighting functions $K(\mathbf{x}; \mathbf{x}_s, \mathbf{\Sigma}_s)$, where $\mathbf{x}_s$ is a location vector and $\mathbf{\Sigma}_s$ a covariance matrix for the sth function. A representation of $(\mathbf{x})$ is

$$\hat{f}(\mathbf{x}) = \frac{1}{n} \sum_{s=1}^{n} K(\mathbf{x} \,|\, \mathbf{x}_s, \mathbf{\Sigma}_s). \tag{1}$$

Another approach is to represent $f(\mathbf{x})$ by

$$\hat{f}(\mathbf{x}) = K(\mathbf{x} \,|\, \hat{\mathbf{m}}, \hat{\mathbf{\Sigma}}), \tag{2}$$

where

$$\hat{\mathbf{m}} = \frac{1}{n} \sum_{s=1}^{n} \mathbf{x}_s,$$

$$\hat{\mathbf{\Sigma}} = \frac{1}{n} \sum_{s=1}^{n} (\mathbf{x}_s - \hat{\mathbf{m}})(\mathbf{x}_s - \hat{\mathbf{m}})^t.$$

The disadvantages of Eq. (1) are

1. No complexity-reduction results for subsequent decision making.
2. Estimation of $\mathbf{\Sigma}_s$ requires additional assumptions similar to the definition of approach (2); thus researchers frequently assume that $\mathbf{\Sigma}_s = \sigma^2 \mathbf{I}$.
3. Essentially it is just empirical density estimation with a weighting function $K(\mathbf{x})$ which is other than a delta function.
4. No direct provision is made for inserting an a priori uncertain local covariance matrix which can subsequently be updated.

2-24 Information Function

Suppose that a random vector $\mathbf{x}$ can be one of k points $\mathbf{x}^{(1)}, \mathbf{x}^{(2)}, \ldots, \mathbf{x}^{(k)}$ in an observation space. Then the average uncertainty removed (or information conveyed) by revealing the value of $\mathbf{x}$ is defined as

$$H(\mathbf{x}) = -\sum_{i=1}^{k} \ln\left[p(\mathbf{x}^{(i)})\right]p(\mathbf{x}^{(i)}), \tag{1}$$

which is the expected value of the function $\ln p(\mathbf{x})$. When $\mathbf{x}$ is continuous,

$$H(\mathbf{x}) = -\int \ln[f(\mathbf{x})]f(\mathbf{x})\, d\mathbf{x}. \tag{2}$$

A distance measure related to $H(\mathbf{x})$ which naturally arises in Bayes estimation is

$$\eta(\mathbf{b}, \mathbf{b}^*) = \int \ln[f(\mathbf{x}\,|\,\mathbf{b})]f(\mathbf{x}\,|\,\mathbf{b}^*)\, d\mathbf{x}, \tag{3}$$

where $\mathbf{b}$ is a point in the parameter space characterizing $\mathcal{F}$. The function $\eta(\mathbf{b}, \mathbf{b}^*)$ is a measure of distance between $\mathbf{b}$ and $\mathbf{b}^*$ and may be maximum when $\mathbf{b} = \mathbf{b}^*$. Note that

$$\eta(\mathbf{b}, \mathbf{b}) = -H(\mathbf{x}), \qquad f(\mathbf{x}) = f(\mathbf{x}\,|\,\mathbf{b}). \tag{4}$$

Thus, maximizing $\eta(\mathbf{b}, \mathbf{b}^*)$ at $\mathbf{b} = \mathbf{b}^*$ minimizes the uncertainty function $H(\mathbf{x})$.

The joint uncertainty of two vectors $\mathbf{x}_1$ and $\mathbf{x}_2$ is defined as

$$H(\mathbf{x}_1, \mathbf{x}_2) = -\int\int f(\mathbf{x}_1, \mathbf{x}_2) \ln f(\mathbf{x}_1, \mathbf{x}_2)\, d\mathbf{x}_1\, d\mathbf{x}_2; \tag{5}$$

in general, for n vectors, the joint uncertainty of its components is

$$H(\mathbf{x}_1, \mathbf{x}_2, \ldots, \mathbf{x}_n)$$

$$= \int \cdots \int f(\mathbf{x}_1, \mathbf{x}_2, \ldots, \mathbf{x}_n) \ln f(\mathbf{x}_1, \mathbf{x}_2, \ldots, \mathbf{x}_n)\, d\mathbf{x}_1\, d\mathbf{x}_2 \cdots d\mathbf{x}_n. \tag{6}$$

Similarly, the difference in uncertainty for a vector with density $f(\mathbf{x})$ and a vector with density $\hat{f}(\mathbf{x})$ is

$$\Delta H = -\hat{H}(\mathbf{x}) + H(\mathbf{x}) = \int \hat{f}(\mathbf{x}) \ln \hat{f}(\mathbf{x})\, d\mathbf{x} - \int f(\mathbf{x}) \ln f(\mathbf{x})\, d\mathbf{x}. \tag{7}$$

Distance Between Classes

Suppose that there are two densities $p(\mathbf{x}\,|\,\omega_1)P_1$ and $p(\mathbf{x}\,|\,\omega_2)P_2$ used in a minimum-risk decision rule. The one possible measure that approximates the probability of error for these densities is

$$K = \int f(\mathbf{x}|\omega_1)P_1 \ln\left[\frac{f(\mathbf{x}|\omega_2)P_2}{f(\mathbf{x}|\omega_1)P_1}\right] dx + \int f(\mathbf{x}|\omega_2)P_2 \ln\left[\frac{f(\mathbf{x}|\omega_1)P_1}{f(\mathbf{x}|\omega_2)P_2}\right] dx$$

$$= \int [f(\mathbf{x}|\omega_1)P_1 - f(\mathbf{x}|\omega_2)P_2][\ln f(\mathbf{x}|\omega_2)P_2 - \ln f(\mathbf{x}|\omega_1)P_1]\, dx \tag{8}$$

or, in a discretized observation space,

$$K = \sum_{i=1}^{R} [p(\mathbf{x}^{(i)}|\omega_1)P_1 - p(\mathbf{x}^{(i)}|\omega_2)P_2][\ln p(\mathbf{x}^{(i)}|\omega_2)P_2 - \ln p(\mathbf{x}^{(i)}|\omega_1)P_1].$$

Also, continuing from (8),

$$K = \int f(\mathbf{x}|\omega_1)P_1 \ln f(\mathbf{x}|\omega_2)P_2\, dx - \int f(\mathbf{x}|\omega_1)P_1 \ln f(\mathbf{x}|\omega_1)P_1\, dx$$

$$+ \int f(\mathbf{x}|\omega_2)P_2 \ln f(\mathbf{x}|\omega_1)P_1\, dx - \int f(\mathbf{x}|\omega_2)P_2 \ln f(\mathbf{x}|\omega_2)P_2\, dx$$

$$\triangleq \eta(\omega_1, \omega_2) - \eta(\omega_1, \omega_1) + \eta(\omega_2, \omega_1) - \eta(\omega_2, \omega_2).$$

The notation $\eta(\omega_i, \omega_j)$ is nonparametric, where ω_i and ω_j denote the respective classes without requiring a parameteric representation; i.e.,

$$\eta(\omega_i, \omega_j) \triangleq \int f(x|\omega_i)P_i \ln f(\mathbf{x}|\omega_j)P_j\, dx.$$

Another relationship, denoted $K(\mathbf{b}, \mathbf{b}^*)$, places in evidence the parameters characterizing the respective densities, where $\mathbf{b}$ contains $\mathbf{b}_1$ and $\mathbf{b}_2$, the parameters characterizing the densities $f(\mathbf{x}|\omega_1)$ and $f(\mathbf{x}|\omega_2)$, respectively.

$$K(\mathbf{b}, \mathbf{b}^*) = \int f(\mathbf{x}|\mathbf{b}_1^*, \omega_1)P_1^* \ln f(\mathbf{x}|\mathbf{b}_2, \omega_2)P_2\, dx$$

$$- \int f(\mathbf{x}|\mathbf{b}_1^*, \omega_1)P_1^* \ln f(\mathbf{x}|\mathbf{b}_1, \omega_1)P_1\, dx$$

$$+ \int f(\mathbf{x}|\mathbf{b}_2^*, \omega_2)P_2^* \ln f(\mathbf{x}|\mathbf{b}_1, \omega_1)P_1\, dx \tag{10}$$

$$- \int f(\mathbf{x}|\mathbf{b}_2^*, \omega_2)P_2^* \ln f(\mathbf{x}|\mathbf{b}_2, \omega_2)P_2\, dx$$

$$= -\eta(\mathbf{b}_1, \mathbf{b}_1^*) - \eta(\mathbf{b}_2, \mathbf{b}_2^*) + \eta(\mathbf{b}_1, \mathbf{b}_2^*) + \eta(\mathbf{b}_2, \mathbf{b}_1^*).$$

By using the relationships

$$\int f_1^*(\mathbf{x})P_1^* \ln f_2(\mathbf{x})P_2 \, d\mathbf{x}$$

$$= \int f_1^*(\mathbf{x})P_1^* \ln f_2^*(\mathbf{x})P_2^* + \int f_1^*(\mathbf{x})P_1^* \ln \frac{f_2(\mathbf{x})P_2}{f_2^*(\mathbf{x})P_2^*} \, d\mathbf{x},$$

$$\int f_2^*(\mathbf{x})P_2^* \ln f_1(\mathbf{x})P_1 \, d\mathbf{x}$$

$$= \int f_2^*(\mathbf{x})P_2^* \ln f_1^*(\mathbf{x})P_1^* + \int f_2^*(\mathbf{x})P_2^* \ln \frac{f_1(\mathbf{x})P_1}{f_1^*(\mathbf{x})P_1^*} \, d\mathbf{x},$$

(11)

Eq. (10) can be put in the form

$$K(\mathbf{b}, \mathbf{b}^*) = -\eta(\mathbf{b}_1, \mathbf{b}_1^*) - \eta(\mathbf{b}_2, \mathbf{b}_2^*) + \eta(\mathbf{b}_1^*, \mathbf{b}_2^*) + \eta(\mathbf{b}_2^*, \mathbf{b}_1^*)$$
$$+ \int f(\mathbf{x}\,|\,\mathbf{b}_1^*)P_1^* \ln \frac{f(\mathbf{x}\,|\,\mathbf{b}_2)P_2}{f(\mathbf{x}\,|\,\mathbf{b}_2^*)P_2} \, d\mathbf{x} + \int f(\mathbf{x}\,|\,\mathbf{b}_2^*)P_2^* \ln \frac{f(\mathbf{x}\,|\,\mathbf{b}_1)P_1}{f(\mathbf{x}\,|\,\mathbf{b}_1^*)P_1^*} \, d\mathbf{x}.$$

(12)

We conclude the following for expression (12):
$\eta(\mathbf{b}_j, \mathbf{b}_j^*)$ terms measure the quality of $\mathbf{b}_j$ as a point estimator for $\mathbf{b}_j^*$;
$\eta(\mathbf{b}_i, \mathbf{b}_j^*)$, $i \neq j$, terms measure the distance of a point estimator $\mathbf{b}_i$ from $\mathbf{b}_j^*$.
Concerning the integrals in (12), note that they are near zero if $\mathbf{b}_j \cong \mathbf{b}_j^*$.

A consistent estimate for the terms in Eq. (10) are sample means as follows:

$$\hat{K}(\mathbf{b}, \mathbf{b}^*) = -\frac{1}{n_1}\sum_{s=1}^{n_1} \ln f(\mathbf{x}_s^1\,|\,\mathbf{b}_1)P_1 - \frac{1}{n_2}\sum_{s=1}^{n_2} \ln f(\mathbf{x}_s^2\,|\,\mathbf{b}_2)P_2$$
$$+ \frac{1}{n_1}\sum_{s=1}^{n_1} \ln f(\mathbf{x}_s^1\,|\,\mathbf{b}_2)P_2 + \frac{1}{n_2}\sum_{s=1}^{n_2} \ln f(\mathbf{x}_s^2\,|\,\mathbf{b}_1)P_1,$$

(13)

where $\mathbf{x}_s^i$, $s = 1, 2, \ldots, n_i$, are n_i samples from the ith category. The vector $\mathbf{b}$ contains $\mathbf{b}_1$ and $\mathbf{b}_2$, the parameters characterizing the respective class densities.

It may be possible to use $\hat{K}(\mathbf{b}, \mathbf{b}^*)$ as a regression function and search for the parameter $\mathbf{b}$ maximizing this function. Such a solution would thus correspond to minimizing the uncertainty function or maximizing the distance between the two classes.

We could begin with other distance functions than that advocated by Eq. (8). For example, consider the following:

     Elementary Properties of Estimators   Chap. 2

Discrete space	*Continuous space*

$$\sum_{j=1}^{k} (P_1 p_{1j} - P_2 p_{2j})^2 \qquad\qquad \int (P_1 f(\mathbf{x}\,|\,\omega_1) - P_2 f(\mathbf{x}\,|\,\omega_2))^2 \, d\mathbf{x}$$

$$\sum_{j=1}^{k} \min_{i=1,2} [P_i p_{ij}] \qquad\qquad \int \min_{i=1,2} [P_i f(\mathbf{x}\,|\,\omega_i)] \, d\mathbf{x}$$

$$\sum_{j=1}^{k} (P_1 p_{1j})(P_2 p_{2j}) \qquad\qquad P_1 P_2 \int f(\mathbf{x}\,|\,\omega_1) f(\mathbf{x}\,|\,\omega_2) \, d\mathbf{x}$$

where $p_{ij} = p(\mathbf{x}^j\,|\,\omega_i)$, $P_i = P(\omega_i)$, and $\mathbf{x}^j$ is an observation from class j.

2-25 Topological Properties of $\eta(\mathbf{b}, \mathbf{b}^*)$ and $\gamma(\mathbf{b}, \mathbf{b}^*)$

$\eta(\mathbf{b}, \mathbf{b}^*)$

Explicit evaluation of $\eta(\mathbf{b}, \mathbf{b}^*)$, even for a Gaussian family, is unavailable. A numerical evaluation has been made for $h(\mathbf{x})$, a mixture of two ($M = 2$) one-dimensional ($L = 1$) Gaussian densities, where the common variance $(\sigma^*)^2 = 1$ and $P_1^* = P_2^* = \frac{1}{2}$ are known, but the true means, m_1^* and m_2^*, are unknown. The objective then is to plot contours of constant $\eta(\mathbf{b}, \mathbf{b}^*)$, where $\eta(\mathbf{b}, \mathbf{b}^*) = \eta(m_1, m_2, \mathbf{b}^*)$ is defined as

$$\eta(m_1, m_2, \mathbf{b}^*) = \int_{-\infty}^{\infty} [\ln \sum_{i=1}^{2} \tfrac{1}{2} f(x\,|\,m_i, (\sigma^*)^2] \sum_{j=1}^{2} \tfrac{1}{2} f(x\,|\,m_i^*, (\sigma^*)^2) \, dx.$$

The above was evaluated for $m_1^* = 5$, $m_2^* = 2$ at signal-to-noise ratios,

$$\mathrm{SNR} = \left(\frac{m_1^* - m_2^*}{\sigma^*}\right)^2,$$

of 4.0 and 9.0; the results are plotted in Figures 2.3a and 2.3b.

At SNR $= 4.0$, the mixture density is unimodal; at SNR $= 9.0$, the class densities are beginning to become separable (although there is still considerable overlap).

$\gamma(\mathbf{b}, \mathbf{b}^*)$

The function $\gamma(\mathbf{b}, \mathbf{b}^*)$,

$$\gamma(\mathbf{b}, \mathbf{b}^*) = 2E[h(\mathbf{x}\,|\,\mathbf{b})] - ||\,h(\mathbf{x}\,|\,\mathbf{b})\,||^2$$
$$= ||\,h(\mathbf{x}\,|\,\mathbf{b}^*)\,||^2 - e^2(\mathbf{b}),$$

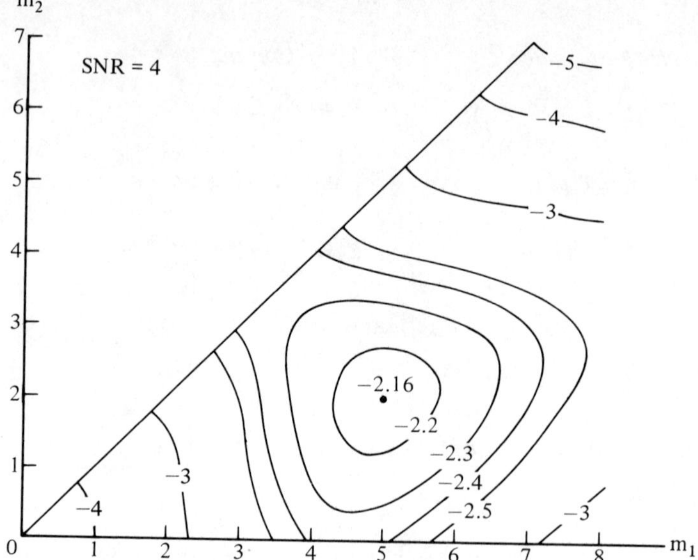

Fig. 2.3a Contour plots of constant $\eta(\mathbf{b})$ with $\left(\dfrac{m_1 - m_2}{\sigma}\right)^2 = 4$

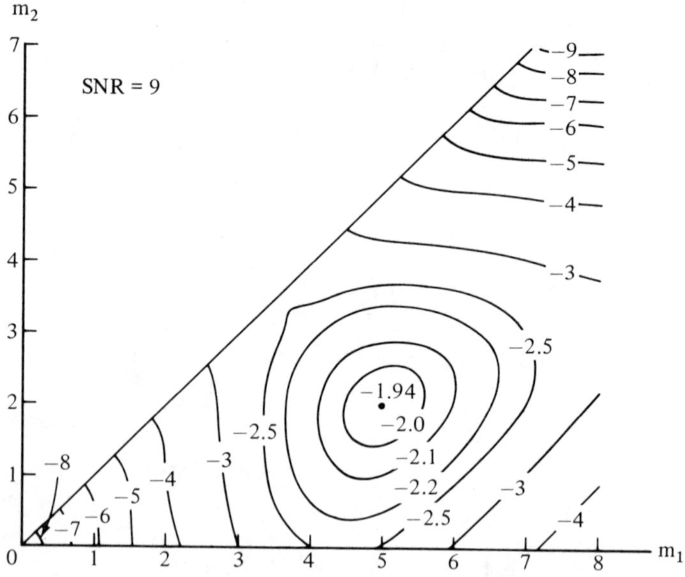

Fig. 2.3b Contour plots of constant $\eta(\mathbf{b})$ with $\left(\dfrac{m_1 - m_2}{\sigma}\right)^2 = 9$

154

where

$$e^2(\mathbf{b}) = \|h(\mathbf{x}\,|\,\mathbf{b}) - h(\mathbf{x}\,|\,\mathbf{b}^*)\|^2,$$

is easier to conceptualize. For example, $\gamma(\mathbf{b})$ versus the norm square error $e^2(\mathbf{b})$ is as shown in Figure 2.4. The term $e^2(\mathbf{b})$ is evaluated as follows:

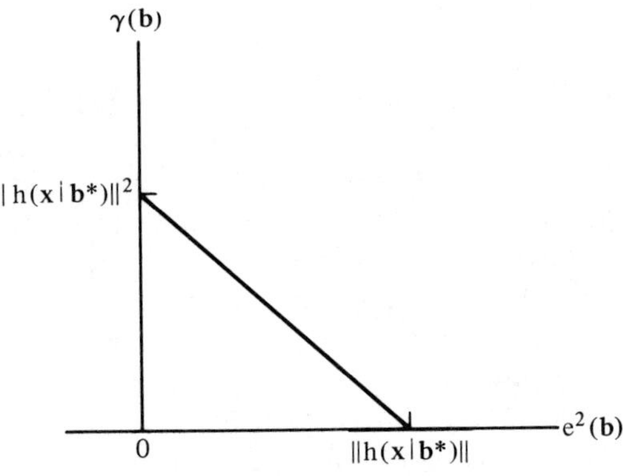

Fig. 2.4 $\gamma(\mathbf{b})$ vs. $e^2(\mathbf{b})$

$$e^2(\mathbf{b}) = \int \left[\sum_{i=1}^{M} P_i f(\mathbf{x}\,|\,i, \mathbf{b}_i) - \sum_{j=1}^{M^*} P_j^* f(\mathbf{x}\,|\,j, \mathbf{b}_j^*) \right]^2 dx$$

$$= \sum_{i=1}^{M} \sum_{k=1}^{M} \int P_i P_k f(\mathbf{x}\,|\,i, \mathbf{b}_i) f(\mathbf{x}\,|\,k, \mathbf{b}_k)\, dx$$

$$+ \sum_{j=1}^{M^*} \sum_{k=1}^{M^*} P_j^* P_k^* f(\mathbf{x}\,|\,j, \mathbf{b}_j^*) f(\mathbf{x}\,|\,k, \mathbf{b}_k^*)\, dx$$

$$- 2 \sum_{i=1}^{M} \sum_{j=1}^{M^*} P_i P_j^* f(\mathbf{x}\,|\,i, \mathbf{b}_i) f(\mathbf{x}\,|\,j, \mathbf{b}_j^*)\, dx.$$

Define

$$c_{rs}^{ij} = P_i P_j \int f(\mathbf{x}\,|\,i, \mathbf{b}_i^r) f(\mathbf{x}\,|\,j, \mathbf{b}_j^s)\, dx,$$

where r and s are either * or blank (indicated -):

$$e^2(\mathbf{b}) = \sum_{i=1}^{M} \sum_{j=1}^{M} c_{--}^{ij} + \sum_{i=1}^{M^*} \sum_{j=1}^{M^*} c_{**}^{i\,j} - 2 \sum_{i=1}^{M} \sum_{j=1}^{M^*} c_{-*}^{i\,j}.$$

If

$$f(\mathbf{x}\,|\,i, \mathbf{b}_i) = \left(\frac{1}{\sqrt{2\pi}\,\sigma} \right)^{L} \exp\left(-\frac{1}{2\sigma^2} \|\mathbf{x} - \mathbf{m}_i\|^2 \right),$$

then

$$c_{rs}^{ij} = P_i P_j \left(\frac{1}{\sqrt{2\pi}\,\sigma}\right)^L \exp\left(-\frac{1}{4\sigma^2}\|\mathbf{m}_i^r - \mathbf{m}_j^s\|^2\right),$$

and we observe that c_{-*}^{ij} increases as $\|\mathbf{m}_i - \mathbf{m}_j^*\|$ decreases.

Comment

The parameter-estimation procedures (especially Bayes) presented in this chapter are indispensable for an understanding of pattern recognition. A limitation of maximum-likelihood estimation and stochastic approximation is that the problem model must be made available in terms of functionals so that the procedures can be applied. Bayes, on the other hand, is a framework that conceptually can be applied to problems where a functional model cannot be defined. Bayes deals with a set of points $\mathbf{b}$ and probability attached to these points. Because the frontier of pattern recognition is how to insert problem knowledge into the decision rule, the Bayes framework is very appealing. This suggests the need for work more topologically oriented.

2-26 Proof that a posteriori Density Maximizes Entropy

The a posteriori density of $\mathbf{b} \in \mathscr{B}$ is computed as (as discussed in Section 2-8)

$$f(\mathbf{b}\,|\,\dot{\mathbf{x}}_n) = \frac{f(\dot{\mathbf{x}}_n\,|\,\mathbf{b})f_0(\mathbf{b})}{f(\dot{\mathbf{x}}_n)} \tag{1}$$

when samples $\mathbf{x}_1,\ \mathbf{x}_2,\ \ldots,\ \mathbf{x}_n$ are parameter conditionally independent and each distributed as $h(\mathbf{x}\,|\,\mathbf{b}^*) \in \mathscr{F}$. It is desirable that

$$\lim_{n\to\infty} f(\mathbf{b}\,|\,\dot{\mathbf{x}}_n) = \delta(\mathbf{b},\mathbf{b}^*). \tag{2}$$

Conditions will be explored in Chapter 5 under which this occurs; but, what can be said about $f(\mathbf{b}\,|\,\dot{\mathbf{x}}_n)$ for small sample size? Is there anything special about the form (1)?

It will be shown that $f(\mathbf{b}\,|\,\dot{\mathbf{x}}_n)$ given by (1) is least biased in the sense that it maximizes the entropy

$$d(f(\mathbf{b}\,|\,\dot{\mathbf{x}}_n)) \triangleq -\int \ln f(\mathbf{b}\,|\,\dot{\mathbf{x}}_n) f(\mathbf{b}\,|\,\dot{\mathbf{x}}_n)\, d\mathbf{b} \tag{3}$$

at every stage n subject to constraints to be specified. The first constraint,

$$\int_{\mathscr{B}} f(\mathbf{b} \mid \mathbf{x}_n) \, d\mathbf{b} = 1, \tag{4a}$$

requires that the a posteriori function $f(\mathbf{b} \mid \dot{\mathbf{x}}_n)$ in (2) be a probability density function. Next, defining

$$\eta(\mathbf{b}^*) \triangleq \int_{\mathscr{B}} \ln h(\mathbf{x} \mid \mathbf{b}^*) h(\mathbf{x} \mid \mathbf{b}^*) \, d\mathbf{x},$$

the second constraint will follow because

$$\eta(\mathbf{b}^*) - \lim_{n \to \infty} \frac{1}{n} \int_{\mathscr{B}} [\ln(f_0(\mathbf{b}) f(\dot{\mathbf{x}}_n \mid \mathbf{b}))] f(\mathbf{b} \mid \dot{\mathbf{x}}_n) \, d\mathbf{b} \xrightarrow{\text{w.p.1}} 0, \tag{4b}$$

which is equivalent to (2) and the fact that

$$\frac{1}{n} \sum_{s=1}^{n} \ln h(\mathbf{x}_s \mid \mathbf{b}^*) \xrightarrow{\text{w.p.1}} \eta(\mathbf{b}^*),$$

where it is assumed that the family of densities $\mathscr{F} = \{h(\mathbf{x} \mid \mathbf{b})\}$ have the following properties:

$$E[|\ln h(\mathbf{x} \mid \mathbf{b})|] < \infty, \tag{5a}$$

$$E[\ln h(\mathbf{x} \mid \mathbf{b})] = \eta(\mathbf{b}), \tag{5b}$$

$$\eta(\mathbf{b}) < \eta(\mathbf{b}^*) \; \forall \; \mathbf{b} \neq \mathbf{b}^*. \tag{5c}$$

The second constraint will be

$$\eta(\mathbf{b}^*) - \frac{1}{n} \int_{\mathscr{B}} [\ln(f_0(\mathbf{b}) f(\dot{\mathbf{x}}_n \mid \mathbf{b}))] f(\mathbf{b} \mid \dot{\mathbf{x}}_n) \, d\mathbf{b} = 0.$$

Using Lagrange's maximization procedure [50], the solution $f(\mathbf{b} \mid \dot{\mathbf{x}}_n)$ maximizing (3) subject to constraints (4) satisfies

$$\frac{\partial}{\partial f(\mathbf{b} \mid \dot{\mathbf{x}}_n)} \left\{ - \int_{\mathscr{B}} \ln f(\mathbf{b} \mid \dot{\mathbf{x}}_n) f(\mathbf{b} \mid \dot{\mathbf{x}}_n) \, d\mathbf{b} \right.$$

$$+ \lambda \left[\eta(\mathbf{b}^*) - \frac{1}{n} \int_{\mathscr{B}} [\ln f_0(\mathbf{b}) f(\dot{\mathbf{x}}_n \mid \mathbf{b})] f(\mathbf{b} \mid \dot{\mathbf{x}}_n) \, d\mathbf{b} \right]$$

$$\left. + \gamma \left[\int_{\mathscr{B}} f(\mathbf{b} \mid \dot{\mathbf{x}}_n) \, d\mathbf{b} - 1 \right] \right\} = 0.$$

Thus a sufficient solution is

$$-\ln f(\mathbf{b}\,|\,\dot{\mathbf{x}}_n) - \frac{\lambda}{n}\ln[f_0(\mathbf{b})f(\dot{\mathbf{x}}_n\,|\,\mathbf{b})] + \gamma - 1 = 0.$$

Solving for $f(\mathbf{b}\,|\,\dot{\mathbf{x}}_n)$,

$$f(\mathbf{b}\,|\,\dot{\mathbf{x}}_n) = e^{\{\lambda/n\,\ln\,[f_0(\mathbf{b})f(\dot{\mathbf{x}}_n|\mathbf{b})] + (1-\gamma)\}}. \tag{6}$$

Equation (6) is the form of the solution for $f(\mathbf{b}\,|\,\dot{\mathbf{x}}_n)$ maximizing entropy (3). Now, however, we will use the constraints in order to evaluate γ and λ. Substituting (6) into (4a), it follows that

$$e^{\gamma-1} = \frac{1}{\displaystyle\int_{\mathscr{B}} e^{\{\lambda/n\,\ln\,f_0(\mathbf{b})f(\dot{\mathbf{x}}_n|\mathbf{b})\}}\,d\mathbf{b}}$$

such that (6) becomes

$$f(\mathbf{b}\,|\,\dot{\mathbf{x}}_n) = \frac{e^{\{\lambda/n\,\ln\,f_0(\mathbf{b})f(\dot{\mathbf{x}}_n|\mathbf{b})\}}}{\displaystyle\int_{\mathscr{B}} e^{\{\lambda/n\,\ln\,f_0(\mathbf{b})f(\dot{\mathbf{x}}_n|\mathbf{b})\}}\,d\mathbf{b}}. \tag{7}$$

At this point it is of interest to observe that (7) is the a posteriori probability density (1) if we choose $\lambda = n$. However, at this point, λ is a free parameter which can be fixed through use of an appropriate constraint. The constraint not yet used is related to (4b) and concerns the asymptotic property of (2).

Equation (2) is equivalent to requiring that as $n \longrightarrow \infty$ the probability mass at $\mathbf{b}$ outside an ϵ neighborhood of $\mathbf{b}^*$ goes to zero. Define

$$\rho_\epsilon(\mathbf{b}^*) \triangleq \{\mathbf{b} : \|\mathbf{b} - \mathbf{b}^*\| < \epsilon\}$$

and

$$\mathscr{B}^* \triangleq \mathscr{B} - \rho_\epsilon(\mathbf{b}^*).$$

For any ϵ

$$\int_{\mathscr{B}^*} f(\mathbf{b}\,|\,\dot{\mathbf{x}}_n)\,d\mathbf{b} \leq \frac{\displaystyle\int_{\mathscr{B}^*} f(\mathbf{b}\,|\,\dot{\mathbf{x}}_n)\,d\mathbf{b}}{\displaystyle\int_{\rho_\epsilon(\mathbf{b}^*)} f(\mathbf{b}\,|\,\dot{\mathbf{x}}_n)\,d\mathbf{b}} = \frac{\displaystyle\int_{\mathscr{B}^*} e^{\lambda/n\,\ln\,f_0(\mathbf{b})f(\dot{\mathbf{x}}_n|\mathbf{b})}\,d\mathbf{b}}{\displaystyle\int_{\rho_\epsilon(\mathbf{b}^*)} e^{\lambda/n\,\ln\,f_0(\mathbf{b})f(\dot{\mathbf{x}}_n|\mathbf{b})}\,d\mathbf{b}}. \tag{8}$$

Define

$$V(\epsilon) \triangleq \int_{\rho_\epsilon(\mathbf{b}^*)} d\mathbf{b}$$

and let $\mathscr{B}_1^*, \mathscr{B}_2^*, \ldots, \mathscr{B}_K^*$ be a finite cover for $\mathscr{B}^*$ and

$$V_e(\epsilon) = \int_{\mathscr{B}^*_e} d\mathbf{b} \leq V(\epsilon),$$

$$\mathscr{B}^* \subset \bigcup_{e=1}^{K} \mathscr{B}_e^*.$$

Finally, for some $\mathbf{b}_e \in \mathscr{B}_e^*$ and $\mathbf{b}' \in \rho_\epsilon(\mathbf{b}^*)$, (8) is equivalent to

$$\int_{\mathscr{B}^*} f(\mathbf{b} \mid \dot{\mathbf{x}}_n)\, d\mathbf{b} < \frac{\sum_{e=1}^{K} V_e(\epsilon) e^{\lambda/n} f_0(\mathbf{b}_e) f(\dot{\mathbf{x}}_n \mid \mathbf{b}_e)}{V(\epsilon) e^{\lambda/n \ln f_0(\mathbf{b}') f(\dot{\mathbf{x}}_n \mid \mathbf{b}')}}$$

or

$$\int_{\mathscr{B}^*} f(\mathbf{b} \mid \dot{\mathbf{x}}_n)\, d\mathbf{b} < c \sum_{e=1}^{K} e^{-\lambda[1/n \ln f_0(\mathbf{b}') f(\dot{\mathbf{x}}_n \mid \mathbf{b}') - 1/n \ln f_0(\mathbf{b}_e) f(\mathbf{x}_n \mid \mathbf{b}_e)]}. \tag{9}$$

As a result of (5), for any $\delta > 0$ and $\xi > 0$ $\exists\, n(\delta)$ such that for all $n > n(\delta)$,

$$\left| \frac{1}{n} \sum_{s=1}^{n} \ln f_0(\mathbf{b}) f(\mathbf{x}_s \mid \mathbf{b}) - \eta(\mathbf{b}) \right| < \delta$$

with probability greater than $1 - \xi$. Choosing

$$\delta = \frac{1}{4} \min_{\substack{\mathbf{b}' \in \rho_\epsilon(\mathbf{b}^*) \\ \mathbf{b}_e \in \mathscr{B}_e^*}} |\eta(\mathbf{b}') - \eta(\mathbf{b}_e)|,$$

it follows from (9) that

$$\int_{\mathscr{B}^*} f(\mathbf{b} \mid \dot{\mathbf{x}}_n)\, d\mathbf{b} < KC\, e^{-\lambda\, 2\delta}. \tag{10}$$

It is apparent from (10) that in order for (2) to be satisfied,

$$\lambda(n) \longrightarrow \infty \text{ as } n \longrightarrow \infty$$

is required. Suppose that

$$\lambda(n) = n^q. \tag{11}$$

Then constraint (2) is satisfied for any $q > 0$. On the other hand, $q \to 0$ maximizes entropy while violating (2). *If $q \to \infty$ the asymptotic rate of convergence would appear to increase but the finite sample size convergence is affected.* Thus it appears that q should be selected such that the asymptotic rate of convergence is neither maximized nor minimized. To search for such a q we examine the bound (10) at successive stages; that is, consider

$$r = \frac{e^{-2\lambda(n)\delta}}{e^{-2\lambda(n+1)\delta}} = e^{-2\delta((n+1)^q - n^q)}. \tag{12}$$

We find from

$$\frac{\partial R}{\partial q} = -2\delta[q(n+1)^{q-1} - qn^{q-1}]e^{-2\delta((n+1)^q - n^q)} = 0$$

that the only critical value of q is 1. Taking the second derivative,

$$\left.\frac{\partial^2 R}{\partial q^2}\right|_{q=1} = 0,$$

indicating that $q = 1$ is a saddle point, a point of neither maximum or minimum. Thus, for $q = 1$,

$$f(\mathbf{b}\,|\,\dot{\mathbf{x}}_n) = \frac{f_0(\mathbf{b})f(\dot{\mathbf{x}}_n\,|\,\mathbf{b})}{\int f_0(\mathbf{b})f(\dot{\mathbf{x}}_n\,|\,\mathbf{b})\,d\mathbf{b}}, \tag{13}$$

which is the a posteriori probability density.

Discussion

We have not considered small sample size performance in arriving at (13) other than maximizing entropy (3) at every stage n. Small sample size performance is probably dependent upon properties of the parameter space and the probability density $h(\mathbf{x}\,|\,\mathbf{b})$.

[1] H. Cramer, *The Elements of Probability Theory*, John Wiley & Sons, Inc., New York, 1962.

[2] H. Cramer, *Mathematical Methods of Statistics*, Princeton University Press, Princeton, N.J., 1963.

[3] S. S. Wilks, *Mathematical Statistics*, John Wiley & Sons, Inc., New York, 1963.

[4] D. A. S. Fraser, *Nonparametric Methods in Statistics*, John Wiley & Sons, Inc., New York, 1963.

[5] M. Fisz, *Probability Theory and Mathematical Statistics*, John Wiley & Sons, Inc., New York, 1963.

[6] E. Parzen, *Modern Probability Theory and Its Applications*, John Wiley & Sons, Inc., New York, 1960.

[7] A. Papoulis, *Probability Random Variables, and Stochastic Processes*, McGraw-Hill Book Company, Inc., New York, 1965.

[8] M. Loève, *Probability Theory*, Van Nostrand Reinhold, New York, 1963.

[9] S. Kullback, *Information Theory and Statistics*, John Wiley & Sons, Inc., New York, 1959.

[10] N. Abramson and D. Braverman, Learning to Recognize Patterns in a Random Environment, *IRE Intern. Symp. Information Theory*, Vol. IT-8, pp. s58–s63, July 1962.

[11] D. G. Keehn, Learning the Mean Vector and Covariance Matrix of Gaussian Signals in Pattern Recognition, *Stanford Electronics Laboratories Tech. Rept.* 2003–6, Stanford, Calif., Feb. 1963.

[12] J. D. Spragins, Reproducing Distributions for Machine Learning, *Stanford Electronics Laboratories Tech. Rept.* 6103–7, Stanford, Calif., Nov. 1963.

[13] J. Kiefer and J. Wolfowitz, Stochastic Estimation of the Maximum of a Regression Function, *Ann. Math. Statistics*, Vol. 23, No. 3, pp. 462–66, Sept. 1952.

[14] J. H. Venter, On Dvoretzky's Stochastic Approximation Theorems, *Ann. Math. Statistics*, Vol. 37, No. 6, pp. 1534–44, 1966.

[15] H. Robbins and S. Monro, A Stochastic Approximation Method, *Ann. Math. Statistics*, Vol. 22, No. 3, pp. 400–407, Sept. 1951.

[16] P. Henrici, *Elements of Numerical Analysis*, John Wiley & Sons, Inc., New York, 1964.

[17] A. Dvoretzky, On Stochastic Approximation, *Proceedings of the Third Berkeley Symposium on Mathematical Statistics and Probability*, Vol. 1, University of California Press, Berkeley, Calif., pp. 39–55, 1956.

[18] L. LeCam, *On Same Asymptotic Properties of Maximum Likelihood Estimates and Related Bayes Estimates* (University of California Publications in Statistics, Vol. 1, No. 11, pp. 277–329), University of California Press, Berkeley, Calif., Jan. 30 1953.

[19] Y. C. Ho and R. C. K. Lee, Identification of Linear Dynamic Systems, *Proceedings of the Third Symposium on Adaptive Processes*, pp. 86–101, Oct. 1964.

[20] G. N. Saridis and G. Stein, Stochastic Approximation Algorithms for Linear Discrete-Time System Identification, *IEEE Trans. Automatic Controls*, Vol. AC-13, No. 5, pp. 513–523, Oct. 1968.

[21] L. E. Dubins and L. J. Savage, A Tchebysheff-like Inequality for Stochastic Processes, *Proc. Natl. Acad. Sci.*, Vol. 53, No. 2, pp. 274–275, Feb. 1965.

[22] D. J. Sakrison, Stochastic Approximation, a Recursive Method of Solving Regression Problems, *Advances in Communication Theory*, Vol. 2, A. V. Balabrishnan, ed., Academic Press, Inc., New York, 1966.

[23] G. N. Saridis, Z. J. Nikolic, and K. S. Fu, Stochastic Approximation Algorithms for System Identification, Estimation and Decomposition of Mixtures, *IEEE Trans. System Science and Cybernetics*, Vol. SSC-5, No. 1, pp. 8–151, Jan. 1969.

[24] M. A. Aizerman, E. M. Braverman, and L. I. Rozonoer, The Probability Problem of Pattern Recognition Learning and the Method of Potential Functions, *Avtomatika i Telemekhanika*, Vol. 25, No. 9, pp. 1307–1323, Sept. 1964.

[25] Y. Z. Tsypkin, Use of the Stochastic Approximation Method in Estimating Unknown Distribution Densities from Observations, *Avtomatika i Telemekhanika*, Vol. 27, No. 3, pp. 94–96, March 1966.

[26] R. L. Kashyap and C. C. Blaydon, Estimation of Probability Density and Distribution Functions, *IEEE Trans. Information Theory*, Vol. IT-14, No. 4, pp. 549–556, July 1968.

[27] M. Rosenblatt, Remark on Some Nonparametric Estimates of a Density Function, *Ann. Math. Statistics*, Vol. 27, No. 3, pp. 832–837, Sept. 1956.

[28] E. Parzen, On Estimation of a Probability Density Function and Mode, *Ann. Math. Stat.*, Vol. 33, No. 3, pp. 1065–1076, Sept. 1962.

[29] V. K. Murthy, Nonparametric Estimation of Multivariate Densities with Applications, *Multivariate Analysis*, P. R. Krishnaiah, ed., Academic Press, Inc., New York, pp. 43–56, 1966.

[30] P. Whittle, On the Smoothing of Probability Density Functions, *J. Roy. Statistical Soc.*, Ser. B, Vol. 20, No. 2, pp. 334–343, 1958.

[31] G. S. Watson and M. R. Leadbetter, On the Estimation of the Probability Density, *Ann. Math. Statistics*, Vol. 34, No. 2, pp. 480–491, June 1963.

[32] G. R. Cooper and J. A. Tabczynski, Estimation of Probability Density and Distribution Functions, *Purdue University School of Electrical Engineering Tech. Rept.* EE 65–15, Aug. 1965.

     Elementary Properties of Estimators   Chap. 2

[33] D. O. Loftsgaarden and C. P. Quesenberry, A Nonparametric Estimate of a Multivariate Density Function, *Ann. Math. Statistics*, Vol. 36, No. 3, pp. 1049–1051, 1965.

[34] S. S. Wilks, Determination of Sample Sizes for Setting Tolerance Limits, *Ann. Math. Statistics*, Vol. 12, No. 1, pp. 91–96, March 1941.

[35] J. H. B. Kemperman, Generalized Tolerance Limits, *Ann. Math. Statistics*, Vol. 27, No. 1, pp. 180–186, March 1956.

[36] J. W. Tukey, Nonparametric Estimation, II. Statistically Equivalent Blocks and Tolerance Regions—The Continuous Case, *Ann. Math. Statistics*, Vol. 18, No. 4, pp. 529–539, Dec. 1947.

[37] J. R. Blum, Multidimensional Stochastic Approximation Methods, *Ann. Math. Statistics*, Vol. 25, No. 4, pp. 734–744, Dec. 1954.

[38] J. R. Blum, Approximation Methods Which Converge with Probability One, *Ann. Math. Statistics*, Vol. 25, No. 2, pp. 382–386, June 1954.

[39] J. Wolfowitz, On the Stochastic Approximation Method of Robbins and Monro, *Ann. Math. Statistics*, Vol. 23, No. 3. pp. 457–461, Sept. 1952.

[40] R. V. Hogg and A. T. Craig, *Introduction to Mathematical Statistics*, 2nd ed., The Macmillian Company, New York, 1965, pp. 156–157.

[41] D. Wilde, *Optimum Seeking Methods*, Prentice-Hall, Inc., Englewood Cliffs, N.J., 1964, pp. 159–192.

[42] H. Kesten, Accelerated Stochastic Approximation, *Ann. Math. Statistics*, Vol. 29, No. 1, pp. 41–59, March 1958.

[43] K. S. Fu, *Sequential Methods in Pattern Recognition and Machine Learning*, Academic Press, Inc., New York, 1968.

[44] T. Y. Young and Giorgio Coraluppi, Stochastic Estimation of a Mixture of Normal Density Functions Using an Information Criterion, *IEEE Trans. Information Theory*, Vol. IT-16, pp. 258–263, May 1970.

[45] E. A. Patrick, Asymptotic Distribution of Maximum Likelihood Estimators for Nonsupervised Adaptive Receiver, *IEEE Intern. Communications Conf. Record*, Philadelphia, June 1966.

[46] J. H. Wolfe, NORMIX: Computational Methods for Estimating the Parameters of Multivariate Normal Mixtures of Distributions, *U.S. Naval Personnel Research Activity, Research Memorandum SRM 68–6*, San Diego, Calif., Aug. 1967.

[47] M. Schwartz, *Information Transmission, Modulation and Noise*, McGraw-Hill Book Company, Inc., New York, 1959.

[48] D. A. S. Fraser, Sequentially Determined Statistically Equivalent Blocks, *Ann. Math. Statistics*, Vol. 22, No. 3, pp. 372–381, Sept. 1957.

[49] T. S. Ferguson, *Mathematical Statistics: A Decision Theoretical Approach*, Academic Press, Inc., New York, 1967.

[50] W. Kaplan, *Advanced Calculus*, Addison-Wesley Publishing Co., Inc., Reading, Mass., pp. 128–129, 1952.

[51] M. W. Anderson and R. D. Benning, A Distribution-Free Discrimination Procedure Based on Clustering, *IEEE Transaction Information Theory*, Vol. IT-16, No. 5, pp. 541–548, Sept. 1970.

[52] E. B. Dynkin, Necessary and Sufficient Statistics for a Family of Probability Distributions, *Selected Translations in Mathematical Statistics and Probability*, Vol. 1, pp. 17–40, 1961.

Problems

[1] It is shown by Kullback [9] that, for a function denoted $I(1, 2)$,

$$I(1, 2) \triangleq \int \ln \frac{h(\mathbf{x})}{h'(\mathbf{x})} h(\mathbf{x}) \, d\mathbf{x} \geq 0,$$

with equality if and only if $h(\mathbf{x}) = h'(\mathbf{x})$. Show that

$$\int \ln h(\mathbf{x}) h(\mathbf{x}) \, d\mathbf{x} \geq \int \ln h'(\mathbf{x}) h(\mathbf{x}) \, d\mathbf{x},$$

with equality if and only if $h(\mathbf{x}) = h'(\mathbf{x})$.

[2] Let $\mathbf{x}_1, \mathbf{x}_2, \ldots, \mathbf{x}_n$ be statistically independent and identically distributed random vectors. Prove that if $|\mathbf{x}_s| < c$, a finite number, for all s, then the sample mean converges to $E[\mathbf{x}]$ in probability and with probability 1.

[3] Show that under the conditions listed in Problem 2, the sample mean
(a) is a consistent (simple consistency) estimate for $E[\mathbf{x}]$.
(b) is a squared-error consistent estimator for $E[\mathbf{x}]$.

[4] Let $f(\mathbf{x}|\mathbf{b}) \in \mathscr{F}$, the family of Gaussian distributions, where $\mathbf{b} = (\mathbf{m}, \boldsymbol{\Sigma})$.
(a) Show that $f(\mathbf{x}|\mathbf{b})$ is regular with respect to its first $\mathbf{m}$ derivative.
(b) Show that $f(\mathbf{x}|\mathbf{b})$ is regular with respect to its first $\boldsymbol{\Sigma}$ derivative.
(c) Show that $f(\mathbf{x}|\mathbf{b})$ is regular with respect to its second $\mathbf{m}$ derivative.
(d) Show that $f(\mathbf{x}|\mathbf{b})$ is regular with respect to its second $\boldsymbol{\Sigma}$ derivative.

[5] Let $h(\mathbf{x}|\mathbf{b}) = \sum_{i=1}^{M} f(\mathbf{x}|\mathbf{b}_i) P_i$, where $f(\mathbf{x}|\mathbf{b}_i) \in \mathscr{F}$, the family of Gaussian distribution, where $\mathbf{b}_i = [\mathbf{m}_i, \boldsymbol{\Sigma}_i]$.
(a) Verify the first regularity conditions.
(b) Verify the second regularity conditions.

[6] Let $\mathbf{x}_1, \mathbf{x}_2, \ldots, \mathbf{x}_n$ be from $f(\mathbf{x}|\mathbf{b})$, where $f(\mathbf{x}|\mathbf{b}) \in \mathscr{F}$, the family of Gaussian distributions, $\mathbf{b} = (\mathbf{m}, \boldsymbol{\Sigma})$. Assuming that $\boldsymbol{\Sigma}$ is known,
(a) Compute the Cramèr–Rao lower bound for the variance of the maximum-likelihood estimator of $\mathbf{m}$.
(b) Show that

$$\frac{\partial}{\partial \mathbf{m}} \ln f(\dot{\mathbf{x}}_n|\mathbf{b}) = k \left[\frac{1}{n} \sum_{s=1}^{n} \mathbf{x}_s - \mathbf{m} \right],$$

where $\mathbf{b} = (\mathbf{m}, \boldsymbol{\Sigma})$.
(c) Show that if the maximum-likelihood estimator for $\mathbf{m}$ is unique for $n \geq$ some n_0, then it converges with probability 1.

[7] If $f(\mathbf{x}|\mathbf{b}) \in \mathscr{F}$, the family of Gaussian density functions, compute the Bayes estimator for $\mathbf{m}$ with the a priori density $f(\mathbf{b})$ arbitrary. Show that this estimator is easily implemented in practice.

[8] If $h(\mathbf{x}\,|\,\mathbf{b}) = \sum_{i=1}^{M} f(\mathbf{x}\,|\,\mathbf{b}_i)P_i$, where $f(\mathbf{x}\,|\,\mathbf{b}_i) \in \mathscr{F}$, the family of Gaussian density functions, find the Bayes estimator for each $\mathbf{m}_i$, $i = 1, 2, \ldots, M$. Show that this estimator cannot be implemented in practice.

[9] Show that the Gaussian reproduces itself under Bayes iteration for (a) one-dimensional spaces; (b) for L-dimensional spaces.

[10] Verify using induction that (8) of Section 2-9 is the extension of (6) of Section 2-9 when n samples are processed.

[11] Verify using induction that (10) of Section 2-9 is the extension of (9) of Section 2-9 when n samples are processed.

[12] Show that if $\mathbf{x}_1, \mathbf{x}_2, \ldots, \mathbf{x}_n$ are statistically independent and identically distributed as $f(\mathbf{x}\,|\,\mathbf{b})$, Gaussian, then

$$\boldsymbol{\mu}_n = E[\mathbf{m}\,|\,\mathbf{x}_1, \mathbf{x}_2, \ldots, \mathbf{x}_n]$$

is the Bayes estimator of $\mathbf{m}^*$ using the quadratic loss function.

[13] Show that the multinomial family of density functions is reproducing with respect to Bayes iteration.

[14] If $\mathbf{x}_1, \mathbf{x}_2, \ldots, \mathbf{x}_n$ are statistically independent and identically distributed as $N(\mathbf{x}\,|\,\mathbf{m}^*, \boldsymbol{\Phi})$ with $\boldsymbol{\Phi}$ known but $\mathbf{m}^*$ unknown, show that

$$p(\mathbf{x}\,|\,\mathbf{x}_1, \mathbf{x}_2, \ldots, \mathbf{x}_n) = \int p(\mathbf{x}\,|\,\mathbf{m})p(\mathbf{m}\,|\,\mathbf{x}_1, \mathbf{x}_2, \ldots, \mathbf{x}_n)\,d\mathbf{m}$$

is $N(\mathbf{x}\,|\,\boldsymbol{\mu}_n, \boldsymbol{\Sigma}_n + \boldsymbol{\Phi})$, where $\boldsymbol{\mu}_n$ is the Bayes estimate of $\mathbf{m}^*$ and has uncertainty $\boldsymbol{\Sigma}_n$.

[15] The purpose of this problem is to provide an illustration of the difference between convergence in probability and convergence with probability 1. Suppose you have a population of people with each individual named η, $\eta = 1, 2, \ldots$. Let $\gamma_s(\eta)$ be the "health" of person η at the sth microsecond of his life and $\gamma(\eta)$ his "health" at 60 years of age. If all people only get seriously ill for very short periods of time, then any particular person η has "health" converging *in probability* (or very nearly) to $\gamma(\eta)$. On the other hand, if only a few (one or two) people die at age 30, then any particular person η converges to $\gamma(\eta)$ *with probability 1* (or very nearly). Do you agree? Why?

[16] Show that for $\mathbf{x}_1, \mathbf{x}_2, \ldots, \mathbf{x}_n$ distributed as $h(\mathbf{x}_1, \mathbf{x}_2, \ldots, \mathbf{x}_n\,|\,\mathbf{b}^*) = c \exp[-\frac{1}{2}\sum_{s=1}^{n}(x_s - m)^2]$, i.e., $\mathbf{b}^* = m$, $L = 1$, $f(x\,|\,\mathbf{b}^*) = N(x\,|\,m)$, then

(a) $h(x_1, x_2, \ldots, x_n\,|\,m) = d\exp[-\frac{1}{2}\sum_{s=1}^{n}(x_s - x)^2]\exp[-\frac{1}{2}n(\bar{x} - \mu)^2]$
and thus

$$(b)_n = \frac{1}{n}\sum_{s=1}^{n}x_s$$

is a sufficient statistic for estimating μ.

(b) Show that $h(m \mid \mathbf{x}_1, \mathbf{x}_2, \ldots, \mathbf{x}_n)$ is completely characterized by

$$(b_n) = \frac{1}{n} \sum_{s=1}^{n} x_s.$$

(c) Do you believe that a sufficient statistic for $\mathbf{b}^*$ exists only if that statistic completely characterizes $h(\mathbf{m} \mid \mathbf{x}_1, \mathbf{x}_2, \ldots, \mathbf{x}_n)$?

[17] Show that $h(\mathbf{b})$ is, in general, not reproducing with respect to $h(\mathbf{x} \mid \mathbf{b})$ if $h(\mathbf{x} \mid \mathbf{b})$ is a mixture.

[18] Can you show that a sufficient statistic does not in general exist for estimating $\mathbf{b}^*$ if $h(\mathbf{x} \mid \mathbf{b}^*)$ is a mixture?

[19] In a clustering approach to resolving a mixture of Gaussian functions, the mean vector and covariance matrix for each cluster are estimated using the clustering procedure. Are these estimates sufficient, in an engineering sense, for estimating $\mathbf{b}^*$?

[20] (a) Show that if $h(\mathbf{x} \mid \mathbf{b})$ satisfies the first regularity condition, then the information function $\eta(\mathbf{b}, \mathbf{b}^*)$ is an extremum at $\mathbf{b} = \mathbf{b}^*$.
(b) Show that if $h(\mathbf{x} \mid \mathbf{b})$ satisfies both the first and second regularity conditions, then $\eta(\mathbf{b}, \mathbf{b}^*)$ is a maximum at $\mathbf{b} = \mathbf{b}^*$.

[21] In conjunction with the Cramèr–Rao lower bound, show that

$$E\left[\left(\frac{\partial}{\partial b} \sum_{s=1}^{n} \ln h(\mathbf{x}_s \mid b)\right)^2\right] = nE\left[\left(\frac{\partial}{\partial b} \ln h(\mathbf{x}_s \mid b)\right)^2\right]$$

when the first regularity condition holds and the samples $\mathbf{x}_1, \mathbf{x}_2, \ldots, \mathbf{x}_n$ are parameter conditionally independent.

[22] Show that the second regularity condition is not required for the Cramèr–Rao bound to hold.

[23] Let $x_1, x_2, \ldots, x_n$ be conditionally independent samples from $N(x \mid m, \sigma^2)$.
(a) Show that $1/n \sum_{s=1}^{n} x_s$ is the maximum-likelihood estimator form m.
(b) Show that $1/n \sum_{s=1}^{n} x_s$ achieves the Cramèr–Rao lower bound.
(c) Show that $1/n \sum_{s=1}^{n} x_s$ is an estimator from stochastic approximation.
(d) Show that $1/n \sum_{s=1}^{n} x_s$ is a Bayes estimator (actually, to be strictly correct, an ϵ Bayes estimator).

[24] Given samples $x_1, x_2, \ldots, x_n$ from

$$f(x \mid a, b) = \begin{cases} \dfrac{1}{b - a}, & a < x < b, \\ 0, & \text{otherwise.} \end{cases}$$

(a) Show that $f(x_1, x_2, \ldots, x_n \mid a, b) = 1/(b - a)^n$.
(b) For $\max_s \{x_s\}$ and $\min_s \{x_s\}$ the maximum and minimum ordered samples, respectively, show that

$$f(\max_s \{x_s\}, \min_s \{x_s\}) = \frac{n(n-1)(\max_s \{x_s\} - \min_s \{x_s\})^{n-2}}{(b-a)^n},$$

where

$$a < \min_s \{x_s\} \leq \max_s \{x_s\} < b.$$

(c) Show that the density $1/(b-a)^n$ factors into a product of a term that is a function of sufficient statistics for estimating a and b and a term that is independent of the sufficient statistic.

[25] Is $\eta(\mathbf{b}, \mathbf{b}^*) = \int \ln h(\mathbf{x}\,|\,\mathbf{b})h(\mathbf{x}\,|\mathbf{b})^* \, d\mathbf{x}$

    (a) a metric?

    (b) an inner product?

[26] Is $\int [P_1 f(\mathbf{x}\,|\,\omega_1) - P_2 f(\mathbf{x}\,|\,\omega_2)]^2 \, d\mathbf{x}$

    (a) a metric?

    (b) an inner product?

[27] Is $\int \min_{i=1,2} [P_i f(\mathbf{x}\,|\,\omega_i)] \, d\mathbf{x}$

    (a) a metric?

    (b) an inner product?

[28] Is $P_1 P_2 \int f(\mathbf{x}\,|\,\omega_1)f(\mathbf{x}\,|\,\omega_2) \, d\mathbf{x}$

    (a) a metric?

    (b) an inner product?

[29] This problem compares Blum's extension of the Kiefer–Wolfowitz procedure for multiparameters,

$$(\mathbf{b})_{n+1} = (\mathbf{b})_n + a_n \frac{\boldsymbol{\delta}_{\mathbf{x}_{n+1},\,(\mathbf{b})_n,\,c_n}}{c_n} \tag{1}$$

with $\boldsymbol{\delta}_{\mathbf{x}_{n+1},\,(\mathbf{b})_n,\,c_n}$ given by (23) of Section 2-12, with the following Bayes-solution-utilizing auxiliary parameter (Section 2-19):

$$(\mathbf{b})_{n+1} = [(\mathbf{b}_1)_{n+1}, (\mathbf{b}_2)_{n+1}, \ldots, (\mathbf{b}_M)_{n+1}, (P_1)_{n+1}, (P_2)_{n+1}, \ldots, (P_M)_{n+1}], \tag{2}$$

with

$$(\mathbf{b}_k)_{n+1} = \left[\sum_{i \neq k} (w_i)_{n+1} \right](\mathbf{b}_k)_n$$

$$+ \,[(w_k)_{n+1}] \int \mathbf{b}_k \frac{f(\mathbf{x}_{n+1}\,|\,k,\,\mathbf{b}_k)}{f(\mathbf{x}_{n+1}\,|\,\dot{\mathbf{x}}_n)} f(\mathbf{b}_k\,|\,\dot{\mathbf{x}}_n) \, d\mathbf{b}_k,$$

$$(P_k)_{n+1} = \left[\sum_{i \neq k} (w_i)_{n+1} \right] (P_k)_n$$

$$+ \left[(w_k)_{n+1} \right] \int \frac{P_k}{\int P_k f(P_k \,|\, (\mathbf{b}_k)_n, \, \dot{\mathbf{x}}_n) \, dP_k} f(P_k \,|\, \dot{\mathbf{x}}_n).$$

(a) How does the updating of $(\mathbf{b}_k)_n$ in (1) depend on whether the sample $\mathbf{x}_{n+1}$ is "close" to the region of the measurement space where class k has relatively large probability density?

(b) How does the updating of $(\mathbf{b}_k)_n$ in (2) depend on whether the sample $\mathbf{x}_{n+1}$ is "close" to the region of the measurement space where class k has relatively large probability density?

(c) Indicate from the Bayes suggested estimator (2) how weighting coefficients might be used with the two terms on the right-hand side of (1).

CHAPTER 3

Decision Rules for Use in Pattern Recognition

3-1 Introduction

Early work in communications and information theory involved analysis of decision rules. This research essentially was centered around a decision rule that minimizes risk. The *minimum-risk decision rule* is implemented in terms of a class-conditional density function $f(\mathbf{x}|i)$ for the ith class, a corresponding class probability P_i, loss L_{ji} assigned when $\mathbf{x}$ is decided to be from class j but, in fact, is from class i, $i = 1, 2, \ldots, M$, where M is the number of classes. This minimum-risk decision rule is derived in Section 3-2.1, the result being Eq. (5). When a loss of 1 is assigned for an incorrect decision and a loss of zero is assigned for a correct decision, the minimum-risk decision rule reduces to the *minimum-probability-of-error decision rule* given by Eq. (7a) or (7b). Such a decision rule is considered by many authors including Wilks [1], Helstrom [2], Hancock and Wintz [3], Weiss [5], Wozencraft and Jacobs [7], Sebestyen [9], Thomas [11], Raemer [12], Kailath [13, 14], and Van Trees [6].

The nature of these rules is that there are natural decision boundaries in the measurement space. These boundaries determine M regions or sets of points $\mathscr{D}_1, \mathscr{D}_2, \ldots, \mathscr{D}_M$; if an observation vector is in $\mathscr{D}_i$, then it is decided that the observation comes from class i. An example involving two decision regions for the two-class ($M = 2$) problem is presented in Section 3-2.3. There, false-alarm probability P_F, detection probability P_D, and miss probability P_M

so often used in radar and sonar detection are presented. These rules are also having impact in computer-assisted medical diagnosis and treatment, sonar target classification, and other problem areas. For the purpose of historical continuity it is shown in that section how an incorrect guess at the parameters characterizing $f(\mathbf{x}|i)$ (including P_i), $i = 1, 2, \ldots, M$, can lead to considerably increased risk (one of the early books considering this problem is the first edition of Helstrom [2]). A more direct vantage point is to ask for the *minimum-conditional-risk decision rule*, i.e., a decision rule having minimum risk when conditioned on n training samples $\dot{\mathbf{x}}_n = [\mathbf{x}_1, \mathbf{x}_2, \ldots, \mathbf{x}_n]$, the family $\mathscr{F}$ of class-conditional density functions, and other a priori knowledge about the parameters $\mathbf{b}_1, \mathbf{b}_2, \ldots, \mathbf{b}_M$ and $P_1, P_2, \ldots, P_M$.

The minimum-conditional-risk decision rule is derived in Section 3-2.4 using the Bayes approach. A significant aspect of this approach is that one should calculate the a posteriori probability density $f(\mathbf{b}|\dot{\mathbf{x}}_n)$, where $\mathbf{b}$ is in the parameter space of fixed but unknown parameters. When each sample $\mathbf{x}$ is from a mixture probability density $h(\mathbf{x}) = \sum_{i=1}^{M} f(\mathbf{x}|i, \mathbf{b}_i)$, the problem becomes more complicated.

An approximation to the minimum-conditional-probability-of-error decision rule is to obtain an estimator $(\mathbf{b}_i)_n$ for the parameters characterizing $f(\mathbf{x}|i)$, assuming the family $\mathscr{F}$ known, and form the estimated density $f(\mathbf{x}|i, (\mathbf{b}_i)_n)$, $i = 1, 2, \ldots, M$. For example, when $\mathbf{x}_1, \mathbf{x}_2, \ldots, \mathbf{x}_n$ are from a mixture (i.e., unsupervised) and M is unknown, these parameters might be estimated using careful application of clustering techniques discussed in Chapter 5. This appears to present a very nice solution to many problems requiring decision making. *One thing is certain: The ability to utilize a priori starting vectors $(\mathbf{b}_1)_0, (\mathbf{b}_2)_0, \ldots, (\mathbf{b}_M)_0$ for the M classes and then update these starting vectors using training samples is a powerful facility for such applications as computer-assisted medical diagnosis, sonar target classification, etc.*

In Section 3-2.5, the optimum approach to decision making is formulated for the case where samples $\mathbf{x}_1, \mathbf{x}_2, \ldots, \mathbf{x}_n$ can be statistically dependent. This is a complicated problem, but an important one.

The *decision rule that minimizes point risk* is discussed in Section 3-2.6. When there are loss functions assigning no loss to a correct decision and a loss of 1 to an incorrect decision, the decision rule says simply that one should decide that $\mathbf{x}$ is from the class having highest probability density at $\mathbf{x}$ (assuming equal a priori class probabilities). This concept of point risk or point probability of error leads nicely to the k-nearest-neighbor type of decision rule, discussed in Chapter 4.

A slightly different approach to decision making is referred to in Section 3-3 as the "sample-based decision rule." Here M regions $\mathscr{D}_1(\dot{\mathbf{x}}_n), \mathscr{D}_2(\dot{\mathbf{x}}_n), \ldots, \mathscr{D}_M(\dot{\mathbf{x}}_n)$ are created using the n samples $\mathbf{x}_1, \mathbf{x}_2, \ldots, \mathbf{x}_n$. These regions are such that a decision rule $d(\mathbf{x}; \dot{\mathbf{x}}_n) = \omega_i$ if $\mathbf{x} \in \mathscr{D}_i(\dot{\mathbf{x}}_n)$. The reader might suspect that the region $\mathscr{D}_i(\dot{\mathbf{x}}_n)$ is a region of the measurement space where we estimate that samples from $f(\mathbf{x}|i)$ are denser than from any other class. There are various ways to construct these regions: for example, clustering. Sample-based decision rules are those where all the a priori problem knowledge has not been used because otherwise they would be the minimum conditional risk rule (Bayes). By examining a sample-based decision rule and various sets of samples, it may be possible to see ways to improve the distribution of risk of the rule because of the nature of the training sets.

In Section 3-4 we return to a minimum-probability-of-error decision rule for when the family is Gaussian. This elementary but instructive and important decision rule is basic to an understanding of pattern recognition.† The quadratic-form distance measure $(\mathbf{x} - \mathbf{m}_i)^t \, \Sigma_i^{-1}(\mathbf{x} - \mathbf{m}_i)$ for the ith class demonstrates the importance of knowing the "local distance" measure. Lack of use of such local measures has led to poor performance in the application of many decision rules, such as the nearest-neighbor decision rule. In Chapter 5 a clustering technique is presented whereby an a priori guess for Σ_i and $\mathbf{m}_i$, with specified confidence, can be provided for the ith class. This is an elementary procedure for interactively providing problem knowledge. These guesses are then updated using training samples $\mathbf{x}_1, \mathbf{x}_2, \ldots, \mathbf{x}_n$.

In Section 3-4.4 the decision rule for the case where each class density $f(\mathbf{x}|i)$ is itself a mixture of M densities is presented. This is an important decision rule in pattern recognition.

Some decision rules of the "sample-based" type are presented in Chapter 4. Included are three kinds of k-nearest-neighbor decision rules including some of the work by Cover and Hart [15], Cover [16], Hart [17], Patrick and Fischer [18, 19], Patrick [25], Fix and Hodges [26], Cover [27], and Peterson [28]. When the local distance measure used in these rules is the quadratic form, the rules have similarities with the minimum conditional probability of error decision rules (when $\mathscr{F}$ is the Gaussian family).

A discussion of decision rules would not be complete if we did not mention that there are some pattern-recognition problems in which the decision-making problem essentially is simple and obvious. For example, suppose that $L = 2$ (i.e., $\mathbf{x}$ has two components) and the pattern samples from the respective classes are easily separated by a straight line. *One must be careful not to overly experiment with decision-making rules when some acceptably practical preprocessing technique (feature extraction) renders the problem such as to require an elementary form of decision making.*‡ The reader may

---

†It is one of the easiest to get programmed or implemented with hardware. It often fails because the statistics of $\mathbf{x}$ for the respective classes are not Gaussian.

‡Feature extraction, discussed in Chapter 6, is a process of providing relationships among measurements (components of $\mathbf{x}$) to create features. Features may be constructed for each class individually using a priori knowledge about the problem. In constructing features one should be guided by estimation and decision theory.

be interested in a survey paper by Nagy [20] and another by Ho and Agrawala [21], a book by Kullback [10], and different viewpoints from Rosenblatt [8].

3-2 Decision Rules Minimizing Risk and Conditional Risk

3-2.1 Minimizing Risk

We begin the discussion given n samples $\dot{\mathbf{x}}_n = \mathbf{x}_1, \mathbf{x}_2, \ldots, \mathbf{x}_n$ each distributed as $\mathbf{x}$ with density $h(\mathbf{x})$. Let $d(\mathbf{x})$ be a rule that is a member of a known class of rules denoted D. A loss $L(j, i)$ (sometimes written L_{ji}) is incurred by placing $\mathbf{x}$ in the category j using $d(\mathbf{x}) = j$ when $\mathbf{x}$ belongs to category i. Assume that class densities $f(\mathbf{x}|i)$, $i = 1, 2, \ldots, M$, are known along with a priori class probabilities P_i, $i = 1, 2, \ldots, M$.

Risk. The loss at $\mathbf{x}$ when $\mathbf{x}$ belongs to class i and the decision rule decides $d(\mathbf{x})$ is just the loss $L(d(\mathbf{x}), i)$. The *point risk* at $\mathbf{x}$ is defined as

$$
\begin{aligned}
r(d(\mathbf{x})) &= \sum_{i=1}^{M} L(d(\mathbf{x}), i) p(i \mid \mathbf{x}) \\
&= \sum_{i=1}^{M} L(d(\mathbf{x}), i) \frac{f(\mathbf{x}\mid i)P_i}{h(\mathbf{x})},
\end{aligned}
\tag{1}
$$

which is the average loss at point $\mathbf{x}$. The *average*, or *global*, *risk*, denoted $R(d)$, is

$$
R(d) = \int r(d(\mathbf{x}))h(\mathbf{x})\, d\mathbf{x},
\tag{2}
$$

which, upon inserting (1), becomes

$$
R(d) = \int \sum_{i=1}^{M} L(d(\mathbf{x}), i) f(\mathbf{x}\mid i)P_i\, d\mathbf{x}.
\tag{3}
$$

The global risk (2) could have been immediately written, by definition, as the loss averaged over the M categories and the observation space:

$$
\begin{aligned}
R(d) &= \int \sum_{i=1}^{M} L(d(\mathbf{x}), i) f(\mathbf{x}, i)\, d\mathbf{x} \\
&= \int \sum_{i=1}^{M} L(d(\mathbf{x}), i) f(\mathbf{x}\mid i)P_i\, d\mathbf{x}.
\end{aligned}
\tag{4}
$$

The classical objective is to find the decision rule $d(\mathbf{x})$ that minimizes the global risk (2). This is achieved by selecting $d^*(\mathbf{x})$ from D such that the point risk is minimized at each point $\mathbf{x}$. From (2) we conclude, because $h(\mathbf{x})$ is nonnegative: Risk $R(d)$ is minimized by selecting $d^*(\mathbf{x})$ from D such that $d^*(\mathbf{x}) = $ category for which

$$\sum_{i=1}^{M} L(d^*(\mathbf{x}), i) f(\mathbf{x}|i) P_i$$

$$< \sum_{i=1}^{M} L(d(\mathbf{x}), i) f(\mathbf{x}|i) P_i, \qquad \forall \; d(\mathbf{x}) \in D; \qquad \text{for each } \mathbf{x}. \qquad (5)$$

Students sometimes have difficulty realizing that (5) is the defining equation for the minimum-risk decision rule $d^*(\mathbf{x})$ because the equation is a function of $d^*(\mathbf{x})$.

3-2.2 Zero–One Loss Matrix Solutions

A straightforward solution of (5) for $d^*(\mathbf{x})$ can be obtained. When there are M categories, the average loss at $\mathbf{x}$ resulting for the zero–one loss matrix,

$$L = [L_{ji}]_{MM}, \qquad L_{ji} = 1 - \delta_{ij}, \qquad (6)$$

for decisions $d^*(\mathbf{x}) = 1, 2, \ldots, M$, respectively, is

$$
\begin{array}{cc}
d^*(\mathbf{x}) & \textit{Average loss at } \mathbf{x} \\
1 & \displaystyle\sum_{i \neq 1} \frac{P_i f(\mathbf{x}|i)}{h(\mathbf{x})} = 1 - P_1 f(\mathbf{x}|1)/h(\mathbf{x}), \\
2 & \displaystyle\sum_{i \neq 2} \frac{P_i f(\mathbf{x}|i)}{h(\mathbf{x})} = 1 - P_2 f(\mathbf{x}|2)/h(\mathbf{x}), \\
\vdots & \\
M & \displaystyle\sum_{i \neq M} \frac{P_i f(\mathbf{x}|i)}{h(\mathbf{x})} = 1 - P_M f(\mathbf{x}|M)/h(\mathbf{x}).
\end{array}
$$

Thus, for a minimum average loss (risk) decision at point $\mathbf{x}$, decide category j $(d^*(\mathbf{x}) = j)$ if

$$P_j f(\mathbf{x}|j) = \max \{P_i f(\mathbf{x}|i)\}_{i=1}^{M}, \qquad (7a)$$

since that is equivalent to $1 - P_j f(\mathbf{x}|j)/h(\mathbf{x}) = \min_i \{1 - P_i f(\mathbf{x}|i)/h(\mathbf{x})\}$.

It is not difficult to show that application of (7a) results in minimum probability of error at point $\mathbf{x}$. To show this, observe that $p(i|\mathbf{x})$ is the probability, given $\mathbf{x}$, that $\mathbf{x}$ is from category i. To maximize the detection probability, decide that $\mathbf{x}$ is from category j, where

$$p(j\,|\,\mathbf{x}) = \max\,\{p(i\,|\,\mathbf{x})\}_{i=1}^{M}. \tag{7b}$$

But since

$$p(j\,|\,\mathbf{x}) = \frac{f(\mathbf{x}\,|\,j)P_j}{h(\mathbf{x})},$$

Eq. (7b) is equivalent to Eq. (7a), since $h(\mathbf{x})$ is common to the M terms. Thus, the decision rule given by Eq. (7a) maximizes the detection probability or minimizes the probability of error: The minimum-risk decision rule for a zero–one loss matrix maximizes the probability of detection at any point $\mathbf{x}$ in the observation space.

The above statement concerns point probability of error. Global probability or error is discussed in the following section.

3-2.3 Decision Boundary and Probability of Error

The set of points for which equality holds in (5) defines a decision boundary; this boundary separates the observation space into two regions, $\mathscr{D}_1$ and $\mathscr{D}_2$, corresponding to categories 1 and 2, respectively. The global risk R for a two-category problem ($M = 2$) is

$$R = \sum_{j=1}^{2} \sum_{i=1}^{2} L_{ji}\,p(j, i), \tag{8}$$

where $p(j, i)$ is the probability of deciding category j with category i being active and L_{ji} is an associated loss. In terms of $f(\mathbf{x}\,|\,i)$, $p(j, i)$ is

$$p(j, i) = \int_{\mathscr{D}_j} P_i f(\mathbf{x}\,|\,i)\,d\mathbf{x}, \tag{9}$$

and R becomes

$$
\begin{aligned}
R &= \sum_{j=1}^{2} \sum_{i=1}^{2} P_i L_{ji} \int_{\mathscr{D}_j} f(\mathbf{x}\,|\,i)\,d\mathbf{x} \\
&= P_1 L_{11} \int_{\mathscr{D}_1} f(\mathbf{x}\,|\,1)\,d\mathbf{x} + P_2 L_{12} \int_{\mathscr{D}_1} f(\mathbf{x}\,|\,2)\,d\mathbf{x} \\
&\quad + P_1 L_{21} \int_{\mathscr{D}_2} f(\mathbf{x}\,|\,1)\,d\mathbf{x} + P_2 L_{22} \int_{\mathscr{D}_2} f(\mathbf{x}\,|\,2)\,d\mathbf{x}.
\end{aligned}
\tag{10}
$$

Add and subtract

$$P_1 L_{21} \int_{\mathscr{D}_1} f(\mathbf{x}\,|\,1)\,d\mathbf{x} + P_2 L_{22} \int_{\mathscr{D}_1} f(\mathbf{x}\,|\,2)\,d\mathbf{x}$$

to obtain

$$R = P_1 L_{21} + P_2 L_{22}$$

$$+ \int_{\mathscr{D}_1} [P_2(L_{12} - L_{22})f(\mathbf{x}|2) - P_1(L_{21} - L_{11})f(\mathbf{x}|1)]\,d\mathbf{x}, \quad (11)$$

because $\mathscr{D}_1 + \mathscr{D}_2 = \mathscr{V}_L$, the measurement space. From (11) we conclude that risk is minimized by making the integrand of the integral negative for all $\mathbf{x}$. This establishes the region $\mathscr{D}_1$:

$$\mathscr{D}_1 = \left\{ \mathbf{x}:\; \frac{f(\mathbf{x}|1)}{f(\mathbf{x}|2)} > \frac{P_2(L_{12} - L_{22})}{P_1(L_{21} - L_{11})} \right\} \quad (12)$$

assuming that†

$$L_{12} > L_{22}, \qquad L_{21} > L_{11}.$$

For a loss matrix

$$\mathbf{L} = \begin{bmatrix} 0 & 1 \\ 1 & 0 \end{bmatrix},$$

the risk R (10) reduces to

$$R = P_1 \int_{\mathscr{D}_2} f(\mathbf{x}|1)\,d\mathbf{x} + P_2 \int_{\mathscr{D}_1} f(\mathbf{x}|2)\,d\mathbf{x} = P_e, \quad (13)$$

which is the global probability of error P_e.

Extensions of this global-risk approach to the multicategory problem are found in Van Trees [6]. Also, the global risk for a class of decision rules, called "sample-based" decision rules, is discussed in Section 3-3. These sample-based rules may include the k-nearest-neighbor type of rule and rules based on estimating local density using tolerance regions.

Probabilities of False Alarm, Detection, and Miss

Let ω_1 index the category corresponding to a target and ω_2 a nontarget. The probabilities of false alarm, detection, and miss are as follows:

false-alarm probability: $\quad P_F = \int_{\mathscr{D}_1} f(\mathbf{x}|\omega_2)\,d\mathbf{x}\,P_2;$ $\hspace{2cm}$ (14a)

†Mathematically these assumptions need to be made but in practice they may be satisfied automatically.

detection probability:
$$P_D = \int_{\mathscr{D}_1} f(\mathbf{x}|\omega_1)\, d\mathbf{x}\, P_1; \tag{14b}$$

miss probability:
$$P_M = \int_{\mathscr{D}_2} f(\mathbf{x}|\omega_1)\, d\mathbf{x}\, P_1. \tag{14c}$$

From (11), in terms of P_F, P_D, and P_1 the risk is

$$R = P_1 L_{21} + (1 - P_1)L_{22} + (L_{12} - L_{22})P_F - (L_{21} - L_{11})P_D,$$

or, emphasizing dependence on P_1,

$$R(P_1) = [L_{22} + (L_{12} - L_{22})P_F - (L_{21} - L_{11})P_D] \\ + P_1[L_{21} - L_{22}]. \tag{15}$$

Suppose that the decision rule implied by (12) is designed on the a priori assumption that $\tilde{P}_1$ is the true a priori probability of category ω_1, when, in fact, the true value is P_1^*. Then the regions $\mathscr{D}_1$ and $\mathscr{D}_2$, and consequently P_F and P_D, will be determined by this assumed value of $\tilde{P}_1$; denote the estimated region $\tilde{\mathscr{D}}_1$ and $\tilde{\mathscr{D}}_2$. The actual risk, however, depends upon the true value P_1^*. This suggests writing (15) as

$$R(\tilde{P}_1, P_1^*) = [L_{22} + (L_{12} - L_{22})\tilde{P}_F - (L_{12} - L_{11})\tilde{P}_D] \\ + P_1^*(L_{21} - L_{22}),$$
$$= \left[L_{22} + (L_{12} - L_{22})\int_{\tilde{\mathscr{D}}_1} f(\mathbf{x}|\omega_2)\, d\mathbf{x}\, (1 - P_1^*) \right. \\ \left. - (L_{12} - L_{11})\int_{\tilde{\mathscr{D}}_1} f(\mathbf{x}|\omega_1)\, d\mathbf{x}\, P_1^* + P_1^*(L_{21} - L_{22}) \right]. \tag{16}$$

Defining

$$c_1 = L_{22} + (L_{12} - L_{22})\int_{\tilde{\mathscr{D}}_1} f(\mathbf{x}|\omega_2)\, d\mathbf{x}$$

$$c_2 = \left[(L_{21} - L_{22}) - (L_{12} - L_{11})\int_{\tilde{\mathscr{D}}_1} f(\mathbf{x}|\omega_1)\, d\mathbf{x} \right] \\ - \left[L_{22} + (L_{12} - L_{22})\int_{\tilde{\mathscr{D}}_1} f(\mathbf{x}|\omega_2)\, d\mathbf{x} \right]$$

Eq. (16) can be reexpressed

$$R(\tilde{P}_1, P_1^*) = c_1 + P_1^* c_2. \tag{17}$$

The risk when P_1^* is used to determine the decision boundary and thus also determine P_F^*, P_D^* is

$$R(P_1^*, P_1^*) = [L_{22} + (L_{12} - L_{22})P_F^* - (L_{12} - L_{11})P_D^*] + P_1^*(L_{21} - L_{22}), \tag{18}$$

which is sketched in Figure 3.1. The risk when a fixed value of $\tilde{P}_1$ is used to determine the decision boundary and thus $\tilde{P}_F$ and $\tilde{P}_D$ is expressed by (17) and sketched as the straight line in Figure 3.1. It is obvious that

$$R(\tilde{P}_1, P_1^*) \geq R(P_1^*, P_1^*),$$

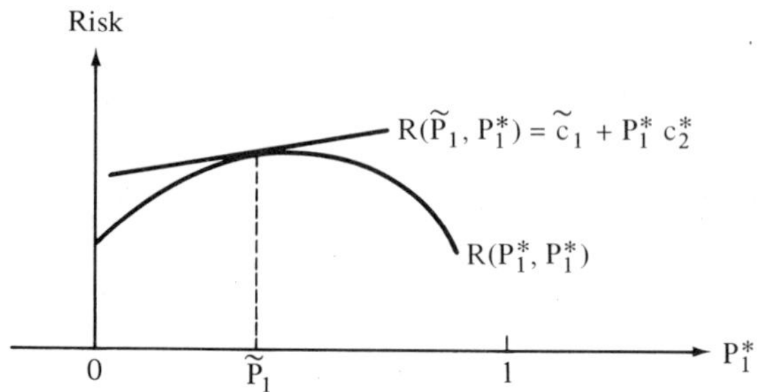

Fig. 3.1 Example of $R(\tilde{P}_1, P_1^*) \; R(P_1^*, P_1^*)$

since P_1^* is the true value. It follows from the above that as estimation of P_1^* improves, risk may decrease.

Several investigators, including Cooper and Cooper [22] and Patrick and Carayannopoulos [23], have devised unsupervised estimators for P_1^*.

Just as risk depends upon the estimate $\tilde{P}_1$ of P_1^*, it depends upon estimates $\tilde{\mathbf{b}}_1$ and $\tilde{\mathbf{b}}_2$ for $\mathbf{b}_1^*$ and $\mathbf{b}_2^*$, respectively. Thus there must be expressions obeying

$$R(\tilde{P}_1, \tilde{\mathbf{b}}_1, \tilde{\mathbf{b}}_2; P_1^*, \mathbf{b}_1^*, \mathbf{b}_2^*) \geq R(P_1^*, \mathbf{b}_1^*, \mathbf{b}_2^*; P_1^*, \mathbf{b}_1^*, \mathbf{b}_2^*),$$

because in general $\tilde{P}_F$ and $\tilde{P}_D$ are functions of $\tilde{P}_1, \tilde{\mathbf{b}}_1, \tilde{\mathbf{b}}_2, P_1^*, \mathbf{b}_1^*,$ and $\mathbf{b}_2^*$. That is, the decision regions $\mathscr{D}_1$ and $\mathscr{D}_2$ used in the decision rule (12) are computed using $\tilde{P}_1, \tilde{\mathbf{b}}_1,$ and $\tilde{\mathbf{b}}_2$. Yet, the actual risk depends upon the true value, P_1^*.

Discussion

The decision regions $\mathscr{D}_1$ and $\mathscr{D}_2$ are determined using, in general, an a priori guess at the parameter point $\mathbf{b}^*$, where the guess is denoted $\tilde{\mathbf{b}}$. There are not many theoretical results available showing how large $R(\tilde{\mathbf{b}}, \mathbf{b}^*) - R(\mathbf{b}^*, \mathbf{b}^*)$ can be as a function of dimensionality L and the number of parameters in $\mathbf{b}^*$. The world of pattern recognition abounds with problems of this sort; it is likely that because of the enormous number of such examples, few results have been published. Some results for general L are found in a paper by Patrick and Costello [24].

The facility for using an a priori starting point $\tilde{\mathbf{b}}$ and then updating it using training samples is very important. Imagine the educational experience acquired by a research-oriented physician who could enter his a priori knowledge $\tilde{\mathbf{b}}$ about classes of diseases, and then observe updated versions of $\tilde{\mathbf{b}}$ after using patient patterns as training data. The techniques discussed in this book are strongly directed toward such an application. The future undoubtedly holds many exciting experiences for the professional who makes use of interactive pattern recognition.

3-2.4 Minimizing Conditional Risk

The decision rule given by (5) minimizing risk is for the statistics $f(\mathbf{x}\,|\,i)$, $P_i,\ i = 1, 2, \ldots, M$ known. In Chapters 4 and 5 methods are presented for estimating these statistics for supervised and unsupervised samples $\dot{\mathbf{x}}_n$, respectively. Although estimators for these statistics can be substituted directly into (5), it is desirable to avoid this two-step process (at least for theoretical purposes) and seek a decision rule minimizing conditional risk. By conditional risk† is meant risk conditioned on the samples $\dot{\mathbf{x}}_n$ and, of course, on any other a priori knowledge.

A direct extension of the derivation of (1) gives a conditional risk

$$r^n(d(\mathbf{x}), i) \triangleq r(d(\mathbf{x}), i\,|\,\dot{\mathbf{x}}_n) = L(d(\mathbf{x}), i)f(\mathbf{x}, i\,|\,\dot{\mathbf{x}}_n), \qquad (19)$$

$$r^n(d(\mathbf{x})) = \sum_{i=1}^{M} r^n(d(\mathbf{x}), i). \qquad (20)$$

By a development similar to that in Section 3-2.1, the decision rule minimizing risk conditioned on $\dot{\mathbf{x}}_n$ is: $d^*(\mathbf{x}) = $ category for which

$$\sum_{i=1}^{M} L(d^*(\mathbf{x}), i)f(\mathbf{x}, i\,|\,\dot{\mathbf{x}}_n) < \sum_{i=1}^{M} L(d(\mathbf{x}), i)f(\mathbf{x}, i\,|\,\dot{\mathbf{x}}_n), \qquad \forall\ d(\mathbf{x}) \in D. \qquad (21)$$

Clearly, $d(\mathbf{x})$ depends on $\dot{\mathbf{x}}_n$ such that $d(\mathbf{x}; \dot{\mathbf{x}}_n)$ is a better notation. Because the parameter points $\{\mathbf{b}_i\}_{i=1}^{M}$ are unknown (where there are exactly N parameter points in the parameter space), they are not shown in (21); rather they are "integrated out."

---

†Conditional risk is a random variable depending on the training samples $\dot{\mathbf{x}}_n$. It is presumed that all a priori knowledge about the underlying statistics $f(\mathbf{x}\,|\,i)$, P_i, for all i, is to be used in calculating this conditional risk. That is, for the set of training samples $\dot{\mathbf{x}}_n$, all possible is known about the a posteriori density of fixed but unknown parameters.

Assume that $\mathbf{x}_1, \mathbf{x}_2, \ldots, \mathbf{x}_n$ are parameter conditionally independent† and the category probabilities P_i are fixed but unknown. Then

$$f(\mathbf{x}_n \mid \mathbf{b}, \dot{\mathbf{x}}_{n-1}) = f(\mathbf{x}_n \mid \mathbf{b}), \tag{22}$$

$$p(i \mid P_i, \dot{\mathbf{x}}_{n-1}) = P_i. \tag{23}$$

Observe that $f(\mathbf{x}, i \mid \dot{\mathbf{x}}_n)$ is calculated from the a posteriori density $f(\mathbf{b} \mid \dot{\mathbf{x}}_n)$ as follows:

$$f(\mathbf{x}, i \mid \dot{\mathbf{x}}_n) = \int f(\mathbf{x}, i, \mathbf{b} \mid \dot{\mathbf{x}}_n) \, d\mathbf{b}$$

$$= \int f(\mathbf{x}, i \mid \mathbf{b}, \dot{\mathbf{x}}_n) f(\mathbf{b} \mid \dot{\mathbf{x}}_n) \, d\mathbf{b}$$

$$= \int f(\mathbf{x} \mid i, \mathbf{b}, \dot{\mathbf{x}}_n) p(i \mid \mathbf{b}, \dot{\mathbf{x}}_n) f(\mathbf{b} \mid \dot{\mathbf{x}}_n) \, d\mathbf{b}.$$

since $\mathbf{b}_i \in \mathbf{b}$ and $P_i \in \mathbf{b}$, applying (22) and (23), respectively, reduces the last equation to

$$f(\mathbf{x}, i \mid \dot{\mathbf{x}}_n) = \int [f(\mathbf{x} \mid i, \mathbf{b}_i) P_i] f(\mathbf{b} \mid \dot{\mathbf{x}}_n) \, d\mathbf{b}. \tag{24}$$

Thus, $f(\mathbf{x}, i \mid \dot{\mathbf{x}}_n)$ is the Bayes estimator of $[f(\mathbf{x} \mid i, \mathbf{b}_i) P_i]$ for quadratic loss function (see Section 2-8).

$f(b \mid \dot{\mathbf{x}}_n)$ is computed as follows: Denote by $\mathbf{b}^k$ the kth set of points in the parameter space $\mathscr{B}^{M'}$ according to the notation of Section 1-3. This kth set is for M_k classes with respective parameter points $\mathbf{b}_i^k$, $i = 1, 2, \ldots, M_k$. Thus

$$\mathbf{b}^k = \{\mathbf{b}_1^k, \mathbf{b}_2^k, \ldots, \mathbf{b}_{M_k}^k, P_1^k, P_2^k, \ldots, P_{M_k}^k\}.$$

Then

$$f(\mathbf{b}^k \mid \dot{\mathbf{x}}_n) = \frac{f(\mathbf{x}_n \mid \mathbf{b}^k, \dot{\mathbf{x}}_{n-1}) f(\mathbf{b}^k \mid \dot{\mathbf{x}}_{n-1})}{f(\mathbf{x}_n \mid \dot{\mathbf{x}}_{n-1})}.$$

But, using (22),

$$f(\mathbf{x}_n \mid \mathbf{b}^k, \dot{\mathbf{x}}_{n-1}) = f(\mathbf{x}_n \mid \mathbf{b}^k),$$

---

†To remind the reader, parameter conditional independence means that $f(\mathbf{x}_1, \mathbf{x}_2, \ldots, \mathbf{x}_n \mid \mathbf{b}) = f(\mathbf{x}_1 \mid \mathbf{b}) f(\mathbf{x}_2 \mid \mathbf{b}) \cdots f(\mathbf{x}_n \mid \mathbf{b})$.

and because $(\mathbf{x}_n, i)$, $i = 1, 2, \ldots, M_k$, are mutually exclusive and exhaustive events,

$$f(\mathbf{x}_n \mid \mathbf{b}^k) = \sum_{i=1}^{M_k} f(\mathbf{x}_n, i \mid \mathbf{b}^k)$$

$$= \sum_{i=1}^{M_k} f(\mathbf{x}_n \mid \mathbf{b}_i^k, i) P_i^k.$$

Thus,

$$f(\mathbf{b}^k \mid \dot{\mathbf{x}}_n) = \frac{\left[\sum_{i=1}^{M_k} f(\mathbf{x}_n \mid \mathbf{b}_i^k, i) P_i^k \right] f(\mathbf{b}^k \mid \dot{\mathbf{x}}_{n-1})}{\int [\text{numerator}] \, d\mathbf{b}^k}, \tag{25}$$

where we have used the result

$$f(\mathbf{x}_n \mid \dot{\mathbf{x}}_{n-1}) = \int f(\mathbf{x}_n \mid \mathbf{b}^k, \dot{\mathbf{x}}_{n-1}) f(\mathbf{b}^k \mid \dot{\mathbf{x}}_{n-1}) \, d\mathbf{b}^k.$$

Simplified Approach

The computation of $f(\mathbf{b} \mid \dot{\mathbf{x}}_n)$ for use in (24) may be impractical. For this reason, many different simplifying approaches are considered in this book. Perhaps the simplified approach most often used in practice essentially involves obtaining an estimator $(\mathbf{b})_n$ and substituting it directly into (24) to obtain

$$f(\mathbf{x}, i \mid \dot{\mathbf{x}}_n) \triangleq f(\mathbf{x} \mid i, (\mathbf{b}_i)_n)(P_i)_n, \tag{26}$$

which is an approximation in most cases.

3-2.5 Introducing Parameter-Conditional Dependence and Nonstationary Class Probabilities

We now return to the problem of computing $f(\mathbf{x}_n, i \mid \dot{\mathbf{x}}_{n-1})$ without assuming that the samples $\mathbf{x}_1, \mathbf{x}_2, \ldots, \mathbf{x}_n$ are parameter conditionally independent and allowing P_i to depend on the samples; i.e., it is no longer necessarily true that $p(i \mid P_i, \dot{\mathbf{x}}_{n-1}) = P_i$.

The assumption that samples are parameter conditionally independent is not always justified in practice. On the other hand, neither is the assumption that $\mathbf{x}_n$ is dependent on all previous samples; therefore, it is reasonable to assume that $\mathbf{x}_n$ is parameter conditionally dependent only on the previous $v - 1$ samples, where v is any integer, $v \leq n$.

Since there are $(M_k)^v$ ways the categories can occur to cause the last v samples, let

$$W_k = (M_k)^v. \tag{27}$$

The objective, as before, is to compute $f(\mathbf{x}_n, i \mid \dot{\mathbf{x}}_{n-1})$. In terms of sequences π_r,

$$f(\mathbf{x}_n, i \mid \dot{\mathbf{x}}_n) = \sum_{\pi_r \in \mathscr{R}} f(\mathbf{x}, \pi_r \mid \dot{\mathbf{x}}_n), \tag{28}$$

where $\mathscr{R}$ is the set of all sequences for which $\mathbf{x}$ is from category i. Thus the problem is to compute $f(\mathbf{x}_n, \pi_r \mid \dot{\mathbf{x}}_{n-1})$ as

$$
\begin{aligned}
f(\mathbf{x}_n, \pi_r \mid \dot{\mathbf{x}}_n) &= \int f(\mathbf{x}_n, \pi_r, \mathbf{c} \mid \dot{\mathbf{x}}_{n-1}) \, d\mathbf{c} \\
&= \int f(\mathbf{x}_n, \pi_r, \mid \mathbf{c}, \dot{\mathbf{x}}_{n-1}) f(\mathbf{c} \mid \dot{\mathbf{x}}_{n-1}) \, d\mathbf{c} \\
&= \int f(\mathbf{x}_n \mid \pi_r, \dot{\mathbf{x}}_{n-1}, \mathbf{c}) p(\pi_r \mid \dot{\mathbf{x}}_{n-1}, \mathbf{c}) f(\mathbf{c} \mid \dot{\mathbf{x}}_{n-1}) \, d\mathbf{c} \\
&= \int [f(\mathbf{x}_n \mid \pi_r, \dot{\mathbf{x}}_{n-1}, \mathbf{c}) P(\pi_r)] f(\mathbf{c} \mid \dot{\mathbf{x}}_{n-1}) \, d\mathbf{c},
\end{aligned} \tag{29}
$$

where we have used the fact that

$$p(\pi_r \mid \dot{\mathbf{x}}_{n-1}, \mathbf{c}) = P(\pi_r), \tag{30}$$

which follows because $\mathbf{c}$ contains $P(\pi_r)$. Thus the merit of sequence probabilities is obvious.

Because $\mathbf{x}_n$ is parameter conditionally dependent only on $\mathbf{x}_{n-1}$, $\mathbf{x}_{n-2}$, $\ldots$, $\mathbf{x}_{n-v+1}$,

$$
\begin{aligned}
f(\mathbf{x}_n \mid \pi_r, \mathbf{c}^k, \dot{\mathbf{x}}_{n-1}) &= f(\mathbf{x}_n \mid \pi_r, \mathbf{c}^k, \mathbf{x}_{n-1}, \mathbf{x}_{n-2}, \ldots, \mathbf{x}_{n-v+1}) \\
&= \frac{f(\mathbf{x}_n, \ldots, \mathbf{x}_{n-v+1} \mid \pi_r, \mathbf{c}^k)}{f(\mathbf{x}_{n-1}, \ldots, \mathbf{x}_{n-v+1} \mid \pi_r, \mathbf{c}^k)},
\end{aligned} \tag{31}
$$

which is used in (29). The final computation is

$$f(\mathbf{c}^k \mid \dot{\mathbf{x}}_n) = \frac{\left[\sum_{r=1}^{W_k} f(\mathbf{x}_n \mid \pi_r, \mathbf{c}^k, \mathbf{x}_{n-1}, \ldots, \mathbf{x}_{n-v+1}) P(\pi_r) \right] f(\mathbf{c}^k \mid \dot{\mathbf{x}}_{n-1})}{\int [\text{numerator}] \, d\mathbf{c}^k}, \tag{32}$$

$$f(\mathbf{c}^k \mid \dot{\mathbf{x}}_n) = \frac{\left[\sum_{r=1}^{W_k} \dfrac{f(\mathbf{x}_n, \ldots, \mathbf{x}_{n-v+1} \mid \pi_r, \mathbf{c}^k)}{f(\mathbf{x}_{n-1}, \ldots, \mathbf{x}_{n-v+1} \mid \pi_r, \mathbf{c}^k)} P(\pi_r) \right] f(\mathbf{c}^k \mid \mathbf{x}_{n-1})}{\int [\text{numerator}] \, d\mathbf{c}^k}, \tag{33}$$

and we observe that the mixture for this problem ($\mathbf{c}^k$ can be replaced with $\mathbf{c}_r^k$) is

$$\sum_{r=1}^{W_k} \frac{f(\mathbf{x}_n, \ldots, \mathbf{x}_{n-v+1} \mid \pi_r, \mathbf{c}_r^k)}{f(\mathbf{x}_{n-1}, \ldots, \mathbf{x}_{n-v+1} \mid \pi_r, \mathbf{c}_r^k)} P(\pi_r). \tag{34}$$

Example

To use the minimum conditional risk decision rule (21) when the samples $\mathbf{x}_1, \mathbf{x}_2, \ldots, \mathbf{x}_n$ are not parameter conditionally independent or the class probabilities are not fixed, one computes $f(\mathbf{x}, i \mid \dot{\mathbf{x}}_n)$ according to (28) and (29), noting the use of sequence probabilities $P(\pi_r)$ rather than class probabilities.

Observe that properties of the rth sequence affect $f(\mathbf{x} \mid \pi_r, \dot{\mathbf{x}}_n, \mathbf{c})$ through the structure of the family of these functions as well as through $f(\mathbf{c} \mid \dot{\mathbf{x}}_n)$. This is illustrated by the following examples:

(i) Suppose it is known that $M = 2$ and $\mathbf{x}_1, \mathbf{x}_2, \ldots, \mathbf{x}_n$ are consistent for class 1 and not for class 2. A feature y which measures the consistency of the sequence could be constructed and the density of y for each of the two classes estimated and used in the decision rule. In this way "consistency structure" is inserted in a relatively simple way.

(ii) As a separate example, suppose it is known that all n samples are from either class 1 or class 2, but not both. Then there are two sequences $\pi_1 = [1, 1, \ldots, 1]$ and $\pi_2 = [2, 2, \ldots, 2]$ and the sequence probabilities which are nonzero are $P(\pi_1)$ and $P(\pi_2)$. Clearly, one of these sequences may "fit the sample $\mathbf{x}_1, \mathbf{x}_2, \ldots, \mathbf{x}_n$ best." To see this, suppose that

$$f(\mathbf{c} \mid \dot{\mathbf{x}}_n) = \frac{f(\dot{\mathbf{x}}_n \mid \mathbf{c}) f(\mathbf{c})}{f(\dot{\mathbf{x}}_n)} = \frac{\sum\limits_{r=1}^{2} f(\dot{\mathbf{x}}_n \mid \mathbf{c}_r, \pi_r) P(\pi_r)}{f(\dot{\mathbf{x}}_n)} f(\mathbf{c}); \tag{35a}$$

and $\dot{\mathbf{x}}_n$ is such that $f(\dot{\mathbf{x}}_n \mid \mathbf{c}_1, \pi_1) P(\pi_1) \gg f(\dot{\mathbf{x}}_n \mid \mathbf{c}_2, \pi_2) P(\pi_2)$; then

$$f(P(\pi_1), P(\pi_2) \mid \dot{\mathbf{x}}_n) \simeq \frac{f(\dot{\mathbf{x}}_n \mid \pi_1) P(\pi_1)}{f(\dot{\mathbf{x}}_n)} f(P(\pi_1), P(\pi_2)). \tag{35b}$$

For convenience assume that $f(P(\pi_1), P(\pi_2))$ is uniform, $P(\pi_1) + P(\pi_2) = 1$,

$$f(P(\pi_1), P(\pi_2)) = 2\delta(P(\pi_1) - (1 - P(\pi_2))), \tag{35c}$$

$0 < P(\pi_1) < 1$, $0 < P(\pi_2) < 1$, where $\delta(\cdot)$ is the dirac delta function. Then

$$f(P(\pi_1), P(\pi_2) \mid \dot{\mathbf{x}}_n) = 2P(\pi_1)\delta(P(\pi_1) - (1 - P(\pi_2))).$$

The marginal a posteriori densities are

$$f(P(\pi_1)|\dot{\mathbf{x}}_n) = \int_0^1 2P(\pi_1)\delta(P(\pi_1) - (1 - P(\pi_2))\,dP(\pi_2) = 2P(\pi_1), \qquad (35\text{d})$$

$$f(P(\pi_2)|\dot{\mathbf{x}}_n) = \int_0^1 2P(\pi_1)\delta(P(\pi_1) - (1 - P(\pi_2))\,dP(\pi_1)$$
$$= 2(1 - P(\pi_2)). \qquad (35\text{e})$$

Obviously from (35d) and (35e),

$$E[P(\pi_1)|\dot{\mathbf{x}}_n] > E[P(\pi_2)|\dot{\mathbf{x}}_n] \qquad (35\text{f})$$

because $f(P(\pi_1)|\dot{\mathbf{x}}_n)$ has more density near the upper end of the interval than $f(P(\pi_2)|\dot{\mathbf{x}}_n)$.

The Bayes estimators for $P(\pi_1)$ and $P(\pi_2)$, using the square law loss functions, are

$$(P(\pi_1))_1 = \int_0^1 P(\pi_1)2P(\pi_1)\,dP(\pi_1) = \tfrac{2}{3},$$
$$(P(\pi_2))_1 = \int_0^1 P(\pi_2)2(1 - P(\pi_2))\,dP(\pi_2) = \tfrac{1}{3}. \qquad (35\text{g})$$

Note that we have seen only one sample of the sequence $\dot{\mathbf{x}}_n$ and this explains why the above estimators do not depend on n.

It is of interest to observe that

$$f(\mathbf{x}_{n+1}, \pi_i|\dot{\mathbf{x}}_n) = f(\mathbf{x}_{n+1}|\pi_i, \dot{\mathbf{x}}_n)p(\pi_i|\dot{\mathbf{x}}_n)$$
$$= f(\mathbf{x}_{n+1}|\pi_i)\int_0^1 (P(\pi_i)f(P(\pi_i)|\dot{\mathbf{x}}_n)\,dP(\pi_i)$$
$$= \begin{cases} \tfrac{2}{3}f(\mathbf{x}_{n+1}|\pi_1), & i = 1 \\ \tfrac{1}{3}f(\mathbf{x}_{n+1}|\pi_2), & i = 2. \end{cases} \qquad (35\text{h})$$

Thus if $\mathbf{x}_{n+1}$ is from class 1 we expect that $f(\mathbf{x}_{n+1}, \pi_1|\dot{\mathbf{x}}_n) > f(\mathbf{x}_{n+1}, \pi_2|\dot{\mathbf{x}}_n)$ with the inequality resulting both from the effect shown in (35g) and the fact that we expect $f(\mathbf{x}_{n+1}|\pi_1) > f(\mathbf{x}_{n+1}|\pi_2)$.

A decision rule for this problem would compute

$$p(\pi_i|\dot{\mathbf{x}}_{n+1}) = \frac{p(\dot{\mathbf{x}}_{n+1}|\pi_i)p(\pi_i)}{f(\dot{\mathbf{x}}_{n+1})},$$

which means that a decision is made by comparing $f(\dot{\mathbf{x}}_{n+1}|\pi_1)p(\pi_1)$ with $f(\dot{\mathbf{x}}_{n+1}|\pi_2)p(\pi_2)$. Note the significant merit of the latter comparison.

In the example (ii) there could have been $W = M^n$ sequences but we supposed there were only two. It is felt, for example, by some physicians that in medical diagnosis they accomplish what amounts to quickly eliminating many of the large number of sequences in coming up with a diagnosis based on a set of symptoms. This medical diagnosis problem is complicated, however, by the fact that classes of disease are not well defined.

Probably a good example of where (ii) applies is in sonar automatic detection and classification where there are two classes, subs and nonsubs, and $\dot{\mathbf{x}}_n$ is a sequence of target echos at the receiver.

3-2.6 *Risk in Terms of Decision Probabilities*

A slightly different approach from that presented in previous sections is to express point risk in terms of decision probabilities. As before, let L_{ji} be the loss incurred by placing $\mathbf{x}$ (here $\mathbf{x}$ is generic for $\mathbf{x}_n$) in category j by using decision rule $d(\mathbf{x}) = j$, when in truth $\mathbf{x}$ belongs to category i. Define by $p(d(\mathbf{x}) = j; i, \mathbf{x} \mid \dot{\mathbf{x}}_{n-1})$ the joint probability, conditioned on samples $\dot{\mathbf{x}}_{n-1}$, that $\mathbf{x}$ is the observation and is placed in category j, but category i is truth.

When $d(\mathbf{x}) = j$, the point risk at observation $\mathbf{x}$ is

$$r_j(\mathbf{x}) = \sum_{i=1}^{M} L_{ji} p(d(\mathbf{x}) = j; i, \mathbf{x} \mid \dot{\mathbf{x}}_{n-1}). \tag{36}$$

But since

$$p(d(\mathbf{x}) = j; i, \mathbf{x} \mid \dot{\mathbf{x}}_{n-1}) = p(d(\mathbf{x}) = j \mid \dot{\mathbf{x}}_{n-1}, i, \mathbf{x}) p(i, \mathbf{x} \mid \dot{\mathbf{x}}_{n-1}),$$

it follows that (36) is equivalent to

$$r_j(\mathbf{x}) = \sum_{i=1}^{M} L_{ji} p(d(\mathbf{x}) = j \mid \dot{\mathbf{x}}_{n-1}, i, \mathbf{x}) \eta_i^n(\mathbf{x}), \tag{37}$$

where

$$\eta_i^n(\mathbf{x}) \triangleq p(i, \mathbf{x} \mid \dot{\mathbf{x}}_{n-1}).$$

Thus, the point risk at observation $\mathbf{x}$ is

$$r(\mathbf{x}) = \sum_{j=1}^{M} r_j(\mathbf{x}) = \sum_{j=1}^{M} \sum_{i=1}^{M} p(d(\mathbf{x}) = j \mid \dot{\mathbf{x}}_{n-1}, i, \mathbf{x}) L_{ji} \eta_i^n(\mathbf{x}). \tag{38}$$

Point risk at observation $\mathbf{x}$ is minimized by making a decision that minimizes (38). Suppose that M nonoverlapping regions are formed which cover $\mathcal{X}$ such that $d(\mathbf{x}) = j, j = 1, 2, \ldots, M$, respectively, in the regions. Then,

$p(d(\mathbf{x}) = j \,|\, \dot{\mathbf{x}}_{n-1}, i, \mathbf{x}) = 1$ when $\mathbf{x}$ is in the jth region and zero otherwise. Then (38) simplifies according to the following summary: If $p(d(\mathbf{x}) = j \,|\, \dot{\mathbf{x}}_{n-1}, i, \mathbf{x}) = 1$ when $\mathbf{x}$ is in the jth region and zero otherwise, point risk $r(\mathbf{x})$ at observation $\mathbf{x}$ is minimized by $d(\mathbf{x}) = j$ if

$$\sum_{i=1}^{M} L_{ji}\eta_i^n(\mathbf{x}) = \min_r \left\{ \sum_{\xi=1}^{M} L_{r\xi}\eta_\xi^n(\mathbf{x}) \right\}_{r=1}^{M}$$

In Chapter 4 nonparametric decision rules, in particular k-nearest-neighbor rules, are considered. For these rules we are interested in computing $p(d(\mathbf{x}) = j \,|\, \dot{\mathbf{x}}_{n-1}, i)$. We shall find it necessary, however, *to perform such calculations assuming the existence of specific underlying densities $f(\mathbf{x}\,|\,i)$. In other words, the performance of distribution-free decision rules may not be distribution-free.* This makes one wonder sometimes if the distribution-free or nonparametric approaches are really theoretically basic for pattern recognition. They may primarily be implementation conveniences.

In terms of (38), the overall or global risk R is

$$R = \int r(\mathbf{x})h(\mathbf{x})\, d\mathbf{x}, \tag{39}$$

where

$$h(\mathbf{x}) = \sum_{i=1}^{M} f(\mathbf{x}\,|\,i)P_i.$$

3-3 Risk of Sample-Based Decision Rules

3-3.1 Introduction

A different approach from the minimum conditional risk approach is to define a *sample-based decision rule*, denoted $d(\mathbf{x}; \dot{\mathbf{x}}_n)$, as a rule that maps points in the $(n+1)$th product space $\mathscr{X} \times \mathscr{X}^n$ to only one of the elements $\omega_1, \omega_2, \ldots, \omega_M$.

The ith training set $\dot{\mathbf{x}}_{n_i}^i = [\mathbf{x}_1^i, \mathbf{x}_2^i, \ldots, \mathbf{x}_{n_i}^i]$ is a collection of n_i independent vectors in $\mathscr{X}$ identically distributed† as $F(\mathbf{x}\,|\,\omega_i)$. The training sets are collectively denoted by $\dot{\mathbf{x}}_{\mathbf{n}} \triangleq [\dot{\mathbf{x}}_{n_1}^1, \dot{\mathbf{x}}_{n_2}^2, \ldots, \dot{\mathbf{x}}_{n_M}^M]$, where $\sum_{i=1}^{M} n_i = n$, and $\mathbf{n} = [n_1, n_2, \ldots, n_M]$.

The decision rule $d(\mathbf{x}; \dot{\mathbf{x}}_{\mathbf{n}})$ induces M sets $\{\mathscr{D}_1(\dot{\mathbf{x}}_{\mathbf{n}}), \mathscr{D}_2(\dot{\mathbf{x}}_{\mathbf{n}}), \ldots, \mathscr{D}_M(\dot{\mathbf{x}}_{\mathbf{n}})\}$, where $\mathbf{x} \in \mathscr{D}_i(\dot{\mathbf{x}}_{\mathbf{n}})$ if and only if $d(\mathbf{x}; \dot{\mathbf{x}}_{\mathbf{n}}) = \omega_i$.

Given the observation point $\mathbf{x}$, the probability of assigning $\mathbf{x}$ to class

---

†To be mathematically precise, we let $\mathscr{B}$ denote the Borel σ field on $\mathscr{X}$. On $(\mathscr{X} \times \mathscr{B})$ there are M probability distributions $F(\mathbf{x}\,|\,\omega)_i$; $i = 1, 2, \ldots, M$.

ω_j when $\mathbf{x}$ is distributed $F(\mathbf{x}|\omega_i)$ is denoted a_{ji}:

$$a_{ji} = \int_{\mathscr{D}_j(\dot{\mathbf{x}}_n)} dF(\mathbf{x}|\omega_i) = \int_{\mathscr{X}} D_j(\mathbf{x};\dot{\mathbf{x}}_\mathbf{n}) \, dF(\mathbf{x}|\omega_i), \tag{1}$$

where

$$D_j(\mathbf{x};\dot{\mathbf{x}}_\mathbf{n}) = \begin{cases} 1, & \text{when } \mathbf{x} \in \mathscr{D}_j(\dot{\mathbf{x}}_\mathbf{n}), \\ 0, & \text{otherwise.} \end{cases} \tag{2}$$

The risk or expected loss using $d(\mathbf{x};\dot{\mathbf{x}}_\mathbf{n})$ given $\dot{\mathbf{x}}_\mathbf{n}$ is

$$R(\dot{\mathbf{x}}_n) = \sum_{i=1}^{M} P_i \sum_{j=1}^{M} L_{ji} \int_{\mathscr{X}} D_j(\mathbf{x};\dot{\mathbf{x}}_n) \, dF(\mathbf{x}|\omega_i). \tag{3}$$

Of course it is not possible that risk $R(\dot{\mathbf{x}}_\mathbf{n})$ is less than R^*, the natural lower bound (Bayes risk for known statistics) of the risk of all rules.

The risk $R(\dot{\mathbf{x}}_\mathbf{n})$ is a random variable since $\dot{\mathbf{x}}_\mathbf{n}$ is a random vector with distribution function $\dot{F}(\dot{\mathbf{x}}_\mathbf{n})$,

$$\dot{F}(\dot{\mathbf{x}}_\mathbf{n}) = \prod_{i=1}^{M} \prod_{j=1}^{n_i} F(\dot{\mathbf{x}}_j^i|\omega_i). \tag{4}$$

$R(\dot{\mathbf{x}}_\mathbf{n})$ is a random real number that ranges between R^* (the Bayes risk) and some upper bound R^{**}. A typical distribution of $R(\dot{\mathbf{x}}_\mathbf{n})$ for a prescribed set of underlying distributions $\{F(\mathbf{x}|\omega_i)\}$ is illustrated in Figure 3.2 for several values of sample size. As n increases, the mean of $R(\dot{\mathbf{x}}_\mathbf{n})$ might decrease to a value not less than R^*, while the variance of $R(\dot{\mathbf{x}}_\mathbf{n})$ might decrease to zero.

After selecting a statistical model and using it in defining the risk of

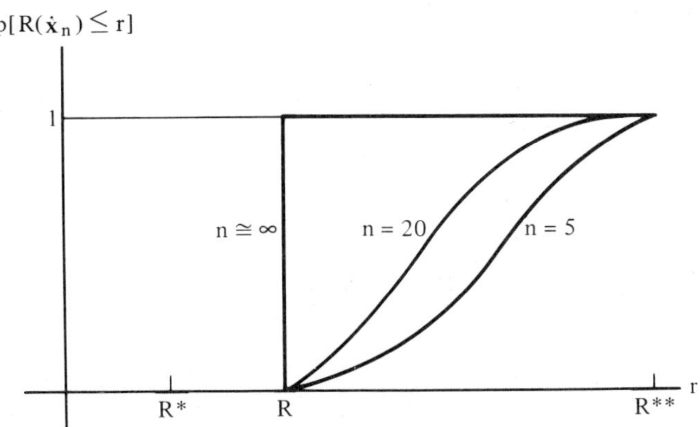

Fig. 3.2 Example: Distribution of risk of sample-based rule

the corresponding sample-based decision rule, the distribution function of $R(\dot{\mathbf{x}}_\mathbf{n})$ can be described as a function of sample size, decision rule, and underlying statistics. However, since the sequence of (finite) moments of a distribution of a random variable specifies the distribution function everywhere except on its set of discontinuity functions, it is sufficient to describe the moments of the distribution function of $R(\dot{\mathbf{x}}_\mathbf{n})$ as a function of sample size, decision rule, and underlying statistics.

3-3.2 Moments of Risk of Sample-Based Rules

Since the risk of a sample-based rule given $\dot{\mathbf{x}}_\mathbf{n}$ is bounded below by finite R^* and above by finite R^{**}, the δth moment of this risk for any positive integer μ exists and is defined as

$$\mu_\mathbf{n}^\delta \triangleq E_{\dot{\mathbf{x}}_\mathbf{n}}[[R(\dot{\mathbf{x}}_\mathbf{n})]^\delta], \tag{5}$$

where the expectation is with respect to the randomly drawn training set. Substituting (3) in (5) results in

$$\mu_\mathbf{n}^\delta = \int_{\mathcal{X}^n} \left\{ \sum_{i=1}^{M} P_i \sum_{j=1}^{M} L_{ji} \int_{\mathcal{X}} D_j(\mathbf{x}, \dot{\mathbf{x}}_\mathbf{n})\, dF(\mathbf{x}\,|\,\omega_i) \right\}^\delta d\dot{F}(\dot{\mathbf{x}}_\mathbf{n}). \tag{6}$$

Equation (6) is a final result, but if knowledge is available from the statistical model specifying values for $\int_{\mathcal{X}} D_j(\mathbf{x}, \dot{\mathbf{x}}_\mathbf{n})\, dF(\mathbf{x}\,|\,\omega_i)$ for certain $(\mathbf{x}, i, j)$, this knowledge should, of course, be usable. In what follows, (6) is rewritten to demonstrate this idea.

Express the term $\{\cdot\}^\delta$ in (6) as the product of δ expressions with integration variables and summation indices subscripted by v, obtaining

$$\mu_\mathbf{n}^\delta = \int_{\mathcal{X}^n} \prod_{v=1}^{\delta} \left[\sum_{i_v=1}^{M} \sum_{j_v=1}^{M} P_{i_v} L_{j_v i_v} \int_{\mathcal{X}} D_{j_v}(\mathbf{x}^{(v)}; \dot{\mathbf{x}}_\mathbf{n})\, dF(\mathbf{x}^{(v)}\,|\,\omega_{i_v}) \right] d\dot{F}(\dot{\mathbf{x}}_\mathbf{n}), \tag{7}$$

$$\mu_\mathbf{n}^\delta = \int_{\mathcal{X}^n} \sum_{i_1=1}^{M} \sum_{j_1=1}^{M} \cdots \sum_{i_\delta=1}^{M} \sum_{j_\delta=1}^{M}$$
$$\times \left\{ \prod_{v=1}^{\delta} \left[P_{i_v} L_{j_v i_v} \int_{\mathcal{X}} D_{j_v}(\mathbf{x}^{(v)}; \dot{\mathbf{x}}_\mathbf{n})\, dF(\mathbf{x}^{(v)}\,|\,\omega_{i_v}) \right] \right\} d\dot{F}(\dot{\mathbf{x}}_\mathbf{n}). \tag{8}$$

By two applications of Fubini's theorem ([29], p. 136), which allows equating a product of integrals to a multiple integral of a product, it results that

$$\int_{\mathscr{X}^n} \prod_{v=1}^{\delta} \left[\int_{\mathscr{X}} D_{j_v}(\mathbf{x}^{(v)}; \dot{\mathbf{x}}_n)\, dF(\mathbf{x}^{(v)}|\omega_{i_v}) \right] d\dot{F}(\dot{\mathbf{x}}_n)$$

$$= \int_{\mathscr{X}^n} \int_{\mathscr{X}} \cdots \int_{\mathscr{X}} \prod_{v=1}^{\delta} [D_{j_v}(\mathbf{x}^{(v)}; \dot{\mathbf{x}}_n)]\, dF(\mathbf{x}^{(1)}|\omega_{i_1}) \cdots$$

$$\times\, dF(\mathbf{x}^{(\delta)}|\omega_{i_\delta})\, d\dot{F}(\dot{\mathbf{x}}_n) \tag{9}$$

$$= \int_{\mathscr{X}} \cdots \int_{\mathscr{X}} q_{j_1 \cdots j_\delta}^n(\mathbf{x}^{(1)}, \ldots, \mathbf{x}^{(\delta)}; \dot{\mathbf{x}}_n)\, dF(\mathbf{x}^{(1)}|\omega_{i_1}) \cdots$$

$$\times\, dF(\mathbf{x}^{(\delta)}|\omega_{i_\delta}), \tag{10}$$

where

$$q_{j_1 \cdots j_\delta}^n(\mathbf{x}^{(1)}, \ldots, \mathbf{x}^{(\delta)}) \triangleq \int_{\mathscr{X}^n} \prod_{v=1}^{\delta} [D_{j_v}(\mathbf{x}^{(v)}; \dot{\mathbf{x}}_n)]\, d\dot{F}(\dot{\mathbf{x}}_n) \tag{11}$$

is the probability that the random training set $\dot{\mathbf{x}}_n$ results in a sample-based rule that assigns vector point $\mathbf{x}^{(1)}$ to ω_{j_1}, vector point $\mathbf{x}^{(2)}$ to $\omega_{j_2}, \ldots$, vector point $\mathbf{x}^{(\delta)}$ to ω_{j_δ}. That is,

$$q_{j_1 \cdots j_\delta}^n(\mathbf{x}^{(1)}, \ldots, \mathbf{x}^{(\delta)}) = p[d(\mathbf{x}^{(v)}; \dot{\mathbf{x}}_n) = \omega_{j_v}, v = 1, 2, \ldots, \delta] \tag{12}$$

for the specific δ points $\mathbf{x}^{(1)}, \mathbf{x}^{(2)}, \ldots, \mathbf{x}^{(\delta)}$ in the observation space. Hence by substituting (10) into (8), it has been shown that

$$\mu_n^\delta = \sum_{i_1=1}^{M} \sum_{j_1=1}^{M} \cdots \sum_{i_\delta=1}^{M} \sum_{j_\delta=1}^{M} \left\{ \prod_{v=1}^{\delta} [P_{i_v} L_{j_v i_v}] \right.$$

$$\times \left. \int_{\mathscr{X}} \cdots \int_{\mathscr{X}} q_{j_1 \cdots j_\delta}^n(\mathbf{x}^{(1)}, \ldots, \mathbf{x}^{(\delta)})\, dF(\mathbf{x}^{(1)}|\omega_{i_1}) \cdots dF(\mathbf{x}^{(\delta)}|\omega_{i_\delta}) \right\}.$$

$$\tag{13}$$

Writing the δth moment of risk as in (13) is like "going after an ant with a telephone pole" unless it is subsequently useful because the moments of risk can be evaluated straightforwardly as in Section 3-3.5. The reader should be aware of (13), however, as a method for evaluating risk moments for $k\mathrm{NN}_3$ rules given underlying statistics.

Conclusion

From (13) we can conclude that the δth moment of risk of a sample-based rule is not distribution-free but depends on the respective true class distribution functions $F(\mathbf{x}|\omega_i)$, $i = 1, 2, \ldots, M$. We also can conclude that, if there are regions in $\mathscr{X}$ containing significant probability mass, then the decision regions $\{\mathscr{D}_1(\dot{\mathbf{x}}_n), \mathscr{D}_2(\dot{\mathbf{x}}_n), \ldots, \mathscr{D}_M(\dot{\mathbf{x}}_n)\}$ should be chosen [and thus

$q_{j_1 \cdots j_\delta}(\mathbf{x}^{(1)}, \ldots, \mathbf{x}^{(\delta)}; \dot{\mathbf{x}}_\mathbf{n})$ determined] such as to reduce the moments μ_n^δ of risk to small values.

3-3.3 Central Moments of Risk of Sample-Based Rules

The δth central moment, or moment about the first moment, is defined by

$$\bar{\mu}_n^\delta \triangleq E_{\mathbf{x}_\mathbf{n}}[R(\dot{\mathbf{x}}_\mathbf{n}) - \mu_n^1]^\delta \tag{14a}$$

$$= \sum_{w=0}^{\delta} (-1)^{\delta-w} \binom{\delta}{w} (\mu_n^1)^{\delta-w} E_{\dot{\mathbf{x}}_\mathbf{n}}[R(\dot{\mathbf{x}}_\mathbf{n})^w]. \tag{14b}$$

It is straightforward to show using (13), the result from Problem 6, and Fubini's theorem that

$$\bar{\mu}_n^\delta = \sum_{i_1=1}^{M} \sum_{j_1=1}^{M} \cdots \sum_{i_\delta=1}^{M} \sum_{j_\delta=1}^{M} \left\{ \prod_{v=1}^{\delta} [P_{i_v} L_{j_v i_v}] \right.$$

$$\times \int_{\mathcal{X}} \cdots \int_{\mathcal{X}} \sum_{w=0}^{\delta} \left\{ (-1)^{\delta-w} \binom{\delta}{w} q_{j_1 \cdots j_w}^n (\mathbf{x}^{(1)}, \ldots, \mathbf{x}^{(w)}) \right. \tag{15}$$

$$\left. \times q_{w+1}^n(\mathbf{x}^{(w+1)}) \cdot \cdots \cdot q_{j_\delta}^n(\mathbf{x}^{(\delta)}) \right\} dF(\mathbf{x}^{(1)} | \omega_{i_1}) \cdots dF(\mathbf{x}^{(\delta)} | \omega_{i_\delta}) \Big\} .$$

Example of a Sample-Based Rule

An example of a sample-based decision rule is described now, but a detailed presentation is left for Chapter 4. Suppose n training samples $\mathbf{x}_1, \mathbf{x}_2, \ldots, \mathbf{x}_n$ are available with $\{\mathbf{x}_s^i\}_{s=1}^{n_i}$ from class i, $\sum_{i=1}^{M} n_i = n$. A decision is made to classify a vector point $\mathbf{x} \in \mathcal{X}$ to one of the classes. First, we estimate probability density $f(\mathbf{x}|i)$ at $\mathbf{x}$ for class i, $i = 1, 2, \ldots, M$:

$$(f(\mathbf{x}|i))_n = \frac{k_i}{(n_i + 1)\Phi_i}.$$

In this estimation of density, a "neighborhood" denoted $\mathcal{I}_i$ centered at $\mathbf{x}$ is constructed for each class containing k_i of class i's n_i samples; Φ_i is the volume of the neighborhood. A sample-based decision rule is: Decide class ω_a if

$$\frac{P_a k_a}{(n_a + 1)\Phi_a} = \max_i \left\{ \frac{P_i k_i}{(n_i + 1)\Phi_i} \right\}_{i=1}^{M} .$$

This rule is a special case of the $k\mathrm{NN}_3$ rule discussed in Chapter 4. If $\Phi_1 = \Phi_2 = \Phi_3 = \cdots = \Phi_M$ the rule simplifies to: Decide class ω_a if

$$\frac{P_a k_a}{n_a + 1} = \max_i \left\{ \frac{P_i k_i}{n_i + 1} \right\}_{i=1}^{M} .$$

3-3.4 Point Risk of a Sample-Based Rule

In Section 3-2.6 it is shown that the point risk (risk in classifying a single point $\mathbf{x}$) is

$$r(\mathbf{x}) = \sum_{j=1}^{M} \sum_{i=1}^{M} p(d(\mathbf{x}) = j \,|\, \dot{\mathbf{x}}_{n-1}, i, \mathbf{x}) L_{ji} \eta_i^n(\mathbf{x}). \qquad (16a)$$

There were no restrictions placed on $d(\mathbf{x})$ in Section 3-2.6, which prevents it from being a sample-based rule. Therefore, the above is the point risk of a sample-based rule.

If the sample-based rule is: $d(\mathbf{x}) = j$ with probability 1 if

$$\sum_{i=1}^{M} L_{ji} \eta_i^n(\mathbf{x}) = \min_{r} \left\{ \sum_{\xi=1}^{M} L_{r\xi} \eta_\xi^n(\mathbf{x}) \right\}_{r=1}^{M}, \qquad r = 1, 2, \ldots, M,$$

then the above point risk reduces to

$$r(\mathbf{x}) = \min_{j} \left\{ \sum_{i=1}^{M} L_{ji} \eta_i^n(\mathbf{x}) \right\}. \qquad (16b)$$

3-3.5 Small Sample Size Risk

Suppose that there are N separate training sets $\dot{\mathbf{x}}_n^{(k)}$, $k = 1, 2, \ldots, N$. Denote the samples in the kth training set from the ith class, $\mathbf{x}_1^{i(k)}$, $\mathbf{x}_2^{i(k)}$, $\ldots, \mathbf{x}_{n_i}^{i(k)}$ assuming all training sets for the ith class have n_i samples and $n = n_1 + n_2 + \cdots + n_M$. Then an estimate for μ_n^δ in (6) is given by

$$\hat{\mu}_n^\delta = \frac{1}{N} \sum_{k=1}^{N} \left\{ \sum_{i=1}^{M} P_i \sum_{j=1}^{M} L_{ji} \sum_{s=1}^{n_i} D_j(\mathbf{x}_s^{i(k)}, \dot{\mathbf{x}}_n^{(k)}) \right\}^\delta. \qquad (17)$$

Likewise, an estimate for $\bar{\mu}_n^\delta$, the δth central moment (14a), is

$$\hat{\bar{\mu}}_n^\delta = \frac{1}{N} \sum_{k=1}^{N} \left\{ \sum_{i=1}^{M} P_i \sum_{j=1}^{M} L_{ji} \sum_{s=1}^{n_i} D_j(\mathbf{x}_s^{i(k)}, \dot{\mathbf{x}}_n^{(k)}) \right.$$
$$\left. - \frac{1}{N} \sum_{k=1}^{N} \sum_{i=1}^{M} P_i \sum_{j=1}^{M} L_{ji} \sum_{s=1}^{n_i} D_j(\mathbf{x}_s^{i(k)}, \dot{\mathbf{x}}_n^{(k)}) \right\}^\delta, \qquad \delta = 2, 3, \ldots. \qquad (18)$$

Of course, $D_j(\mathbf{x}, \dot{\mathbf{x}}_n)$ describes a decision boundary as a function of $\mathbf{x}$ which depends on the particular decision rule being used. This decision boundary could vary greatly if there is a great variety of training sets and the decision rule was not prepared a priori to take this into account. There are several cases of interest worthwhile mentioning.

Case 1. μ_n^1 very large
$\bar{\mu}_n^2$ very small

This would be the case when there is large risk for all training sets.

Case 2. μ_n^1 moderately large
$\bar{\mu}_n^2$ large

This would be the case when there is large variation among the training sets, some giving low conditional risk μ_n^1 and some very high conditional risk μ_n^1.

Case 3. $R(\dot{\mathbf{x}}_n)$ has a bimodal distribution, one mode centered at a large value, and another mode centered at a small value
$\bar{\mu}_n^2$ thus is large

This would be the case where there are some training sets with large risk and some training sets with small risk.

An example of case 3 would be a group of physicians diagnosing disease with small risk and another group diagnosing disease with large risk. It obviously would be desirable to identify the presence of these two groups as the reason for the large variance in risk.

An example of case 2 is a problem where the features are so ineffective that risk is generally large.

The minimum conditional risk decision rule (Bayes) introduced in Section 3-2.4 is designed to be optimum for any training set because it uses all a priori knowledge about the underlying statistics. This Bayes framework provides us with direction as to how to repair a sample-based decision rule which is inconsistent with problem knowledge or whose performance "does not make sense." The sample-based decision rule is the way one may frequently approach a problem when he has little problem knowledge. Using the sample-based decision rule for interactive analysis, he may then proceed using the Bayes framework to design a better decision rule.

3-3.6   Asymptotic Distribution of Risk of Sample-Based Rules

It is always of interest to conjecture how well a sample-based decision rule will perform if the training set size approaches infinity. Because the performance of such a rule is implicitly characterized by the distribution function of risk by the admission of loss functions and prior probabilities, the performance of a rule as n tends to infinity can be described by the manner in which its distribution function behaves in the limit. Five natural classifications of limiting behavior are listed below in order of increasing strength:

1. $R(\dot{\mathbf{x}}_n)$ does not converge in distribution.
2. The δth moment of $R(\dot{\mathbf{x}}_n)$ converges to a constant for some δ.

3. $R(\dot{\mathbf{x}}_n)$ converges in distribution to a distribution $H(r)$.
4. $R(\dot{\mathbf{x}}_n)$ converges in probability to a constant R.
5. $R(\dot{\mathbf{x}}_n)$ converges with probability 1 to a constant R.

The literature related to the kNN type of rule is now briefly reviewed to indicate the state of theoretical research with regard to the distribution of risk. Fix and Hodges [26] essentially proved that the risk of the kNN$_1$ rule converges in probability to the Bayes risk R^* if k is permitted to increase slowly with n.

Fix and Hodges [26] determined the asymptotic expected risk for fixed k in terms of the underlying densities. Cover and Hart [15], in addition to determining the asymptotic expected risk of the kNN$_2$ rule for fixed k, demonstrated that the asymptotic expected risk is bounded by a function of R^* and obtained bounds on the rate of convergence of expected risk. Cover [27] later refined the rate of convergence of expected risk to be n^{-2} for the 1NN$_2$ rule with univariate distributions.

Peterson [28] considered in more detail some properties of convergence of expected risk by examining a term not unlike $q_j^n(\mathbf{x})$. If $q_j(\mathbf{x})$ is the limit of $q_j^n(\mathbf{x})$, it was shown that under suitable restrictions, analogously $q_j^n(\mathbf{x}) - q_j(\mathbf{x})$ converges with probability 1 to zero when $\mathbf{x}$ and the training samples are drawn at random.

3-4 Gaussian Decision Rule

3-4.1 Introduction

When $f(\mathbf{x}\,|\,i)$ is a Gaussian function with known mean $\mathbf{m}_i$ and covariance matrix $\boldsymbol{\Sigma}_i$, the minimum-probability-of-error decision rule for P_i and the number of categories M also known is: Decide class a if

$$
\frac{P_a}{|\boldsymbol{\Sigma}_a|^{1/2}(2\pi)^{L/2}} \exp[-\tfrac{1}{2}(\mathbf{x} - \mathbf{m}_a)^t\boldsymbol{\Sigma}_a^{-1}(\mathbf{x} - \mathbf{m}_a)]
$$
$$
= \max_i \left\{ \frac{P_i}{|\boldsymbol{\Sigma}_i|^{1/2}(2\pi)^{L/2}} \exp[-\tfrac{1}{2}(\mathbf{x} - \mathbf{m}_i)^t\boldsymbol{\Sigma}_i^{-1}(\mathbf{x} - \mathbf{m}_i)] \right\}_{i=1}^{M}. \tag{1}
$$

Because $\ln(\xi)$ is a monotonically increasing function of its argument ξ, the comparison in (1) is equivalent to: Decide class a if

$$
\ln P_a - \ln|\boldsymbol{\Sigma}_a|^{1/2} - \tfrac{1}{2}(\mathbf{x} - \mathbf{m}_a)^t\boldsymbol{\Sigma}_a^{-1}(\mathbf{x} - \mathbf{m}_a)
$$
$$
= \max_i \{\ln P_i - \ln|\boldsymbol{\Sigma}_i|^{1/2} - \tfrac{1}{2}(\mathbf{x} - \mathbf{m}_i)^t\boldsymbol{\Sigma}_i^{-1}(\mathbf{x} - \mathbf{m}_i)\}. \tag{2}
$$

When $M = 2$, Eq. (2) is equivalent to

$$\ln \frac{P_1 |\mathbf{\Sigma}_2|^{1/2}}{(1 - P_1)|\mathbf{\Sigma}_1|^{1/2}} - \tfrac{1}{2}[\mathbf{m}_1^t \mathbf{\Sigma}_1^{-1}\mathbf{m}_1 - \mathbf{m}_2^t \mathbf{\Sigma}_2^{-1}\mathbf{m}_2] + \tfrac{1}{2}[\mathbf{x}^t \mathbf{\Sigma}_2^{-1}\mathbf{x} - 2\mathbf{m}_2^t \mathbf{\Sigma}_2^{-1}\mathbf{x}]$$

$$- \tfrac{1}{2}[\mathbf{x}^t \mathbf{\Sigma}_1^{-1}\mathbf{x} - 2\mathbf{m}_1^t \mathbf{\Sigma}_1^{-1}\mathbf{x}] \begin{cases} > 0: & \text{decide class 1,} \\ < 0: & \text{decide class 2.} \end{cases}$$

$$(3)$$

The first term, $\ln(P_1 |\mathbf{\Sigma}_2|^{1/2}/P_2 |\mathbf{\Sigma}_1|^{1/2})$, in (3) is a "bias" term which is nonzero, for example, when $P_1 \neq \tfrac{1}{2}$ and/or $\mathbf{\Sigma}_2 \neq \mathbf{\Sigma}_1$; the second term is also a "bias" term. The terms $\mathbf{m}_i^t \mathbf{\Sigma}_i^{-1}\mathbf{x}$ represent the outputs of *matched filters* operating on $\mathbf{x}$.

Case: $\mathbf{\Sigma}_1 = \mathbf{\Sigma}_2$

When $\mathbf{\Sigma}_1 = \mathbf{\Sigma}_2 = \mathbf{\Sigma}$, terms can be conveniently grouped in (3) to produce the equivalent result,

$$2(\mathbf{m}_2 - \mathbf{m}_1)^t \mathbf{\Sigma}^{-1}\left(\mathbf{x} - \frac{\mathbf{m}_1 + \mathbf{m}_2}{2}\right) \quad \left.\right\} \underset{\omega_1}{\overset{\omega_2}{\gtrless}} b, \qquad (4)$$

where

$$b \triangleq \ln \frac{P_1}{1 - P_1}. \qquad (5)$$

Equation (4) with an equality sign is the equation of a hyperplane, $(\mathbf{m}_1 + \mathbf{m}_2)/2$ is a point on the hyperplane, and $(\mathbf{m}_2 - \mathbf{m}_1)^t \mathbf{\Sigma}^{-1}$ is a normal to the hyperplane. This hyperplane is a separating surface between the two categories for making decisions that minimize the probability of error.

Case: Diagonal Covariances

When

$$\mathbf{\Sigma}_i = \begin{bmatrix} \sigma_{i_1}^2 & 0 & \cdots & 0 \\ 0 & \sigma_{i_2}^2 & & \\ \vdots & & \ddots & \vdots \\ 0 & & & \sigma_{i_L}^2 \end{bmatrix},$$

the decision rule (2) reduces to: Decide ω_a if

$$\ln P_a - \ln\left[\prod_{j=1}^{L} \sigma_{aj}^2\right]^{1/2} - \frac{1}{2}\sum_{j=1}^{L}\frac{(x_j - m_{aj})^2}{\sigma_{aj}^2}$$

$$= \max_i\left\{\ln P_i - \ln\left[\prod_{j=1}^{L} \sigma_{ij}^2\right]^{1/2} - \frac{1}{2}\sum_{j=1}^{L}\frac{(x_j - m_{ij})^2}{\sigma_{ij}^2}\right\}_{i=1}^{M}. \qquad (6)$$

Case: **Equal Diagonal Covariances**

When the covariances are equal and diagonal,

$$\boldsymbol{\Sigma}_i = \boldsymbol{\Sigma} = \begin{bmatrix} \sigma_1^2 & 0 & \cdots & 0 \\ 0 & \sigma_2^2 & & \\ \vdots & & & \vdots \\ & & & \\ 0 & \cdots & 0 & \sigma_L^2 \end{bmatrix},$$

Eq. (6) becomes: Decide ω_a if

$$\ln P_a - \frac{1}{2}\sum_{j=1}^{L}\frac{(x_j - m_{aj})^2}{\sigma_j^2} = \max_i \left\{ \ln P_i - \frac{1}{2}\sum_{j=1}^{L}\frac{(x_j - m_{ij})^2}{\sigma_j^2}\right\}_{i=1}^{L}. \tag{7}$$

For two categories (7) is equivalent to

$$2\sum_{j=1}^{L}\frac{m_{2j} - m_{1j}}{\sigma_j^2}\left[x_j - \frac{m_{2j} + m_{1j}}{2}\right] \underset{\omega_1}{\overset{\omega_2}{\gtrless}} b. \tag{8}$$

Case: **Equal Mean Vectors**

When the mean vectors are identical, $\mathbf{m}_i$ in (2) is replaced by $\mathbf{m}$ for all i. For two categories, the decision rule simplifies to

$$(\mathbf{x} - \mathbf{m})'[-\boldsymbol{\Sigma}_1^{-1} + \boldsymbol{\Sigma}_2^{-1}](\mathbf{x} - \mathbf{m}) \underset{\omega_2}{\overset{\omega_1}{\gtrless}} 2\ln\frac{|\boldsymbol{\Sigma}_1|^{1/2}P_2}{|\boldsymbol{\Sigma}_2|^{1/2}P_1} = b'. \tag{9}$$

3-4.2 *Gaussian Decision Rule Implemented with Filters*

A philosophy in designing a communications receiver is that terms in (2) of the form

$$\ln\frac{P_i}{|\boldsymbol{\Sigma}_i|^{1/2}} - \frac{\mathbf{m}_i'\boldsymbol{\Sigma}_i^{-1}\mathbf{m}_i}{2}$$

can be computed a priori† and thus a bias term,

$$b_i = \ln\frac{P_i}{|\boldsymbol{\Sigma}_i|^{1/2}} - \tfrac{1}{2}\mathbf{m}_i'\boldsymbol{\Sigma}_i^{-1}\mathbf{m}_i \tag{10}$$

stored for the ith category. Now we shall interpret the terms

$$\mathbf{x}'\boldsymbol{\Sigma}_i^{-1}\mathbf{x}, \qquad \mathbf{m}_i'\boldsymbol{\Sigma}_i^{-1}\mathbf{x} \tag{11}$$

†In this section we are assuming that all parameters are known.

as filtering operations. From a pattern-recognition standpoint, the filtering interpretation adds little insight.

We begin by assuming a channel model: Suppose that for the ith category,

$$\mathbf{x} = \mathbf{s}_i + \mathbf{n}_i, \tag{12}$$

where $\mathbf{s}_i$ is a Gaussian signal vector with mean $\mathbf{m}_i$ and covariance $\boldsymbol{\Sigma}_{si}$ and $\mathbf{n}_i$ is a Gaussian noise vector with zero mean and covariance $\boldsymbol{\Sigma}_{ni}$. Assuming that $\mathbf{s}_i$ and $\mathbf{n}_i$ are uncorrelated, the covariance matrix $\boldsymbol{\Sigma}_i$ of $\mathbf{x}$ is

$$\boldsymbol{\Sigma}_i = E[(\mathbf{s}_i + \mathbf{n}_i)(\mathbf{s}_i + \mathbf{n}_i)^t] = \boldsymbol{\Sigma}_{si} + \boldsymbol{\Sigma}_{ni};$$

next observe that

$$\boldsymbol{\Sigma}_i^{-1} = (\boldsymbol{\Sigma}_{si} + \boldsymbol{\Sigma}_{ni})^{-1}$$

and define a matrix filter $\mathbf{H}_i$,

$$\mathbf{H}_i \triangleq \boldsymbol{\Sigma}_{si}(\boldsymbol{\Sigma}_{si} + \boldsymbol{\Sigma}_{ni})^{-1}. \tag{13}$$

Lemma

$$\boldsymbol{\Sigma}_i^{-1} = \boldsymbol{\Sigma}_{ni}^{-1}(\mathbf{I} - \mathbf{H}_i). \tag{14}$$

Proof:

$$
\begin{aligned}
\boldsymbol{\Sigma}_i^{-1} &= \boldsymbol{\Sigma}_{ni}^{-1}\boldsymbol{\Sigma}_{ni}\boldsymbol{\Sigma}_i^{-1} \\
&= \boldsymbol{\Sigma}_{ni}^{-1}[\boldsymbol{\Sigma}_i - \boldsymbol{\Sigma}_{si}]\boldsymbol{\Sigma}_i^{-1} \\
&= \boldsymbol{\Sigma}_{ni}^{-1}[\mathbf{I} - \boldsymbol{\Sigma}_{si}\boldsymbol{\Sigma}_i^{-1}] \\
&= \boldsymbol{\Sigma}_{ni}^{-1} - \boldsymbol{\Sigma}_{ni}^{-1}\boldsymbol{\Sigma}_{si}\boldsymbol{\Sigma}_i^{-1} \\
&= \boldsymbol{\Sigma}_{ni}^{-1} - \boldsymbol{\Sigma}_{ni}^{-1}\mathbf{H}_i.
\end{aligned}
$$

Applying the lemma to the terms (11),

$$
\begin{aligned}
\mathbf{x}^t\boldsymbol{\Sigma}_i^{-1}\mathbf{x} &= \mathbf{x}^t\boldsymbol{\Sigma}_{ni}^{-1}\mathbf{x} - \mathbf{x}^t\boldsymbol{\Sigma}_{ni}^{-1}\mathbf{H}_i\mathbf{x}, \\
\mathbf{m}_i^t\boldsymbol{\Sigma}_i^{-1}\mathbf{x} &= \mathbf{m}_i^t\boldsymbol{\Sigma}_{ni}^{-1}\mathbf{x} - \mathbf{m}_i^t\boldsymbol{\Sigma}_{ni}^{-1}\mathbf{H}_i\mathbf{x}.
\end{aligned} \tag{15}
$$

With b_i given by (10) and using the definition of H_i, the decision rule (2) is equivalent to: Decide class ω_a if

$$c_a = \max_i \{c_i\}_{i=1}^M,$$

where c_i is obtained for each class according to Figure 3.3. In the figure the

    Decision Rules for Use in Pattern Recognition   Chap. 3

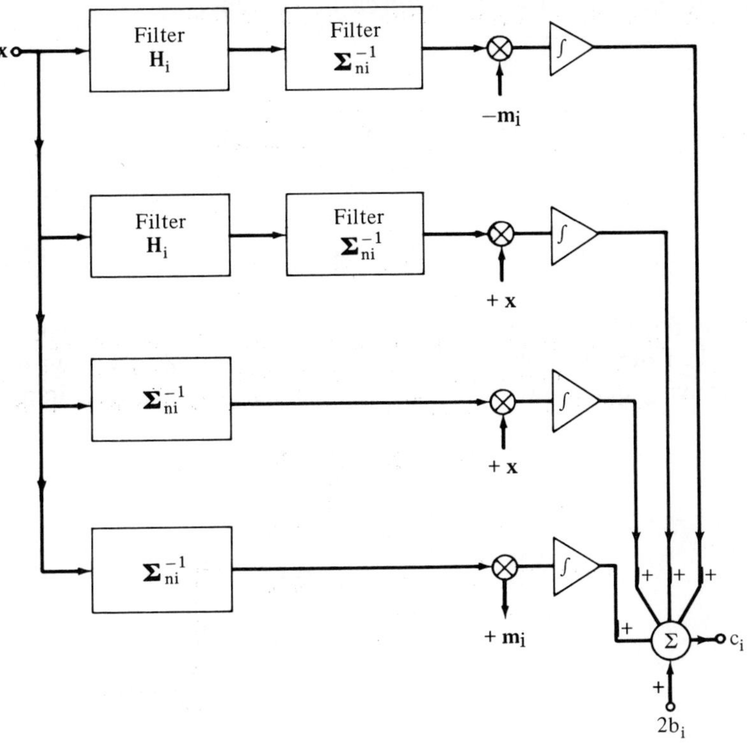

Fig. 3.3 Gaussian Decision Rule implemented with filters

operation denoted

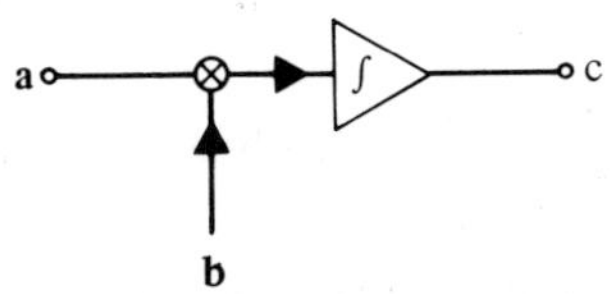

means

$$c = \mathbf{a}^t\mathbf{b}$$

and Fig. 3.BB adds

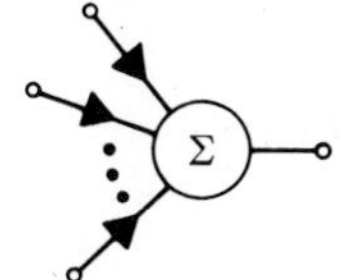

scalars. A filter, shown below, performs the operation

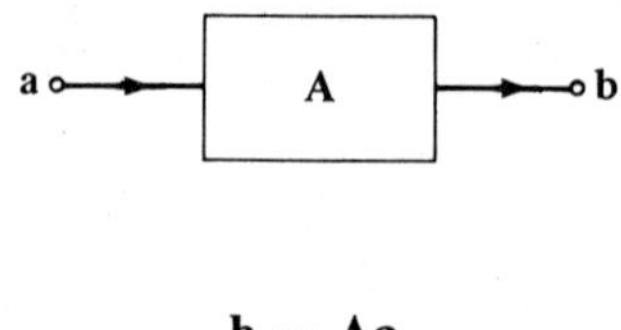

$$\mathbf{b} = \mathbf{Aa}.$$

The filter implementation shown in Figure 3.3 does not seem to offer much when digital implementation is used because the Gaussian decision rule involving quadratic forms (2) (see Figure 3.4) is simpler to implement.

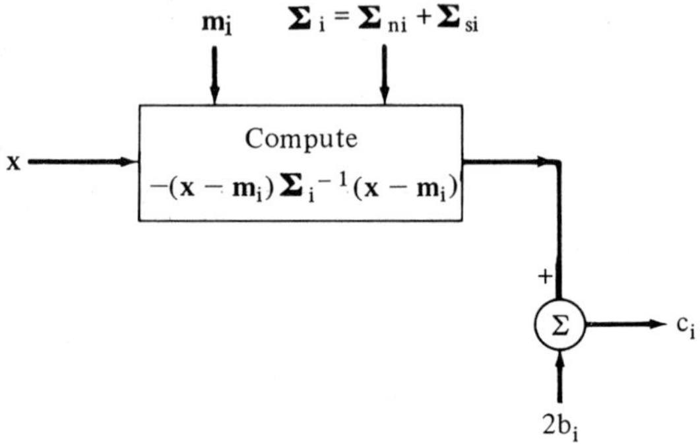

Fig. 3.4 Gaussian Decision Rule implemented with quadratics

The quadratic form $(\mathbf{x} - \mathbf{m}_i)\mathbf{\Sigma}^{-1}(\mathbf{x} - \mathbf{m}_i) = (\mathbf{x} - \mathbf{m}_i)\mathbf{A}(\mathbf{x} - \mathbf{m}_i)$ is simply

$$\sum_{k=1}^{L} \sum_{j=1}^{L} (x_k - m_{ik})(x_j - m_{ij})a_{kj}$$

and is easily computed using software or special-purpose hardware implementation. The most time-consuming operation involves obtaining the inverse covariance matrix $\mathbf{A}$ from $\mathbf{\Sigma}$.

It is worthwhile to point out that when $\mathbf{\Sigma}_{si} = \mathbf{0}$ (fixed signal), $\mathbf{\Sigma}_{ni} = \mathbf{I}$ (white noise),

$$c_i = \mathbf{x}'\mathbf{m}_i,$$

which is the classical *matched filter*.

     Decision Rules for Use in Pattern Recognition   Chap. 3

Example

As a communications example,† let

$$\mathbf{x} = \mathbf{n}: \qquad \omega_1,$$
$$\mathbf{x} = \mathbf{n} + \mathbf{s}: \qquad \omega_2,$$

$$\text{Cov}\,[\mathbf{x}\,|\,\omega_1] = \mathbf{K}_n = \sigma_n^2\mathbf{I},$$
$$\text{Cov}\,[\mathbf{x}\,|\,\omega_2] = \mathbf{K}_s + \mathbf{K}_n.$$

Then

$$\mathbf{A}_1 = \frac{1}{\sigma_n^2}\mathbf{I},$$

$$\mathbf{A}_2 = (\mathbf{K}_s + \sigma_n^2\mathbf{I})^{-1} = \frac{1}{\sigma_n^2}\left(\mathbf{I} + \frac{\mathbf{K}_s}{\sigma_n^2}\right)^{-1}.$$

If

$$\mathbf{H} = \mathbf{K}_s(\sigma_n^2\mathbf{I} + \mathbf{K}_s)^{-1}, \tag{16}$$

then

$$\left(\mathbf{I} + \frac{\mathbf{K}_s}{\sigma_n^2}\right)^{-1} = \left[\mathbf{I} + \left(\frac{\mathbf{K}_s}{\sigma_n^2} - \frac{\mathbf{K}_s}{\sigma_n^2}\right)\right]\left(\mathbf{I} + \frac{\mathbf{K}_s}{\sigma_n^2}\right)^{-1}$$

$$= \left[\left(\mathbf{I} + \frac{\mathbf{K}_s}{\sigma_n^2}\right) - \frac{\mathbf{K}_s}{\sigma_n^2}\right]\left(\mathbf{I} + \frac{\mathbf{K}_s}{\sigma_n^2}\right)^{-1} \tag{17}$$

$$= [\mathbf{I} - \mathbf{K}_s(_n^2\mathbf{I} + \mathbf{K}_s)^{-1}] = \mathbf{I} - \mathbf{H}.$$

In terms of (17),

$$\mathbf{A}_2 = \frac{\mathbf{I} - \mathbf{H}}{\sigma_n^2},$$

$$\Delta\mathbf{A} = \frac{-\mathbf{H}}{\sigma_n^2};$$

thus

$$d(\mathbf{x}) = \frac{-\mathbf{x}'\mathbf{H}\mathbf{x}}{\sigma_n^2} \underset{\omega_2}{\overset{\omega_1}{\gtrless}} b'. \tag{18}$$

Now if

$$\mathbf{K}_s = \sigma_s^2\mathbf{I},$$

†Class ω_1 is noise only and class ω_2 is signal and noise. The distribution of s is Gaussian with **0** mean. (Although a signal may be nonzero, the average signal is zero.)

then

$$\mathbf{H} = (\sigma_n^2 \mathbf{I} + \sigma_s^2 \mathbf{I})^{-1} \sigma_s^2 \mathbf{I}$$

$$= \frac{\sigma_s^2}{\sigma_n^2 + \sigma_s^2} \mathbf{I},$$

$$d(\mathbf{x}) = \frac{-\sigma_s^2}{\sigma_n^2(\sigma_n^2 + \sigma_s^2)} \mathbf{x}^t \mathbf{x}$$

$$= \frac{-\sigma_s^2}{\sigma_n^2(\sigma_n^2 + \sigma_s^2)} \sum_{i=1}^{L} x_i^2 \underset{\omega_2}{\overset{\omega_1}{\gtrless}} b'. \tag{19}$$

If

$$\mathbf{K}_s = \begin{bmatrix} \sigma_{s_1}^2 & & & & \\ & \sigma_{s_2}^2 & & & \\ & & \cdot & & \\ & & & \cdot & \\ & & & & \sigma_{s_L}^2 \end{bmatrix},$$

then

$$\mathbf{H} = \begin{bmatrix} \dfrac{\sigma_{s_1}^2}{\sigma_n^2 + \sigma_{s_1}^2} & & & \\ & \cdot & & \\ & & \cdot & \\ & & & \dfrac{\sigma_{s_L}^2}{\sigma_n^2 + \sigma_{s_L}^2} \end{bmatrix}, \tag{20}$$

$$d(\mathbf{x}) = \sum_{j=1}^{L} \frac{-\sigma_{s_j}^2}{\sigma_n^2(\sigma_n^2 + \sigma_{s_j}^2)} x_j^2 \underset{\omega_2}{\overset{\omega_1}{\gtrless}} b'.$$

3-4.3 *Performance of Gaussian Decision Rule, M = 2*
A. $\boldsymbol{\Sigma}_1 = \boldsymbol{\Sigma}_2$

Again considering two categories ($M = 2$), rewrite (4) as

$$(\mathbf{m}_2 - \mathbf{m}_1)^t \mathbf{A} \mathbf{x} \underset{\omega_1}{\overset{\omega_2}{\gtrless}} \tfrac{1}{2}(\mathbf{m}_2^t \mathbf{A} \mathbf{m}_2 - \mathbf{m}_1^t \mathbf{A} \mathbf{m}_1 + b) = b'', \tag{21}$$

where we have let $\mathbf{A} = \boldsymbol{\Sigma}^{-1}$ and b is given by (5). Define

$$\Delta \mathbf{m} = \mathbf{m}_2 - \mathbf{m}_1. \tag{22}$$

Then the decision equation in terms of $\mathbf{\Delta m}$ is

$$d(\mathbf{x}) = \mathbf{\Delta m}^t \mathbf{A} \mathbf{x} \underset{\omega_1}{\overset{\omega_2}{\gtrless}} b'', \tag{23}$$

where $d(\mathbf{x})$ used here is a distance measure. Since $d(\mathbf{x})$ is a result of linear operations on $\mathbf{x}$, it is a Gaussian random variable with the mean vector and variance depending on whether ω_1 or ω_2 is active (refer to Fig. 3.5).

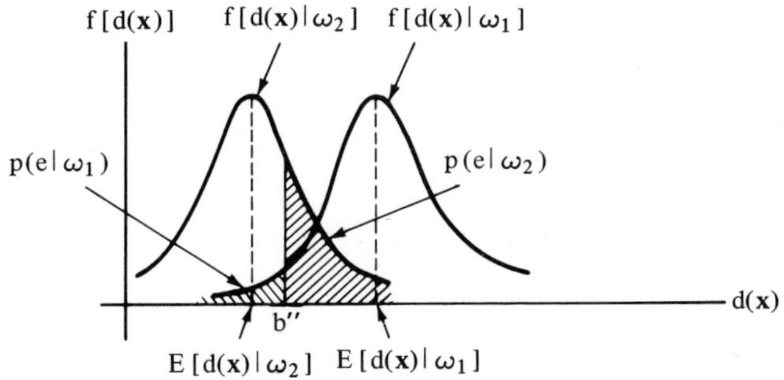

Fig. 3.5 Density function of $d(\mathbf{x})|\omega_i$

Observe that

$$E[d(\mathbf{x})|\omega_i] = \mathbf{\Delta m}^t \mathbf{A} E[\mathbf{x}|\omega_i] = \mathbf{\Delta m}^t \mathbf{A} \mathbf{m}_i, \tag{24}$$

and

$$
\begin{aligned}
\mathrm{Var}[d(\mathbf{x})|\omega_1] &= E\{[\mathbf{\Delta m}^t \mathbf{A}(\mathbf{x} - \mathbf{m}_i)]^2\} \\
&= E\{[\mathbf{\Delta m}^t \mathbf{A}(\mathbf{x} - \mathbf{m}_i)][(\mathbf{x} - \mathbf{m}_i)^t \mathbf{A} \mathbf{\Delta m}\} \\
&= \mathbf{\Delta m}^t \mathbf{A} \Sigma_i \mathbf{A} \mathbf{\Delta m} \\
&= \mathbf{\Delta m}^t \mathbf{A} \mathbf{\Delta m}.
\end{aligned}
\tag{25}
$$

Let $p(e)$, $p(e|\omega_1)$, and $p(e|\omega_2)$ denote, respectively, the probability of error, the probability of error if ω_1 is active, and the probability of error if ω_2 is active. To calculate $p(e|\omega_i)$, define c_i

$$c_i = \frac{b'' - E[d(\mathbf{x})|\omega_i]}{\sqrt{\mathrm{Var}[d(\mathbf{x})|\omega_i]}}.$$

Then,

$$p(e|\omega_1) = \int_{-\infty}^{b''} \frac{1}{\sqrt{2\pi\,\mathrm{Var}[d(\mathbf{x})|\omega_1]}} \exp\left(-\frac{1}{2}\frac{\{\xi - E[d(\mathbf{x})|\omega_1]\}^2}{\mathrm{Var}[d(\mathbf{x})|\omega_1]}\right) d\xi$$

$$= \mathrm{erf}_*(c_1) \tag{26a}$$

and

$$p(e\,|\,\omega_2) = \int_{b''}^{\infty} \frac{1}{\sqrt{2\pi\,\operatorname{Var}[d(\mathbf{x})\,|\,\omega_2]}}\,\exp\!\left(-\frac{1}{2}\frac{\{\xi - E[d(\mathbf{x})\,|\,\omega_2]\}^2}{\operatorname{Var}[d(\mathbf{x})\,|\,\omega_2]}\right)d\xi$$
$$= \operatorname{erfc}_*(c_2), \tag{26b}$$

where

$$\operatorname{erf}_*(y) = \int_{-\infty}^{y} \frac{1}{\sqrt{2\pi}}\,\exp(-\tfrac{1}{2}\xi^2)\,d\xi$$

and

$$\operatorname{erfc}_*(y) = \int_{y}^{\infty} \frac{1}{\sqrt{2\pi}}\,\exp(-\tfrac{1}{2}\xi^2)\,d\xi$$

are tabulated functions related by

$$\operatorname{erf}_*(-y) = \operatorname{erfc}_*(y).$$

The probability of error is

$$\begin{aligned}
p(e) &= P_1\,p(e\,|\,\omega_1) + P_2\,p(e\,|\,\omega_2) \\
&= P_1\,\operatorname{erf}_*(c_1) + P_2\,\operatorname{erfc}_*(c_2).
\end{aligned} \tag{27}$$

When $P_1 = P_2 = \tfrac{1}{2}$, it is useful to define the normalized $(\operatorname{Var}[d(\mathbf{x})\,|\,\omega_1] = \operatorname{Var}[d(\mathbf{x})\,|\,\omega_2])$ distance between means,

$$\begin{aligned}
r &= \frac{E[d(\mathbf{x})\,|\,\omega_1] - E[d(\mathbf{x})\,|\,\omega_2]}{\sqrt{\operatorname{Var}[d(\mathbf{x})\,|\,\omega_1]}} = \Delta\mathbf{m}^t\mathbf{A}\mathbf{m}_1 - \Delta\mathbf{m}^t\mathbf{A}\mathbf{m}_2 \\
&= (\Delta\mathbf{m}^t\mathbf{A}\Delta\mathbf{m})^{1/2}.
\end{aligned} \tag{28}$$

It follows that

$$-c_1 = \frac{r}{2} = c_2$$

and thus

$$\begin{aligned}
p(e) &= \frac{1}{2}\operatorname{erf}_*\!\left(-\frac{r}{2}\right) + \frac{1}{2}\operatorname{erfc}_*\!\left(\frac{r}{2}\right) \\
&= \operatorname{erfc}_*\!\left(\frac{r}{2}\right).
\end{aligned} \tag{29}$$

   Decision Rules for Use in Pattern Recognition   Chap. 3

Thus the performance of the Gaussian decision rule for two categories with equal covariances is entirely determined by the quadratic form $\Delta\mathbf{m}'\mathbf{A}\,\Delta\mathbf{m}$ and b''. An example of performance calculation using this result will be presented shortly.

Orthogonal Transformation

If $\mathbf{y} = \mathbf{Bx}$, then

$$\begin{aligned}
\mathbf{\Sigma}^y &\triangleq E[(\mathbf{y} - E[\mathbf{y}])(\mathbf{y} - E[\mathbf{y}])'] \\
&= E[\mathbf{B}(\mathbf{x} - E[\mathbf{x}])(\mathbf{x} - E[\mathbf{x}])'\mathbf{B}'] \\
&= \mathbf{B}\mathbf{\Sigma}^x\mathbf{B}' \triangleq \mathbf{D}.
\end{aligned}$$

If $\mathbf{B}$ is an orthogonal matrix whose columns are eigenvectors of $\mathbf{\Sigma}^x$, then

$$\mathbf{\Sigma}^y = \begin{bmatrix} \lambda_1 & & & & \\ & \lambda_2 & & & \\ & & \cdot & & \\ & & & \cdot & \\ & & & & \lambda_L \end{bmatrix},$$

where $\lambda_1, \lambda_2, \ldots, \lambda_L$ are eigenvalues of $\mathbf{\Sigma}^x$. Then for the two-category case with $\mathbf{\Sigma}_1 = \mathbf{\Sigma}_2 = \mathbf{\Sigma}^x$,

$$\Delta\mathbf{m} = \mathbf{B}^{-1}E[\mathbf{y}\,|\,\omega_2] - \mathbf{B}^{-1}E[\mathbf{y}\,|\,\omega_1] = \mathbf{B}^{-1}[\mathbf{\mu}_2 - \mathbf{\mu}_1] = \mathbf{B}^{-1}\,\Delta\mathbf{m}',$$

where $\Delta\mathbf{m}' = [\mathbf{\mu}_2 - \mathbf{\mu}_1]$, and

$$\begin{aligned}
d(\mathbf{y}) &= \Delta\mathbf{m}'(\mathbf{\Sigma}^x)^{-1}\mathbf{B}^{-1}\mathbf{y} \\
&= (\Delta\mathbf{m}')'(\mathbf{B}^{-1})'(\mathbf{\Sigma}^x)^{-1}\mathbf{B}^{-1}\mathbf{y} \\
&= (\Delta\mathbf{m}')'\mathbf{D}^{-1}\mathbf{y} \\
&= \sum_{j=1}^{L} \frac{\Delta m'_j}{\lambda_j}\, y_j.
\end{aligned} \tag{30}$$

Note that (30) is identical in form to that for $d(\mathbf{x})$ when $\mathbf{\Sigma}$ is a diagonal covariance matrix; then

$$d(\mathbf{x}) = \sum_{j=1}^{L} \frac{\Delta m_j}{\sigma_j^2}\, x_j. \tag{31}$$

If $\Delta m_j = \Delta m$ and $\sigma_j^2 = \sigma^2$, we have that

$$r^2 = L\frac{\Delta m^2}{\sigma^2},$$

which shows the basic result—that the distance between categories goes up linearly as dimensionality goes up if the signal-to-noise ratio is the same in each dimension. In practice, however, researchers have observed that increasing dimensionality can "degrade performance." It should be stressed that the above results presume that the parameters (means and variances) are known; if not known, they can be a "nuisance." Thus, one must be sure that *the increasing number of parameters are being properly estimated as dimensionality increases.*

B. Equal Mean Vectors

If $\mathbf{m}_1 = \mathbf{m}_2 = \mathbf{m}$ but $\boldsymbol{\Sigma}_1 \neq \boldsymbol{\Sigma}_2$ and we define

$$\Delta\mathbf{A} \triangleq \boldsymbol{\Sigma}_2^{-1} - \boldsymbol{\Sigma}_1^{-1},$$

$$\mathbf{y} = (\mathbf{x} - \mathbf{m}),$$

then, from (9),

$$d(\mathbf{y}) = \mathbf{y}^t \Delta\mathbf{A} \mathbf{y} \underset{\omega_2}{\overset{\omega_1}{\gtrless}} b'.$$

Performance can be evaluated under certain conditions on $\boldsymbol{\Sigma}_1$ and $\boldsymbol{\Sigma}_2$ leading to $d(\mathbf{y})$ having a Γ distribution. (Do problem 17).

C. Example of Performance Calculation

When

$$M = 2,$$

$$P_1 = P_2 = \frac{1}{2}$$

$$\Delta m_i \triangleq \Delta m,$$

$$\boldsymbol{\Sigma}_i = \sigma^2 \mathbf{I},$$

$$\frac{m_{2j} + m_{1j}}{2} = x_B, \text{ for all } j,$$

then in terms of the decision boundary x_B,

$$d(\mathbf{x}) = \sum_{j=1}^{L} \frac{\Delta m}{2} \left[x_j - \frac{m_{2j} + m_{1j}}{2} \right] \underset{\omega_1}{\overset{\omega_2}{\gtrless}} b,$$

or

$$d(x) = \left[\sum_{j=1}^{L} \frac{\Delta m}{\sigma^2} x_j \right] - \frac{L \, \Delta m x_B}{2\sigma^2} \underset{\omega_1}{\overset{\omega_2}{\gtrless}} b,$$

and

$$r^2 = \frac{L\,\Delta m^2}{\sigma^2}.$$

Thus the probability of error is $\mathrm{erfc}_*\!\left(\dfrac{\sqrt{L}\,\Delta m}{2\sigma}\right).$

Antipodal Mean Vectors

Suppose $\mathbf{m}_1 = \mathbf{m}$ and $\mathbf{m}_2 = -\mathbf{m}$, $\boldsymbol{\Sigma}_1 = \boldsymbol{\Sigma}_2 = \sigma^2\mathbf{I}$, and average signal energy is

$$E = \sum_{i=1}^{L} m_i^2 = \mathbf{m}^t\mathbf{m}.$$

Then

$$r^2 = \frac{2\mathbf{m}^t 2\mathbf{m}}{\sigma^2} = \frac{4\mathbf{m}^t\mathbf{m}}{\sigma^2} = \frac{4E}{\sigma^2}.$$

Thus

$$P[e] = \mathrm{erfc}_*\!\left(\frac{\sqrt{E}}{\sigma}\right). \tag{32}$$

Orthogonal Signals

If $\mathbf{m}_2$ and $\mathbf{m}_1$ are orthogonal, then $\mathbf{m}_2^t\mathbf{m}_1 = 0$. Assuming $\boldsymbol{\Sigma}_1 = \boldsymbol{\Sigma}_2 = \sigma^2\mathbf{I}$, $E = \mathbf{m}_2^t\mathbf{m}_2 = \mathbf{m}_1^t\mathbf{m}_1$, then

$$r^2 = \frac{(\mathbf{m}_2 - \mathbf{m}_1)^t(\mathbf{m}_2 - \mathbf{m}_1)}{\sigma^2} = \frac{\mathbf{m}_2^t\mathbf{m}_2 + \mathbf{m}_1^t\mathbf{m}_1}{\sigma^2} = \frac{2E}{\sigma^2}.$$

Thus

$$P[e] = \mathrm{erfc}_*\!\left(\frac{\sqrt{E}}{\sqrt{2}\,\sigma}\right). \tag{33}$$

3-4.4 Decision Rule for Each Category a Mixture of Gaussians

Suppose that

$$f(\mathbf{x}\,|\,i) = \sum_{j=1}^{M_i} f(\mathbf{x}\,|\,\mathbf{m}_{ij},\,\boldsymbol{\Sigma}_{ij})P_{ij}$$

such that the minimum probability of error decision rule is: Decide class ω_a if

$$\sum_{j=1}^{M_a} \frac{P_{aj}}{|\boldsymbol{\Sigma}_{aj}|^{1/2}(2\pi)^{L/2}} \exp[-\tfrac{1}{2}(\mathbf{x} - \mathbf{m}_{aj})'\boldsymbol{\Sigma}_{aj}^{-1}(\mathbf{x} - \mathbf{m}_{aj})]$$

$$= \max_{i}\left\{ \sum_{j=1}^{M_i} \frac{P_{ij}}{|\boldsymbol{\Sigma}_{ij}|^{1/2}(2\pi)^{L/2}} \exp[-\tfrac{1}{2}(\mathbf{x} - \mathbf{m}_{ij})'\boldsymbol{\Sigma}_{ij}^{-1}(\mathbf{x} - \mathbf{m}_{ij})]\right\}_{i=1}^{M}.$$

If the decision rule is implemented using filters, for the ith category, M_i systems, each of the form shown in Figure 3.3, are required. If the decision rule is implemented using quadratics, for the ith category, M_i systems, each of the form shown in Figure 3.4 are required.

If M_i and the parameters characterizing the M_i quadratics are unknown, they must be determined from samples with distribution $f(\mathbf{x}\mid i)$ using unsupervised estimation techniques. Some of the most practical techniques are clustering techniques for accomplishing this.

Suggested Reading for Chapter 3

[1] S. S. Wilks, *Mathematical Statistics*, John Wiley & Sons, Inc., New York, 1963.

[2] C. W. Helstrom, *Statistical Theory of Signal Detection*, Vol. 9, 2nd ed., Pergamon Press, Oxford, 1968, p. 470.

[3] J. C. Hancock and P. A. Wintz, *Signal Detection Theory*, McGraw-Hill Book Company, Inc., New York, p. 247, 1966.

[4] N. J. Nilsson, *Learning Machines*, McGraw-Hill Book Company, Inc., New York, 1965.

[5] Lionel Weiss, *Statistical Decision Theory*, McGraw-Hill Book Company, Inc., New York, 1961.

[6] H. L. Van Trees, *Detection, Estimation, and Modulation Theory*, John Wiley & Sons, Inc., New York, 1968.

[7] J. M. Wozencraft and I. M. Jacobs, *Principles of Communication Engineering*, John Wiley & Sons, Inc., New York, 1965.

[8] F. Rosenblatt, *Principles of Neurodynamics: Perceptrons and the Theory of Brain Mechanism*, Spartan Books, Washington, D.C., 1962.

[9] G. S. Sebestyen, *Decision Making Processes in Pattern Recognition*, The Macmillan Company, New York, 1962.

[10] S. Kullback, *Information Theory and Statistics*, John Wiley & Sons, Inc., New York, 1959.

[11] J. B. Thomas, *An Introduction to Statistical Communication Theory*, John Wiley & Sons, Inc., New York, 1969.

[12] H. R. Raemer, *Statistical Communication Theory and Applications*, Prentice-Hall, Inc., Englewood Cliffs, N.J., 1969.

[13] T. Kailath, A General Likelihood-Ratio Formula for Random Signals in Gaussian Noise, *IEEE Trans. Information Theory*, Vol. IT-15, pp. 350–361, May 1960.

[14] T. Kailath, Likelihood Ratios for Gaussian Processes, *IEEE Trans. Information Theory*, Vol. IT-16, pp. 276–288, May 1970.

[15] T. M. Cover and P. E. Hart, Nearest Neighbor Pattern Classification, *IEEE Trans. Information Theory*, Vol. IT-13, No. 1, pp. 21–27, Jan. 1967.

[16] T. M. Cover, Estimation by the Nearest Neighbor Rule, *IEEE Trans. Information Theory*, Vol. IT-14, No. 1, pp. 50–55, 1968.

[17] P. E. Hart, The Condensed Nearest Neighbor Rule, *IEEE Trans. Information Theory*, Vol. IT, pp. 515–516, May 1968.

[18] E. A. Patrick and F. P. Fischer, II, A Generalization of the k-Nearest Neighbor Decision Rule, presented at the 1969 International Joint Conference on Artificial Intelligence, May 1969.

[19] E. A. Patrick and F. P. Fischer, A Generalized k-Nearest Neighbor Decision Rule, *Information and Control*, Vol. 16, No. 2, pp. 128–152, Apr. 1970.

[20] G. Nagy, State of the Art in Pattern Recognition, *Proc. IEEE*, Vol. 56, No. 5, pp. 836–862, May 1968.

[21] Y.-C. Ho and A. K. Agrawala, On Pattern Classification Algorithms—Introduction and Survey, *Proc. IEEE*, Vol. 56, No. 12, pp. 2101–2114, Dec. 1968.

[22] D. B. Cooper and P. W. Cooper, Nonsupervised Adaptive Signal Detection and Pattern Recognition, *Information and Control*, Vol. 7, No. 3, pp. 416–444, Sept. 1964.

[23] E. A. Patrick and G. Carayannopoulos, Codes for Unsupervised Learning of Source and Binary Channel Probabilities, *Information and Control*, Vol. 14, No. 4, pp. 358–375, April 1969.

[24] E. A. Patrick and J. P. Costello, Asymptotic Probability of Error Using Two Decision Directed Estimators for Two Unknown Mean Vectors, *IEEE Trans. Information Theory*, Vol. IT-14, No. 1, pp. 160–162, Jan. 1968.

[25] E. A. Patrick, Distribution Free, Minimum Conditional Risk Learning Systems, *Purdue University School of Electrical Engineering Tech. Rept.* EE 68–18, Nov. 1966.

[26] E. Fix and J. L. Hodges, Jr., Discriminatory Analysis: Nonparametric Discrimination: Consistency Properties, *USAF School of Aviation Medicine, Project 21–49–004, Rept. 4*, Randolph Field, Texas, Feb. 1951.

[27] T. M. Cover, Rates of Convergence for Nearest Neighbor Procedures, *First Annual International Conference on System Sciences*, B. K. Kinariwala, ed., University of Hawaii Press, Honolulu, Hawaii, Jan. 1968.

[28] D. W. Peterson, Some Convergence Properties of a Nearest Neighbor Decision Rule, *IEEE Trans. Information Theory*, Vol. IT-16, No. 1, pp. 26–31, 1970.

[29] E. S. McShane and T. A. Botts, *Real Analysis*, Van Nostrand Reinhold, New York, 1956.

[30] K. Pearson, *Tables of the Incomplete Γ-Function*, Cambridge University Press, Cambridge, 1934.

Problems

[1] Let $M = 2$, $L = 1$, and $\mathscr{F}$ be a Gaussian family of density functions and assume a loss matrix.

   (a) Construct the decision regions $\mathscr{D}_1$ and $\mathscr{D}_2$ for the minimum-risk decision rule [Eq. (12) of Section 3-2.3] using estimated values $\tilde{m}_1, \tilde{\sigma}_1, P_1$, and $\tilde{m}_2, \tilde{\sigma}_2, P_2$ for the class 1 and class 2 parameters, respectively.

   (b) Suppose the true parameters are m_1^*, σ_1^*, P_1^* and m_2^*, σ_2^*, P_2^*. Obtain an expression for risk, $R(\tilde{P}_1, \tilde{m}_1, \tilde{m}_2, \tilde{\sigma}_1, \tilde{\sigma}_2; P_1^*, m_1^*, m_2^*, \sigma_1^*, \sigma_2^*)$, introduced in Section 3-2.3.

   (c) Determine if

$$R(\tilde{P}_1, \tilde{m}_1, \tilde{m}_2, \tilde{\sigma}_1, \tilde{\sigma}_2; P_1^*, m_1^*, m_2^*, \sigma_1^*, \sigma_2^*)$$

$$\geq R(P_1^*, m_1^*, m_2^*, \sigma_1^*, \sigma_2^*; P_1^*, m_1^*, m_2^*, \sigma_1^*, \sigma_2^*).$$

[2] (a) For the example in Problem 1, compute the decision regions $\mathscr{D}_1$ and $\mathscr{D}_2$ first using estimated parameters,

$$\tilde{\mathbf{b}} = (\tilde{m}_1, \tilde{\sigma}_1, \tilde{P}_1, \tilde{m}_2, \tilde{\sigma}_2, \tilde{P}_2)$$

and next using true parameters,

$$\mathbf{b}^* = (m_1^*, \sigma_1^*, P_1^*, m_2^*, \sigma_2^*, P_2^*).$$

   (b) Using $\tilde{\mathbf{b}}$ for the decision rule, compute the risk $R(\tilde{\mathbf{b}}, \mathbf{b}^*)$. Using $\mathbf{b}^*$ for the decision rule, compute the risk $R(\mathbf{b}^*, \mathbf{b}^*)$.

   (c) Show that $R(\tilde{\mathbf{b}}, \mathbf{b}^*) \geq R(\mathbf{b}^*, \mathbf{b}^*)$.

[3] When decision regions $\mathscr{D}_1$ and $\mathscr{D}_2$ are constructed using estimated parameters $\tilde{\mathbf{b}}$, the increase in risk $R(\tilde{\mathbf{b}}, \mathbf{b}^*) - R(\mathbf{b}^*, \mathbf{b}^*)$ over using the true parameter should be a function of dimensionality L and the number of parameters in $\mathbf{b}^*$. Discuss the seriousness of using a bad a priori guess $\tilde{\mathbf{b}}$, as dimensionality L increases and as the number of parameters increases.

[4] (a) Show that

$$\left[\sum_{i=1}^{M} \sum_{j=1}^{M} c_{ji} \int_{\mathscr{x}} d_{ji}(\mathbf{x})\, d\mathbf{x} \right]^{\delta} \tag{a1}$$

$$= \prod_{v=1}^{\delta} \left[\sum_{i_v=1}^{M} \sum_{j_v=1}^{M} c_{j_v i_v} \int d_{j_v i_v}(\mathbf{x}^{(v)})\, d\mathbf{x}^{(v)} \right] \tag{a2}$$

$$= \sum_{i_1=1}^{M} \sum_{j_1=1}^{M} \cdots \sum_{i_\delta=1}^{M} \sum_{j_\delta=1}^{M} \left[\prod_{v=1}^{\delta} c_{j_v i_v} \int d_{j_v i_v}(\mathbf{x}^{(v)})\, d\mathbf{x}^{(v)} \right] \tag{a3}$$

by using a result that a product of sums equals a sum of products.

(b) Convince yourself that Eq. (6) of Section 3-3.2 can be greatly simplified. Form (a3) has merit when $\int_{\mathbf{x}} d_{jvi_v}(\mathbf{x}^v)\, d\mathbf{x}^v$ is, say, zero for certain values of $(j_v, i_v, \mathbf{x}^v)$.

[5] Show that because $\prod_{v=1}^{\delta} D_{j_v}(\mathbf{x}^{(v)}; \dot{\mathbf{x}}_n)$ is a $\beta^{\delta+n}$-measurable, nonnegative function on $\mathcal{X}^{\delta+n}$, Fubini's theorem ([29], p. 136) can be applied to obtain (9) and (10) from (8), Section 3-3.2.

. [6] Show that

$$(\mu_n^1)^{\delta-w} = \sum_{i_{w+1}=1}^{M} \sum_{j_{w+1}=1}^{M} \cdots \sum_{i_{\delta}=1}^{M} \sum_{j_{\delta}=1}^{M} \left\{ \prod_{v=w+1}^{\delta} [P_{i_v} L_{j_v i_v}] \right.$$

$$\times \int_{\mathcal{X}}^{\delta-w} \cdots \int_{\mathcal{X}} q_{j_{w+1}}(\mathbf{x}^{(w+1)}) \cdots q_{j_{\delta}}(\mathbf{x}^{(\delta)})$$

$$\times \left. dF(\mathbf{x}^{(w+1)}\,|\,\omega_{i_{w+1}}) \cdots dF(\mathbf{x}^{(v)}\,|\,\omega_{i_v}) \right\}.$$

[7] Verify Eq. (15) for the δth central moment $\bar{\mu}_n^{\delta}$ obtained in Section 3-3.3.

[8] Write a Fortran IV computer program implementing the minimum-probability-of-error decision rule for $\mathcal{F}$ Gaussian and all parameters $\{P_i, \Sigma_i, \mathbf{m}_i\}_{i=1}^{M}$ known [Eq. (1) of Section 3-4.1]: Decide class ω_a if

$$\frac{P_a}{|\Sigma_a|^{1/2}(2\pi)^{L/2}} \exp[-\tfrac{1}{2}(\mathbf{x} - \mathbf{m}_a)^t \Sigma_a^{-1}(\mathbf{x} - \mathbf{m}_a)]$$

$$= \max_i \left\{ \frac{P_i}{|\Sigma_i|^{1/2}(2\pi)^{L/2}} \exp[-\tfrac{1}{2}(\mathbf{x} - \mathbf{m}_i)^t \Sigma_i^{-1}(\mathbf{x} - \mathbf{m}_i)] \right\}_{i=1}^{M}.$$

[9] Write a Fortran IV computer program implementing the above Gaussian decision rule for $M = 2$, $\Sigma_1 = \Sigma_2 = \Sigma$:

$$2(\mathbf{m}_2 - \mathbf{m}_1)^t \Sigma^{-1} \left(\mathbf{x} - \frac{\mathbf{m}_1 + \mathbf{m}_2}{2} \right) \underset{\omega_1}{\overset{\omega_2}{\gtrless}} b,$$

where

$$b = \ln \frac{P_1}{1 - P_1}.$$

[10] (a) Write a Fortran IV computer program implementing the $k\text{NN}_3$ decision rule for $\Phi_1 = \Phi_2$, but $\{k_i, n_i, P_i\}_{i=1}^{M}$ all arbitrary. Use a distance measure $d_i(\mathbf{x}, \mathbf{y}) = |\mathbf{x} - \mathbf{y}|$ for class i, $i = 1, 2, \ldots, M$, to determine the neighborhood.

(b) Suppose that $d_i(\mathbf{x}, \mathbf{y}) = (\mathbf{y} - \mathbf{x})^t \Sigma_i^{-1}(\mathbf{y} - \mathbf{x})$ for Σ_i an appropriately defined covariance matrix "at point $\mathbf{x}$." Can you suggest a way to estimate Σ_i and use $d_i(\mathbf{x}, \mathbf{y})$ in this $k\text{NN}_3$ rule?

[11] Suppose you are given n samples $\mathbf{x}_1, \mathbf{x}_2, \ldots, \mathbf{x}_n$ with $\{\mathbf{x}_s^i\}_{i=1}^{n_i}$ from class i, $i = 1, 2, \ldots, M$. Then given the M decision regions $D_j(\mathbf{x}, \dot{\mathbf{x}}_n)$, $j = 1, 2, \ldots,$

M, and estimated distribution $\hat{F}(\mathbf{x}\,|\,\omega_i)$, $i = 1, 2, \ldots, M$, the risk for this training set is

$$\sum_{i=1}^{M} P_i \sum_{j=1}^{M} L_{ji} \int_{\mathscr{X}} D_j(\mathbf{x}, \dot{\mathbf{x}}_n)\, d\hat{F}(\mathbf{x}\,|\,\omega_i).$$

(a) Show that the above risk can be estimated as

$$\sum_{i=1}^{M} P_i \sum_{j=1}^{M} L_{ji} \frac{1}{n_i} \sum_{s=1}^{n_i} D_j(\mathbf{x}_s^i, \dot{\mathbf{x}}_n).$$

(b) The risk in (a) is for the specific training set $\dot{\mathbf{x}}_n$ and decision rule creating the regions $\{D_j(\mathbf{x}, \dot{\mathbf{x}}_n)\}_{j=1}^{M}$. Discuss why it is possible to adapt this decision rule by selecting the rule resulting in the smallest risk in (a).

(c) Suppose that an unlimited number of statistically independent training sets $\dot{\mathbf{x}}_n$ are available and that a decision rule is found which minimizes the risk [in (a)] averaged over all these training sets [risk given by Eq. (6) of Section 3-3.2 with $\delta = 1$]. It is suggested that you have accomplished little since given an infinite number of training samples, it is not difficult in theory to achieve the minimum-risk rule. Discuss carefully.

[12] Discuss why

$$q_{j_1, \, \cdots \, j_\delta}(\mathbf{x}^{(1)}, \ldots, \mathbf{x}^{(\delta)}) = \int_{\mathscr{X}^n} \prod_{v=1}^{\delta} [D_{j_v}(\mathbf{x}^{(v)}; \dot{\mathbf{x}}_n)]\, d\dot{F}(\dot{\mathbf{x}}_n)$$

is not conditioned on the training samples $\dot{\mathbf{x}}_n$.

[13] (a) Starting with the expression for $\mu_{\mathbf{n}}^1$, the expected risk, show that

$$\text{expected risk} = \sum_{i=1}^{M} P_i \sum_{j=1}^{M} L_{ji}\, p(\text{decide } j;\ \text{class } i \text{ active})$$

independent of the training set $\dot{\mathbf{x}}_n$ and the decision rule. Realize that $p(\text{decide } j;\ \text{class } i \text{ active})$ does depend upon the decision rule.

(b) Suppose that

$$\int_{\mathscr{X}^n} D_j(\mathbf{x}, \dot{\mathbf{x}}_n)\, dF(\dot{\mathbf{x}}_n) \longrightarrow p(\text{classify } \mathbf{x} \text{ in category } j)$$
$$\triangleq d_j(\mathbf{x}).$$

Show that

$$\mu_{\infty}^1 = \sum_{i=1}^{M} P_i \sum_{j=1}^{M} L_{ji} \int_{x} d_j(\mathbf{x}) \eta_i(\mathbf{x})\, dx,$$

where

$$\eta_i(\mathbf{x}) = \frac{P_i f_i(\mathbf{x})}{\displaystyle\sum_{j=1}^{M} P_j f_j(\mathbf{x})}.$$

(c) Suppose $L_{ji} = 1 - \delta_{ji}$, and

$$d_j(\mathbf{x}) = \begin{cases} 1, & \eta_j(\mathbf{x}) = \max_i \{\eta_i(\mathbf{x})\}_{i=1}^M, \\ 0, & \text{otherwise.} \end{cases}$$

Show that

$$\mu_\infty = \sum_{\substack{i=1 \\ i \neq j}}^M P_i \eta_i(\mathbf{x}),$$

where sample $\mathbf{x}$ is classified into category j.

[14] Indicate conditions under which

(a) $(\sum_{i=1}^M a_i)(\sum_{i=1}^M b_i)(\sum_{i=1}^M c_i) = \sum_{i=1}^M \sum_{j=1}^M \sum_{k=1}^M a_i b_j c_k$.

(b) $\int f(z)\,dz \int g(y)\,dy = \int\int f(z)g(y)\,dz\,dy$.

[15] Show that, although it may not be true that $p(\omega_i \,|\, \dot{\mathbf{x}}_n, \mathbf{b}) = P_i$, it is always true that $p(\pi_r \,|\, \dot{\mathbf{x}}_n, \mathbf{c}) = P(\pi_r)$. When is the former true?

[16] Show that $p(\pi_r \,|\, \dot{\mathbf{x}}_n) = E[p(\pi_i \,|\, \dot{\mathbf{x}}_n)]$.

[17] The probability of error of the two-class, L-dimensional Gaussian decision rule with equal mean vectors is not difficult to calculate if both classes have scalar covariance matrices. For example, let $\mathbf{\Sigma}_1 = \sigma_1^2 \mathbf{I}$ and $\mathbf{\Sigma}_2 = \sigma_2^2 \mathbf{I}$.

(a) Show that the decision equation can be written as

$$d(\mathbf{y}\,|\,\omega_i) = \mathbf{y}^t\mathbf{y} \underset{\omega_2}{\overset{\omega_1}{\gtrless}} b'''$$

and find the expression for b''' in terms of P_1, P_2, σ_1^2, and σ_2^2.

(b) Show that the density of $d(\mathbf{y}\,|\,\omega_i)$ is

$$f(d\,|\,\omega_i) = \frac{d^{(L/2-1)} \exp(-L/2\sigma_i^2)}{2^{L/2}\sigma_i^L \Gamma(L/2)}.$$

(c) For $L = 2$ show that $f(d\,|\,\omega_i)$ is an exponential density, and find the probability of error.

(d) Find the probability of error for general L in terms of the incomplete gamma integral,

$$I_\Gamma(u, M) = \int_0^{u\sqrt{M+1}} \frac{\xi^M}{M!} \exp(-\xi)\,d\xi$$

which was tabulated by Pearson [30].

CHAPTER 4

Supervised Estimation

4-1 Introduction

It is clear as a result of studying decision rules in Chapter 3 that density estimation is important to implement the decision rule. Basically, however, a decision rule is characterized by decision boundaries in the observation space $\mathscr{X} = \mathscr{V}_L$. Therefore, it would seem that direct estimation of decision boundaries is a reasonable approach; however, numerous difficulties arise.

The reader may be interested in results for layered machines discussed in a book, *Learning Machines*, by Nilsson [1]. A more complicated approach was considered by Patrick and Bechtel [2], where a *partition of the observation space* is modified with training to maximize a criterion related to performance. Even though the approach operates with fixed storage, it is complex to implement, especially for multidimensional problems where $L \geq 2$. Although little performance theory is available, it appears that the performance of approaches using direct estimation of decision boundaries is not as good as that of procedures utilizing local density estimation (utilizing an appropriate distance measure). Another approach was suggested by Fu and Henrichon [3].

There are decision rules that may not appear to involve density estimation, such as the nearest-neighbor decision rule. It can be shown, however, that these rules do fit into the framework of decision rules utilizing local density estimation.

When a decision rule is designed for M categories and samples from the respective categories are unsupervised, and in addition each category can have multiple modes, the problem of estimating each category density can be a difficult one. In this chapter we are concerned with estimating the density function for a category where supervised training samples are available from that category. Even with supervised samples from the category, it is possible that the category density is multimodal such that unsupervised estimation techniques (for example, clustering) are still required to estimate the category density.

If the locations of category modes could be determined, then these modes could (for example) be fitted with multivariate density functions from an appropriate family. If the family is Gaussian, the mean vector and covariance matrix characterizing each mode are estimated. The estimated covariance matrix provides a distance measure for local distance measurement when decision making. An alternative approach is to measure local density using tolerance regions†; this leads to the generalized k-nearest-neighbor decision rule discussed in this chapter. Unfortunately, it is possible that the required tolerance-region shape will vary over the observation space or even be different for each possible observation vector. Because of this, it may be impossible to estimate the ideal tolerance-region shape at each point in the observation space.

Thus, we are led back to the approach of locating category modes and fitting each mode with a member density from a prescribed family. The unsupervised technique of clustering is one practical way to locate these modes, and possibly even of determining the mean vector and covariance matrix characterizing the mode. Another advantage of the clustering approach is complexity reduction, since it is not necessary to retain the samples in storage.

It is the author's opinion that a good solution to estimation and decision making is to estimate a density function by locating its modes using clustering. There are pattern-recognition problems, however, where the simplicity of the k-nearest-neighbor rules has appeal. Much of the recent material on k-nearest-neighbor rules is presented in this chapter.

The problems of estimating the distributions $F(\mathbf{x}|\omega_i)$, $i = 1, 2, \ldots, M$, given supervised training samples from each class has been considered from the following vantage points:

1. $F(\mathbf{x}|\omega_i)$, $i = 1, 2, \ldots, M$, is known. This is the vantage point taken in developing minimum-risk decision rules in Chapter 3.
2. $F(\mathbf{x}|\omega_i)$, $i = 1, 2, \ldots, M$, are known to belong to a parametric family $\mathscr{F}$, where the ith member is characterized by a parameter vector $\mathbf{b}_i$, $i = 1, 2, \ldots, M$; these vectors are unknown and must

†Tolerance regions were defined in Chapter 2.

be estimated. Estimation of parameter vectors for both supervised and unsupervised problems are considered in Chapter 2 and in more detail for unsupervised problems in Chapter 5.

3. $F(\mathbf{x} \mid \omega_i)$ is unknown, or at most nonparametric information such as continuity or symmetry is known. This is the case for which the k-nearest-neighbor rules are developed.

Case 1 is considered in Chapter 3. Concerning case 2: In reference [4] it is shown that the conditional probability of error (the probability of error conditioned on $\dot{\mathbf{x}}_n$) is minimized for the supervised problem and Gaussian statistics if the a posteriori probabilities

$$f(\mathbf{b}_i \mid \dot{\mathbf{x}}_n), \qquad i = 1, 2, \ldots, M, \tag{1}$$

are calculated and then used to calculate $f(\mathbf{x} \mid i, \dot{\mathbf{x}}_n)$ according to

$$f(\mathbf{x} \mid i, \dot{\mathbf{x}}_n) = \int f(\mathbf{x} \mid i, \mathbf{b}_i) f(\mathbf{b}_i \mid \dot{\mathbf{x}}_n) \, d\mathbf{b} \triangleq (f(\mathbf{x} \mid i))_n. \tag{2}$$

The parametric nature of this case means that $f(\mathbf{x} \mid i, \mathbf{b}_i)$ is a known functional form, although $\mathbf{b}_i$ is an unknown vector point. Abramson and Braverman [5] and Keehn [6] used this approach when $\mathscr{F}$ is Gaussian. A suboptimum approach is to use an estimate of the parameters $\mathbf{b}_i^*$, based on a training set, and substitute this estimate into (1). Fischer's discriminant function [7] is a good example of this for Gaussian statistics. Fix and Hodges [8] showed that if $(\mathbf{b}_i)_n \xrightarrow{P} \mathbf{b}_i$, then the risk resulting from a rule obtained by substituting $(f(\mathbf{x} \mid i, (\mathbf{b}_i))_n$ for $f(\mathbf{x} \mid i, \mathbf{b}_i)$ is a random variable that converges in probability to the risk of the optimum rule.

Case 3 problems are, in my opinion, difficult to document because even nonparametric approaches utilize a priori knowledge. Procedures using the training observations to obtain estimates of the densities $f(\mathbf{x} \mid i)$ in the Bayes decision rule were later given the title "empirical Bayes procedures" by Robbins [37]. Perhaps the "empirical Bayes procedures" are in this third category. An engineering approach to the nonparametric density-estimation problem is to assume that the density can be well approximated using a linear combination of functions from some family $\mathscr{F}$. One approach is to assume that the functions are completely known, except that a subset of them must be selected for use in the approximation. A second approach is to estimate parameters characterizing the functions to obtain the approximation. A third approach is to partition the observation space using tolerance regions. We shall discuss these three approaches for representing densities in the next section.

4-2 Introduction to Nonparametric Density Estimation

A degenerate case is where $h(\mathbf{x})$ is estimated using a single density from a family $\mathscr{F}$. For example, as discussed in Chapter 2, Abramson and Braverman [5] considered the assumption

$$h(\mathbf{x}) = N(\mathbf{x} \,|\, \mathbf{m}, \boldsymbol{\Sigma})$$

and estimated the mean vector $\mathbf{m}$. Subsequently Keehn [6] estimated both the mean vector $\mathbf{m}$ and covariance matrix $\boldsymbol{\Sigma}$. As also discussed in Chapter 2, Aizerman, Braverman, and Rozonoer [9] use a set of complete orthonormal basis functions $\{\{\psi_{ji}(\mathbf{x})\}\}$ which *are all known a priori.* Tsypkin [10] uses a set of orthonormal basis functions which do not necessarily span a complete space where the density function $h(\mathbf{x})$ is in the space; he assumes that the basis functions are known a priori. Kashyap and Blaydon [11] also assume that the set of basis functions is known a priori, but then require that this set of basis functions be linearly independent. The histogram approach also uses basis functions which are assumed known a priori.

In my opinion an approach well suited to many pattern-recognition problems is to let

$$h(\mathbf{x}) = \sum_{i=1}^{M} P_i f(\mathbf{x} \,|\, i, \mathbf{b}_i), \tag{1}$$

where $f(\mathbf{x} \,|\, i, \mathbf{b}_i)$ is, for example, in a Gaussian family† and $\{P_i, \mathbf{b}_i\}_{i=1}^{M}$ and M all are estimated. Practical techniques for estimating these parameters when dimensionality L is large are clustering techniques discussed in Chapter 5. Clustering approaches provide for replacing the n samples with estimated parameters $\{(P_i)_n, (\mathbf{b}_i)_n\}_{i=1}^{M}$. It would appear that if nL is less than the total number of parameters used, it may be better to use an approach based on retaining the samples. This would be an acceptable case except that we probably cannot accept such a small n situation because of poor ultimate performance. An alternative is for the a priori knowledge about local clusters to be supplied interactively, possibly utilizing problem knowledge. The importance of this interaction cannot be stressed enough!

The following sections are devoted to decision rules which have frequently been referred to as k-nearest-neighbor decision rules. To put these rules in the perspective of the previous discussion, consider an estimate of $f(\mathbf{x} \,|\, i)$,

---

†It is easy to show that there are examples where a $k\text{NN}_3$ type of rule should be used, given observations are within that mode, using a quadratic-form distance measure. This allows a potential other than the Gaussian potential to be constructed.

$$
(f(\mathbf{x}\,|\,i))_{n_i} = \begin{cases} \dfrac{k_i}{(n_i + 1)\Phi_i}, & \mathbf{x} \in \mathscr{I}_i, \\ 0, & \text{otherwise,} \end{cases} \tag{2}
$$

where Φ_i is the volume of the region $\mathscr{I}_i$ which contains k_i samples and distance is measured using an appropriately defined distance measure $d(\mathbf{x}, \mathbf{y})$.

4-3 Decision Rules Using Local Density Estimation

4-3.1 $k\mathrm{NN}_1$: First k-Nearest-Neighbor Decision Rule

In 1951 Fix and Hodges [8] described a decision rule for two categories which is based on nonparametric estimation of probability density. The estimation procedure used can be motivated by the now-standard concept that the number of samples which fall in a small neighborhood about a vector point $\mathbf{x}$ can be used to estimate the density at $\mathbf{x}$. Specifically, Fix and Hodges stated the following result: If $f(\mathbf{x})$ is continuous at $\mathbf{x}$ and if $\{\mathscr{I}_s\}_{s=1}^n$ is a sequence of sets with corresponding volumes $\{\Phi_s\}_{s=1}^n$ such that

1. $\lim\limits_{n\to\infty} \sup\limits_{\mathbf{y}\in\mathscr{I}_n} \|\mathbf{x} - \mathbf{y}\| = 0,$
2. $\lim\limits_{n\to\infty} n\Phi_n = \infty,$
3. k is the number of statistically independent random samples $\mathbf{x}_1, \mathbf{x}_2,$ $\ldots, \mathbf{x}_n$ of $f(\mathbf{x})$ that lie in $\mathscr{I}_n$, $k \longrightarrow \infty$ as $n \longrightarrow \infty$;

then

$$
(f(\mathbf{x}))_n = \frac{k}{n\Phi_n} \xrightarrow{P} f(\mathbf{x}). \tag{1}
$$

Essentially, in summary, if the sequence of neighborhoods $\{\mathscr{I}_s\}_{s=1}^n$ shrinks in size about $\mathbf{x}$ slow enough so that the expected number of samples falling in $\mathscr{I}_n$ approaches infinity as $n \longrightarrow \infty$, a consistent density estimate results.

It should be kept in mind that asymptotic ($n \longrightarrow \infty$) estimation of density may be of little value in practice since there never are an infinite number of samples. Thus, it becomes important, for small sample sizes, to have the regions $\{\mathscr{I}_s\}_{s=1}^n$ "match" the local density. It does not appear practical to try to match the density at every point $\mathbf{x}$, an extension the reader might think we mean to imply. Rather, matching in local, finite-size regions is practical, and this involves the concept of clustering to obtain the regions.

With the theoretical result (1), theoretical research essentially branched into three directions. One direction was initiated by Rosenblatt [38], who analyzed the mean and variance of the above $(f(\mathbf{x}))_n$ for the case where the sets $\{\mathscr{I}_s\}_{s=1}^n$ took the form

$$\mathscr{I}_n = \{\mathbf{y} : \|\mathbf{y} - \mathbf{x}\| \leq h_n\},$$

$$\lim_{n \to \infty} h_n = 0.$$

$$(2)$$

The concept of local density estimation was generalized by Whittle [12] and later Parzen [13] by replacing the set $\mathscr{I}_n$ with a weighting function $K_n(\mathbf{y}, \mathbf{x})$. For $\mathscr{I}_n$ of the Rosenblatt type, $K_n(\mathbf{y}, \mathbf{x}) = 1$ whenever $|\mathbf{y} - \mathbf{x}| \leq h_n$ and zero otherwise. More generally, $K_n(\mathbf{y}, \mathbf{x})$ can have other nonnegative values, the objective being to obtain a "smoother" density estimate. The local density estimate of $\mathbf{x}$ is obtained, using generalized definitions of Φ_n and k, as follows:

$$\Phi_n = \int_{\mathscr{X}} K_n(\mathbf{x}, \mathbf{y}) \, d\mathbf{y},$$

$$k = n \int_{\mathscr{X}} K_n(\mathbf{x}, \mathbf{y}) f_n(\mathbf{y}) \, d\mathbf{y},$$

$$(3)$$

where $f_n(\mathbf{x})$ is the empirical density function of the n observations. Thus,

$$k = \sum_{s=1}^{n} K_n(\mathbf{x}, \mathbf{x}_s);$$

$$(4)$$

thus

$$(f(\mathbf{x}))_n = \frac{k}{n\Phi_n} = \frac{\sum_{s=1}^{n} K_n(\mathbf{x}, \mathbf{x}_s)}{n\Phi_n}.$$

$$(5)$$

Watson and Leadbetter [14] determined the best kernel functions $K_n(\mathbf{x}, \mathbf{y})$ which minimized integral square error for several specific densities $f(\mathbf{x})$. It appears that Cacoullus [15] generalized the Parzen estimator to the multivariate case. Van Ryzin [16] finally demonstrated that the estimator (5), when used in an empirical Bayes decision rule, approaches the Bayes risk in probability.

Sebestyen [17] considered the use of estimators similar to Parzen's in an empirical Bayes context from the engineering viewpoint. He did not have as much concern with theoretical performance as the above-mentioned investigators. Rather, he considered engineering methods for creating local regions characterized by location and variance parameters. Attached to each of these local regions was a Parzen-type weighting function.

Subsequently, Sebestyen and Edie [18] considered an artful approach†combining concepts of clustering, weighting functions, and nearest neighbor.

---

†Ball and Hall [19] considered a more complex scheme whereby the density $f(\mathbf{x} \mid i)$ is represented by a mixture of Gaussians.

The observation space is partitioned using clustering, where a cluster is located at a cluster point. Regions of the observation space relatively near a cluster point utilize density estimators of the Parzen type. In regions of the observation space outside clusters, a vector $\mathbf{x}$ is classified according to the class of its nearest cluster point. *The measurement of distance is changed at each cluster point to reflect local conditions.*

This above-mentioned procedure of clustering, determining local distance criteria, and then obtaining an engineering estimate of density is a fundamental theme of this book. Chapter 5 contains a detailed presentation of unsupervised estimation (including clustering) techniques. That is not to say that the k-nearest-neighbor rules shortly presented may not be the best in the engineering sense for certain problems.

The second direction which appears to have precipitated from the result (1) is the adaptive histogram concept, where the observation space is partitioned into cells of predetermined shape.† If the number of cells increases with sample size, a density estimate of the form (5) can be applied where $\mathscr{I}_n$ is the particular cell containing $\mathbf{x}$.

The third direction appears to have been started by Fix and Hodges [8], who realized that the size of $\mathscr{I}_n$ should depend on the samples $\mathbf{x}_1, \mathbf{x}_2, \ldots, \mathbf{x}_n$ "close" to $\mathbf{x}$ and not just on the sample size n. To achieve this dependence, they suggested that $\mathscr{I}_n$ be defined as a "ball," with respect to some arbitrary distance measure‡ $d(\mathbf{x}, \mathbf{y})$ centered at $\mathbf{x}$, just large enough to contain k samples from the population. For the M category case, M sets of regions $\{\mathscr{I}_{1s}\}_{s=1}^{n_1}, \{\mathscr{I}_{2s}\}_{s=1}^{n_2}, \ldots, \{\mathscr{I}_{Ms}\}_{s=1}^{n_M}$ are used where the first set depends upon n_1 samples from category 1, the second depends upon n_2 samples from category 2, etc., $n = n_1 + n_2 + \cdots + n_M$. It appears that, at that time, Fix and Hodges questioned the consistency of decision rules resulting from such estimators because the sets $\{\mathscr{I}_{is}\}$ are random and not fixed. Much later, Loftsgaarden and Quesenberry [20] proved that the estimators were consistent under appropriate restrictions.

The vantage point taken by Fix and Hodges is to use a single set, $\{\mathscr{I}_s\}_{s=1}^{n}$, for the two-category problem. The set is determined by letting $\mathscr{I}_n$ be the smallest ball centered at $\mathbf{x}$ which contains k of the "pooled" observations $\mathbf{x}_1, \mathbf{x}_2, \ldots, \mathbf{x}_n$ from the two categories. We summarize the procedure as follows and will call it $k\mathrm{NN}_1$, the first k-nearest-neighbor decision rule.

$k\mathrm{NN}_1$: First k-Nearest-Neighbor Decision Rule

1. There is a single sequence of regions $\{\mathscr{I}_s\}_{s=1}^{n}$ which are "balls" centered at $\mathbf{x}$. $\mathscr{I}_n$ contains k of the "pooled" samples $\mathbf{x}_1, \mathbf{x}_2, \ldots, \mathbf{x}_n$, $n = n_1 + n_2$. $\mathscr{I}_n$ contains k_i samples from i, $k = k_1 + k_2$.

†There are numerous papers utilizing a histogram approach.
‡It may be desirable that $d(\mathbf{x}, \mathbf{y})$ be a metric as defined in Chapter 1.

2. The distance measure $d(\mathbf{x}, \mathbf{y})$ is arbitrary† *but not dependent on the classification of the training sample.*
3. $M = 2$ and $\boldsymbol{\Phi}_1 = \boldsymbol{\Phi}_2 = \boldsymbol{\Phi}$ because of the single sequence of sets $\{\mathscr{I}_s\}_{s=1}^n$.
4. A consistent estimate of $f_i(\mathbf{x})$ is

$$(f(\mathbf{x}\,|\,i))_{n_i} = \frac{k_i}{n_i \boldsymbol{\Phi}}, \qquad i = 1, 2.$$

The $k\mathrm{NN}_1$ decision rule is, assign $\mathbf{x}$ to class j if

$$(f(\mathbf{x}\,|\,j))_{n_j} > (f(\mathbf{x}\,|\,i))_{n_i}, \qquad i \neq j, i = 1, 2, \tag{6}$$

or, introducing an arbitrary constant c, a more general form is

$$\frac{k_j}{n_j} > c\frac{k_i}{n_i}, \qquad i \neq j, i = 1, 2. \tag{7}$$

Note that

5. If $c = L_{ji} P_i / L_{ij} P_j$, then the decision rule (6) or (7) is an estimate of a minimum-risk rule (an empirical Bayes rule) considered in Chapter 3.

Subsequently, Fix and Hodges [21] examined the small-sample-size properties of rule (7) for the special case of Gaussian statistics. Using numerical integration techniques, they found theoretical probability of error when $k = 1$ for both univariate and bivariate Gaussian assumptions. The distance measure used was $d(\mathbf{x}, \mathbf{y}) = \max_i |x_i - y_i|$. Performance when $k > 1$ was obtained for asymptotic sample size. The results are for global performance rather than performance at a single point $\mathbf{x}$.

4-3.2 $k\mathrm{NN}_2$: Second k-Nearest-Neighbor Decision Rule

Beginning in 1966, Cover and Hart [22, 23] published papers on a decision rule that will be denoted $k\mathrm{NN}_2$, the second k-nearest-neighbor decision rule. The rule is described as follows: A set of n statistically independent vector samples $\mathbf{x}_1, \mathbf{x}_2, \ldots, \mathbf{x}_n$ is drawn with the correct classification of each sample known. An unclassified vector $\mathbf{x}$ is assigned to the category most heavily represented among its k nearest neighbors.

A summary of properties of this rule is as follows:

1. There is a single sequence of regions $\{\mathscr{I}_s\}_{s=1}^n$, each region a "ball" centered at $\mathbf{x}$. $\mathscr{I}_n$ contains k of the "pooled" samples $\mathbf{x}_1, \mathbf{x}_2, \ldots, \mathbf{x}_n$; $n = \sum_{i=1}^M n_i$.

†Performance depends upon the distance measure chosen.

2. Distance is measured using an arbitrary† distance measure $d(\mathbf{x}, \mathbf{y})$ *which is not dependent on the training samples.*

3. M is any value and $\Phi_1 = \Phi_2 = \cdots = \Phi_M$.

4. n_i/n is assumed representative of P_i.

The $k\mathrm{NN}_2$ rule is: Assign $\mathbf{x}$ to category j if

$$k_j > k_i, \qquad j \neq i, \, i = 1, 2, \ldots, M. \tag{8}$$

Note that the $k\mathrm{NN}_2$ rule (8) has the form (6) with‡

$$(f(\mathbf{x}\,|\,i))_{n_i} = \frac{k_i}{n_i \Phi}$$

but with the implied constraint $P_i = n_i/n$. Also note that the $k\mathrm{NN}_2$ rule considered by Cover and Hart is not restricted to two categories ($M = 2$) as is the $k\mathrm{NN}_1$ rule.

In 1966 Whitney and Dwyer [24], with references to earlier papers than Cover and Hart, considered the $k\mathrm{NN}_2$ rule for "quasi-supervised" samples; they assumed that a given training set contained vectors which are correctly classified with a probability§ $\beta > \frac{1}{2}$ (Cover and Hart's analysis lets $\beta = 1$).

It is widely known by researchers in estimation and decision making that estimation of parameters using training samples and classifying samples into categories are related. Thus, there has been a desire to try to avoid the two-step procedure of estimating parameters characterizing probability densities and then substituting the resulting estimated densities into a decision rule [for example, (6)]. In 1968 Cover [25] modified the $k\mathrm{NN}_2$ decision rule to include estimation of parameters as follows: Let $[\mathbf{x}_1, \boldsymbol{\alpha}_1]$, $[\mathbf{x}_2, \boldsymbol{\alpha}_2]$, $\ldots, [\mathbf{x}_n, \boldsymbol{\alpha}_n]$ be a sequence of n two-component vectors where $\boldsymbol{\alpha}_i$ is the parameter vector characterizing the category to which the training sample $\mathbf{x}_i$ belongs; store these two component vectors. Then, given an observation vector $\mathbf{x}$, assign it to the category of the stored training vector $\mathbf{x}_a$ (and thus an estimate for the parameter corresponding to $\mathbf{x}$ is $\boldsymbol{\alpha}_a$) closest to $\mathbf{x}$ with respect to an arbitrary distance measure $d(\mathbf{x}, \mathbf{x}_a)$. It is likely that $d(\mathbf{x}, \mathbf{x}_a)$ would be chosen the familiar Euclidean distance for lack of a priori knowledge. Clearly, this shows how estimation of parameters and decision making have similarities. Also, it provides a good example of how such a nonparametric classification procedure can have a degraded performance for lack of utilizing a priori knowledge. (Do Problem 3.)

---

†Performance depends on the distance measure.

‡When convenient, notation $f_i(\mathbf{x})$ will be used in place of $(f(\mathbf{x}\,|\,i))_{n_i}$.

§This has some application for the analysis of decision-directed estimators presented in Chapter 5.

It is not difficult to find examples for which (nonparametric) kNN rules give a poor performance, whereas a parametric rule with estimated parameters shows very good performance for the same problem.† Nevertheless, there are problems where the kNN rules have a clear advantage when n is not too large (to cause storage and time problems) and the data are not such as to require several different local distance measures. For example, if each category is spherically symmetric and nonoverlapping with other categories, there can be zero probability of error using the kNN rules. (Do Problem 4.)

4-3.3 kNN$_3$: Third k-Nearest-Neighbor Decision Rule

A review of the literature covering kNN decision rules‡ seems to indicate that research on the kNN$_1$ and kNN$_2$ rules is partially a result of the concentration of Fix and Hodges on using a single sequence of sets $\{\mathscr{I}_s\}_{s=1}^n$ about $\mathbf{x}$. The next decision rule, suggested by Patrick in 1966 [26], however, propagates from Fix and Hodges's initial idea of allowing a sequence $\{\mathscr{I}_{is}\}_{s=1}^{n_i}$ for the ith category, $i = 1, 2, \ldots, M$.

For $\mathbf{x}$ and $\mathbf{y}$ in $\mathscr{X}$, a distance measure $d_i(\mathbf{y}, \mathbf{x})$ mapping $\mathscr{X} \times \mathscr{X}$ to the nonnegative real line is defined an acceptable distance measure if:

1. Definition of $d_i(\mathbf{y}, \mathbf{x})$:
   (a) $\lim_{\epsilon \to 0} [\max_{\mathbf{y} \in \mathscr{X}} \{\|\mathbf{x} - \mathbf{y}\| : d_i(\mathbf{x}, \mathbf{y}) < \epsilon\}] = 0, \qquad \forall\, \mathbf{x} \in \mathscr{X}$,
   (b) The set $\{\mathbf{y} : d_i(\mathbf{y}, \mathbf{x}) = \epsilon\}$ has zero volume for all $\epsilon > 0$ and all $\mathbf{x} \in \mathscr{X}$,
   (c) $k_i(\mathbf{x})$ is a positive integer-valued function of $\mathbf{x}$, $\mathscr{I}_i(\mathbf{x}; \dot{\mathbf{x}}_n)$ is a neighborhood of $\mathbf{x}$ (containing $k_i(\mathbf{x})$ samples) with size and shape depending on $\dot{\mathbf{x}}_n$, and $\Phi_i(\mathbf{x}; \dot{\mathbf{x}}_n)$ is the volume of $\mathscr{I}_i(\mathbf{x}; \dot{\mathbf{x}}_n)$, $i = 1, 2, \ldots, M$.

Next:

2. Thus there is a sequence of regions $\{\mathscr{I}_{is}\}_{s=1}^{n_i}$ *for each category,* $i = 1, 2, \ldots, M$.
3. $\{P_i\}_{i=1}^M$ and loss functions $\{L_{ji}\}_{i=1}^M$, $j = 1, 2, \ldots, M$, are supplied as a priori knowledge.

---

†Performance of the kNN type of rule can be improved by proper choice of distance measure. The kNN$_3$ rule discussed in the next section allows for a different distance measure for each class. In a sense, distance measures introduce a parametric tone.

‡"kNN decision rules" is a phrase used in this book to refer to nonparametric rules using a measurement of distance from an unclassified sample $\mathbf{x}$ to each stored training sample.

The kNN_3 decision rule is: Assign $\mathbf{x}$ to category j if

$$\sum_{i=1}^{M} P_i L_{ji} \frac{k_i(\mathbf{x})}{(n_i + 1)\Phi_i(\mathbf{x}; \dot{\mathbf{x}}_n)} < \sum_{i=1}^{M} P_i L_{mi} \frac{k_i(\mathbf{x})}{(n_i + 1)\Phi_i(\mathbf{x}; \dot{\mathbf{x}}_n)}, \tag{9}$$

$$m \neq j, \ m = 1, 2, \ldots, M.$$

For the special case that

1. $k_1 = k_2 = \cdots = k_M = k,$
2. $n_1 = n_2 = \cdots = n_M = n/M,$
3. $d_i(\mathbf{y}, \mathbf{x}) = \|\mathbf{y} - \mathbf{x}\|, i = 1, 2, \ldots, M,$
4. $L_{ji} = 0$ if $j = i$; otherwise, $L_{ji} = 1,$
5. $P_1 = P_2 = \cdots = P_M = 1/M,$

the kNN_3 rule is simply stated as follows: Assign $\mathbf{x}$ to the category ω_j corresponding to the jth training set $\dot{\mathbf{x}}_j$ whose kth nearest neighbor to $\mathbf{x}$ is closest to $\mathbf{x}$ (in "common everyday Euclidean distance") than for any other training set.

The decision rule (9) was introduced by Patrick [26] in a report and subsequently appeared in a conference record [27]. In a paper by Patrick and Fischer [28], the rule was called the generalized k-nearest-neighbor decision rule. In this book, for historical perspective, it is called the kNN_3 rule.

4-3.4 Comparison of kNN_1, kNN_2, and kNN_3

A disadvantage of these kNN rules described thus far is that the training observations must be retained in storage.† Other versions of the kNN decision rule concept which incorporate a memory constraint are discussed later in this chapter (for example, the condensed nearest-neighbor rule by Hart [29]).

Another possibly very serious disadvantage of the three kNN rules discussed so far is that they do not directly provide for estimating the local distance measure $d(\mathbf{x}, \mathbf{y})$ for each category. The kNN_3 rule does, however, have the framework for including an estimate of a local distance measure for each category.

The kNN_3 rule has the following advantages over the kNN_2 rule:

1. For k even, ties when announcing decisions can occur using the kNN_2 rule because there is only one "ball" $\mathscr{I}_n$ containing $\mathbf{x}$ for the M categories. Ties can be resolved, however, by randomly selecting

---

†This disadvantage does not appear as serious when one realizes that one alternative is to store estimates of local density functions, such as Gaussian functions.

one of the categories or, say, selecting the category nearest $\mathbf{x}$. For $M = 2$ and k odd, ties when using the $k\text{NN}_2$ rule are impossible. Ties occur frequently, in practice, however, for $M > 2$ and small k, causing the $k\text{NN}_2$ rule to have poor performance. The $k\text{NN}_3$ rule does not have ties in the above sense; this is because the ith category uses a set of regions $\{\mathscr{I}_{is}\}_{s=1}^{n_i}$, and the probability of equal values of $(f(\mathbf{x}\,|\,i))_{n_i}$ for two or more categories is small.

2. For the $k\text{NN}_2$ rule it is assumed that the sample size n_i is representative of P_i. The $k\text{NN}_3$ rule provides for inserting the a priori probabilities P_i if available; of course, $P_i = n_i/n$ is allowed.

The reader is referred to Problem 5 for further comparisons of these rules.

4-3.5   *Rules Related to the* $k\text{NN}$ *Rules*

A $k\text{NN}_2$ type of rule with a reject option was described by Hellman [30] in 1970. He modified the $k\text{NN}_2$ rule such that if at least k' of the k nearest neighbors to $\mathbf{x}$ is of the same category, then $\mathbf{x}$ is assigned to that category; otherwise, decision is withheld (i.e., $\mathbf{x}$ is rejected). Thus, we could define the $k\text{NN}_2$ *rule with reject option.*

It has been noted by Specht [31] that if the kernel function $K_n(\mathbf{x}, \mathbf{y})$ used in the Parzen approach to density estimation (Section 4-3.1) is of the form

$$K_n(\mathbf{x}, \mathbf{y}) = \frac{1}{(2\pi\sigma^2)^{L/2}} \exp\left(-\frac{\frac{1}{2}\|\mathbf{x} - \mathbf{y}\|^2}{\sigma^2}\right), \tag{10}$$

then a decision rule using the Parzen estimator $(f(\mathbf{x}))_n$ with σ sufficiently small is the same as the 1NN_2 rule. This result follows since the Parzen approach involves a sum of effects, each due to one of the observations in the training set. As $\sigma \longrightarrow 0$, the effect of the nearest training observations to $\mathbf{x}$ overwhelms the effects of all other observations. Proceeding along this line, modify the Parzen estimator by replacing the summation of effects by the vth largest effect. Let $\max_{1 \leq j \leq n_i} (v) \{n_i^{-1} K_n(\mathbf{x}, \mathbf{x}_j^i)\}$ denote the vth largest of $n_i^{-1} K_n(\mathbf{x}, \mathbf{x}_j^i)$, $j = 1, 2, \ldots, n_i$. Then define

$$(f(\mathbf{x}\,|\,i))_{n_i} = \max_{1 \leq j \leq n_i} (v) \{n_i^{-1} K_n(\mathbf{x}, \mathbf{x}_j^i)\Phi_n^{-1}\}. \tag{11}$$

Define a distance function

$$d(\mathbf{x}, \mathbf{y}) = K_n(\mathbf{x}, \mathbf{x}) - K_n(\mathbf{x}, \mathbf{y}). \tag{12}$$

Then for zero–one loss functions, $M = 2$, $P_1/n_1 = P_2/n_2$, the empirical Bayes decision rule resulting using density estimator (11) is equivalent to the $k\text{NN}_1$

and kNN_2 rules using distance function (12) for every $\mathbf{x}$ when $k = 2v - 1$.†
To show this, suppose that the empirical Bayes rule using (11) assigns $\mathbf{x}$ to
class ω_1:

$$P_1(f(\mathbf{x}|1))_{n_1} > P_2(f(\mathbf{x}|2))_{n_2} \tag{13a}$$

or

$$P_1 \max_{1 \leq j \leq n_1} (v)\left\{\frac{K_n(\mathbf{x}, \mathbf{x}_j^1)}{n_1 \Phi_n}\right\} > P_2 \max_{1 \leq j \leq n_2} (v)\left\{\frac{K_n(\mathbf{x}, \mathbf{x}_j^2)}{n_2 \Phi_n}\right\} \tag{13b}$$

or

$$\max_{1 \leq j \leq n_1} (v)\{-K_n(\mathbf{x}, \mathbf{x}_j^1) + K_n(\mathbf{x}, \mathbf{x})\} < \max_{1 \leq j \leq n_2} (v)\{-K_n(\mathbf{x}, \mathbf{x}_j^2) + K_n(\mathbf{x}, \mathbf{x})\} \tag{13c}$$

or

$$\max_{1 \leq j \leq n_1} (v)\{d(\mathbf{x}, \mathbf{x}_j^1)\} < \max_{1 \leq j \leq n_2} (v)\{d(\mathbf{x}, \mathbf{x}_j^2)\} \tag{13d}$$

or

$$\frac{1}{\max_{1 \leq j \leq n_1} (v)\{d(\mathbf{x}, \mathbf{x}_j^1)\}} > \frac{1}{\max_{1 \leq j \leq n_2} (v)\{d(\mathbf{x}, \mathbf{x}_j^2)\}}. \tag{14}$$

Thus, the vth closest vector to $\mathbf{x}$ among the class ω_1 training samples is
closer to $\mathbf{x}$ than the vth closest vector to $\mathbf{x}$ among the class ω_2 training samples. Hence, among the $2v - 1$ pooled nearest neighbors to $\mathbf{x}$ [with respect
to the distance measure (12)] there must be more class ω_1 samples than class
ω_2 samples. As a result, the kNN_2 rule with $k = 2v - 1$ will also decide
class ω_1. Furthermore, the kNN_1 rule will choose class ω_1 since

$$\frac{P_1 k_1}{n_1} > \frac{P_2 k_2}{n_2}$$

because k_i is the number of samples of class ω_i among the $2v - 1$ pooled
nearest vectors to $\mathbf{x}$ and it was assumed that $P_1/n_1 = P_2/n_2$. The conclusion
is that the kNN approach and an approach using potential functions for
local density estimation are related.

4-4 Cover–Hart Bounds for the $1NN_2$ Rule for Two Categories

Proceeding with the second k-nearest-neighbor rule, kNN_2 bounds on the
asymptotic risk for this rule are presented. As usual there are M classes or

---

†An empirical Bayes decision rule is defined as where estimates $(f(\mathbf{x}|i))_n$ and $(P_i)_n$
are used in place of true densities and class probabilities in the minimum-risk decision rule.

categories, $\mathbf{x}$ is an L-dimensional vector in the observation space, and the corresponding densities are $f_1(\mathbf{x}), f_2(\mathbf{x}), \ldots, f_M(\mathbf{x})$. Let $L(j, i)$ be the loss incurred by assigning an observation from category i to category j. The prior probabilities of the M categories are $P_1, P_2, \ldots, P_M$ with $\sum_{i=1}^{M} P_i = 1$.

The probability $\eta_i(\mathbf{x})$ that a pattern with observation $\mathbf{x}$ belongs to category i is

$$\eta_i(\mathbf{x}) \triangleq p(i \mid \mathbf{x}) = \frac{P_i f_i(\mathbf{x})}{\sum\limits_{j=1}^{M} P_j f_j(\mathbf{x})}, \qquad i = 1, 2, \ldots, M. \tag{1}$$

The point loss at $\mathbf{x}$ incurred by placing a pattern with observation $\mathbf{x}$ into category j is

$$r_j(\mathbf{x}) = \sum_{i=1}^{M} \eta_i(\mathbf{x}) L(j, i), \qquad j = 1, 2, \ldots, M. \tag{2}$$

Denote by $r^*(\mathbf{x})$ the point loss (2) which is minimum over the M categories. Selecting the category j with minimum point loss is, of course, the Bayes decision procedure. The global or overall minimum expected risk R^* is defined

$$R^* = E[r^*(\mathbf{x})] = \int_{\mathscr{X}} r^*(\mathbf{x}) \left[\sum_{i=1}^{M} P_i f_i(\mathbf{x}) \right] d\mathbf{x}. \tag{3}$$

Either $r^*(\mathbf{x})$ or R^* can be computed given P_i, $f_i(\mathbf{x})$, $i = 1, 2, \ldots, M$. In the 1NN_2 rule, as in all nonparametric rules, these probabilities are not completely known (however, they may be directly or indirectly estimated in the rule).

Define the n sample 1NN_2 risk R_n by the expectation

$$R_n = E[L(\omega^{[1]}, \omega)], \tag{4}$$

where $\omega^{[1]}$ is the category of $\mathbf{x}^{[1]} \in \{\mathbf{x}_1, \mathbf{x}_2, \ldots, \mathbf{x}_n\}$ which is the nearest neighbor to the observation $\mathbf{x}$ whose category is denoted ω. The large sample 1NN_2 risk R is

$$R = \lim_{n \to \infty} R_n. \tag{5}$$

We now restrict attention to two categories ($M = 2$) and a zero–one loss matrix:

$$\mathbf{L} = \begin{bmatrix} 0 & 1 \\ 1 & 0 \end{bmatrix}.$$

It also is assumed that, given $f_1(\mathbf{x})$ and $f_2(\mathbf{x})$, the samples $\mathbf{x}_1^1, \mathbf{x}_2^1, \ldots, \mathbf{x}_{n_1}^1$ are statistically independent and the samples $\mathbf{x}_1^2, \mathbf{x}_2^2, \ldots, \mathbf{x}_{n_2}^2$ are statistically independent.

Theorem. Cover–Hart $1NN_2$ Bounds

Let $\mathscr{X}$ be a separable metric space. Let $f_1(\mathbf{x})$ and $f_2(\mathbf{x})$ be such that, with probability 1, $\mathbf{x}$ is either (1) a continuity point of $f_1(\mathbf{x})$ and $f_2(\mathbf{x})$ or (2) a point of nonzero probability measure. Then the $1NN_2$ risk R (probability of error because of zero–one loss matrix) has the bounds

$$R^* \le R \le 2R^*(1 - R^*). \tag{6}$$

Proof: The point risk is conditioned on the test observation $\mathbf{x}$ and its nearest neighbor $\mathbf{x}^{[1]}$. This risk is

$$
\begin{aligned}
r(\mathbf{x}^{[1]}, \mathbf{x}) &= E[L(\omega^{[1]}, \omega) \mid \mathbf{x}, \mathbf{x}^{[1]}] \\
&= p[\omega^{[1]} = 2 \mid \mathbf{x}^{[1]}] p[\omega = 1 \mid \mathbf{x}] \\
&\quad + p[\omega^{[1]} = 1 \mid \mathbf{x}^{[1]}] p[\omega = 2 \mid \mathbf{x}].
\end{aligned} \tag{7}
$$

By the development of (1), the above may be written

$$r(\mathbf{x}^{[1]}, \mathbf{x}) = \eta_2(\mathbf{x}^{[1]})\eta_1(\mathbf{x}) + \eta_1(\mathbf{x}^{[1]})\eta_2(\mathbf{x}). \tag{8}$$

It can be shown that under quite general conditions [22, 23]

$$\lim_{n \to \infty} \eta(\mathbf{x}^{[1]}) \stackrel{\text{w.p. 1}}{=} \eta(\mathbf{x}). \tag{9}$$

Hence, with probability 1,

$$r(\mathbf{x}^{[1]}, \mathbf{x}) = r(\mathbf{x}) = 2\eta_1(\mathbf{x})\eta_2(\mathbf{x}). \tag{10}$$

The Bayes risk at $\mathbf{x}$ is

$$r^*(\mathbf{x}) = \min\{\eta_1(\mathbf{x}), \eta_2(\mathbf{x})\} = \min\{\eta_1(\mathbf{x}), 1 - \eta_1(\mathbf{x})\}. \tag{11}$$

Now because $r(\mathbf{x}) = 2\eta_1(\mathbf{x})\eta_2(\mathbf{x})$, it follows that

$$r(\mathbf{x}) = 2r^*(\mathbf{x})(1 - r^*(\mathbf{x})). \tag{12}$$

The large sample overall or global risk is the limit of the expectation of $r(\mathbf{x}^{[1]}, \mathbf{x})$ with respect to $\mathbf{x}^{[1]}$ and $\mathbf{x}$:

$$R = \lim_{n \to \infty} E[r(\mathbf{x}^{[1]}, \mathbf{x})] = E[\lim_{n \to \infty} r(\mathbf{x}^{[1]}, \mathbf{x})], \tag{13}$$

where the latter results from an application of the dominated convergence theorem. Thus, using (10), the above becomes

$$R = E[r(\mathbf{x})] = E[2\eta_1(\mathbf{x})\eta_2(\mathbf{x})] = E[2r^*(\mathbf{x})(1 - r^*(\mathbf{x}))]. \tag{14}$$

Since the Bayes risk R^* is the expectation of r^*, we have

$$R = 2R^*(1 - R^*) - 2 \operatorname{Var} r^*(\mathbf{x}).$$ (15)

Hence

$$R \leq 2R^*(1 - R^*)$$ (16)

with equality iff $\operatorname{Var} r^* = 0$, which holds iff the point Bayes risk equals the global Bayes risk (i.e., $r^* = R^*$) with probability 1. The lower bound is achieved by rewriting (14) as

$$
\begin{aligned}
R &= E[r^*(\mathbf{x}) + r^*(\mathbf{x})(1 - 2r^*(\mathbf{x}))] \\
&= R^* + E[r^*(\mathbf{x})(1 - 2r^*(\mathbf{x}))] \\
&\geq R^*
\end{aligned}
$$

with equality iff $r^*(\mathbf{x})(1 - 2r^*(\mathbf{x})) = 0$ for almost every $\mathbf{x}$.

The Cover–Hart bounds for the $1\mathrm{NN}_2$ rule do not depend upon the distance measure $d(\mathbf{x}, \mathbf{y})$ used in finding the nearest sample $\mathbf{x}^{[1]}$ to $\mathbf{x}$.

4-5 $k\mathrm{NN}_2$ Rule with a Reject Option

4-5.1 Rejects

Hellman [30] suggested a $k\mathrm{NN}_2$ type of rule with a reject option. Let there be two categories ($M = 2$) and zero–one loss functions such that the Bayes point risk is

$$r^*(\mathbf{x}) = \min \{\eta_1(\mathbf{x}), \eta_2(\mathbf{x})\},$$ (1)

which is also the probability of error. When $r^*(\mathbf{x})$ is near $\frac{1}{2}$, the decision is not much better than a guess; in that case it may be better to reject[†]—i.e., make no decision. Suppose that t is the ratio of the cost of a reject to the cost of an error and that a correct decision has zero loss. Then overall cost is minimized by rejecting whenever

$$r^*(\mathbf{x}) \geq t.$$ (2)

The probability of a reject $R_{[k]}$ is

$$R_{[k]} = p[r^*(\mathbf{x}) \geq t] = \int_t^{1/2} f(r)\, dr$$ (3)

[†]In communications, also called an erasure.

and the probability of an error $P_{[k]}$ is

$$P_{[k]} = \int_0^t rf(r)\,dr. \tag{4}$$

The $k\mathrm{NN}_2$ rule with a reject option is now defined as a rule where the k nearest neighbors to $\mathbf{x}$ are examined and a decision made only if all k are from the same category.†

4-5.2 Calculation of Error Rate $P_{[k]}$ and Reject Rate $R_{[k]}$

First consider $k = 2$ and make a decision only if both neighbors are from the same category. If ω, $\omega^{[1]}$, and $\omega^{[2]}$ denote the true classes of $\mathbf{x}$, its NN ($\mathbf{x}^{[1]}$), and second NN ($\mathbf{x}^{[2]}$), respectively, then

$$\begin{aligned}
p[\text{reject} \mid \mathbf{x}, \mathbf{x}^{[1]}, \mathbf{x}^{[2]}] &= p[\omega^{[1]} \neq \omega^{[2]} \mid \mathbf{x}, \mathbf{x}^{[1]}, \mathbf{x}^{[2]}] \\
&= \eta_1(\mathbf{x}^{[1]})\eta_2(\mathbf{x}^{[2]}) + \eta_2(\mathbf{x}^{[1]})\eta_1(\mathbf{x}^{[2]}),
\end{aligned} \tag{5}$$

$$\begin{aligned}
p[\text{error} \mid \mathbf{x}, \mathbf{x}^{[1]}, \mathbf{x}^{[2]}] &= P_r[\omega^{[1]} = \omega^{[2]} \neq \omega \mid \mathbf{x}, \mathbf{x}^{[1]}, \mathbf{x}^{[2]}] \\
&= \eta_1(\mathbf{x}^{[1]})\eta_1(\mathbf{x}^{[2]})\eta_2(\mathbf{x}) + \eta_2(\mathbf{x}^{[1]})\eta_2(\mathbf{x}^{[2]})\eta_1(\mathbf{x}).
\end{aligned} \tag{6}$$

Since $\eta_i(\mathbf{x}^{[1]}) \to \eta_i(\mathbf{x})$ and $\eta_i(\mathbf{x}^{[2]}) \to \eta_i(\mathbf{x})$ with probability 1 as $n \to \infty$, then with probability 1,

$$p[\text{reject} \mid \mathbf{x}, \mathbf{x}^{[1]}, \mathbf{x}^{[2]}] \to 2\eta_1(\mathbf{x})\eta_2(\mathbf{x}) \triangleq R_2(\mathbf{x}), \tag{7}$$

$$\begin{aligned}
p[\text{error} \mid \mathbf{x}, \mathbf{x}^{[1]}, \mathbf{x}^{[2]}] &\to [\eta_1(\mathbf{x})]^2 \eta_2(\mathbf{x}) + \eta_1(\mathbf{x})[\eta_2(\mathbf{x})]^2 \\
&= \eta_1(\mathbf{x})\eta_2(\mathbf{x}) \triangleq P_{[2]}(\mathbf{x}).
\end{aligned} \tag{8}$$

In summary,

$$R_{[2]}(\mathbf{x}) = 2r^*(\mathbf{x})[1 - r(\mathbf{x})], \tag{9}$$

$$P_{[2]}(\mathbf{x}) = r^*(\mathbf{x})[1 - r(\mathbf{x})], \tag{10}$$

for the $2\mathrm{NN}_2$ rule with a reject option. From (9) and (10) we conclude that

$$R_{[2]}(\mathbf{x}) = 2P_{[2]}(\mathbf{x}). \tag{11}$$

Comparing (9) and (10) with the asymptotic probability of error for the $1\mathrm{NN}_2$ rule, we see that

$$R_{[2]} = \text{probability of error of } 1\mathrm{NN}_2 \text{ rule}, \tag{12}$$

---

†For small sample size, this rule can have poor performance because it does not have provision for using different distance measures for the respective classes.

$$P_{[2]} = \tfrac{1}{2}[\text{probability of error of 1NN}_2 \text{ rule}].\qquad(13)$$

Thus if errors are at least twice as costly as rejects, the 2NN_2 rule with reject option has lower total cost than the 1NN_2 rule.

To show this, note that if c_r is the cost of reject and c_e is the cost of error, then the cost when using the 2NN_2 rule with reject option is

$$R_{[2]}c_r + P_{[2]}c_e = P_{[2]}[2c_r + c_e].$$

The cost using the 1NN_2 rule is

$$2P_{[2]}c_e.$$

Thus, it is advantageous to use the 2NN_2 rule with reject option rather than the 1NN_2 rule if $2c_r < c_e$.

Next consider general k where a decision is made only if all kNN's are from the same category. Then, asymptotically,

$$\begin{aligned}
R_{[k]}(\mathbf{x}) &= p[\text{reject}\,|\,\mathbf{x}, \mathbf{x}^{[1]}, \mathbf{x}^{[2]}, \ldots, \mathbf{x}^{[k]}] = 1 - [\eta_1(\mathbf{x})]^k - [\eta_2(\mathbf{x})]^k \\
&= 1 - [r^*(\mathbf{x})]^k - [1 - r^*(\mathbf{x})]^k,
\end{aligned}\qquad(14)$$

and thus

$$R_{[k]} = E[1 - [r(\mathbf{x})]^k - [1 - r(\mathbf{x})]^k].\qquad(15)$$

Similarly,

$$\begin{aligned}
P_{[k]}(\mathbf{x}) &= [\eta_1(\mathbf{x})]^k[1 - \eta_1(\mathbf{x})] + [\eta_2(\mathbf{x})]^k[1 - \eta_2(\mathbf{x})] \\
&= [r^*(\mathbf{x})]^k[1 - r^*(\mathbf{x})] + r^*(\mathbf{x})[1 - r^*(\mathbf{x})]^k,
\end{aligned}\qquad(16)$$

$$P_{[k]} = E[P_{[k]}(\mathbf{x})].\qquad(17)$$

Modification Allowing $k - k'$ Discrepancies

Consider a rule where $\mathbf{x}$ is decided from category i if k' or more of the nearest neighbors to $\mathbf{x}$ are from category i. If k is even, then k' must be greater than or equal to $(k/2) + 1$ to ensure a nonzero reject rate. If k is odd, $k' \geq (k + 3)/2$ is sufficient. The reject rate for this rule, denoted $R_{k,k'}(\mathbf{x})$, is

$$R_{k,k'}(\mathbf{x}) = \sum_{i=[(k+3)/2]^-}^{k'-1} \binom{k}{i}\{[r^*(\mathbf{x})]^i[1 - r^*(\mathbf{x})]^{k-i} + [r^*(\mathbf{x})]^{k-i}[1 - r^*(\mathbf{x})]^i\},\quad(18)$$

where $[\xi]^-$ denotes the largest integer, smaller than or equal to ξ. The probability of error for the rule, denoted $P_{k,k'}(\mathbf{x})$, is

$$P_{k,k'}(\mathbf{x}) = \sum_{i=k'}^{k} \binom{k}{i} \{[r^*(\mathbf{x})]^i [1 - r^*(\mathbf{x})]^{k-i} + [r^*(\mathbf{x})]^{k-i} [1 - r^*(\mathbf{x})]^k. \qquad (19)$$

$k\mathrm{NN}_3$ Rule with a Reject Option

The $k\mathrm{NN}_3$ rule with a reject option will be defined similar to Hellman's definition for the $k\mathrm{NN}_2$ rule with a reject option. Let t be the ratio of the cost of a reject to the cost of an error and a correct decision has zero loss. Then overall cost is minimized by rejecting whenever $r(\mathbf{x}) \geq t$, the same as for the $k\mathrm{NN}_2$ rule.

The $k\mathrm{NN}_3$ rule with a reject option is now defined as a rule where the terms $P_i(f(\mathbf{x}|i))_{n_i}$, $i = 1, 2, \ldots, M$, are examined for each category. Category a is decided if

$$\frac{P_a(f(\mathbf{x}|a))_{n_a}}{P_i(f(\mathbf{x}|i))_{n_i}} > \alpha, \qquad \text{for all } i \neq a, \alpha > 1$$

where α is a constant and

$$(f(\mathbf{x}|i))_{n_i} = \frac{k_i}{(n_i + 1)\Phi_i},$$

and the distance measure $d_i(\mathbf{x}, \mathbf{y})$ is specified at $\mathbf{x}$ for the ith class to fit the problem.

4-6 Upper Bound for Risk of $k\mathrm{NN}_3$ Rule

Restricting attention to two categories ($M = 2$) and a zero–one loss matrix,

$$\mathbf{L} = \begin{bmatrix} 0 & 1 \\ 1 & 0 \end{bmatrix},$$

the point risk $r(\mathbf{x})$ of the $k\mathrm{NN}_3$ rule reduces to (see Section 3-2.6)

$$r(\mathbf{x}) = \eta_1(\mathbf{x})q_2^n(\mathbf{x}) + \eta_2(\mathbf{x})q_1^n(\mathbf{x}), \qquad (1)$$

with $q_j^n(\mathbf{x})$ given by

$$q_j^n(\mathbf{x}) = p\left[\frac{P_i k_i}{(n_i + 1)\Phi_i} < \frac{P_j k_j}{(n_j + 1)\Phi_j}, \; i \neq j\right]. \qquad (2)$$

In Section 4-3.1 conditions for

$$\frac{k_i}{(n_i + 1)\Phi_i} \xrightarrow{P} f(\mathbf{x}|i) \tag{3}$$

were given. In terms of these conditions, the following theorem is stated.

Theorem.   If for $i = 1, 2$, $f_i(\mathbf{x})$ is continuous at $\mathbf{x}$, regions $\{\mathscr{I}_{is}\}_{s=1}^{n_i}$ with corresponding volumes $\{\Phi_{is}\}_{s=1}^{n_i}$ satisfy

1. $\lim\limits_{n_i \to \infty} \sup\limits_{\mathbf{y} \in \mathscr{I}_{in_i}} |\mathbf{x} - \mathbf{y}| = 0,$
2. $\lim\limits_{n_i \to \infty} n_i \Phi_{in_i} = \infty,$
3. k_i is the number of statistically independent random samples $\mathbf{x}_1^i$, $\mathbf{x}_2^i, \ldots, \mathbf{x}_{n_i}^i$ from $f_i(\mathbf{x})$ which lie in $\mathscr{I}_{in_i}$,

then

$$\lim_{\substack{n_1 \to \infty \\ n_2 \to \infty}} r(\mathbf{x}) = \begin{cases} \eta_1(\mathbf{x}), & P_1 f_1(\mathbf{x}) < P_2 f_2(\mathbf{x}), \\ \eta_2(\mathbf{x}), & P_2 f_2(\mathbf{x}) < P_1 f_1(\mathbf{x}). \end{cases}$$

Outline of Proof.   As a result of conditions 1, 2, and 3, Eq. (3) applies and $q_j^n(\mathbf{x})$ converges to 1 or zero except when $P_1 f_1(\mathbf{x}) = f_2(\mathbf{x})P_2$. Then Eq. (1) follows. It follows that

$$R = \lim_{\substack{n_1 \to \infty \\ n_2 \to \infty}} E[r(\mathbf{x})] = E\left[\lim_{\substack{n_1 \to \infty \\ n_2 \to \infty}} r(\mathbf{x})\right] = R^*$$

by using the dominated convergence theorem (see [40]) for interchanging the limit and expectation operations. Thus, the global risk of the $k\mathrm{NN}_3$ rule converges to the Bayes risk $R^* : R = R^*$.

4-7   Example of Estimating Distance Measures for the $k\mathrm{NN}_3$ Rules

The $k\mathrm{NN}_3$ decision rule requires that

$$(f_i(\mathbf{x}))_{n_i} = \frac{k_i}{(n_i + 1)\Phi_i} \tag{1}$$

be computed for each category. For spherical tolerance regions centered at $\mathbf{x}$, Φ_i is the volume of the smallest sphere (with distance function d_i) which contains k_i of the n_i samples. A distance measure similar to the one implicit in the multivariate Gaussian density function is

$$d_i(\mathbf{x}, \mathbf{y}; \mathbf{A}_i) = (\mathbf{x} - \mathbf{y})^t \mathbf{A}_i^t \mathbf{A}_i (\mathbf{x} - \mathbf{y}) \tag{2}$$

with (for $L = 2$)

$$\mathbf{A}_i = \begin{bmatrix} a_i \cos \theta_i & a_i \sin \theta_i \\ -\sin \theta_i & \cos \theta_i \end{bmatrix}, \qquad 0 \leq \theta_i \leq \pi, \ 1 \leq a_i < \infty.$$

Use of this distance measure d_i for determining k_i nearest samples to $\mathbf{x}$, for use in (1), is equivalent to linearly transforming the samples from category i by a nonsingular transformation $\mathbf{A}_i$ and then using the Euclidean distance measure $d_i(\mathbf{x}, \mathbf{y}) = \| \mathbf{x} - \mathbf{y} \|$ in the $k\mathrm{NN}_3$ rule applied to the transformed vectors. Figure 4.1 is a sketch of $d_i(\mathbf{x}, \mathbf{y}; \mathbf{A}_i) = $ constant. The following

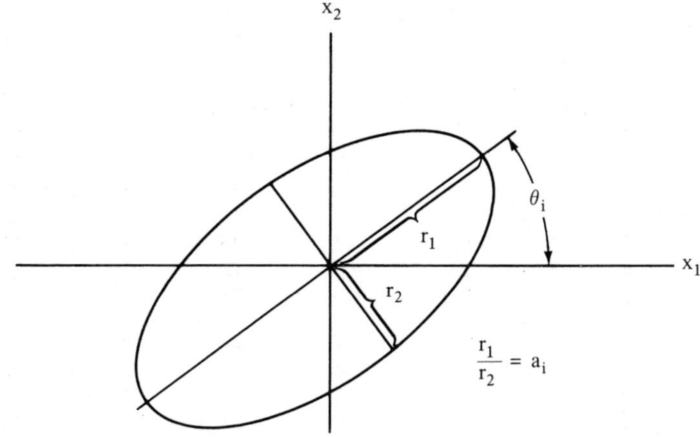

Fig. 4.1 Locus of points $d_i(\mathbf{x}, \mathbf{y}) = $ constant

computer-simulated examples illustrate how $\mathbf{A}_i$ can be estimated to improve performance of the $k\mathrm{NN}_3$ rule for small sample size.

Example 1 For a first example there are two categories ($M = 2$), $P_1 = P_2 = \frac{1}{2}$ and known, $k_1 = k_2 = k$, and $\mathbf{A}_i = \mathbf{A}$, $i = 1, 2$. Pseudo-random vectors are generated from two bivariate Gaussian densities with means and covariances,

$$\mathbf{m}_1 = [-\tfrac{3}{2}, 0], \qquad \mathbf{\Sigma}_1 = \mathbf{I},$$

$$\mathbf{m}_2 = [\tfrac{3}{2}, 0], \qquad \mathbf{\Sigma}_2 = \mathbf{I}.$$

The Bayes error can be calculated using results from Chapter 2 and is 6.7 percent. For the experiment, $n_1 = n_2 = 50$ for training and 250 additional samples are generated from each category to serve as a recognition set.

The total number of errors in misclassifying the 500 recognition samples based on the 100 training samples was determined for 35 distance measures corresponding to $a = 1, 2, 5, 10, 20, 50, 100$ and $\theta = 0, \pi/8, \pi/4, 3\pi/8$, and $\pi/2$. The 35 distance measures were applied for $k = 1, 3$, and 10. The results are shown in Table 4.1.

Table 4.1 Number of k-NN$_3$ errors as function of Metric parameters a and θ for 50 training samples per class

	a	$\theta = 0$	$\theta = \pi/8$	$\theta = \pi/4$	$\theta = 3\pi/8$	$\theta = \pi/2$
	1	47	47	47	47	47
	2	50	44	48	47	46
	5	51	56	55	42	30
$k = 1$	10	61	64	59	44	36
	20	79	79	61	42	39
	50	123	113	76	40	43
	100	172	135	89	46	43
	1	29	29	29	29	29
	2	31	33	29	29	26
	5	40	37	37	35	23
$k = 3$	10	47	63	44	37	25
	20	112	88	46	32	27
	50	206	138	72	35	25
	100	245	161	75	35	23
	1	23	23	23	23	23
	2	23	26	27	25	22
	5	48	46	39	31	22
$k = 10$	10	114	91	53	34	20
	20	200	134	62	34	20
	50	240	157	63	34	20
	100	243	162	63	34	20

The same experiment was repeated with $n_1 = n_2 = 250$; the results are shown in Table 4.2. Conclusions from the two experiments are as follows:

1. The choice of distance measure affects performance and the Euclidean metric ($\mathbf{A} = \mathbf{I}$) is not "too bad."
2. Experimental performance tends to be highest for θ near $\pi/2$ and large a.
3. The peak in performance is broad near $\theta = \pi/2$ and the valley in performance is narrow near $\theta = 0$.
4. The peak in performance becomes broader as $n_1 = n_2$ increases.

In conclusion, an acceptable transformation is

$$\mathbf{A} \cong \begin{bmatrix} 1 & 0 \\ 0 & 0 \end{bmatrix},$$

Table 4.2 Number of errors as function of Metric parameters a and θ for 250 samples/class

	a	$\theta = 0$	$\theta = \pi/8$	$\theta = \pi/4$	$\theta = 3\pi/8$	$\theta = \pi/2$
	1	46	46	46	46	46
	2	43	38	38	44	42
	5	46	42	38	42	38
$k = 1$	10	46	43	36	34	33
	20	47	49	45	35	26
	50	67	62	45	35	28
	100	91	69	49	40	29
	1	25	25	25	25	25
	2	23	25	25	26	28
	5	29	26	29	30	28
$k = 3$	10	35	27	31	33	30
	20	41	33	40	34	24
	50	67	53	47	35	25
	100	114	83	55	35	25
	1	27	27	27	27	27
	2	25	30	32	28	26
	5	29	33	35	29	27
$k = 10$	10	36	42	38	29	28
	20	58	56	47	33	27
	50	120	93	53	37	25
	100	213	129	60	37	24

which indicates that only the first dimension (or feature) should be used for classification; the Bayes decision rule for this problem would use only the first dimension for classification.

Example 2 (Computer Homework Problem, do Problem 20)
    Consider the following example:

$$\mathbf{m}_1 = [-1, 0], \qquad \Sigma_1 = \begin{bmatrix} 10 & 0 \\ 0 & 1 \end{bmatrix},$$

$$\mathbf{m}_2 = [1, 0], \qquad \Sigma_2 = \begin{bmatrix} 10 & 0 \\ 0 & 1 \end{bmatrix}.$$

Example 3 (Computer Homework Problem, do Problem 20)
    Consider the following example:

$$\mathbf{m}_1 = [-1, 0], \qquad \Sigma_1 = \begin{bmatrix} 5 & 0 \\ 0 & 1 \end{bmatrix},$$

$$\mathbf{m}_2 = [1, 0], \qquad \Sigma_2 = \begin{bmatrix} 1 & 0 \\ 0 & 1 \end{bmatrix}.$$

Example 4 (Computer Homework Problem, do Problem 20)
Consider the following example:

$$\mathbf{m}_1 = [-2, 0], \qquad \Sigma_1 = \begin{bmatrix} 1 & 0 \\ 0 & 3 \end{bmatrix},$$

$$\mathbf{m}_2 = [2, 0], \qquad \Sigma_2 = \begin{bmatrix} 3 & 0 \\ 0 & 1 \end{bmatrix}.$$

4-8 Consistency of $k\mathrm{NN}_3$ Rule for Increasing k_i

If $k_i(\mathbf{x})$ is allowed to be a slowly increasing function of n_i, it is relatively simple to prove that the risk of the $k\mathrm{NN}_3$ rule converges in probability to the Bayes risk R^* (type 4 convergence of Section 3-3.6).

Theorem. Let $k_i(\mathbf{x})$ be such that $\lim_{n_i \to \infty} k_i(\mathbf{x}) = \infty$, and $\lim_{n_i \to \infty} k_i(\mathbf{x})/n_i = 0$. If $f(\mathbf{x}|\omega_i)$ are continuous functions of $\mathbf{x}$, then the risk of the $k\mathrm{NN}_3$ rule converges in probability to the Bayes risk R^* as $n_1, n_2, \ldots, n_M \to \infty$.

Outline of Proof. Since the distance function $d_i(\mathbf{y}, \mathbf{x})$ induces a continuous distribution for fixed $\mathbf{x}, \mathbf{y}$ and $f(\mathbf{x}|\omega_i)$ is continuous at $\mathbf{x}$, an argument identical to that of Loftsgaarden and Quesenberry [20] can be used to show that the density estimator $k_i(\mathbf{x})/((n_i + 1)\Phi_i(\mathbf{x}; \dot{\mathbf{x}}_n))$ converges in probability to $f(\mathbf{x}|\omega_i)$.

Let $D_j^*(\mathbf{x}) = 1$ if and only if the Bayes decision rule assigns $\mathbf{x}$ to class ω_j and 0 otherwise; then for each $\epsilon > 0$ and $\mathbf{x}$ there is a number $n(\epsilon, \mathbf{x})$ such that for $n > n(\epsilon, \mathbf{x})$, $|q_j^n(\mathbf{x}) - D_j^*(\mathbf{x})| < \epsilon$ for all classes for which the Bayes decision is unique. For $\epsilon > 0$, let $\tau_{n,\epsilon}$ be the set of $\mathbf{x}$ for which $n(\epsilon, \mathbf{x}) < n$. Then, from Section 3-3.2,

$$
\begin{aligned}
E_{\mathbf{x_n}}[R(\dot{\mathbf{x}}_n)] &= \sum_{i=1}^{M} P_i \sum_{j=1}^{M} L_{ji} \int_{\tau_{n,\epsilon}} q_j^n(\mathbf{x}) \, dF(\mathbf{x}|\omega_i) \\
&\quad + \sum_{i=1}^{M} P_i \sum_{j=1}^{M} L_{ji} \int_{\tau_{n,\epsilon}^c} q_j^n(\mathbf{x}) \, dF(\mathbf{x}|\omega_i) \\
&\leq \sum_{i=1}^{M} P_i \sum_{j=1}^{M} L_{ji} \int_{\tau_{n,\epsilon}} D_j^*(\mathbf{x}; \dot{\mathbf{x}}_n) \, dF(\mathbf{x}|\omega_i) \\
&\quad + \sum_{i=1}^{M} P_i \sum_{j=1}^{M} L_{ji} \int_{\tau_{n,\epsilon}} \epsilon \, dF(\mathbf{x}|\omega_i) \\
&\quad + \sum_{i=1}^{M} P_i \sum_{j=1}^{M} L_{ji} \int_{\tau_{n,\epsilon}^c} q_j^n(\mathbf{x}) \, dF(\mathbf{x}|\omega_i),
\end{aligned}
\tag{1}
$$

where $\tau_{n,\epsilon}^c$ is the set of $\mathbf{x}$ for which $n(\epsilon, \mathbf{x}) \geq n$. The first term is always less than R^*. The second term can be made smaller than some positive $\eta/2$ by choosing ϵ small enough. Since for fixed $\epsilon > 0$, $\tau_{n,\epsilon}$ monotonically increases to $\mathscr{X}$, let $n(\eta/2)$ be a number such that if $n > n(\eta/2)$, the third term is less than $\eta/2$. Hence, for any $\eta > 0$, there exists an $n(\eta/2)$ such that if $n > n(\eta/2)$, $R^* \leq E_{\mathbf{x_n}}[R(\dot{\mathbf{x}}_n)] < R^* + \eta$. Hence, $E_{\mathbf{x_n}}[R(\dot{\mathbf{x}}_n)]$ converges to R^*, the lower bound of the random variable $R(\dot{\mathbf{x}}_n)$. This, and the fact that $R(\dot{\mathbf{x}}_n) \leq R^{**}$, a constant, implies that the variance of risk converges to 0, yielding convergence in mean square and hence in probability.

A question that immediately arises is: How fast should $k_i(\mathbf{x})$ be allowed to go to infinity with n_i to obtain the fastest convergence rate? Loftsgaarden and Quesenberry [20] indicated that if $k_i(\mathbf{x})$ is near $n_i^{1/2}$, the density estimator (1) of Section 4-3.1 appears to give good results on the basis of some empirical work. Patrick and Fischer [28] found that the "best" choice of $k_i(\mathbf{x})$ also is a function of L and the irregularity of the underlying density functions, also on the basis of empirical work. Another question often is asked about the choice of distance function. Clearly, if the distance function is acceptable such that the density estimates converge, then the $k\mathrm{NN}_3$ rule is consistent. The choice of $d_i(\mathbf{y}, \mathbf{x})$ can affect the rate of convergence. How is the "best" distance function chosen? The choice is made on the basis of the smoothness of the underlying densities and on other a priori knowledge concerning relationships among the measurements.

4-9 Moments of $k\mathrm{NN}_3$ Risk

The δth moment of the distribution of the $k\mathrm{NN}_3$ rule is now examined as a function of k_i, n_i, and the underlying statistics. From Section 3-2.8, the δth moment of risk of any sample-based rule can be specified if $q^n_{j_1,\ldots,j_\delta}(\mathbf{x}^{(1)}, \ldots, \mathbf{x}^{(\delta)})$ can be found for any δ-tuple $(\mathbf{x}^{(1)}, \ldots, \mathbf{x}^{(\delta)})$.

From Section 3-2.8 and previous results in the present chapter,

$$
\begin{aligned}
q^n_{j_1,\ldots,j_\delta}(\mathbf{x}^{(1)}, \ldots, \mathbf{x}^{(\delta)}) &= p[d(\mathbf{x}^{(v)}; \dot{\mathbf{x}}_n) = \omega_{j_v}; v = 1, 2, \ldots, \delta] \\
&= p\Bigg[\sum_{i=1}^{M} P_i L_{j_v i} \frac{k_i(\mathbf{x}^{(v)})}{(n_i + 1)\Phi_i(\mathbf{x}^{(v)}; \dot{\mathbf{x}}_n)} \\
&\quad < \sum_{i=1}^{M} P_i L_{m_i} \frac{k_i(\mathbf{x}^{(v)})}{(n_i + 1)\Phi_i(\mathbf{x}^{(v)}; \dot{\mathbf{x}}_n)}, \\
&\qquad m = 1, \ldots, M; m \neq j_v; v = 1, 2, \ldots, \delta \Bigg],
\end{aligned}
$$

(1)

where $\Phi_i(\mathbf{x}^{(v)}; \dot{\mathbf{x}}_n)$ is the volume of the neighborhood $\mathscr{I}_i(\mathbf{x}^{(v)}; \dot{\mathbf{x}}_n) = \{\mathbf{y} : d_i(\mathbf{y}, \mathbf{x}^{(v)}) \leq \epsilon_i(\mathbf{x}^{(v)}; \dot{\mathbf{x}}_n)\}$ about $\mathbf{x}^{(v)}$.

Define the "coverage" of $\mathscr{I}_i(\mathbf{x}^{(v)}; \dot{\mathbf{x}}_\mathbf{n})$ to be u_i^v, where

$$u_i^v \triangleq u_i^v(\mathbf{x}^{(v)}, \dot{\mathbf{x}}_\mathbf{n}) \triangleq H_i(\Phi_i(\mathbf{x}^{(v)}; \dot{\mathbf{x}}_\mathbf{n}), \mathbf{x}^{(v)})$$

$$\triangleq \int_{\mathscr{I}_i(\mathbf{x}^{(v)}; \dot{\mathbf{x}}_\mathbf{n})} dF(\mathbf{x} \,|\, \omega_i). \tag{2}$$

H_i is a nondecreasing function of $\Phi_i(\mathbf{x}^{(v)}; \dot{\mathbf{x}}_\mathbf{n})$ which takes into account the underlying density and the distance function. The inverse is defined

$$H_i^{-1}(u_i^v; \mathbf{x}^{(v)}) = \min \{\Phi : u_i^v = H_i(\Phi, \mathbf{x}^{(v)})\}. \tag{3}$$

Thus, (1) becomes

$$
\begin{aligned}
q_{j_1,\ldots,j_\delta}(\mathbf{x}^{(1)}, \ldots, \mathbf{x}^{(\delta)}) = p\Bigg[&\sum_{i=1}^{M} P_i L_{j_v i} \frac{k_i(\mathbf{x}^{(v)})}{(n_i + 1)H_i^{-1}(u_i^v; \mathbf{x}^{(v)})} \\
&< \sum_{i=1}^{M} P_i L_{mi} \frac{k_i(\mathbf{x}^{(v)})}{(n_i + 1)H_i^{-1}(u_i^v; \mathbf{x}^{(v)})}; \\
&m = 1, \ldots, M,\ m \neq j_v,\ v = 1, 2, \ldots, \delta \Bigg].
\end{aligned}
\tag{4}
$$

Let $G_i(u_i^1, \ldots, u_i^\delta)$ denote the joint distribution of the δ coverages $(u_i^1, \ldots, u_i^\delta)$. Since u_i^v is independent of u_j^w for $j \neq i$ irrespective of w and v due to one class training set being independent of another class training set, (4) can be written

$$
\begin{aligned}
q_{j_1,\ldots,j_\delta}^n(\mathbf{x}^{(1)}, \ldots, \mathbf{x}^{(\delta)}) = \int \cdots \int &\prod_{v=1}^{\delta} [Q_{j_v}^n(u_1^v, \ldots, u_M^v; \mathbf{x}^{(v)})] \\
&\times \prod_{i=1}^{M} [dG_i(u_i^1, \ldots, u_i^\delta)],
\end{aligned}
\tag{5}
$$

where $Q_{j_v}^r$ is the indicator function of $\mathscr{D}_{j_v}^n(\mathbf{x}^v)$:

$$
\begin{aligned}
\mathscr{D}_{j_v}^n(\mathbf{x}^v) = \Bigg\{ (u_1^v, \ldots, u_M^v) : &\sum_{i=1}^{M} P_i L_{j_v i} \frac{k_i(\mathbf{x}^{(v)})}{(n_i + 1)H_i^{-1}(u_i^v; \mathbf{x}^{(v)})} \\
&< \sum_{i=1}^{M} P_i L_{mi} \frac{k_i(\mathbf{x}^{(v)})}{(n_i + 1)H_i^{-1}(u_i^v; \mathbf{x}^{(v)})};\ m = 1, \ldots, M,\ m \neq j_v \Bigg\}.
\end{aligned}
\tag{6}
$$

The problem remains to determine $G_i(u_i^1, \ldots, u_i^\delta)$. The distribution will be found on a portion of the δ-dimensional unit cube by showing similarity to another sequence of coverages of nonoverlapping sets, denoted $\{\underline{\mathscr{I}}_i(\mathbf{x}^{(v)}, \dot{\mathbf{x}}_\mathbf{n})\}$, constructed from the training sets. These latter regions are the familiar tolerance regions from studies in order statistics which are introduced in Section 2-21.

These tolerance regions are defined as follows: Let

$$\varphi_{i_v}(\mathbf{y}) = d_i(\mathbf{y}; \mathbf{x}^{(v)}); \quad v = 1, 2, \ldots, \delta, \tag{7}$$

$$k_i(\mathbf{x}^{(v)}) = \text{number of class } i \text{ samples in } \mathscr{I}_i(\mathbf{x}^{(v)}; \dot{\mathbf{x}}_{\mathbf{n}}) \tag{8}$$

Using Tukey's tolerance region construction procedure† ([33], p. 152) with the above-defined functions, construct the regions:

$$\mathscr{I}_i(\mathbf{x}^{(1)}; \dot{\mathbf{x}}_{\mathbf{n}}) = \{\mathbf{y} : \varphi_{i_1}(\mathbf{y}) \leq \min_j \, (k_i(\mathbf{x}^{(1)}))[\varphi_{i_1}(\mathbf{x}_j^i) : 1 \leq j \leq n_i]\},\ddagger \tag{9a}$$

$$\begin{aligned}
\mathscr{I}_i(\mathbf{x}^{(2)}; \mathbf{x}_{\mathbf{n}}) = \{\mathbf{y} : \mathbf{y} &\notin \mathscr{I}_i(\mathbf{x}^{(1)}; \dot{\mathbf{x}}_{\mathbf{n}}) \text{ and} \\
\varphi_{i_2}(\mathbf{y}) &\leq \min_j \, (k_i(\mathbf{x}^{(2)}))[\varphi_{i_2}(\mathbf{x}_j^i) : 1 \leq j \leq n_i, \text{ and} \\
\mathbf{x}_j^i &\notin \mathscr{I}_i(\mathbf{x}^{(1)}; \dot{\mathbf{x}}_{\mathbf{n}})]\},
\end{aligned} \tag{9b}$$

$$\begin{aligned}
\mathscr{I}_i(\mathbf{x}^{(\delta)}; \dot{\mathbf{x}}_{\mathbf{n}}) = \{\mathbf{y} : \mathbf{y} &\notin \mathscr{I}_i(\mathbf{x}^{(v)}; \dot{\mathbf{x}}_{\mathbf{n}}), \, v = 1, 2, \ldots, \delta - 1 \text{ and} \\
\varphi_{i_v}(\mathbf{y}) &\leq \min_j \, (k_i(\mathbf{x}_j^v))[\varphi_{i_v}(\mathbf{x}_j^i) : 1 \leq j \leq n_i, \text{ and} \\
\mathbf{x}_j^i &\notin \mathscr{I}_i(\mathbf{x}^{(v)}; \dot{\mathbf{x}}_{\mathbf{n}}), \, v = 1, 2, \ldots, \delta - 1]\},
\end{aligned} \tag{9c}$$

where $\min \, (k_i(\mathbf{x}^{(v)}))$ means the $k_i(\mathbf{x}^v)$th minimum.

An illustration is provided in Figure 4.2 for such a construction for the ith class when $k_i(\mathbf{x}) = 4$, $n_i = 26$, $d_i(\mathbf{y}, \mathbf{x}) = |\mathbf{y} - \mathbf{x}|$, $\delta = 4$, and a particular training set. For comparison, the similar regions $\{\mathscr{I}_i(\mathbf{x}^{(v)}; \dot{\mathbf{x}}_{\mathbf{n}})\}$ are illustrated in Figure 4.3 under identical conditions.

Denote by $\underline{u}_i^v$ the coverage of $\mathscr{I}_i(\mathbf{x}^{(v)}; \dot{\mathbf{x}}_{\mathbf{n}})$ defined in a manner similar to u_i^v. Under the assumption that $F(\mathbf{x}\,|\,\omega_i)$ are such that $d_i(\mathbf{y}, \mathbf{x})$ induces continuous distributions for fixed $\mathbf{x}$, by Fraser's theorem 3.2 [32], the coverages $\underline{u}_i^1, \ldots, \underline{u}_i^\delta$ have the γ-variate Dirichlet distribution ([33], p. 238) $\underline{G}_i(\underline{u}_i^1, \ldots, \underline{u}_i^\delta)$:

$$\begin{aligned}
\underline{G}_i(\underline{u}_i^1, \underline{u}_i^2, \ldots, \underline{u}_i^\delta) = \, &\frac{n_i!}{(k_i(\mathbf{x}^{(1)}) - 1)! \cdots (k_i(\mathbf{x}^{(v)}) - 1)! \cdots (k_i(\mathbf{x}^{(\delta)}))!} \\
&\times (\underline{u}_i^1)^{k_i(\mathbf{x}^{(1)}) - 1} \cdots (\underline{u}_i^\delta)^{k_i(\mathbf{x}^{(\delta)}) - 1} \\
&\times (1 - \underline{u}_i^1 - \cdots - \underline{u}_i^\delta)^{n_i - k_i(\mathbf{x}^{(1)}) - \cdots - k_i(\mathbf{x}^{(\delta)})}
\end{aligned} \tag{10}$$

†See Chapter 2.

‡$\min_j \, (k_i(\mathbf{x}^{(v)}))[\varphi_{i_v}(\mathbf{x}_j^i) : 1 \leq j \leq n_i]$ in words means that for class i samples, the order functions $\varphi_{i_v}(\mathbf{x}_j^i)$ of these samples are taken and the $k_i(\mathbf{x}^{(v)})$ from the smallest taken as the first-order function.

defined on the simplex $\underline{u}_i^1 + \cdots + \underline{u}_i^\delta \leq 1$. The regions $\mathcal{I}_i(\mathbf{x}^{(v)}; \dot{\mathbf{x}}_\mathbf{n})$ are called "distribution-free tolerance regions" (discussed in Chapter 2) because the distribution of their coverages is free of the functional form of the underlying densities.

Comparing Figures 4.2 and 4.3 it is clear that the regions $\{\mathcal{I}_i(\mathbf{x}^{(v)}, \dot{\mathbf{x}}_\mathbf{n})\}$ (tolerance regions) and their respective coverages $\{\underline{u}_i^v\}$ are identical to† $\{\mathcal{I}_i(\mathbf{x}^{(v)}, \dot{\mathbf{x}}_\mathbf{n})\}$ (nontolerance regions) and their respective coverages $\{u_i^v\}$ if the latter regions are disjoint.

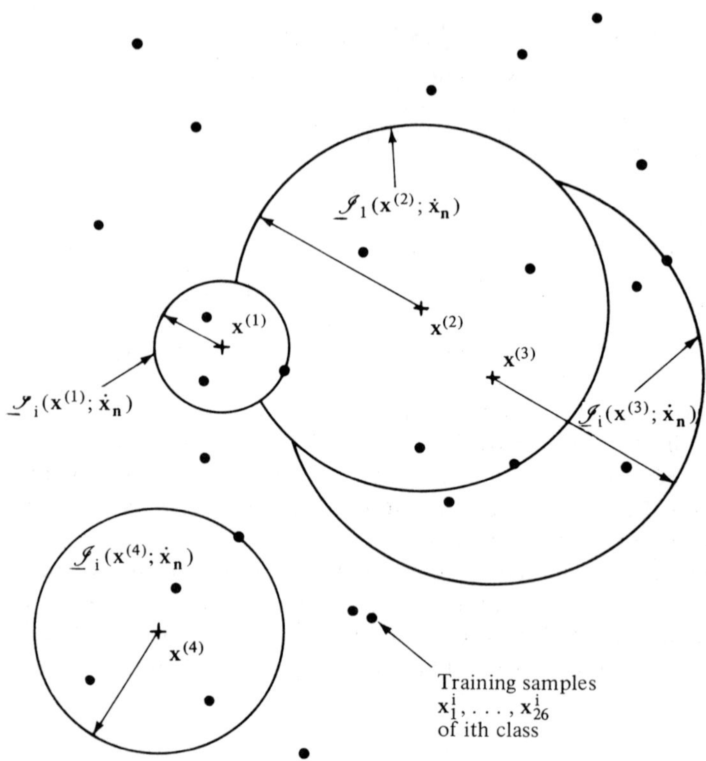

Fig. 4.2 Tolerance regions

Denote by $\mathcal{A}_i(\mathbf{x}^{(v)}, \ldots, \mathbf{x}^{(\delta)}) \triangleq \mathcal{A}_i^\delta$ the set of all δ-tuples $(u_i^1, \ldots, u_i^\delta)$ resulting from coverages of possible nonintersecting regions $\mathcal{I}_i(\mathbf{x}^{(1)}; \dot{\mathbf{x}}_\mathbf{n})$, $\ldots, \mathcal{I}_i(\mathbf{x}^{(\delta)}; \dot{\mathbf{x}}_\mathbf{n})$. $\mathcal{A}_i^\delta$ has the easily proved but temporarily unessential

---

†The regions $\mathcal{I}_i(\mathbf{x}^{(v)}, \mathbf{x}_\mathbf{n})$ have been used in the definition of the kNN_3 rule. The existence of multiple regions for $v = 1, 2, \ldots, \delta$ exists because of our consideration of the moments of risk.

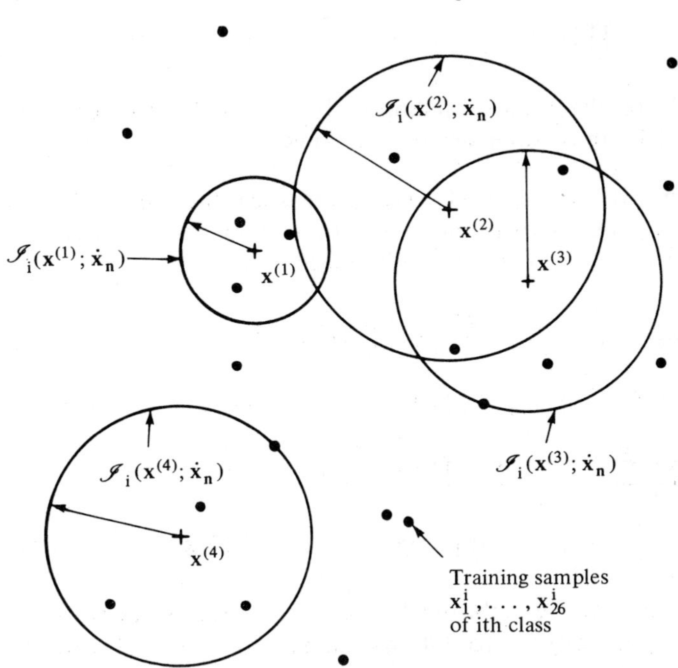

Fig. 4.3 Nontolerance regions

properties that:

1. Its boundary is a simple closed surface including the origin.
2. If $(a_1, \ldots, a_\delta)$ is in $\mathscr{A}_i^\delta$, then so is $(\alpha_1, \ldots, \alpha_\delta)$, where $0 \le \alpha_v \le a_v$, $v = 1, 2, \ldots, \delta$.
3. $a_i(\mathbf{x}^{(1)})$ equals the entire interval between 0 and 1;
4. $\mathscr{A}_i^\delta$ contains only the origin if $\mathbf{x}^{(i)} = \mathbf{x}^{(j)}$ for some i and j.

It is not difficult to show that $(u_i^1, \ldots, u_i^\delta)$ is in $\mathscr{A}_i^\delta$ if and only if $(\underline{u}_i^1, \ldots, \underline{u}_i^\delta)$ is in $\mathscr{A}_i^\delta$, and in that event $u_i^v = \underline{u}_i^v$. Hence $(u_i^1, \ldots, u_i^\delta)$ is Dirichlet distributed over $\mathscr{A}_i^\delta$. If $p_i(\mathbf{x}^{(1)}, \ldots, \mathbf{x}^{(\delta)})$ denotes the probability that $(u_i^1, \ldots, u_i^\delta)$ is contained in $\mathscr{A}_i^\delta$ with respect to $G_i(u_i^1, \ldots, u_i^\delta)$, and $A_i(u_i^1, \ldots, u_i^\delta; \mathbf{x}^{(1)}, \ldots, \mathbf{x}^{(\delta)})$ is the indicator function of $\mathscr{A}_i^\delta$, then it results that

$$0 \le q_{j_1 \ldots j_\delta}^n(\mathbf{x}^{(1)}, \ldots, \mathbf{x}^{(\delta)}) - q_{j_1 \ldots j_\delta}^{\prime n}(\mathbf{x}^{(1)}, \ldots, \mathbf{x}^{(\delta)})$$

$$\le 1 - \prod_{i=1}^{M} p_i(\mathbf{x}^{(1)}, \ldots, \mathbf{x}^{(\delta)}), \tag{11}$$

where

$$q'^n_{j_1 \ldots j_\delta}(\mathbf{x}^{(1)}, \ldots, \mathbf{x}^{(\delta)}) = \int \cdots \int \prod_{v=1}^{\delta} [Q^n_{j_v}(u_1^v, \ldots, u_M^v; \mathbf{x}^{(v)})]$$

$$\times \prod_{i=1}^{M} [A_i(u_i^1, \ldots, u_i^\delta; \mathbf{x}^{(1)}, \ldots, \mathbf{x}^{(\delta)})] \times \prod_{i=1}^{M} [dGu_i^1, \ldots, u_i^\delta)]. \qquad (12)$$

The results of the preceding analysis of the δth moment of the distribution of risk can be summarized as follows:

Theorem. If $F(\mathbf{x}|\omega_i)$ and $d_i(\mathbf{y}, \mathbf{x})$ are such that the order functions (8) induce continuous distribution functions, then the δth moment of risk of the $k\mathrm{NN}_3$ decision rule can be bounded:

$$0 \leq \mu_n^\delta - \sum_{i_1=1}^{M} \sum_{j_1=1}^{M} \cdots \sum_{i_\delta=1}^{M} \sum_{j_\delta=1}^{M} \left\{ \prod_{v=1}^{\delta} [P_{i_v} L_{j_v i_v}] \right.$$

$$\times \int_{\mathscr{X}} \cdots \int_{\mathscr{X}} q'^n_{j_1, \ldots, j_\delta}(\mathbf{x}^{(1)}, \ldots, \mathbf{x}^{(\delta)}) \, dF(\mathbf{x}^{(1)}|\omega_{i_1}) \cdots dF(\mathbf{x}^{(\delta)}|\omega_{i_\delta}) \right\}$$

$$\leq \sum_{i_1=1}^{M} \sum_{j_1=1}^{M} \cdots \sum_{i_\delta=1}^{M} \sum_{j_\delta=1}^{M} \left\{ \prod_{v=1}^{\delta} [P_{i_v} L_{j_v i_v}] \right.$$

$$\times \int_{\mathscr{X}} \cdots \int_{\mathscr{X}} 1 - \prod_{i=1}^{M} [p_i(\mathbf{x}^{(1)}, \ldots, \mathbf{x}^{(\delta)})] \, dF(\mathbf{x}^{(1)}|\omega_{i_1}) \cdots dF(\mathbf{x}^{(\delta)}|\omega_{i_\delta}) \right\}$$

$$(13)$$

with a zero on the right-hand side if the regions (nontolerance regions) $\mathscr{I}_i(\mathbf{x}^{(v)}, \dot{\mathbf{x}}_n)$ are disjoint for all possible $\dot{\mathbf{x}}_n$. This result (13) will be used as a framework for showing the limit of $q_{j_1, j_2, \ldots, j_\delta}(\mathbf{x}^{(1)}, \ldots, \mathbf{x}^{(\delta)})$ in Section 4-11.1 and convergence rate in Section 4-12.

It should be noticed that since $p_i(\mathbf{x}^{(1)})$ equals 1, the first moment is described explicitly. In a subsequent section it will be shown that for any δ, $p_i(\mathbf{x}^{(1)}, \ldots, \mathbf{x}^{(\delta)})$ can be made as close to 1 as desired by taking n_i large enough.

Example

To illustrate the calculation of the first moment of the $k\mathrm{NN}_3$ risk, a test problem considered by Cover and Hart [22, 23] and later by Peterson [34] will be examined.† In that one-dimensional, two-class example, the classes are equally likely ($p_1 = p_2 = \frac{1}{2}$), and in the interval $(0, 1)$, $f(x|\omega_1) = 2x$ while $f(x|\omega_2) = 2 - 2x$, as is indicated in Figure 4.4. Let the loss incurred by an error be 1 while a correct decision has 0 loss. A $k\mathrm{NN}_3$ rule based on $n_1 = n_2 = n/2$ samples per training set will be used, where $k_1 = k_2 = 1$. The

---

†Although this will illustrate the $k\mathrm{NN}_3$ rule expected risk for specific underlying statistics, it does not make use of the framework just set up for evaluating higher-order moments of risk.

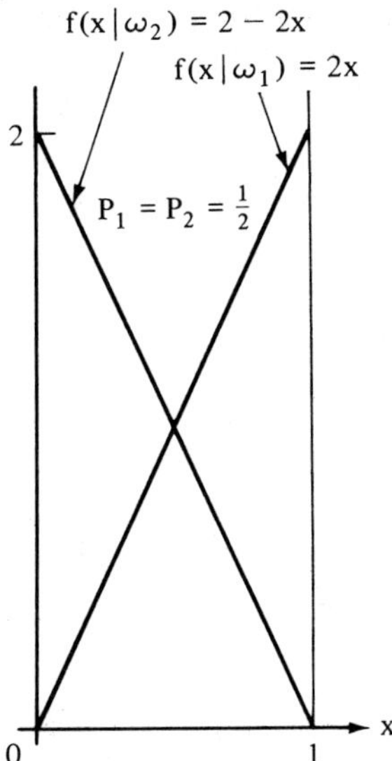

Fig. 4.4 Triangular density test problem

first moment of risk μ_n^1 will be determined using (13), where for simplicity we drop the superscript $\delta = 1$:

$$\mu_n = \sum_{i_1=1}^{2} \sum_{j_1=1}^{2} P_{i_1} L_{j_1 i_1} \int_{\mathscr{X}} q_{j_1}^n(\mathbf{x})\, dF(\mathbf{x}|\omega_{i_1}) \tag{14}$$

$$= \tfrac{1}{2} \int_{\mathscr{X}} q_1^n(\mathbf{x})\, dF(\mathbf{x}|\omega_2) + \tfrac{1}{2} \int_{\mathscr{X}} q_2^n(\mathbf{x})\, dF(\mathbf{x}|\omega_1). \tag{15}$$

Because of the problem symmetry, $q_1^n(\tfrac{1}{2} - x) = q_2^n(\tfrac{1}{2} + x)$. Since $q_1^n(x) + q_2^n(x) = 1$ and substituting $f(\mathbf{x}|\omega_1)$ and $f(\mathbf{x}|\omega_2)$, it results that

$$\mu_n = \tfrac{1}{4} + 2 \int_0^{1/2} (1 - 2x) q_1^n(x)\, dx, \tag{16}$$

where

$$q_1^n(x) = \int_0^1 \int_0^1 Q_1^n(u_1, u_2; \mathbf{x}) \prod_{i=1}^{2} [n_i(1 - u_i)^{n_i-1}\, du_i^1] \tag{17}$$

and where, for $0 \le x \le \tfrac{1}{2}$, $Q_1^n(u_1, u_2; \mathbf{x})$ is the indicator function for

$$Q_1^n(u_1, u_2; \mathbf{x}) = \left\{ u_1, u_2; \mathbf{x} \ge 2(u_1)^{1/2} - u_1 \text{ or } u_2 \ge \frac{1-x}{x} \right\}. \tag{18}$$

The primary requirements of obtaining the region Q_1^n used for evaluating the integral in (17) is to obtain a relationship between u_1 and u_2. To do this, consider a volume 2Δ about the point x as shown below:

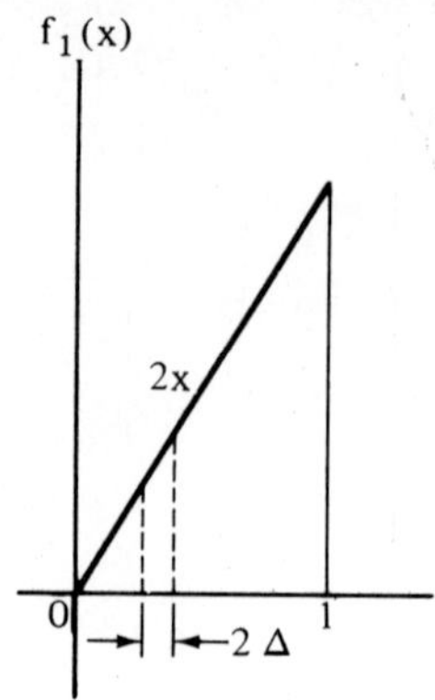

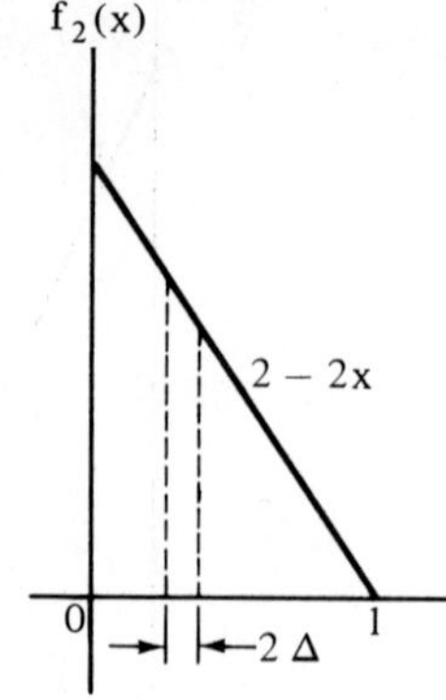

Then

$$u_1 = \int_{x-\Delta}^{x+\Delta} 2x\, dx = 4\Delta x, \qquad \Delta \leq x,$$

$$= \int_{0}^{x+\Delta} 2x\, dx = (x + \Delta)^2, \qquad x \leq \Delta \leq 1 - x,$$

and

$$u_2 = (2 - 2x)(2\Delta), \qquad \Delta \leq x,$$

$$= \int_{0}^{x+\Delta} (2 - 2x)\, dx = 2(x + \Delta)^2, \qquad x \leq \Delta \leq 1 - x.$$

Now, $Q_1(x^{(1)}) = H_1^{-1}(u_1^1, x^{(1)}) \leq H_2^{-1}(u_2^1, x^{(1)})$ or equality corresponds to the decision boundary. Thus, using a volume of Δ for each class as above,

$$u_2 = \frac{2 - 2x}{2x} u_1 = \frac{1 - x}{x}, \qquad u_1 \leq 4x^2,$$

$$u_2 = 2u_1^{1/2} - u_1, \qquad 4x^2 \leq u_1 \leq 1.$$

From the above it is possible to sketch

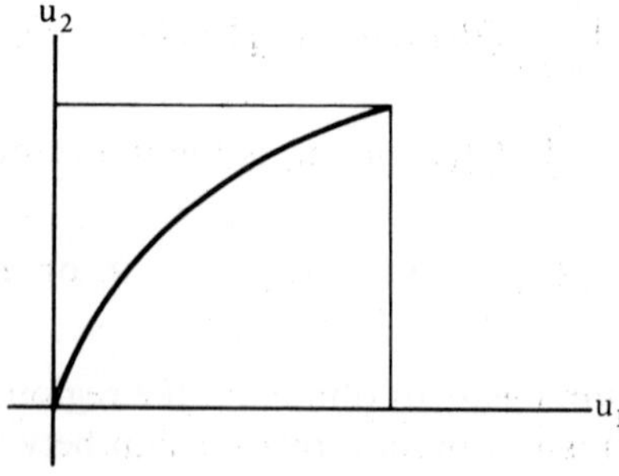

which corresponds to equal volumes for the tolerance region of each class in a $k\text{NN}_3$ rule. Thus the probability that the $k\text{NN}_3$ rule chooses class i can be evaluated, the results shown in Figure 4.5 for the example.

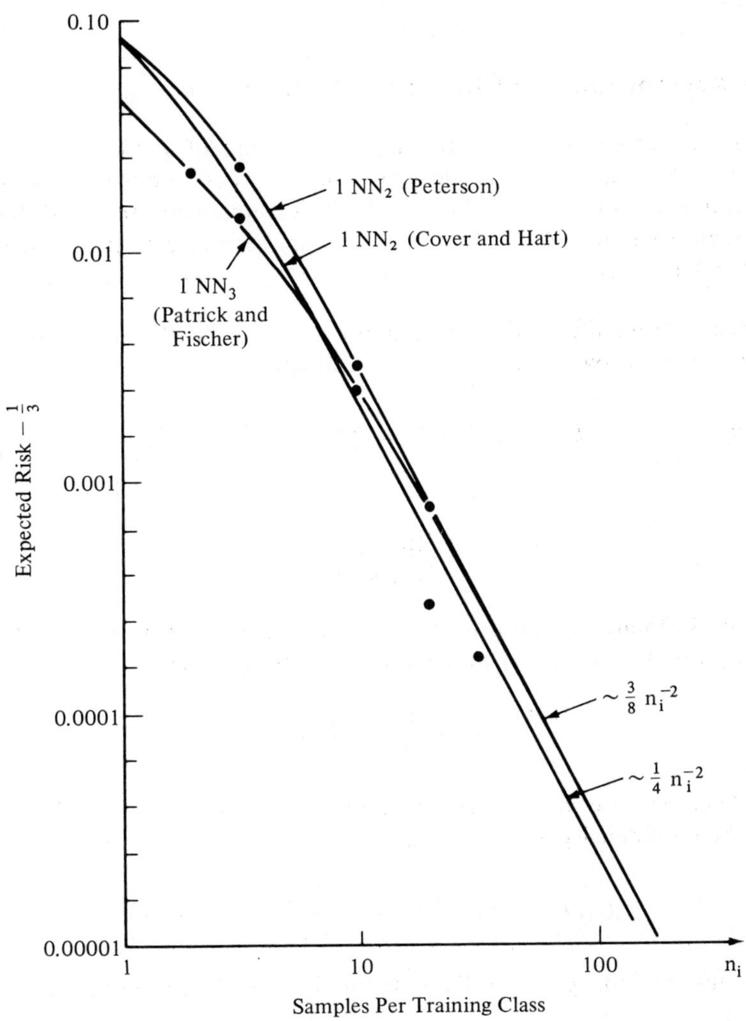

Fig. 4.5 Triangular test problem; small sample expected risk

These results suggest that an ideally designed $k\text{NN}_3$ rule should have a linear curve u_2 versus u_1 near $u_1, u_2 \longrightarrow 0$.

The reader should use this one-dimensional example to help him visualize a multidimensional problem where the metrics used to measure distances in the $k\text{NN}_3$ rule may not match the underlying statistics.

Even for this relatively simple problem, the upper and lower bounds of the second and higher moments are extremely difficult to evaluate (even numerically).

4-10 Asymptotic Point Risk of $k\mathrm{NN}_3$ Rule

In this section we determine the asymptotic limit of $q_j^n(\mathbf{x})$, the probability that the $k\mathrm{NN}_3$ decision rule decides category j conditioned on samples $\dot{\mathbf{x}}$. Constraints are that as n_1 and $n_2 \longrightarrow \infty$, the k_j remain constant and the tolerance-region volumes $\Phi_j \longrightarrow 0$. The results are restricted to the two-category problem ($M = 2$).

Theorem.   If $\partial u_i / \partial \Phi_i = f(\mathbf{x} | \omega_i)$ at $\mathbf{x}$ for $i = 1, 2$, then the asymptotic value of $q_1^n(\mathbf{x})$ is given by the incomplete beta function:

$$q_1(\mathbf{x}) = \int_0^{1/(1+w)} B_e(y; k_1, k_2)\, dy = \sum_{m=0}^{k_2-1} \binom{m + k_1 - 1}{m} \frac{w^m}{(1 + w)^{m+k_1}}, \quad (1)$$

where

$$w = \frac{f(\mathbf{x} | \omega_2) L_{12} P_2 k_2}{f(\mathbf{x} | \omega_1) L_{21} P_1 k_1}. \quad (2)$$

Outline of Proof.   Because u_i has the beta density $B_e(t_i; k_i, n_i - k_i + 1)$, it follows that $t_i = (n_i + 1)u_i$ has the scaled beta density

$$\frac{B_e[t_i/(n_i + 1); k_i, n_i - k_i + 1]}{n_i + 1}.$$

Then because the two sets of training samples are statistically independent, the joint density of t_1 and t_2 is

$$g_n(t_1, t_2) = \prod_{i=1}^{2} \frac{B_e(t_i/(n_i + 1); k_i, n_i - k_i + 1)}{n_i + 1}, \quad (3)$$

which has the limit $g(t_1, t_2)$. Because the limit of the scaled beta is gamma, $\gamma(t_j; k_i)$,

$$g(t_1, t_2) = \prod_{i=1}^{2} \gamma(t_i; k_i) \quad (4)$$

with

$$E[t_i] = k_i.$$

Now there exists relationships between u_i and Φ_i, although they are not known to the $k\mathrm{NN}_3$ decision rule, as shown in Figure 4.6. The decision

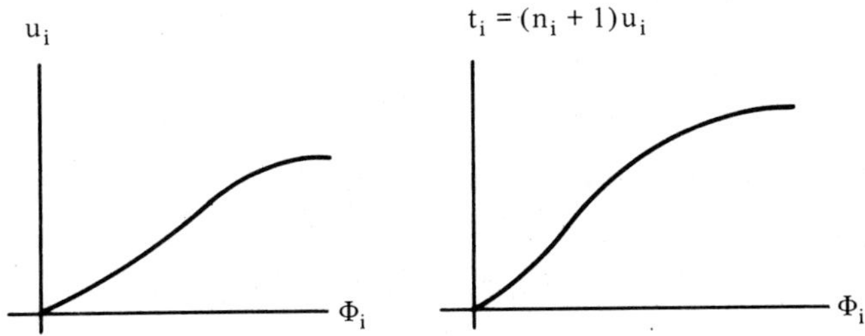

Fig. 4.6 Relations not known by $k\mathrm{NN}_3$ decision rule but known by statistician

boundary at point $\mathbf{x}$ is determined by the respective volumes Φ_1 and Φ_2 of the tolerance regions containing $\mathbf{x}$:

$$\frac{k_1 P_1 L_{21}}{\Phi_1(n_1 + 1)} = \frac{k_2 P_2 L_{12}}{\Phi_2(n_2 + 1)}. \tag{5}$$

Because t_i is a function of Φ_i, there exists a decision boundary in the t_1, t_2 plane as shown in Figure 4.7. We denote by T_n the region where the statistician

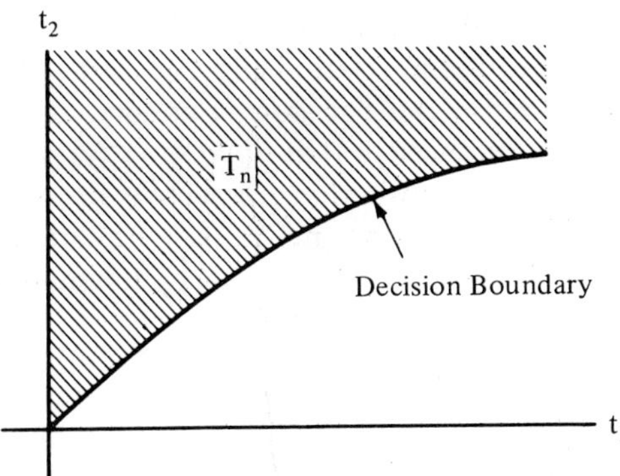

Fig. 4.7 Decision boundary in t_1, t_2 plane

knows that the $k\mathrm{NN}_3$ rule decides category 1, assuming that the statistician knows the relationship† u_i versus Φ_i shown in Figure 4.6. T_n is the region of t_1, t_2 plane where the statistician knows that the $k\mathrm{NN}_3$ rule decides category 1 (assuming that the statistician knows the relationships u_i versus Φ_i in Figure 4.7). The region to which T_n converges in the limit is T. On the boundary

†The $k\mathrm{NN}_3$ rule operates with values of Φ_1 and Φ_2. If the statistician knows the relationships u_i versus Φ_i and thus t_i versus Φ_i, he can construct the decision boundary in the t_1, t_2 plane as a function of these relationships.

of T_n,

$$\frac{k_1 P_1 L_{21}}{\Phi_1(n_1 + 1)} = \frac{k_2 P_2 L_{12}}{\Phi_2(n_2 + 1)}$$

and there exists a relationship $u_2 = \psi(u_1)$. By the chain rule,

$$\frac{\partial t_2}{\partial t_1}\bigg|_{\text{decision boundary, }\mathbf{x}} = \frac{\partial t_2}{\partial u_2}\frac{\partial u_2}{\partial u_1}\bigg|_{\text{d.b.,}\mathbf{x}}\frac{\partial u_1}{\partial t_1} = \frac{n_2 + 1}{n_1 + 1}\frac{\partial u_2}{\partial u_1}\bigg|_{\text{d.b.,}\mathbf{x}},$$

$$\frac{\partial u_2}{\partial u_1}\bigg|_{\text{d.b.,}\mathbf{x}} = \frac{\partial u_2}{\partial \Phi_2}\bigg|_{\mathbf{x}}\frac{\partial \Phi_2}{\partial \Phi_1}\bigg|_{\text{d.b.,}\mathbf{x}}\frac{\partial \Phi_1}{\partial u_1}\bigg|$$

$$= \frac{f(\mathbf{x}\,|\,\omega_2)}{f(\mathbf{x}\,|\,\omega_1)}\frac{L_{12}P_2k_2(n_1 + 1)}{(n_2 + 1)L_{21}P_1k_1},$$

where we use the assumption in the theorem statement that $\partial u_i/\partial \Phi_i = f(\mathbf{x}\,|\,\omega_i)$ at $\mathbf{x}$. Thus,

$$\frac{\partial t_2}{\partial t_1}\bigg|_{\text{d.b.,}\mathbf{x}} = \frac{f(\mathbf{x}\,|\,\omega_2)L_{12}P_2k_2}{f(\mathbf{x}\,|\,\omega_1)L_{21}P_1k_1}$$

and, integrating,

$$t_2 = wt_1; \qquad w = \frac{f(\mathbf{x}\,|\,\omega_2)L_{12}P_2k_2}{f(\mathbf{x}\,|\,\omega_1)L_{21}P_1k_1} \tag{6}$$

because the integration constant is zero.

In summary, Eq. (6) is the relationship between t_2 and t_1 in the t_1, t_2 plane corresponding to $\mathbf{x}$ on the decision boundary using the $k\text{NN}_3$ rule. The statistician has used knowledge that $\partial u_i/\partial \Phi_i = f(\mathbf{x}\,|\,\omega_i)$ at $\mathbf{x}$.

Because the statistician knows that (6) is the expression on the decision boundary (which the $k\text{NN}_3$ rule does not know), he can proceed to evaluate how the $k\text{NN}_3$ rule performs [because t_1 and t_2 are random variables with density (4) when $n \rightarrow \infty$]. Thus, asymptotically,

$$q_1(\mathbf{x}) = \int_{t_1=0}^{\infty}\int_{t_2=wt_1}^{\infty} \gamma(t_1; k_1)\gamma(t_2; k_2)\,dt_2\,dt_1$$

$$= \int_{t_1=0}^{\infty}\int_{t_2=wt_1}^{\infty}\prod_{j=1}^{2}\left\{\frac{1}{(k_j - 1)!}t_j^{k_j-1}e^{-t_j}\right\}dt_2\,dt_1.$$

From Gradshtyen and Ryzkik ([39], p. 100, 3.351.2)

$$\int_{t_2=wt_1}^{\infty}\frac{t_2^{k_2-1}e^{-t_2}}{(k_2 - 1)!}\,dt_2 = \exp\left[-wt_1\sum_{m=0}^{k_2-1}\frac{(wt_1)^m}{m!}\right],$$

and it follows that

$$q_1(\mathbf{x}) = \sum_{m=0}^{k_2-1}\frac{w^m}{(m!)(k_1 - 1)!}\int_{t_1=0}^{\infty}t_1^{m+k_1-1}e^{-t_1(1+m)}\,dt_1.$$

Using 3.351.3 in [39], the above integral is evaluated, resulting in

$$q_1(\mathbf{x}) = \sum_{m=0}^{k_2-1} \binom{m + k_1 - 1}{m} \frac{w^m}{(1 + w)^{m+k_1}}. \tag{7}$$

Example

Let $L_{ij} = 1 - \delta_{ij}$; then

$$w = \frac{f(\mathbf{x}\,|\,\omega_2)P_2\,k_2}{f(\mathbf{x}\,|\,\omega_1)P_1\,k_1} = \frac{k_2(1 - \eta_1(\mathbf{x}))}{k_1\eta_1(\mathbf{x})}, \tag{8}$$

where

$$\eta_1(\mathbf{x}) = \frac{P_1 f(\mathbf{x}\,|\,\omega_1)}{\sum\limits_{i=1}^{2} P_i f(\mathbf{x}\,|\,\omega_i)} \tag{9}$$

is the probability $\mathbf{x}$ is from category ω_1. The point risk $r(\mathbf{x})$ at $\mathbf{x}$ is

$$r(\mathbf{x}) = q_1(\mathbf{x})[1 - \eta_1(\mathbf{x})] + \eta_1(\mathbf{x})[1 - q_1(\mathbf{x})]. \tag{10}$$

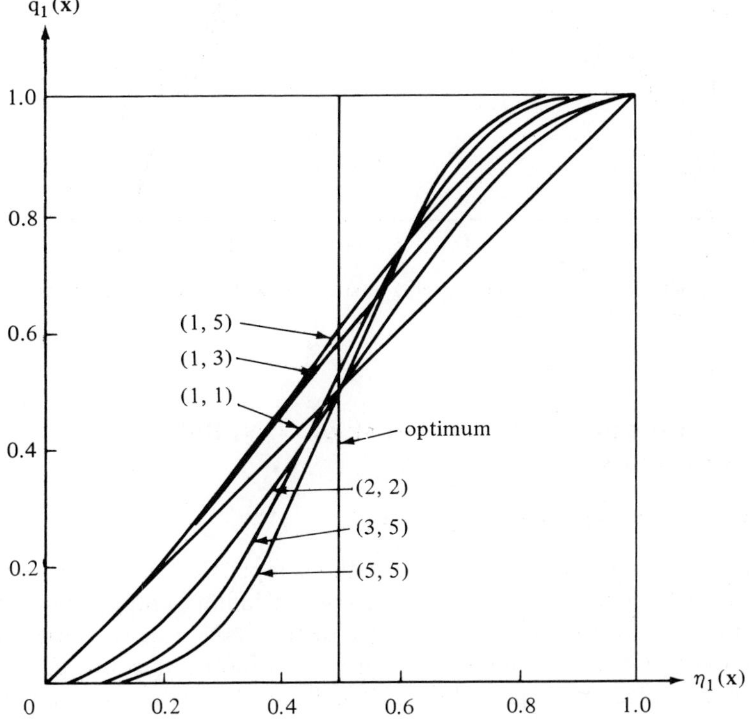

Fig. 4.8 Asymptotic $q_1(\mathbf{x})$ versus $\eta_1(\mathbf{x})$ with k_1, k_2 as parameters, for $k\mathrm{NN}_3$ rule

Thus, w and $q_1(\mathbf{x})$ are functions of $\eta_1(\mathbf{x})$, k_1, and k_2. In Figure 4.8, $q_1(\mathbf{x})$ is plotted versus η_1 with k_1 and k_2 as parameters. In Figure 4.9, the point risk $r(\mathbf{x})$ (10) is plotted versus $\eta_1(\mathbf{x})$, k_1, and k_2.

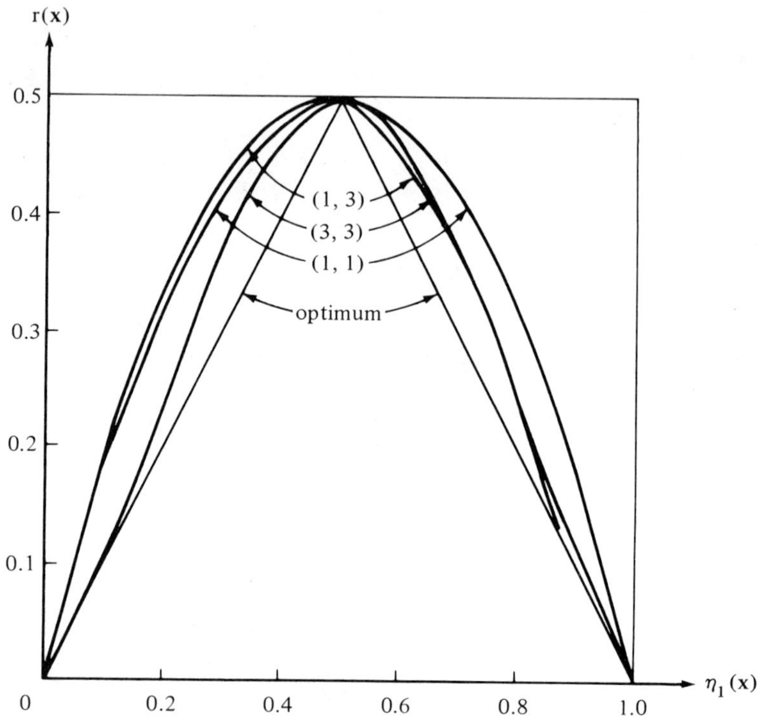

Fig. 4.9 Asymptotic point risk $r(\mathbf{x})$ versus $\eta_1(\mathbf{x})$ with k_1, k_2 as parameters, for $k\mathrm{NN}_3$ rule

4-11 Asymptotic Moments of Risk of $k\mathrm{NN}_3$ Rule for Fixed k_i

4-11.1 Convergence of $q^n_{j_1,\ldots,j_\delta}(\mathbf{x}^{(1)}, \ldots, \mathbf{x}^{(\delta)})$

In Section 4-8 it is shown that if the sample size increases to infinity in such a way as to ensure that n_i also goes to infinity and k_i tends slowly to infinity with n_i, then the expected risk of the $k\mathrm{NN}_3$ rule converges to the Bayes risk[†]; and the second and higher central moments converge to zero, yielding convergence in probability. It will be shown in this section that

[†]That result in Section 4-8 is based on an argument by Loftsgaarden and Quesenberry [20] used to show that $[k_i(\mathbf{x})/((n_i + 1)\Phi_i(\mathbf{x}; \dot{\mathbf{x}}_n))]$ converges in probability to $f(\mathbf{x}\,|\,i)$.

     Supervised Estimation   Chap. 4

under certain conditions the risk for a *fixed k_i* rule also converges in probability to a constant that is a function of the underlying densities and k_i. These results essentially are an extension of Section 4-10.

Theorem.   If

1. the order functions (7) of Section 4-9 admit continuous distribution functions for $\mathbf{x}^{(v)}$, $v = 1, 2, \ldots, \delta$,
2. $\lim_{\epsilon \to 0} H_i(\epsilon, \mathbf{x}^{(v)})/\epsilon = h_i(\mathbf{x}^{(v)}) < \infty$ for all $\mathbf{x}$, $i = 1, 2, \ldots, M$, $v = 1, 2, \ldots, \delta$,

then $q_{j_v}(\mathbf{x}^{(v)})$, the limit of $q_{j_v}^n(\mathbf{x}^{(v)})$, exists and

$$q_{j_v}(\mathbf{x}^{(v)}) = \int_0^\infty \cdots \int_0^\infty \tilde{Q}_{j_v}(t_1^v, \ldots, t_M^v; \mathbf{x}^{(v)}) \prod_{i=1}^M \left[\frac{(t_i^v)^{k_i^v - 1} e^{-t_i^v}}{(k_i^v - 1)!} \right]$$
$$\times \, dt_1^v \ldots dt_M^v, \tag{1}$$

where

$$\tilde{Q}_{j_v}(t_1^v, \ldots, t_M^v; \mathbf{x}^{(v)}) \triangleq \left\{ (t_1^v, \ldots, t_M^v) : \sum_{i=1}^M \frac{L_{j_v i} P_i k_i^v h_i(\mathbf{x}^{(v)})}{t_i^v} \right.$$
$$\left. \leq \sum_{i=1}^M \frac{L_{m i} P_i k_i^v h_i(\mathbf{x}^{(v)})}{t_i^v}, \begin{array}{c} m = 1, \ldots, M \\ m \neq j_v \end{array} \right\}. \tag{2}$$

Further, if

3. there exists an $a > 0$ such that if $u_i^j \leq a$, $j = 1, 2, \ldots, \delta$, $i = 1, 2, \ldots, M$, then $(u_i^1, \ldots, u_i^\delta) \in \mathcal{A}_i(\mathbf{x}^1, \ldots, \mathbf{x}^\delta)$, and

$$q_{j_1, \ldots, j_\delta}(\mathbf{x}^{(1)}, \ldots, \mathbf{x}^{(\delta)}) = \lim_{n \to \infty} q_{j_1, \ldots, j_\delta}^n(\mathbf{x}^{(1)}, \ldots, \mathbf{x}^{(\delta)})$$

$$= \prod_{v=1}^\delta q_{j_v}(\mathbf{x}^{(v)}). \tag{3}$$

Proof: Since, asymptotically, the Dirichlet distribution $\underline{G}_i(u_i^1, \ldots, u_i^\delta)$ becomes concentrated close to the origin,† the following transformation is made to stabilize the limiting distribution:

$$t_i^v = (n_i + 1)u_i^v; \, v = 1, 2, \ldots, \delta, \, i = 1, 2, \ldots, M. \tag{4}$$

Let $\mathcal{A}_i^n(\mathbf{x}^{(1)}, \ldots, \mathbf{x}^{(\delta)})$ and $\tilde{\mathcal{Q}}_{j_v}^n(\mathbf{x}^{(1)}, \ldots, \mathbf{x}^{(\delta)})$ denote the induced sets of $\mathcal{A}_i^n(\mathbf{x}^{(1)}, \ldots, \mathbf{x}^{(\delta)})$ and $\mathcal{Q}_{j_v}^n(\mathbf{x}^{(1)}, \ldots, \mathbf{x}^{(\delta)})$, respectively, under the transformation; and let $\tilde{A}_i^n(t_i^1, \ldots, t_i^\delta; \mathbf{x}^{(1)}, \ldots, \mathbf{x}^{(\delta)})$ and $\tilde{Q}_{j_v}^n(t_1^v, \ldots, t_M^v; \mathbf{x}^{(1)}, \ldots, \mathbf{x}^{(\delta)})$ be the corresponding indicator functions defined in the $\mathbf{t}$ space. Then

---

†Because k_i is fixed, small values of u_i are more likely as the region $\mathcal{I}_i$ decreases in size.

from† [(11) and (12) of Section 4-9],

$$0 \leq q^n_{j_1,\ldots,j_\delta}(\mathbf{x}^{(1)},\ldots,\mathbf{x}^{(\delta)}) - \int \cdots \int \prod_{v=1}^{\delta} [\tilde{Q}^n_{j_v}(t^v_1,\ldots,t^v_M; \mathbf{x}^{(1)},\ldots,\mathbf{x}^{(\delta)})]$$

$$\times \prod_{i=1}^{M} [\tilde{A}^n_i(t^1_i,\ldots,t^\delta_i; \mathbf{x}^{(1)},\ldots,\mathbf{x}^{(\delta)})]$$

$$\times \prod_{i=1}^{M} \left[d\underline{G}_i\left(\frac{t^1_i}{n_i+1},\ldots,\frac{t^\delta_i}{n_i+1}; \mathbf{x}^{(1)},\ldots,\mathbf{x}^{(\delta)}\right) \middle/ (n_i+1)^\delta \right] \qquad (5)$$

$$\leq 1 - \prod_{i=1}^{M} \left[\int \tilde{A}^n_i(t^1_i,\ldots,t^\delta_i; \mathbf{x}^{(1)},\ldots,\mathbf{x}^{(\delta)}) \right.$$

$$\left. \times d\underline{G}_i\left(\frac{t^1_i}{n_i+1},\ldots,\frac{t^\delta_i}{n_i+1}; \mathbf{x}^{(1)},\ldots,\mathbf{x}^{(\delta)}\right) \right].$$

The proof consists of showing that with the stabilizing transformation, the limit of the integral on the right above equals the integral of the limit of its integrand, and the integral tends to zero as $n \longrightarrow \infty$. The dominated convergence theorem ([40], p. 125) can be applied if the integrand of an integral is uniformly bounded by an integrable function, and converges pointwise (or almost everywhere) to a limit.

An outline of the rest of the proof is as follows:

1. $\tilde{\mathcal{Q}}^n_{j_v}(t^v_1,\ldots,t^v_M; \mathbf{x}^{(v)})$ converges pointwise to $\tilde{\mathcal{Q}}_{j_v}(t^v_1,\ldots,t^v_M; \mathbf{x}^{(v)})$.
2. As a result of Problem 16,

$$g_i\left(\frac{t^1_i}{n_i+1},\ldots,\frac{t^\delta_i}{n_i+1}\right) \middle/ (n_i+1)^\delta < c \times \prod_{v=1}^{\delta} \gamma(t^v_i; k^v_i)$$

for all $n_i > k^v_i$, $v = 1, 2, \ldots, \delta$, and c a finite constant.
3. The limit of $q^n_{j_v}(\mathbf{x}^{(v)})$ equals the integral of the limit of the integrand.
4. $\tilde{A}^n_i(\mathbf{x}^{(1)},\ldots,\mathbf{x}^{(v)})$ converges pointwise to 1 with n_i.
5. The integral after the first $\leq$ in (5) converges to zero, whereas the integral after the second $\leq$ in (5) converges to the integral of the limit of integrand in step 2 above, after applying Fubini's theorem [40].

4-11.2   Convergence of Moments

Theorem. If

1. the order functions (7) of Section 4-9 admit continuous distributions,

†We note that

$$d\underline{G}_i\left(\frac{t^1_i}{n_i+1},\ldots,\frac{t^\delta_i}{n_i+1}; \mathbf{x}^{(1)},\ldots,\mathbf{x}^{(\delta)}\right) = d\underline{G}_i\left(\frac{t^1_i}{n_i+1},\ldots,\frac{t^\delta_i}{n_i+1}\right)$$

since the Dirichlet distribution does not depend on the sample values.

2. $\lim_{\epsilon \to 0} H_i(\epsilon, \mathbf{x})/\epsilon = h_i(\mathbf{x})$, $\forall\, \mathbf{x}$, $i = 1, 2, \ldots, M$,

then†

$$\mu = \lim_{n \to \infty} \mu_n^1 = \sum_{i_1=1}^{M} \sum_{j_1=1}^{M} P_{i_1} L_{j_1 i_1} \int q_{j_1}(\mathbf{x}^{(1)})\, dF(\mathbf{x}^{(1)} \mid \omega_{i_1}). \tag{6}$$

Further, if

3. the probability of drawing $\mathbf{x}^{(1)}, \ldots, \mathbf{x}^{(\delta)}$, independently distributed as $F(\mathbf{x}^{(1)} \mid \omega_{i_1}), \ldots, F(\mathbf{x}^{(\delta)} \mid \omega_{i_\delta})$, which does not satisfy condition 3 of the preceding theorem, is zero for any sequence $i_1, \ldots, i_\delta$,

or, if

4. $h_i(\mathbf{x}) = f(\mathbf{x} \mid \omega_i)$ almost everywhere with respect to $F(\mathbf{x} \mid \omega_i)$, $i = 1, 2, \ldots, M$, and the supports of $h_i(\mathbf{x})$ are disjoint, then

$$\mu^\delta = \lim_{n \to \infty} \mu_n^\delta = [\mu]^\delta, \tag{7}$$

and $R(\dot{\mathbf{x}}_n)$ converges in probability to μ.

Outline of Proof. $q_{j_1}^n(\mathbf{x}^{(1)})$ is bounded by unity and, further, converges pointwise to $q_{j_1}(\mathbf{x}^{(1)})$. Hence (6) follows by an application of the dominated convergence theorem [40].

In like manner, if condition 3 is satisfied,

$$\mu^\delta = \sum_{i_1=1}^{M} \sum_{j_1=1}^{M} \cdots \sum_{i_\delta=1}^{M} \sum_{j_\delta=1}^{M} \prod_{v=1}^{\delta} [P_{i_v} L_{j_v i_v}]$$

$$\times \int_{\mathscr{X}^{(1)}} \cdots \int_{\mathscr{X}^{(\delta)}} \prod_{v=1}^{\delta} [q_{j_v}(\mathbf{x}^{(v)})]\, dF(\mathbf{x}^{(1)} \mid \omega_{i_1}) \cdots dF(\mathbf{x}^{(\delta)} \mid \omega_{i_\delta}). \tag{8}$$

After expressing the above integral of products as products of integrals and then expressing the sum of products as products of sums, the result (7) is obtained.

Since, then, all moments are finite and converge to the moments of the degenerate random variable μ, the distribution of risk converges to the degenerate distribution, placing all probability at the point $R(\dot{\mathbf{x}}_n) = \mu$; hence $R(\dot{\mathbf{x}}_n)$ converges in probability to μ.

If condition 4 is satisfied, the limiting expected risk μ is zero. Because risk cannot be less than zero nor exceed some R^{**}, this implies that all moments must converge to zero. Thus, the risk converges in probability to zero, and the last part of the theorem is proved.

†This is the same result (derived using a different approach) as in Section 4-10.

4-12 Rate of Convergence of Risk

In this section rate of convergence of $q^n_{j_1, j_2, \ldots, j_\delta}$ defined in Section 3-3.2, and hence the rate of convergence of the δth moment, is examined. Assume a zero–one loss matrix, $M = 2$, $k_1(\mathbf{x}) = k_2(\mathbf{x}) = k$, and $n_1 = n_2 = n/2$.

The function H_i governs the convergence rate. This is because moments are a function of the "q" functions [Eq. (10) of Section 3-2.8], which in turn are a function of their regions of integration $\mathscr{Q}$ [Eq. (5) of Section 4-9], which in turn are dependent on the decision equations and H_i [Eq. (2) of Section 4-9]. H_i is a function that expresses the convergence of a region as a function of the region's volume, and the distance function, which establishes the shape of the region. Recall that the $k\mathrm{NN}_3$ decision rule utilizes local volumes established with a priori distance measures for the respective classes. In this section we shall consider the convergence rate of the $k\mathrm{NN}_3$ rule when the underlying statistics have a specific relationship between coverage and volume established by the same distance measure used by the $k\mathrm{NN}_3$ rule.

Property (B, α)

A probability distribution $F(\mathbf{x})$ and distance measure $d(\mathbf{y}, \mathbf{x})$ will be said to have property (B, α) at $\mathbf{x}$ for some positive B and α if there exists some functions $h(\mathbf{x})$ and $B(\mathbf{x}, \boldsymbol{\Phi})$ such that the probability u assigned by $F(\mathbf{x})$ to the neighborhood $\{\mathbf{y} : d(\mathbf{y}, \mathbf{x}) < \epsilon\}$ at $\mathbf{x}$ of volume $\boldsymbol{\Phi}$ can be written as

$$u = h(\mathbf{x})\boldsymbol{\Phi} + B(\mathbf{x}, \boldsymbol{\Phi})\boldsymbol{\Phi}^{1+\alpha} \tag{1}$$

for all $\boldsymbol{\Phi}$ for which $0 \leq u \leq 1$ and where $|B(\mathbf{x}, \boldsymbol{\Phi})| < B$.

A probability distribution $F(\mathbf{x})$ and distance function $d(\mathbf{y}, \mathbf{x})$ will be said to have property (B, α) if they have property (B, α) at $\mathbf{x}$ for all $\mathbf{x}$.

B and α describe in a certain sense the degree of maximum nonlinearity of the coverage–volume relationship over the observation space. It results from theorems following that the convergence rate of moments of the distribution of $k\mathrm{NN}_3$ risk increases with α. On the other hand, the magnitude of the difference between the moment and its limit increases with B.

4-12.1 Convergence Rate of $q^n_{j_1, \ldots, j_\delta}(\mathbf{x}^{(1)}, \ldots, \mathbf{x}^{(\delta)})$

Theorem. Let $M = 2$, $k_1(\mathbf{x}) = k_2(\mathbf{x}) = k$, $n_1 = n_2 = n/2$, 0–1 loss functions and if

1. $F(\mathbf{x} \mid \omega_i)$ and $d_i(\mathbf{y}, \mathbf{x})$ have property (B, α) for some $B, \alpha > 0$, and
2. the distributions of coverages $u_i^{(1)}, \ldots, u_i^{(\delta)}$, $i = 1, 2, \ldots, M$, are continuous,

then $q_j^n(\mathbf{x})$ converges pointwise to $q_j(\mathbf{x})$ defined by Eq. (4) of Section 4-9 with a rate no slower than n^{-e}, where $e = \min(1, \alpha)$. If, in addition to 1 and 2,

> 3. $h_1(\mathbf{x})$ and $h_2(\mathbf{x})$ are never both nonzero at the same $\dot{\mathbf{x}}$,

then $q_j^n(\mathbf{x})$ converges pointwise to $q_j(\mathbf{x})$ with a rate no slower than $n^{-\alpha k}$. If in addition to 1 and 2

> 4. there exists an $a > 0$ such that if $u_i^j \leq a, j = 1, 2, \ldots, \delta, i = 1, 2,$
> $\ldots, M, (u_i^1, \ldots, u_i^\delta)\dagger \in \mathscr{A}_i(\mathbf{x}^1, \ldots, \mathbf{x}^\delta), i = 1, 2,$

then $q_{j_1,\ldots,j_\delta}^n(\mathbf{x}^1, \ldots, \mathbf{x}^\delta)$ converges to its limit $q_{j_1,\ldots,j_\delta}(\mathbf{x}^{(1)}, \ldots, \mathbf{x}^{(\delta)})$ with a rate no slower than n^{-e}, where $e = \min(1, \alpha)$.

Proof: Since $f(\mathbf{x}\,|\,\omega_i)$ and $d(\mathbf{y}, \mathbf{x})$ have property (B, α), then

$$\lim_{\Phi \to 0} \frac{u}{\Phi} = \lim_{\Phi \to 0} \frac{h(\mathbf{x})\Phi + B(\mathbf{x}, \Phi)\Phi^{(1+\alpha)}}{\Phi} = h(\mathbf{x}) \tag{2}$$

and condition 2 of the theorem in Section 4-11 is satisfied. From the results in Section 4-11, conditions 1, 2, and 3 of the theorem are sufficient to guarantee $q_{j_1,\ldots,j_\delta}^n(\mathbf{x}^{(1)}, \ldots, \mathbf{x}^{(\delta)}) \longrightarrow q_{j_1,\ldots,j_\delta}(\mathbf{x}^{(1)}, \ldots, \mathbf{x}^{(\delta)})$.

It follows from Eq. (5) of Section 4-11.2 that

$$q_{j_1,\ldots,j_\delta}(\mathbf{x}^{(1)}, \ldots, \mathbf{x}^{(\delta)}) \leq \int \cdots \int \prod_{v=1}^{\delta} \tilde{Q}_{j_v}^n(t_1^v, t_2^v; \mathbf{x}^{(v)})$$

$$\times \prod_{i=1}^{2} \left[dG_i\left(\frac{t_i^1}{n/2 + 1}, \ldots, \frac{t_i^\delta}{n/2 + 1}\right) \middle/ \left(\frac{n}{2} + 1\right)^\delta \right]$$

$$+ \int \cdots \int \left\{ 1 - \prod_{i=1}^{2} [\tilde{A}_i^n(t_i^1, \ldots, t_i^\delta; \mathbf{x}^{(1)}, \ldots, \mathbf{x}^{(\delta)})] \right\} \tag{3}$$

$$\times \prod_{i=1}^{2} \left[dG_i\left(\frac{t_i^1}{n/2 + 1}, \ldots, \frac{t_i^\delta}{n/2 + 1}\right) \middle/ \left(\frac{n}{2} + 1\right)^\delta \right],$$

where $\tilde{Q}_{j_v}^n(t_1^v, t_2^v; \mathbf{x}^{(v)})$ is the indicator function for the set

$$\tilde{\mathscr{Q}}_{j_v}(\mathbf{x}^v) = \{t_j^v, t_l^v; \Phi_j(\mathbf{x}^{(v)}; \dot{\mathbf{x}}_n) < \Phi_l(\mathbf{x}^{(v)}; \dot{\mathbf{x}}_n)\}, \qquad l \neq j, j = 1, 2. \tag{4}$$

Note that $\tilde{A}_i^n(t_i^1, \ldots, t_i^\delta; \mathbf{x}^{(1)}, \ldots, \mathbf{x}^{(\delta)})$ is replaced by 1 in the first integral on the right-hand side of (3) without violating the inequality. As a result of 1. of the theorem and the transformation $t_j^v/(n_j + 1) = u_j^v = h_j(\mathbf{x})\Phi + B(\mathbf{x}, \Phi)\Phi^{1+\alpha}$,

$$\frac{t_j^v}{n/2 + 1} \leq h_j(\mathbf{x}^{(v)})\Phi + B\Phi^{1+\alpha}, \tag{5a}$$

†Recall that $u_i^1, u_i^2, \ldots, u_i^\delta$ are coverages of tolerance regions.

$$\frac{t_l^v}{n/2 + 1} \geq h_l(\mathbf{x}^{(v)})\Phi - B\Phi^{1+\alpha}. \tag{5b}$$

Then it is straightforward to verify that, for any $w > 0$, either

$$t_j^v + t_l^v > w \tag{6a}$$

or $t_j^v + t_l^v < w$, and therefore

$$t_j^v < \left[\frac{h_j(\mathbf{x}^{(v)}) + B\left(\dfrac{w/(n/2 + 1)}{h_1(\mathbf{x}^{(v)}) + h_2(\mathbf{x}^{(v)})}\right)^\alpha}{h_l(\mathbf{x}^{(v)}) - B\left(\dfrac{w/(n/2 + 1)}{h_1(\mathbf{x}^{(v)}) + h_2(\mathbf{x}^{(v)})}\right)^\alpha}\right] t_l^v \triangleq W^v(w) t_l^v. \tag{6b}$$

Thus, the region of integration in (3) can be bounded:

$$\tilde{\mathcal{Q}}_{j_v}^n \subset \mathcal{W}^v(w) \triangleq \{(t_j^v, t_l^v) : t_j^v, t_l^v > 0, \text{ and } t_j^v + t_l^v > w \text{ or } t_j^v < W^v(w) t_l^v\}. \tag{7}$$

Because the univariate Dirichlet distribution is bounded from above by a scalar multiple of the gamma distribution (do Problem 16)

$$\frac{g_i\left(\dfrac{t_i^1}{n/2 + 1}, \ldots, \dfrac{t_i^\delta}{n/2 + 1}\right)}{\left(\dfrac{n}{2} + 1\right)^\delta} \leq \prod_{v=1}^\delta \left[\frac{1}{\left(1 - \dfrac{k + 1}{n/2 + 1}\right)^{k+1}} \gamma(t_i^v; k)\right]. \tag{8}$$

Thus, the first term on the right-hand side of (3) can be bounded:

$$\int \cdots \int \prod_{v=1}^\delta \tilde{Q}_{j_v}^n(t_j^v, t_l^v; \mathbf{x}^{(v)}) \times \prod_{i=1}^2 \left[dG_i\left(\frac{t_i^1}{n/2 + 1}, \ldots, \frac{t_i^\delta}{n/2 + 1}\right)\Big|\left(\frac{n}{2} + 1\right)^\delta\right]$$

$$\leq \prod_{v=1}^\delta \left[\int_{\mathcal{W}^v(w)} \prod_{i=1}^2 \left[\frac{\gamma(t_i^v, k)}{\left(1 - \dfrac{k + 1}{n/2 + 1}\right)^{k+1}}\right] dt_j^v \, dt_l^v\right]. \tag{9}$$

Note that

$$q_j(\mathbf{x}^{(v)}) = \int \cdots \int \prod_{i=1}^2 \gamma(t_i^v, k) \, dt_1^v \, dt_2^v$$

$$\times \left\{(t_j^v, t_l^v) : t_j^v < \frac{h_j(\mathbf{x}^{(v)})}{h_l(\mathbf{x}^{(v)})} t_l^v\right\} \tag{10}$$

and the range of integration is entirely within $\mathcal{W}^v(w)$. Thus,

$$\int_{\mathcal{W}^v(w)} \prod_{i=1}^2 [\gamma(t_i^v; k)] \, dt_i^v$$

$$\leq q_j(\mathbf{x}^{(v)}) + p\left[t_j^v + t_l^v \leq w \text{ or } \frac{h_j(\mathbf{x}^{(v)})}{h_l(\mathbf{x}^{(v)})} t_l^v < t_j^v < W^v(w) t_l^v\right], \tag{11}$$

where t_j^v and t_l^v are independent and identically distributed with the gamma distribution $\gamma(t_i^v; k)$. From Wilks ([33], p. 188), $t_j^v + t_l^v$ is gamma distributed with parameter $2k$, and $t_l^v/(t_j^v + t_l^v)$ is beta distributed. Hence,

$$p\left[t_j^v + t_l^v > w \text{ or } \frac{h_j(\mathbf{x}^{(v)})}{h_l(\mathbf{x}^{(v)})} t_l^v < t_j^v < W^v(w)t_l^v \right] \tag{12}$$

$$= p\left[t_j^v + t_l^v > w \text{ or } c_1 \triangleq [1 + W^v(w)]^{-1} \leq \frac{t_l^v}{t_l^v + t_j^v} \right.$$

$$\leq \left. \left[1 + \frac{h_j(\mathbf{x}^{(v)})}{h_l(\mathbf{x}^{(v)})} \right]^{-1} \triangleq c_2 \right] \tag{13}$$

$$< \int_w^\infty \gamma(y; 2k)\, dy + \int_{c_1}^{c_2} B_e(y; k, k)\, dy.$$

Since $B_e(y; k, k)$ has a peak at $y = \frac{1}{2}$, and

$$c_2 - c_1 = B \frac{[w/(n/2 + 1)]^\alpha}{[h_1(\mathbf{x}^{(v)}) + h_2(\mathbf{x}^{(v)})]^{1+\alpha}},$$

making use of an expansion used in Section 4-10 (Gradshtyen and Ryzhik [39], p. 100) we obtain

$$p\left[t_j' + t_l' > w \text{ or } \frac{f(x \mid \omega_j)}{f(x \mid \omega_l)} t_l' < t_j' < W^v(w)t_l' \right] \tag{14}$$

$$< e^{-w} \sum_{m=0}^{2k-1} \frac{w^m}{m!} + (c_2 - c_1)B_e\left(\frac{1}{2}; k, k\right).$$

Thus,

$$\iint_{\mathcal{W}^v(w)} \prod_{i=1}^{2} [\gamma(t_i^v, k)]\, dt_1^v\, dt_2^v \leq q_j(\mathbf{x}^v) + e^{-w} \sum_{m=0}^{2k-1} \frac{w^m}{m!}$$

$$+ \frac{B[w/(n/2 + 1)]^\alpha}{[h_1(\mathbf{x}^{(v)}) + h_2(\mathbf{x}^{(v)})]^{1+\alpha}}. \tag{15}$$

Hence the first right-hand term of (3) can be bounded:

$$\int \cdots \int \prod_{v=1}^{\delta} \tilde{Q}_{j_v}^n(t_1^v, t_2^v; \mathbf{x}^{(v)}) \times \prod_{i=1}^{2} \left[d\underline{G}_i\left(\frac{t_i^1}{n/2 + 1}, \cdots, \frac{t_i^\delta}{n/2 + 1} \right) \middle/ \left(\frac{n}{2} + 1 \right)^\delta \right]$$

$$\leq \left\{ \prod_{v=1}^{\delta} \left[q_{j_v}(\mathbf{x}^{(v)}) + e^{-w} \sum_{m=0}^{2k-1} \frac{w^m}{m!} \right. \right. \tag{16}$$

$$\left. \left. + \frac{B[w/(n/2 + 1)]^\alpha}{[h_1(\mathbf{x}^{(v)}) + h_2(\mathbf{x}^{(v)})]^{1+\alpha}} \right] \right\} \left(1 - \frac{k + 1}{n/2 + 1} \right)^{-(k+1)2\delta}.$$

Also, the second integral on the right-hand side of (3) can be bounded. For the case $\delta = 1$, $A_i^n(u_i^1, \ldots, u_i^\delta; \mathbf{x}^{(1)}, \ldots, \mathbf{x}^{(\delta)}) = 1$ for all possible values of $u_i^1, \ldots, u_i^\delta$, and the second right-hand term of (3) is identically zero. Otherwise, substituting (8) into (3),

$$\int \cdots \int \left(1 - \prod_{i=1}^{2} \left[A_i^n\left(\frac{t_i^1}{n/2+1}, \ldots, \frac{t_i^\delta}{n/2+1}; \mathbf{x}^{(1)}, \ldots, \mathbf{x}^{(\delta)}\right)\right]\right)$$

$$\times \prod_{i=1}^{2} \left[d\underline{G}_i\left(\frac{t_i^1}{n/2+1}, \ldots, \frac{t_i^\delta}{n/2+1}\right) \Big/ \left(\frac{n}{2}+1\right)^\delta\right]$$

$$\leq \int \cdots \int \left(1 - \prod_{i=1}^{2} \left[A_i^n\left(\frac{t_i^1}{n/2+1}, \ldots, \frac{t_i^\delta}{n/2+1}; \mathbf{x}^{(1)}, \ldots, \mathbf{x}^{(\delta)}\right)\right]\right) \quad (17)$$

$$\times \prod_{i=1}^{2} \prod_{v=1}^{\delta} \left[\frac{1}{(1-(k+1)/(n/2+1))^{k+1}} \gamma(t_i^v; k)\right] dt_1^1 \ldots \ldots dt_2^\delta$$

$$= \left[\frac{1}{(1-(k+1)/(n/2+1))^{k+1}}\right]^{2\delta} \left\{1 - \int \cdots \int \prod_{i=1}^{2} \left[A_i^n\left(\frac{t_i^1}{n/2+1}, \ldots, \right.\right.\right.$$

$$\left.\left.\left. \frac{t_i^\delta}{n/2+1}; \mathbf{x}^{(1)}, \ldots, \mathbf{x}^{(\delta)}\right) \times \prod_{v=1}^{\delta} \gamma(t_i^v; k)\right] dt_1^1 \ldots \ldots dt_2^\delta\right\}.$$

Now, by condition 4 of the theorem there exists an a such that

$$\int \cdots \int \prod_{i=1}^{2} \left[A_i^n\left(\frac{t_i^1}{n/2+1}, \ldots, \frac{t_i^\delta}{n/2+1}; \mathbf{x}^{(1)}, \ldots, \mathbf{x}^{(\delta)}\right)\right]$$

$$\times \prod_{v=1}^{\delta} [\gamma(t_i^v; k)] \, dt_1^1 \ldots \ldots dt_2^\delta$$

$$= \prod_{i=1}^{2} \left[\int \cdots \int A_i^n\left(\frac{t_i^1}{n/2+1}, \ldots, \frac{t_i^\delta}{n/2+1}; \mathbf{x}^{(1)}, \ldots, \mathbf{x}^{(\delta)}\right)\right.$$

$$\left. \times \prod_{v=1}^{\delta} [\gamma(t_i^v; k)] \, dt_i^1 \ldots \ldots dt_i^\delta\right] \quad (18)$$

$$\leq \prod_{i=1}^{2} \left[\int_0^{a(n+1)} \cdots \int_0^{a(n+1)} \prod_{v=1}^{\delta} [\gamma(t_i^v; k)]\right] dt_i^1 \ldots \ldots dt_i^\delta \quad (19)$$

$$= \Gamma(a(n+1); k)^{2\delta}. \quad (20)$$

Hence, the second right-hand term of (3) is always less than

$$\left(1 - \frac{k+1}{n/2+1}\right)^{(k+1)2\delta} [1 - \Gamma(a(n+1); k)^{2\delta}]. \quad (21)$$

Cumulating results from (16) and (21), for any $w > 0$,

$$q_{j_1, \ldots, j_\delta}^n(\mathbf{x}^{(1)}, \ldots, \mathbf{x}^{(\delta)})$$

$$\leq \left(1 - \frac{k+1}{n/2+1}\right)^{-(k+1)2\delta} \left\{\prod_{v=1}^{\delta} \left[q_{j_v}(\mathbf{x}^{(v)}) + e^{-w} \sum_{m=0}^{2k-1} \frac{w^m}{m!}\right.\right.$$

$$\left.\left. + \frac{B[w/(n/2+1)]^\alpha}{[h_1(\mathbf{x}^{(v)}) + h_2(\mathbf{x}^{(v)})]^{1+\alpha}}\right] + [1 - \Gamma(a(n+1); k)^{2\delta}]\right\}. \quad (22)$$

The above inequality involves the free parameter w. The inequality holds for any choice of w. To obtain the tightest upper bound, it is desirable to choose the value of w that minimizes the upper bound. Clearly, there is such a unique value, for $e^{-w} \sum_{m=0}^{2k-1} w^m/m!$ decreases with positive w while w increases without bound with w.

Suppose w is permitted to slowly increase as an arbitrarily small power of n:

$$w = n^{\xi}.$$

The multiplicative term $[1 - (k+1)/(n/2+1)]^{-(k+1)/2\delta}$ tends to decrease to unity as n^{-1}. The expression $e^{-w} \sum_{m=0}^{2k-1} w^m/m!$ within brackets tends exponentially to zero with w. Hence, that expression decreases to zero faster than n^{-1}, as does the last expression, involving the incomplete gamma integral. The second term within the brackets, involving w^{α}, decreases to zero as $n^{+\alpha(\xi-1)}$.

Hence, the upper bound of $q^n_{j_1,\ldots,j_\delta}(\mathbf{x}^{(1)}, \ldots, \mathbf{x}^{(\delta)})$ converges to $q_{j_1}(\mathbf{x}^{(1)})$, $\ldots, q_{j_\delta}(\mathbf{x}^{(\delta)}) = q_{j_1,\ldots,j_\delta}(\mathbf{x}^{(1)}, \ldots, \mathbf{x}^{(\delta)})$ as n^{-p}, where p is the minimum of 1 and $\alpha(1-\xi)$ for any positive ξ. This completes proof of part 3 of the theorem concerning convergence rate.

Discussion

The effect of large values of B is to reduce the value of w minimizing the upper bound and to increase the upper bound. Thus, B^{-1} is a figure of merit of how well the distance function "matches" the underlying statistics at $\mathbf{x}^{(1)}, \ldots,$ $\mathbf{x}^{(\delta)}$. If the distance functions happen to "match" the density functions so that B is zero, then the terms above which are associated with the free parameter w vanish:

$$q^n_{j_1,\ldots,j_\delta}(\mathbf{x}^{(1)}, \ldots, \mathbf{x}^{(\delta)})$$

$$\leq \left(1 - \frac{k+1}{n/2+1}\right)^{-(k+1)2\delta} \{q_{j_1,\ldots,j_\delta}(\mathbf{x}^{(1)},\ldots,\mathbf{x}^{(\delta)}) + [1 - \Gamma(a(n+1);k)^{2\delta}]\}.$$

In this case the convergence is not affected by arbitrarily small values of $h_1(\mathbf{x}^{(v)}) + h_2(\mathbf{x}^v)$ in regions of low density mixtures.

For the case $\delta = 1$ (when $a = 1$) the term

$$\min_{0<w<\infty} \left(1 - \frac{k+1}{n/2+1}\right)^{-2(k+1)} \left\{e^{-w} \sum_{m=0}^{2k-1} \frac{w^m}{m!} + B \frac{[w/(n/2+1)]^{\alpha}}{[h_1(\mathbf{x}^{(v)}) + h_2(\mathbf{x}^{(v)})]^{1+\alpha}}\right\}$$

can be thought of as being contributed due to the use of inappropriate distance functions at $\mathbf{x}^{(v)}$.

4-13 Preprocessing for Nearest-Neighbor Decision Rules

Clustering techniques presented in Chapter 5 are preprocessing techniques in that a cluster of samples is, say, replaced by a mean vector and covariance matrix. Without some form of preprocessing, the kNN type of rule may be complex in terms of computer storage and decision time. Hart [29], for example, considered finding a subset of the training set so that a 1NN$_2$ rule based on that subset would correctly classify all the training samples. In the following section a construction procedure is presented which can be used as preprocessing for kNN rules.

4-13.1 Preprocessing Procedure

Let $\mathbf{x}_1, \mathbf{x}_2, \ldots, \mathbf{x}_n$ be n (not necessarily distinct) vectors. The objective is to reorder the n vectors to obtain a new sequence,† $\mathbf{x}^1, \mathbf{x}^2, \ldots, \mathbf{x}^n$.

The first element, $\mathbf{x}^1$, is chosen arbitrarily from the sequence $\mathbf{x}_1, \mathbf{x}_2, \ldots, \mathbf{x}_n$. Assuming that m vectors have been ordered, $m < n$, the $(m + 1)$st vector is determined as follows: Define the sphere $S_r(\mathbf{x})$ as the set of all vectors $\mathbf{z}$ that are a distance of r or less from $\mathbf{x}$ with respect to a Euclidean distance measure d:

$$S_r(\mathbf{x}) = \{\mathbf{z} : d(\mathbf{x}, \mathbf{z}) \le r\}. \tag{1}$$

Let $R(m)$ denote the smallest common radius of the m spheres centered on the first m ordered vectors such that the union of spheres covers all the n vectors:

$$R(m) \triangleq \min\left\{r : \mathbf{x}_i \in \bigcup_{j=1}^{m} S_r(\mathbf{x}^j),\ i = 1, 2, \ldots, n\right\} \tag{2}$$

and denote the cover of the first m regions C_m:

$$C_m = \bigcup_{j=1}^{m} S_r(\mathbf{x}^j), \qquad \text{where } r = R(m). \tag{3}$$

By construction there must be at least one‡ $\mathbf{x}_i$ on the boundary of C_m (which is denoted $\bar{C}_m$) not a member of $\mathbf{x}^1, \mathbf{x}^2, \ldots, \mathbf{x}^m$. Define $\mathbf{x}^{m+1}$ to be the vector on the boundary.§

---

†Because it is possible that two vectors in $\mathbf{x}_1, \mathbf{x}_2, \ldots, \mathbf{x}_n$ are identical, it is more general to denote the reordered sequence $\mathbf{x}_{s(1)}, \mathbf{x}_{s(2)}, \ldots, \mathbf{x}_{s(n)}$, where $s(i)$ will be called the "serial number" of the ith element in the new sequence. For convenience we let $\mathbf{x}^i = \mathbf{x}_{s(i)}$.

‡If $R(m) \ne 0$, then all $\mathbf{x}_i \in \bar{C}_m$ are not equal to any of the first reordered vectors.

§If there is more than one vector in $\bar{C}_m$, pick the one with smallest index.

Let $N(m + 1)$ be the (smallest) index of the vector in the set of reordered vectors $\mathbf{x}^1, \mathbf{x}^2, \mathbf{x}^m$ which is nearest to $\mathbf{x}^{m+1}$; and set $N(1) = 0$.

This construction procedure is very similar to the *maximin* clustering procedure described in Chapter 5, due to Batchelor and Wilkens [41]. Observe that $\mathbf{x}_i \in \bigcup_{j=1}^m S_r(\mathbf{x}^j)$ is equivalent to the statement that $\mathbf{x}_i$ is within a distance $R(m)$ to at least one of the first m reordered vectors for all i, or that $\min\{d(\mathbf{x}_i, \mathbf{x}^j) : 1 \leq j \leq m\} \leq r$. Hence

$$R(m) = \min \{r : \min_{1 \leq j \leq m} d(\mathbf{x}_i, \mathbf{x}^j) \leq r, \text{ all } i\} \tag{4}$$

or

$$R(m) = \max_{1 \leq i \leq n} \min_{1 \leq j \leq m} d(\mathbf{x}_i, \mathbf{x}^j), \tag{5}$$

which is a *maximum minimum distance*. Hence the name *maximin* can be used to denote this procedure.

An iterative algorithmic procedure can be developed from the above expression which reduces the effort in calculating $R(m)$; Eq. (5) can be written†

$$R(m) = \max_{\mathbf{x}_i : \mathbf{x}_i \notin \{\mathbf{x}^j\}_{j=1}^{m-1}} \{\min [d(\mathbf{x}_i, \mathbf{x}^m), \min_{1 \leq j \leq m-1} d(\mathbf{x}_i, \mathbf{x}^j)]\}$$

$$\triangleq \max_{\mathbf{x}_i : \mathbf{x}_i \notin \{\mathbf{x}^j\}_{j=1}^{m-1}} \{A(m, \mathbf{x}_i)\}, \tag{6a}$$

where

$$A(m, \mathbf{x}_i) \triangleq \begin{cases} \min [d(\mathbf{x}_i, \mathbf{x}^m), A(m - 1, \mathbf{x}_i)], & \text{all } \mathbf{x}_i; \, m \neq 1, \\ \infty, & \text{all } \mathbf{x}_i; \, m = 1. \end{cases} \tag{6b}$$

Thus, the reordering can be facilitated by updating the n coefficients $A(m, \mathbf{x}_i)$, $\ldots, A(m, \mathbf{x}_n)$ at each stage, requiring storage of n real numbers.

4-13.2 Properties of the Procedure

1. Given the reordered sequence of vectors $\mathbf{x}^1, \mathbf{x}^2, \ldots, \mathbf{x}^n$, the sequences‡ $N(i)$ and $R(i)$ can be constructed:

$$N(i) = \begin{cases} \min \{k; d(\mathbf{x}^k, \mathbf{x}^i) \leq d(\mathbf{x}^j, \mathbf{x}^i); 1 \leq j, k \leq i - 1\}, & i \neq 1, \\ 0, & i = 1, \end{cases}$$

$$\tag{7a}$$

$$R(i) = \begin{cases} d(\mathbf{x}^{i+1}, \mathbf{x}^{N(i+1)}), & i \neq n, \\ 0, & i = n. \end{cases}$$

---

†A slight modification is required when two samples can be the same.
‡$N(i)$ simply is the index of the reordered sample closest to $\mathbf{x}^i$ having order less than i.

2. The sequence $R(m)$ is nonincreasing, because

$$R(m) = \max_{1 \le i \le n} \min_{1 \le j \le m} d(\mathbf{x}_i, \mathbf{x}^j). \tag{7b}$$

3. The sequence $\mathbf{x}^1, \mathbf{x}^2, \ldots, \mathbf{x}^n$ can be truncated after the mth vector with the assurance that the samples $\mathbf{x}^m, \mathbf{x}^{m+1}, \ldots, \mathbf{x}^n$ are within a distance $R(m-1)$ of at least one of the vectors $\mathbf{x}^1, \mathbf{x}^2, \ldots, \mathbf{x}^{m-1}$.

4. There are not two vectors in the ordered sequence $\mathbf{x}^1, \mathbf{x}^2, \ldots, \mathbf{x}^m$ which are closer together than $R(m-1)$. This follows, simply, because $R(i)$ is decreasing as i increases.

5. If $R(m) < \frac{1}{2}R(m-1)$, then all observations can be covered with m disjoint spheres of common radius, where each sphere contains at least one vector. This follows because, by the construction, spheres centered at $\mathbf{x}^1, \mathbf{x}^2, \ldots, \mathbf{x}^m$ are pairwise distant by at least $R(m-1)$. Since $R(m) \le \frac{1}{2}R(m-1)$ there are no points $\mathbf{x}$ in the space which are simultaneously closer to some $\mathbf{x}^i$ and $\mathbf{x}^j$ than $R(m)$, for $1 \le i$, $j \le m$. Hence the spheres are disjoint.

6. If there are M disjoint groups of vectors where the maximum intragroup distance is less than one half the minimum intergroup† distance, then $R(m) < \frac{1}{2}R(m-1)$.

7. Let $\mathbf{y}$ be a vector not necessarily distinct from any $\mathbf{x}_i$, $i = 1, 2, \ldots,$ n. Define $\mathbf{x}_m^{[k]}$ to be the vector in the set $\mathbf{x}^1, \mathbf{x}^2, \ldots, \mathbf{x}^m$, which is the kth nearest to $\mathbf{y}$.

    If $d(\mathbf{x}_m^{[1]}, \mathbf{y}) < R(m)/2$, then $\mathbf{x}^{m+1} \ne \mathbf{x}_m^{[1]}$, indicating that $\mathbf{x}^{m+1}$ cannot be the nearest neighbor to $\mathbf{y}$. Thus, by storing $d(\mathbf{y}, \mathbf{x}_m^1)$, the distance of $\mathbf{y}$ to its current nearest neighbor and referring to the number $R(m)$, it can be determined whether the vector $\mathbf{x}^{m+1}$ has a possibility of being the first nearest neighbor to $\mathbf{y}$ before calculating the distance $d(\mathbf{y}, \mathbf{x}^{m+1})$.

8. Another approach is to determine, prior to the calculation of $d(\mathbf{y}, \mathbf{x}^{m+1})$, if $\mathbf{x}^{m+1}$ could possibly be one of the k nearest vectors among $\mathbf{x}^1, \ldots, \mathbf{x}^n$ to $\mathbf{y}$. The idea is to update and store best (largest) lower bounds of the distance from $\mathbf{y}$ to $\mathbf{x}^i$, $i = 1, 2, \ldots, n$, as the vectors are reordered. Then based on knowledge of $R(m)$, $N(m+1)$, and the current greatest lower bounds on $d(\mathbf{y}, \mathbf{x}^i)$, the necessity of the calculation of $d(\mathbf{y}, \mathbf{x}^{m+1})$ can be determined.

Let $D(i)$ be the current best (largest) lower bound on all the distances $d(\mathbf{y}, \mathbf{x}^i)$, $i = 1, 2, \ldots, n$; and let $\mathbf{x}_m^{[k]}$ denote the kth nearest neighbor to $\mathbf{y}$ among $\mathbf{x}^1, \ldots, \mathbf{x}^m$ (provided that $m \ge k$). Before the computation of the kth nearest vector to $\mathbf{y}$, $d(\mathbf{y}, \mathbf{x}^i)$, $i = 1, 2, \ldots, n$, are all unknown and hence

---

†The intergroup distance between groups 1 and 2 is the smallest distance $d(\mathbf{x}_i, \mathbf{x}_j)$, where $\mathbf{x}_i$ is from group 1 and $\mathbf{x}_j$ is from group 2.

Supervised Estimation   *Chap. 4*

initially can be set to zero. The procedure is started by computing $d(\mathbf{y}, \mathbf{x}^i)$, $i = 1, 2, \ldots, k$. Hence, on the basis of those calculations, $D(1), \ldots, D(k)$ can be updated to equal $d(\mathbf{y}, \mathbf{x}^1), \ldots, d(\mathbf{y}, \mathbf{x}^k)$, respectively.

Since $R(k)$ is available $[R(k) = d(\mathbf{x}^{k+1}, \mathbf{x}^{N(k+1)})]$, then as a result of the simple vector relationship,

$$d(\mathbf{y}, \mathbf{x}^{k+1}) \geq d(\mathbf{y}, \mathbf{x}^{N(k+1)}) - d(\mathbf{x}^{k+1}, \mathbf{x}^{N(k+1)}),$$

$$d(\mathbf{y}, \mathbf{x}^{N(k+1)}) \geq D(N(k+1)),$$

it follows that

$$d(\mathbf{y}, \mathbf{x}^{k+1}) \geq D(N(k+1)) - R(k).$$

Now the largest lower bound on $d(\mathbf{y}, \mathbf{x}^{k+1})$ can be adjusted†:

$$D(k+1) = \max\{0, D(N(k+1)) - R(k)\}.$$

The question is asked: Can $\mathbf{x}^{k+1}$ be one of the kth nearest neighbors to $\mathbf{y}$ among $\mathbf{x}^1, \ldots, \mathbf{x}^n$? Certainly, if $d(\mathbf{y}, \mathbf{x}^{k+1})$ is greater than the distance from $\mathbf{y}$ to its kth nearest neighbor among $\mathbf{x}^1, \ldots, \mathbf{x}^k$. That is, if

$$d(\mathbf{y}, \mathbf{x}_k^{[k]}) < D(k),$$

$\mathbf{x}^{k+1}$ cannot possibly be one of the k nearest neighbors to $\mathbf{y}$. Consequently, $d(\mathbf{y}, \mathbf{x}^{k+1})$ is not calculated and one distance calculation is eliminated from the recognition process. On the other hand, if

$$d(\mathbf{y}, \mathbf{x}_k^{[k]}) \geq D(k),$$

then according to these considerations, $\mathbf{x}^{k+1}$ might be one of the kth nearest neighbor to $\mathbf{y}$, and the distance $d(\mathbf{y}, \mathbf{x}^{k+1})$ must be calculated as a final check. In that case, $D(k+1)$ is updated to be equal to $d(\mathbf{y}, \mathbf{x}^{k+1})$. The last step in this stage is to update $D(k+2)$ as was done before:

$$D(k+2) = \max(0, D(N(k+2)) - R(k+1)).$$

The process is repeated, now testing for the calculation of $\mathbf{x}^{k+2}, \ldots, \mathbf{x}^n$.

The general procedure for checking $\mathbf{x}^m$ (after processing $\mathbf{x}^1, \mathbf{x}^2, \ldots, \mathbf{x}^{m-1}, m \geq k$) is specified as follows: If

$$d(\mathbf{y}, \mathbf{x}_{m-1}^{[k]}) < D(m),$$

---

†At this point, $D(i)$, $i = 1, 2, \ldots, n$, might also be sequentially updated; however, the same result is achieved if these coefficients are not readjusted at this time.

the calculation of the distance $d(\mathbf{y}, \mathbf{x}^m)$ can be omitted. If

$$d(\mathbf{y}, \mathbf{x}^{[k]}_{m-1}) \geq D(m),$$

$d(\mathbf{y}, \mathbf{x}^m)$ must be computed, and set $D(m) = d(\mathbf{y}, \mathbf{x}^m)$. In either case, update the greatest lower bound on $d(\mathbf{y}, \mathbf{x}^{m+1})$:

$$D(m+1) = \max(0, D(N(m+1)) - R(m)).$$

It is worthwhile to note that a slight improvement can be made to the above procedure. Every time a distance calculation *is* made, say between $\mathbf{y}$ and $\mathbf{x}^m$, coefficients $D(i)$ can be readjusted for i *less than* m (as well as for i greater than m). For if $d(\mathbf{y}, \mathbf{x}^m)$ is calculated and $R(m-1) = d(\mathbf{x}^m, \mathbf{x}^{N(m)})$ is known and

$$d(\mathbf{y}, \mathbf{x}^{N(m)}) > D(m) - R(m-1),$$

then the $D(N(m))$ can be updated by replacing the old value of $D(m)$ by $D(m) - R(m-1)$ if the latter is larger than $D(N(m))$. Likewise, $D(N(N(m)))$, etc., can be updated. The advantage of this modification is that in checking for the calculation of the distance between $\mathbf{y}$ and other vectors $\mathbf{x}^i$ further down in the list, $D(N(i))$ may be too large as a lower bound for $d(\mathbf{y}, \mathbf{x}^{N(i)})$ for the indicator to permit omission of the distance calculation. By updating, more omissions will be allowed.

Example of Preprocessing

To determine how many distance calculations can be omitted in a practical situation as a function of the vector set size n, the following simulation was completed for $n = 50, 100, 200, 500,$ and 1000. The n vector observations were drawn from the bivariate Gaussian distribution with unity covariance matrix. Using the preprocessing procedure developed in Section 4-13.1, the vector set was reordered to obtain the sequences $\mathbf{x}^i$, $R(i)$, and $N(i)$, $i = 1, 2, \ldots, n$. Another independent set of test vectors numbering 1000 was drawn from the same distribution. Each test vector was sequentially considered as the vector $\mathbf{y}$, and the number of distance calculations necessary to find the first nearest neighbor ($k = 1$) to $\mathbf{y}$ among $\mathbf{x}^1, \mathbf{x}^2, \ldots, \mathbf{x}^n$ was determined. This resulted in 1000 integers for each value of n.

Instead of graphing the average and standard deviation of the 1000 integers as a function of n, the empirical 10, 50, and 90 percentiles were obtained and graphed in Figure 4.10. The graph is interpreted as in the following: For a sample size of $n = 1000$, 900 of the 1000 test vectors required less than 86 distance calculations to determine the nearest neighbor, a computation normally requiring 1000 distance calculations.

Note that in this simulation the complexity reduction resulting from preprocessing does not linearly increase with the vector set size. As the

                                                                     Supervised Estimation   Chap. 4

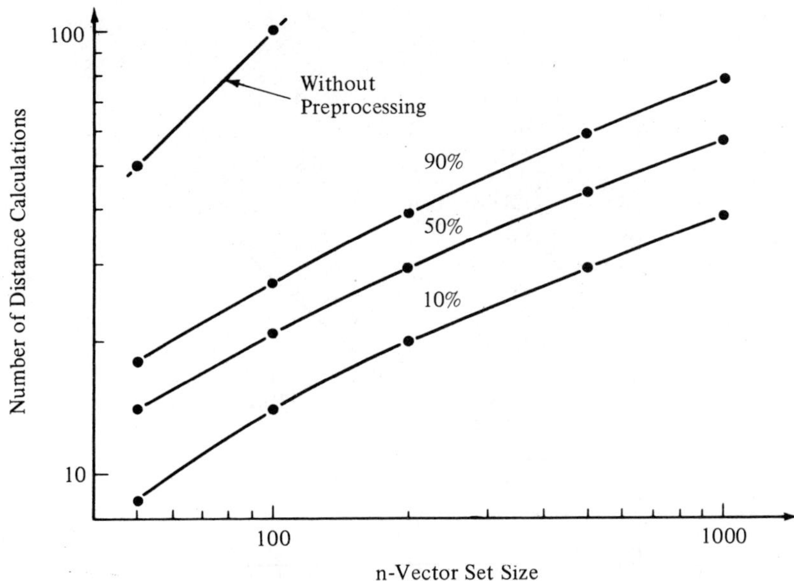

Fig. 4.10 Empirical upper bound on distance calculations for $1NN_2$ rule with confidences of 10, 50 and 90%

vector set size n increases, the ratio of actual number of distance calculations to the number normally required without preprocessing tends to zero. This also applies to reduce the complexity of nearest-neighbor type of rule discussed shortly.

For this simulation, it can be empirically projected how many distance calculations would be required if r rather than 1000 test vectors are used. It results from these projections that if the test size r is greater than the function of the reordered set size n indicated in Figure 4.11, then with a projected empirical confidence of 90 percent, it is better from the standpoint of total number of distance calculations to preprocess the vector set [$n(n + 1)/2$ calculations] prior to finding nearest neighbors using the preprocessed-list procedure.†

4-13.3 Application to Clustering

Properties 4, 5, and 6 suggest how this construction procedure can be used to locate clusters by observing $R(m)$. This is very similar to the maximin

†The reader should verify in his thinking that the number of distance calculations can be reduced further by supplying a priori knowledge about the underlying statistics. For example, if regions of equal density can be determined, it is sufficient to test for a sample being in such a region.

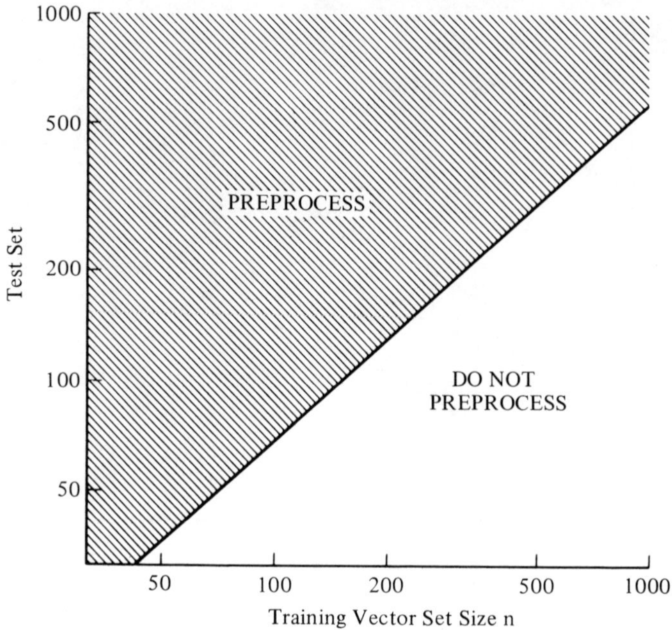

Fig. 4.11 Test example policy which minimizes total complexity for $1NN_2$ with at least an empirical confidence of 90%

clustering procedure discussed in Chapter 5. One disadvantage of using the procedure to locate clusters is that it utilizes the Euclidean distance measure; therefore, the presence of nonspherical clusters may cause the procedure to fail. The cluster-growing technique of Section 5-4.9 was developed after realizing these difficulties.

4-13.4 Application to kNN Rules

The kNN_2 rule [22, 25] investigated by Cover has the disadvantage that the entire data set has to be stored to implement the decision rule. Hart [23] later proposed a "condensed nearest-neighbor rule" which preprocessed the data set in such a way as to obtain a subset that correctly classifies (by the $1NN_2$ rule) the remaining vectors. The general approach was to reduce the size of the training set used at recognition time so as to reduce the number of distance calculations as well as to reduce storage requirements.

The procedure presented in this section can be used to reduce the number of calculations made at recognition time. This is accomplished by using the reordered samples $\mathbf{x}^1, \mathbf{x}^2, \ldots, \mathbf{x}^m$ and associated sequences $N(i)$, $R(i)$, $i = 1, 2, \ldots, m$, generated during preprocessing. The example in the following subsection will help to illustrate.

$k\mathrm{NN}_3$ *Rules*

The basic difference between $k\mathrm{NN}_2$ rules discussed in the last section and $k\mathrm{NN}_3$ rules is that for $k\mathrm{NN}_3$ rules the training set is separated as to class, instead of operating on the pooled training set. Hence, to apply this preprocessing to $k\mathrm{NN}_3$-type rules, each training set must be separately preprocessed.

For $k\mathrm{NN}_3$ rules, an additional device can be used to reduce complexity. As described in the last section, as each vector in a reordered list is sequentially examined, the region in which the kth nearest neighbor to y lies monotonically decreases. More explicitly, after the nth vector in the reordered list is processed, it is known that

$$\underline{B}_m \leq d(\mathbf{y}, \mathbf{x}^{[k]}) \leq \bar{B}_m,$$

where

$$\underline{B}_m = \begin{cases} 0, & m = 1, 2, \ldots, k, \\ \max\,[\underline{B}_{m-1}, d(\mathbf{y}, \mathbf{x}_m^{[k]}) - R(m-1)], & k < m \leq n, \end{cases}$$

and where

$$\bar{B}_m = d(\mathbf{y}, \mathbf{x}_m^{[k]}).$$

Thus the estimate density function $k_i/(n_i + 1)\Phi_i$ for the ith class, used in the $k\mathrm{NN}_3$ decision rule, can be upper-bounded and lower-bounded.† Hence the estimated risk of deciding class ω_j active can be upper- and lower-bounded at each stage for each class, since it is a function of tolerance-region volumes. If the training sets are processed in parallel, there will be a stage at which the estimate risk will be less than some value and the parallel processing may terminate before all training samples have been examined.

As an illustration, let $\underline{r}_m(i)$ and $\bar{r}_m(i)$ denote the lower and upper bounds of the empirical risk of the $k\mathrm{NN}_3$ rule obtained by utilizing $\underline{B}_m$ and $\bar{B}_m$. Figure 4.12 indicates in an idealized manner how the bounds on risk converge to a limit. In this illustration there is no need to consider 400 of the training samples, as the $k\mathrm{NN}_3$ decision will be unchanged.

Example. A two-class ($M = 2$) example was simulated using pseudo-random-number generators. For class 1, 500 vectors were drawn from the bivariate Gaussian distribution with covariance matrix $\delta^2\mathbf{I}$ and mean vector $[-2, -2]$; class 2 had 500 observations with covariance matrix $\sigma^2\mathbf{I}$ and mean vector $[2, 2]$. These two vector sets were independently processed, resulting in a sequence of reordered vectors and associated sequences $\{R(i)\}$, $\{N(i)\}$ for each class. Then 1000 test vectors were drawn at random from the two distributions.

The experimental results for the $1\mathrm{NN}_2$ rule are that the 10, 50, and 90

---

†Theoretically, the estimate density functions at $\mathbf{x}$ used in the $k\mathrm{NN}_3$ rule can be upper-bounded and lower-bounded *before all training samples have been examined.*

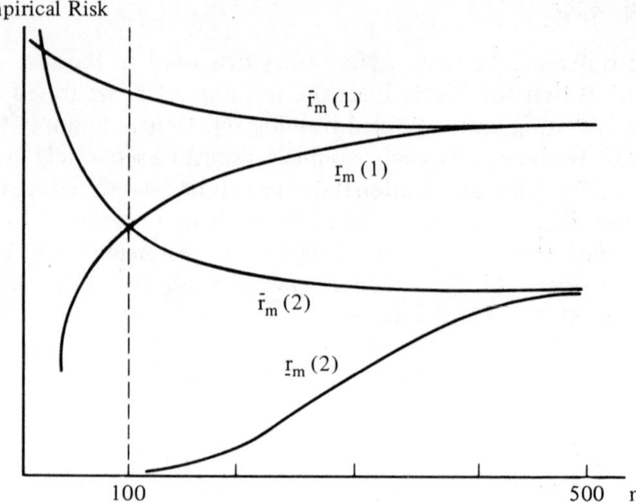

Fig. 4.12 Hypothetical bounds on empirical risks as function of the number of samples parallel processed

percentiles on the number of distance calculations required to classify a test vector were 3, 10, and 19, respectively. The average number of distance calculations was 8.2 (1000 distance calculations would be required without preprocessing). As a comparison, the condensed nearest-neighbor rule selected 16 samples to represent the $1NN_2$ rule.

4-14 Adaptive Threshold Elements

4-14.1 Linear Discriminant Function

The use of boundaries to separate categories is the approach taken by Nilsson in his book, *Learning Machines* [1]. In this section we will briefly present certain aspects of this approach to show how it relates to previous results in this chapter.

The minimum probability of error decision rule for $f(\mathbf{x}|i) \in \mathscr{F}$ Gaussian and two categories ($M = 2$) is given by Eq. (2) in Section 3-4.1. When the covariance matrices of the respective classes are equal, i.e., $\boldsymbol{\Sigma}_1 = \boldsymbol{\Sigma}_2 = \boldsymbol{\Sigma}$, the decision rule reduces to

$$2(\mathbf{m}_2 - \mathbf{m}_1)'\boldsymbol{\Sigma}^{-1}\left(\mathbf{x} - \frac{\mathbf{m}_1 + \mathbf{m}_2}{2}\right) \begin{cases} > \ln \dfrac{P_1}{1 - P_1}: & \text{decide } \omega_2, \\[3mm] < \ln \dfrac{P_1}{1 - P_1}: & \text{decide } \omega_1. \end{cases} \tag{1}$$

This suggests defining a vector $\mathbf{d}$,

$$\mathbf{d}^t = (\mathbf{m}_2 - \mathbf{m}_1)^t \mathbf{\Sigma}^{-1}, \tag{2}$$

and a scalar,

$$d_0 = -\frac{1}{2}\mathbf{d}^t(\mathbf{m}_1 + \mathbf{m}_2) - \frac{1}{2}\ln\frac{P_1}{1 - P_1}. \tag{3}$$

Then (1), in terms of (2) and (3), is equivalent to

$$d = \mathbf{d}^t\mathbf{x} + d_0 \begin{cases} > 0: & \text{decide } \omega_2, \\ < 0: & \text{decide } \omega_1. \end{cases} \tag{4}$$

It may be possible to use samples $\mathbf{x}_1^1, \mathbf{x}_2^1, \ldots, \mathbf{x}_{n_1}^1$ from class 1 and samples $\mathbf{x}_1^2, \mathbf{x}_2^2, \ldots, \mathbf{x}_{n_2}^2$ from class 2 to estimate $\mathbf{d}$ and d_0 such that

$$\mathbf{d}^t\mathbf{x} + d_0 = 0 \tag{5}$$

is the equation of a hyperplane separating the two categories. An illustration of Eq. (5) is shown in Figure 4.13.

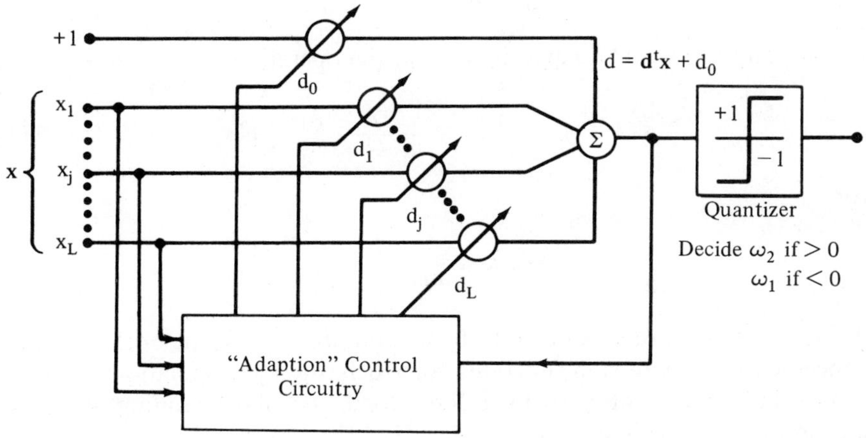

Fig. 4.13 Linear threshold element

Training

Let d^1 and d^2 be desired values of d for the two respective categories. Define the error in classifying sample $\mathbf{x}_s^i$,

$$e_s^i = d_s^i - d^i. \tag{6}$$

Define

$$\mathbf{y}_s^i \triangleq \begin{bmatrix} \mathbf{x}_s^i \\ 1 \end{bmatrix}, \tag{7a}$$

$$\mathbf{d}^t \triangleq (\mathbf{d}, d_0) \tag{7b}$$

and a *mean-error function,*

$$g(\dot{\mathbf{d}}) \triangleq \frac{1}{n_1 + n_2} \sum_{i=1}^{2} \sum_{s=1}^{n_i} g^i(e_s^i), \tag{8}$$

where $g^i(\cdot)$ is a function to be specified. It may not be possible to search for a value of $\dot{\mathbf{d}}$ minimizing (8).

Example. Let $d^i = (-1)^i$ and

$$g^i(e_s^i) = (\dot{\mathbf{d}}^t y_s^i - (1)^i)^2. \tag{9}$$

Then (8) becomes

$$g(\dot{\mathbf{d}}) = \frac{1}{n_1 + n_2} \sum_{i=1}^{2} \sum_{s=1}^{n_i} (\dot{\mathbf{d}}^t y_s^i - (1)^i)^2. \tag{10}$$

Koford and Groner [35] have shown that the operation

$$\dot{\mathbf{d}}^i(\lambda + 1) = \dot{\mathbf{d}}(\lambda) - \frac{2\mu}{n_1 + n_2} \sum_{i=1}^{2} \sum_{s=1}^{n_1} g_s^i \mathbf{y}_s \tag{11}$$

for

$$0 < \mu < \frac{1}{\max [\| \mathbf{y}_s \|^2]}$$

will converge toward a value of $\dot{\mathbf{d}}$ which minimizes $g(\dot{\mathbf{d}})$. Some of the research concerned with regression functions for stochastic approximation (Chapter 2) may have been motivated by a desire for better understanding of "training procedures" such as above.

4-14.2 Nonlinear Discriminant Function

A more general form than (4) for discriminating between two categories is

$$h(\mathbf{x}, \mathbf{d}) + d_0 \begin{cases} > 0: & \text{decide } \omega_2, \\ < 0: & \text{decide } \omega_1, \end{cases}$$

where h is a nonlinear function. For example,

$$h(\mathbf{x}, \mathbf{d}) = \sqrt{\sum_{j=1}^{L} (x_j - d_j)^2},$$

or, for $L = 2$,

$$h(\mathbf{x}, \mathbf{d}) = \frac{x_2 - d_2}{x_1 - d_1},$$

or, for $L = 2$,

$$h(\mathbf{x}, \mathbf{d}) = \tan^{-1} \frac{x_2}{x_1}.$$

Training rules for estimating $\mathbf{d}$ using nonlinear functions as above undoubtedly merit study. These nonlinear functions can reflect problem knowledge and thus enhance performance. They are discussed in more detail in Chapter 6.

4-14.3 Polynomial Discriminant Function

A nonlinear decision boundary can be approximated by a polynomial. In this section a procedure for estimating the parameters characterizing a polynomial decision boundary is presented (see Specht [31] for further discussion).

Let there be two classes ($M = 2$), $f_i(\mathbf{x})$ not necessarily Gaussian, and training samples $\{\mathbf{x}_s^i\}_{s=1}^{n_i}$, $i = 1, 2$ available. Let the estimate of $f_i(\mathbf{x})$ be

$$\hat{f}_i(\mathbf{x}) = \frac{1}{n_i} \sum_{s=1}^{n_i} \frac{1}{(\sqrt{2\pi})^L \sigma^L} \exp\left(-\frac{1}{2\sigma^2} \sum_{j=1}^{L} (x_j - x_{sj}^i)^2\right). \tag{12}$$

The objective is to form a polynomial $\hat{p}(\mathbf{x})$,

$$\hat{p}(\mathbf{x}) = P_1 \hat{f}_1(\mathbf{x}) - P_2 \hat{f}_2(\mathbf{x}) \tag{13}$$

such that

$$\hat{p}(\mathbf{x}) \begin{cases} > 0: & \text{decide class } \omega_1, \\ < 0: & \text{decide class } \omega_2. \end{cases} \tag{14}$$

To obtain a polynomial form, begin by rewriting the exponent in (12) as

$$-\frac{1}{2\sigma^2} \sum_{j=1}^{L} (x_j - x_{sj}^i)^2 = -\frac{1}{2\sigma^2}[\mathbf{x}^t\mathbf{x} - 2\mathbf{x}^t\mathbf{x}_s^i + (\mathbf{x}_s^i)^t\mathbf{x}_s^i],$$

giving

$$\hat{f}_i(\mathbf{x}) = \frac{1}{(2\pi)^{L/2}\sigma^L} \exp\left(-\frac{\mathbf{x}^t\mathbf{x}}{2\sigma^2}\right)\left[\frac{1}{n_i} \sum_{s=1}^{n_i} \exp\left(\frac{\mathbf{x}^t\mathbf{x}_s^i}{\sigma^2}\right) \times \exp(c_s^i)\right],$$

where

$$c_s^i = -\frac{1}{2\sigma^2}(\mathbf{x}_s^i)^t \mathbf{x}_s^i.$$

Next, expand $\exp(\mathbf{x}^t \mathbf{x}_s^i/\sigma^2)$ about 0:

$$\exp\left(\frac{\mathbf{x}^t \mathbf{x}_s^i}{\sigma^2}\right) = 1 + \frac{\mathbf{x}^t \mathbf{x}_s^i}{\sigma^2} + \frac{1}{2!}\left[\frac{\mathbf{x}^t \mathbf{x}_s^i}{\sigma^2}\right]^2 + \cdots$$

$$= 1 + \frac{1}{\sigma^2}\sum_{k=1}^{L} x_k x_{sk}^i + \frac{1}{2!\sigma^4}\sum_{k_1=1}^{L}\sum_{k_2=1}^{L} x_{k_1} x_{k_2} x_{sk_1}^i x_{sk_2}^i.$$

The hth-degree term in the above expression is

$$\frac{1}{h!\,\sigma^{2h}}\left[\sum_{k=1}^{L} x_k x_{sk}^i\right]^h = \frac{1}{h!\,\sigma^{2k}}\sum_{z_1,z_2,\ldots,z_L}\frac{h!}{z_1!\,z_2!\cdots z_L!}(x_1 x_{s_1}^i)^{z_1}\cdots(x_L x_{s_L}^i)^{z_L}$$

with

$$\sum_{k=1}^{L} z_k = h.$$

Thus,

$$\hat{f}_i(\mathbf{x}) = \frac{1}{(2\pi)^{L/2}\sigma^L}\exp\left(-\frac{\mathbf{x}^t \mathbf{x}}{2\sigma^2}\right)\left[\frac{1}{n_i}\sum_{s=1}^{n_i}\exp(c_s^i)\right.$$

$$\left.\times \sum_{h=0}^{\infty}\frac{1}{\sigma^{2h}}\sum_{z_1,z_2,\ldots,z_L}\frac{1}{z_1!\,z_2!\cdots z_L!}\prod_{j=1}^{L}(x_j x_{sj}^i)^{z_j}\right]$$

with

$$\sum_{k=1}^{L} z_k = h.$$

The above expression for $\hat{f}_i(\mathbf{x})$ is more conveniently written

$$\hat{f}_i(\mathbf{x}) = \frac{1}{(2\pi)^{L/2}\sigma^L}\exp\left(-\frac{\mathbf{x}^t \mathbf{x}}{2\sigma^2}\right)p^i(\mathbf{x}), \tag{15}$$

where

$$p^i(\mathbf{x}) = d_0^i + \sum_{k=1}^{L} d_k^i x_k + \sum_{k_2=k_1}^{L}\sum_{k_1=1}^{L} d_{k_1,k_2}^i x_{k_1} x_{k_2} + \cdots$$

$$+ \sum_{k_h=k_{h-1}}^{L}\cdots\sum_{k_1=1}^{L} d_{k_1,k_2,\ldots,k_h}^i x_{k_1} x_{k_2}\cdots x_{k_h} + \cdots, \tag{16}$$

where

$$d_0^i = \frac{1}{n_i}\sum_{s=1}^{n_i}\exp\left(\frac{c_s^i}{\sigma^2{}_2}\right)$$

$$$$

$$\tag{17}$$

$$d_{k_1,k_2,\ldots,k_h}^i = \frac{1}{n_i}\sum_{s=1}^{n_i}\exp\left(\frac{c_s^i}{\sigma^2{}_2}\right)\left[\frac{1}{\sigma^{2h}}\frac{1}{z_1!\,z_2!\cdots z_L!}\right]\prod_{j=1}^{L}(x_{sj}^i)^{z_j}$$

with

$$\sum_{k=1}^{L} z_k = h.$$

The polynomial discriminant function is

$$p(\mathbf{x}) = P_1 p^1(\mathbf{x}) - P_2 p^2(\mathbf{x}) \tag{18}$$

with $p^i(\mathbf{x})$ given by (16) and the estimated parameters characterizing (16) given by (17).

It is left as a problem to show that $p^i(\mathbf{x})$ is a Taylor-series expansion about $\mathbf{x} = \mathbf{0}$.

A Priori Knowledge

In the spirit of Bayes's estimation, one could presume that n_i^1, $i = 1, 2$, samples are available a priori to produce estimates

$$\begin{gathered} (d_0^i)_{n_i^1} \\ \cdot \\ \cdot \\ \cdot \\ (d_{k_1, k_2, \ldots, k_h}^i)_{n_i^1}. \end{gathered} \tag{19}$$

Then with n_i^2, $i = 1, 2$, current samples, estimates

$$\begin{gathered} (d_0^i)_{n_i^2} \\ \cdot \\ \cdot \\ \cdot \\ (d_{k_1, k_2, \ldots, k_h}^i)_{n_i^2} \end{gathered} \tag{20}$$

are formed. The a posteriori estimates are, with $n = n_i^1 + n_i^2$,

$$\begin{gathered} (d_0^i) = \frac{n_i^1}{n_i^1 + n_i^2}(d_0^i)_{n_i^2} + \frac{n_i^2}{n_i^1 + n_i^2}(d_0^i)_{n_i^2} \\ \cdot \quad \cdot \\ \cdot \quad \cdot \\ \cdot \quad \cdot \\ (d_{k_1, k_2, \ldots, k_h}^i)_n = \frac{n_i^1}{n_i^1 + n_i^2}(d_{k_1, k_2, \ldots, k_h}^i)_{n_i^1} + \frac{n_i^2}{n_i^1 + n_i^2}(d_{k_1, k_2, \ldots, k_h}^i)_{n_i^2}. \end{gathered} \tag{21}$$

The polynomial discriminant function does, in theory, allow for introducing nonlinear problem knowledge. It is, however, a complex nonlinear function; and it is likely that other simple nonlinear decision boundaries will find more application. It is hard to imagine problems where problem knowledge could be easily obtained in the form of (16). But, research is so unpredictable that this may not be true very long.

4-15 Adaptive Sample Set Construction

"Adaptive sample set construction" was discussed earlier in Section 4-3.1 with regard to how it fit in with the development of classification operations in pattern recognition. Good references are Sebestyen [17] and Sebestyen and Edie [18].

Let there be n_i supervised observations from class ω_i, $i = 1, 2, \ldots, M$. Samples from class ω_i are grouped into subsets or subclasses ω_{ij}, $j = 1, 2, \ldots, M_i$. The subset ω_{ij} is characterized by its mean vector $\mathbf{m}_i(j)$ and a (as yet undefined) radius t. The sets are created as follows:

> When the first observation vector from class ω_i is encountered it is assigned to subset ω_{i1}; $\mathbf{m}_i(1)$ is set equal to this first vector. The number of samples in the neighborhood of $\mathbf{m}_i(1)$, M_{i1}, is set equal to 1.
>
> If the second observation vector from class ω_i is within a Euclidean distance† t of $\mathbf{m}_i(1)$, it is assigned to the subset ω_{i1}, $\mathbf{m}_i(1)$ is updated, and $M_{i1} = 2$. If the second observation is a distance greater than t from $\mathbf{m}_i(1)$, the observation is assigned to a new subset ω_{i2} with mean $\mathbf{m}_i(2)$ equal to the second observation, $M_{i2} = 1$.

This procedure is continued until all n_i samples are processed for each of the M classes.

The p.d.f. for class ω_i is approximated by a sum of multivariate Gaussian functions where the jth function has covariance matrix $\sigma^2\mathbf{I}$, mean vector $\mathbf{m}_i(j)$, and weighting M_{ij}:

$$\hat{f}_i(\mathbf{x}) = \sum_{j=1}^{M_i} M_{ij} \exp\left[-\frac{1}{2\sigma^2} \sum_{k=1}^{L} (x_k - m_{ik}(j))^2 \right], \tag{1}$$

where $m_{ik}(j)$ is the kth component of $\mathbf{m}_i(j)$. The decision rule is then the usual one:

$$\text{decide class } \omega_a \text{ if } \hat{f}_a(\mathbf{x})P_a = \max_j \{\hat{f}_j(\mathbf{x})P_j\}_{j=1}^{M}. \tag{2}$$

Disadvantages of this approach are the following:

1. The threshold t must be set a priori.‡

---

†The Euclidean distance between two vectors $\mathbf{x}$ and $\mathbf{y}$ is $\sqrt{\sum_{i=1}^{L} (x_i - y_i)^2}$.
‡This may be an advantage for the practitioner of interactive pattern recognition.

2. The Gaussian weighting function may violate a priori p.d.f. $f_i(\mathbf{x})$, but a practical alternative is difficult.

4-16 Piecewise Linear Discriminant Functions

In Section 4-14.1 a linear discriminant function was discussed. In this section a piecewise linear discriminant function [1] is discussed. For convenience let $M = 2$. We introduce the approach by an example shown in Figure 4.14 in

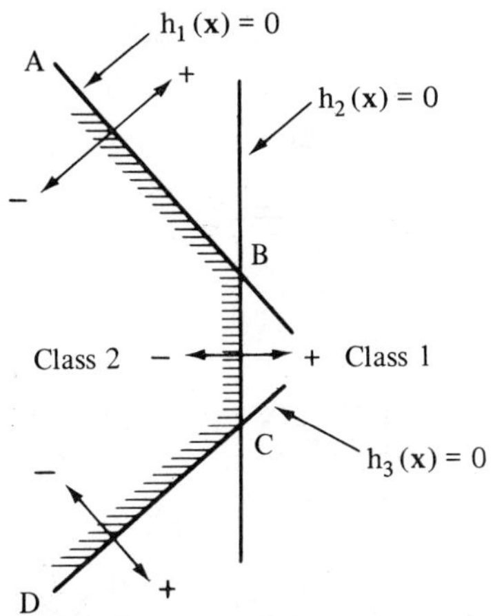

Fig. 4.14 A piecewise linear discriminant function

which there are three linear functions $h_1(\mathbf{x})$, $h_2(\mathbf{x})$, $h_3(\mathbf{x})$. The piecewise linear function $h(\mathbf{x})$ is represented by the broken line $ABCD$.

The functions $h_i(\mathbf{x})$ are such that

$$h_i(\mathbf{x}) \geq 0, \text{ decide } \omega_1,$$
$$h_i(\mathbf{x}) < 0, \text{ decide } \omega_2. \tag{1}$$

In general the piecewise linear discriminant function is expressed as

$$h(\mathbf{x}) = \max_i \{h_i(\mathbf{x})\}_{i=1}^K \tag{2}$$

Each discriminant function $h_i(\mathbf{x})$ separates the observation space into two parts. Therefore given K functions $h_i(\mathbf{x})$ (called subsidiary discriminant functions), the observation space can be partitioned into 2^K regions. Assign a code (1 or -1) to each class (ω_1 or ω_2) for each of these 2^K regions.

The decision boundary (2) can be implemented using threshold logic units (TLUs). A TLU for $h_i(\mathbf{x})$ realizes sign $[h_i(\mathbf{x})]$. For the example in Figure 4.14,

$$h(\mathbf{x}) \geq 0 \text{ if } h_1(\mathbf{x}) \geq 0 \text{ or } h_2(\mathbf{x}) \geq 0 \text{ or } h_3(\mathbf{x}) \geq 0 \tag{3}$$

which is implemented by a switching function known as OR:

$$\text{sign}[h(\mathbf{x})] = \text{sign}[\text{sign}[h_1(\mathbf{x})] + \text{sign}[h_2(\mathbf{x})] + \text{sign}[h_3(\mathbf{x})] + 2].$$

In general, (2) is implemented by the following OR:

$$\text{sign}[h(\mathbf{x})] = \text{sign}\left[\sum_{i=1}^{K} \text{sign}[h_i(\mathbf{x})] + (K - 1)\right]. \tag{4}$$

A TLU implementation of (4) is shown in Figure 4.15.

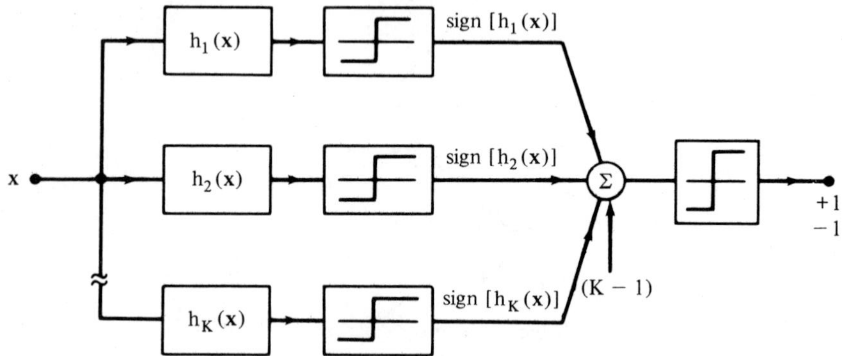

Fig. 4.15 Block diagram of TLU implementation of piecewise linear discriminant function

An alternative implementation of $h_i(\mathbf{x})$ is the adaptive threshold element,

$$\begin{aligned}
\mathbf{d}_i^t\mathbf{x} + d_{i0} > 0, \text{ decide } \omega_1, \\
\mathbf{d}_i^t\mathbf{x} + d_{i0} < 0, \text{ decide } \omega_2.
\end{aligned} \tag{5}$$

It is easy to show that under certain conditions a piecewise linear discriminator is equivalent to a minimum distance classifier which uses Euclidean distance. Let $d(\mathbf{x}, \mathbf{x}^i)$ be the smallest distance between an unclassified vector $\mathbf{x}$ and the training observations from class ω_i. Then

$$\begin{aligned}
d(\mathbf{x}, \mathbf{x}^i) &= \min_{j=1,2,\ldots,M} (\mathbf{x} - \mathbf{x}^j)^t(\mathbf{x} - \mathbf{x}^j) \\
&= \min (\mathbf{x}^t\mathbf{x} - 2(\mathbf{x}^j)^t\mathbf{x} + (\mathbf{x}^j)^t\mathbf{x}^j). \tag{6}
\end{aligned}$$

A decision can be made by

$$h(\mathbf{x}) = d(\mathbf{x}, \mathbf{x}^2) - d(\mathbf{x}, \mathbf{x}^1) \geq 0, \text{ decide } \omega_1,$$
$$h(\mathbf{x}) = d(\mathbf{x}, \mathbf{x}^2) - d(\mathbf{x}, \mathbf{x}^1) < 0, \text{ decide } \omega_2. \tag{7}$$

Substituting (6) into (7) gives

$$h(\mathbf{x}) = -2(\mathbf{x}^2)^t \mathbf{x} + (\mathbf{x}^2)^t (\mathbf{x}^2) + 2(\mathbf{x}^1)^t \mathbf{x} - (\mathbf{x}^1)^t \mathbf{x}^1$$

or, in general,

$$h(\mathbf{x}) = \max \{-2(\mathbf{x}^j)^t \mathbf{x} + (\mathbf{x}^j)^t \mathbf{x}^j\}_{j=1}^M. \tag{8}$$

Clearly, Eq. (8) has the form of (5).

There do not yet exist any general training procedures for piecewise linear functions. Early proposals for training were made by Rosenblatt [36]. More recently, Fu and Henrichon [3] and Patrick and Bechtel [2] have taken approaches which essentially lead to considerable complexity.

The piecewise linear function approach has appeal if a priori knowledge is available about where the K boundaries should be placed.

A disadvantage of the piecewise linear function approach is that it does not directly provide for introducing local correlation information. A piecewise nonlinear function approach would directly provide for local correlation information. Of course, nonlinear functions can be approximated by piecewise linear functions.

Suggested Reading for Chapter 4

[1] N. J. Nilsson, *Learning Machines*, McGraw-Hill Book Company, Inc., New York, 1965.

[2] E. A. Patrick and F. P. Bechtel, A Nonparametric Recognition Procedure with Storage Constraint, *Purdue University School of Electrical Engineering Tech. Rept. EE 69–24*, Lafayette, Ind., Aug. 1969.

[3] K. S. Fu and E. G. Henrichon, Jr., On Non-parametric Methods for Pattern Recognition, *Purdue University School of Electrical Engineering Tech. Rept. EE 69–24*, Lafayette, Ind., Aug. 1969.

[4] D. Braverman, Learning Filters for Optimum Pattern Recognition, *IRE Trans. Information Theory*, Vol. IT-8, pp. 280–285, July 1962.

[5] N. Abramson and D. Braverman, Learning to Recognize Patterns in a Random Environment, *IRE Trans. Information Theory*, Vol. IT-8, No. 5, pp. 58–63, Sept. 1962.

[6] D. G. Keehn, A Note on Learning for Gaussian Properties," *IEEE Trans. Information Theory*, Vol. IT-11, pp. 126–132, Jan. 1965.

[7] R. A. Fischer, Use of Multiple Measurements in Taxonomic Problems, *Ann. Eugenics*, Vol. 7, pp. 179–188, 1936.

[8] E. Fix and J. L. Hodges, Jr., Discriminatory Analysis; Nonparametric, Discrimination: Consistency Properties, *USAF School of Aviation Medicine Project Number 21–49–004, Rept. No. 4*, Randolph Field, Texas, Feb. 1951.

[9] M. A. Aizerman, E. M. Braverman, and L. I. Rozonoer, The Probability Problem of Pattern Recognition Learning and the Method of Potential Functions, *Automation and Remote Control*, Vol. 26, pp. 1175–1190, Sept. 1964.

[10] Y. Z. Tsypkin, Use of the Stochastic Approximation Method in Estimating Unknown Distribution Densities from Observations, *Avtomatika i Telemekhanika*, Vol. 27, No. 3, pp. 94–96, March 1966.

[11] R. L. Kashyap and C. C. Blaydon, Estimation of Probability Density and Distribution Functions, *IEEE Trans. Information Theory*, Vol. IT-14, No. 4, pp. 549–556, July 1968.

[12] P. Whittle, On the Smoothing of Probability Density Functions, *J. Royal Statistical Soc.*, Ser. B, Vol. 20, pp. 334–343, 1958.

[13] E. Parzen, On Estimation of a Probability Density Function and Mode, *Ann. Math. Statistics*, Vol. 33, No. 3, pp. 1065–1076, Sept. 1962.

[14] G. S. Watson and M. R. Leadbetter, On the Estimation of the Probability Density, *Ann. Math. Statistics*, Vol. 34, No. 2, pp. 480–491, June 1963.

[15] T. Cacoullus, Estimation of a Multivariate Density, *Tech. Rept. No. 40*, Dept. of Statistics, University of Minnesota, Minneapolis, May 1964.

[16] J. Van Ryzin, The Sequential Compound Decision Problem with $m \times n$ Finite Loss Matrix, *Ann. Math. Statistics*, Vol. 37, pp. 954–975, 1966.

[17] G. Sebestyen, Pattern Recognition by an Adaptive Process of Sample Set Construction, *IRE Trans. Information Theory*, Vol. IT-8, No. 5, pp. 582–591, Sept. 1962.

[18] G. Sebestyen and J. Edie, An Algorithm for Non-parametric Pattern Recognition, *IEEE Trans. Electronic Computers*, Vol. EC-15, No. 6, pp. 908–915, Dec. 1966.

[19] G. H. Ball and D. J. Hall, ISODATA, An Iterative Method of Multivariate Analysis and Pattern Classification, *1966 IEEE the International Communications Conference, Philadelphia*, Digest of Technical Papers, pp. 116–117. Lewis Winner, New York, N. Y. June 1966.

[20] D. O. Loftsgaarden and C. P. Quesenberry, A Nonparametric Estimate of a Multivariate Density Function, *Ann. Math. Statistics*, Vol. 36, No. 3, pp. 1049–1051, 1965.

[21] E. Fix and J. L. Hodges, Jr., Discriminatory Analysis; Non-parametric Discrimination: Small Sample Performance, *USAF School of Aviation Medicine Project Number 21–49–004, Rept. No. 11*, Randolph Field, Texas, Aug. 1952.

[22] T. M. Cover and P. E. Hart, Nearest Neighbor Pattern Classification, *IEEE Trans. Information Theory*, Vol. IT-13, No. 1, pp. 21–27, Jan. 1967.

[23] P. E. Hart, An Asymptotic Analysis of the Nearest Neighbor Decision Rule, *Stanford Tech. Rept. No. 1828–2*, Stanford Electronics Laboratories, Stanford, Calif., May 1966.

[24] A. W. Whitney and S. J. Dwyer, III, Performance and Implementation of the k-Nearest Neighbor Decision Rule with Incorrectly Identified Training Samples, *Proceedings of the Fourth Annual Allerton Conference on Circuit Theory and System Theory*, Champaign, Ill., Oct. 1966.

[25] T. M. Cover, Estimation by the Nearest Neighbor Rule, *IEEE Trans. Information Theory*, Vol. IT-14, No. 1, pp. 50–55, Jan. 1968.

[26] E. A. Patrick, Distribution Free, Minimum Conditional Risk Learning Systems, *Purdue University School of Electrical Engineering Technical Rept. EE66-18*, Lafayette, Ind., Nov. 1966.

[27] E. A. Patrick, Distribution Free, Minimum Conditional Risk Learning Systems, *Proceedings of the 1967 International Conference on Communication, Minneapolis, Minn.*, Institute of Electrical and Electronics Engineers, New York, June 1967.

[28] E. A. Patrick and F. P. Fischer, Generalized k Nearest Neighbor Decision Rule, *J. Information and Control*, Vol. 16, No. 2, pp. 128–152, April 1970.

[29] P. E. Hart, The Condensed Nearest Neighbor Rule, *IEEE Trans. Information Theory*, Vol. IT-14, pp. 515–516, May 1968.

[30] M. E. Hellman, The Nearest Neighbor Classification Rule with a Reject Option, presented at IEEE International Convention on Information Theory, Nourwisk, Holland, June 1970.

[31] D. F. Specht, Generation of Polynomial Discriminant Functions for Pattern Recognition, presented at IEEE Pattern Recognition Workshop, Puerto Rico, Oct. 1966.

[32] D. A. S. Fraser, *Nonparametric Methods in Statistics*, John Wiley & Sons, New York, 1957.

[33] S. S. Wilks, *Mathematical Statistics*, John Wiley & Sons, New York, 1962.

[34] D. W. Peterson, Some Convergence Properties of a Nearest Neighbor Decision Rule, *IEEE Trans. Information Theory*, Vol. IT-16, No. 1, pp. 26–31, Jan. 1970.

[35] J. S. Koford and G. F. Groner, The Use of an Adaptive Threshold Element to Design a Linear Optimum Pattern Classifier, *IEEE Trans. Information Theory*, Vol. IT-12, No. 1, pp. 42–50, Jan. 1966.

[36] F. Rosenblatt, *Principles of Neurodynamics: Perceptrons and the Theory of Brain Mechanism*, Spartan Books, New York, 1962.

[37] H. Robbins, An Empirical Bayes Approach to Statistics, *Proc. Third Berkeley Symp. Math. Statistics Prob.*, Vol. 4, pp. 157–163, 1955.

[38] M. Rosenblatt, Remarks on Some Nonparametric Estimates of a Density Function, *Ann. Math. Statistics*, Vol. 27, No. 3, pp. 832–837, Sept. 1956.

[39] I. S. Gradshtyen and I. W. Ryzhik, *Tables of Integrals, Series and Products*, Academic Press, Inc., New York, 1965.

[40] M. Loeve, *Probability Theory*, Van Nostrand Reinhold, New York, 1963.

[41] B. G. Batchelor and R. B. Wilkins, Method for Location of Clusters of Patterns to Initialize a Learning Machine, *Electronics Letters*, Vol. 5, No. 20, pp. 481–483, Oct. 1969.

Problems

[1] Let an estimate of the minimum conditional risk rule with loss functions $L_{ij} = 1 - \delta_{ij}$ be, decide class a if

$$P_a \hat{f}_a(\mathbf{x}) = \max_i \{P_i \hat{f}_i(\mathbf{x})\}.$$

(a) Show that $P_i = n_i/n$ is implied in the $k\mathrm{NN}_2$ decision rule, thus verifying property 4 of this rule.

[2] Suppose that $L = 2$, $M = 2$, and the two categories have samples as shown below.

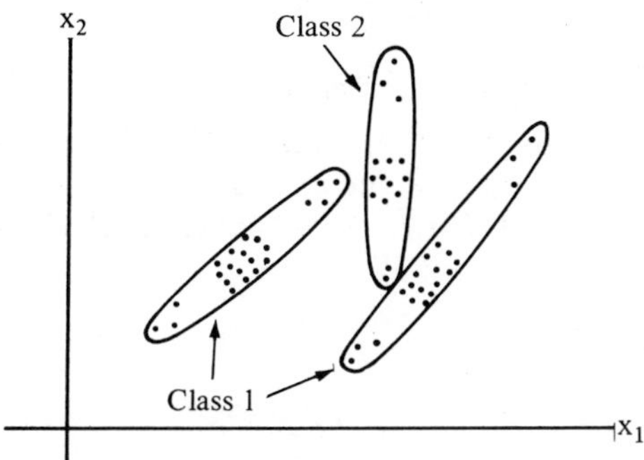

(a) If $d(\mathbf{x}, \mathbf{y}) = [\sum_{i=1}^{L} (x_i - y_i)^2]^{1/2} = |\mathbf{x} - \mathbf{y}|$ in the $k\mathrm{NN}_1$ or $k\mathrm{NN}_2$ rule, what samples are likely to be misclassified?

(b) Assume that category 2 is multivariate Gaussian and category 1 is a mixture of two multivariate Gaussian and that all mean vectors and covariance matrices have been estimated. Show that there are effectively three distance measures determined by category number and region of the observation space concerned.

(c) State conditions for n, L, and M where you would use a $k\mathrm{NN}_1$ or $k\mathrm{NN}_2$ rule for this type of problem and conditions where you would take an approach as in (b).

[3] Let $\mathbf{x}_1, \mathbf{x}_2, \ldots, \mathbf{x}_n$ be n training samples in a two-dimensional space as sketched below. Suppose an operation is available for associating a parameter vector $\boldsymbol{\alpha}_i$ with sample $\mathbf{x}_i$, and the pair $(\mathbf{x}_i, \boldsymbol{\alpha}_i)$ is stored, $i = 1, 2, \ldots, n$. Suppose that there are only $M = 6$ distinct $\boldsymbol{\alpha}_i$ and $n/6$ training samples for each $\boldsymbol{\alpha}_i$. Let the samples for each $\boldsymbol{\alpha}_i$ have a truncated multivariate Gaussian distribution. The density of each cluster is relatively dense in the center.

(a) Show why the $1\mathrm{NN}_2$ rule would have poor performance using distance measure $d(\mathbf{x}, \mathbf{x}_k) = |\mathbf{x} - \mathbf{x}_k|$, $k = 1, 2, \ldots, n$, even though the categories (parameter vectors) $\boldsymbol{\alpha}_1, \boldsymbol{\alpha}_2, \ldots, \boldsymbol{\alpha}_6$ are separated.

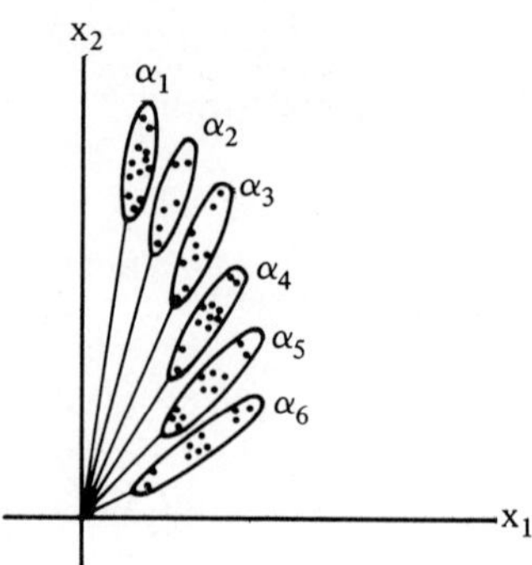

(b) Show using results from Chapter 2 that if 6 distance measures of the form

$$d_i(\mathbf{x}, \boldsymbol{\alpha}_i) = (\mathbf{x} - \boldsymbol{\alpha}_i)^t \boldsymbol{\Sigma}_i^{-1}(\mathbf{x} - \boldsymbol{\alpha}_i), \; i = 1, 2, \ldots, 6,$$

are used, zero probability of error results.

[4] (a) Show that the $k\mathrm{NN}_1$, $k\mathrm{NN}_2$, and $k\mathrm{NN}_3$ rules can have zero probability of error for arbitrary L, M and n if $f(\mathbf{x}|i)$ is spherical and symmetrical and $(f(\mathbf{x}|i), f(\mathbf{x}|j)) = 0$, $i \neq j$. A two-dimensional illustration with $M = 3$ is shown below:

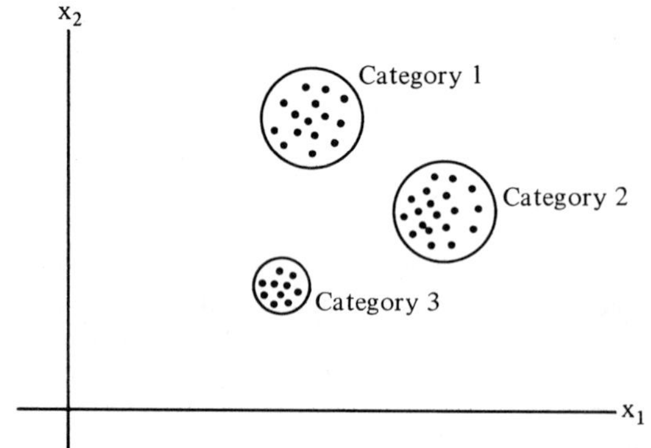

(b) Is it possible to have resulting errors for some values of k and P_i, $i = 1, 2, \ldots, M$, for the $k\mathrm{NN}_1$ rule?

(c) Repeat (b) for the $k\mathrm{NN}_2$ rule.

(d) Repeat (b) for the $k\mathrm{NN}_3$ rule considering possible values of k_1, k_2, and k_3.

(e) Show precisely when it is more economical to store the n sample in order to use the $k\mathrm{NN}$ rules rather than a condensed set of mean vectors and scalar covariance matrices in order to use a parametric decision rule based on Gaussian statistics.

[5] Suppose one uses the $k\mathrm{NN}_2$ decision rule with a priori knowledge that $P_1 = P_2 = \cdots = P_M$ but $n_1 \neq n_2 \neq \cdots \neq n_M$.

(a) Then show that the kNN$_2$ decision rule would be forced to operate using only n samples, where

$$n = \min (n_1, n_2, \ldots, n_M).$$

(b) Show that the kNN$_1$ rule is not affected by the constraint of equal prior probabilities and unequal sample sizes for the respective categories.

[6] Suppose $\mathbf{x}_1, \mathbf{x}_2, \ldots, \mathbf{x}_n$ are samples with probability density $h(\mathbf{x})$ where

$$h(\mathbf{x}) = \sum_{i=1}^{M} f_i(\mathbf{x})P_i.$$

If $P_1, P_2, \ldots, P_M$ are unknown, they must be estimated from the samples $\mathbf{x}_1, \mathbf{x}_2, \ldots, \mathbf{x}_n$.

(a) Show that if $\mathbf{x}_1, \mathbf{x}_2, \ldots, \mathbf{x}_n$ are supervised (i.e., classified into M categories) and we take $P_i = n_i/n$ because $n = \sum_{i=1}^{M} n_i$, then $P_1, P_2, \ldots, P_M$ must actually have been known a priori!

(b) Discuss, why, if $\mathbf{x}_1, \mathbf{x}_2, \ldots, \mathbf{x}_n$ are supervised, then $P_i = n_i/n$ is an unnecessarily overconstraining assumption.

(c) Why is the assumption of equal volumes in the kNN$_1$ and kNN$_2$ rules often a bad assumption?

(d) What conclusion do you reach about the kNN$_2$ decision rule as a result of the solutions to (a) and (b) above?

[7] (a) Show that

$$\eta_i(\mathbf{x}) = \frac{P_i f_i(\mathbf{x})}{\sum_{j=1}^{M} P_j f_i(\mathbf{x})}$$

is the probability that a pattern with observation $\mathbf{x}$ belongs to category i.

(b) Show that the point loss at $\mathbf{x}$ incurred by placing a pattern with observation $\mathbf{x}$ into category j is

$$r_j(\mathbf{x}) = \sum_{i=1}^{M} \eta_i(\mathbf{x})L_{ji}.$$

(c) Show that for the Bayes decision rule, probability of error when classifying a vector point $\mathbf{x}$ is $r^*(\mathbf{x})$,

$$r^*(\mathbf{x}) = 1 - \max \{\eta_1(\mathbf{x}), \eta_2(\mathbf{x}), \ldots, \eta_M(\mathbf{x})\}$$

[8] State sufficient conditions for

$$\lim_{n \to \infty} \eta(\mathbf{x}^1) \overset{\text{w.p.1}}{=} \eta(\mathbf{x}).$$

[9] Verify starting with

$$R = E[2r^*(\mathbf{x})(1 - r^*(\mathbf{x}))]$$

that

$$R = 2R^*(1 - R^*) - 2 \operatorname{Var} r^*(\mathbf{x})$$

and hence

$$R \leq 2R^*(1 - R)^*.$$

[10] Extend the Cover–Hart bounds to the M category problem.

[11] Consider a two-category problem ($M = 2$) with 5 training samples from each category as shown below:

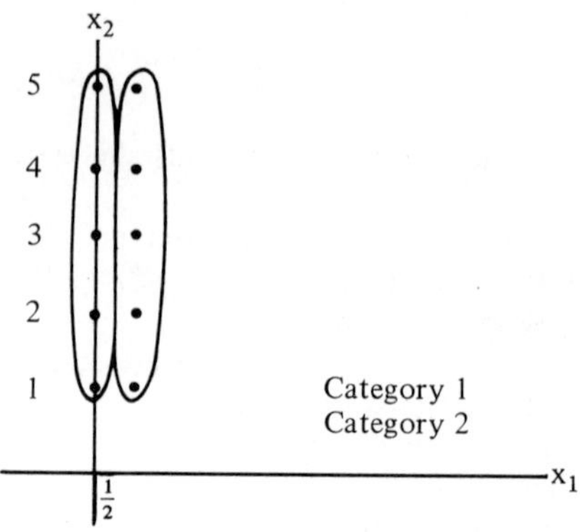

(a) Show that the $1NN_2$ rule with Euclidean distance measure will always make an error. Let the sample classified $\mathbf{x}$ be one of the ten sample points shown, and let training samples be the remaining nine samples.

(b) Show that the $1NN_3$ decision rule with respective distance measures for the two categories

$$d_i(\mathbf{y}, \mathbf{x}) = \sum_{i=1}^{2} \frac{(x_i - y_i)^2}{\sigma_i^2} \qquad \begin{cases} \sigma_1 = \frac{1}{4} \\ \sigma_2 = 4 \end{cases}$$

will never make errors.

[12] In Section 4-9, a function $u_i = H_i(\Phi_i(\mathbf{x}; \dot{\mathbf{x}}_n), \mathbf{x})$ is defined as a nondecreasing function of volume $\Phi_i(\mathbf{x}; \dot{\mathbf{x}}_n)$ which takes into account the underlying density and the distance function.

(a) If $\mathscr{I}_i(\mathbf{x}; \dot{\mathbf{x}}_n)$ is a region centered at $\mathbf{x}$, show that

$$u_i = \int_{\mathscr{I}_i(\mathbf{x}, \dot{\mathbf{x}})} dF(\mathbf{x} \mid \omega_i)$$

independent of the distance function.

(b) Suppose $f(\mathbf{x} \mid \omega_i)$ is uniform over $\mathscr{I}_i(\mathbf{x}, \dot{\mathbf{x}}_n)$, the latter being defined by the distance function $d(\mathbf{y}, \mathbf{x}) = (\sum_{i=1}^{L} (x_i - y_i)^2)^{1/2}$. Compute u_i as a function of r where $\mathscr{I}_i(\mathbf{x}, \dot{\mathbf{x}}_n)$ is the set of all $\mathbf{y}$ for which $d(\mathbf{y}, \mathbf{x}) \leq r$.

[13] Show that the definition, in Section 4-9,

$$H_i^{-1}(u_i; \dot{\mathbf{x}}_n) = \min\{\Phi : u_i = H_i(\Phi, \mathbf{x})\}$$

is sufficient to guarantee uniqueness of H_i^{-1} for functions $H_i(\Phi, \mathbf{x})$ which are nonincreasing with Φ over certain domains of Φ.

[14] Tolerance-region construction is based on ordering a sequence of samples $\mathbf{x}_1, \mathbf{x}_2, \ldots, \mathbf{x}_n$; coverages of these tolerance regions have the Dirichlet distribution. Show that if the procedure for constructing the regions is chosen after given samples $\mathbf{x}_1, \mathbf{x}_2, \ldots, \mathbf{x}_n$, then the regions are not in general distribution free tolerance regions.

[15] Show that although the $k\mathrm{NN}_3$ decision rule utilizes distance measures for the respective classes, the distribution of coverages of tolerance regions does not depend upon a priori knowledge of the underlying statistics.

[16] Show that if $k = k_1 + k_2 + \cdots + k_\delta$ and

$$r_n(t^1, t^2, \ldots, t^\delta)$$
$$= \begin{cases} \dfrac{g(t^1/(n+1), \ldots, t^\delta/(n+1); k_1, \ldots, k_\delta; n-k)|(n+1)^\delta}{\prod\limits_{v=1}^{\delta} \gamma(t^v; k^v)}, & t \leq n+1, \\[6pt] 0, & t > n+1, \end{cases}$$

where

$$g(u^1, \ldots, u^\delta; k^2, \ldots, k^\delta; n-k)$$
$$= \frac{n!}{\prod\limits_{v=1}^{\delta} [(k^v - 1)!](n-k)!} (u^1)^{k^1-1}, \ldots, (k^\delta)^{k^\delta - 1}(1 - u^1 - \cdots - u^\delta)^{n-k},$$
$$0 \leq u^i \leq 1, \ \sum_{i=1}^{\delta} u^i \leq 1,$$

and where

$$\gamma(t^v; k^v) = \frac{(t^v)^{k-1} e^{-t^v}}{(k^v - 1)!}, \ t^v \geq 0,$$

then

(a) $$r_n(t^1, \ldots, t^\delta) \begin{cases} \leq \dfrac{1}{(1 - (k+1)/(n+1))^{k+1}}, & t \leq n+1, \\[6pt] = 0, & t > n+1, \end{cases}$$

and

(b) $$r_n(t^1, \ldots, t^\delta) \xrightarrow{n} 1 \text{ for } t_i \geq 0, \qquad i = 1, 2, \ldots, \delta.$$

[17] Verify that all samples $\mathbf{x}_1, \mathbf{x}_2, \ldots, \mathbf{x}_n$ are covered by m globular regions with common radius

$$R(m) = \max_{1 \leq i \leq n} \min_{1 \leq j \leq n} d(\mathbf{x}_i, \mathbf{x}^j)$$

as presented in Section 4-13.1.

[18] Eq. (6) of Section 4-13.1 is a mathematical description of the relatively straight-forward "maximum distance" clustering procedure.
   (a) How much savings in storage results by storing $A(m, i), i = 1, 2, \ldots, n$, rather than all samples?
   (b) How is the reordering faciliated by using Eq. (6)?

[19] Verify using the preprocessing procedure of Section 4-13 that the sequence $\mathbf{x}^1, \mathbf{x}^2, \ldots, \mathbf{x}^n$ can be truncated after the mth vector with the assurance that the samples $\mathbf{x}^m, \mathbf{x}^{m+1}, \ldots, \mathbf{x}^n$ are within a distance $R(m - 1)$ of at least one of the vectors $\mathbf{x}^1, \mathbf{x}^2, \ldots, \mathbf{x}^{m-1}$.

[20] This problem concerns several computer simulations to show how estimating a local metric can improve performance of the $k\mathrm{NN}_3$ decision rule.
   (a) Complete Example 2 of Section 4-7 analogous to Example 1.
   (b) Complete Example 3 of Section 4-7 analogous to Example 1.
   (c) Complete Example 4 of Section 4-7 analogous to Example 1.

CHAPTER 5

Unsupervised Estimation

5-1 Introduction

Unsupervised estimation has application in determining the number of signals being transmitted over a communications channel, estimating the locations and shapes of modes in a probability density function, estimating the locations of objects in pictures such as biological cells in photomicrographs, and elsewhere. There have been two primary areas of research that may be considered unsupervised estimation. One area involves techniques that are parameter-estimation techniques; these techniques center around the Bayes approach but include maximum likelihood, stochastic approximation, stochastic hill climb, pseudo-deterministic hill climb, decision-directed estimators, and the method of moments. The other area involves clustering techniques; a clustering technique incorporates in a natural way a priori knowledge specialized to the problem being solved in order to find groups of samples in the data. Although in this book clustering techniques are naturally developed out of the Bayes framework, they could be considered as an individual area of research. For example, several techniques which are clustering-like techniques are evolving for use in image processing without using the Bayes framework as a guide. An understanding of how clustering relates to the Bayes approach gives the practitioner of pattern recognition more perspective. He is able to use clustering as an aid in estimating the class-conditional densities used in the Bayes decision rule.

A warning is in order to those who would want to use clustering or other unsupervised estimation techniques in processing measurement vectors of high dimensionality. First, a priori problem knowledge should be used to reflect known relationships among measurements to obtain feature vectors of lower dimensionality. Elementary clustering procedures then can be applied to these feature vectors.

In Chapter 1 the unsupervised estimation problem was formulated in terms of a parameter vector $\mathbf{b}$ characterizing a density $h(\mathbf{x})$ given samples $\mathbf{x}_1, \mathbf{x}_2, \ldots, \mathbf{x}_n$ each identically distributed as $h(\mathbf{x})$. The classification of the samples $\dot{\mathbf{x}}_n = [\mathbf{x}_1, \mathbf{x}_2, \ldots, \mathbf{x}_n]$ may be unknown. In Chapter 1 the mixture model was presented where the density function $h(\mathbf{x})$ is expressed as a linear combination of density functions from a *known* family whose members are characterized by a parameter vector; this is called *parametric structure*. We have seen in previous chapters that an often-used parametric family is the family of Gaussian density functions, where each member is characterized by a mean vector and a covariance matrix. Another structure, more difficult to define precisely, is what could be called "mode" or "cluster" structure, where samples that are close in some sense are defined to be in a "cluster."

An early application of unsupervised estimation or clustering was considered by Pearson in 1894 [1] and 1902 [2]. Pearson "clustered" species of animals into one category he felt was becoming extinct and another category he felt was destined to survive; $\mathbf{x}$ consisted of measurements from a representative sample of the species. Undoubtedly Darwin would have been greatly assisted by a computer programmed with clustering algorithms which he could have used in studying the evolution of the species.

A complete review of the literature on unsupervised estimation is not presented here; for additional references see the Suggested Reading List at the end of this chapter. In this section, we concentrate on work leading to the Bayes minimum-conditional-risk solution.

An early pioneering approach to the minimum-conditional-risk solution was formulated by Daly [6]. His approach for $M = 2$ classes is based on the fact that for n samples $\dot{\mathbf{x}}_n$ there are M^n possible sequences, considering all the ways the samples can be classified. Given one of these sequences, the samples for that sequence may be considered classified or supervised. Suppose, for example, that $\mathscr{F}$ is Gaussian; then, given a particular sequence, the respective class means $\{\mathbf{m}_i\}$ can be updated as if the samples are classified. Of course, we have as many different sets of mean estimators as there are sequences, and there are M^n sequences. This solution has been called the "growing-complexity solution," for obvious reasons. It is not practical and hides the fundamental properties of the Bayes process.

Fralick [7], under an assumption that the a posteriori density $f(\mathbf{b} \mid \dot{\mathbf{x}}_n)$ of the parameters characterizing M classes (M is known) factors into the product of the a posteriori densities of the parameters characterizing each class, found an iterative form without the growing-complexity problem.

Patrick and Hancock [8, 13] found the general iterative Bayes solution and showed the equivalence between Daly's work and the general solution [9].

Unsupervised estimation arises in a class of problems [10] including nonstationary class probabilities, statistically dependent measurement vectors $\mathbf{x}_1, \mathbf{x}_2, \ldots, \mathbf{x}_n$, and unknown synchronization (for waveforms, and sometimes, in the case of images, called unknown registration). The general problems were formulated in a Bayesian minimum-conditional-risk framework by Patrick [10], with the mixture concept emphasized. Combined with similar work by Hilborn and Lainiotis [11], this provides a precise formal definition of the problem. The mixture concept is introduced in Chapter 1 of this book, used in Chapter 2 when developing estimation procedures, and used in Chapter 3 when developing minimum-conditional-risk decision rules.

Again, emphasizing mixtures, Patrick and Costello [12] showed that the Bayes minimum-conditional-risk solution involves the information function $\eta(\mathbf{b}, \mathbf{b}^*) = \int \ln h(\mathbf{x}|\mathbf{b}) h(\mathbf{x}|\mathbf{b}^*)\, d\mathbf{x}$, where $h(\mathbf{x}|\mathbf{b}^*)$ is the true density and $h(\mathbf{x}|\mathbf{b})$ is a mixture probability density characterized by $\mathbf{b}$. *They showed that an estimate of $\eta(\mathbf{b})$,*

$$\hat{\eta}(\mathbf{b}) = \frac{1}{n} \sum_{s=1}^{n} \ln h(\mathbf{x}_s | \mathbf{b}) \tag{1}$$

should be evaluated at every $\mathbf{b}$ in the parameter space. The Bayes solution with mean square error loss then uses $\hat{\eta}(\mathbf{b})$ indirectly to weight $\mathbf{b}$ to form the average estimator $(\mathbf{b})_n$, which is a Bayes estimator. This averaging property of the Bayes approach can be contrasted with a stochastic-approximation approach [based on some starting value $(\mathbf{b})_0$ which searches for the maximum of $\eta(\mathbf{b})$ with respect to $\mathbf{b}$.] *Stochastic approximation is starting-point-dependent, whereas Bayes can "average out" the starting points. The "quasi-Bayes" approach discussed in Section 5-3.6 was developed to incorporate the desirable Bayes averaging effect with the desirable stochastic-approximation property of reduced complexity.*

Properties of mixtures were first considered in the statistical literature [15–18, 68] and applied to the unsupervised estimation problem by engineers [8, 13, 14]. The problem of unsupervised estimation is to resolve an unknown mixture into the underlying categories or, equivalently, to find the indices (parameter vectors) and weights (mixing parameters) that express the unknown mixture density as a linear combination of density functions.

Implicit in the solution of unsupervised estimation problems is the concept of *identifiability*—that there should be a one-to-one mapping or relationship between a set of mixing parameters and the resulting mixtures. Teicher's work on finite mixtures [16] was reduced by Yakowitz and Spragins to a sufficiency theorem that a necessary and sufficient condition for identifiability of a class of finite mixtures is linear independence of the density functions in each finite mixture [19]. They showed also that a large number of parametric families (including Gaussian) are identifiable as discussed in Chapter 2.

Cooper and Cooper† [21] showed how simple, easily calculated statistics can be used for certain problems. For example, they showed how the sample mean of the mixture measurement vectors,

$$\hat{\mathbf{m}} = \frac{1}{n} \sum_{s=1}^{n} \mathbf{x}_s,$$

is a consistent estimator for the decision boundary $(\mathbf{m}_1 + \mathbf{m}_2)/2$ for the two-category, minimum-risk decision rule when $\mathscr{F}$ is the Gaussian family, $f_1(\mathbf{x})$ and $f_2(\mathbf{x})$ have equal covariance matrices, and the a priori category probabilities are equal. From the results developed in Chapter 3, it follows that this decision boundary completely characterizes the decision rule under the above conditions. Patrick and Hancock [14] showed that, when $|\mathbf{m}_2 - \mathbf{m}_1|$ is large compared with σ^2, where $\mathbf{\Sigma} = \sigma^2 \mathbf{I}$, sample quantiles of the mixture density provide estimates for $\mathbf{m}_1$ and $\mathbf{m}_2$ resulting in a better estimate for $(\mathbf{m}_1 + \mathbf{m}_2)/2$. In [21] Cooper and Cooper also showed how the eigenvector corresponding to the largest eigenvalue of the sample space can be used to estimate an optimum two-class decision boundary for a wide variety of statistics. Moment estimators for the parameters characterizing a two-category, Gaussian decision rule are presented by Cooper and Cooper [21] and Patrick and Hancock [14].

Maximum-likelihood-estimator equations for the two-category problem where $\mathscr{F}$ is Gaussian were developed by Cooper and Cooper [21] for the case of a single unknown parameter. Patrick [13, 24] extended the estimators to more than one unknown parameter. These results were for M (the number of categories) equal to 2 and known. Numerical methods for the multicategory problem and M unknown are presented by Wolfe [25].

Stochastic-approximation algorithms which seek the maximum of the average likelihood function are defined by Sakrison [26] for a normalized problem. A maximum-likelihood estimator $\hat{\mathbf{b}}$ for $\mathbf{b}^*$, where $\mathbf{x}_1, \mathbf{x}_2, \ldots, \mathbf{x}_n$ have density $h(\mathbf{x}|\mathbf{b}^*)$, is obtained essentially as a solution of

$$\hat{\mathbf{b}} = \arg\left\{\max_{\mathbf{b}} \ln f(\mathbf{x}_1, \mathbf{x}_2, \ldots, \mathbf{x}_n | \mathbf{b})\right\}$$

$$= \arg\left\{\max_{\mathbf{b}} \ln \prod_{s=1}^{n} h(\mathbf{x}_s | \mathbf{b})\right\}$$

$$= \arg\left\{\max_{\mathbf{b}} \sum_{s=1}^{n} \ln h(\mathbf{x}_s | \mathbf{b})\right\}$$

$$= \arg\left\{\max_{\mathbf{b}} n\hat{\eta}(\mathbf{b})\right\}.$$

†See also Cooper [22]; Cooper [23]; and Cooper [81].

The decision-directed approach† to unsupervised estimation can be well illustrated by an M-category example where $\mathscr{F}$ is Gaussian. Suppose that, a priori, M mean vectors, covariance matrices, and a priori category probabilities are given:

$$(\mathbf{m}_i)_0, \ (\boldsymbol{\Sigma}_i)_0, \ (P_i)_0, \qquad i = 1, 2, \ldots, M.$$

When sample $\mathbf{x}_1$ is received, the Gaussian decision rule is applied: Decide that $\mathbf{x}_1$ is from category i if

$$\ln \frac{(P_i)_0}{|(\boldsymbol{\Sigma}_i)_0|^{1/2}} - [\mathbf{x}_1 - (\mathbf{m}_i)_0]'[(\boldsymbol{\Sigma}_i)_0]^{-1}[\mathbf{x}_1 - (\mathbf{m}_i)_0]$$

is larger than for any other category i. Then $\mathbf{x}_1$ is used to update $(\mathbf{m}_i)_0$ [and $(\boldsymbol{\Sigma}_i)_0$] to become $(\mathbf{m}_i)_1$ [and $(\boldsymbol{\Sigma}_i)_1$] using the updating procedures discussed in Chapter 2 (except that $n_a = 1$). Also, $(P_i)_0$ can be updated. *Thus, the decision-directed approach may be considered a good tracking procedure under certain conditions.*

For most unsupervised estimation problems, a direct implementation of the Bayes solution utilizing a posteriori density $p(\mathbf{b}\,|\,\dot{\mathbf{x}}_n)$ developed in Section 5-2 (previously in Chapter 3 and originally by Patrick [8, 13]) requires the approximation of the parameter space with a finite number V of vector points. In Section 5-2 the Bayes estimator for $\mathbf{b}^*$ is proved to converge to an asymptotic vector with probability 1 and in mean square; the asymptotic estimator and asymptotic rate of convergence are also found. These results lead to the information criteria $\boldsymbol{\eta}(\mathbf{b})$. In Section 5-3.1 the convergence rate of the Bayes estimator is obtained; in Section 5-3.2 conditions giving an exponential convergence rate are presented. An alternative view of the asymptotic Bayes a posteriori density is developed in Section 5-3.3; an alternative view of the variance of the Bayes estimator for finite parameter set is given in Section 5-3.4. In Section 5-3.5, a minimum-norm-square-error estimator for $\mathbf{b}^*$ leads to the definition of a criterion $\Gamma(\mathbf{b})$,

$$\begin{aligned}
\Gamma(\mathbf{b}) &= 2E[h(\mathbf{x}\,|\,\mathbf{b}) - \|\,h(\mathbf{x}\,|\,\mathbf{b})\,\|^2 \\
&= 2 \int h(\mathbf{x}\,|\,\mathbf{b})h(\mathbf{x}\,|\,\mathbf{b}^*)\,d\mathbf{x} - \int h^2(\mathbf{x}\,|\,\mathbf{b})\,d\mathbf{x} \\
&= \|\,h(\mathbf{x}\,|\,\mathbf{b}^*)\,\|^2 - e^2(\mathbf{b}),
\end{aligned}$$

where

$$e^2(\mathbf{b}) = \|\,h(\mathbf{x}\,|\,\mathbf{b}) - h(\mathbf{x}\,|\,\mathbf{b}^*)\,\|^2.$$

---

†In addition to references cited previously, see also Jakowatz, Shuey, and White [4] and Hinich [5]. See how decision directed is suggested by the Bayes framework in Chapter 2.

In Section 5-3.6 an estimator called "quasi-Bayes" is developed using both criterion $\eta(\mathbf{b})$ and criterion $\Gamma(\mathbf{b})$. The quasi-Bayes estimator has the desirable averaging of Bayes and some of the desirable simplicity of stochastic approximation.

In Section 5-3.7 an empirical estimate of $\Gamma(\mathbf{b})$ is formed, denoted $\Gamma_n(\mathbf{b})$; deterministic hill climb is then used to search for $\mathbf{b}$ minimizing $\Gamma_n(\mathbf{b})$.

5-2 Introduction to the Bayes Solution

Constraints placed on admissible $\mathbf{b}^k$ define a set of admissible points denoted $\mathscr{B}^{M'}$. Let the number of points $\mathbf{b}^k$ or possible solution vectors be V and the number of classes in the kth solution be M_k. The respective class parameters for the kth solution are $\mathbf{b}_1^k, \mathbf{b}_2^k, \ldots, \mathbf{b}_{M_k}^k$ and $\mathbf{b}^k = [\mathbf{b}_1^k, \mathbf{b}_2^k, \ldots, \mathbf{b}_{M_k}^k, P_1^k, P_2^k, \ldots, P_{M_k}^k]$.

The Bayes estimator for the true parameter $\mathbf{b}^*$ characterizing $h(\mathbf{x})$ computes the a posteriori density of each point $\mathbf{b}^k$ in $\mathscr{B}^{M'}$ using Bayes theorem,

$$p(\mathbf{b}^k \mid \mathbf{x}_1) = \frac{\left[\sum_{i=1}^{M_k} f(\mathbf{x}_1 \mid \mathbf{b}_i^k) P_i^k\right] p_0(\mathbf{b}^k)}{\sum [\text{numerator}]},$$

$$k = 1, 2, \ldots, V, \text{ all } \mathbf{b}^k \in \mathscr{B}^{M'} \qquad (1)$$

given one sample $\mathbf{x}_1$, an a priori density $\{p_0(\mathbf{b}^k)\}_{k=1}^{V}$, and the family $\mathscr{F}$ of densities.† For a given sequence of n samples $\dot{\mathbf{x}}_n$, an a priori density, and family $\mathscr{F}$, the a posteriori density is

$$p(\mathbf{b}^k \mid \dot{\mathbf{x}}_n) = \frac{\left[\sum_{i=1}^{M_k} f(\mathbf{x}_n \mid \mathbf{b}_i^k) P_i^k\right] p(\mathbf{b}^k \mid \dot{\mathbf{x}}_{n-1})}{\sum [\text{numerator}]},$$

$$k = 1, 2, \ldots, V, \text{ all } \mathbf{b}^k \in \mathscr{B}^{M'}. \qquad (2)$$

For the above computation, samples $\mathbf{x}_1, \mathbf{x}_2, \ldots, \mathbf{x}_n$ are assumed parameter conditionally independent and the prior probabilities P_i^k (or mixing parameters) are assumed independent of the samples (i.e., these probabilities are fixed or stationary). Extensions that include a broad class of unsupervised estimation problems are included in reference [10].

To implement (2) utilizing either hardware or software, it is necessary that $\mathscr{B}^{M'}$ be a finite set of V vector points $\{\mathbf{b}^k\}_{k=1}^{V}$. For a quadratic loss func-

---

†Rigorously, $f(\mathbf{x}_1 \mid \mathbf{b}_i^k, i)$ should be used instead of $f(\mathbf{x}_1 \mid \mathbf{b}_i^k)$. We have dropped the i for convenience where this will not cause confusion in this chapter.

tion and this discretized parameter space, the Bayes estimator is

$$(\mathbf{b})_n = \sum_{k=1}^{V} \mathbf{b}^k p(\mathbf{b}^k \mid \dot{\mathbf{x}}_n) \tag{3}$$

with $p(\mathbf{b}^k \mid \dot{\mathbf{x}}_n)$ calculated according to (2).

Denoting the true mixture density by $h(\mathbf{x})$, define a function $\eta(\mathbf{b}^k)$,

$$\eta(\mathbf{b}^k) = E[\ln h(\mathbf{x} \mid \mathbf{b}^k)] = \int [\ln h(\mathbf{x} \mid \mathbf{b}^k)] h(\mathbf{x}) \, d\mathbf{x}. \tag{4}$$

In Sections 5-3.1 and 5-3.2 it will be shown how the convergence properties of $p(\mathbf{b}^k \mid \dot{\mathbf{x}}_n)$ and $(\mathbf{b})_n$ depend on $\eta(\mathbf{b}^k)$, which is a measure of the projection of $\ln h(\mathbf{x} \mid \mathbf{b}^k)$ onto $h(\mathbf{x})$.

5-3 Bayes Solution

5-3.1 Convergence Utilizing an Information Function

Convergence properties of the Bayes estimator for a finite set $\mathscr{B}^{M'}$ will be established in this section. It is shown that under certain conditions the Bayes estimator converges in mean square and with probability 1 to an asymptotic vector point; furthermore, it is shown that the Bayes estimator converges faster than $1/n$ if $E[|\ln h(\mathbf{x} \mid \mathbf{b}^*)|^s] < \infty$ for some $s < 3$. One of the required conditions is that $\mathbf{b}^*$ corresponds to a unique maximum of $\eta(\mathbf{b})$. Another viewpoint of this faster than $1/n$ convergence is given in Section 5-3.3 and is considerably easier mathematically.

The following list of assumptions is used as needed in the different parts of the theorem.

1. $h(\mathbf{x}_n \mid \mathbf{x}_1, \mathbf{x}_2, \ldots, \mathbf{x}_{n-1}, \mathbf{b}) = h(\mathbf{x}_n \mid \mathbf{b})$.
2. There exists a positive integer $s > 1$ such that $E[|\ln h(\mathbf{x} \mid \mathbf{b}^k)|^s] < \infty$ for all $\mathbf{b}^k \in \mathscr{B}^{M'}$.

Denote by s^* the largest even integer for which this absolute moment exists.

3. The probability measures corresponding to $\{h(\mathbf{x} \mid \mathbf{b}^k)\}$ are absolutely continuous with respect to Lebesque measure v.
4. $v[\mathbf{x}: |h(\mathbf{x} \mid \mathbf{b}^k) - h(\mathbf{x} \mid \mathbf{b}^j)| > 0] > 0$ for all $\mathbf{b}^k, \mathbf{b}^j, j \neq k$.

The last two conditions require that there be no diracs in the mixture and that pairs of mixture densities be different on an open set. They are satisfied for such functional families used in practice as the Gaussian, binomial, and Cauchy.

5. $\{h(\mathbf{x}\,|\,\mathbf{b}^k)\}$ contains the true mixture $h(\mathbf{x})$.

In the proof of the theorem, the sample conditional independence (when given the parameter vector point $\mathbf{b}$) and absolute moment existence assumptions (1 and 2) will allow application of the strong law of large numbers.

If assumptions 3 and 4 are not satisfied, the projection $\eta(\mathbf{b}^k)$ of ln $h(\mathbf{x}\,|\,\mathbf{b}^k)$ onto $h(\mathbf{x})$ for the different $h(\mathbf{x}\,|\,\mathbf{b}^k)$ will not be unique. These two conditions, together with 5, will be used to establish a uniqueness property of the Bayes estimator.

An additional requirement that no points $\mathbf{b}^k$ are ruled out as the true point $\mathbf{b}^*$,

6. the a priori probabilities $p_0(\mathbf{b}^k)$ are nonzero,

will be utilized in proving the theorem.

Theorem 1   If 3, 4, and 5 are satisfied, then†
(a) $\mathbf{b}^* = \arg[\max_{\mathbf{b}^k \in \mathscr{B}^{M'}} \{\eta(\mathbf{b}^k)\}]$ is unique.

If, in addition, 1, 2, and 6 are satisfied, then the Bayes estimator $(\mathbf{b})_n$ defined by (3) of Section 5-2 has the properties:

(b) $p[\lim_{n \to \infty} (\mathbf{b})_n = \mathbf{b}^*] = 1$.

(c)   There exists a positive number $c < \infty$ such that for n large enough,

$$E[\|(\mathbf{b})_n - \mathbf{b}^*\|^2] \leq cn^{-s^*/2}.$$

Proof: It is well known (see Kullback [56], p. 14, for example) that under conditions 3 and 4, if $h(\mathbf{x}) \in \{h(\mathbf{x}\,|\,\mathbf{b}^k)\}$, only $h(\mathbf{x}\,|\,\mathbf{b}^*) = h(\mathbf{x})$ maximizes $E[\ln h(\mathbf{x}\,|\,\mathbf{b}^k)]$. Also, 4 implies uniqueness of the mixture densities (such a unique mapping between the $\{\mathbf{b}^k\}$ and the $\{h(\mathbf{x}\,|\,\mathbf{b}^k)\}$ is called identifiability). See references [8, 15–20] for discussions of identifiability. Hence there is only one $\mathbf{b}^*$ such that $h(\mathbf{x}\,|\,\mathbf{b}^*) = h(\mathbf{x})$, proving (a).

To prove (b), Eqs. (2) and (3) of Section 5-2 are used to express the Bayes estimator,

---

†$\mathbf{b}^* = \arg[\max_{\mathbf{b}^k \in \mathscr{B}^{M'}} \{\eta(\mathbf{b}^k)\}]$ means that $\mathbf{b}^*$ is the parameter point maximizing $\eta(\mathbf{b})$.

$$(\mathbf{b})_n = \sum_{k=1}^{V} \mathbf{b}^k \frac{\prod_{s=1}^{n} h(\mathbf{x}_s \mid \mathbf{b}^k) p_0(\mathbf{b}^k)}{\sum_{i=1}^{V} \prod_{s=1}^{n} h(\mathbf{x}_s \mid \mathbf{b}^i) p_0(\mathbf{b}^i)}$$

$$= \sum_{k=1}^{V} \mathbf{b}^k \frac{\left[\exp\left(\frac{1}{n} \sum_{s=1}^{n} \ln h(\mathbf{x}_s \mid \mathbf{b}^k)\right)\right]^n p_0(\mathbf{b}^k)}{\sum_{i=1}^{V} \left[\exp\left(\frac{1}{n} \sum_{s=1}^{n} \ln h(\mathbf{x}_s \mid \mathbf{b}^i)\right)\right]^n p_0(\mathbf{b}^i)}. \tag{1}$$

The strong law of large numbers (see Chapter 2) can be applied because of conditions 1 and 2 to give the result

$$p\left[\lim_{n\to\infty} \frac{1}{n} \sum_{s=1}^{n} \ln h(\mathbf{x}_s \mid \mathbf{b}^k) = \eta(\mathbf{b}^k)\right] = 1. \tag{2}$$

Thus,

$$p\left[\lim_{n\to\infty} \exp\left(\frac{1}{n} \sum_{s=1}^{n} \ln h(\mathbf{x}_s \, \mathbf{b}^k)\right) = \exp(\eta(\mathbf{b}^k)\right] = 1 \tag{3}$$

and, with probability 1,

$$\lim_{n\to\infty} \left\{\frac{p(\mathbf{b}^k \mid \dot{\mathbf{x}}_n)}{p(\mathbf{b}^* \mid \dot{\mathbf{x}}_n)}\right\}^{1/n} = \frac{\exp[\eta(\mathbf{b}^k)]}{\exp[\eta(\mathbf{b}^*)]} \lim_{n\to\infty} \left[\frac{p_0(\mathbf{b}^k)}{p_0(\mathbf{b}^*)}\right]^{1/n}.$$

Now because of condition 6, $p_0(\mathbf{b}^k)$ and $p_0(\mathbf{b}^*)$ are nonzero and

$$\lim_{n\to\infty} \left[\frac{p_0(\mathbf{b}^k)}{p_0(\mathbf{b}^*)}\right]^{1/n} = 1,$$

$$p\left[\lim_{n\to\infty} \frac{p(\mathbf{b}^k \mid \dot{\mathbf{x}}_n)}{p(\mathbf{b}^* \mid \dot{\mathbf{x}}_n)} = 0\right] = 1, \qquad \mathbf{b}^k \neq \mathbf{b}^*.$$

So as a consequence of (a) it follows that $p[\lim_{n\to\infty} (\mathbf{b})_n = \mathbf{b}^*] = 1$, proving assertion (b) of the theorem.

To prove (c), first expand the mean square error

$$E[\|(\mathbf{b})_n - \mathbf{b}^*\|^2] = E\left[\sum_{k=1}^{V} \sum_{j=1}^{V} (\mathbf{b}^k - \mathbf{b}^*)^t (b^j - \mathbf{b}^*) p(\mathbf{b}^k \mid \dot{\mathbf{x}}_n) p(\mathbf{b}^j \mid \dot{\mathbf{x}}_n)\right]$$

$$= \sum_{k=1}^{V} \sum_{j=1}^{V} (\mathbf{b}^k - \mathbf{b}^*)^t (b^j - \mathbf{b}^*) E[p(\mathbf{b}^k \mid \dot{\mathbf{x}}_n) p(\mathbf{b}^j \mid \dot{\mathbf{x}}_n)]. \tag{4}$$

For notational convenience assume that the vectors $\{\mathbf{b}^k\}_{k=1}^{V}$ are ordered so that $\mathbf{b}^1 = \mathbf{b}^*$. The mean square error then can be bounded,

$$E[\| (\mathbf{b})_n - \mathbf{b}^* \|^2] \le \sum_{k=2}^{V} \sum_{j=2}^{V} (\mathbf{b}^k - \mathbf{b}^*)^t (\mathbf{b}^j - \mathbf{b}^*)$$

$$\times \min \{ E[p(\mathbf{b}^k \,|\, \dot{\mathbf{x}}_n)], E[p(\mathbf{b}^j \,|\, \dot{\mathbf{x}}_n)] \}. \tag{5}$$

The next several steps will be used to show that for $\mathbf{b}^k \ne \mathbf{b}^*$, $E[p(\mathbf{b}^k \,|\, \dot{\mathbf{x}}_n)] \le 0\,(n^{-s^*/2})$, which along with (5) allows us to conclude (c).

For $\mathbf{b}^k \ne \mathbf{b}^*$, the random variable $p(\mathbf{b}^k \,|\, \dot{\mathbf{x}}_n)$ can be bounded by the random variable

$$z_n^k \triangleq \begin{cases} \dfrac{p(\mathbf{b}^k \,|\, \dot{\mathbf{x}}_n)}{p(\mathbf{b}^* \,|\, \dot{\mathbf{x}}_n)}, & \dfrac{p(\mathbf{b}^k \,|\, \dot{\mathbf{x}}_n)}{p(\mathbf{b}^* \,|\, \dot{\mathbf{x}}_n)} < e^{-nd^k/2}, \\ 1, & \text{elsewhere,} \end{cases} \tag{6}$$

where

$$(d^k) = \eta(\mathbf{b}^*) - \eta(\mathbf{b}^k). \tag{7}$$

Then the expectation of the random variable z_n^k bounds the expectation of the random variable $p(\mathbf{b}^k \,|\, \dot{\mathbf{x}}_n)$,

$$E[p(\mathbf{b}^k \,|\, \dot{\mathbf{x}}_n)] \le E[z_n^k]. \tag{8}$$

Defining

$$r_n^k = \frac{p(\mathbf{b}^k \,|\, \dot{\mathbf{x}}_n)}{p(\mathbf{b}^* \,|\, \dot{\mathbf{x}}_n)},$$

the expectation of z_n^k can be expanded,

$$E[z_n^k] = \int_0^\infty z_n^k p(z_n^k) \, dz_n^k$$

$$= \int_0^{\exp\,[-nd^k/2]} r^k p(r^k) \, dr^k + \int_{\exp\,[-nd^k/2]}^\infty p(r^k) \, dr^k. \tag{9}$$

The second integral in (9) is the probability that r_n^k is greater than or equal to $e^{-nd^k/2}$. Reexpressing this integral as a probability,

$$p\left[\frac{p(\mathbf{b}^k \,|\, \dot{\mathbf{x}}_n)}{p(\mathbf{b}^* \,|\, \dot{\mathbf{x}}_n)} \ge e^{-nd^k/2} \right]$$

$$= p\left[\frac{1}{n} \sum_{s=1}^{n} [\ln h(\mathbf{x}_s \,|\, \mathbf{b}^k) - \ln h(\mathbf{x}_s \,|\, \mathbf{b}^*)] \ge -\frac{d^k}{2} - \frac{1}{n} \ln \frac{p_0(\mathbf{b}^k)}{p_0(\mathbf{b}^*)} \right]$$

$$= p\left[\frac{1}{n} \sum_{s=1}^{n} [\ln h(\mathbf{x}_s \,|\, \mathbf{b}^k) - \ln h(\mathbf{x}_s \,|\, \mathbf{b}^*) + d^k] \ge \frac{d^k}{2} - \frac{1}{n} \ln \frac{p_0(\mathbf{b}^k)}{p_0(\mathbf{b}^*)} \right]$$

$$\le p\left[\left| \frac{1}{n} \sum_{s=1}^{n} [\ln h(\mathbf{x}_s \,|\, \mathbf{b}^k) - \ln h(\mathbf{x}_s \,|\, \mathbf{b}^*) + d^k] \right| \ge \frac{d^k}{3} \right] \tag{10}$$

for $n > 6 |\ln (p_0(\mathbf{b}^k)/p_0(\mathbf{b}^*))| / d^k$.

Using the Markov inequality (see Loeve [57], p. 158) Eq. (10) can be bounded, giving

$$\int_{\exp[-nd^k/2]}^{\infty} p(r^k)\, dr^k$$

$$\leq \left(\frac{3}{d^k}\right)^s E\left[\left|\frac{1}{n}\sum_{j=1}^{n}[\ln h(\mathbf{x}_j\,|\,\mathbf{b}^k) - \ln h(\mathbf{x}_j\,|\,\mathbf{b}^*) + d^k]\right|^s\right]$$

$$= \left(\frac{3}{d^k}\right)^s \frac{1}{n^s} E\left[\left|\sum_{j=1}^{n}[\ln h(\mathbf{x}_j\,|\,\mathbf{b}^k) - \ln h(\mathbf{x}_j\,|\,\mathbf{b}^*) + d^k]\right|^s\right]. \qquad (11)$$

It is left as a problem† (Problem 4) to show that

$$E\left[\left|\sum_{j=1}^{n}[\ln h(\mathbf{x}_j\,|\,\mathbf{b}^k) - \ln h(\mathbf{x}_j\,|\,\mathbf{b}^*) + d^k]\right|^s\right]$$

$$\leq n^{s/2}\,\frac{s + 2^{s-1} - 1}{s/2!}\sum_{i=0}^{s}\binom{s}{i}(d^k)^{s-i}E[|\ln h(\mathbf{x}\,|\,\mathbf{b}^k) - \ln h(\mathbf{x}\,|\,\mathbf{b}^*)|^i].$$

Using the triangle-inequality relationship (see Chapter 1),

$$|\mathbf{a} - \mathbf{b}| \leq |\mathbf{a}| + |\mathbf{b}|,$$

and the Minkowski inequality (see Rudin [58], p. 62),

$$E[(|\mathbf{a}| + |\mathbf{b}|)^k]^{1/k} \leq (E[|\mathbf{a}|^k])^{1/k} + (E[|\mathbf{b}|^k])^{1/k}$$

$$E[z_n^k] \leq e^{-nd^k/2} + n^{-s^*/2}\left(\frac{3}{d^k}\right)^{s^*}\frac{s^* + 2^{s^*-1} - 1}{s^*/2!}$$

$$\times\left[(d^k)^{s^*} + \sum_{i=1}^{s^*}\binom{s^*}{i}(d^k)^{s^*-i}((E[|\ln h(\mathbf{x}\,|\,\mathbf{b}^k)|^i])^{1/i}\right.$$

$$\left. + (E[|\ln h(\mathbf{x}\,|\,\mathbf{b}^*)|^i])^{1/i})\right]. \qquad (12)$$

As a consequence of (8) this proves (c).

If R denotes

$$R = \max_{\mathbf{b}^k} \|\mathbf{b}^k - \mathbf{b}^*\|,$$

then the constant c in the theorem statement is

$$c = R^2(V - 1)^2\left(\frac{3}{d^k}\right)^{s^*}\frac{s^* + 2^{s^*-1} - 1}{s^*/2!}$$

$$\times\left\{(d^k)^{s^*} + \sum_{i=1}^{s^*}\binom{s}{i}(d^k)^{s^*-1}((E[|\ln h(\mathbf{x}\,|\,\mathbf{b}^k)|^i])^{1/i} + (E[|\ln h(\mathbf{x}\,|\,\mathbf{b}^*)|^i])^{1/i})\right\}.$$

$$(13)$$

†See also reference [12].

Corollary 1   If condition 1 for Theorem 1 in Section 5-3.1 is satisfied and, in addition, if

2. $\sup\limits_{\mathbf{x}\in\mathscr{D}}|\ln h(\mathbf{x}\,|\,\mathbf{b}^k)|\le c$ for some $c<\infty$ for all $\mathbf{b}^k\in\mathscr{B}^{M'}$, where the set $\mathscr{D}$ is the support of the true mixture $h(\mathbf{x})$ (i.e., $\mathscr{D}$ equals the closure of the set $\{\mathbf{x}\!:h(\mathbf{x})>0,\ \mathbf{x}\in\mathscr{V}_L\})$,
3. $\mathbf{b}^*=\arg\max_{\mathbf{b}^k}\{\eta(\mathbf{b}^k)\}$ is unique,
4. $R=\max_k\|\,\mathbf{b}^k-\mathbf{b}^*\,\|$,

then

$$E[\|\,(\mathbf{b})_n-\mathbf{b}^*\,\|]\le R^2(V-1)^2\rho^{n^{1/2}},\qquad \rho<1 \text{ for } n \text{ large enough.}$$

Proof: From the proof of Theorem 1, it is sufficient to find an exponential bound on $p[\sum_{s=1}^{n}[\ln h(\mathbf{x}_s\,|\,\mathbf{b}^k)-\ln h(\mathbf{x}_s\,|\,\mathbf{b}^*)+nd^k]>nd^k/3]$. Since the random variable $[\ln h(\mathbf{x}_s\,|\,\mathbf{b}^k)-\ln h(\mathbf{x}_s\,|\,\mathbf{b}^*)]$ is bounded because of condition 2,

$$(\sigma_k)^2\triangleq E[|\ln h(\mathbf{x}\,|\,\mathbf{b}^k)-\ln h(\mathbf{x}\,|\,\mathbf{b}^*)|^2]\tag{14}$$

is finite. Define

$$c'\triangleq\sup_{\mathbf{x}}\sup_{\mathbf{b}^k\in\mathscr{B}^{M'}}|\ln h(\mathbf{x}\,|\,\mathbf{b}^k)-\ln h(\mathbf{x}\,|\,\mathbf{b}^*)+d^k\tag{15}$$

and observe that $c'<\infty$.

As a consequence of Kolmogorov's inequalities (see Loeve [57], p. 254), for arbitrary $\epsilon<0$ and $(c'/\sigma_k)\,\epsilon>1$,

$$p\left\{\frac{1}{n^{1/2}\sigma_k}\left[\sum_{s=1}^{n}\ln h(\mathbf{x}_s|\ \mathbf{b}^k)-\ln h(\mathbf{x}_s\,|\,\mathbf{b}^*)+nd^k\right]>\epsilon\right\}$$

$$<\exp\left[-\frac{\epsilon\sigma_k}{4c'}\right].\tag{16}$$

Letting $\epsilon=n^{1/2}(d^k/3\sigma_k)$, (16) is bounded for $n>[3(\sigma_k)^2/c'd^k]^2$ such that

$$p\left\{\left[\sum_{s=1}^{n}\ln h(\mathbf{x}_s\,|\,\mathbf{b}^k)-\ln h(\mathbf{x}_s\,|\,\mathbf{b}^*)+nd^k\right]>nd^k/3\right\}$$

$$<\exp\left[-\frac{n^{1/2}d^k}{12c'}\right]\cdot\rho_k^{n^{1/2}},$$

where

$$\rho_k=e^{-d^k/12c'}<1.$$

Finally,

$$E[\|(\mathbf{b})_n - \mathbf{b}^*\|^2] \le R^2(V-1)^2 \rho^{n^{1/2}},$$

where

$$\rho = \max_k \{\rho_k\}.$$

5-3.3 Alternative View of Asymptotic Form of Bayes a posteriori Density Function

The result obtained in this section is summarized below as a theorem stating conditions under which the Bayes a posteriori probability density lying outside an ϵ neighborhood of $\mathbf{b}^*$ diminishes to zero at an exponential rate. Denote by $\mathscr{H}$ a family of density functions (mixtures) indexed by a vector of parameters $\mathbf{b} \in \mathscr{B}'$, where $\mathscr{B}'$ is the set† of admissible values of $\mathbf{b}$. Let $\mathbf{x}$ be an L-dimensional observation having density $h(\mathbf{x}\,|\,\mathbf{b}^*)$. Individual observations of $\mathbf{x}$ are denoted $\mathbf{x}_1, \mathbf{x}_2, \ldots, \mathbf{x}_n$ and are parameter conditionally independent and identically distributed.

Assumptions

1. The function $\eta(\mathbf{b}) = E[\ln h(\mathbf{x}\,|\,\mathbf{b})]$ is uniquely maximum at $\mathbf{b} = \mathbf{b}^*$; i.e.,

$$\mathbf{b} \ne \mathbf{b}^* \Longrightarrow \eta(\mathbf{b}) < \eta(\mathbf{b}^*).$$

2. A practical bound on $\mathscr{B}$ is available; i.e., it is known that $\mathbf{b} \in \mathscr{B}' \subset \mathscr{B}$ and that for all $\mathbf{b} \in \mathscr{B}'$,

$$\|\mathbf{b} - \mathbf{b}^*\| \le R < \infty.$$

3. $E[(\ln h(\mathbf{x}\,|\,\mathbf{b}) - \eta(\mathbf{b}))^2] < \infty, \; \forall \mathbf{b}.$

Assumption 1 guarantees that the Bayes estimator converges to the true parameter $\mathbf{b}^*$. Assumption 2 is a practical constraint, and assumption 3 permits the use of the strong law of large numbers.

Theorem 2 Let ϵ be an arbitrarily small positive constant and let $\mathscr{I}_{(\epsilon)}$ denote an ϵ neighborhood of $\mathbf{b}^*$; i.e., $\mathbf{b} \in \mathscr{I}_{(\epsilon)}$: $\|\mathbf{b} - \mathbf{b}^*\| < \epsilon$. If for the family $\mathscr{H}$, assumptions 1 through 3 hold, then for n sufficiently large,

$$\int_{\mathscr{B}' - \mathscr{I}_{(\epsilon)}} p(\mathbf{b}\,|\,\dot{\mathbf{x}}_n)\,d\mathbf{b} < K \exp(-n2\delta), \tag{17}$$

where $\delta > 0$ and K is an integer depending on ϵ.

> †$\mathscr{B}'$ is used, for simplicity, in place of $\mathscr{B}^{M'}$ defined in Chapter 1.

Proof

$$\int_{\mathscr{B}'-\mathscr{I}_{(\epsilon)}} p(\mathbf{b}\,|\,\dot{\mathbf{x}}_n)\,d\mathbf{b} < \frac{\int_{\mathscr{B}'-\mathscr{I}_{(\epsilon)}} p(\mathbf{b}\,|\,\dot{\mathbf{x}}_n)\,d\mathbf{b}}{\int_{\mathscr{I}_{(\epsilon/2)}} p(\mathbf{b}\,|\,\dot{\mathbf{x}}_n)\,d\mathbf{b}} \tag{18}$$

$$= \frac{\left[\int_{\mathscr{B}'-\mathscr{I}_{(\epsilon)}} \prod_{s=1}^{n} h(\mathbf{x}_s\,|\,\mathbf{b})\,d\mathbf{b}\right] p_0(\mathbf{b}) \int_{\mathscr{B}'} \prod_{s=1}^{n} h(\mathbf{x}_s\,|\,\mathbf{b})\,d\mathbf{b}}{\left[\int_{\mathscr{I}_{(\epsilon/2)}} \prod_{s=1}^{n} h(\mathbf{x}_s\,|\,\mathbf{b})\,d\mathbf{b}\right] p_0(\mathbf{b}) \int_{\mathscr{B}'} \prod_{s=1}^{n} h(\mathbf{x}_s\,|\,\mathbf{b})\,d\mathbf{b}}. \tag{19}$$

Assumption 1 guarantees that $\eta(\mathbf{b})$ is locally unimodal on $\mathscr{I}_{(\epsilon)}$, provided that ϵ is not too large; i.e., $\mathbf{b}' \in \mathscr{I}_{(\epsilon/2)}$, $\mathbf{b} \in \mathscr{B}' - \mathscr{I}_{(\epsilon/2)}$, $\eta(\mathbf{b}') > \eta(\mathbf{b})$. By the mean-value theorem,

$$\int_{\mathscr{I}_{(\epsilon/2)}} \prod_{s=1}^{n} h(\mathbf{x}_s\,|\,\mathbf{b})\,d\mathbf{b} = \prod_{s=1}^{n} h(\mathbf{x}_s\,|\,\mathbf{b}^\epsilon) V(\mathscr{I}_{(\epsilon/2)}), \qquad \text{where } \mathbf{b}^\epsilon \in \mathscr{I}_{(\epsilon/2)}, \tag{20}$$

and $V(\mathscr{I}_{(\epsilon/2)})$ is the volume of $\mathscr{I}_{(\epsilon-2)}$. The region $\mathscr{B}' - \mathscr{I}_{(\epsilon)}$ can be partitioned into K regions $\mathscr{B}_1, \mathscr{B}_2, \ldots, \mathscr{B}_K$ such that

$$\bigcup_{k=1}^{K} \mathscr{B}_k = \mathscr{B}' - \mathscr{I}_{(\epsilon)}, \mathscr{B}_i \cap \mathscr{B}_j = \varnothing, \qquad i \neq j, \tag{21}$$

no region has volume greater than $V(\mathscr{I}_{(\epsilon/2)})$, where K is finite because $\mathscr{B}'$ is bounded. Thus,

$$\int_{\mathscr{B}'-\mathscr{I}_{(\epsilon)}} \prod_{s=1}^{n} h(\mathbf{x}_s\,|\,\mathbf{b})\,d\mathbf{b} = \sum_{k=1}^{K} \int_{\mathscr{B}_k} \prod_{s=1}^{K} h(\mathbf{x}_s\,|\,\mathbf{b}^k)\,d\mathbf{b}^k. \tag{22}$$

Using the mean-value theorem on each of the K integrals in (22), we obtain

$$\int_{\mathscr{B}'-\mathscr{I}_{(\epsilon)}} \prod_{s=1}^{n} h(\mathbf{x}_s\,|\,\mathbf{b})\,d\mathbf{b} \leq \sum_{k=1}^{K} \prod_{s=1}^{n} h(\mathbf{x}_s\,|\,\mathbf{b}^k) V(\mathscr{I}_{(\epsilon/2)}), \tag{23}$$

where

$$\mathbf{b}^k \in \mathscr{B}_k; \tag{24}$$

thus,

$$\int_{\mathscr{B}'-\mathscr{I}_{(\epsilon)}} p(b\,|\,\dot{x}_n)\,db < \frac{\sum_{k=1}^{K} \prod_{s=1}^{n} h(\mathbf{x}_s\,|\,\mathbf{b}^k)}{\prod_{s=1}^{K} h(\mathbf{x}_s|\,\mathbf{b}^\epsilon)}$$

$$= \sum_{k=1}^{K} \exp\left[n\left\{ \frac{1}{n} \sum_{s=1}^{n} \ln h(\mathbf{x}_s\,|\,\mathbf{b}^k) - \frac{1}{n} \sum_{s=1}^{n} \ln h(\mathbf{x}_s\,|\,\mathbf{b}^\epsilon) \right\} \right]. \tag{25}$$

Because of assumption 3, the strong law of large numbers applies to give

$$\frac{1}{n}\sum_{s=1}^{n}\ln h(\mathbf{x}_s\,|\,\mathbf{b}) \xrightarrow{\text{w.p.1}} \eta(\mathbf{b}), \qquad \forall\,\mathbf{b}\in\mathscr{B}'. \tag{26}$$

Since, by assumption 1, the positive quantity $\eta(\mathbf{b}^\epsilon) - \eta(\mathbf{b}^k)$ is bounded away from 0, we can choose

$$4\delta = \min_{\mathbf{b}^k}\{\eta(\mathbf{b}^\epsilon) - \eta(\mathbf{b}^k)\},\ \mathbf{b}^k\in\mathscr{B}' - \mathscr{I}_{(\epsilon)},\ \mathbf{b}^\epsilon\in\mathscr{I}_{(\epsilon/2)}. \tag{27}$$

In view of (26), for given δ, $\exists\,n(\delta)$ such that

$$\left|\frac{1}{n}\sum_{s=1}^{n}\ln h(\mathbf{x}_s\,|\,\mathbf{b}) - \eta(\mathbf{b})\right| < \delta, \qquad n > n(\delta). \tag{28}$$

Then, for $n > n(\delta)$, the right-hand side of (18) can be bounded as follows:

$$\int_{\mathscr{B}' - \mathscr{I}_{(\epsilon)}} p(\mathbf{b}\,|\,\dot{\mathbf{x}}_n)\,d\mathbf{b} < K\exp(-n2\delta). \tag{29}$$

Equation (27) reveals that the "time constant" of the convergence rate depends upon the magnitude of the gradient of $\eta(\mathbf{b})$ near $\mathbf{b}^*$; the rate is enhanced the more sharply peaked the function η is at $\mathbf{b}^*$. Also, (29) shows that the rate depends, through the number K, upon the tightness of the bound on $\mathscr{B}$. The more we are able to restrict the region of search $\mathscr{B}'$, the smaller K will be for fixed ϵ.

Corollary 2 Let $\|\mathbf{b} - \mathbf{b}^*\| < R$; then for the Bayes estimator $(\mathbf{b})_n = \int_{\mathscr{B}'}\mathbf{b}\,p(\mathbf{b}\,|\,\dot{\mathbf{x}}_n)\,d\mathbf{b}$,

$$\sigma_n^2 = E[\|(\mathbf{b})_n - \mathbf{b}^*\|^2] < KR(R + \epsilon)\times\exp(-n2\delta) + \epsilon^2. \tag{30}$$

Proof

$$E[\|(\mathbf{b})_n - \mathbf{b}^*\|^2]$$

$$= E\left[\int_{\mathscr{B}'}d\mathbf{b}'\int_{\mathscr{B}'}(\mathbf{b} - \mathbf{b}^*)'(\mathbf{b}' - \mathbf{b}^*)p(\mathbf{b}'\,|\,\dot{\mathbf{x}}_n)p(\mathbf{b}\,|\,\dot{\mathbf{x}}_n)\,d\mathbf{b}\right]$$

$$= E\left[\int_{\mathscr{B}'}d\mathbf{b}'\int_{\mathscr{B}' - \mathscr{I}_\epsilon}(\mathbf{b} - \mathbf{b}^*)'(\mathbf{b}' - \mathbf{b}^*)p(\mathbf{b}\,|\,\dot{\mathbf{x}}_n)p(\mathbf{b}'\,|\,\dot{\mathbf{x}}_n)\,d\mathbf{b}\right]$$

$$+ E\left[\int_{\mathscr{B}'}d\mathbf{b}'\int_{\mathscr{I}_\epsilon}(\mathbf{b} - \mathbf{b}^*)'(\mathbf{b}' - \mathbf{b}^*)p(\mathbf{b}\,|\,\dot{\mathbf{x}}_n)p(\mathbf{b}'\,|\,\mathbf{x}_n)\,d\mathbf{b}\right]$$

$$\triangleq E_1 + E_2. \tag{31}$$

Because $(\mathbf{b} - \mathbf{b}^*)^t(\mathbf{b}' - \mathbf{b}^*) \leq R^2$,

$$E_1 \leq R^2 \int_{\mathscr{B}' - \mathscr{I}_\epsilon} p(\mathbf{b} \,|\, \dot{\mathbf{x}}_n)\, d\mathbf{b} \int_{\mathscr{B}} p(\mathbf{b}' \,|\, \dot{\mathbf{x}}_n)\, d\mathbf{b}' = R^2$$

$$\times \int_{\mathscr{B}' - \mathscr{I}_\epsilon} p(\mathbf{b} \,|\, \dot{\mathbf{x}}_n)\, d\mathbf{b}. \tag{32}$$

Observe that

$$E_2 = E\!\left[\int_{\mathscr{B}' - \mathscr{I}_\epsilon} d\mathbf{b}' \int_{\mathscr{I}_\epsilon} (\mathbf{b} - \mathbf{b}^*)^t(\mathbf{b}' - \mathbf{b}^*) p(\mathbf{b} \,|\, \dot{\mathbf{x}}_n) p(\mathbf{b}' \,|\, \dot{\mathbf{x}}_n)\, d\mathbf{b}\right]$$

$$+ E\!\left[\int_{\mathscr{I}_\epsilon} d\mathbf{b}' \int_{\mathscr{I}_\epsilon} (\mathbf{b} - \mathbf{b}^*)^t(\mathbf{b}' - \mathbf{b}^*) p(\mathbf{b} \,|\, \dot{\mathbf{x}}_n) p(\mathbf{b}' \,|\, \dot{\mathbf{x}}_n)\, d\mathbf{b}\right].$$

Because

$$(\mathbf{b} - \mathbf{b}^*)^t(\mathbf{b}' - \mathbf{b}^*) \leq \epsilon R, \qquad \mathbf{b} \in \mathscr{I}_\epsilon, \mathbf{b}' \in \mathscr{B}' - \mathscr{I}_\epsilon,$$

$$(\mathbf{b} - \mathbf{b}^*)^t(\mathbf{b}' - \mathbf{b}^*) \leq \epsilon^2, \qquad \mathbf{b} \in \mathscr{I}_\epsilon, \mathbf{b}' \in \mathscr{I}_\epsilon,$$

$$E_2 \leq \epsilon R E\!\left[\int_{\mathscr{B}' - \mathscr{I}_\epsilon} p(\mathbf{b}' \,|\, \dot{\mathbf{x}}_n)\, d\mathbf{b}' \int_{\mathscr{I}_\epsilon} p(\mathbf{b} \,|\, \dot{\mathbf{x}}_n)\, d\mathbf{b}\right] + \epsilon^2$$

$$< \epsilon R E\!\left[\int_{\mathscr{B}' - \mathscr{I}_\epsilon} p(\mathbf{b}' \,|\, \dot{\mathbf{x}}_n)\, d\mathbf{b}'\right] + \epsilon^2, \tag{33}$$

where the last inequality follows because

$$\int_{\mathscr{I}_\epsilon} p(\mathbf{b} \,|\, \dot{\mathbf{x}}_n)\, d\mathbf{b} < 1.$$

Thus, these two upper bounds, (32) and (33), on E_1 and E_2 give

$$\sigma_n^2 < R(R + \epsilon) E\!\left[\int_{\mathscr{B}' - \mathscr{I}_\epsilon} p(\mathbf{b}' \,|\, \dot{\mathbf{x}}_n)\, d\mathbf{b}'\right] + \epsilon^2. \tag{34}$$

Using (29) we obtain

$$\sigma_n^2 < R(R + \epsilon) K \exp(-n2\delta) + \epsilon^2.$$

5-3.4 Bayes Estimator on a Finite Parameter Set

Let $\mathbf{x}$ be an L-dimensional observable random vector having density function $h(\mathbf{x} \,|\, \mathbf{b}^*)$ indexed by an s-dimensional vector of parameters $\mathbf{b}^*$ and belonging to a known family $\{h(\mathbf{x} \,|\, \mathbf{b})\}$, $\mathbf{b} \in \mathscr{B}$, where $\mathscr{B}$ is the admissible set of parameters. Observations of $\mathbf{x}$ are as always denoted by $\mathbf{x}_1, \ldots, \mathbf{x}_n$. For convenience use $\dot{\mathbf{x}}_n = \{\mathbf{x}_k\}_{k=1}^n$. Let $\mathscr{B}^V$ denote a finite set of points in $\mathscr{B}$; i.e., $\mathscr{B}^V = \{\mathbf{b}^r\}_{r=1}^V$. The Bayes estimator $(\mathbf{b})_n$ minimizing average risk on

$\mathscr{B}$ for a quadratic loss function (see, e.g., Lehmann [59], p. 23) is defined as in previous sections by

$$(\mathbf{b})_n = \sum_{r=1}^{V} \mathbf{b}^r p(\mathbf{b}^r | \dot{\mathbf{x}}_n), \tag{35}$$

where $p(\mathbf{b}^r | \dot{\mathbf{x}}_n)$ is the a posteriori probability mass on $\mathbf{b}^r$ computed as

$$p(\mathbf{b}^r | \dot{\mathbf{x}}_n) = \frac{\prod_{k=1}^{n} h(\mathbf{x}_k \, \mathbf{b}^r)}{\sum_{r=1}^{V} \prod_{s=1}^{n} h(\mathbf{x}_s | \mathbf{b}^r)}, \qquad r = 1, 2, \ldots, V. \tag{36}$$

For simplicity, it has been assumed in (36) that the a priori density on $\mathscr{B}^V$ is uniform.

Define the regression function (which was shown in previous sections to naturally arise in the Bayes solution),

$$\eta(\mathbf{b}) = E[\ln h(\mathbf{x} | \mathbf{b})]. \tag{37}$$

Denote by $\mathbf{b}^m$ the point in $\mathscr{B}^V$ at which η is maximized; i.e,

$$\eta(\mathbf{b}^m) = \max_{r=1, 2, \ldots, V} \{\eta(\mathbf{b}^r)\}. \tag{38}$$

In this section it is shown that $p(\mathbf{b}^r | \dot{\mathbf{x}}_n)$, $r \neq m$, defined in (36) diminishes to zero at exponential rate for large enough n with probability 1. Then as a corollary it is shown that the average norm square error σ_n^2 approaches zero at asymptotically exponential rate, where

$$\sigma_n^2 \triangleq E[\| (\mathbf{b})_n - \mathbf{b}^m \|^2]. \tag{39}$$

That is, the Bayes estimator on a finite parameter set is asymptotically superefficient.† LeCam [30] pointed out that‡ an estimator can be superefficient only on a set of parameters of Lebesque measure zero. The first of the above results is contained in the following theorem.

Theorem 3   If assumption 3 holds, then the a posteriori probability mass $p(\mathbf{b}^r | \dot{\mathbf{x}}_n)$ defined in (36) is bounded for n sufficiently large by

$$p(\mathbf{b}^r | \dot{\mathbf{x}}_n) < \exp(-n\delta_r), \qquad r \neq m, \tag{40}$$

with probability 1, where

$$\delta_r = \tfrac{1}{3} [\eta(\mathbf{b}^m) - \eta(\mathbf{b}^r)]. \tag{41}$$

†An estimator is said to be superefficient if it has variance smaller than $0(1/n)$.
‡See also reference [29].

Proof: Since $p(\mathbf{b}^m \mid \dot{\mathbf{x}}_n) < 1$,

$$p(\mathbf{b}^r \mid \dot{\mathbf{x}}_n) < \frac{p(\mathbf{b}^r \mid \dot{\mathbf{x}}_n)}{p(\mathbf{b}^m \mid \dot{\mathbf{x}}_n)}. \tag{42}$$

Using (36) and the identity $w = \exp(\ln w)$ in (42) yields the bound

$$p(\mathbf{b}^r \mid \dot{\mathbf{x}}_n) < \exp\left\{ -n\left[\frac{1}{n} \sum_{s=1}^{n} \ln h(\mathbf{x}_s \mid \mathbf{x}^m) - \frac{1}{n} \sum_{s=1}^{n} \ln h(\mathbf{x}_s \mid \mathbf{b}^r) \right] \right\}. \tag{43}$$

Again, invoking the strong law of large numbers and letting $\delta_r = \frac{1}{3}\,[\eta(\mathbf{b}^m) - \eta(\mathbf{b}^r)]$, we conclude that for $n > n(\delta_r)$,

$$p(\mathbf{b}^r \mid \dot{\mathbf{x}}_n) < \exp(-n\delta_r)$$

with probability 1.

Corollary 3 For $n > \max_r \{n(\delta_r)\}$, the mean norm-square error denoted σ_n^2 defined in (39) is bounded above as

$$\sigma_n^2 < \sum_{j \neq m} \sum_{k \neq m} (\mathbf{b}^j - \mathbf{b}^m)^t(\mathbf{b}^k - \mathbf{b}^m)\exp(-n\delta_j) \tag{44}$$

$$\sigma_n^2 < C\exp(-n\delta'), \tag{45}$$

with probability 1, where δ_j and C are positive constants and

$$\delta' = \min_{j \neq m} \{\delta_j\}. \tag{46}$$

Proof: The average norm-square error can be expanded as

$$\sigma_n^2 = \sum_{j \neq m} \sum_{k \neq m} (\mathbf{b}^j - \mathbf{b}^m)^t(\mathbf{b}^k - \mathbf{b}^m)E[p(\mathbf{b}^j \mid \dot{\mathbf{x}}_n)p(\mathbf{b}^k \mid \dot{\mathbf{x}}_n)]. \tag{47}$$

Noting that $p(\mathbf{b}^r \mid \dot{\mathbf{x}}_n)p(\mathbf{b}^r \mid \dot{\mathbf{x}}_n) < p(\mathbf{b}^r \mid \dot{\mathbf{x}}_n)$ and, using Theorem 3, we conclude that for $n > \max_j \{n(\delta_j)\}$,

$$\sigma_n^2 < \sum_{j \neq m} \sum_{k \neq m} (\mathbf{b}^j - \mathbf{b}^m)^t(\mathbf{b}^k - \mathbf{b}^m)\exp(-n2\delta_j) \tag{48}$$

with probability 1. Define

$$C = \sum_{j \neq m} \sum_{k \neq m} (\mathbf{b}^j - \mathbf{b}^m)^t(\mathbf{b}^k - \mathbf{b}^m). \tag{49}$$

Then, noting the definition of δ', we conclude that

$$\sigma_n^2 < C\exp(-n\delta').$$

Although this concludes the corollary proof, note that if $R = \max_r\{\|\mathbf{b}^r - \mathbf{b}^m\|\}$, then as a result of the corollary and (49),

$$\sigma_n^2 < (V-1)^2 R^2 \exp(-n\delta'). \tag{50}$$

The foregoing corollary says that the Bayes estimator converges in quadratic mean to the point in $\mathscr{B}^V$ at which η is greatest. However, since for some family $\mathscr{H}$ and some values of $\mathbf{b}^*$, η may be multimodal, there is no guarantee that $\mathbf{b}^m$, the limit of the estimator, is close to $\mathbf{b}^*$. The bound on σ_n^2 obtained in the corollary can be compared with the result $\sigma_n^2 < C(v)n^{-v}$, for $n > v$, where v is the order of the highest finite moment of $\ln h(\mathbf{x}\,|\,\mathbf{b})$ and $C(v)$ is monotonically increasing in v; the latter result is in Section 5-3.1.

5-3.5 Minimum-Norm-Square-Error Estimator

The foregoing discussion of the asymptotic properties of the Bayes estimator on a finite parameter set reveals that the aspects of the estimator giving rise to the superefficient performance are twofold: The exponential rate stems from the product form of the estimator; convergence to the true parameter is a consequence of the fact that the function η achieves its maximum at the true parameter. Thus, the form of the Bayes a posteriori probability density suggests that there may be other product-type functions which can be utilized similar to that for Bayes. One such function results in what will be called the minimum-norm-square-error estimator, which for brevity will be referred to as the m.n.s.e. estimator. The form of the m.n.s.e. estimator motivates the second regression function, the Γ function, discussed in this section.

Continuous Parameter Set

The m.n.s.e. estimator, denoted $(\mathbf{a})_n$, is defined on $\mathscr{B}'$ as

$$(\mathbf{a})_n = \int_{\mathscr{B}'} \mathbf{b} q(\mathbf{b}\,|\,\dot{\mathbf{x}}_n)\, d\mathbf{b}, \tag{51}$$

where

$$q(\mathbf{b}\,|\,\dot{\mathbf{x}}_n) = \frac{\exp\left\{ \sum_{s=1}^{n} [2h(\mathbf{x}_s\,|\,\mathbf{b}) - \|(\mathbf{x}\,|\,\mathbf{b})\|^2] \right\}}{\int_{\mathscr{B}'} [\text{numerator}]\, d\mathbf{b}}, \tag{52}$$

and the norm is defined as

$$\| f(\mathbf{x}) \|^2 = \int f^2(\mathbf{x})\, d\mathbf{x}.$$

Note that $q(\mathbf{b}\,|\,\dot{\mathbf{x}}_n) \geq 0$ and $\int_{\mathscr{B}'} q(\mathbf{b}\,|\,\dot{\mathbf{x}}_n)\,d\mathbf{b} = 1$, which are properties of a density function on $\mathscr{B}'$.

Denote the norm-square error between $h(\mathbf{x}\,|\,\mathbf{b})$ and true density function $h(\mathbf{x}\,|\,\mathbf{b}^*)$ by $e^2(\mathbf{b})$,

$$e^2(\mathbf{b}) = \|\,h(\mathbf{x}\,|\,\mathbf{b}) - h(\mathbf{x}\,|\,\mathbf{b}^*)\|^2$$
$$= \|\,h(\mathbf{x}\,|\,\mathbf{b})\|^2 - 2E\{h(\mathbf{x}\,|\,\mathbf{b})\} + \|\,h(\mathbf{x}\,|\,\mathbf{b}^*)\|^2. \tag{53}$$

The above expression can be put in a form described as the expected fractional squared error,

$$e^2(\mathbf{b}) = \int \left\{ \frac{[h(\mathbf{x}\,|\,\mathbf{b}) - h(\mathbf{x}\,|\,\mathbf{b}^*)]^2}{h(\mathbf{x}\,|\,\mathbf{b}^*)} \right\} h(\mathbf{x}\,|\,\mathbf{b}^*)\,dx$$
$$= E\left\{ \frac{[h(\mathbf{x}\,|\,\mathbf{b}) - h(\mathbf{x}\,|\,\mathbf{b}^*)]^2}{h(\mathbf{x}\,|\,\mathbf{b})} \right\}. \tag{54}$$

A regression function $\Gamma(\mathbf{b})$ is defined as

$$\Gamma(\mathbf{b}) \triangleq 2E[h(\mathbf{x}\,|\,\mathbf{b})] - \|\,h(\mathbf{x}\,|\,\mathbf{b})\|^2$$
$$= \|\,h(\mathbf{x}\,|\,\mathbf{b}^*)\|^2 - e^2(\mathbf{b}). \tag{55}$$

In view of this definition of $\Gamma(\mathbf{b})$, it is clear that as long as $h(\mathbf{x}\,|\,\mathbf{b}^*)$ is identifiable [i.e., $h(\mathbf{x}) = h(\mathbf{x}\,|\,\mathbf{b}^*)$ is unique], then $\Gamma(\mathbf{b})$ is uniquely maximized at $\mathbf{b}^*$; this follows because $e^2(\mathbf{b}) \geq 0$ with equality if and only if $h(\mathbf{x}\,|\,\mathbf{b}) = h(\mathbf{x}\,|\,\mathbf{b}^*)$ with probability 1. That is, identifiability guarantees that $e^2(\mathbf{b}) = 0$ implies that $h(\mathbf{x}\,|\,\mathbf{b})$ and $h(\mathbf{x}\,|\,\mathbf{b}^*)$ can differ only on a set of measure zero.

Considering the numerator of (52), note that because $h(\mathbf{x}\,|\,\mathbf{b})$ has finite mean, the strong law of large numbers can be applied, resulting in

$$\frac{1}{n}\sum_{s=1}^{n} 2h(\mathbf{x}_s\,|\,\mathbf{b}) - \|\,h(\mathbf{x}\,|\,\mathbf{b})\|^2 \xrightarrow{\text{w.p.1}} \|\,h(\mathbf{x}\,|\,\mathbf{b}^*)\|^2 - e^2(\mathbf{b}) = \Gamma(\mathbf{b}). \tag{56}$$

Theorem 4 Let $\mathscr{I}_{(\epsilon)}$ denote an ϵ neighborhood of $\mathbf{b}^*$. If $h(\mathbf{x}\,|\,\mathbf{b})$ has finite mean for all $\mathbf{b} \in \mathscr{B}'$, then with probability 1, for n sufficiently large,

$$\int_{\mathscr{B}' - \mathscr{I}_{(\epsilon)}} q(\mathbf{b}\,|\,\dot{\mathbf{x}}_n)\,d\mathbf{b} < K\exp[-\tfrac{1}{2}(e^2(\mathbf{b}') - e^2(\mathbf{b}^\epsilon))], \tag{57}$$

where $\mathbf{b}' \in \mathscr{B}' - \mathscr{I}_{(\epsilon)}$, $\mathbf{b}^\epsilon \in \mathscr{I}_{(\epsilon)}$, and K is a finite number. That is, the probability mass defined by lying outside the ball $\|\,\mathbf{b} - \mathbf{b}^*\| \leq \epsilon$ shrinks to zero asymptotically at an exponential rate. The proof parallels that of Theorem 2, with

$$\delta_m \text{ chosen as } \tfrac{1}{2}\,[\Gamma(\mathbf{b}^\epsilon) - \Gamma(\mathbf{b}^m)].$$

The m.n.s.e. estimator $(\mathbf{a})_n$ on a finite parameter set $\mathscr{B}^V$ is defined by the discrete version of (51); i.e.,

$$(\mathbf{a})_n \triangleq \sum_{r=1}^{V} \mathbf{b}^r q(\mathbf{b}_r \,|\, \dot{\mathbf{x}}_n), \tag{58}$$

where

$$q(\mathbf{b}^r \,|\, \dot{\mathbf{x}}_n) = \frac{\exp\left\{ \sum_{s=1}^{n} [2h(\mathbf{x}_s \,|\, \mathbf{b}^r) - \|h(\cdot \,|\, \mathbf{b}^r)\|^2] \right\}}{\sum_{r=1}^{V} [\text{numerator}]}. \tag{59}$$

Let $\mathbf{b}^m$ denote, again, the point in $\mathscr{B}^V$ at which the regression function is maximized; i.e.,

$$\Gamma(\mathbf{b}^m) = \max_{r} \{\Gamma(\mathbf{b}^r)\}. \tag{60}$$

The asymptotic properties of $(\mathbf{a})_n$ are indicated in the following theorem and corollary.

Theorem 5 For n sufficiently large,

$$p(\mathbf{b}^r \,|\, \dot{\mathbf{x}}_n) < \exp\{-n \cdot [e^2(\mathbf{b}^r) - e^2(\mathbf{b}^m)]\},$$
$$r \neq m, \text{ with probability 1.} \tag{61}$$

The proof of Theorem 5 follows the proof of Theorem 3, with δ_j chosen as

$$\delta_j = \tfrac{1}{3} [\Gamma(\mathbf{b}^m) - \Gamma(\mathbf{b}^j)].$$

Corollary 3 Define the expected norm-square error in $(\mathbf{a})_n$ by $\sigma^2(n)$; i.e.,

$$\sigma^2(n) \triangleq E[\|(\mathbf{a})_n - \mathbf{b}^m\|^2]. \tag{62}$$

For n sufficiently large,

$$\sigma^2(n) < C \exp\{-n \cdot [e^2(\mathbf{b}') - e^2(\mathbf{b}^m)]\}, \tag{63}$$

with probability 1, where $0 < C < \infty$, $\mathbf{b}' \in \{\mathbf{b}^r\}_{r \neq m}$.

Equation (61) points up that the convergence rate depends both upon how close $h(\mathbf{x} \,|\, \mathbf{b}^r)$, $r \neq m$, is to $h(\mathbf{x} \,|\, \mathbf{b}^*)$ relative to $h(\mathbf{x} \,|\, \mathbf{b}^m)$, and also upon how close $h(\mathbf{x} \,|\, \mathbf{b}^m)$ is to $h(\mathbf{x} \,|\, \mathbf{b}^*)$, in the norm-square sense. That is, the probability mass at $\mathbf{b}^r$, $r \neq m$, will diminish to zero faster the closer $\mathbf{b}^m$ is to $\mathbf{b}^*$.

Theoretical results that compare the convergence rate using $\Gamma(\mathbf{b})$ versus the rate using $\eta(\mathbf{b})$ are not available. Although such results would be useful, it must be remembered that pragmatic assumptions may lead to estimators that make such theoretical results unnecessary. For example, the clustering techniques discussed in Section 5-4 utilize a priori knowledge not easily inserted when using the approaches presented thus far involving $\Gamma(\mathbf{b})$ and $\eta(\mathbf{b})$. Yet these clustering techniques may provide very practical solutions for many problems.

The regression function Γ has appeal over η because the former involves $h(\mathbf{x}\,|\,\mathbf{b})$ rather than $\ln h(\mathbf{x}\,|\,\mathbf{b})$. A clustering procedure utilizing Γ under a high signal-to-noise assumption is presented in Section 5-4.6.

5-3.6 Quasi-Bayes Estimator (Finite Parameter Set)

Stochastic approximation (s.a.) techniques introduced in Chapter 2 may be described as stochastic versions of either zero-seeking or peak-seeking (hill-climbing) methods of numerical analysis. The function whose zero or peak is sought is called the *regression function*. The regression function is usually unknown, but measurements of it may be made. Typically a starting point is chosen for the estimator arbitrarily, and thereafter the estimator is incremented according to a procedure that involves the latest noisy observation of the regression function. Although convergence is assured regardless of the starting point, the starting point strongly affects the convergence rate. This section contains a method for enhancing the performance of s.a. estimators by deemphasizing the starting point. The method involves computing several s.a. estimates, all using the same observables, but having different starting points, and then forming a weighted average in which the weighting coefficients of all the estimates except the one closest (according to a criterion) to the true parameter point diminish to zero rapidly. Before delineating the method, a few key papers, some already mentioned in Chapter 2, are discussed for continuity in this section.

The advent of the s.a. method was marked by the pioneer paper of Robbins and Monroe [61], in which the authors presented an iterative scheme for determining the zero of a regression function. The following year, Kiefer and Wolfowitz [62] reported a stochastic hill-climbing technique for determining the maximum of a regression function having one unknown parameter. Later Blum [63] extended Kiefer and Wolfowitz's approach to accommodate several unknown parameters. All these results were subsequently unified, strengthened, and generalized by Dvoretzky [64]. A very readable discussion of the mechanisms underlying these methods may be found in the book by Wilde ([65], Chap. 6).

Two of the initial approaches to the problem of improving the performance of s.a. techniques include one presented by Kesten [66]. His method is to reduce the step size only when the estimator changes sign—the idea being that when the estimator is far from the zero point or peak, no sign changes are expected; whereas when the estimator is close to the zero point, frequent sign changes will occur. A second approach is that of Cruz-Dias (see [67], p. 178). That approach is to use only the sign of the noisy measurement of the regression function rather than the actual value. In this way the estimator takes larger steps in the regions beyond inflectional points.

The method presented in this section differs in nature from these two performance-improving methods in that the current method does not accelerate the convergence of the s.a. scheme. Rather the current method, in effect, "singles out" the best of several s.a. estimators.

The mechanism underlying the current method is the superefficiency of the Bayes estimator on a finite parameter set. An estimator is said to be superefficient if its variance is smaller than $O(1/n)$. LeCam [28] pointed out that superefficiency is possible on a parameter set of Lebesque measure zero. The averaging method is motivated by the Bayes solution for finite-size parameter space presented in Section 5-3.4.

The Bayes estimator on a finite parameter space requires that $\eta(\mathbf{b}^k)$ be estimated at each point $\mathbf{b}^k$, $k = 1, 2, \ldots, V$, in the parameter space. In particular, stochastic-approximation-type estimators

$$\hat{\eta}(\mathbf{b}^k) = \frac{1}{n} \sum_{s=1}^{n} \ln h(\mathbf{x}_s \,|\, \mathbf{b}^k), \qquad k = 1, 2, \ldots, V, \tag{64}$$

must be obtained. The objective of quasi-Bayes is to reduce the number of points V, introducing the facility to move the selected points closer to the true point $\mathbf{b}^*$. Because one of the selected points will be started nearest to $\mathbf{b}^*$, we expect that point to more quickly move to the true parameter point $\mathbf{b}^*$ than the other initial points. Because of this we expect the Bayes estimator defined using these selected points to be less sensitive to the a priori selected starting values.

Method

Assume that $\mathbf{b}^*$ is contained in a known bounded set $\mathscr{B}'$ so that the ith component b_i^* of $\mathbf{b}^*$ lies in the interval $[\alpha_i, \beta_i]$, with α_i and β_i, $i = 1, 2, \ldots, q$, known. The set $\mathscr{B}'$ is decomposed into V cells formed by equally subdividing the interval $[\alpha_i, \beta_i]$ into V_i subintervals, where $\prod_{i=1}^{q} V_i = V$. After the nth observation $\mathbf{x}_n$ of $\mathbf{x}$ is obtained, V s.a. estimates $(\mathbf{b}^r)_{n+1}$, $r = 1, 2, \ldots, V$, are computed, the starting points $(\mathbf{b}^r)_0$, $r = 1, 2, \ldots, V$, being the centers of the cells in $\mathscr{B}'$.

The ith component $(b_i^r)_{n+1}$ is computed by means of the expression

$$(b_i^r)_{n+1} = (b_i^r)_n + \frac{a_n}{c_n}(y_{r,2n}^i - y_{r,2n-1}^i), \qquad r = 1, 2, \ldots, V, \qquad (65)$$

where $\{a_n\}$ and $\{c_n\}$ are infinite sequences satisfying

$$\lim_{n \to \infty} c_n = 0, \qquad (66a)$$

$$\sum_{n=1}^{\infty} a_n = \infty, \qquad (66b)$$

$$\sum_{n=1}^{\infty} a_n c_n < \infty, \qquad (66c)$$

$$\sum_{n=1}^{\infty} a_n^2 c_n^{-2} < \infty; \qquad (66d)$$

and $y_{r,2n}^i$ and $y_{r,2n-1}^i$ are noisy measurements of the regression function:

$$y_{r,2n}^i = \ln h(\mathbf{x} \mid (\mathbf{b}^r)_n + c_n \mathbf{e}_i), \qquad (67a)$$

$$y_{r,2n-1}^i = \ln h(\mathbf{x}_n \mid (\mathbf{b}^r)_n - c_n \mathbf{e}_i). \qquad (67b)$$

The vector $\mathbf{e}_i$ is a column vector having 1 in the ith row and zeros elsewhere. If $(b_i^r)_{n+1}$ as computed in (65) falls outside the rth cell, i.e., if

$$|(b_i^r)_{n+1} - (b_i^r)_0| > \frac{\tfrac{1}{2}(\beta_i - \alpha_i)}{V_i}, \qquad (68)$$

then $(b_i^r)_{n+1}$ is moved to the nearer end point:

$$(b_i^r)_0 \pm \frac{\tfrac{1}{2}(\beta_i - \alpha_i)}{V}.$$

Thus, $(b_i^r)_{n+1}$ will differ in absolute value from its starting point $(b_i^r)_0$ by at most $\tfrac{1}{2}(\beta_i - \alpha_i)/V_i$. The relationships among these quantities are schematized in Figure 5.1 for $q = 2$, $V_1 = 4$, and $V_2 = 5$.

Having incremented the V s.a. estimates according to (65), next form the "quasi-Bayes" estimator $(\mathbf{b})_{n+1}$ as

$$(\mathbf{b})_{n+1} = \sum_{r=1}^{V} (\mathbf{b}^r)_{n+1} p((\mathbf{b}^r)_0 \mid \dot{\mathbf{x}}_n), \qquad (69)$$

where $p((\mathbf{b}^r)_0 \mid \dot{\mathbf{x}}_n)$ is the a posteriori probability mass defined† in (36) of

---

†The reader might consider why we have not used $p((\mathbf{b}^r)_n \mid \dot{\mathbf{x}}_n)$ in Eq. (69).

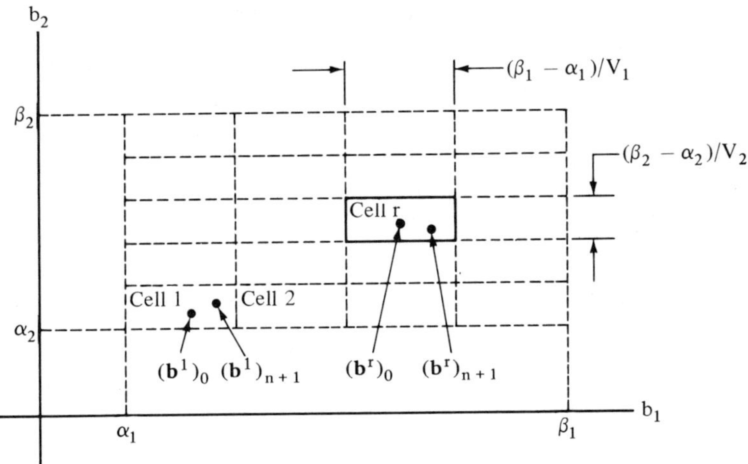

Fig. 5.1 Set $\mathscr{B}$, containing $\mathbf{b}^*$

Section 5-3.4. Thus, $(\mathbf{b})_{n+1}$ is a weighted average of the V s.a. estimates, the weighting coefficient of the rth s.a. estimate being the Bayes a posteriori probability mass at the center of the rth cell. Forming V s.a. estimates in this way effectively divides the interval of search for b_i^* by V_i. By allowing n to become sufficiently large, $(\mathbf{b})_{n+1}$ can be made to differ from $\mathbf{b}^m$ by as little as desired. However, practical implementation of the standard Bayes method incurs a quantization error no matter how large n becomes. Since the weights for $r \neq m$ converge rapidly to zero, only $(\mathbf{b}^m)_{n+1}$, the s.a. estimator that is best in the sense of maximizing η, survives. Accordingly, it is shown next that for large n the expected norm-square error in $(\mathbf{b})_n$ is arbitrarily close to the expected norm-square error in $(\mathbf{b}^m)_n$.

Performance

The average norm-square error in $(\mathbf{b})_n$ is

$$\sigma^2(n) \triangleq E\{\|(\mathbf{b})_n - \mathbf{b}^*\|^2\}$$

$$= \sum_{r=1}^{V} \sum_{t=1}^{V} E\{[(\mathbf{b}^r)_n - \mathbf{b}^*]^t[(\mathbf{b}^t)_n - \mathbf{b}^*]$$

$$\times p((\mathbf{b}^r)_0 \mid \dot{\mathbf{x}}_n)p((\mathbf{b}^t)_0 \mid \dot{\mathbf{x}}_n)\}. \tag{70}$$

Adding and subtracting $(\mathbf{b}^m)_n$ in the bracketed terms within the sum yields

$$\sigma^2(n) = \sum_{\substack{r=1 \\ r,t \neq m}}^{V} \sum_{t=1}^{V} E\{[(\mathbf{b}^r)_n - (\mathbf{b}^m)_n]^t[(\mathbf{b}^t)_n - (\mathbf{b}^m)_n]$$

$$\times p((\mathbf{b}^r)_0 \mid \dot{\mathbf{x}}_n) p((\mathbf{b}^t)_0 \mid \dot{\mathbf{x}}_n)\}$$

$$+ 2E\{[(\mathbf{b}^m)_n - \mathbf{b}^*]^t \sum_{r \neq m}^{V} [(\mathbf{b}^r)_n - (\mathbf{b}^m)_n] p((\mathbf{b}^r)_0 \mid \dot{\mathbf{x}}_n)\}$$

$$+ E\{\|(\mathbf{b}^m)_n - \mathbf{b}^*\|^2\}. \tag{71}$$

Since the parameter set is bounded,

$$\|(\mathbf{b}^r)_n - (\mathbf{b}^m)_n\| \leq R < \infty.$$

Using this fact and the Schwarz inequality (see Chapter 1) and letting

$$\sigma_m^2(n) \triangleq E\{\|(\mathbf{b}^m)_n - \mathbf{b}^*\|^2\},$$

the right side of (71) can be bounded by

$$\sigma^2(n) < (V - 1)R^2 \sum_{r \neq m}^{V} E\{p(\mathbf{b}^r)_0 \mid \dot{\mathbf{x}}_n)\}$$

$$+ 2R\sigma_m(n)\left(E\left\{\left[\sum_{r \neq m}^{V} p((\mathbf{b}^r)_0 \mid \dot{\mathbf{x}}_n)\right]^2\right\}\right)^{1/2} + \sigma_m^2(n) \tag{72}$$

$$< (V - 1)R^2 \sum_{r \neq m}^{V} E\{p(\mathbf{b}^r)_0 \mid \dot{\mathbf{x}}_n)\}$$

$$+ 2R\sigma_m(n)\left(\sum_{r \neq m}^{V} E\{p((\mathbf{b}^r)_0 \mid \dot{\mathbf{x}}_n)\}\right)^{1/2} + \sigma_m^2(n). \tag{73}$$

As shown in Section 5-3.4, for large n, $p((\mathbf{b}^r)_0 \mid \dot{\mathbf{x}}_n) < 0[\exp(-n\delta_r)]$, a.s., whereas by the Rao–Cramer lower bound, $\sigma_m^2(n) > 0(n^{-1})$, so that for large n,

$$\sigma^2(n) \approx \sigma_m^2(n). \tag{74}$$

That is, the performance of the quasi-Bayes estimator is asymptotically indistinguishable from that of the s.a. estimator, which is best in the sense of having the starting point at which the regression function is greatest.

The reason it is meaningful to form the weighted average in (69) is that the Bayes algorithm converges much faster than the s.a. estimators upon which it is superimposed. In turn, the rapid convergence of the Bayes technique stems from the product form of the estimator and from the fact that the function η is maximized at $\mathbf{b}^*$. This suggests that the same behavior might be expected of any product-type algorithm whose solution is characterized as maximizing some function defined on $\mathscr{B}'$. With this idea in mind, we discuss in the following subsection an alternative realization of the averaging technique. The alternative approach is formulated in terms of regression function, $\Gamma(\mathbf{b})$, defined by (69) in Section 5-3.5.

An alternative way of implementing the averaging technique is to use $\mathbf{\Gamma}(\mathbf{b})$, defined in Section 5-3.5, as the hill for the s.a. estimators to climb, and then form the average with $q((\mathbf{b}^r)_0 \mid \dot{\mathbf{x}}_n)$, $1 \leq r \leq V$, as the weighting coefficients (see Section 5-3.5). Specifically, the ith component of $(\mathbf{b}^r)_{n+1}$ is computed as

$$(\mathbf{b}_i^r)_{n+1} = (\mathbf{b}_i^r)_n + \frac{a_n}{c_n}(\mathbf{u}_{r,2n}^i - u_{r,2n-1}^i), \tag{75}$$

$u_{r,2n}^i$ and $u_{r,2n-1}^i$ being the noisy measurements of the regression function $\mathbf{\Gamma}$; i.e.,

$$u_{r,2n}^i = 2h(\mathbf{x}_n \mid (\mathbf{b}^r)_n + c_n \mathbf{e}_i) - \|h(\cdot \mid (\mathbf{b}^r)_n + c_n \mathbf{e}_i)\|^2, \tag{76a}$$

$$u_{r,2n-1}^i = 2h(\mathbf{x}_n \mid (\mathbf{b}^r)_n - c_n \mathbf{e}_i) - \|h(\cdot \mid (\mathbf{b}^r)_n - c_n \mathbf{e}_i)\|^2. \tag{76b}$$

With $(\mathbf{b}^r)_{n+1}$, $r = 1, 2, \ldots, V$, computed by means of (75), the average is then computed as

$$(\mathbf{b})_{n+1} = \sum_{r=1}^{V} (\mathbf{b}^r)_{n+1} q(\mathbf{b}^r)_0 \mid \dot{\mathbf{x}}_n). \tag{77}$$

Using arguments paralleling those in Section 3-3.4, it is concluded that the averaged estimator defined by (77) singles out the s.a. estimator whose starting point is best, in the sense that the corresponding density function is "closest" in the norm-square-error sense to the true density.

Computer-Simulated Results

A computer simulation of the averaging scheme incorporating each of the regression functions $\eta(\mathbf{b})$ and $\mathbf{\Gamma}(\mathbf{b})$ has been carried out with the true density a mixture of three one-dimensional Gaussian density functions,

$$h(\mathbf{x} \mid \mathbf{b}^*) = \sum_{i=1}^{3} P_i N(\mathbf{x} \mid m_i, \sigma). \tag{78}$$

The parameters were chosen as follows:

$$P_i = \tfrac{1}{3} \text{ and known,}$$
$$m_1 = -3 \text{ and unknown,}$$
$$m_2 = 0 \text{ and unknown,}$$
$$m_3 = 3 \text{ and unknown,}$$
$$\sigma = 1 \text{ and known,}$$
$$V = 36.$$

The computer-simulation results are shown in Figures 5.2 and 5.3. Figure 5.2 compares the norm-square error in the quasi-Bayes estimator with that of two of the underlying s.a. estimators, one being the s.a. estimator having

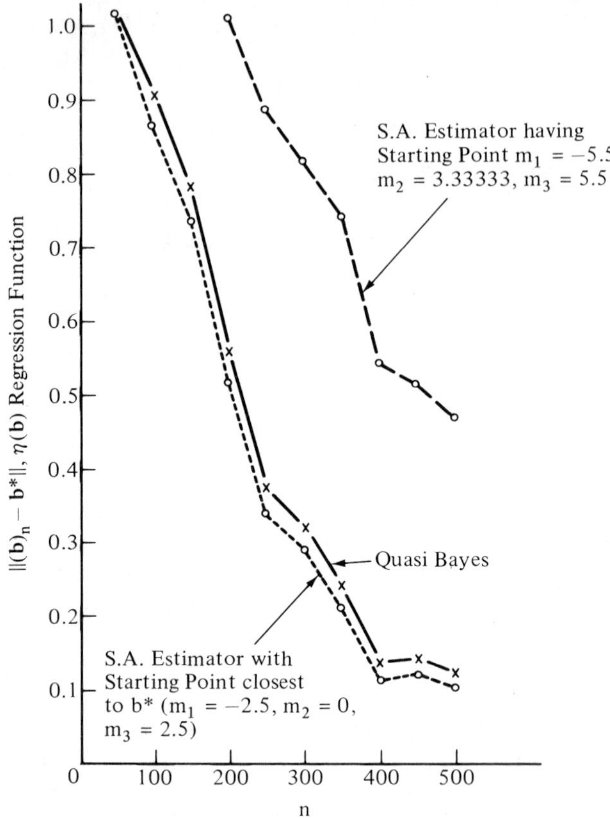

Fig. 5.2 Performance of quasi-Bayes estimator

starting point closest to $\mathbf{b}^*$. Similarly, Figure 5.3 compares the norm-square error in the average estimator based on $\Gamma(\mathbf{b})$ with that of the s.a. estimator [based on $\mathbf{a}(\mathbf{b})$] having starting point closest to $\mathbf{b}^*$. The curves for the other s.a. estimators based on $\Gamma(\mathbf{b})$ fell outside the range of the figure.

Conclusions

By superimposing a superefficient estimator upon the s.a. scheme by means of forming an average of several s.a. estimators, it is possible to deemphasize the starting point and improve the performance of the s.a. method over that obtainable with one s.a. estimator whose starting point is chosen at random.

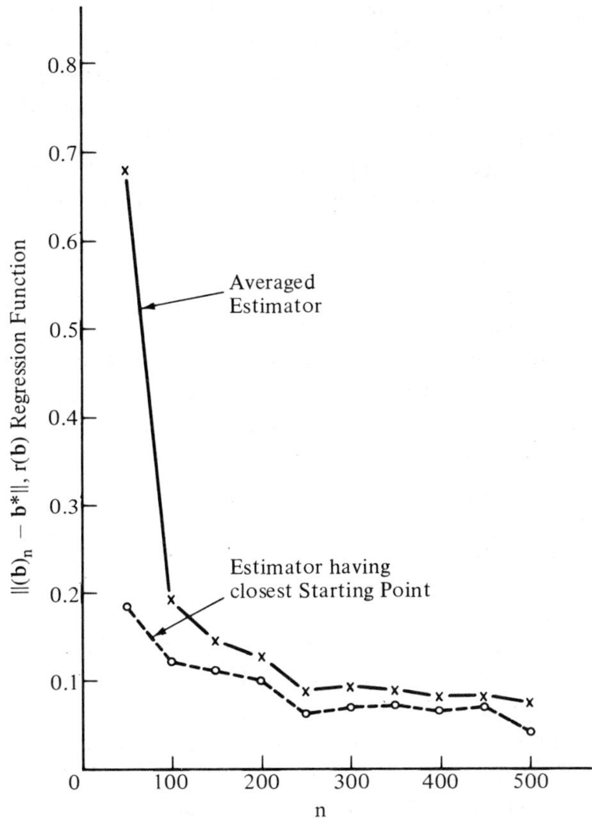

Fig. 5.3 Performance of averaged estimator based on $\Gamma(\mathbf{b})$

Although the averaging technique was discussed in connection with Kiefer–Wolfowitz type of s.a. method, it applies to the Robbins–Monro method as well.

If for a particular family of density functions, the regression function is multimodal, then the averaging technique may be employed to prevent convergence to a local maximum other than the global maximum, provided that V is large enough. That is, in addition to singling out the s.a. estimator having the best starting point, the averaging technique is also an automatic parallel-processing algorithm.

5-3.7 Pseudo-Deterministic Hill Climb

The merit of the Bayes approach is that, for one thing, it shows that $p(\mathbf{b}\,|\,\mathbf{x}_n)$ must be computed for each point $\mathbf{b}$ in the parameter space; of course, this can be impractical when there are many points in the parameter space. Because this a posteriori density is computed at each point $\mathbf{b}$, the Bayes estimator $(\mathbf{b})_n = \int \mathbf{b}p(\mathbf{b}|\mathbf{x}_n)\,d\mathbf{b}$ need not be starting-point-dependent. Stochastic approximation is, on the other hand, starting-point-dependent; given n iterations in the stochastic approximation algorithm, the estimator's performance may be expected to be very poor. An advantage of stochastic approximation is that it can be implemented with relatively little computation complexity.

Quasi-Bayes, introduced in the last section, is an attempt to combine the simplicity of stochastic approximation with the averaging effect of Bayes, which reduces starting-point dependence.

Another approach, actually suggested indirectly by the Bayes approach, which has increased computation time but is not so dependent on starting point, is developed as follows: Realize that the slow convergence of stochastic approximation stems partially from the fact that the sequences $\{a_s\}_{s=1}^n$ and $\{c_s\}_{s=1}^n$ that monitor the step sizes diminish to zero too rapidly to overcome the bias of the starting point. This, by the way, suggests that the sequences should be chosen based on an estimate of how close the starting point is to the true parameter. This is precisely one of the things that Bayes estimation accomplishes.

The stochastic approximation hill-climbing methods discussed in Chapter 2 increment estimators by an amount determined by an estimate of the gradient of the regression function. The gradient estimate, in turn, requires two noisy measurements of the regression function in the neighborhood of the parameter estimator. Each such measurement is based on one observation and has "some variance." If instead, each measurement of the regression function is a sample mean based on n observations, the variance will be multiplied by n^{-1}. The idea underlying the pseudo-deterministic hill climb, therefore, is simply to estimate† $\Gamma(\mathbf{b})$ by means of all n observations $\mathbf{x}_1$, $\mathbf{x}_2$, $\ldots$, $\mathbf{x}_n$, and then to employ a gradient-directed algorithm to determine the stationary point.

Denote the estimate of $\Gamma(\mathbf{b})$ based on $\mathbf{x}_1$, $\mathbf{x}_2$, $\ldots$, $\mathbf{x}_n$ by $\Gamma_n(\mathbf{b})$ computed as

$$\Gamma_n(\mathbf{b}) = \frac{1}{n}\sum_{s=1}^{n}\{2h(\mathbf{x}_s|\mathbf{b}) - \|h(\cdot|\mathbf{b})\|^2\}$$

$$= \frac{2}{n}\sum_{s=1}^{n}h(\mathbf{x}_s|\mathbf{b}) - \|h(\cdot|\mathbf{b})\|^2. \tag{79}$$

Let e be some prespecified allowable error in the parameter estimate and let c and d be positive constants with c smaller than e. Denote by $(\mathbf{b})_{n,k}$ the

---

†$\eta(\mathbf{b})$ could be used in place of $\Gamma(\mathbf{b})$.

kth recursive estimate of $\mathbf{b}^*$ based on n observations. The jth component $(b_j)_{n,\,k}$ is computed by means of the expression

$$(b_j)_{n,\,k+1} = (b_j)_{n,\,k} + \frac{d}{c}\,\Gamma((\mathbf{b})_{n,\,k} + c\mathbf{e}_j) - \Gamma_n((\mathbf{b})_{n,\,k})],\qquad(80)$$

where $\mathbf{e}_j$ is the unit vector with jth component 1 and other components zero.

Informally stated, the algorithm increments the estimator in the direction of the gradient by an amount proportional to the gradient. The iterations on k terminate when

$$\|(\mathbf{b})_{n,\,k+1} - (\mathbf{b})_{n,\,k}\| < e.\qquad(81)$$

The algorithm (80) does not present a storage problem; however, for large L, it may be impossible to search over all possible values of $\mathbf{b}$. The algorithm may have application as a follow-up to clustering where the starting vector point $(\mathbf{b}_j)_{n,\,1}$ has been determined using a clustering algorithm.

It must be emphasized that the estimator resulting from stochastic hill climb is generally not as good as the Bayes estimator. At best, the estimator $(\mathbf{b})_{n,\,\infty}$ *is the solution maximizing* $\Gamma_n(\mathbf{b})$ *or* $\eta_n(\mathbf{b})$ *if the information function is used. The Bayes estimator evaluates*

$$\eta_n(\mathbf{b}) = \frac{1}{n}\sum_{s=1}^{n}\ln h(\mathbf{x}_s\,|\,\mathbf{b})$$

for each point $\mathbf{b}$ *in the parameter space and then takes an average.*

5-3.8 A Class of Minimum-Integral-Square-Distance Algorithms

The class of minimum-integral-square-difference algorithms requires the restriction of $\mathscr{A}$ to a finite set $\{\boldsymbol{\alpha}^k\}_{k=1}^{N}$ of N vector points.

The *empirical distribution* of the mixture from n samples $\{\mathbf{x}_k\}_{k=1}^{n}$ is defined as†

$$C_n(\mathbf{x}) = \frac{1}{n}\sum_{k=1}^{n}\varkappa_{(\mathbf{x}_k,\,\infty)}(\mathbf{x})\qquad(82)$$

and the *empirical density* as

$$c_n(\mathbf{x}) = \frac{1}{n}\sum_{k=1}^{n}\delta(\mathbf{x} - \mathbf{x}_k),\qquad(83)$$

†The multidimensional cases can also use the tolerance-region approach defined in Chapter 3 and used to define the $k\mathrm{NN}_3$ rule of Chapter 4.

where $\varkappa$ and δ are the usual characteristic† and delta functions, respectively, and ∞ denotes an L-dimensional vector of infinities. Equations (82) and (83) will be generically referred to as *empirical mixture functions* and are estimates of what will be referred to as the *mixture functions*. Digital implementation of (82) or (83) implies storage of the $\{\mathbf{x}_k\}_{k=1}^n$ samples.

Another type of estimate of the mixture functions is the histogram of the distribution or density of the mixture. Defining N^* ordered regions $\{\mathscr{I}_k\}_{k=1}^{N^*}$ on a bounded portion of the observation space $\mathscr{V}_L$, where $\bigcup_{k=1}^{N^*} \mathscr{I}_k = \mathscr{V}_L$, $\mu(\mathscr{I}_k \cap \mathscr{I}_j) = 0$, $k \neq j$ (μ denotes Lebesque measure, and the ordering is arbitrary), the histogram estimate of the mixture density is

$$c_n(\mathbf{x}) = \sum_{k=1}^{N^*} \varkappa_{\mathscr{I}_k}(\mathbf{x})a_{k_n} \tag{84}$$

with

$$a_{k_n} = \left(\frac{n-1}{n}\right)a_{k_{n-1}} + \frac{1}{n}\varkappa_{\mathscr{I}_k}(\mathbf{x}_n), \qquad k = 1, \ldots, N^*. \tag{85}$$

The distribution histogram estimate is

$$C_n(\mathbf{x}) = \sum_{k=1}^{N^*} \varkappa_{\mathscr{I}_k}(\mathbf{x}) \sum_{t=1}^{k} a_{t_n}. \tag{86}$$

Equations (84) and (86) will be generically referred to as the *histogram mixture functions*. Digital implementation of (84) or (86) requires storage of the N^* coefficients $\{a_{k_n}\}$ and, either implicitly or explicitly, the regions $\{\mathscr{I}_k\}$.

We are interested in unbiased estimators of the mixing parameters of $\mathscr{F}$ which are contained‡ in $L_1 \cap L_2$ and which are optimum in the sense that they minimize the squared norm of the difference between the estimated mixture function using the finite family of functions and either the histogram mixture function or the empirical mixture function. The unbiased vector estimator $\hat{P}_n = (P_n(\boldsymbol{\alpha}^1), P_n(\boldsymbol{\alpha}^2), \ldots, P_n(\boldsymbol{\alpha}^N))$, which minimizes

$$\int \| c_n(\mathbf{x}) - \sum_{i=1}^{N} f(\mathbf{x}\,|\,\boldsymbol{\alpha}^i)P_n(\boldsymbol{\alpha}^i)\|^2 \, d\mathbf{x}, \tag{87}$$

is an example. Robbins functions [43] will be used in two simple stochastic-approximation algorithms that estimate mixing parameters. Each of these

---

†The characteristic function is defined as

$$\varkappa_{\mathscr{A}}(\mathbf{x}) = \begin{cases} 1, & \mathbf{x} \in \mathscr{A}, \\ 0, & \text{otherwise.} \end{cases}$$

‡L_1 denotes the space of absolute integrable functions and L_2 the space of square integrable functions.

two types of algorithms is combined into systems of algorithms. The construction, convergence in mean square, and the asymptotic limit of the mixing-parameter estimators when the assumed finite family does not contain all the active classes are discussed in this section.

The minimum-integral-square-difference algorithms presented use linear operators which are linear combinations of functions from the particular finite family. Because of this, as will be seen later, it is necessary for the functional family to be contained in $L_1 \cap L_2$. To obtain some different forms of these systems of algorithms, three new families of functions in $L_1 \cap L_2$ are derived from $\mathscr{F}$ (family of densities) and $\mathscr{F}'$ (family of distributions).

Although $\mathscr{F}'$ is not in $L_1 \cap L_2$, there exists a finite number $\gamma_0 > 0$ such that for any finite $\gamma > \gamma_0$ the family $\mathscr{F}^* = \{F^*(\mathbf{x}\,|\,\boldsymbol{\alpha}^i)\}_{i=1}^N$,

$$F^*(\mathbf{x}\,|\,\boldsymbol{\alpha}^i) = \begin{cases} F(\mathbf{x}\,|\,\boldsymbol{\alpha}^i), & \|\mathbf{x}\| < \gamma, \\ 0, & \text{otherwise,} \end{cases}$$

$$\mathbf{x} \in \mathscr{V}_L,\, i = 1, 2, \ldots, N, \qquad (88)$$

is in $L_1 \cap L_2$ and composed of linearly independent functions (i.e., if $\{F(\mathbf{x}\,|\,\boldsymbol{\alpha}^i)\}_{i=1}^N$ are linearly independent, then they are linearly independent on some bounded region, in particular $\|\mathbf{x}\| < \gamma_0$). The empirical distribution (82) of the mixture is similarly redefined zero outside $\{\mathbf{x}: \|\mathbf{x}\| < \gamma\}$.

The other two families are *intervalized* forms of the families $\mathscr{F}$ and $\mathscr{F}^*$†. These families have applications for systems that require storage of an estimate of the mixture function because use of these intervalized functions instead of $\mathscr{F}$ and $\mathscr{F}^*$ can result in less storage for the digital implementations of the systems.

Taking the set of regions $\{\mathscr{I}_j\}_{j=1}^{N^*}$, define a new family of functions (we assume that $\bigcup_{k=1}^{N^*} \mathscr{I}_k$ contains those points $\mathbf{x}: \|\mathbf{x}\| < \gamma$)

$$d(\mathbf{x}\,|\,\boldsymbol{\alpha}^i) = \sum_{j=1}^{N^*} \varkappa_{\mathscr{I}_j}(\mathbf{x}) b_{ij}, \qquad i = 1, 2, \ldots, N, \qquad (89)$$

where

$$b_{ij} = \int_{\mathscr{I}_j} f(\mathbf{x}\,|\,\boldsymbol{\alpha}^i)\, dx, \qquad i = 1, 2, \ldots, N, j = 1, 2, \ldots, N^*. \qquad (90)$$

The corresponding family of cumulative densities may be defined using (89) and (90),

$$D(\mathbf{x}\,|\,\boldsymbol{\alpha}^i) = \sum_{t=1}^{N^*} \varkappa_{\mathscr{I}_t}(\mathbf{x}) \sum_{j=1}^{t} b_{ij}, \qquad i = 1, 2, \ldots, N. \qquad (91)$$

†We are considering two possibilities: The empirical density approximating the mixture density is used in (87); now we are preparing to use a histogram approximation to the mixture density.

The functions $\{D(\mathbf{x}\,|\,\boldsymbol{\alpha}^i)\}_{i=1}^N$ are not in $L_1 \cap L_2$. However, we can retain their important properties in the cases of interest by requiring that

$$\mathscr{I}_{N^*} = \{\mathbf{x}: \|\mathbf{x}\| < \gamma, \mathbf{x} \in \mathscr{V}^L\},$$

$$b_{iN^*} = 0, \quad i = 1, 2, \ldots, N. \tag{92}$$

The resulting family, denoted $\{D^*(\mathbf{x}\,|\,\boldsymbol{\alpha}^i)\}_{i=1}^N$, is in $L_1 \cap L_2$. The histogram estimate (86) of the mixture distribution is similarly redefined on $\mathscr{I}_{N^*}$.

Linear independence of the functions $\{F(\mathbf{x}\,|\,\boldsymbol{\alpha}^i)\}_{i=1}^N$ on $\mathscr{V}^l - \mathscr{I}_{N^*}$ is a necessary and sufficient condition for the existence of at least one partition of $\mathscr{V}^l - \mathscr{I}_{N^*}$ into $N^* - 1$ disjoint regions $\{\mathscr{I}_i\}_{i=1}^{N^*}$ such that for $N^* > N$, the class of all finite mixtures of $\{D^*(\mathbf{x}\,|\,\boldsymbol{\alpha}^i)\}_{i=1}^N$ is identifiable (a consequence of Theorem 1 in [16]). Hence, the class of all finite mixtures of $\{d(\mathbf{x}\,|\,\boldsymbol{\alpha}^i)\}_{i=1}^N$ defined on this set $\{\mathscr{I}_i\}_{i=1}^{N^*}$ is also identifiable.†

The following description of the construction of systems of algorithms is with respect to the family $\mathscr{F}$; however, any of the defined families could be used with the corresponding interpretation of the system.

Unsupervised Estimation Systems Using Robbins Functions

The functions $\{f(\mathbf{x}\,|\,\boldsymbol{\alpha}^i)\}_{i=1}^{M'}$ from $\mathscr{F}$ span an M'-dimensional subspace U in $L_1 \cap L_2$.† Let $U_j^\perp$ be the orthogonal complement of the subspace spanned by $\{f(\mathbf{x}\,|\,\boldsymbol{\alpha}^i)\}_{i=1, i \neq j}^M$ in $L_1 \cap L_2$. Define the function

$$\varphi^i(\mathbf{x}) = \frac{f^\perp(\mathbf{x}\,|\,\boldsymbol{\alpha}^i)}{\|f^\perp(\mathbf{x}\,|\,\boldsymbol{\alpha}^i)\|^2}, \qquad i = 1, 2, \ldots, M', \tag{93}$$

where $f^\perp(\mathbf{x}\,|\,\boldsymbol{\alpha}^i)$ is the component of $f(\mathbf{x}\,|\,\boldsymbol{\alpha}^i) \in U_i^\perp$ and $\|\cdot\|^2$ the usual L_2 norm squared. The $\mathbf{x}$ functions have been called "Robbins functions" and have the property‡

$$\int \varphi^j(\mathbf{x}) f(\mathbf{x}\,|\,\boldsymbol{\alpha}^i)\, d\mathbf{x} = \delta_{ji}, \tag{94}$$

where δ_{ji} is the Kronecker delta. Assuming that the mixture density function $h(\mathbf{x})$ contains only functions in $\{f(\mathbf{x}\,|\,\boldsymbol{\alpha}^i)\}$,

$$\int \varphi^j(\mathbf{x}) h(\mathbf{x})\, d\mathbf{x} = \int \varphi^i(\mathbf{x}) \sum_{j=1}^{M'} f(\mathbf{x}\,|\,\boldsymbol{\alpha}^j) P(\boldsymbol{\alpha}^j)\, d\mathbf{x}$$

$$= P(\boldsymbol{\alpha}^i), \qquad i = 1, 2, \ldots, M'. \tag{95}$$

---

†Note that N is the number of points in the parameter space and N^* is the number of ordered regions in the observation space.

‡This is the property that required the redefinition of $\mathscr{F}$ and $\{D(\mathbf{x}\,|\,\boldsymbol{\alpha}^i)\}$ into functional families contained in $L_1 \cap L_2$.

Let $\alpha^{i(j,k)}$ be one of the parameter points $\alpha^1, \alpha^2, \ldots, \alpha^N$. In particular, it is the jth member of the kth possible subset of the N parameter points. If each subset is of size M', there are $\binom{N}{M'}$ subsets of parameters, and k denotes the kth subset. Equation (95) suggests the following algorithm for estimating $P(\alpha^{i(j,k)})$, the jth mixing parameter for the kth subset:

Algorithm 1

$$P_n(\alpha^{i(j,k)}) = \int \varphi^{i(j,k)}(\mathbf{x}) c_n(\mathbf{x}) \, d\mathbf{x}, \qquad i = 1, 2, \ldots, M', \qquad (96)$$

where c_n is the empirical probability density function of the samples defined by (83). The combination of the M' algorithms implicit in (96), where the φ functions are constructed over the subfamily, forms a subsystem whose structure is illustrated in Figure 5.4. This subsystem can be interpreted as an estimated mixture function which is processed by a blank of matched filters.

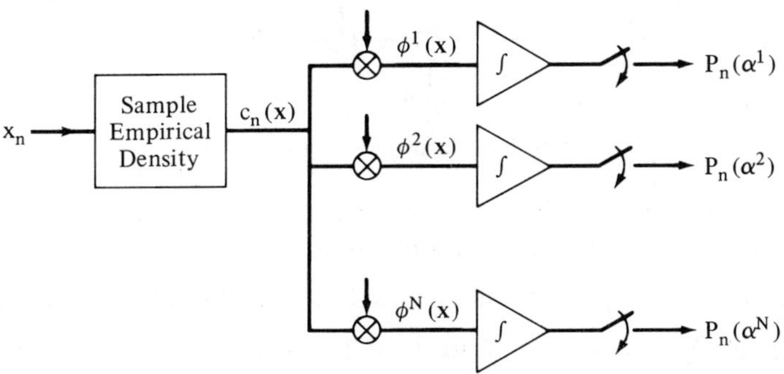

Fig. 5.4 Unsupervised estimation

Equation (94) shows a property of the expectation of the φ functions with respect to the $f(\mathbf{x}|\alpha^i)$. This suggests the basis of the second algorithm due to Robbins [43],

$$P_n(\alpha^{i(j,k)}) = \frac{1}{n} \sum_{s=1}^{n} \varphi^{i(j,k)}(\mathbf{x}_s), \qquad i = 1, 2, \ldots, M', \qquad (97)$$

or in terms of the last estimate of $P(\alpha^{i(j,k)})$,

Algorithm 2

$$P_n(\alpha^{i(j,k)}) = \frac{n-1}{n} P_{n-1}(\alpha^{i(j,k)}) + \frac{1}{n} \varphi^{i(j,k)}(\mathbf{x}_n),$$

$$i = 1, 2, \ldots, M'. \qquad (98)$$

The structure of the subsystem of M' algorithms implicit in (98) is shown in Figure 5.5.

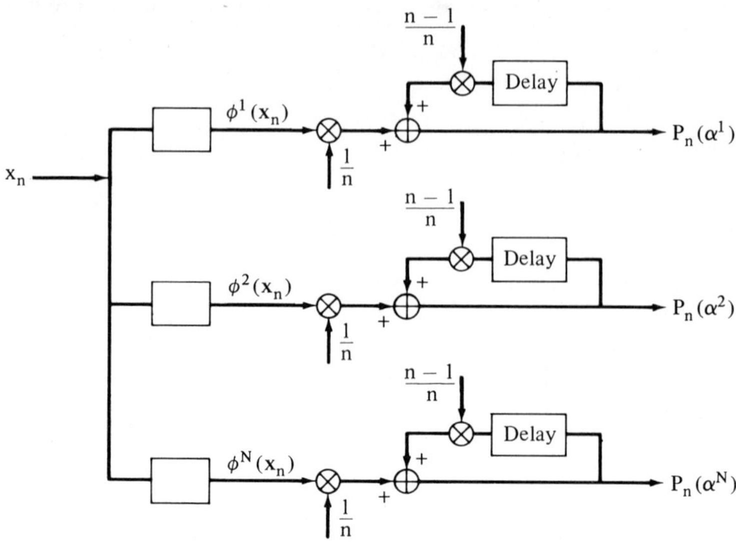

Fig. 5.5 Unsupervised estimation

The subsystems utilizing either algorithm 1 or 2 are now combined into the full unsupervised estimation system.

Each of the $\binom{N}{M'}$ subsystems has a mixture estimate after the nth sample given by $\sum_{j=1}^{M} f(\mathbf{x}\,|\,\alpha^{i(j,k)})P_n(\alpha^{i(j,k)})$. The system-mixture parameter estimate is defined as the parameters from the "closest" subfamily-mixture estimate to the empirical probability density function of the samples,

$$\{\alpha^{i(j,*)}P_n(\alpha^{i(j,*)})\}_{i=1}^{M'} = \arg\left[\min_k \int \|c_n(\mathbf{x}) - \sum_{j=1}^{M'} f(\mathbf{x}\,|\,\alpha^{i(j,k)})\right.$$

$$\left. \times P_n(\alpha^{i(j,k)})\|^2\, d\mathbf{x}\right], \tag{99}$$

where $*$ denotes the subfamily index minimizing (99). The structure of these systems of $\binom{N}{M'}$ subsystems is shown in Figures 5.6 and 5.7 for the algorithms defined by (96) and (98), respectively.

We now establish that the systems given by (99) using algorithms 1 or 2 minimize (87), as previously required. Taking the kth subfamily of $\mathscr{F}$ as before, the estimated mixture density function can be factored relative to $\{f(\mathbf{x}\,|\,\alpha^{i(j,k)})\}$ into $c'_{n_k}(\mathbf{x}) + c^{\perp}_{n_k}(\mathbf{x})$, where $c'_{n_k}(\mathbf{x})$ is the component of $c_n(\mathbf{x})$ in

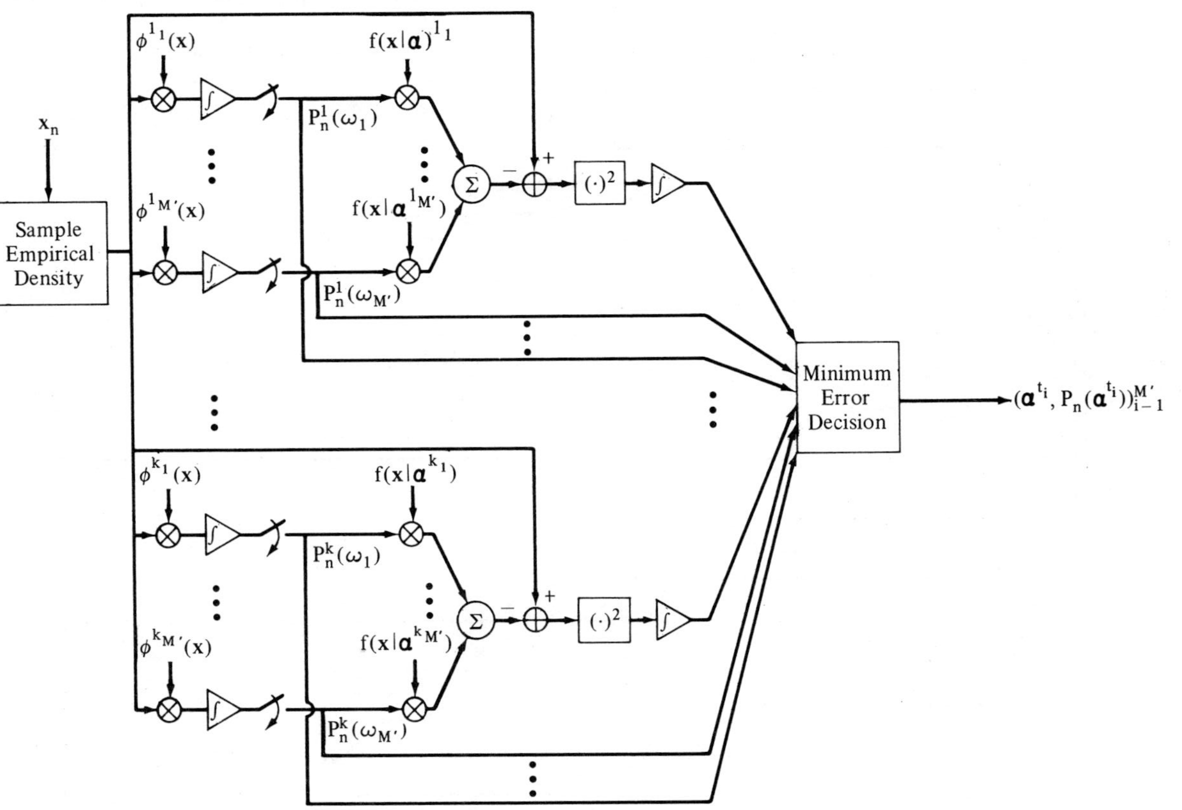

Fig. 5.6 Unsupervised estimation system using Algorithm 1, the family of densities $\mathscr{F}'$

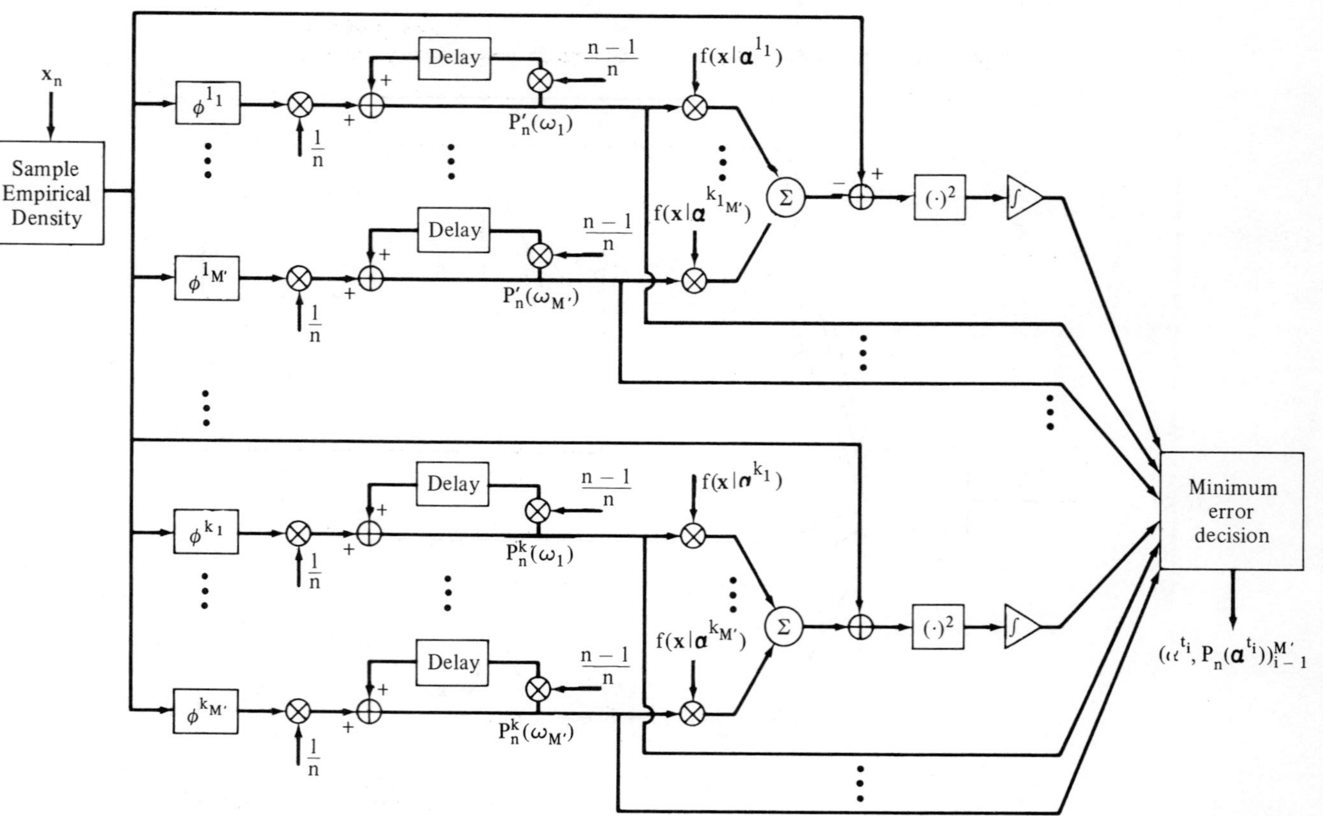

Fig. 5.7 Unsupervised estimation system using Algorithm 2, the family of densities $\mathscr{F}'$

the subspace spanned by $\{f(\mathbf{x}|\boldsymbol{\alpha}^{i(j,k)})\}_{j=1}^{M'}$ and $c_{n_k}^{\perp}(\mathbf{x})$ the perpendicular component. Evaluating the integral square difference,

$$\int (c_n(\mathbf{x}) - \sum_{j=1}^{M'} f(\mathbf{x}|\boldsymbol{\alpha}^{i(j,k)})P_n(\boldsymbol{\alpha}^{i(j,k)}))^2 \, d\mathbf{x}$$

$$= \int [c'_{n_k}(\mathbf{x}) + c_{n_k}^{\perp}(\mathbf{x}) - \sum_{j=1}^{M'} f(\mathbf{x}|\boldsymbol{\alpha}^{i(j,k)})]^2 \, d\mathbf{x}$$

$$= \int \| c_{n_k}^{\perp}(\mathbf{x}) \|^2 \, d\mathbf{x}. \tag{100}$$

As a consequence of (99) and (100), the integral square difference is minimized relative to the $\{f(\mathbf{x}|\boldsymbol{\alpha}^{i(j,k)})\}$ subfamilies.

Robbins-Function Construction

In the following discussion we let $M' = N$ and denote the Robbins functions $\{\varphi^k\}$ for notational simplicity. From their definition in (93), the φ^k functions are linear combinations of $\{f(\mathbf{x}|\boldsymbol{\alpha}^i)\}_{i=1}^{N}$,

$$\varphi^k(\mathbf{x}) = \sum_{i=1}^{N} a_{ki} f(\mathbf{x}|\boldsymbol{\alpha}^i). \tag{101}$$

Let $\mathbf{Q}$ denote an $N \times N$ matrix and define

$$q_{ij} = \int f(\mathbf{x}|\boldsymbol{\alpha}^i)f(\mathbf{x}|\boldsymbol{\alpha}^j) \, d\mathbf{x}. \tag{102}$$

Then (94) is satisfied if in matrix form

$$\mathbf{AQ} = \mathbf{I}, \tag{103}$$

$$\mathbf{A} = \mathbf{Q}^{-1}. \tag{104}$$

The row vectors of $\mathbf{A}$ give the coefficients for (101).

Convergence

If

$$\mathbf{p}_n = \left[\frac{1}{n} \sum_{s=1}^{n} \varphi^1(\mathbf{x}_s), \frac{1}{n} \sum_{s=1}^{n} \varphi^2(\mathbf{x}_s), \dots, \frac{1}{n} \sum_{s=1}^{n} \varphi^N(\mathbf{x}_s) \right]^t$$

is the vector of mixing parameter estimates based on n samples of a system with $M' = N$ and P_0 is the vector of true mixing parameters,

$$\mathbf{p}_0 = [P(\boldsymbol{\alpha}^1), P(\boldsymbol{\alpha}^2), \dots, P(\boldsymbol{\alpha}^N)]^t,$$

the mean-square error is

$$E[\|\mathbf{p}_n - \mathbf{p}_0\|^2] = \frac{1}{n} \sum_{k=1}^{N} E[\varphi^k(\mathbf{x}) - P(\boldsymbol{\alpha}^k)]^2, \tag{105}$$

using the results that $E[\varphi^k(\mathbf{x})] = P(\boldsymbol{\alpha}^k)$ and $\varphi^k(\mathbf{x}_s)$ is statistically independent of $\varphi^k(\mathbf{x}_j)$ for $j \neq s$.

Using the strong law of large numbers it can be concluded that $\mathbf{p}_n$ converges to $\mathbf{p}_0$ with probability 1.

Asymptotic Estimates

For many problems representing the parameter space with the finite set, $\{\boldsymbol{\alpha}^i\}_{i=1}^{N}$ may be an approximation. Nevertheless, with probability 1 the values obtained by sequential application of the algorithm converge at a rate $0(1/n)$, although not necessarily to the true parameter. To investigate the limits, let $\sum_{i=1}^{M} f_i(\mathbf{x})P_i$ denote the *true mixture*. Then the estimator for $P(\boldsymbol{\alpha}^{i(j,k)})$, denoted $P_n(\boldsymbol{\alpha}^{i(j,k)})$, has a limit,

$$\begin{aligned}
\lim_{n \to \infty} P_n(\boldsymbol{\alpha}^{i(j,k)}) &= \int \varphi^{i(j,k)}(\mathbf{x}) \sum_{s=1}^{M} f_s(\mathbf{x})P_s \, d\mathbf{x} \\
&= \sum_{s=1}^{M} P_s \int \varphi^{i(j,k)}(\mathbf{x})f_s(\mathbf{x}) \, d\mathbf{x}.
\end{aligned} \tag{106}$$

It might be useful also to observe that if $h(\mathbf{x}) \notin \mathrm{span}\{f(\mathbf{x}\,|\,\boldsymbol{\alpha}^{i(j,k)})\}$, then, with probability 1,

$$\lim_{n \to \infty} \sum_{i=1}^{n} P_n(\boldsymbol{\alpha}^i) < 1. \tag{107}$$

5-3.9 Consistent Estimators for Finite Mixtures of an Infinite Family

The unsupervised estimation algorithms discussed in the previous two sections required the restriction of $\mathscr{A}$ to a finite set, a pragmatic assumption that can be eliminated. In this section we present two variations of a search algorithm which provide consistent estimators for finite mixtures of an infinate family. Assumptions made include boundedness of $\mathscr{A}$ and a finite upper bound M' on the number of active classes, both sets of bounds known.

Because $\mathscr{A}$ is bounded, $(\mathscr{A} \times \mathscr{P})^{M'}$ is bounded and there exists a finite set of vectors $\mathbf{b}^{k_a}$ such that

$$\mathbf{b}^{k_a} \in (\mathscr{A} \times \mathscr{P})^{M'}, \tag{108}$$

$$\bigcup_{\{\mathbf{b}^{k_a}\}} N\left(\mathbf{b}^{k_a}, \frac{1}{a}\right) \supset (\mathscr{A} \times \mathscr{P})^{M'}, \tag{109}$$

where

$$N_{\frac{1}{a}}(\mathbf{b}^{k_a}) = \left\{\mathbf{b}: \|\mathbf{b} - \mathbf{b}^{k_a}\| < \frac{1}{a}, \mathbf{b}^{k_a} \in (\mathscr{A} \times \mathscr{P})^{M'}\right\}. \tag{110}$$

Equations (109) and (110) simply state that a finite number of spheres with radius $1/a$ cover the product parameter space as illustrated in Figure 5.8. Denote the set of points consisting of the centers of the spheres:

$$\mathscr{B}^{Ma'} = \{\mathbf{b}^{k_a}\}. \tag{111}$$

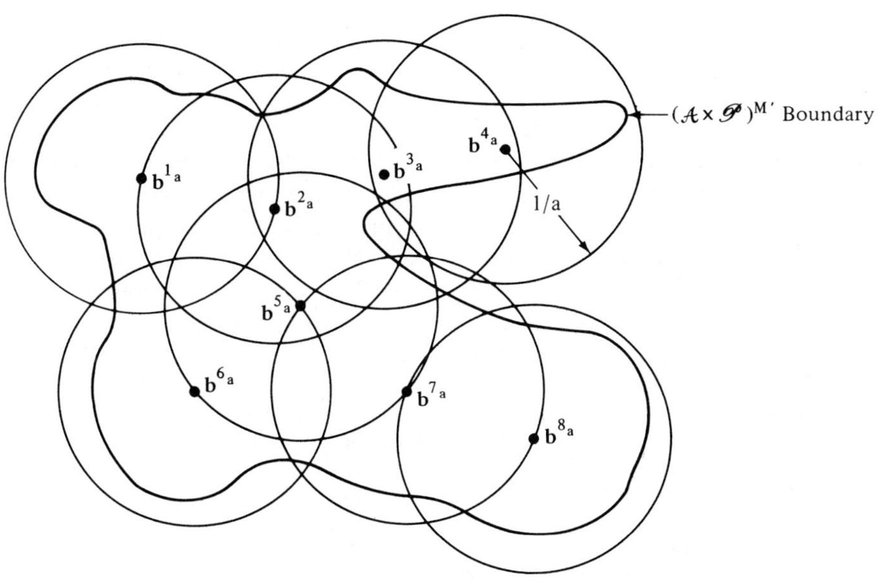

Fig. 5.8 Coverage of the product parameter space by a set of spheres with radius $1/a$

The solution vector $\mathbf{b}^* \in \mathscr{B}^{M'}$ and $\min\limits_{\mathbf{b}^{k_a}} \|\mathbf{b}^0 - \mathbf{b}^{k_a}\| < 1/a$. The construction of a $1/a$ net satisfying (108) through (110) is extremely simple.† If $\mathscr{A}$ is rectangular, for example, a computer program can index the entire net while storing only the base or starting point and the step size for each of the different vector components.

†As n becomes large, the number of computations becomes unwieldly, however. For fixed a, required memory is relatively simple for "small" n sample size, but we soon shall see that the required memory increases linearly with n.

Define the estimator

$$(\mathbf{b})_{n,a} = \arg\{\min_{\mathbf{b}^k}[\sup_{\mathbf{x}}|\,C_n(\mathbf{x}) - H(\mathbf{x}\,|\,\mathbf{b}^k)\,|]\, \mathbf{b}^k \in \mathscr{B}^{M_{a'}} \cap \mathscr{B}^{M'}\}, \qquad (112)$$

where C_n is defined by (82) and the parameter conditional mixture distribution function $H(\mathbf{x}\,|\,\mathbf{b}^k)$ in Chapter 2. This estimator finds the "closest" acceptable point in the $1/a$ net to the empirical distribution function of the samples. A similar problem where α is one-dimensional and $\alpha \in (-\infty, \infty)$ has been solved by Robbins [43]. Although he did not specifically allow a $1/a$ net, it can be used with his formulation of the problem. Robbins's proof requires completeness of the mixture functional space, and the class of all finite mixtures of an infinite family is not complete. Yakowitz and Spragins [19] have constructed a necessarily complex argument for convergence of an estimator similar to that of (112) (however, with a net on $\mathscr{A}$ only) for the class of all finite mixtures.† For such an estimator to be implementable, of course, either the mixing parameters must be known or the net extended to them. In contrast to Yakowitz and Spragins's argument, the convergence proof given below for the class of finite mixtures with an upper bound on the number of classes considered possibly active is extremely simple—in practice, any implementation will require such a bound either explicitly (e.g., a priori bound) or implicitly (e.g., the total available storage). We now show that $(\mathbf{b})_{n,a}$ converges to $\mathbf{b}^*$ with probability 1.

Theorem. Defining the distance between any two distribution functions F_1 and F_2

$$\rho(F_1, F_2) = \sup_{\mathbf{x}}|\,F_1(\mathbf{x}) - F_2(\mathbf{x})\,|, \qquad (113)$$

if

1. for every fixed $\mathbf{x}$, $F(\mathbf{x}\,|\,\boldsymbol{\alpha})$ is continuous (e) with respect to $\boldsymbol{\alpha}$,
2. an upper bound M' is known,
3. $\mathscr{B}^{M'}$ is closed and contains the true vector $\mathbf{b}^*$,
4. $\{\mathscr{H} : H(\mathbf{x}\,|\,\mathbf{b}), \mathbf{b} \in \mathscr{B}^{M'}\}$ is identifiable,

then

$$p[\lim_{\substack{n\to\infty \\ a\to\infty}} (\mathbf{b})_{n,a} = \mathbf{b}^*] = 1.$$

Proof: Because of the continuity (ρ) of $F(\mathbf{x}\,|\,\boldsymbol{\alpha})$ with respect to $\boldsymbol{\alpha}$, $H(\mathbf{x}\,|\,\mathbf{b})$ is continuous (ρ) in $\mathbf{b}$, so letting

†See also [69].

$$\mathbf{b}_{\min_n} = \arg\{\min_{\mathbf{b}^k} \rho(H(\mathbf{x}\,|\,\mathbf{b}^k), C_n(\mathbf{x})); \mathbf{b}^k \in \mathcal{B}^{M'}\},$$

$$\epsilon_{n,r} = \rho(H(\mathbf{x}\,|\,\mathbf{b}_{\min_n}), H(\mathbf{x}\,|\,(\mathbf{b})_{n,a})), \tag{114}$$

then $\epsilon_{n,a} \longrightarrow 0$ as $a \longrightarrow \infty$. By the Glivenko–Cantelli theorem,

$$p[\lim_{n\to\infty} \rho(C_n(\mathbf{x}), H(\mathbf{x}\,|\,\mathbf{b}^*)) = 0] = 1 \tag{115}$$

and since

$$\rho(H(\mathbf{x}\,|\,(\mathbf{b})_{n,a}), H(\mathbf{x}\,|\,\mathbf{b}^*)) \leq 2\rho(H(\mathbf{x}\,|\,\mathbf{b}^*), C_n) + \epsilon_{n,a}, \tag{116}$$

then from [40] with probability 1 the sequence $\mathbf{x}_1, \mathbf{x}_2, \ldots$ is such that

$$\lim_{\substack{n\to\infty \\ a\to\infty}} H(\mathbf{x}\,|\,(\mathbf{b})_{n,a}) = H(\mathbf{x}\,|\,\mathbf{b}^*). \tag{117}$$

Now fix the sequence $\mathbf{x}_1, \mathbf{x}_2, \ldots$, satisfying (117) and choose any convergent subsequence from the sequence of $(\mathbf{b})_{n,a}$ estimates that it generates. Because of assumptions 3 and 4, the limit point of this subsequence is $\mathbf{b}^*$. Since this holds for any convergent subsequence,

$$p[\lim_{\substack{n\to\infty \\ a\to\infty}} \mathbf{b}_{n,a} = \mathbf{b}^*] = 1, \tag{118}$$

which completes the proof.

Comments. Although the boundedness condition of $\mathcal{B}^{M'}$ was not needed in the theorem to prove convergence, it is necessary to implement $(\mathbf{b})_{n,a}$. Also, the manner in which $a \longrightarrow \infty$ was not specified. Examples of possible sequences include $a = n$, $a = n^{1/2}$, etc. Similar comments about $\mathcal{B}^{M'}$ and the net can be made on the next algorithm. In a practical system it may be necessary to stop a at some $a = a'$. The asymptotic estimate is then given by

$$(\mathbf{b})_{\infty,a'} = \arg\{\min_{\mathbf{b}^k}[\sup_{\mathbf{x}}|H(\mathbf{x}) - H(\mathbf{x}\,|\,\mathbf{b}^k)|]\,\mathbf{b}^k \in \mathcal{B}^{M'a'} \cap \mathcal{B}^{M'}\}, \tag{119}$$

where $H(\mathbf{x})$ is the true mixture distribution. Incidentally, one family satisfying condition 1 of the theorem is the L-dimensional Gaussian family.

This algorithm requires storage of the empirical conditional density function of the mixture. Although the tolerance-region approach defined in Chapter 3 and used in Chapter 4 in the $k\mathrm{NN}_3$ decision rule may be used to reduce the number of samples stored, it is not very difficult to construct examples† that for reasonable n give a poor performance in terms of

---

†One such example is a moderate signal-to-noise ratio case, where there is significant overlap of the class densities. Experience indicates that the decision-directed method can perform well for this example (see Section 5-5), whereas the sample-space minimization technique may not.

$\| (\mathbf{b})_{n,a} - \mathbf{b}^* \|$, particularly compared to an a posteriori approach. A block diagram for this method of minimum-distance unsupervised estimation† is shown in Figure 5.9.

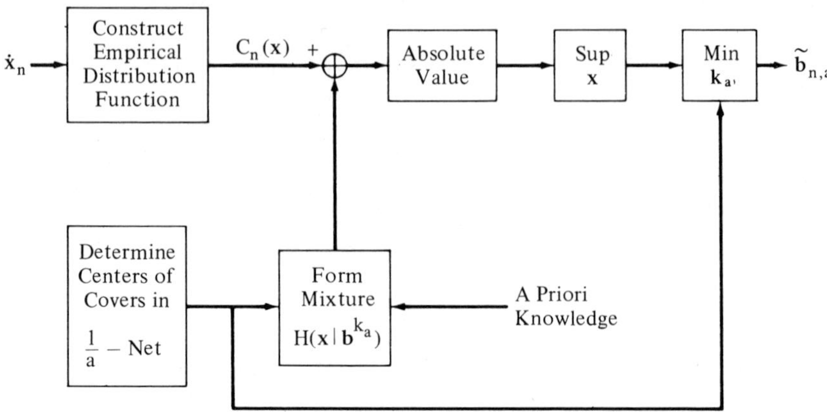

Fig. 5.9 $1/a$—Net sample space minimum distance, unsupervised estimation

Parameter-Space Maximization

The second variation of the search algorithm maximizes the weighted likelihood function over $\mathscr{B}_{M_{a'}}$. Define the estimator

$$(\bar{\mathbf{b}})_{n,a} = \arg\left\{\max_{\mathbf{b}^k}\left[\prod_{j=1}^{n} h(\mathbf{x}_j \mid \mathbf{b}^k)p_0(\mathbf{b}^k)\right]; \mathbf{b}^k \in \mathscr{B}^{M_{a'}} \cap \mathscr{B}^{M'}\right\} \qquad (120)$$

where $p_0(\cdot)$ is the a priori parameter density function on $\mathscr{B}^{M'}$. This algorithm selects as the estimate the point in the $1/a$ net for which the a posteriori density is maximum. In the following theorem for any function $g(\mathbf{x})$ define

$$E_{\mathbf{b}^*}[g(\mathbf{x})] \triangleq \int g(\mathbf{x})h(\mathbf{x} \mid \mathbf{b}^*)\, d\mathbf{x}, \qquad (121)$$

where $h(\mathbf{x} \mid \mathbf{b}^*)$ is the true mixture function.

Theorem. If

1. $\mathscr{B}^{M'}$ is closed and $p_0(\mathbf{b})$ is continuous on $\mathscr{B}^{M'}$ with $p_0(\mathbf{b}^*) > 0$,
2. $h(\mathbf{x} \mid \mathbf{b})$ is jointly measurable $[\mu]$ in $\mathbf{x}$, $\mathbf{b}$,

---

†The idea of a search over the parameter space minimizing the distance measure of (119) was initially suggested by Patrick ([13], p. 44–45).

        Unsupervised Estimation   Chap. 5

3. the first- and second-order partials of $\ln h(\mathbf{x}\,|\,\mathbf{b})$ with respect to the components θ_k of $\mathbf{b}$ exist and are continuous,
4. $E_{\mathbf{b}^*}[\sup\{\partial^2 \ln h(\mathbf{x}\,|\,\mathbf{b})/\partial\theta_i\,\partial\theta_j : \|\mathbf{b}-\mathbf{b}^*\| < \epsilon, \mathbf{b} \in \mathscr{B}^{M'}] < \infty$ for some radius $\epsilon > 0$; conditions 3 and 4 imply that

$$E_{\mathbf{b}^*}\left[\frac{\partial \ln h(x\,|\,\mathbf{b})}{\partial\theta_k}\bigg|_{\mathbf{b}^*}\right] = 0,$$

$$c_{ij}(\mathbf{b}^*) = -E_{\mathbf{b}^*}\left[\frac{\partial^2 \ln h(x\,|\,\mathbf{b})}{\partial\theta_i\,\partial\theta_j}\bigg|_{\mathbf{b}^*}\right] = E_{\mathbf{b}^*}\left[\frac{\partial \ln h}{\partial\theta_i}\frac{\partial \ln h}{\partial\theta_j}\bigg|_{\mathbf{b}^*}\right],$$

5. $\mathbf{C}(\mathbf{b}^*)$ is a positive definite matrix,
6. $E_{\mathbf{b}^*}[\sup\{\ln h(\mathbf{x}\,|\,\mathbf{b}) - \ln h(\mathbf{x}\,|\,\mathbf{b}^*)\} : \|\mathbf{b}-\mathbf{b}^*\| > \epsilon, \mathbf{b} \in \mathscr{B}^{M'}] < 0$ for $\epsilon > 0$,
7. a bound M' on the number of active classes is known,
8. $\{h(\mathbf{x}\,|\,\mathbf{b}^k) : \mathbf{b}^k \in \mathscr{B}_{M'}\}$ is identifiable,

then

$$p[\lim_{\substack{n\to\infty \\ a\to\infty}}(\bar{\mathbf{b}})_{n,\,a} = \mathbf{b}^*] = 1.$$

Proof: Letting

$$\mathbf{b}_{\max_n} = \arg\left\{\max_{\mathbf{b}^k \in \mathscr{B}^{M'}} \prod_{j=1}^{n} h(\mathbf{x}_j\,|\,\mathbf{b}^k)p_0(\mathbf{b}^k)\right\}, \tag{122}$$

$$\epsilon_{n,\,a} = \|\mathbf{b}_{\max_n} - (\bar{\mathbf{b}})_{n,\,a}\|, \tag{123}$$

then from conditions 1 and 3, $\prod_{j=1}^{n} h(\mathbf{x}_j\,|\,\mathbf{b})p_0(\mathbf{b})$ is uniformly continuous with respect to $\mathbf{b}$. Hence

$$\lim_{a\to\infty} \epsilon_{n,\,a} = 0. \tag{124}$$

Since $\mathbf{b}_{\max_n}$ is the maximum-likelihood estimator on the continuous parameter space, as a consequence of results in [7] (p. 308, Theorem 6), under assumptions of this theorem,

$$p[\lim_{n\to\infty} \|\mathbf{b}_{\max_n} - \mathbf{b}^*\| = 0] = 1. \tag{125}$$

Using the triangle inequality,

$$\|(\bar{\mathbf{b}})_{n,\,a} - \mathbf{b}^*\| \le \|\mathbf{b}_{\max_n} - \mathbf{b}^*\| + \|(\bar{\mathbf{b}})_{n,\,a} - \mathbf{b}_{\max_n}\|, \tag{126}$$

and from (124) and (125) we obtain

$$p[\lim_{\substack{n\to\infty \\ a\to\infty}}(\bar{\mathbf{b}})_{n,\,a} = \mathbf{b}^*] = 1, \tag{127}$$

proving the theorem.

The class of minimum-integral-square-difference algorithms defined in Section 5-3.8 involves approximating the parameter space with a finite set of vector points $\{\boldsymbol{\alpha}^k\}_{k=1}^N$. Although the orthogonal φ^i functions can be computed a priori with any degree of precision, the values of the q_{ij} are between zero and 1; resulting round-off-error problems in computing the higher-dimensionality inverse matrices are easily complicated. Systems using the degenerate cases where $M' = N$ have a lower storage requirement than most systems with $1 < M' < N$. However, as the a priori upper bound M' is increased, the φ^i functions become more complex and discrimination between mixture functions becomes more difficult (implying slower convergence). Since the limit (with $M' = N$) of the $\binom{N}{M'}$ subsystems is the degenerate system, its relatively low complexity may be at a cost of slower convergence. Algorithms using this degenerate form of the unsupervised estimation system have a storage advantage over discretized a posteriori density approaches because only the parameter space $\mathscr{A}$ is discretized rather than the product parameter space $(\mathscr{A} \times \mathscr{P})^{M'}$. However, the structure $h(\mathbf{x}|\mathbf{b})$ is not used in forming the empirical mixture function (either explicitly in algorithm 1 or implicitly in algorithm 2). This results, for example, in poor small-sample performance relative to a posteriori approaches for problems of moderate signal-to-noise ratio, where a few samples from each class adequately define the statistics. It is the author's opinion that the most practical use of the orthogonal-functions concept appears to be in a suboptimum system utilizing convolutional functional forms combined with adaptive binning of samples.

The assumptions used in the second theorem of Section 5-8 are a slight specialization of the mixture equivalent to LeCam's [30] results establishing asymptotic normality of the a posteriori density and asymptotic properties of the maximum-likelihood estimator. These assumptions are somewhat stronger than the weakest needed to prove convergence. If it should be necessary to truncate the net at some $a = a'$, the asymptotic estimate can be obtained from the theorem in Section 5-3.1.

The algorithm producing the estimate $(\bar{\mathbf{b}})_{n,\,a}$ is not iterative and requires storage of the samples. Again an adaptive bin approach may significantly reduce the storage problem while yielding useful results. Several other algorithms using the $1/a$-net are immediately obvious. For example, the Bayes estimator for a quadratic loss function could be found under the conditions of the second theorem in Section 5-8. Another method might be to use a net with a fixed number of points but adaptive spacing in an a posteriori approach.

A block diagram of the parameter-space maximization system using the $1/a$ net is shown in Figure 5.10.

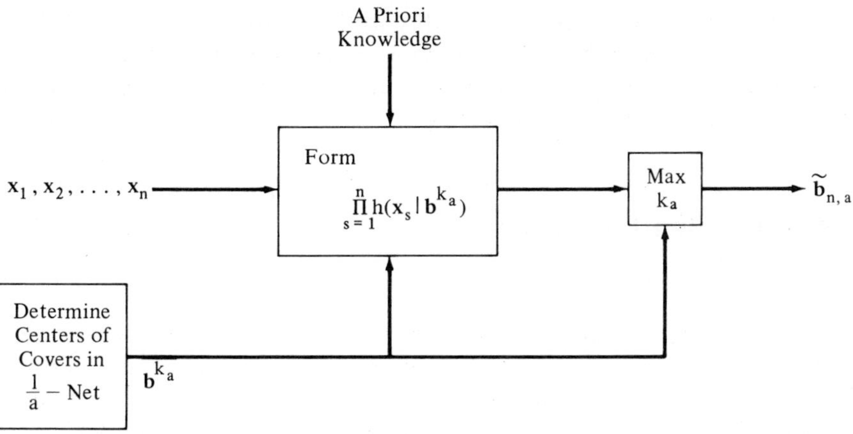

Fig. 5.10 $1/a$—Net parameter space maximization, unsupervised estimation

Implementation Limitations of 1/a-Net Approaches

Storage is proportional to the product nL but may not be a valid measure of implementation difficulty for $1/a$-net algorithms. As the net spacing is reduced, the number of points for which (112) or (120) must be evaluated grows as a *power of a*. The limitation of implementing the algorithms can thus be *time* as well as *storage*. The exchange of increased computing time for a decrease in required storage for "small" a may be very desirable for some applications.

The section on Bayes estimates using a discretized subset of the product parameter space $\mathscr{B}^{M'}$ established strong convergence properties of the estimators with the rate of convergence to the asymptotic vector depending on the largest even power of $E[|\ln h(\mathbf{x} \mid \mathbf{b}^k)|^s]$, $\mathbf{b}^k \in \mathscr{B}^{M'}$, which is finite. The asymptotic estimate was shown to be the point that maximized the measure of information. The convergence proof indicated conditions under which the asymptotic vector estimate is the closest point in $\mathscr{B}^{M'}$ to $\mathbf{b}^0$ (true parameter vector) in the distance measure determined by the Fisher information matrix.

The $1/a$-net approaches discussed in Section 5-3.8 search a bounded subset of the product parameter space in a systematic way and have the advantage of a relatively low initial storage. However, the storage grows with n and the time to compute the (n, a)th estimate also grows with a power of a. There does appear to be a possibility of using an adaptive spacing with a fixed number of points in an a posteriori approach, but the storage and computation time still grow with the number of samples.

Clustering algorithms can have enormously lower complexity requirements than the ones considered in this section. Essentially, this is because most clustering algorithms involve the a priori assumption that the density functions in the mixture are separable and do not utilize a criterion that evaluates the quality of the clustering.

5-4 Clustering Techniques

5-4.1 Introduction

Clustering techniques provide practical solutions to unsupervised estimation for many problems. First there are clustering techniques that must locate the modes of a category density function $f_i(\mathbf{x})$ when dimensionality L is large. Next there are clustering techniques suited for two- and three-dimensional problems in image processing.

Again using the Bayes framework, we shall introduce the concept of clustering with the information function $\eta(\mathbf{b})$, which naturally arose in the Bayes minimum-conditional-risk solution.

5-4.2 Clustering Technique Derived from $\eta(b)$

In this section $\eta(\mathbf{b})$ is investigated under the assumption that the categories are Gaussian and "separated." In a subsequent section $\Gamma(\mathbf{b})$ is utilized in a similar manner. In a certain sense $\Gamma(\mathbf{b})$ is easier to utilize to achieve the clustering concept. The procedure developed is to search for a partition of the observation space for which $\eta(\mathbf{b})$ is maximum. The $\mathbf{b}$ associated with this partition involves the mean, covariance, and number of samples of each category in the respective regions of the partition.

This approach presumes a search over the admissible partitions and thus admissible $\mathbf{b}$ given n samples. The approach can be made interactive by updating the partition upon receipt of sample $n+1$ without having stored the previous n samples. Advantages and disadvantages of the approach are summarized as follows:

Advantages

1. A criterion such as $\eta(\mathbf{b})$ evaluates the goodness of the clustering. The use of a criterion may be necessary when the number of categories M is unknown.
2. The partition based on n samples is updated with the $n+1$st sample without need to store the first n samples.
3. A priori knowledge about P_i and the other category parameters can be utilized. This is important for human interaction, especially when the number of categories is unknown.

                                    Unsupervised Estimation   Chap. 5

Disadvantages

1. The procedure may not work well when the "separable" criterion is violated.
2. The procedure does not provide for assuming (if true) that the categories are widely separated; consequently, the partition adjustment procedure may be more complex than necessary for the problem concerned.

A procedure having the above properties is now developed.

Asymptotic Minimum-Risk Solutions Under a Separable Assumption

For an asymptotic minimum-risk solution it is necessary to find the parameter vector $\mathbf{b} \in \mathscr{B}^{M'}$, with M nonzero mixing parameters $M < M'$, that maximizes

$$\eta(\mathbf{b}) = \int \ln h(\mathbf{x} \mid \mathbf{b}) h(\mathbf{x}) \, d\mathbf{x}$$

$$= \int \ln \left[\sum_{k=1}^{M} f(\mathbf{x} \mid \mathbf{b}_k) P_k \right] h(\mathbf{x}) \, d\mathbf{x} \tag{1}$$

In this section the sample space is partitioned into M disjoint regions, where the regions are defined†

$$S^k \triangleq \{\mathbf{x} : f(\mathbf{x} \mid \mathbf{b}_k) P_k > f(\mathbf{x} \mid \mathbf{b}_j) P_j \text{ all } j \neq k\},$$

$$k = 1, 2, \ldots, M, \tag{2}$$

given a parameter vector $\mathbf{b}$. It is assumed that over each partitioned set the class density is Gaussian having mean vector $\mathbf{m}_k$, covariance matrix $\mathbf{\Sigma}_k$, with the density truncated at the partition boundary.‡ The true mixture $h(\mathbf{x})$ is assumed bounded.

Under these assumptions $\eta(\mathbf{b})$ in (1) can be expanded,

$$\eta(\mathbf{b}) = \sum_{k=1}^{M} \int_{S^k} \ln[f(\mathbf{x} \mid \mathbf{b}_k) P_k] h(\mathbf{x}) \, d\mathbf{x}$$

$$= \sum_{k=1}^{M} \left[\int_{S^k} h(\mathbf{x}) \, d\mathbf{x} \right] \left\{ \ln P_k + \ln \left[\frac{1}{(2\pi)^{L/2} |\mathbf{\Sigma}_k|^{1/2}} \right] \right.$$

$$\left. - \frac{1}{2} \frac{\int_{S^k} (\mathbf{x} - \mathbf{m}_k)^t (\mathbf{\Sigma}_k)^{-1} (\mathbf{x} - \mathbf{m})_k h(\mathbf{x}) \, d\mathbf{x}}{\int_{S^k} h(\mathbf{x}) \, d\mathbf{x}} \right\}. \tag{3}$$

†Also see Ruspini [86].
‡Separability results from this truncation assumption.

In this section we assume a value for M, and then $\mathbf{b}$, and evaluate $\eta(\mathbf{b})$. Then we vary M and $\mathbf{b}$, to see if $\eta(\mathbf{b})$ increases or decreases.

General-Case Maximization of Separable $\eta(\mathbf{b})$

Ignoring for now the definition of the $\{S^k\}_{k=1}^M$ regions in (2), take a *fixed* set of regions characterized by independent parameters. It can be shown by taking partial derivatives with respect to each parameter under the constraint $\sum_{k=1}^M P_k = 1$ that for this fixed partition, (3) is maximized if the parameters are defined,

$$P_k = \int_{S^k} h(\mathbf{x})\,d\mathbf{x},$$

$$\mathbf{m}_k = \int_{S^k} \mathbf{x}h(\mathbf{x})\,d\mathbf{x} \bigg/ \int_{S^k} h(\mathbf{x})\,d\mathbf{x},$$

$$\boldsymbol{\Sigma}_k = \int_{S^k} (\mathbf{x} - \mathbf{m}_k)(\mathbf{x} - \mathbf{m}_k)^t h(\mathbf{x})\,d\mathbf{x} \bigg/ \int_{S^k} h(\mathbf{x})\,d\mathbf{x},$$

$$k = 1, 2, \ldots, M. \qquad (4)$$

Since these definitions maximize (3) for any partition into M regions, they maximize $\eta(\mathbf{b})$ for the regions satisfying (2). If the parameters are defined as in (4), then maximizing $\eta(\mathbf{b})$ is equivalent to finding the partition and the value of M which maximizes

$$\eta(\mathbf{b}) = \sum_{k=1}^M P_k \ln\left[\frac{P_k}{(2\pi)^{L/2}|\boldsymbol{\Sigma}_k|^{1/2}}\right] - \frac{L}{2}. \qquad (5)$$

This equation illustrates the advantage of the separable approach. Equation (5) for $\eta(\mathbf{b})$ may be useful for determining the quality of M or the significance of relatively small mixing-parameter estimates. There is a cost associated with the separable Gaussian assumption—the inability to resolve mixtures having low signal-to-noise ratios except in some cases where M is known. One aspect of the resolution problem for M unknown is investigated in [70].

If the complexity-reducing assumption that $\boldsymbol{\Sigma}_k = (\sigma_k)^2\mathbf{I}$ is made, it can be shown, by taking partial derivatives as discussed previously, that $(\sigma_k)^2$ should be defined as

$$(\sigma_k)^2 = \frac{\int_{S^k} \|\mathbf{x} - \mathbf{m}_k\|^2 h(\mathbf{x})\,d\mathbf{x}}{\int_{S^k} h(\mathbf{x})\,d\mathbf{x}}, \qquad k = 1, 2, \ldots, M. \qquad (6)$$

This subsection has been concerned with determining a criterion for evaluating the quality of estimated parameters and the corresponding partition [defined by (2)]. The following subsection presents one approach for maximizing $\eta(\mathbf{b})$ using estimators corresponding to (4); the reader may think of other approaches.

Unsupervised Estimation Algorithm for Maximizing $\eta(\mathbf{b})$ Under a Separable Gaussian Assumption

This unsupervised estimation algorithm is designed to maximize the $\eta(\mathbf{b})$ criterion (5) given an upper bound M' on the number of classes. Since the algorithm operates without knowledge of the number of classes M which maximizes (5), it is always possible that M' is not chosen large enough. This algorithm will provide an indication when M' should be increased so that the maximum of $\eta(\mathbf{b})$ can be reached. The algorithm utilizes $\eta(\mathbf{b})$ to determine whether $\eta(\mathbf{b})$ is maximized by assigning a sample to one of M' classes, or maximized by combining two classes and defining the sample as a new class. No convergence proof has been presented.

A distinction is maintained in the algorithm between two types of statistical classes: *isolated points* and *clusters*. A cluster is a collection of samples; an isolated point is a single sample which potentially generates a new cluster. The number of clusters which the algorithm determines as maximizing $\eta(\mathbf{b})$ is M^*. The $M' - M^*$ isolated points have no effect on $\eta(\mathbf{b})$. If the number of isolated points becomes too small, M' can be increased to obtain more isolated points provided there is sufficient storage available. An isolated point at $\mathbf{x}$ is defined to have the statistics (1) zero probability mass, (2) mean vector $\mathbf{m} = \mathbf{x}$, and (3) correlation matrix $\mathbf{C} = \mathbf{x}\mathbf{x}'$; the convention used when calculating $\eta(\mathbf{b})$ is that $[0 \ln (0/0)] \triangleq 0$. The kth cluster has the statistics (1) $n^k \triangleq$ total number of samples assigned to this class and $P_k = n^k/n$, (2) mean vector $\mathbf{m}_k$, and (3) correlation matrix $\mathbf{C}_k$.

The following rules define the manner in which the statistics of two combined classes is updated. It is assumed that classes r and s are combined into class j. The following are rules for combining clusters.

Case A Two clusters:

1. $n^j = n^r + n^s$.

2. $\mathbf{m}_j = \dfrac{n^r\mathbf{m}_r + n^s\mathbf{m}_s}{n^r + n^s}$.

3. $\mathbf{C}_j = \dfrac{n^r\mathbf{C}_r + n^s\mathbf{C}_s}{n^r + n^s}$.

Case B A cluster (class r) and an isolated point (class s):

1. $n^j = n^r + 1$.

2. $\mathbf{m}_j = \dfrac{n^r\mathbf{m}_r + \mathbf{m}_s}{n^r + 1}$.

3. $\mathbf{C}_j = \dfrac{n^r\mathbf{C}_r + \mathbf{C}_s}{n^r + 1}$.

Case C   Two isolated points:

1. $n^j = 2.$

2. $\mathbf{m}_j = \dfrac{\mathbf{m}_r + \mathbf{m}_s}{2}.$

3. $\mathbf{C}_j = \dfrac{\mathbf{C}_r + \mathbf{C}_s}{2}.$

The rules for updating the statistics of the rth class with a sample presumed from that class are cases D and E, which follow.

Case D   A cluster (class r) and the nth sample:

1. $n^r = n^r + 1.$

2. $\mathbf{m}_r = \dfrac{n^r \mathbf{m}_r + \mathbf{x}_n}{n^r + 1}.$

3. $\mathbf{C}_r = \dfrac{n^r \mathbf{C}_r + \mathbf{x}_n \mathbf{x}_n^t}{n^r + 1}.$

Case E   An isolated point (class r) and the nth sample:

1. $n^r = 2.$

2. $\mathbf{m}_r = \dfrac{\mathbf{m}_r + \mathbf{x}_n}{2}.$

3. $\mathbf{C}_r = \dfrac{\mathbf{C}_r + \mathbf{x}_n \mathbf{x}_n^t}{2}.$

Figure 5.11 shows a flow chart of the algorithm. The algorithm is started by using the first M' samples as M' isolated points. Then, given sample $\mathbf{x}_n$, there are two types of possible actions:

1. Assign $\mathbf{x}_n$ to one of the M' classes (M' possible actions).
2. Combine two of the M' classes and make $\mathbf{x}_n$ a new class (isolated point) $\left[\binom{M'}{2} \text{ possible actions} \right].$

The $\eta(\mathbf{b})$ criterion of (5) is calculated for each of the $M' + \binom{M'}{2}$ possible actions. The update corresponding to the action which maximizes $\eta(\mathbf{b})$ is then performed. Effectively, the favorable action produces the largest estimated $\eta(\mathbf{b})$ by accepting classes having large estimated values of

$$P_k \ln P_k |\mathbf{\Sigma}^k|^{1/2}.$$

This procedure can be compared with such clustering techniques as cluster map (Section 5-4.2) [80], chain map (Section 5-4.3), and isodata [71]. However, the latter algorithms do not utilize a criterion such as $\eta(\mathbf{b})$ derived from an optimum approach.

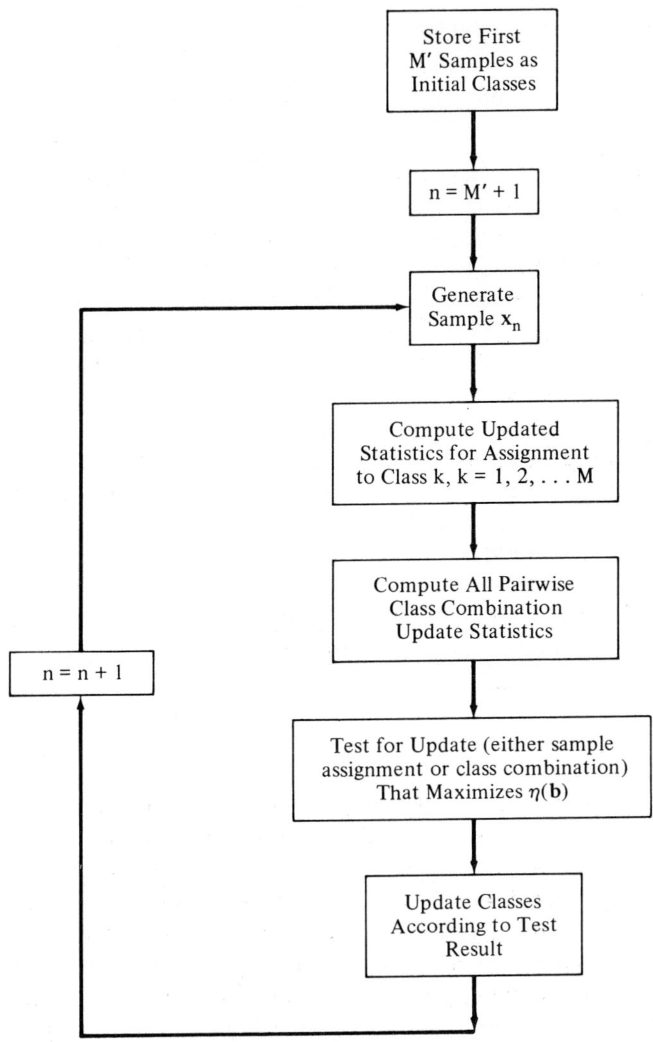

Fig. 5.11 Flow chart of algorithm to maximize $\eta(\mathbf{b})$ under a separable Gaussian assumption.

Special Case: $\Sigma_k = (\sigma)^2 I$ *and* $P_k = 1/M$, *Where M is Known*

Under these conditions the $\eta(\mathbf{b})$ expression in (3) becomes

$$\eta(\mathbf{b}) = \ln\left[\frac{1}{M(2\pi)^{L/2}(\sigma)^L}\right] - \frac{1}{2(\sigma)^2}\sum_{k=1}^{M}\int_{S^k}\|\mathbf{x} - \mathbf{m}_k\|^2 h(\mathbf{x})\,d\mathbf{x}, \qquad (7)$$

and maximizing $\eta(\mathbf{b})$ is equivalent to finding

$$\min_{\{\mathbf{m}_k\}_{k=1}^{M}} \sum_{k=1}^{M} \int_{S^k} \|\mathbf{x} - \mathbf{m}_k\|^2 h(\mathbf{x})\, d\mathbf{x}. \tag{8}$$

This criterion, or the slight generalization for P_k not identical, is relevant to the class of decision-directed algorithms. It is extremely easy to implement an algorithm to asymptotically minimize risk under the a priori assumptions that lead to (8). One disadvantage of the criterion of (8) is that it cannot be used to determine M if this knowledge is not available. This drawback occurs because (8) does not incorporate a cost for adding additional categories, as does the criterion of (7). Parallel processing suggested by MacQueen [31] for $M = 1, 2, \ldots, M'$ can produce more classes than there really are. For example, suppose $h(\mathbf{x})$ is composed of a single one-dimensional Gaussian density function with mean zero, variance $(\sigma)^2$. If it is assumed that $M = 2$, the solution of (8) is a partition through $\mathbf{x} = 0$. Denoting the variances on either side of this solution partition by $(\sigma_i)^2$, $i = 1, 2$, the strict inequality $(\sigma_1)^2 + (\sigma_2) < (\sigma)^2$ holds. This shows that even though there was only one class, (8) is less for $M = 2$ than for $M = 1$, and the use of (8) to determine M failed. For certain applications, knowledge of M may not be an unreasonable assumption, and the criterion of (8) motivates one of the simplest unsupervised estimation algorithms currently in existence† (see [35]).

Discussion

The procedure presented in this section has the disadvantage that parallel processing is involved; i.e., all the samples are involved in computation at each stage. It may be advantageous to concentrate on constructing a single cluster as in Sections 5-4.2, 5-4.3, and 5-4.5. An advantage of the approach is that it tries to apply a global criterion, $\eta(\mathbf{b})$, for evaluating the quality of choice for M and a partition of the samples into clusters. Since no procedure has been given for breaking up a cluster into two or more clusters, it may be necessary to begin the process from the beginning for samples in some part of the observation space. This problem of determining if a cluster should be decomposed into two or more clusters is a difficult one. First, it is difficult because any procedure is dependent on the criterion chosen [such as $\eta(\mathbf{b})$ for evaluating the decomposition]; *second, it is difficult because for a finite number of samples there are many different ways to decompose a cluster into more than one cluster.*

†See Section 5-5.

5-4.3 Clustering Utilizing "Portable Magnifying Glass" (Cluster Map)

The clustering approach described in Section 5-4.1 involves searching for a solution $\mathbf{b}$ which maximizes $\eta(\mathbf{b})$. This search can take a relatively long time and especially is undesirable for use in an interactive data-processing system where computer output display of category properties should be fast. It is equally undesirable where the clustering technique is being used to estimate the modes or clusters in a multimodal density function, either $h(\mathbf{x})$ or $f_i(\mathbf{x})$.

A faster solution to clustering may be achieved if a criterion [such as $\eta(\mathbf{b})$] is not used to measure the quality of the clustering solution. Because the criterion $\eta(\mathbf{b})$ results from the Bayes solution, it provides for introducing a priori knowledge and, when a separability assumption is not made, for unsupervised estimation of category parameters even when the categories have overlapping probability densities.

Suppose that you are given a function $t(\mathbf{x}\,|\,\mathbf{x}_s, \boldsymbol{\Phi})$ which is the multivariate Gaussian density function having mean vector $\mathbf{x}_s$ and covariance matrix $\boldsymbol{\Phi}$. Visualize a "neighborhood" about $\mathbf{x}_s$ as a set of points within the region of concentration of t; this function t will be called the *test function*.

Suppose $\mathbf{x}$ has a density $h(\mathbf{x})$ which is a mixture of M functions from the Gaussian family $\mathscr{F}$:

$$h(\mathbf{x}) = \sum_{i=1}^{M} P_i f(\mathbf{x}\,|\,\mathbf{m}_i, \boldsymbol{\Sigma}_i). \tag{9}$$

If the covariance matrix of the test function is carefully chosen and the M categories in (9) reasonably separated, it can be assumed that the test function $t(\mathbf{x}\,|\,\mathbf{x}_s, \boldsymbol{\Phi})$ "singles out" the dth member in (9) if $f(\mathbf{x}\,|\,\mathbf{m}_d, \boldsymbol{\Sigma}_d)$ is the dominant cluster near $\mathbf{x}_s$ (see Figure 5.12):

$$t(\mathbf{x}\,|\,\mathbf{x}_s, \boldsymbol{\Phi})h(\mathbf{x}) = t(\mathbf{x}\,|\,\mathbf{x}_s, \boldsymbol{\Phi})P_d f(\mathbf{x}\,|\,\mathbf{m}_d, \boldsymbol{\Sigma}_d). \tag{10}$$

Under the assumption that produced (10), $t(\mathbf{x})h(\mathbf{x})$ is itself Gaussian; denote this as a Gaussian function with mean vector $\boldsymbol{\gamma}_s$ and covariance matrix $\mathbf{C}_s$. The procedure for estimating the parameters $\mathbf{m}_d$ and $\boldsymbol{\Sigma}_d$ characterizing the dth cluster is as follows:

1. Estimate $\boldsymbol{\gamma}_s$ and $\mathbf{C}_s$ utilizing a method described shortly, after selecting a point $\mathbf{x}_s$.
2. Supply P_d and $\boldsymbol{\Phi}$ interactively.
3. Calculate $\mathbf{m}_d$ and $\boldsymbol{\Sigma}_d$ in terms of $\boldsymbol{\gamma}_s$, $\mathbf{C}_s$, $\boldsymbol{\Phi}$, P_d, and $\mathbf{x}_s$.
4. Repeat steps 1 and 3 using another point $\mathbf{x}_s$.

The procedure takes an unusual turn: *Find the mean and covariance*

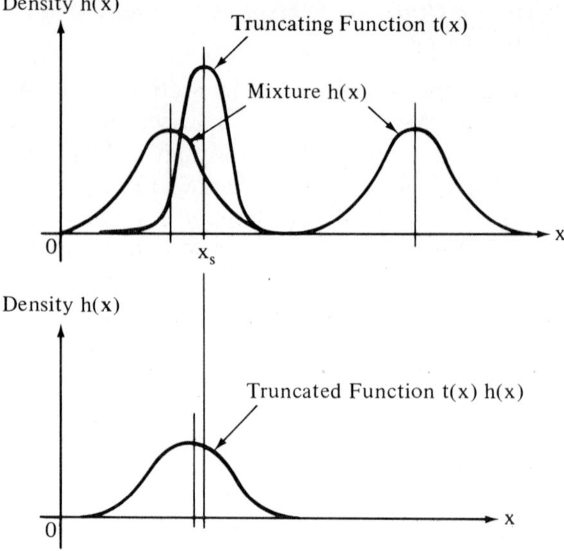

Fig. 5.12 A truncating function

matrix of the category to which $\mathbf{x}_s$ *belongs.* It is expected that samples $\mathbf{x}_s$ close to each other will produce means and covariances, respectively, close to each other; thus, this is a kind of clustering in the parameter space.

Using a theorem in Miller ([75], p. 24), it results that

$$\mathbf{\Sigma}_d = (\mathbf{C}_s^{-1} - \mathbf{\Phi}^{-1})^{-1}, \tag{11}$$

$$\mathbf{m}_d = (\mathbf{\Sigma}_d\mathbf{\Phi}^{-1} + \mathbf{I})(\mathbf{\gamma}_s - \mathbf{x}_s) + \mathbf{x}_s. \tag{12}$$

Moments of $t(\mathbf{x}\,|\,\mathbf{x}_s, \mathbf{\Phi})\hat{h}(\mathbf{x})$ are estimated next, where $\hat{h}(\mathbf{x})$ is

$$\hat{h}(\mathbf{x}) = \frac{1}{n}\sum_{s=1}^{n}\delta(\mathbf{x} - \mathbf{x}_s); \qquad \delta(\mathbf{x}) \text{ is the Dirac delta function.}$$

The moments are

$$\hat{a}_s = \frac{1}{n}\sum_{j=1}^{n}t(\mathbf{x}_j\,|\,\mathbf{x}_s, \mathbf{\Phi}), \tag{13a}$$

$$\hat{a}_{s\mu} = \frac{1}{n}\sum_{j=1}^{n}x_{j\mu}t(\mathbf{x}_j\,|\,\mathbf{x}_s, \mathbf{\Phi}), \qquad \mu = 1, 2, \ldots, L, \tag{13b}$$

$$\hat{a}_{s\mu v} = \frac{1}{n}\sum_{j=1}^{n}(x_{j\mu} - \hat{a}_{l\mu})(x_{jv} - \hat{a}_{sv})t(\mathbf{x}_j\,|\,\mathbf{x}_s, \mathbf{\Phi}),$$
$$\mu, v = 1, 2, \ldots, L, \tag{13c}$$

Unsupervised Estimation   *Chap. 5*

and then

$$\hat{\boldsymbol{\gamma}}_s = \begin{bmatrix} \hat{a}_{s1} \\ \hat{a}_{s2} \\ \cdot \\ \cdot \\ \cdot \\ \hat{a}_{sL} \end{bmatrix}, \tag{14}$$

$$\hat{\mathbf{C}}_s = \begin{bmatrix} \hat{a}_{s11} & \hat{a}_{s12} & \cdots & \\ \hat{a}_{s21} & \hat{a}_{s22} & \cdots & \\ \cdot & & \cdot & \\ \cdot & & & \cdot \\ \cdot & & & \cdot \\ & & \cdots & \hat{a}_{sLL} \end{bmatrix}, \tag{15}$$

$$\hat{\boldsymbol{\Sigma}}_{sd} = (\hat{\mathbf{C}}_s - \boldsymbol{\Phi}^{-1})^{-1}, \tag{16}$$

$$\hat{\mathbf{m}}_{sd} = (\hat{\boldsymbol{\Sigma}}_{sd}\boldsymbol{\Phi}^{-1} + \mathbf{I})(\hat{\boldsymbol{\gamma}}_s - \mathbf{x}_s) + \mathbf{x}_s. \tag{17}$$

By (17) a set of parameters $(\hat{\boldsymbol{\Sigma}}_{sd}, \hat{\mathbf{m}}_{sd})$ may be associated with sample $\mathbf{x}_s, s = 1, 2, \ldots, n$. If the assumption of separability leading to (10) is reasonably well satisfied, the set of points $(\hat{\boldsymbol{\Sigma}}_{sd}, \hat{\mathbf{m}}_{sd})$, $s = 1, 2, \ldots, n$, may be expected to form clusters in the parameter space. Now, if the procedure is repeated, this time using $(\hat{\boldsymbol{\Sigma}}_{sd}, \hat{\mathbf{m}}_{sd})$, $s = 1, 2, \ldots, n$, as the data base rather than $\mathbf{x}_1, \mathbf{x}_2, \ldots, \mathbf{x}_n$, it is an experimentally observed result that the clusters in the parameter space get "tighter." The theoretical explanation for this is the "product effect" resulting from Eq. (10); this product effect is very familiar to anyone experienced with the a posteriori density of parameters using the Bayes approach.

For some special applications it may be sufficient to assume $\boldsymbol{\Sigma}_i = \boldsymbol{\Sigma}$, for all categories $i = 1, 2, \ldots, M$, where $\boldsymbol{\Sigma}$ is known and supplied as a priori knowledge. Then it remains to estimate the means. Under these assumptions (17) reduces to

$$\hat{\mathbf{m}}_{sd} = (\boldsymbol{\Sigma}\boldsymbol{\Phi}^{-1} + \mathbf{I})(\hat{\boldsymbol{\gamma}}_s - \mathbf{x}_s) + \mathbf{x}_s. \tag{18}$$

If $\boldsymbol{\Sigma}$ is chosen to be an a^{-1} multiple of $\boldsymbol{\Phi}$, then

$$\hat{\mathbf{m}}_{sd} = -a\mathbf{x}_s + (1 + a)\hat{\boldsymbol{\gamma}}_s. \tag{19}$$

When dimensionality of the parameter space is greater than two, a problem remains as how to display the clustered points on a computer output display screen. One way is to use a *chain map*, described in Section 5-4.3; another is to use a *maximin map*, described in Section 5-4.4; another is to use a *continuity map*, described in Section 5-4.6; and another is to use the *cluster grow technique*, described in Section 5-4.7.

If $\boldsymbol{\Sigma}_d$ is unknown, it may be reasonable to use the estimation procedure discussed in Chapter 3. Let $\boldsymbol{\Sigma}_{ad}$ be an a priori guess for $\boldsymbol{\Sigma}_d$ with confidence of n_a samples,

$$\boldsymbol{\Sigma}_{sd} = \frac{n_a}{n_d + n_a}\boldsymbol{\Sigma}_{ad} + \frac{n_d}{n_d + n_a}(\hat{\mathbf{C}}_s - \boldsymbol{\Phi}^{-1})^{-1},$$

and n_d is the number of samples within some distance of $\mathbf{x}_s$.

The reader may wish to compare "cluster map" just presented with an approach by Butler [76].

Examples using a cluster map with clusters displayed on the display screen are presented below; for each example, the test function covariance matrix was determined interactively.

Example 1   The first example is chosen so that there are three well-separated clusters. Specifically, the mixture density (9) is

$$h(\mathbf{x}) = \sum_{i=1}^{3} \tfrac{1}{3} f(\mathbf{x} \,|\, \mathbf{m}_i, \boldsymbol{\Sigma}_i), \tag{20}$$

where $f(\mathbf{x}\,|\,\mathbf{m}_i, \boldsymbol{\Sigma}_i)$ is the bivariate Gaussian distribution with parameters:

$$\boldsymbol{\Sigma}_i = \begin{bmatrix} 1.5 & 0 \\ 0 & 1.5 \end{bmatrix}, \qquad i = 1, 2, 3,$$

$$\mathbf{m}_1 = [0, 0], \tag{21}$$

$$\mathbf{m}_2 = [5, -5],$$

$$\mathbf{m}_3 = [-5, 5].$$

Two hundred and fifty observations were independently drawn from a random vector generator designed to have the density (20). These observations are shown in Figure 5.13.

The clustering transformation [(16) and (17)] was then used to map the 250 observations to the parameter space of means and covariances. The result was that the observations became more tightly clustered in the parameter space.

The transformation was reapplied to the points in the parameter space which resulted from the transformation of points in the observation space;

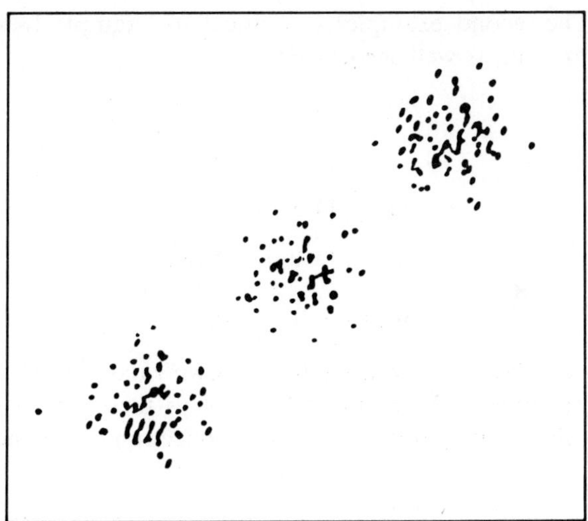

Fig. 5.13 Original data

then the transformation was sequentially applied four times to the points in the parameter space. Figure 5.14 shows the results after the fifth application of the clustering transformation. Approximately 10 seconds of computation time was required to transform all the observations once using the CDC 6500 computer.

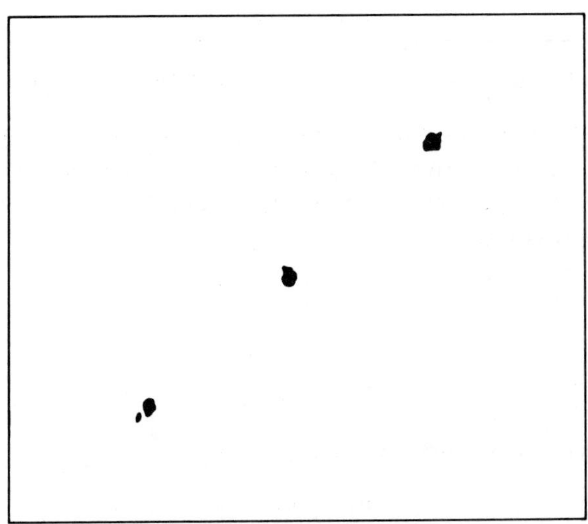

Fig. 5.14 After fifth mapping

Example 2 The second example is identical to Example 1 except that the three classes are not as well separated:

$$\Sigma_i = \begin{bmatrix} 2.25 & 0 \\ 0 & 2.25 \end{bmatrix}, \qquad i = 1, 2, 3,$$

$$\mathbf{m}_1 = [4.0, 0], \tag{22}$$

$$\mathbf{m}_2 = [-4.0, -2.0],$$

$$\mathbf{m}_3 = [4.0, -2.0].$$

One hundred and fifty observations were drawn randomly with density (20) with parameter values (22). Figure 5.15 displays these observations. Figure 5.16 indicates the results after the seventh application of the modified cluster algorithm.

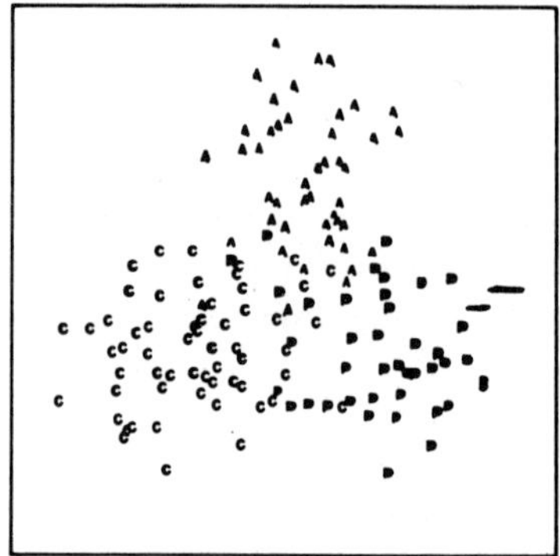

Fig. **5.15** Labeled original data   Fig. **5.16** After seventh mapping

Example 3 This third example is a two-class, two-dimensional problem in which class 1 has a relatively large variance in dimension two, while class 2 has a relatively large variance in dimension one. Specifically, the respective covariance matrices are

$$\Sigma_1 = \begin{bmatrix} \frac{1}{4} & 0 \\ 0 & 4 \end{bmatrix},$$

$$\Sigma_2 = \begin{bmatrix} 4 & 0 \\ 0 & 4 \end{bmatrix},$$

the respective mean vectors are

$$\mathbf{m}_1 = (0, -2),$$

$$\mathbf{m}_2 = (0, 5),$$

and the respective class probabilities are equal.† A total of 100 observations were independently drawn from a random vector generator designed to have density (20) for each class. A computer-output display of the 100 samples is shown in Figure 5.17. A's identify observations from class 1; B's identify

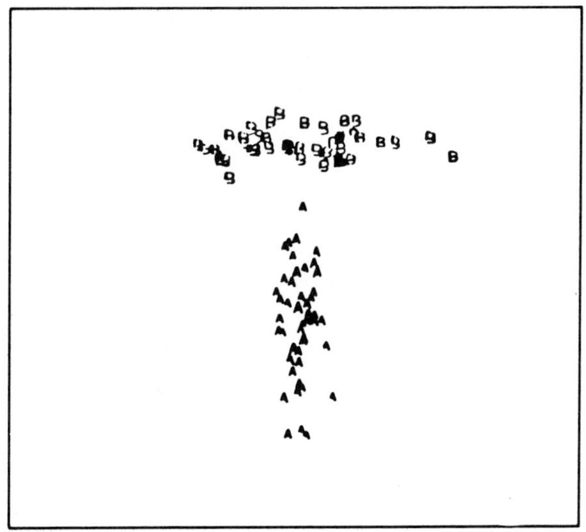

Fig. 5.17 Original data

observations from class 2. The mapped samples after five applications of the mapping are shown in Figure 5.18.

Discussion

If the test function $t(\mathbf{x} \mid \mathbf{x}_s, \boldsymbol{\Phi})$ is not truncated (i.e., if it is nonzero over the observation space), there will be a tendency, once clusters have formed, for the clusters to attract each other. This may present no problem if the cluster map is stopped after a predetermined number of applications. Another possibility is to use a truncated test function. Another suggestion is to use a $\sin(x/x)$ function, which has the effect of causing points close to attract but points farther apart to repel. A force-field interpretation of "clustering" has been suggested by Butler [76], resembling the cluster-map or test-function approach.‡

Advantages and disadvantages of the cluster-map approach are the

†The two mean vectors and covariance matrices are unknown and estimated according to (16) and (17).

‡See also [87].

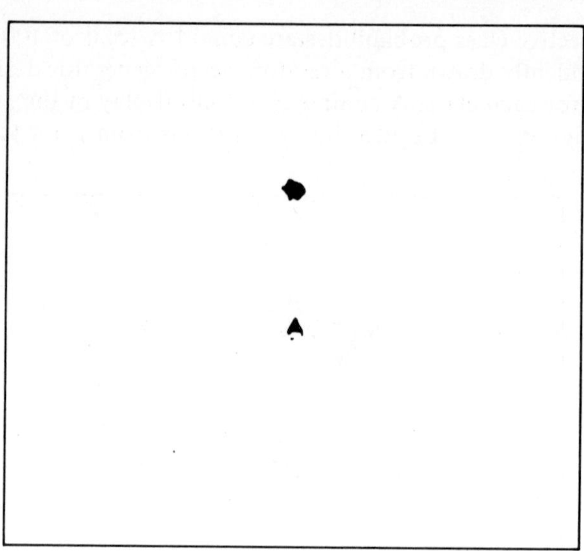

Fig. 5.18 After fifth mapping

following:

Advantages

1. Search for an optimum partition is not the objective of the procedure. This is an advantage from a time and complexity viewpoint but a possible disadvantage as described in point 1 below.
2. Clusters are displayed in the parameter space. By successive applications of the mapping, these clusters get tighter.

Disadvantages

1. A criterion such as $\eta(\mathbf{b})$ for evaluating cluster quality is not utilized. This could be a disadvantage if it is necessary to know the precise number of clusters, which is a difficult problem.
2. The category covariance matrix must be provided by interaction; this can be an advantage if it is supplied as a result of problem knowledge.
3. Means and covariances are not directly estimated but displayed as clusters in the parameter space. A subsequent mapping is required to extract means and covariances or to display the cluster in one-, two-, or three-dimensional space.
4. To obtain the parameter estimates ($\hat{\boldsymbol{\Sigma}}_{sd}$, $\hat{\mathbf{m}}_{sd}$) corresponding to the individual sample $\mathbf{x}_s$ requires processing all n samples. Even if the

test function $t(\mathbf{x}\,|\,\mathbf{x}_s, \boldsymbol{\Phi})$ is truncated, it must be determined which samples $\mathbf{x}_1, \mathbf{x}_2, \ldots, \mathbf{x}_n$ are within the influence of the test function.

5-4.4 Chain Map

A relatively simple mapping of clusters in an L-dimensional space to a lower-dimensional space is described in this section and called a *chain map*. Let $\mathbf{x}_1, \mathbf{x}_2, \ldots, \mathbf{x}_n$ be n vector samples as illustrated in Figure 5.19 for

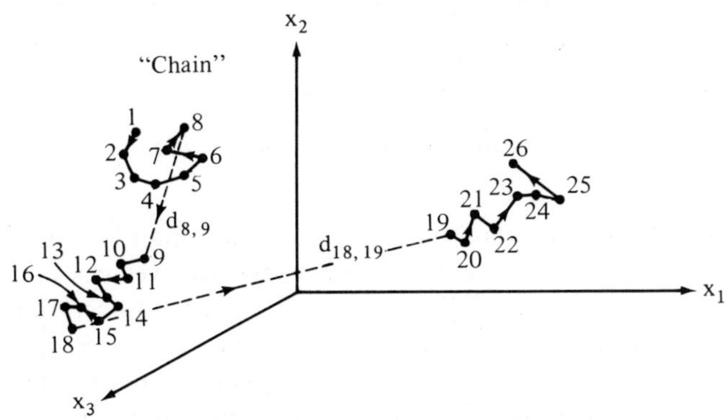

Fig. 5.19 Example of "chain" in $L = 3$ space

a three-dimensional ($L = 3$) example and $n = 26$. Then:

1. Arbitrarily choose any one of the n vectors, say sample $\mathbf{x}_1$, as illustrated in Figure 5.19.
2. Locate the nearest sample to $\mathbf{x}_1$, say $\mathbf{x}_2$ (as illustrated in Figure 5.19), using Euclidean distance measure. Plot the distance between $\mathbf{x}_1$ and $\mathbf{x}_2$, denoted d_{12}, along the y_2 axis as indicated in Figure 5.20; the second point along the y_1 axis corresponds to $\mathbf{x}_2$.
3. Continue this process, producing the "chain" shown in Figure 5.19, and plot distances between elements in the chain as shown in Figure 5.20.

The chain map as illustrated in Figure 5.20 can be very educational when viewed on a computer-output display screen. When categories are well separated with the respective categories "tightly clustered," the clusters can be identified as those samples between large jumps in the mapped space. This is clearly illustrated by the example. If the categories are not tightly clustered, then there may be frequent "small" jumps in the display. This is why it may be advantageous to apply a "cluster tightener" such as a cluster map prior to applying chain map.

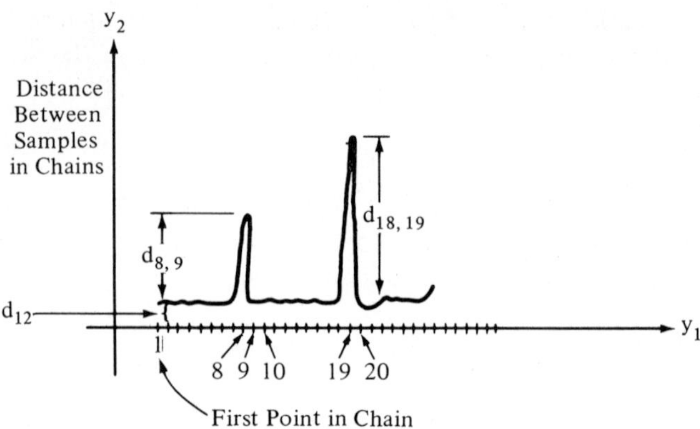

Fig. 5.20 Map of samples in Fig. 5.19

Caution should be exercised in using a chain map because it does not directly provide for a distance measure between two vectors $\mathbf{x}$ and $\mathbf{y}$, other than the Euclidean distance $[\sum_{i=1}^{L} (x_i - y_i)^2]^{1/2}$. A modification found helpful in *some* applications is to compute the global variances $\hat{\sigma}_i^2 = 1/n \sum_{s=1}^{n} (x_{si} - 1/n \sum_{s=1}^{n} x_{si})^2$, $i = 1, 2, \ldots, L$, using the mixture of data from all M categories and then measure the distance between x and y as

$$\sum_{i=1}^{L} \frac{(x_i - y_i)^2}{\hat{\sigma}_i^2}.$$

It would be desirable to have sets of local variances, one set corresponding to each cluster, but a chain map is not a sufficiently complex algorithm to provide for estimating the respective category or subcategory covariance. An algorithm that provides for both interactively inserting a priori knowledge with a prescribed confidence and "growing" the distance measures individually for the respective classes is described in Section 5-4.7.

5-4.5   Maximin (Maximum, Minimum Distance)

An approach to clustering having both resolution and time advantages over a *chain map* was recently suggested by Batchelor and Wilkins [78]. Let there be M categories ω_i, $i = 1, 2, \ldots, M$. Given samples $\mathbf{x}_1, \mathbf{x}_2, \ldots, \mathbf{x}_n$, the objective is to sort them into M categories, where M is unknown. Define a distance measure as simply Euclidean distance,

$$d(\mathbf{x}, \mathbf{y}) = |\mathbf{x} - \mathbf{y}|.$$

We shall illustrate the procedure using the six samples ($n = 6$) shown in the following figure.

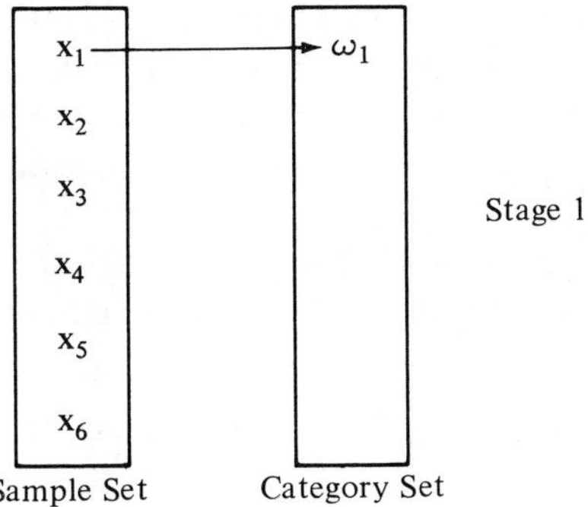

As stage 1, place the *n* vectors in a table as shown and arbitrarily assign class ω_1 to sample $\mathbf{x}_1$. Next, find the sample farthest from ω_1, say x_4; assign class ω_2 to $\mathbf{x}_4$ as shown:

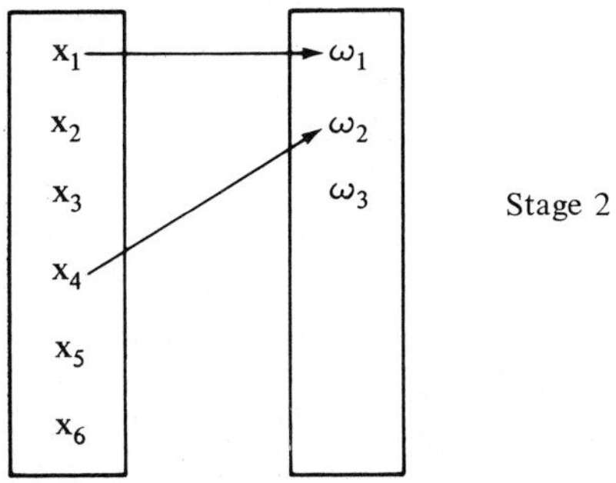

Now, find the class closest to each of the remaining samples and store these *minimum distances*. Find the *maximum among these minimum distances* and assign the corresponding sample to class ω_3. Suppose that sample is $\mathbf{x}_6$, as shown:

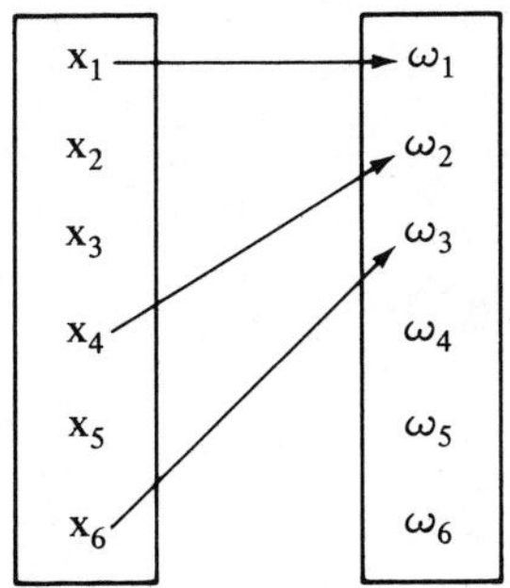

Now, of the remaining samples $\mathbf{x}_2$, $\mathbf{x}_3$, and $\mathbf{x}_5$, find the category among ω_1,

ω_2, or ω_3 which is closest to each sample and store the distances. *Find the maximum of these minimum distances*; we conclude for this example: This fourth measured maximum of the minimum distances is significantly less than the previous "maximum" distances. *This indicates that there are three clusters* ($M = 3$).

The reader will find a procedure utilizing the maximum–minimum distance concept for preprocessing in k-nearest-neighbor rules (Section 4-13).

5-4.6 *Clustering Technique Derived from* $\Gamma(\mathbf{b})$

Let $h(\mathbf{x})$ be a mixture of functions from the Gaussian family:

$$h(\mathbf{x}\,|\,\mathbf{b}^*) = \sum_{i=1}^{M} P_i^* N(\mathbf{x}\,|\,\mathbf{m}_i^*, \mathbf{\Sigma}_i^*). \tag{23}$$

The parameter space $\mathscr{B}$ is the set of points $\{\mathbf{b}_i\}$, where $\mathbf{b}_i = (\mathbf{m}_i, \mathbf{\Sigma}_i)$. Constraints are

$$0 \leq P_i \leq 1,$$

$$\sum_{i=1}^{M} P_i = 1.$$

It follows that†

$$\|\,h(\mathbf{x}\,|\,\mathbf{b})\,\|^2 = \sum_{i=1}^{M} \sum_{j=1}^{M} P_i P_j c_{ij}, \tag{24}$$

where

$$c_{ij} = \int N(\mathbf{x}\,|\,\mathbf{m}_i, \mathbf{\Sigma}_i) N(\mathbf{x}\,|\,\mathbf{m}_j, \mathbf{\Sigma}_j)\, d\mathbf{x}. \tag{25}$$

By completing the square, the integration on the right side of (25) may be obtained, yielding

$$\begin{aligned}
c_{ij} = (2\pi)^{-L/2} |\mathbf{\Sigma}_i|^{-1/2} |\mathbf{\Sigma}_j|^{-1/2} |\mathbf{\Sigma}_i^{-1} + \mathbf{\Sigma}_j^{-1}|^{-1/2} \\
\times \exp\{-\tfrac{1}{2}[(\mathbf{m}_i - \mathbf{m}_{ij})^t \mathbf{\Sigma}_i^{-1}(\mathbf{m}_i - \mathbf{m}_{ij}) \\
+ (\mathbf{m}_j - \mathbf{m}_{ij})^t \mathbf{\Sigma}_j^{-1}(\mathbf{m}_j - \mathbf{m}_{ij})]\},
\end{aligned} \tag{26}$$

where

$$\mathbf{m}_{ij} = (\mathbf{\Sigma}_i^{-1} + \mathbf{\Sigma}_j^{-1})^{-1}(\mathbf{\Sigma}_i^{-1}\mathbf{m}_i + \mathbf{\Sigma}_j^{-1}\mathbf{m}_j). \tag{27}$$

---

†Recall from Section 5-3.5 that the m.n.s.e. estimator required evaluation of $\|\,h(\mathbf{x}\,|\,\mathbf{b})\,\|^2$.

                                     Unsupervised Estimation   Chap. 5

When the covariance matrices are equal, $\mathbf{\Sigma}_i = \mathbf{\Sigma}_j = \mathbf{\Sigma}$,

$$c_{ij} = 2^{-1/2}(2\pi)^{-L/2}|\mathbf{\Sigma}|^{-1/2}\exp\{-\tfrac{1}{2}(\mathbf{m}_i - \mathbf{m}_j)'\mathbf{\Sigma}^{-1}(\mathbf{m}_i - \mathbf{m}_j)\}. \qquad (28)$$

Now, the form (24) for $\|h(\mathbf{x}\,|\,\mathbf{b})\|^2$ simplifies when a high signal-to-noise ratio prevails. Conveniently define a high signal-to-noise ratio as when

$$(\mathbf{m}_i - \mathbf{m}_j)'(\mathbf{\Sigma}_i^{-1} + \mathbf{\Sigma}_j^{-1})(\mathbf{m}_i - \mathbf{m}_j) > \alpha \gg 1. \qquad (29)$$

When (29) is satisfied, the class-conditional d.f.'s are "quasi-orthogonal"; i.e.,

$$c_{ij} = \int N(\mathbf{x}\,|\,\mathbf{m}_i, \mathbf{\Sigma}_i) \times N(\mathbf{x}\,|\,\mathbf{m}_j, \mathbf{\Sigma}_j)\,d\mathbf{x} \cong 0, \qquad i \neq j. \qquad (30)$$

Accordingly,

$$\|h(\,\cdot\,|\,\mathbf{b})\|^2 \cong \sum_{i=1}^{M} P_i^2 c_{ii} \qquad (31)$$

with c_{ii} given by (26). By (31) and (30) of Section 5-3.5, we see that

$$q(\mathbf{b}\,|\,\dot{\mathbf{x}}_n) \cong \prod_{i=1}^{M} q_i(\mathbf{b}\,|\,\dot{\mathbf{x}}_n), \qquad (32)$$

where

$$q_i(\mathbf{b}\,|\,\dot{\mathbf{x}}_n) = \frac{\exp\left\{\sum_{s=1}^{n} 2P_i N(\mathbf{x}_s\,|\,\mathbf{m}_i, \mathbf{\Sigma}_i) - P_i^2 c_{ii}\right\}}{\sum_{i=1}^{M} [\text{numerator}]}. \qquad (33)$$

Thus, according to (32), when the classes "are widely separated," the joint density $q(\mathbf{b}\,|\,\dot{\mathbf{x}}_n)$ on the parameters factors, in an approximate sense, into the M d.f.'s on the parameters for each class, the approximation improving as α [29] increases.

Discussion

The factoring in (32) was conveniently obtained because the m.n.s.e. approach involves $\|h(\mathbf{x}\,|\,\mathbf{b})\|^2$ and thus c_{ij} in (25). It is not as convenient to obtain a "quasi-orthogonal" condition as in (30) when using the Bayes estimator involving $\eta(\mathbf{b})$.

The density $q_i(\mathbf{b}\,|\,\dot{\mathbf{x}}_n)$ involves only parameters from class i. On the other hand, $q(\mathbf{b}\,|\,\dot{\mathbf{x}}_n)$ generally involves parameters from all M classes. The complexity of evaluating $q(\mathbf{b}\,|\,\dot{\mathbf{x}}_n)$ for a fixed number of parameter points $\mathbf{b}$ is prodigious compared with evaluating $q_i(\mathbf{b}\,|\,\dot{\mathbf{x}}_n)$, $i = 1, 2, \ldots, M$.

A clustering algorithm is obtained as follows: Let

$$\hat{\Gamma}(\mathbf{b}) = \frac{1}{n} \sum_{s=1}^{n} h(\mathbf{x}_s \mid \mathbf{b}) = \frac{1}{n} \sum_{s=1}^{n} \sum_{i=1}^{M} P_i f(\mathbf{x}_s \mid \mathbf{b}_i). \tag{34}$$

If $\mathscr{F}$ is Gaussian with $\mathbf{\Sigma}_i$ diagonal,

$$\hat{\Gamma}(\mathbf{b}) = \sum_{i=1}^{M} \frac{1}{n} \sum_{s=1}^{n} \exp\left[-\frac{1}{2} \sum_{r=1}^{L} \frac{(x_{sr} - m_{ir})^2}{(\sigma_{ir})^2} \right], \tag{35}$$

where m_{ir} is the rth component of $\mathbf{m}$ and σ_{ir}^2 is the rth component along the diagonal of $\mathbf{\Sigma}_i$.

Now, suppose that $\mathbf{x}_s$ is a currently unclassified sample; measure the distance

$$\exp\left[-\frac{1}{2} \sum_{r=1}^{L} \frac{(x_{sr} - m_{ir})^2}{(\sigma_{ir})^2} \right], \qquad i = 1, 2. \ldots, M, \tag{36}$$

and classify $\mathbf{x}_s$ as in the class i having smallest distance. Then update the mean vector $\mathbf{m}_i$ and covariance matrix $\mathbf{\Sigma}_i$ using this sample. The reader will notice a "decision-directed" flavor in this approach. (The concept of decision direction is discussed in more detail in Section 5-5.3.)

5-4.7 Continuity Map

Measures of Sample Similarity

Consider a sequence of n L-dimensional vectors $\mathbf{x}_1, \mathbf{x}_2, \ldots, \mathbf{x}_n$ with n_1 from category 1, n_2 from category 2, $\ldots$, n_M from category M; $n = \sum_{i=1}^{M} n_i$. If these M categories are unsupervised or unsorted, then we presume that an unsupervised technique such as a cluster map is used to form the M groups of samples. The objective of a continuity map is to transform these n L-dimensional vectors to n l-dimensional vectors $\mathbf{y}_1, \mathbf{y}_2, \ldots, \mathbf{y}_n$ in such a way that the relationships or similarities among the samples are preserved. For example, if there are M distinct clusters in $\mathscr{V}_L$, then it is desired that there be M distinct clusters in $\mathscr{V}_l$. If $l = 2$, the clusters can be displayed on a computer-output display.

It is desirable that the measure d_{ij} of the *dissimilarity* between two vectors $\mathbf{x}_i$ and $\mathbf{x}_j$ increase with any increase in discrepancy between the two vector components $x_{i,k}$ and $x_{j,k}$ for any k. Two possible distances are the squared Euclidean distance

$$d_{i,j} = \sum_{k=1}^{L} (x_{i,k} - x_{j,k})^2$$

and the "city-block" distance

$$d_{i,j} = \sum_{k=1}^{L} |x_{i,k} - x_{j,k}|^2.$$

Either of these distances reflects the effect resulting when two vector samples that have corresponding components approach each other.

It is desirable that the mapping from $\mathcal{V}_L$ to $\mathcal{V}_l$ be one to one and continuous. The one-to-one property assumes that a sample point in $\mathcal{V}_L$ will not map to more than one sample point in $\mathcal{V}_l$. The continuous property assumes that samples "close" in $\mathcal{V}_L$ are close in $\mathcal{V}_l$. Unfortunately, it can be shown by results in mathematical analysis that a one-to-one, bicontinuous map from $\mathcal{V}_L$ to $\mathcal{V}_l$, $l < L$, is impossible in general [72].

A map suggested by Shepard and Carroll [73] attempts to obtain the continuous property as follows: Let the distance between x_i and x_j be defined as

$$d_{ij}^2 = \sum_{k=1}^{L} (x_{ik} - x_{jk})^2$$

and the distance between the two corresponding mapped samples in $\mathcal{V}_l$ be defined as

$$D_{ij}^2 = \sum_{s=1}^{l} (y_{is} - y_{js})^2.$$

A measure of continuity, considering $\mathbf{x}$ as a function of $\mathbf{y}$, in the vicinity of $\mathbf{y}_i$ and $\mathbf{y}_j$, is

$$\delta_{ij}^2 = \frac{\sum_{k=1}^{L} (x_{ik} - x_{jk})^2}{\sum_{s=1}^{l} (y_{is} - y_{js})^2}.$$

If the mapping of the samples from $\mathcal{V}_L$ to $\mathcal{V}_l$ could be achieved maintaining $\delta_{ij}^2 = 1$ for all i, j, then properties of the categories or clusters would not be lost. Such a juggling for all pairs seems a difficult task; nevertheless, Shepard and Carroll [73] have proposed a measure

$$\delta^2 = \sum_{i \neq j} \sum \frac{d_{ij}^2}{D_{ij}^2} w_{ij},$$

where the weight w_{ij} decreases monotonically with increasing multidimensional distance D_{ij}^2; for example,

$$w_{ij} = \frac{1}{D_{ij}^2}, \text{ or } w_{ij} = \frac{1}{d_{ii}^2}.$$

Perhaps a better weight would be

$$w_{ij} = \begin{cases} 1, & d_{ij}^2 < T \text{ and } D_{ij}^2 < T, \\ 0, & \text{otherwise}, \end{cases}$$

where T is an a priori threshold.

The object is to minimize δ^2 by adjusting the locations of points $\mathbf{x}_i$ in $\mathscr{V}_l$. Obviously a solution is to make all D_{ij}^2 arbitrarily large. To eliminate this possibility, Shepard and Carroll suggested dividing the above δ^2 by

$$\sum_{i \neq j} \sum \frac{1}{D_{ij}^2}$$

to obtain

$$\mathscr{K} = \sum_{i \neq j} \sum \frac{d_{ij}^2}{D_{ij}^4} [\sum_{i \neq j} \sum (D_{ij}^2)^{-1}]^2$$

as the measure to be minimized.

Minimization Algorithm

The measure $\mathscr{K}$ varies continuously with $\mathbf{x}$; therefore, the negative gradiant of $\mathscr{K}$ can be used in an iterative algorithm where the samples $\mathbf{x}_1, \mathbf{x}_2, \ldots, \mathbf{x}_n$ are repeatedly adjusted by the method of *steepest descent* until a configuration for the sequence $\dot{\mathbf{x}}_n$ is reached for which $\mathscr{K}$ is stationary.

It is not expected that the measure $\mathscr{K}$ will be unimodal or have a unique minimum. For this reason, the possibility of a local minimum exists. Standard methods [74] for searching for a global minimum could be applied. A disadvantage of continuity map is that there can be an unlimited number of ways to adjust the $\mathbf{y}_i$ in $\mathscr{V}_l$. Since the form of the mapping from $\mathscr{V}_L$ to $\mathscr{V}_l$ is not specified, the result could be nonlinear. Many researchers are aware that a nonlinear mapping of the observation space to a lower-dimensional space can improve performance. It would not appear, however, that an almost unconstrained procedure, such as a continuity map, is the way to go. Rather, the nonlinearity should result from the insertion of a model reflecting problem knowledge, where a model is the basis for a relationship among the dimensions in $\mathscr{V}_L$.

5-4.8 Interactive Use of Problem Knowledge for Clustering and Decision Making

Introduction

In this section an approach to clustering and decision making is presented where a priori problem knowledge is inserted interactively. Problem knowledge inserted is in the form of subcategory *mean vectors* and *covariance matrices* and *confidence* that these means and covariances accurately characterize the category. Then measurement vectors from the category are used to update these a priori supplied means and covariances. The extent to which new measurement vectors update the a priori values depends upon the expert's a priori confidence.

It is possible for pattern recognition to be accomplished without any training vectors by using a priori supplied subcategory parameters. This is an important consideration because an expert is given an opportunity to insert problem knowledge and observe performance in classifying vectors. Also, the expert can observe his a priori knowledge being modified with training vectors. Through such interaction the expert is in control of the pattern recognition; furthermore, he is likely to learn from the interactive experience.

The approach of inserting a priori mean vectors and covariance matrices is not the only way to insert problem knowledge. For example, problem knowledge can be inserted using nonlinear relationships among measurements. For convenience, attention in this section will be restricted to the former approach.

The Gaussian density is specified by a distance measure from the mean and by the density decreasing as $e^{-d^2/2}$, where d is the distance from the mean. Other densities are characterized by distance measures from a mean and the rate at which the density decreases. In particular, the case of a uniform density on a disc is considered. Although the Gaussian density is a prime example in this section, other densities apply also.

The procedure involves search for one cluster at a time because it permits one to observe the growth of the cluster and to interact if desired. An approach that starts many clusters tends to be difficult for the human mind to follow. In addition to providing an a priori starting point, a priori knowledge is supplied about the family to which the cluster density belongs. The procedure begins by starting a first cluster by successively collecting "nearest" samples. In this cluster, a distance measure used for measuring distance is updated. Hopefully, this distance measure is so suited to the cluster being grown that samples actively from that cluster are "close," whereas samples from other clusters are "farther away." Using an a priori supplied threshold for distance, the first cluster stops accumulating samples when new samples are at a distance greater than the threshold.

Examples presented in this section are primarily for the Gaussian family, where a cluster is characterized by a mean vector and covariance matrix. A few examples are for where the clusters correspond to spherically, uniform densities. The latter family has application in separating touching biological cells in scanned photomicrographs.

There is particular interest as to how well the approach locates clusters

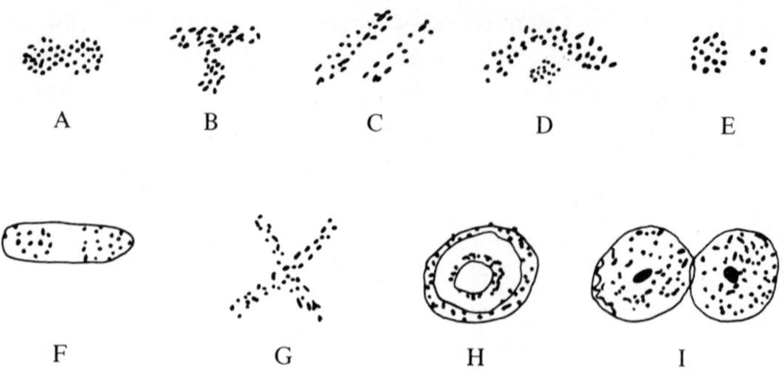

A   B   C   D   E

F   G   H   I

Fig. 5.21 Cluster problems

for the types of problems shown in Figure 5.21. These include several problems outlined by Nagy [79] and are as follows:

A, B: bridges between clusters
C: parallel nonspherical clusters
D: linearly nonspherical clusters
E: unequal cluster populations
F: cluster with a hole (actually two clusters)
G: the x
H: annulus

The growing approach used in this section could be presented without relating it to, say, the Bayes approach to unsupervised estimation. However, the Bayes approach frequently provides insight for extensions so it will be utilized. Let $\mathbf{x} = [x_1, x_2, \ldots, x_L]$ be the L-dimensional observation corresponding to a pattern. Restrict attention to one category of patterns but suppose that the category probability density function is a mixture density,

$$h(\mathbf{x}\,|\,\mathbf{b}) = \sum_{i=1}^{M} f(\mathbf{x}\,|\,\mathbf{b}_i)P_i, \tag{37}$$

where $\mathbf{b}$ is the set of all parameters $\mathbf{b}_i$, P_i, $i = 1, 2, \ldots, M$, characterizing $h(\mathbf{x})$. Since attention is restricted to one category, M is the number of sub-categories. Let $f(\mathbf{x}\,|\,\mathbf{b}_i)$, simply denoted $f_i(\mathbf{x})$, be in the family $\mathscr{F}$. Define $\eta(\mathbf{b})$, as usual, to be the information function (which naturally arises in the Bayes solution),

$$\eta(\mathbf{b}) \triangleq E[\ln h(\mathbf{x}\,|\,\mathbf{b})] = \int \ln h(\mathbf{x}\,|\,\mathbf{b})h(\mathbf{x}\,|\,\mathbf{b}^*)\,d\mathbf{x}, \tag{38}$$

where $\mathbf{b}^*$ is the true set of parameters we are trying to estimate. Note that

$$\eta(\mathbf{b}^*) = \int [\ln h(\mathbf{x}\,|\,\mathbf{b}^*)]h(\mathbf{x}\,|\,\mathbf{b}^*)\,d\mathbf{x}.$$

If the respective densities $f(\mathbf{x}|\mathbf{b}^*)$, $i = 1, 2, \ldots, M^*$, are separated (have no measure in common), then

$$\eta(\mathbf{b}^*) = \sum_{i=1}^{M^*} \int [\ln h(\mathbf{x}|\mathbf{b}^*)] f(\mathbf{x}|\mathbf{b}_i^*) P_i \, d\mathbf{x}. \tag{39}$$

Now, because $\eta(\mathbf{b})$ is maximum when $\mathbf{b} = \mathbf{b}^*$, the above discussion [in particular (39)] suggests that

$$\frac{1}{n_i} \sum_{s=1}^{n_i} \ln[f(\mathbf{x}_s|\hat{\mathbf{b}}_i)\hat{P}_i] \triangleq \hat{\eta}_i, \tag{40}$$

where $\mathbf{x}_1, \mathbf{x}_2, \ldots, \mathbf{x}_{n_i}$ are from $f_i(\mathbf{x})$, is a measure for the ith cluster (the parameters $\hat{\mathbf{b}}_i$ and $\hat{P}_i$ are estimated using these samples). One suspects that as samples from $f_i(\mathbf{x})$ are collected by the ith cluster and $\hat{\mathbf{b}}_i$ and $\hat{P}_i$ updated, then $\hat{\eta}_i$ will continue to increase, indicating that the new samples continue to "match" and should be included in the cluster being grown.

If, for example, $\mathscr{F}$ is the Gaussian family, then (40) becomes

$$\ln \frac{\hat{P}_i}{|\hat{\mathbf{\Sigma}}_i|^{1/2}(2\pi)^{L/2}} - \frac{1}{n} \sum_{s=1}^{n_i} \frac{(\mathbf{x}_s - \hat{\mathbf{m}}_i)^t \hat{\mathbf{\Sigma}}_i^{-1}(\mathbf{x}_s - \hat{\mathbf{m}}_i)}{2} = \hat{\eta}_i, \tag{41}$$

where

$$\begin{aligned}
\hat{\mathbf{m}}_i &= \frac{1}{n_i} \sum_{s=1}^{n_i} \mathbf{x}_s, \\
\hat{\mathbf{\Sigma}}_i &= \frac{1}{n_i} \sum_{s=1}^{n_i} (\mathbf{x}_s - \hat{\mathbf{m}}_i)(\mathbf{x}_s - \hat{\mathbf{m}}_i)^t.
\end{aligned} \tag{42}$$

Suppose that n_i samples have been used to grow the ith cluster with $\hat{\mathbf{m}}_i$ and $\hat{\mathbf{\Sigma}}_i$ estimated for that cluster. Any sample $\mathbf{x}$ not yet included in that cluster would contribute approximately

$$-d(\mathbf{x}, \hat{\mathbf{m}}_i | \hat{\mathbf{\Sigma}}_i) \triangleq - \frac{(\mathbf{x} - \hat{\mathbf{m}}_i)^t \hat{\mathbf{\Sigma}}_i^{-1}(\mathbf{x} - \hat{\mathbf{m}}_i)}{2} \tag{43}$$

to $\hat{\eta}_i$ if that sample were included in the ith cluster.

Thus, the larger the magnitude of d, the more η will be decreased by this sample. This suggests the following procedure for growing a cluster:

1. Let $\mathbf{x}_1, \mathbf{x}_2, \ldots, \mathbf{x}_n$ be n samples from $h(\mathbf{x})$, where the number of clusters M is unknown. Suppose that n_i samples $\mathbf{x}_1, \mathbf{x}_2, \ldots, \mathbf{x}_{n_i}$ already have been used to grow the ith-cluster producing estimates $\hat{\mathbf{m}}_i$ and $\hat{\mathbf{\Sigma}}_i$. Using distance measure (43), find the sample $\mathbf{x}$ of the $n - n_i$ samples not yet in cluster i which has smallest value of $d(\mathbf{x}, \hat{\mathbf{m}}_i | \hat{\mathbf{\Sigma}}_i)$. If $d > T$, where T is an a priori supplied threshold, it is

declared that none of the remaining samples are "sufficiently close" to the ith cluster, a new cluster would be initiated using starting a priori knowledge, as discussed in the next section.

This procedure also arises from an ad hoc approach. In this approach, samples that are close to a mean of a cluster in terms of the covariance are assumed to be from that cluster. Hence they are used to update the means and covariances of that cluster.

Equations (41), (42), and (43) resulted because $\mathcal{F}$ was assumed to be Gaussian. Attention is restricted to the Gaussian family until otherwise indicated. In the subsection to follow, a method for introducing problem knowledge is presented, experimental results for the Gaussian family are presented, a modification of the procedure for uniform spherical clusters is presented, and possible extensions are discussed.

Inserting Problem Knowledge

Either when starting to grow the first cluster or, according to step 1 in the last section, a new cluster is to be begun, a priori knowledge must be supplied. Specifically, the procedure for entering a priori problem knowledge in order to initiate growing a cluster is as follows:

2. Specify a confidence in the a priori parameters to be supplied. Then specify an a priori starting mean $\mathbf{m}_a$ and an a priori covariance matrix $\boldsymbol{\Sigma}_a$. The confidence is proportional to a number n_a, a hypothetical number that could be attributed to previous estimation (learning) samples. Then supply T, a threshold value used in determining when a sample $\mathbf{x}$ is "too far" from the cluster to be included in the cluster.

Given n_i current samples $\mathbf{x}_1, \mathbf{x}_2, \ldots, \mathbf{x}_{n_i}$, a priori confidence n_a, a priori mean vector $\mathbf{m}_a$, and a priori covariance matrix $\boldsymbol{\Sigma}_a$, the mean vector and covariance matrix is updated according to the following equations:

$$(\hat{\mathbf{m}})_{n_i} = \frac{n_a}{n_a + n_i} \mathbf{m}_a + \frac{1}{n_a + n_i} \sum_{s=1}^{n_i} \mathbf{x}_s, \tag{44a}$$

$$(\hat{\boldsymbol{\Sigma}})_{n_i} = \frac{n_a}{n_a + n_i} \boldsymbol{\Sigma}_a + \frac{1}{n_a + n_i} \sum_{s=1}^{n_i} [\mathbf{x}_s - (\hat{\mathbf{m}})_{n_i}][\mathbf{x}_s - (\hat{\mathbf{m}})_{n_i}]^t. \tag{44b}$$

Equations (44) are shown, for example, to produce Bayes estimates for the mean vector and covariance matrix (see Chapter 3).

A computer can be programmed as follows:

3. The computer requests, via typewriter, values of n_a, $\mathbf{m}_a$, $\boldsymbol{\Sigma}_a$, and T. Then the computer grows the cluster-accumulating samples, printing

out current $(\hat{\mathbf{m}})_{n_i}$ and n until there is no sample $\mathbf{x}$ such that $d(\mathbf{x}) \leq$ T. When this happens, the computer requests new a priori values in order to start the next cluster.

Recall that early in this section attention was restricted to one category with M subcategories. Thus, after M clusters are found for the category being processed, the procedure must be repeated for each category. Of course, a category is being represented as a mixture of Gaussian clusters.

Experimental Results

The results of several experiments will be presented for problems of the type illustrated in Figure 5.21.

Example 1 Two categories, each consisting of 20 samples, were used. The first 20 samples, category 2, are the vertical part of the T shown in Figure 5.22.

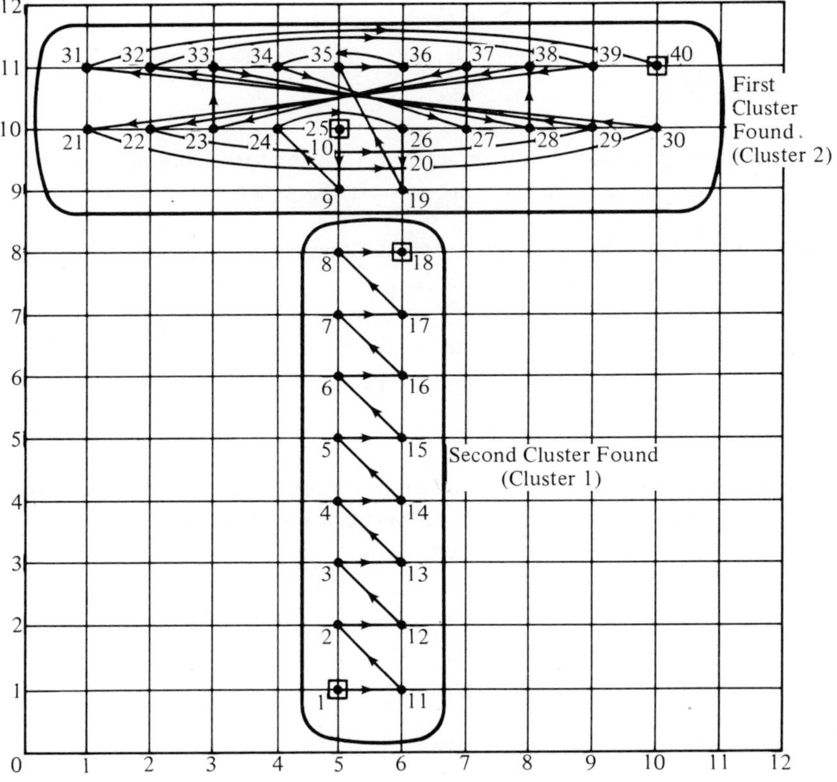

Fig. 5.22 Example 1

The second 20 samples, category 1, are the horizontal part of the T shown in Figure 5.22.

To start, set

$$n_a = 1 \text{ (indicating very little confidence)},$$
$$\mathbf{m}_a = [5, 10],$$
$$\boldsymbol{\Sigma}_a = 2\mathbf{I},$$
$$T = 7.$$

The algorithm proceeded to grow the cluster as shown in Figure 5.22 from the initial sample, 10 or 25. Note how samples are not associated according to their Euclidean distance. This is, of course, because $(\hat{\boldsymbol{\Sigma}})_n$ is being formed according to the distribution of samples across the horizontal arm. After sample 40 was associated with the cluster, no sample $\mathbf{x}$ was such that $d(\mathbf{x}) \leq T$; so the program announced that a new cluster should be started.

For the second cluster, set

$$n_a = 1,$$
$$\mathbf{m}_a = [1, 1],$$
$$\boldsymbol{\Sigma}_a = 1\mathbf{I}.$$

The algorithm proceeded to form a second cluster consisting of the remaining samples. Then there were no more samples to process.

Example 2   If, for the same set of 40 samples, the procedure is begun as,

$$n_a = 1,$$
$$\mathbf{m}_a = [5, 1],$$
$$\boldsymbol{\Sigma}_a = 1\mathbf{I},$$
$$T = 7,$$

then the first cluster formed is as shown in Figure 5.23. Because the covariance matrix being estimated favored the vertical direction, the cluster grew to include the topmost samples. Then, with

$$n_a = 1,$$
$$\mathbf{m}_a = [1, 11],$$
$$\boldsymbol{\Sigma}_a = 1\mathbf{I},$$

the second cluster at the top left was found. Then, with

$$n_a = 1,$$

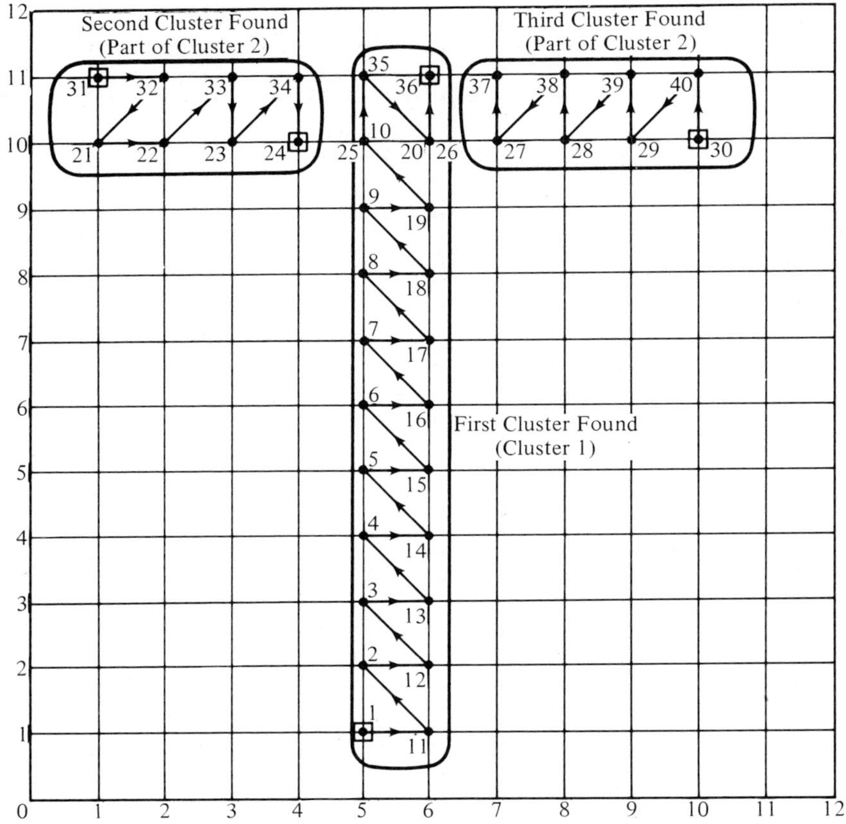

Fig. 5.23 Example 2

$$\mathbf{m}_a = [10, 10],$$
$$\mathbf{\Sigma}_a = 1\mathbf{I},$$

the third cluster at the top right was found.

Of course, the actual horizontal cluster was split into two clusters. *But, this is not serious because, from a decision-making standpoint, this category is adequately characterized* by the three clusters. The question as to whether there are two or three clusters characterizing this category is immaterial for subsequent decision making to recognize samples from this category.

Example 3 For a third example choose 40 samples in the form of a bridge as shown in Figure 5.24. Then a nine-sample, circular cluster is placed under the bridge. There particularly is interest in whether the procedure can find the circular cluster as a separate cluster. To put the procedure to a test, a particularly "bad" starting point was chosen, as shown in Figure 5.24. That

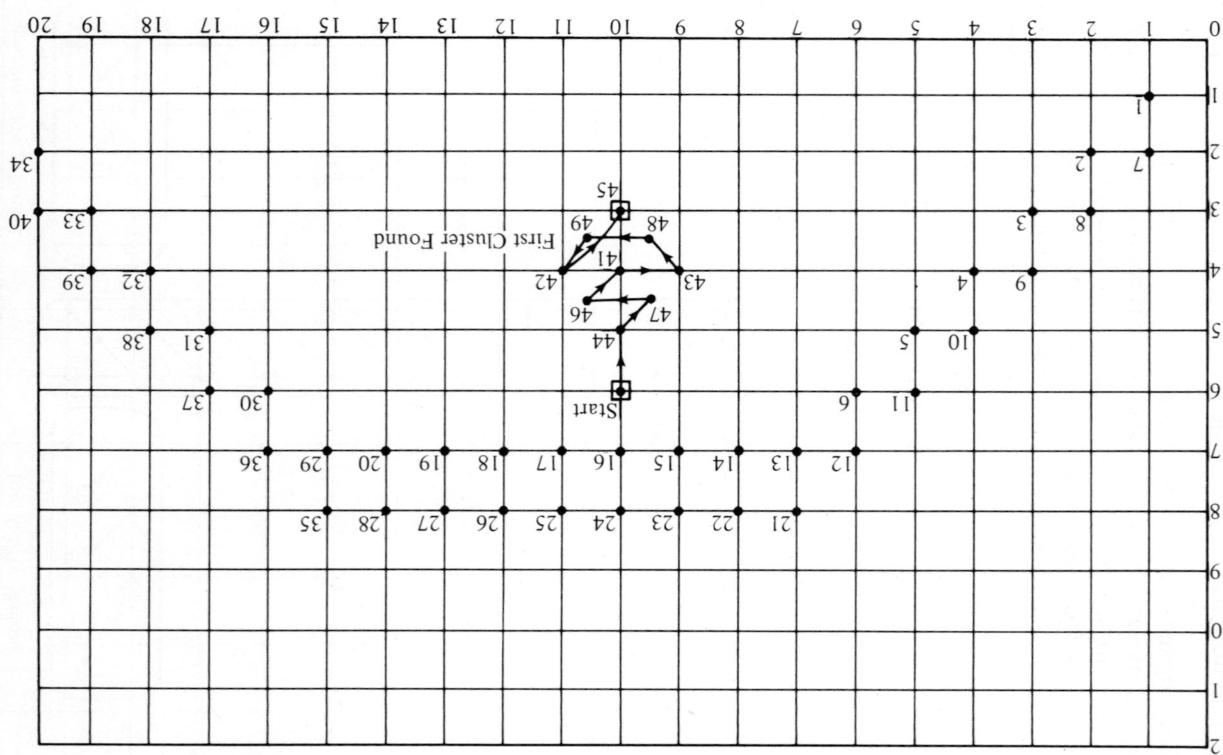

Fig. 5.24 Example 3

is, to find the first cluster, let

$$n_a = 1,$$
$$\mathbf{m}_a = [10, 6],$$
$$\boldsymbol{\Sigma}_a = 1\mathbf{I},$$
$$T = 7.0.$$

Whenever the second sample was in the circular cluster, all samples in the circular cluster were found and collected together as indicated in Figure 5.24. After processing sample 45, there was no sample $\mathbf{x}$ such that $d(\mathbf{x}) \leq T$ so the computer requested that a new cluster be started.

Example 4 For the next example choose the first 20 samples as one leg of an x and the next 20 samples as the other leg of the x. Starting with

$$n_a = 1,$$
$$\mathbf{m}_a = [15, 15],$$
$$\boldsymbol{\Sigma}_a = 15\mathbf{I},$$
$$T = 7.0,$$

the first cluster formed is as shown in Figure 5.25. Of course, the other leg is broken into two clusters, because the center points of this second leg are removed in forming the first cluster.

For subsequent decision making, forming three clusters as indicated is certainly adequate.

It is interesting that even if the procedure was started with $\mathbf{m}_a = [6, 6]$, the center of the x, with $\boldsymbol{\Sigma}_a = 10\mathbf{I}$ (large uncertainty), the procedure still "latches on" to one leg of the x.

Example 5 It was found that the x example can be easily extended to $L = 3$ or $L = 5$; and, insofar as experimented, the first cluster is one of the legs. As L increases, the magnitude of T should be increased. For example, when $L = 5$, $T = 9.0$ works well.

Example 6 How will the growing procedure work for circular clusters as shown in Figure 5.26? With $T = 7$ and the starting mean vector $\mathbf{m}_a$ an extreme point such as 8, the first circular cluster is grown without including any samples from the right circular cluster. However, with a starting point such as 16, the procedure includes all the samples in one cluster (and thus fails!).

When the two circular clusters are bridged such as having 16 and 31 in common as well as 17 and 32 in common, one cluster is almost always formed. This means that the assumption of a Gaussian family is causing the

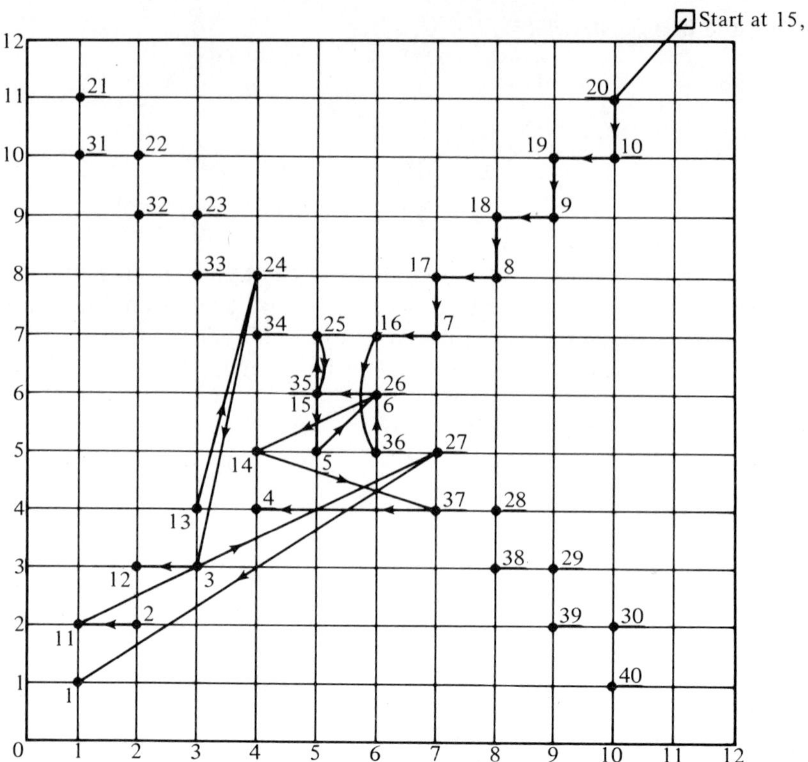

Fig. 5.25 Example 4

procedure to fail! This suggests that the procedure might be modified to a family of spherical and uniform densities as discussed in the following subsection.

Uniform Spherical Clusters

An interesting problem is that of isolating cells in two dimensions on a microscope slide or in three dimensions from a sequence of microscope slides. The slides can be scanned using a flying spot scanner, and the locations of all dark points are stored. Then these dark points are clustered to form dark areas representing cells. The technique presented in the subsection on inserting problem knowledge works well if the cells are sufficiently far apart. If they are close together, however, there is a tendency to combine them both into one cluster, as described in Example 6.

The technique of inserting problem knowledge allows the covariance matrix to change relatively fast, causing the problem of improper clustering.

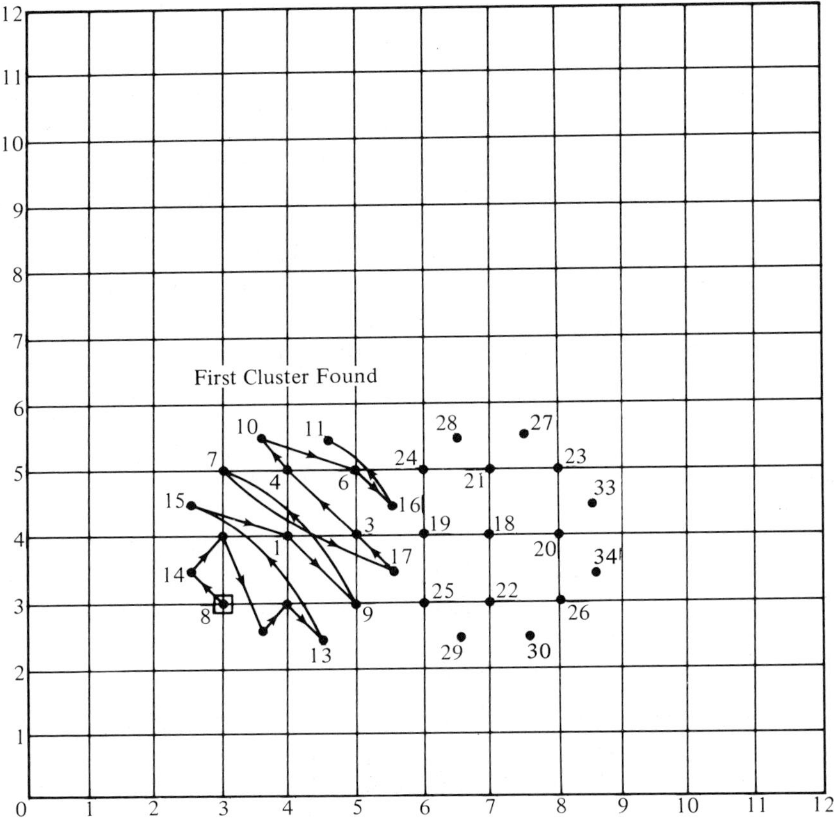

Fig. 5.26 Example 6

A few samples from another cluster may be taken since it is difficult to distinguish samples from the two almost-touching clusters. This taking of samples will alter the covariance enough to let in more samples from the other cluster. Unfortunately, this process continues until all samples of both clusters are taken. The improper clustering occurs because it is too easy to change the covariance matrix.

To get around this problem, distances are measured using old estimates of mean and covariance instead of the current estimate. Thus, the change from one cluster to another is detected before the mean and covariance estimators are corrupted by samples from the second cluster. The actual implementation does not save the old means and covariances. Instead, it compares against the threshold the distance not of the nearest unused sample, but of the kth nearest unused sample. This is equivalent to comparing the distance k samples in the future to the nearest unused sample using the estimates from k samples prior to then.

Combining Clusters   The techniques presented earlier only provide methods of locating clusters. Because of increased complexity in handling large numbers of clusters it is desirable to combine clusters. This combination can be accomplished either with subclusters from within one class at a time or can be done using subclusters from all classes at once.

As an example of combining subclusters from within one class, recall from Example 2 that a "T" was split into three parts: the vertical, the horizontal to the left of center, and the horizontal to the right of center. The two horizontal subclusters could be combined by noting that the subclusters resulting from the combination is as good or even better in representing the density original data than the separate subclusters. One method for checking the desirability of combining is to examine the criterion η in each case. Although it is possible to apply η directly to all possible collections of samples (as in Section 5-4.1), it is computationally much more feasible to apply it only to subclusters.

Combining subclusters from within a class can only be done in terms of how much error is introduced in approximating the density. If information is available between classes, it is desirable to combine even if it causes a bad approximation to the density estimates, as long as the classification based upon the combination is not affected.

Higher Dimensions   When the dimensionality increases in either clustering or decision making, there are three effects. The first effect is that performance may increase, assuming that the dimensions are properly related, while it may decrease if dimensions are incorrectly related. Second, to estimate the required relationships for L-dimensional vectors, the complexity increases as L^2 or faster. Thus, the number of samples required to do a reasonable job of estimation goes up unless a priori relationships between the dimensions are known. Third, the number of computations to handle relationships between dimensions in L-dimensional space increases faster than L^2.

Because of these effects, it is apparent that it is not desirable to work directly with large-dimensional space. Yet, there may be more information in that space than in a smaller space. The major problem is how to get to that information. If good a priori information is available, the problem is greatly simplified.

Clustering and discrimination information appears in two forms. In one form information appears only when more than one dimension is available. An example of this is presented in Figure 5.27. In this two-dimensional example, clustering either x_1 or x_2 gives the wrong information. In the other form, information is present in each dimension. An example for this is given in Figure 5.28. One may cluster first using only x_1. Then he can continue by

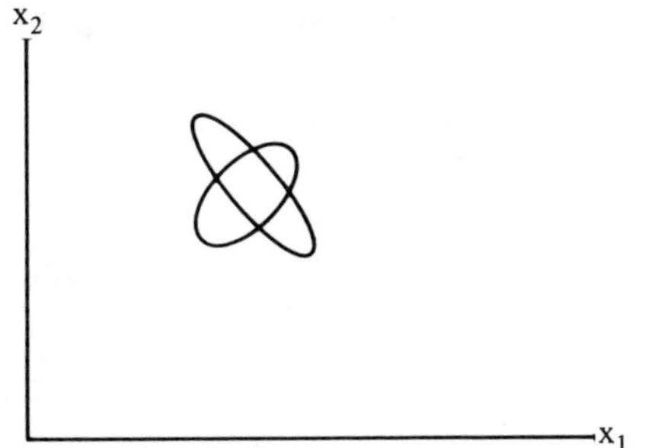

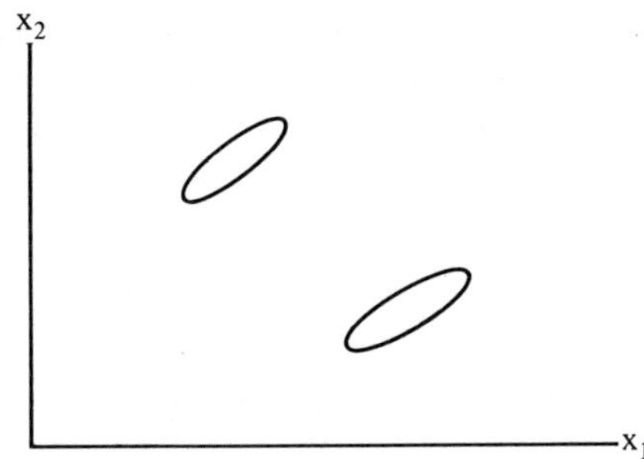

Fig. 5.27 Example needing correlation information to cluster

Fig. 5.28 Example not needing correlation information to cluster

clustering x_2 given some knowledge about x_1. This knowledge may be x_1, or the cluster number of the x_1 space.

Generalizing, note that information can exist in the components of a vector, as in the second example, and in the correlations between components, as in the first example. In dealing with situations where the correlations are important but complexity does not allow use of all dimensions at once, it is desirable to do partial clustering in a subspace and then cluster in other subspaces, providing some knowledge of clustering in the first subspace through a few features. These features may simply tell which cluster in the first subspace a vector fell into, which is a form of conditioning, or may provide more structured information. For example, they may be the features of the cluster center in the first subspace after dimensionality-reducing mappings. The choice of the order in which to process the different dimensions is best made using a priori knowledge.

5-4.9 Growing Clusters from Cluster Centers

Introduction

It has been found advantageous for some problems to initiate growing a cluster from the cluster center; this requires, of course, that an estimate of the cluster center (mean of class-conditional density function) be constructed. The procedure will be to estimate cluster centers using an estimated density. With this in mind define cluster ω_j in the observation space $\mathcal{V}_L$ to be those points $\mathbf{x}_s$ among $\mathbf{x}_1, \mathbf{x}_2, \ldots, \mathbf{x}_n$ for which

$$f_j(\mathbf{x}_s)P_j \geq f_k(\mathbf{x}_s)P_k, \qquad k = 1, 2, \ldots, M. \tag{45}$$

Thus $f_j(\mathbf{x})P_j$ is a measure of the degree of membership of $\mathbf{x}$ in ω_j. If the densities were known, cluster ω_j contains precisely those points $\mathbf{x}$ that would be classified in class j by a Bayes decision rule.

To achieve the above, an estimate of the mixture density is obtained using the potential functions $K(\mathbf{x}, \mathbf{x}_s)$,

$$K(\mathbf{x}, \mathbf{x}_s) \triangleq \frac{1}{1 + \|\mathbf{x} - \mathbf{x}_s\|}, \tag{46}$$

where the norm used here is

$$\|\boldsymbol{\xi}\|^2 = \boldsymbol{\xi}'\boldsymbol{\xi}. \tag{47}$$

Let

$$q(\mathbf{x}) = \sum_{s=1}^{n} K(\mathbf{x}, \mathbf{x}_s). \tag{48}$$

In terms of $q(\mathbf{x})$, an estimate of the mixture density is

$$p_s = \frac{q(\mathbf{x}_s)}{\sum_{j=1}^{n} q(\mathbf{x}_j)}, \qquad s = 1, 2, \ldots, n, \tag{49}$$

defined at the n sample points. Clearly $0 \le p_s$ and $\sum_{s=1}^{n} p_s = 1$, so that $\{p_s\}_{s=1}^{n}$ indeed is a discrete density.

The means $\mathbf{m}_1, \mathbf{m}_2, \ldots, \mathbf{m}_M$ are defined to be the modes of the empirical density on the observed vectors $\mathbf{x}_k$, $k = 1, 2, \ldots, n$.

Assuming multivariate Gaussian class-conditional d.f.'s we define the mean $\mathbf{m}_1$ for cluster ω_1 to be the vector $\mathbf{x}_1^1$ such that p_1^1 is the largest among p_s, $s = 1, 2, \ldots, n$. The mean $\mathbf{m}_2$ for cluster ω_2 is defined to be the vector $\mathbf{x}_1^2$ having greater empirical density than its L nearest neighbors, the observables (excluding $\mathbf{x}_1^1$) being searched in order.† The remaining means are defined similarly so that $\mathbf{x}_1^r \equiv \mathbf{m}_r$ and p_1^r is greater than the L nearest neighbors to $\mathbf{x}_1^r$.

Now, to obtain a nondegenerate initial estimate of the covariance matrix in the canonical coordinate system, the L nearest neighbors to $\mathbf{m}_j$ are appended to cluster ω_j, $j = 1, 2, \ldots, M$. In a two-dimensional space, for example, at least three points are required to obtain a nondegenerate sample covariance matrix; two points will yield a covariance matrix for which one eigenvalue is zero.

With the nearest neighbors appended, each cluster ω_j contains $L + 1$ observables $\mathbf{x}_1^j, \mathbf{x}_2^j, \ldots, \mathbf{x}_{L+1}^j$ at this stage. Thereafter, each observable, denoted $\mathbf{x}_k^j$, is appended to that cluster ω_j for which $(f_j(\mathbf{x}_k^j))_k (P_j)_k$ is greatest,

---

†Although class 1 contains the point $\mathbf{x}_1^1$ with the largest p_j, class 2 does not necessarily contain a point with the next largest p_j not in cluster 1.

     Unsupervised Estimation   *Chap. 5*

where

$$(f_j(\mathbf{x}_k^i))_k(P_j)_k = \frac{(2\pi)^{-L/2}(P_j)_k}{(\sigma_{j1})_k(\sigma_{j2})_k \cdots (\sigma_{jL})_k} \exp[-\tfrac{1}{2}Q_k(\boldsymbol{\xi}_k^j)], \tag{50}$$

$$Q_k(\boldsymbol{\xi}) = \boldsymbol{\xi}^t(\boldsymbol{\Sigma}_j^{-1})_k\boldsymbol{\xi}. \tag{51}$$

$(\boldsymbol{\Sigma}_j)_k$ is the matrix diagonal $[(\sigma_1^2)_k, (\sigma_2^2)_k, \ldots, (\sigma_L^2)_k]$ and $\boldsymbol{\xi}_k^j$ is the vector $\mathbf{x}_k^j$ referred to the canonical orthogonal axes; i.e., the ith component of $\boldsymbol{\xi}_k^j$ is $(\mathbf{x}_k^j - \mathbf{m}_j)^t(\mathbf{e}_i^j)_k$, $(\mathbf{e}_i^j)_k$, being the unit-norm eigenvector belonging to eigenvalue $(\sigma_{ji}^2)_k$. Initially, the mixing-parameter estimates are all set equal to $1/M$. Thereafter, as the clusters are augmented, $(P_j)_k$ is set equal to the relative frequency of elements in cluster j, $j = 1, 2, \ldots, M$.

In the following subsection estimators for the eigenvalues $(\sigma_{ji}^2)_k$ and the eigenvectors $(\mathbf{e}_i^j)_k$, $i = 1, 2, \ldots, L$, are exhibited. These estimators do not involve any matrix operations. Therefore, the problems of small sample size and roundoff error that commonly plague the numerical inversion and diagonalization of matrices are obviated.

Eigenvector and Eigenvalue Estimators

Let $\mathbf{e}$ denote a vector of unit norm. The quadratic form $\mathbf{e}^t\boldsymbol{\Sigma}\mathbf{e}$ is maximized over all vectors $\mathbf{e}$ when $\mathbf{e}$ is an eigenvector belonging to the largest eigenvalue σ_1^2 of $\boldsymbol{\Sigma}$. Note that

$$\begin{aligned}
\mathbf{e}^t\boldsymbol{\Sigma}\mathbf{e} &= E\{\mathbf{e}^t[(\mathbf{x} - \mathbf{m})(\mathbf{x} - \mathbf{m})^t]\mathbf{e}\} \\
&= E\{[\mathbf{e}^t(\mathbf{x} - \mathbf{m})]^2\},
\end{aligned} \tag{52}$$

$\mathbf{m}$ being the expectation of $\mathbf{x}$. Thus, an obvious estimator for the eigenvector $(\mathbf{e}_1^j)_k$ belonging to the largest eigenvalue of the sample covariance matrix is the vector $\mathbf{x}_{(1)}^j - \mathbf{m}_j$ for which the quantity

$$\frac{k^{-1} \sum_{s=1}^{k} [(\mathbf{x}_{(1)}^j - \mathbf{m}_j)^t(\mathbf{x}_s^j - \mathbf{m}_j)]^2}{\| \mathbf{x}_{(1)}^j - \mathbf{m}_j \|^2} \tag{53}$$

is maximized over the k observations currently in ω_j. In turn, the largest eigenvalue $(\sigma_{j1}^2)_k$ is given by (53) with $\mathbf{x}_s^j$ replaced by $\mathbf{x}_{(1)}^j$.

With the largest eigenvalue and its associated eigenvector determined, the next largest eigenvalue $(\sigma_{j2}^2)_k$ and its associated eigenvector $(\mathbf{e}_2^j)_k$ are found by maximizing a quantity similar to (53) in the $(L - 1)$ dimensional orthogonal complement to the span of $(\mathbf{e}_1^j)_k$ (the eigenvectors of a self-adjoint matrix are mutually orthogonal). Specifically,

$$(\mathbf{e}_2^j)_k = \frac{(\mathbf{x}_{(2)}^j - \mathbf{m}_j) - (\mathbf{x}_{(2)}^j - \mathbf{m}_j)^t(\mathbf{e}_1^j)\cdot(\mathbf{e}_1^j)_k}{\| \text{numerator} \|}, \tag{54}$$

where $\mathbf{x}^j_{(2)}$ maximizes

$$\frac{k^{-1} \sum_{s=1}^{k} [(\mathbf{x}^j_s - \mathbf{m}_j)^t(\mathbf{x}^j_{(2)} - \mathbf{m}_j) - (\mathbf{x}^j_{(2)} - \mathbf{m}_j)^t(\mathbf{e}^j_1)_k \cdot (\mathbf{e}^j_1)_k)]^2}{\| (\mathbf{x}^j_{(2)} - \mathbf{m}_j) - (\mathbf{x}^j_{(2)} - \mathbf{m}_j)^t(\mathbf{e}^j_1)_k \cdot (\mathbf{e}^j_1)_k \|^2} \tag{55}$$

over all $\mathbf{x}^j_s: \mathbf{x}^j_s \neq \mathbf{x}^j_{(1)}$.

Proceeding recursively we obtain an estimate $(\mathbf{e}^j_i)_k$ of the eigenvector belonging to the ith largest eigenvalue $(\sigma^2_{ji})_k$ by maximizing a quantity similar to (55) in the $(L - i + 1)$-dimensional orthogonal complement to the span of $(\mathbf{e}^j_1)_k, (\mathbf{e}^j_2)_k, \ldots, (\mathbf{e}^j_{i-1})_k$. Explicitly,

$$(\mathbf{e}^j_i)_k = \frac{(\mathbf{x}^j_{(i)} - \mathbf{m}_j) - \sum_{r=1}^{i-1} (\mathbf{x}^j_r - \mathbf{m}_j)^t(\mathbf{e}^j_r)_k \cdot (\mathbf{e}^j_r)_k}{\| \text{numerator} \|}, \tag{56}$$

where $\mathbf{x}^j_{(i)}$ maximizes

$$k^{-1} \sum_{s=1}^{k} \frac{[(\mathbf{x}^j_s - \mathbf{m}_j)^t((\mathbf{x}^j_s - \mathbf{m}_j) - \sum_{r=1}^{i-1} (\mathbf{x}^j_s - \mathbf{m}_j)^t(\mathbf{e}^j_r)_k \cdot (\mathbf{e}^j_r)_k)]^2}{\| (\mathbf{x}^j_{(i)} - \mathbf{m}_j) - \sum_{r=1}^{i-1} (\mathbf{x}^j_i - \mathbf{m}_j)^t(\mathbf{e}^j_r)_k \cdot (\mathbf{e}^j_r)_k \|^2} \tag{57}$$

over all $\mathbf{x}^j_s: \mathbf{x}^j_s \neq \mathbf{x}^j_{(1)}, \mathbf{x}^j_{(2)}, \ldots, \mathbf{x}^j_{(i-1)}$. Also, $(\sigma^2_{ji})_k$ is given by (57) with $\mathbf{x}^j_s$ replaced by $\mathbf{x}^j_{(i)}$.

The final eigenvector $(\mathbf{e}^j_L)_k$ lies in the one-dimensional orthogonal complement to the span of $(\mathbf{e}^j_1)_k, (\mathbf{e}^j_2)_k, \ldots, (\mathbf{e}^j_{L-1})_k$. Thus

$$(\mathbf{e}^j_L)_k = \frac{\mathbf{x} - \mathbf{m}_j - \sum_{r=1}^{L-1} (\mathbf{x} - \mathbf{m}_j)^t(\mathbf{e}^j_r)_k \cdot (\mathbf{e}^j_r)_k}{\| \text{numerator} \|}, \tag{58}$$

where $\mathbf{x}$ is any vector not contained in the span of $(\mathbf{e}^j_1)_k, (\mathbf{e}^j_2)_k, \ldots, (\mathbf{e}^j_{L-1})_k$. The smallest eigenvalue is computed as

$$(\sigma^2_{jL})_k = k^{-1} \sum_{i=1}^{k} [(\mathbf{x}^j_i - \mathbf{m}_j)^t(\mathbf{e}^j_L)_k]^2. \tag{59}$$

Note that, according to this technique, M is equal to the number of modes in the empirical mixture density and each mode is characterized by the covariance matrix in the canonical coordinate system.

The advantages of the clustering approach presented in this section are

1. Clusters are grown from center points.
2. The use of estimated eigenvectors and associated eigenvalues in estimating $f(\mathbf{x}|\omega_i)P_1$ for computing "distance" may be computa-

tionally less complex than estimating and then inverting a covariance matrix.

3. The criterion of observing $\hat{f}(\mathbf{x}_s \,|\, \omega_i)\hat{P}_1$ decrease and waiting for $q(\mathbf{x}_s)$ to increase may be considered an "adaptive" distance measure.† That is, samples "close" to $\hat{f}(\mathbf{x}_s \,|\, \omega_1)\hat{P}_1$ must be at points of decreasing density with respect to previous points absorbed into the cluster.

Relationship of Clustering to Dimensionality Reduction

In what sense is a clustering procedure accomplishing dimensionality reduction? It is in the sense that finding modes, with associated distance measures, in class-conditional density $f(\mathbf{x} \,|\, \omega_i)$ provides the framework for a nonlinear or linear distance measure for that class. In effect, a nonlinear or linear matched filter for that class is designed with an effective *l*-dimensional space resulting, $l \leq L$.

Complexity reduction associated with the phrase "feature selection" may be achieved by examining interclass density properties.‡ However, this would not be expected to improve performance.

5-4.10 Clustering Using A Priori Supplied Similarity Function

Introduction

In Section 5-4.3 a clustering procedure called "Cluster Map" is considered where a sample $\mathbf{x}$ is said to have a probability density which is characterized by the same parameters characterizing samples "similar to $\mathbf{x}$." Or put differently, $\mathbf{x}$ is from the same probability density as samples which are "similar to $\mathbf{x}$." When using "Cluster Map," samples similar to $\mathbf{x}$ are found using a test function to sift out samples close to $\mathbf{x}$ and this involves a non-Euclidean distance measure. While using this a priori supplied test function, the mean vector and covariance matrix are determined for $\mathbf{x}$ and samples "similar to $\mathbf{x}$."

The similarity concept provides a way to cluster samples which have similar properties; or stated precisely, it provides a way to cluster samples which are judged from the same density because parameters, estimated to characterize the corresponding respective probability densities of these samples, are judged "similar." The procedure "Cluster Map" presumes Gaussian class-conditional densities; therefore, properties correspond to a mean vector and covariance matrix.

In general, a class-conditional density may not be Gaussian; then

---

†This idea of designing a distance measure to fit the a priori knowledge about a problem seems very important.

‡See, for example, [84].

samples from that class should be described by properties other than a mean vector and covariance matrix. This is illustrated by the following examples of the kinds of properties samples from a class-conditional density may have:

1. Gaussian Class-Conditional Density

(a) If $\mathbf{x}_1$ and $\mathbf{x}_2$ are neighbors, then all samples near $\mathbf{x}_1$ should have a *similar* estimated mean vector and covariance matrix as that of all samples near $\mathbf{x}_2$.

(b) If $\mathbf{x}_1$ and $\mathbf{x}_2$ are neighbors, then the k-nearest samples to $\mathbf{x}_1$ should have a mean vector and covariance matrix *most similar* to that of the k-nearest samples to $\mathbf{x}_2$.

(c) If $\mathbf{x}_1$ and $\mathbf{x}_2$ are on an equipotential (determined by an estimated covariance matrix) from an estimated mean vector, then they should have similar local density estimates.

2. Uniform Density on a Circular Domain

(a) Given the mean of the density, there are k samples with a similar Euclidean distance from this mean. This is a statement of symmetry about the mean.

(b) There are k samples on the perimeter of the cluster where the density takes a discontinuous jump to zero. This is a *discontinuous* property at the perimeter.

3. Similarity by Sharing of Near Neighbors

A nonparametric property of a well-behaved class-conditional density is that for any two points $\mathbf{x}_s$, $\mathbf{x}_k$ in $\mathbf{x}_1$, $\mathbf{x}_2$, . . . , $\mathbf{x}_n$, they should share a certain number of neighbors where distance measure is Euclidean. It is not difficult to find class-conditional densities for which this measure of similarity would lead to trouble; nevertheless, it could be an appropriate starting point for exploring data.

The properties of this similarity measure will be

(a) Data points $\mathbf{x}$ are similar if they share a specified number of the same near neighbors using the Euclidean distance measure. In particular, two data points are similar if their respective k-nearest-neighbor lists match.

(b) To avoid the possibility of combining a number of points from a "high-density" class with samples from a "low-density" class, an extra condition is imposed that the k-nearest-neighbor list for $\mathbf{x}_s$ contain $\mathbf{x}_k$ before $\mathbf{x}_s$ and $\mathbf{x}_k$ can be declared similar.

4. Arthritic Diseases

(a) Of 35 features, only the following features are significant for gout:
Occurrence of attacks.
Presence of trophi.
Hyperuricemia.

(b) Of 35 features, only the following are significant for traumatic arthritis:
White cell count/viscosity of synovial fluid.
(White cell count $+$ %polys)/mucin clotting.
Color of synovial fluid.
Clarity of synovial fluid.

(c) Of 35 features, only the following are significant for rheumatic fever:
Viscosity of synovial fluid.
(White cell count $+$ %polys)/mucin clotting.
Color of synovial fluid.
Clarity of synovial fluid

Testing Sample Similarity

Two vector measurements $\mathbf{x}_1$ and $\mathbf{x}_2$ will be said to be in class i (or cluster i) if they have similar properties. Suppose that a relationship exists which, when applied to $\mathbf{x}$, maps points $\mathbf{x}$ of equal class-conditional density to the same point in the new space. Further, suppose that the transformation does not cause samples from another class to overlap samples in this first class. Further, suppose that this function *does not cause samples having equal density of any other class* to map to a same point. Then if this function, designed for one class, is applied to another class, it will not produce points of relatively high density for the latter class as it will for the former. We conclude:

A function g_i designed for class i, mapping L-dimensional measurements to a new space, will

1. Cause samples with similar properties to map to the same point, producing a relatively high density at that point.
2. Even if samples have different class-conditional densities but do have the same properties, they are mapped to the same point.
3. Condition (2) can be relaxed if density variation *is important* for discrimination among classes.
4. When function g_i is applied to class j, because this function does not incorporate properties of class j which are invariant for samples in class j, samples from class j will produce a considerably less dense cluster in another part of the space. These samples from

class j will not overlap samples from class i because they do not have properties built into function g_i.

Constructing a Similarity Matrix

It may be desirable to construct a table where the ith row contains a list of those samples most similar to $\mathbf{x}_i$. Here similarity is measured by comparing $|g_i(\mathbf{x}_i) - g_i(\mathbf{x}_j)|$, for all j not equal to i. Then those K samples most similar to $\mathbf{x}_i$ are stored in the ith row. Two samples $\mathbf{x}_i$, $\mathbf{x}_j$ are said to be from the same class if their rows share a sufficient number of the same samples.

This would seem to be a satisfactory way of grouping these samples if those from class i in this new space now may be assumed to form a globular cluster. However, a simple procedure such as chain map also could probably be used with similar success.

Computer Compiler

It appears desirable to have a basic set of nonlinear relationships which can be called as subroutines or macros for constructing these functions $\{g_i\}_{i=1}^M$. The functions g_i would be constructed much the same way as one writes a Fortran IV program now. Because all problems have a measurement space, and classes have their respective properties, they all fall into this framework.

After clusters are established in the transformed space, it is desirable to be able to extract properties of these clusters such as mean vectors and covariance matrices for use in decision making. Of course, these mean vectors and covariance matrices can be updated with new samples since they are "condensed" properties of the samples. Because, through the g_i, the probability density in the measurement space is converted to a probability density, the functions $\{g_i\}_{i=1}^M$ effectively can be updated using the original $\{g_i\}_{i=1}^M$ as a priori knowledge. The updated estimate could be a weighted sum of the a priori estimate of a density and the current estimate of density.

Example—Similarity by Sharing of Near Neighbors

A clustering procedure using similarity 3 can be constructed as follows:

1. For each point $\mathbf{x}_1$, $\mathbf{x}_2$, $\ldots$, $\mathbf{x}_n$, list its k nearest neighbors, using Euclidean distance measure, by order number $1, 2, \ldots, k$, in a row of a matrix. By regarding each point as its own zeroth neighbor, the first entry in each row is a label indicating to which point the list in that row belongs. Then the raw data can be discarded and the remaining computations are entirely integer.
2. Set up an integer label list of length n with each entry initially set

to the first entry of the corresponding row of the neighborhood matrix.

3. Replace both label entries of two rows of the neighborhood matrix each containing the zeroth neighbor of the other and containing k_t or more neighbor matches. The value of k_t is an interactively supplied number.

4. Clusters for the particular k and k_t are indicated by identical labeling of the points according to 1, 2, and 3 above.

5. Recomputation using new k, k_t can be done by returning to 2.

Because 2 and 3 are integer operations on a set of size $nL \times (k + 1)$, where usually $k \ll L$, computation time is relatively short. Propagating label changes as required in 3 can be made much faster than table search (for large n where it is serious) by using a list-linking procedure; such a procedure forms and utilizes changing information about each group no matter how members of the group are scattered throughout the neighborhood matrix.

To implement 1, two temporary data arrays I, XI, each of size $k + 1$, one integer and the other real, are used to generate each row of the matrix. For each row, initialize all entries in I to zero and all XI entries to a very large number plus a number corresponding to the order in the array; then the last number is the largest and the numbers are monotonically increasing from the first entry to the $(k + 1)$th entry. When a point in $\mathbf{x}_1, \mathbf{x}_2, \ldots, \mathbf{x}_n$ is closer (using Euclidean measure) than the last entry in XI, the last entry is pushed down out of the array and the new distance pushed into the list to maintain monotonic order; the label of the new point replaces the corresponding I entry. When all points have been tested for the list, I entries are transferred to the corresponding main (nontemporary) neighborhood list array. This is done for all points in $\mathbf{x}_1, \mathbf{x}_2, \ldots, \mathbf{x}_n$ producing the n rows of the neighborhood matrix.

Weighted Voting of Near Neighbors

Rather than using Euclidean distance measure in the measurement space, it would be desirable to use a non-Euclidean distance measure, as suggested in the introduction to this subsection, if a priori knowledge about such measures is available. Interactively it may be possible to try different distance measures, preparing neighbor matrices for each distance measure, and then finding which distance measure makes the most sense in terms of the clusters produced.

An approach less nearly optimum than the above (from the theoretical viewpoint) is to provide for different weightings when at step 3 of the procedure of this example. This can be done by weighting the vote of shared neighbors according to their positions in the rows of the neighborhood matrix. Since the ordering in the rows arises naturally in the method of generation, the modification is trivial to implement.

For example, the labels of two rows will be declared identical if a certain weighted comparison of their respective entries is verified. More weight can be given to a match between near neighbors and less to far neighbors. Obviously, this is related to the test function in the cluster mapping procedure of Section 5-4.3, and has the advantage of being significantly faster than the test function applied to the measurements. A disadvantage, however, of weighted voting of near neighbors arises from the fact that near neighbors may not be near if in fact the weights had been used in the measurement space. *Thus the possibility exists that the weighted voting of near neighbors will be working with bad data.* Thus, interactive experience with bad data may not be too rewarding.

Bayes Analysis of Similarity Function Approach

The similarity function essentially is a matched filter and samples are being classified (placed into clusters) using the matched filters. Bayes would suggest that the similarity functions being used have certain fixed but unknown parameters which must be determined.

When a sample is classified to one of the similarity functions an estimate of the parameters characterizing that similarity function results. There will be a distribution on these parameter estimates which is expected to get sharper as the number of samples increases. Eventually the probability density on these parameters should become very sharp at the true parameters characterizing that similarity function. Thus we see how the similarity function approach fits into the Bayes framework.

Concerning the shared nearest neighbor procedure just discussed, the idea essentially is that

$$\hat{f}_i(\mathbf{x}) = \frac{k_i}{(n_i + 1)\Phi_i(\mathbf{x}, \dot{\mathbf{x}}_n)}$$

is an adequate estimate of probability density at $\mathbf{x}$. Two samples $\mathbf{x}_j$, $\mathbf{x}_r$ are classified from the same class if

$$\Phi_i(\mathbf{x}_j, \dot{\mathbf{x}}_n) \sim \Phi_i(\mathbf{x}_r, \dot{\mathbf{x}}_n)$$

where $\sim$ means "similar to," and if the k_i samples in $\Phi_i(\mathbf{x}_j, \dot{\mathbf{x}}_n)$ are similar to the k_i samples in $\Phi_i(\mathbf{x}_j, \mathbf{x}_n)$. Observe that, loosely speaking, the region $\mathscr{I}_i(\mathbf{x}, \dot{\mathbf{x}}_n)$ is being estimated as is $\Phi_i(\mathbf{x}, \dot{\mathbf{x}}_n)$ for samples from this ith class.

In Section 2-18, Eq. (5b), it is shown how the a posteriori probability density $f(\mathbf{b}_k | \dot{\mathbf{x}}_n)$ for parameter vector $\mathbf{b}_k$ characterizing class ω_k is updated from $f(\mathbf{b}_k | \dot{\mathbf{x}}_{n-1})$. In particular, it is shown that updating is weighted by the conditional probability $\mathbf{x}_n$ comes from class ω_k. An approximation is to update only if the conditional probability $\mathbf{x}_n$ is from ω_k is higher than for the other classes; for example, in Section 2-20 a decision-directed estimator suggested by Bayes is

$$f(\mathbf{b}_k \mid \dot{\mathbf{x}}_n) = \begin{cases} f(\mathbf{b}_k \mid \dot{\mathbf{x}}_{n-1}), & \sum_{i \neq k} (w_i)_n > (w_k)_n, \\[2ex] \dfrac{f(\mathbf{x}_n \mid \mathbf{b}_k, k) f(\mathbf{b}_k \mid \dot{\mathbf{x}}_{n-1})}{f(\mathbf{x}_n \mid k)}, & \text{otherwise,} \end{cases}$$

where

$$(w_i)_n = \frac{f(\mathbf{x}_n, i \mid \dot{\mathbf{x}}_{n-1}, \mathbf{b}_k)}{f(\mathbf{x}_n \mid \dot{\mathbf{x}}_{n-1})}.$$

This suggests updating $(\mathbf{b}_k)_{n-1}$ using $\mathbf{x}_n$ as if it were from class ω_k if $(w_k)_n > \sum_{i \neq k} (w_i)_n$.

The reader should also consider the random graphs approach to clustering discussed by Abraham [77] and fuzzy sets discussed by Zadeh [83].

5-5 Decision-Directed Estimation

5-5.1 Introduction

Unless the starting estimators, $(\mathbf{b}_k)_0$, $k = 1, 2, \ldots, M$, used are "reasonably close" to the true parameters, decision-directed parameter estimation for the M-category problem is precarious business. The problem is that "trap states" can cause the grouping of categories (among other problems). Scudder [32] and Patrick and Costello [33] have considered the two-class problem in detail for $\mathscr{F}$ a Gaussian family. The more general M-class problem has been considered by Nagy and Shelton [55], MacQueen [31], and Patrick and Costello [70]. Although MacQueen and Patrick and Costello have produced some conditions for convergence in the M-category case, the conditions are difficult to justify for many practical problems. Besides, the results essentially conclude that if you do not start with estimation "too far off from the true parameter" and the estimation remains "fairly good," then the decision-directed approach may not be a bad procedure to try.

In this section we shall restrict attention to a theoretical discussion of the case where $M = 2$.

5-5.2 The Significant Direction for Two Categories

Scudder [32] used a decision-directed estimator for a single unknown mean vector in a two-category problem. Patrick and Costello [33] extend the approach to a general two-category problem with $\mathscr{F}$ Gaussian and the respective mean vectors unknown. Accordingly, let

$$h(\mathbf{x}) = \sum_{i=1}^{2} N(\mathbf{x} \mid \mathbf{m}_i, \mathbf{\Sigma})P_i. \tag{1}$$

From Chapter 3 the Bayes decision rule classifies $\mathbf{x}_n$ as follows:

$$(\mathbf{m}_1 - \mathbf{m}_2)^t \mathbf{\Sigma}^{-1}(\mathbf{x}_n - \mathbf{x}_0) \begin{cases} > 0: & \text{decide } \omega_1, \\ < 0: & \text{decide } \omega_2, \end{cases} \tag{2}$$

where

$$\mathbf{x}_0 = \frac{\mathbf{\Sigma}(\mathbf{m}_1 - \mathbf{m}_2)}{(\mathbf{m}_1 - \mathbf{m}_2)^t(\mathbf{m}_1 - \mathbf{m}_2)} \ln\left(\frac{1 - P_1}{P_1}\right) + \frac{\mathbf{m}_1 + \mathbf{m}_2}{2}. \tag{3}$$

Letting $\bar{\mathbf{\gamma}} = \mathbf{m}_1 - \mathbf{m}_2$, the above decision equation can be written

$$[\mathbf{\Sigma}^{-1}\bar{\mathbf{\gamma}}]^t(\mathbf{x}_n - \mathbf{x}_0) \begin{cases} > 0: & \text{decide } \omega_1, \\ < 0: & \text{decide } \omega_2, \end{cases} \tag{4}$$

with

$$\mathbf{x}_0 = \frac{\mathbf{\Sigma}\bar{\mathbf{\gamma}}}{(\bar{\mathbf{\gamma}})^t(\bar{\mathbf{\gamma}})} \ln\left(\frac{1 - P_1}{P_1}\right) + \frac{\mathbf{m}_1 + \mathbf{m}_2}{2}. \tag{5}$$

When $\mathbf{\Sigma} = \sigma^2 \mathbf{I}$, the decision equation for classifying $\mathbf{x}_n$ can conveniently be written

$$(\mathbf{m}_1 - \mathbf{m}_2)^t\left(\mathbf{x}_n - \frac{\mathbf{m}_1 + \mathbf{m}_2}{2}\right) > \sigma^2 \ln\left(\frac{P_2}{P_1}\right): \qquad \omega_1. \tag{6}$$

The basic operation involved in this decision equation is taking the inner product of the received sample $\mathbf{x}_n$ with the significant direction and comparing with a threshold (in this case $[\mathbf{\Sigma}^{-1}\bar{\mathbf{\gamma}}]^t\mathbf{x}_n$ and $[\mathbf{\Sigma}^{-1}\bar{\mathbf{\gamma}}]^t\mathbf{x}_0$, respectively).

Since the covariance matrix is known, the decision equation can be simplified by choosing a new set of basis vectors $\{\mathbf{f}_k: k = 1, 2, \ldots, L\}$ composed of the eigenvectors of $\mathbf{\Sigma}$, to represent the decision-equation operation. Letting $\{\mathbf{e}_k: k = 1, 2, \ldots, L\}$ be the basis vectors

$$\mathbf{e}_1 = \begin{bmatrix} 1 \\ 0 \\ 0 \\ \cdot \\ \cdot \\ \cdot \\ 0 \end{bmatrix}, \ \mathbf{e}_2 = \begin{bmatrix} 0 \\ 1 \\ 0 \\ \cdot \\ \cdot \\ \cdot \\ 0 \end{bmatrix}, \ldots, \ \mathbf{e}_L = \begin{bmatrix} 0 \\ 0 \\ 0 \\ \cdot \\ \cdot \\ \cdot \\ 1 \end{bmatrix}, \tag{7}$$

spanning $\mathscr{E}_L$. Define new basis vectors

$$(\mathbf{f}_1, \mathbf{f}_2, \ldots, \mathbf{f}_L) = F(\mathbf{e}_1, \mathbf{e}_2, \ldots, \mathbf{e}_l). \tag{8}$$

But since

$$(\mathbf{e}_1, \mathbf{e}_2, \ldots, \mathbf{e}_l) = \mathbf{I},$$
$$(\mathbf{f}_1, \mathbf{f}_2, \ldots, \mathbf{f}_L) = \mathbf{F}. \tag{9}$$

Since $\mathbf{F}$ is a matrix whose columns are orthogonal eigenvectors of $\boldsymbol{\Sigma}$ and $\boldsymbol{\Sigma}$ is symmetric,

$$\mathbf{F}^t\boldsymbol{\Sigma}\mathbf{F} = [\lambda_i\delta_{ij}] = \boldsymbol{\Lambda}, \tag{10}$$

where $\lambda_1, \lambda_2, \ldots, \lambda_L$ are the corresponding eigenvalues of $\boldsymbol{\Sigma}$. Premultiplying and postmultiplying each side of Eq. (10) by

$$\mathbf{L} = [\lambda_i^{-1/2}\delta_{ij}] = \boldsymbol{\Lambda}^{-1/2} \tag{11}$$

and defining

$$\mathbf{M} = \mathbf{FL}$$
$$= [\mathbf{f}_1\lambda_1^{-1/2}, \mathbf{f}_2\lambda_2^{-1/2}, \ldots, \mathbf{f}_L\lambda_L^{-1/2}] \tag{12}$$

Eq. (10) becomes

$$\mathbf{M}^t\boldsymbol{\Sigma}\mathbf{M} = \mathbf{I}; \tag{13a}$$

hence

$$\boldsymbol{\Sigma} = (\mathbf{MM}^t)^{-1}. \tag{13b}$$

Letting

$$\mathbf{y}_n = \mathbf{M}^t\mathbf{x}_n, \qquad \mathbf{y}_0 = \mathbf{M}^t\mathbf{x}_0, \qquad \boldsymbol{\mu}_i = \mathbf{M}^t\mathbf{m}_i, \tag{14}$$

and substituting Eq. (13b) into the decision equation (4), Eq. (14) gives the transformed decision equation,

$$(\boldsymbol{\mu}_1 - \boldsymbol{\mu}_2)^t(\mathbf{y}_n - \mathbf{y}_0) \begin{cases} > 0: & \text{decide } \omega_1, \\ < 0: & \text{decide } \omega_2, \end{cases}$$

where

$$\mathbf{y}_0 = \frac{\boldsymbol{\mu}_1 - \boldsymbol{\mu}_2}{(\boldsymbol{\mu}_1 - \boldsymbol{\mu}_2)^t(\boldsymbol{\mu}_1 - \boldsymbol{\mu}_2)} \ln\left(\frac{1 - P_1}{P_1}\right) + \frac{\boldsymbol{\mu}_1 + \boldsymbol{\mu}_2}{2}. \tag{15}$$

It is apparent that $(\boldsymbol{\mu}_1 - \boldsymbol{\mu}_2)$ is a "significant direction" and that the components of the random variable $\mathbf{y}_n$ are uncorrelated.

5-5.3 Decision-Directed Estimators

A *decision-directed estimator* $(\mathbf{m}_i)_n$ for $\mathbf{m}_i$ is defined as a weighted sample mean where samples are used that have been classified from class ω_i.

The algorithm for classification of $\mathbf{x}_n$ is the decision equation (6) using $(m_i)_{n-1}$ in the place of the unknown m_i. The set of $\{\alpha_k\}$ weights used in the algorithm definitions below is any sequence of positive numbers satisfying

$$\sum_{k=1}^{\infty} \alpha_k = \infty,$$

$$\sum_{k=1}^{\infty} \alpha_k^2 < \infty. \tag{16}$$

On–Off Case

Let $\mathbf{m}_1 = (\mathbf{m})_n$ and $\mathbf{m}_2 = [0, 0, \ldots, 0]$ in (6). The decision-directed algorithm for $(\mathbf{m})_n$ is then

$$(\mathbf{m})_n = (1 - \rho_n)(\mathbf{m})_{n-1} + \rho_n \mathbf{x}_n, \tag{17}$$

where (at stage $n - 1$, the number of samples classified from class ω_i is N)

$$\rho_n = \begin{cases} \alpha_N, & (\mathbf{m})_{n-1}^t (2\mathbf{x}_n - (\mathbf{m})_{n-1}) \\ & \quad > 2\sigma^2 \ln\left(\dfrac{P_2}{P_1}\right) \text{ and } N = N + 1, \\ 0, & \text{otherwise,} \end{cases} \tag{18}$$

and the P_i are the assumed known.

Binary Case

Using the same approach as in the on–off case, the decision-directed estimators for two unknown mean vectors are expressed as

$$(\mathbf{m}_i)_n = (1 - \rho_{i_n})(\mathbf{m}_i)_{n-1} + \rho_{i_n} \mathbf{x}_n, \qquad i = 1, 2, \tag{19}$$

where (at stage $n - 1$, the number of samples classified from class ω_i is N_i, $i = 1, 2$)

$$\rho_{1_n} = \begin{cases} \alpha_{N_1}, & ((\mathbf{m}_1)_{n-1} - (\mathbf{m}_2)_{n-1})^t \left(\mathbf{x}_n - \dfrac{(\mathbf{m}_1)_{n-1} + (\mathbf{m}_2)_{n-1}}{2}\right) \\ & \quad > \sigma^2 \ln\left(\dfrac{P_2}{P_1}\right) \text{ and } N_1 = N_1 + 1, \\ 0, & \text{otherwise,} \end{cases}$$

$$\rho_{2_n} = \begin{cases} 0, & ((\mathbf{m}_1)_{n-1} - (\mathbf{m}_2)_{n-1})^t \left(\mathbf{x}_n - \dfrac{(\mathbf{m}_1)_{n-1} + (\mathbf{m}_2)_{n-1}}{2}\right) \\ & \quad > \sigma^2 \ln\left(\dfrac{P_2}{P_1}\right), \\ \alpha_{N_2}, & \text{otherwise } N_2 = N_2 + 1. \end{cases}$$

$$\tag{20}$$

The initial vectors $(\mathbf{m})_0$ or $\{(\mathbf{m}_i)_0\}_{i=1}^2$ in (17) and (19), respectively, can be selected arbitrarily utilizing available a priori knowledge or obtained from the samples [for example, in (17), arbitrarily define $(\mathbf{m})_0 = \mathbf{x}_i$]. However, the dynamic performance of the algorithms when $\mathbf{x}_n$ is multidimensional [particularly (19)] is critically dependent on the orientation of $(\mathbf{m}_i)_0$ versus $(\mathbf{m}_i)$ and $((\mathbf{m}_1)_0 - (\mathbf{m}_2)_0)$ versus $(\mathbf{m}_1 - \mathbf{m}_2)$ for (17) and (19), respectively. The orientational "confusion" resulting from a poor choice of the initial vectors is the primary drawback of these algorithms.

A hardware implementation of these algorithms uses $\alpha_k = 1/k$ weighting. The improvement of dynamic performance resulting from other α_k sequences has been studied in [34] and in [70]. It is shown that under certain conditions moderate improvement in performance may be obtained.

As commented upon earlier, knowledge of the P_i, $i = 1, 2$, is of little value unless an ordering is known on $\mathbf{m}_1$ and $\mathbf{m}_2$. For the on–off algorithm there is an implicit ordering since P_2 corresponds to $\mathbf{m}_2 = [0, \ldots, 0]$ and P_1 to the other statistical class; however, there is no such implicit ordering for the binary algorithm.

5-5.4 DEMO-I (Hardware Implementation)

DEMO-I is a hardware implementation of the binary decision-directed algorithms illustrating several design considerations [35]. The system can be operated as a matched filter or in either supervised or unsupervised estimation modes. The number of unknown "signals" that can be "learned" by the receiver is two, and each signal is four-dimensional. The exterior of DEMO-I is shown in Figure 5.29 and a system schematic in Figure 5.30. The

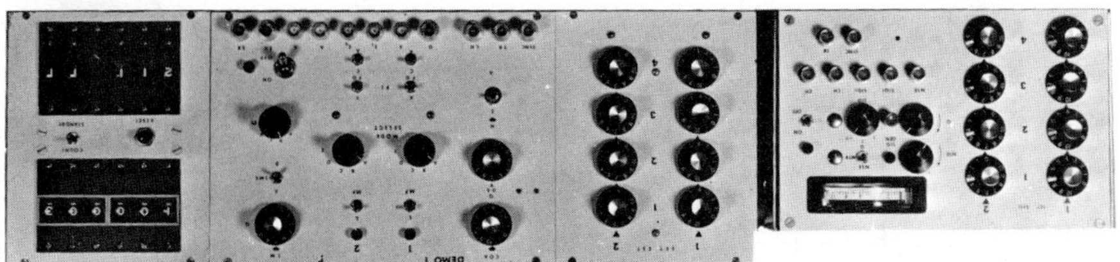

Fig. 5.29 Demo I.

system is composed of two units: a signal generator/channel simulator and a receiver. Pulse-amplitude modulation techniques and time-division multiplexing form the basis of the system design. The basic clock is an astable multivibrator, with bistable multivibrators and other gates and flip-flops providing sample times, sampling pulses, and experiment timings. Integrated circuits are utilized for some of the circuit components. Analog techniques are used in multiplication and addition operations utilizing Hall-effect

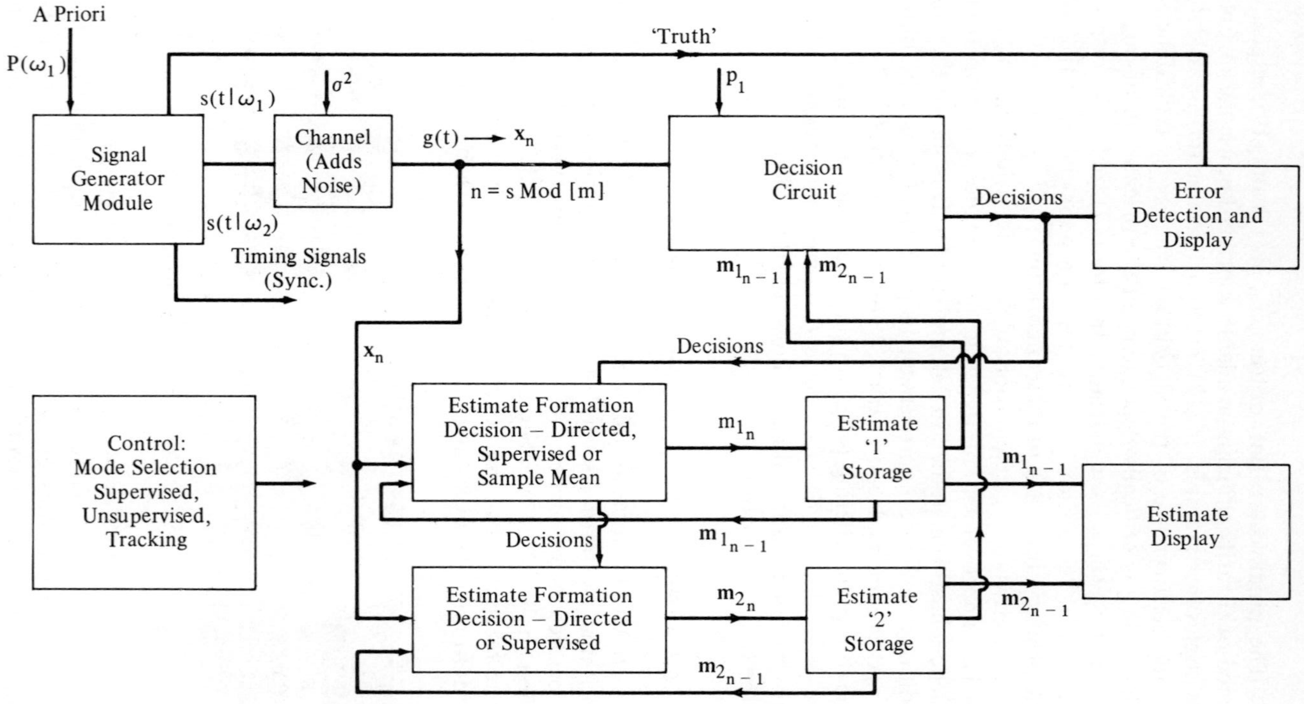

Fig. 5.30 System schematic

multiplier systems. The estimate storage is performed by capacitor stores.

The system has the capability to perform multiple experiments with an experiment length of m samples, where an experiment consists of determining the initial vector(s) or $\{(\mathbf{m}_i)_0\}_{i=1}^{2}$ and updating m times according to the algorithm and mode selected. If $\mathbf{x}_s$ is the sth sample, the corresponding experiment index is $n = s \bmod[m]$.†

Signal Generator and Channel Simulator

The signals consist of four bipolar pulses 2 msec long with amplitudes set on the signal-generator front panel controls. This signal duration has been chosen because of the system's demonstration objective. A comparison of a white-noise generator with an adjustable threshold provides the random selection of the transmitted signal $s(t\,|\,\omega_i)$. The class probabilities are displayed on a front panel meter. The channel simulator adds band-limited white Gaussian noise to the signals, and the adjustable root-mean-square noise value can be read on a meter. A synchronizing signal is provided along with "truth" pulses (telling the true signal classes transmitted) for error detection and supervised estimation.

Receiver

The receiver can be operated as a matched filter with the signal amplitudes set on front panel dials or as a learning system in either supervised or unsupervised estimation modes. The estimate-forming subsystems for each of the two classes have separate controls and can be operated in different modes if desired.

In the learning modes, the estimates can be used in the decision equation as they are formed (iterative operation), or the estimate formed over the last m samples can be used in the decision equation for the next m decisions while a new estimate is being formed (tracking operation). Iterative operation is useful for displaying how learning improves performance with time, while the tracking operation is important when the statistics are nonstationary or where there is storage decay (as in DEMO-I's capacitor stores) and renewed estimation is desirable. The following modes are available on DEMO-I.

1. *Supervised*: In this mode, the true classifications of all samples at the channel output are known, and the receiver calculates the average sample vector for each class ω_i, $i = 1, 2$.
2. *Sample mean*: This mode can be used when the active class is un-

---

†The definition of $a \bmod[b]$ is the smallest positive number obtained from $a - bk$, with k a nonnegative integer.

known (unsupervised estimation) with the class probabilities $P(\omega_i)$, $i = 1, 2$, assumed known and only one class mean vector unknown. Since

$$E[\mathbf{x}_n] = P(\omega_1)\mathbf{m}_1 + [1 - P(\omega_1)]\mathbf{m}_2, \qquad (21)$$

an estimate of m_1, for example, can be obtained by replacing $E[\mathbf{x}_n]$ with the sample mean and $P(\omega_1)$ with the receiver's assumed value P_1, giving

$$\hat{\mathbf{m}}_{1_n} = \frac{1}{P_1}\left[\frac{1}{n}\sum_{k=1}^{n}\mathbf{x}_k - (1 - P_1)\mathbf{m}_2\right]. \qquad (22)$$

The vector $\mathbf{m}_2$ is provided by the signal generator built into the receiver and set by front panel dials.

The starting values for the sample means used in 1 and 2 are normally the first channel output for class ω_1 and the first channel output for class ω_2, respectively, unless a priori knowledge is available.

3. *Decision-directed*: This is the mode of particular interest in this section, implementing the algorithm of (17) or (19) for the on–off or two-unknown mean cases, respectively. The known mean vector in (16) is provided by the receiver internal signal generator. The starting value for each estimate can be the channel output, a first guess, or the estimates of $\mathbf{m}_1$ and $\mathbf{m}_2$ formed over the last m observations using the *tracking mode*. This last method allows a transfer of *labels* from one experiment to the next. The option of starting with one classified sample from each class is also available, providing *supervised starting*.

In the receiver operation, the bipolar-received signals are normalized to negative values within the dynamic range of the receiver. The noise-distorted pulses are sampled approximately at their center for 100 μsec and the component decision equation

$$((m_{1j})_n - (m_{2j})_n)\left(\mathbf{x}_{j_n} - \frac{(m_{1j})_n + (m_{1j})_n}{2}\right), \qquad j = 1, 2, 3, 4, \qquad (23)$$

where† the $(\mathbf{m}_{1j})_n$ are determined by the particular matched filter mode being used (the "known" vectors are set on panel dials, the "unknown" vectors are the appropriate estimates), evaluated for each component sequentially,

†$(\mathbf{m}_{ij})_n$ is the estimate, at stage n, of the jth component in vector $\mathbf{m}_i$, a convenient notation used only here in this section.

and placed in gated capacitor stores. At the end of the signal period the stores are read out, added, and applied to a Schmitt trigger circuit with the threshold set at $\sigma^2 \ln[(1 - P_1)/P_1]$. The output is a pulse on one of two lines depending on the class ω_i declared active.

The updating algorithms are implemented by the estimate-forming subsystems. The subsystems are the same for each vector mean estimate, and a schematic is shown in Figure 5.31. The timing pulses are the same as for decision making. The components of the mean vectors are sequentially updated and stored in "temporary" capacitor stores. The "control" signals (Figure 5.31) step the weight $1/N_i$ after each updating of class ω_i in the various learning modes and transfer the update estimate to "permanent" capacitor storage. A basic constraint of the system is that for each experiment the number of samples used in the experiment must be $m = 8$, 16, 32, or 64, and a panel control is set for one of these four values. At the end of each experiment the contents of the "permanent" estimate stores are transferred to "tracking" stores, erasing the old values.

The receiver also has an error-detection and display subsystem. The "truth" from the signal generator is compared to the receiver decisions at every signal period and an error pulse generated whenever a wrong decision is made. A counter module displays the number of experiments to be performed and the sample number for each experiment at which errors are being counted—both numbers selected manually. Two counters display the current number of experiments performed and errors detected.

5-5.5 Estimator Convergence Theory

The decision-directed estimators were discussed in Section 5-5.3 using the Bayes decision equation for a Gaussian family; however, in general, the family is not actually Gaussian. In [70] it is shown that estimators (20) converge in mean square to the asymptotic vector point under the following conditions:

1. $h(\mathbf{x}_n \mid \mathbf{x}_1, \mathbf{x}_2, \ldots, \mathbf{x}_{n-1}) = h(\mathbf{x}_n)$.
2. The samples $\mathbf{x}_k$ and initial vectors $\{(\mathbf{m}_i)_0\}_{i=1}^{2}$ lie in a closed and bounded convex set $\subset E_L$.
3. $S_1 \triangleq \{\mathbf{x} : ((\mathbf{m}_1)_\infty - (\mathbf{m}_2)_\infty)'[\mathbf{x} - ((\mathbf{m}_1)_\infty + (\mathbf{m}_2)_\infty)/2] > \sigma^2 \ln(P_2/P_1)\}$ is strictly convex function of $(\mathbf{m}_1)_\infty$ and $(\mathbf{m}_2)_\infty$; also, an order relationship between $\mathbf{m}_1$ and $\mathbf{m}_2$ is known if P_1 [the assumed value of $P(\omega_1)$] is not equal to $\frac{1}{2}$. An upper bound B_1 on $\sigma^2 \mid \ln(P_2/P_1) \mid$ is known†

---

†For P_1 [the assumed value of $P(\omega_1)$] not equal to $\frac{1}{2}$, the algorithms defined by (16) and (18) must be modified to include this condition. Samples that would cause the estimators to violate the bound B_1 are ignored.

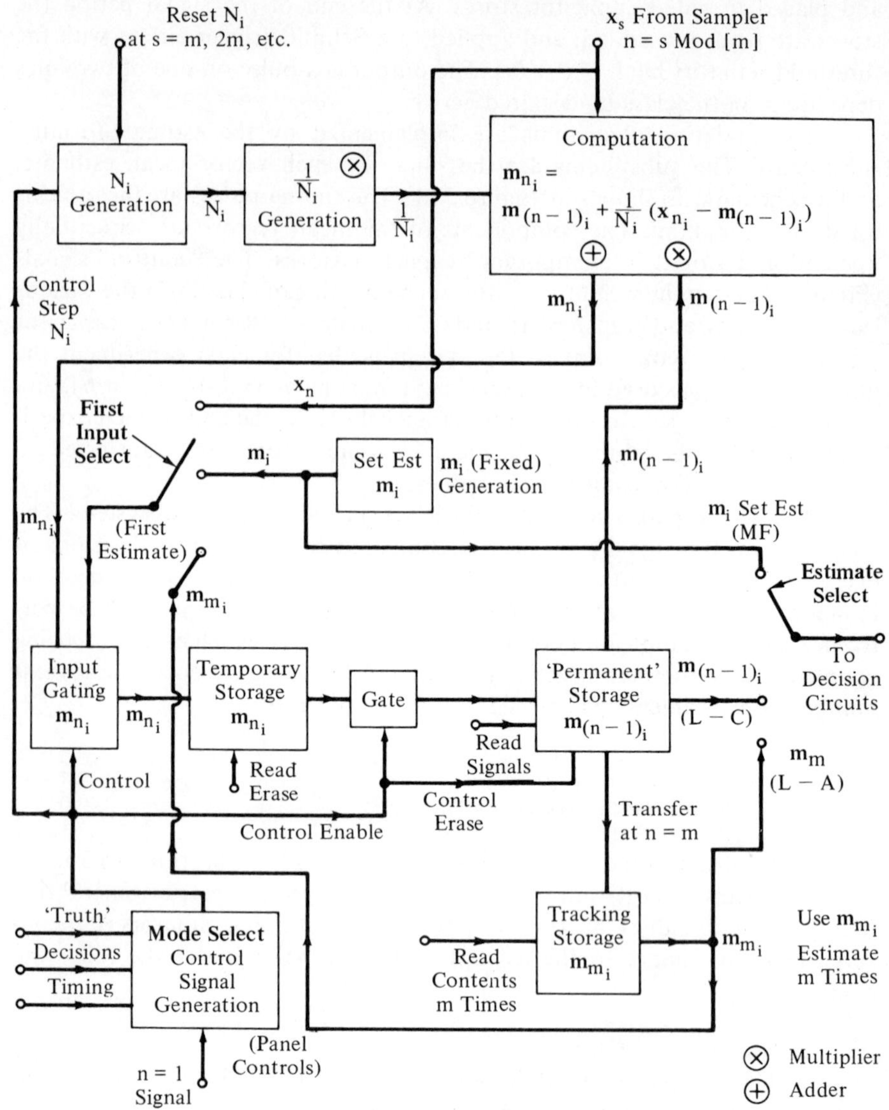

Fig. 5.31 Estimate-making system

such that the mixture density $h(\mathbf{x})$, the bound B_1, and the possible starting vectors $\{(\mathbf{m}_i)_0\}_{i=1}^{2}$ satisfy the integral inequalities

$$\int_{\{\mathbf{x}:\,((\mathbf{m}_1)_0 - \boldsymbol{\mu})^t(\mathbf{x} - (((\mathbf{m}_1)_0 + \boldsymbol{\mu})/2)) > B_1\}} h(\mathbf{x})\, d\mathbf{x} > 0,$$

$$\int_{\{\mathbf{x}:\ (\mathbf{\mu}-(\mathbf{m}_2)_0)^t((\mathbf{x}-(\mathbf{\mu}+(\mathbf{m}_2)_0)/2))<-B_1\}} h(\mathbf{x})\ d\mathbf{x} > 0,$$

where $\mathbf{\mu} \triangleq E[\mathbf{x}]$.

Figure 5.32 contains a plot of the minimum probability of error with

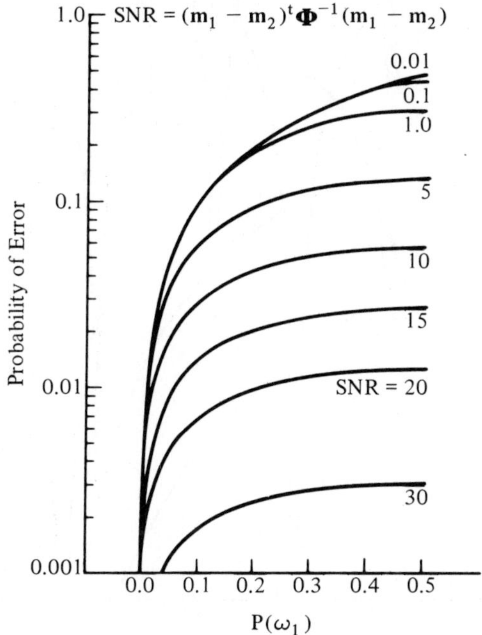

Fig. 5.32 Minimum probability of error vs. $P(\omega_1)$ for several SNR values

all the parameters known. Curves are presented in Figures 5.33 through 5.36 showing ΔP_e versus P_1 [the assumed value of $P(\omega_1)$] with SNR as a parameter for the on–off and binary cases, respectively. Figures 5.33 and 5.35 are with $P_1 = P(\omega_1)$ and an order relationship between $\mathbf{m}_1$ and $\mathbf{m}_2$ known; Figures 5.34 and 5.36 are with $P(\omega_1)$ unknown, but P_1 is assumed to be $\frac{1}{2}$.

Examination of the results shows that the deflections in the value of ΔP_e in Figures 5.33 through 5.36 are due to the relative movements of the optimum and suboptimum decision boundaries as the parameters vary. At certain parameter-set values the boundaries cross, and the optimum and suboptimum systems' probabilities of error are the same.

Figure 5.33 shows that for the class probabilities and an ordering on the $\{\mathbf{m}_i\}_{i=1}^2$ known, the asymptotic performance of the on–off suboptimum system is not much poorer than the system with all parameters known. The

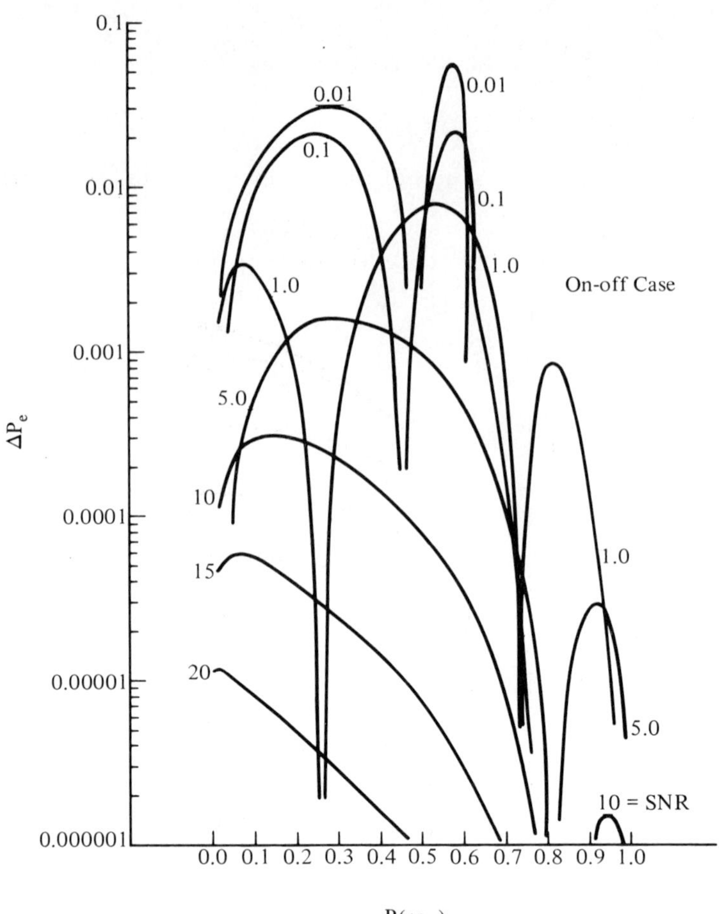

Fig. 5.33 ON-OFF, ΔP_e vs. $P(\omega_1)$, with $P(\omega_1)$ and an ordering $\{\mathbf{m}_i\}_{i=1}^2$ known.

decision-directed estimator for the unknown mean vector is biased, becoming unbiased as the signal-to-noise ratio is increased since the density functions become separable.

The effect of arbitrarily setting P_1 [the assumed value of $P(\omega_1)$] equal to $\frac{1}{2}$ is shown in Figure 5.34 for the on–off system. The curves are nonsymmetric and the rate of degradation of performance is extremely rapid as the differences between the assumed and actual class probabilities increases. However, for higher signal-to-noise ratios, this is an adequate system if $P(\omega_1)$ is not "too close" to the extreme values of zero and 1.

The ΔP_e curves for the two-unknown mean case given in Figures 5.35 and 5.36 are symmetric about $P(\omega_1)$ equal to $\frac{1}{2}$. If $P(\omega_1)$ and an ordering on

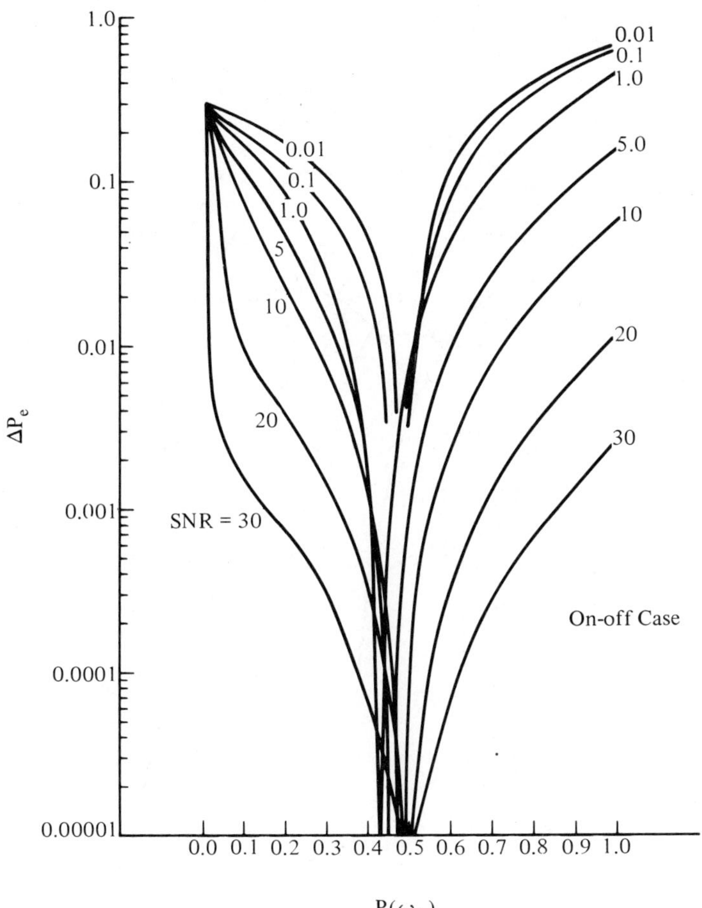

Fig. 5.34 ON-OFF, $\Delta P_e(|P(\omega_1)|$ assumed $\frac{1}{2})$ vs. actual value of $(P(\omega_1))$.

the $\{\mathbf{m}_i\}_{i=1}^2$ are known, Figure 5.35 shows that the asymptotic performance of the system implementing the two-unknown mean algorithm is only slightly worse than that of the optimum system. Although the two decision-directed estimators are biased, for $P(\omega_1) = \frac{1}{2}$, the biases cancel in forming the decision boundary, and this suboptimum decision boundary coincides with the optimum one.

In Figure 5.36 the two-unknown mean vector ΔP_e curves resulting from the system with P_1 set equal to $\frac{1}{2}$ are presented. As stated previously for the corresponding on–off system, for reasonable signal-to-noise ratio and for $P(\omega_1)$ "near" $\frac{1}{2}$, this is an adequate suboptimum system. For $P(\omega_1) = \frac{1}{2}$, the asymptotic probability of error of this two-unknown mean system is the same as the system with all parameters known. From Figure 5.34, this

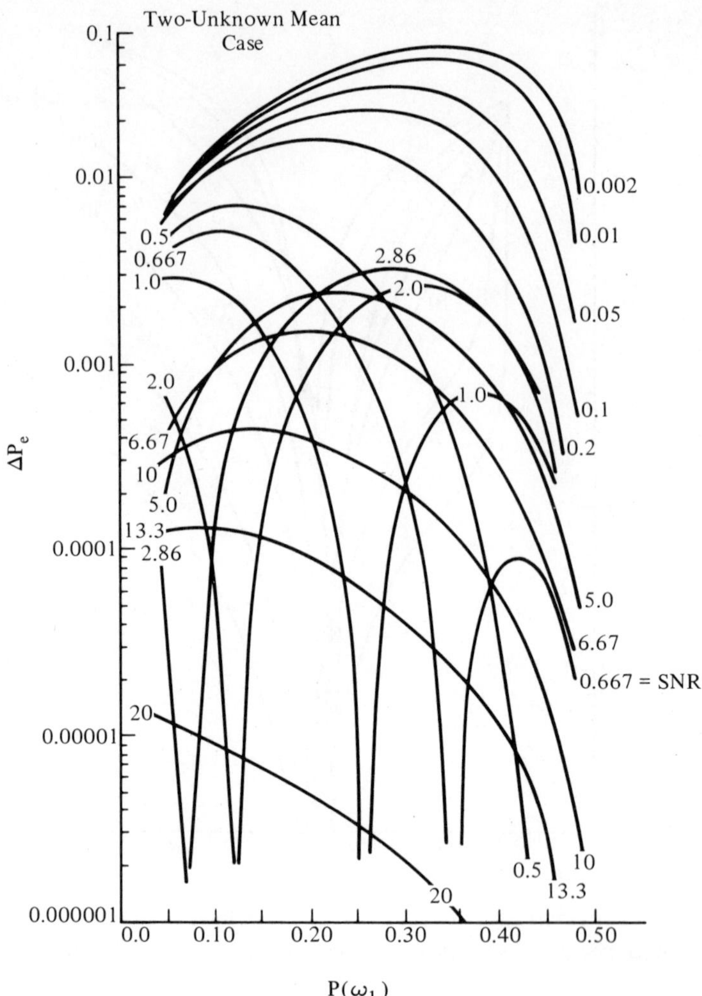

Fig. 5.35 Two-unknown mean, ΔP_e vs. $P(\omega_1)$, with $P(\omega)$ and an ordering on $\{\mathbf{m}_i\}_{i=1}^2$ known.

optimality property is generally not true for the corresponding on–off system.

5-5.6 Experimental-System Performance

As discussed in Section 5-5.4, the special-purpose computer implementing the decision-directed estimators has four-dimensional samples ($L = 4$) and an adjustable decision threshold. For these experimental performance

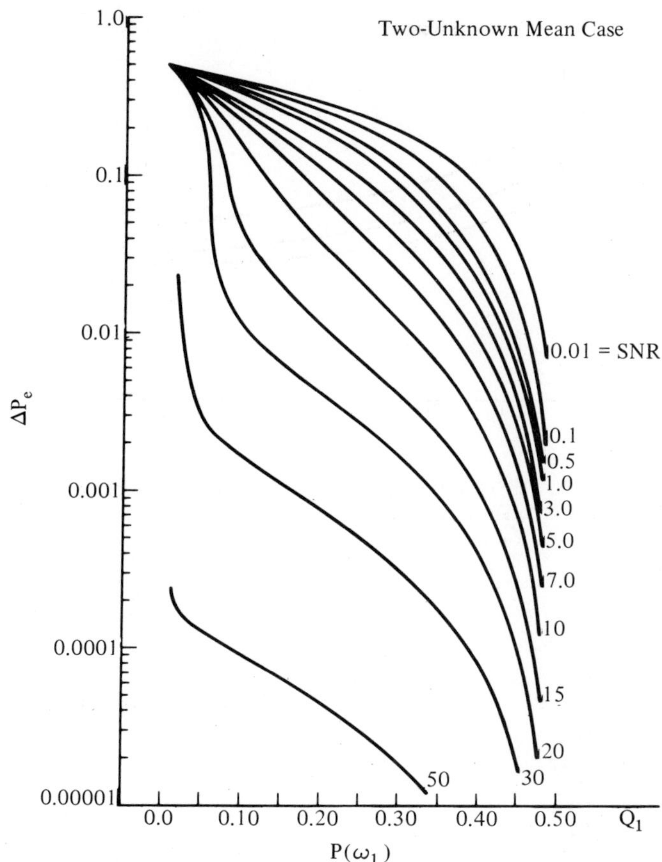

Fig. 5.36 Two-unknown mean, ΔP_e (for $P(\omega_1)$ assumed $\frac{1}{2}$) vs. actual value of $P(\omega_1)$.

results we have defined $P(\omega_1) = \frac{1}{2}$ corresponding to a decision threshold of zero on DEMO-I. No a priori ordering information on the mean vectors is assumed, and the initial vector estimates $(\mathbf{m})_0$ for the on–off algorithm or the $\{(\mathbf{m}_i)_0\}_{i=1}^2$ for the two-unknown mean-case algorithm are defined as the first or first two-channel output vectors, respectively. Five sets of 50 experiments were run for the iterative on–off algorithm, the iterative binary algorithm, and the binary-case algorithm using the tracking mode. The average probability of error for each set of 50 experiments was determined and the median plotted for the various algorithms in Figures 5.37 through 5.39 versus the number of samples n, with signal-to-noise ratio SNR $\triangleq (\mathbf{m}_1 - \mathbf{m}_2)'(\mathbf{m}_1 - \mathbf{m}_2)/\sigma^2$ as a parameter.

The iterative on–off algorithm experimental dynamic average probability of error curves is shown in Figure 5.37. Although not indicated on the

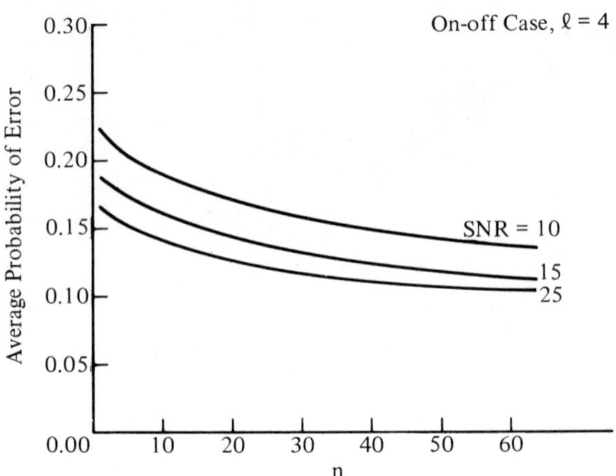

Fig. 5.37 ON-OFF case average probability of error vs. n for several SNR values and a 4-dimensional sample space.

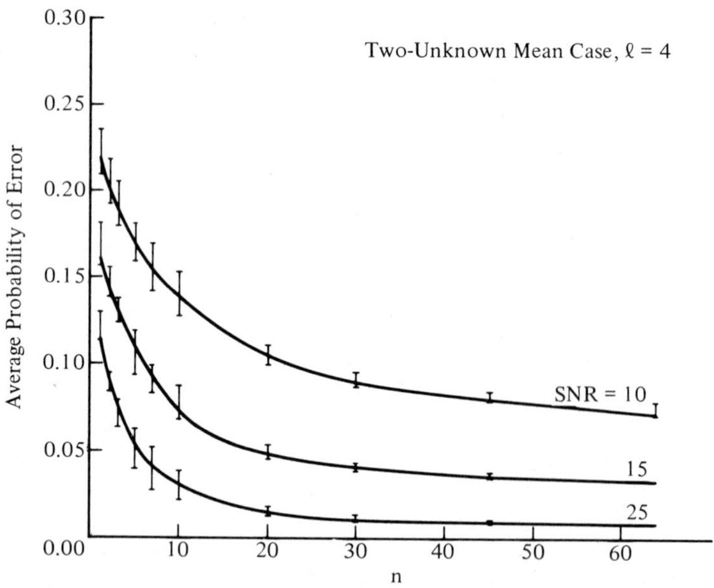

Fig. 5.38 Two-unknown mean case average probability of error vs. n, for several SNR values and a 4-dimensional sample space.

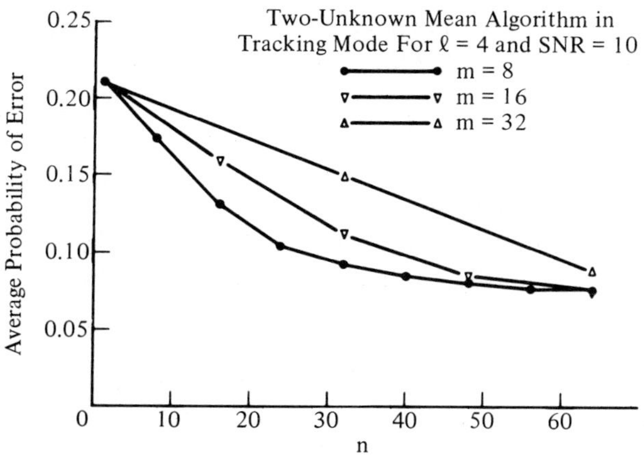

Fig. 5.39 Two-unknown mean tracking mode, average probability of error vs. the number of samples n, for several values of m.

curves, the standard deviation of the probability of error per experiment is approximately 0.2 for the n shown. This high standard deviation is due to the effect of initial vectors $(\mathbf{m})_0$ falling on the "opposite" side of the known vector from the unknown vector. Under certain conditions there results a "trap" state; i.e., $(\mathbf{m})_n$ can never approach the unknown mean vector. Conditions exist such that the system converges eventually, but the time necessary for $(\mathbf{m})_n$ to rotate around the known vector is reflected by the slow convergence in Figure 5.37.

The experimental dynamic average-probability-of-error curves for the two-unknown mean-case algorithm are shown in Figure 5.38. The smallest and largest average probabilities of error of the five sets of 50 experiments are also presented. From these curves, if the two classes are reasonably separated, the convergence is relatively rapid, even with the often poor starting values obtained by using the first two-channel output vectors as the $\{(\mathbf{m}_i)_0\}_{i=1}^2$.

Figure 5.39 shows the experimental average-probability-of-error curves for the two-unknown mean-case algorithm in the tracking mode. The statistics used in the experiments is stationary. In the tracking mode the initial vectors are chosen as the first two-channel output vectors; however, m samples are processed before the decision boundary is updated. The curves show that the smaller the value of m, the more rapid the initial rate of convergence. Since large-sample system performance is better for higher values of m, this indicates the tradeoff involved in the selection of the value of m in a system.

5-5.7 *Clusters on a Minimum Distance Partition Using Decision-Directed Procedure*

It should not be surprising to the reader that a decision-directed estimator for $\mathbf{b}_i$ may fail to converge to $\mathbf{b}_i^*$ characterizing $f(\mathbf{x}\,|\,i)$. A reason for this is that there exist trap states defined as states where no further updating is possible for one or more of the $\mathbf{b}_i$.

Discussion will be restricted to the Gaussian family where $f(\mathbf{x}\,|\,i)$ is characterized by one fixed but unknown mean vector $\mathbf{m}_i$, and the a priori class probability $P_i = 1/M$ and M is known. The number of classes M is unknown but an upper bound $M' > M$ is available.

Define $S_i(\mathbf{m}, \mathbf{p})$ as the region of the observation space $\mathscr{X}$ where a Bayes decision rule would decide class i, given $\mathbf{m}$ and $\mathbf{p}$:

$$S_i(\mathbf{m}, \mathbf{p}) = \{\mathbf{x} : f(\mathbf{x}\,|\,\mathbf{m}_i)P_i > f(\mathbf{x}\,|\,\mathbf{m}_j)P_j, j = 1, 2, \ldots, M', j \neq i\}, \qquad (24)$$

where

$$\mathbf{m} = [\mathbf{m}_1, \mathbf{m}_2, \ldots, \mathbf{m}_{M'}], \qquad (25a)$$

$$\mathbf{p} = [P_1, P_2, \ldots, P_{M'}]. \qquad (25b)$$

Minimum Distance Partition

Given samples $\mathbf{x}_1, \mathbf{x}_2, \ldots, \mathbf{x}_n$ it is possible to select points $(\mathbf{m}_1)_N, (\mathbf{m}_2)_N, \ldots, (\mathbf{m}_M)_N$ such that the average distance from the samples to these points is minimized. Let

$$T_i((\mathbf{m})_N) \triangleq \{\mathbf{x} \in \mathscr{X} : \|\mathbf{x} - (\mathbf{m}_i)_N\| \leq \|\mathbf{x} - (\mathbf{m}_j)_N\|, j = 1, 2, \ldots, M\} \qquad (26)$$

and

$$
\begin{aligned}
S_1((\mathbf{m})_N) &\triangleq T_1((\mathbf{m})_N), \\
S_2((\mathbf{m})_N) &\triangleq T_2((\mathbf{m})_N) \cap (S_1((\mathbf{m})_N))^c, \\
S_3((\mathbf{m})_N) &\triangleq T_3((\mathbf{m})_N) \cap (S_1((\mathbf{m})_N))^c \cap (S_2((\mathbf{m})_N))^c, \\
&\quad\vdots \\
S_M((\mathbf{m})_N) &\triangleq T_M((\mathbf{m})_N) \cap (S_1((\mathbf{m})_N))^c \cap \cdots (S_{M-1}((\mathbf{m})_N))^c
\end{aligned}
\qquad (27)
$$

and define

$$S((\mathbf{m})_N) \triangleq \{S_1((\mathbf{m})_N), S_2((\mathbf{m})_N), \ldots, S_M((\mathbf{m})_N)\}, \qquad (28)$$

which is a minimum distance partition with respect to $(\mathbf{m})_N$.

In the procedure described next, regions $S_i(\mathbf{m}, \mathbf{P})$ are found which, in general, do not satisfy (24). Because $\mathbf{P}$ is assumed known, it is convenient to remove it from notation. The average distance with respect to a density $h(\mathbf{x})$ is

$$W((\mathbf{m})_N) \triangleq \sum_{i=1}^{M} \int_{S_i((\mathbf{m})_N)} \| \mathbf{x} - (\mathbf{m}_i)_N \|^2 h(\mathbf{x}) \, d\mathbf{x}. \tag{29}$$

The mean of $\mathbf{x}$ over a region $S_i(\mathbf{m})$ with respect to $h(\mathbf{x})$ is

$$\boldsymbol{\mu}_i = \int_{S_i(\mathbf{m})} \mathbf{x} \, \frac{h(\mathbf{x})}{\int_{S_i(\mathbf{m})} h(\boldsymbol{\xi}) \, d\boldsymbol{\xi}} \, d\mathbf{x}. \tag{30}$$

McQueen [31] defines $\boldsymbol{\mu}_i$ as "unbiased" for $\mathbf{m}_i$ if $\boldsymbol{\mu}_i = \mathbf{m}_i$ which says nothing about $\boldsymbol{\mu}_i$ being unbiased for $\mathbf{m}_i^*$.

Trap States

Define $(A_i)_N$ as a region of $\mathscr{X}$ where, at stage N, class i can be updated without producing a trap state. Obviously $(A_i)_N$ must be contained in $(S_i)_N$,

$$(A_i)_N \subset (S_i)_N, \tag{31}$$

where it is understood that both $(A_i)_N$ and $(S_i)_N$ depend on $(\mathbf{m})_N$ and $\mathbf{P}$.

We already know that estimators can be constructed for the $\mathbf{m}_i$ when $\mathscr{F}$ is Gaussian, which converge to the $\mathbf{m}_i^*$. Basically, the existence of a uniquely maximized $\eta(\mathbf{b}) = \int \ln h(\mathbf{x}\,|\,\mathbf{b}) h(\mathbf{x}\,|\,\mathbf{b}^*) \, d\mathbf{x}$ makes this possible. The difficulty with a decision-directed estimator, although attractive because of its simplicity, is that it may not involve solution for the argument maximizing $\eta(\mathbf{b})$. There then are numerous ways that decision regions $(S_i)_n$ can be produced for which no further samples $(\mathbf{x}_{n+1}, \mathbf{x}_{n+2}, \ldots)$ will "fall" in the region, resulting in a trap state.

Delayed Updating

To try to avoid a single sample causing the generation of a trap state, a reasonable procedure is to collect k samples, while holding the estimators for $\mathbf{m}_i$ fixed, and then update using all k samples at once. One possible such procedure is described below. Let $\{\mathbf{x}_s\}_{s=Nk+1}^{(N+1)k}$ be k samples collected at stage N, where

$$n = Nk, \text{ at stage } N, \, N = 0, 1, 2, \ldots . \tag{32}$$

Define $(Nk + 1 < n < (N + 1)k)$

$$(\boldsymbol{\xi}_i)_r = (1 - \beta_i(k))(\boldsymbol{\xi}_i)_{k-1} + \beta_i(k)\mathbf{x}_{Nk+r}, \qquad r = 1, 2, \ldots, k, \tag{33a}$$

where

$$(\beta_i)_k = \begin{cases} \dfrac{1}{k_i}, & \mathbf{x}_{nk+r} \in (A_i)_N \\[2mm] & \text{and } k_i = k_i + 1, \\[2mm] 0, & \text{otherwise.} \end{cases} \qquad (33\text{b})$$

After all k samples at stage N have been classified, all $(\xi_i)_r$, $r = 1, 2, \ldots, k$, have been calculated.

Now, at the end of this Nth stage [after processing $n = (N+1)\,k$], the estimate $(\mathbf{m}_i)_N$ is updated:

$$(\mathbf{m}_i)_{N+1} = (1 - \rho_i(N+1))(\mathbf{m}_i)_N$$
$$+ \rho_i(N+1)(\xi_i)_k, \qquad N = 0, 1, 2, \ldots, \qquad (34\text{a})$$

where

$$\rho_i(N+1) = \begin{cases} \alpha_{w_i(N)}, & k_i > 0 \\[1mm] & \text{and } w_i(N+1) = w_i(N) + 1, \\[2mm] 0, & k_i = 0 \\[1mm] & \text{and } w_i(N+1) = w_i(N). \end{cases} \qquad (34\text{b})$$

After $(\mathbf{m}_i)_{N+1}$ is computed, all k_i are reinitialized to zero.

Sufficient Conditions for Convergence

Convergence of $(\mathbf{m}_i)_{N+1}$ to a point, not necessarily $\mathbf{m}_i^*$, can be demonstrated. Here we present sufficient conditions for such convergence and describe the point to which $(\mathbf{m}_i)_{N+1}$ converges under these conditions.

Theorem   If the following conditions 1 through 6 hold,

1. $\mathbf{x}_1, \mathbf{x}_2, \ldots, \mathbf{x}_n$ are statistically independent given $h(\mathbf{x})$, M is assumed known, and it is assumed $P_i = 1/M$.
2. $h(\mathbf{x})$ is absolutely continuous.
3. There exists a closed and bounded convex set $\mathscr{X}' \subset \mathscr{X}$ such that

$$\int_{\mathscr{X}'} h(\mathbf{x})\, d\mathbf{x} = 1.$$

4. For any open set $A \in \mathscr{X}$, $\int_A h(\mathbf{x})\, d\mathbf{x} > 0$.

5. $p\left[\lim_{n \to \infty} \dfrac{p((A_i)_N)}{p((S_i)_N)} = 1 \right] = 1, \; i = 1, 2, \ldots, M.$

then

6. (a) $W((\mathbf{m})_1)$, $W((\mathbf{m})_2)$, ..., $W((\mathbf{m})_N)$ converges with probability 1 if $(\mathbf{m}_i)_0 \in \mathcal{X}'$ and there exists $\mathbf{m}$ such that
   (b) $\lim W((\mathbf{m})\mathbf{b}) = V(\mathbf{m})$,

where

$$V(\mathbf{m}) = \lim_{N \to \infty} \sum_{i=1}^{M} \int_{(S_i)_N} \| \mathbf{x} - \mu_{(S_i)_N} \|^2 h(\mathbf{x})\, d\mathbf{x}$$

with† $\mu_{S_i} = E[\mathbf{x} \mid S_i]$. The proof of this theorem may be found in [70] which is an extension of a result by MacQueen [31].

The reader should observe that $W((\mathbf{m})_N)$ in condition 6 is a criterion which approximates the information function $\int \ln h(\mathbf{x} \mid \mathbf{b}) h(\mathbf{x})\, d\mathbf{x}$ for $\mathcal{F}$ Gaussian, M known, and $P_i = 1/M$.

The result of this theorem is that it is possible to use a decision-directed procedure to obtain a minimum distance partition of the measurement space. It does not demonstrate positive covergence properties for decision-directed estimators.

5-6 Additional Literature

It appears that the earliest unsupervised problem to receive considerable interest in modern communications and information theory was one where a single unknown signal waveform was transmitted through an unknown noisy stationary channel; the problem was to estimate the unknown waveform and to determine when it was present. An energy detector for this problem which evolved into a matched filter was formulated by Glaser [3]. Each time a signal was decided present by the energy detector the signal was averaged into the estimate of the unknown signal waveform and the matched-filter part of the detector for that class was updated.

MacQueen [31] considered a mathematical definition of the decision-directed estimator where the observation space is partitioned into M regions. He proved convergence, with probability 1, of estimators for parameters characterizing the regions. His presentation of the problem clearly shows that, with the decision-directed approach, there can result "trap states" which prevent convergence. In the consideration of the decision-directed estimator definition, the requirement of "good" starting values for the parameters was imposed to avoid the "trap states." For the two-category

---

†There may not be a unique solution $\mathbf{m}$ such that $\mathbf{m}_i = E[\mathbf{x} \mid S_i(\mathbf{m})]$.

problem with $\mathscr{F}$ Gaussian, Scudder [32] evaluated asymptotic probability of error of the decision-directed estimator when there is one unknown mean vector. Patrick and Costello [33] extended the evaluation to the case of two-unknown mean vectors. In these decision-directed estimators, the updating utilizes a uniform weighting sequence (i.e., $1, \frac{1}{2}, \frac{1}{3}, \ldots$). A nonuniform weighting sequence was derived by Gregg and Hancock [34] and resulted from an attempt to find an "optimum" weighting sequence. A special-purpose computer which implements the two-category decision-directed algorithm was built and has been described in a paper by Patrick, Costello, and Monds [35].

It has been discussed elsewhere in this book that an approach to "sample-based† decision making," suboptimum from the Bayes viewpoint, is to use estimated density $f(\mathbf{x}|i)$ for the ith category in the Bayes decision rule. In particular, the performance of decision procedures that use consistent unsupervised estimation algorithms to improve knowledge of the underlying statistics has received considerable study. Decision procedures that classify $\mathbf{x}_1, \mathbf{x}_2, \ldots, \mathbf{x}_n$ only after the unsupervised estimation algorithm has processed an entire finite data set $\{\mathbf{x}_s\}_{s=1}^n$ are called *compound* decision procedures. However, if $\{\mathbf{x}\}_{s=1}^k$ are used to classify only $\mathbf{x}_k$, this is called a *sequential-compound* decision procedure. Most results assume that the samples corresponding to each category come from a known parametric family $\mathscr{F}$ of density functions. The measure of performance used in analyzing compound and sequential-compound decision procedures is called the *regret function*. This is defined as the difference between the average risk of the decision rule using the estimated densities and the minimum average risk computed assuming n supervised samples from the categories. There is a good, brief tutorial on compound and sequential-compound decision procedures by Abend [36].

Assuming a known, fixed finite parametric family, and estimating the unknown mixing parameters, Van Ryzin found uniform bounds on the rate of convergence of the regret function to zero or both compound [37] and sequential-compound [38] decision procedures. These results followed over a decade of work on the problem defined by the fixed, finite family assumption. Van Ryzin's unsupervised estimation procedure uses Robbins functions defined in Section 5-3.8. Alens [39] assumed an infinite known parametric family and showed that the respective regret functions for sequential-compound decision procedures using moment estimators and using maximum-likelihood estimators converge to zero. Other work related to the compound Bayes procedure is that of Samuel [40, 41] and Van Ryzin [42].

These results, related to a compound Bayes and a sequential-compound Bayes, can be summarized as showing that if an unsupervised estimation procedure for the category densities converge, then a Bayes decision rule

†Sample-based decision making is where an empirical approach to density estimation is used. Parameters other than the samples are not necessarily exhibited for classifying the densities $f(\mathbf{x}|i)$.

utilizing these density estimators converges. This is a worthwhile finding, but the estimation procedures developed may be impractical.

The reader may be interested in reading a paper by Robbins [43] entitled The Empirical Bayes Approach to Statistical Decision Problems. A paper by Blischke [44] considered moment estimators for the parameters of a mixture of binomial densities. Patrick and Carayannopoulos [45] extended results in [44] to obtain codes for unsupervised estimation of a priori signal probabilities in a communications system. It is interesting that before this latter work it was not possible to estimate unknown signal probabilities in a communications receiver. A paper by Stewart and Patrick [46] investigated the problem of estimating synchronization parameters in a received waveform; the more general but abstract treatment is found in [10]. Fralick, Slenkorick, and Wilson [47] applied unsupervised estimators to a communications problem where there is an unknown signal frequency. The reader may find a tutorial paper by Spragins [48] written in 1966 instructive in showing the state of unsupervised estimation in 1966. Patrick [49] wrote a paper in 1969 to try to clear up certain misconceptions concerning the difference between estimation and adaption; in this paper the concept of an adaptive estimation system is presented. A book by Fu [50] is available containing much of his work and related work in stochastic approximation with emphasis on sequential pattern recognition. Another book, by Kanal [51], contains material on such topics as compound decision rules as well as image processing. A collection of papers in a book by Watanabe [52] covers approaches to clustering and image processing, and there are some very interesting examples of applications in pattern recognition, such as fingerprint analysis and character recognition. Another collection of papers covering topics in feature selection, for example, is found in a book by Tou [53]. Perhaps the most complete coverage of theoretical image processing is found in a book by Rosenfeld [54]. The reader should also consider Nagy and Shelton [55].

A book by Caceres and Ribli [88] and one by Lusted [89] discuss applications of pattern recognition in computer-assisted diagnosis in medicine. The approaches used do not include such techniques as multidimensional clustering, k-nearest-neighbor decision rules, decision-directed procedures for updating decision rules, or decision rules conditioned on training samples for non-Gaussian statistics. This field of medical diagnosis and treatment appears one of the most fruitful for applying the techniques presented in this book.

Suggested Reading for Chapter 5

[1] K. Pearson, Contributions to the Mathematical Theory of Evolution, *Phil. Trans. Roy. Soc. London*, Vol. 185, p. 71, 1894.

[2] K. Pearson, On the Systematic Fitting of Curves to Observations and Measurements, *Biometricka*, Vol. I, p. 1, 1902.

[3] E. M. Glaser, Signal Detection by Adaptive Filters, *IRE Trans. Information Theory*, Vol. IT-7, No. 2, pp. 87–97, April 1961.

[4] C. V. Jakowatz, R. L. Shuey, and G. M. White, Adaptive Waveform Recognition, *General Electric Research Laboratory Tech. Rept. 60-RL-2353E*, Schenectady, N.Y., May 1960.

[5] M. J. Hinich, A Model for a Self-Adapting Filter, *Information and Control*, Vol. 5, No. 3, pp. 185–203, Sept. 1962.

[6] R. F. Daly, The Adaptive Binary-Detection Problem on the Real Line, *Stanford Electronics Laboratories Tech. Rept. 2003–3*, Stanford, Calif., Feb. 1962.

[7] S. C. Fralick, Learning to Recognize Patterns Without a Teacher, *IEEE Trans. Information Theory*, Vol. IT-13, No. 1, pp. 57–64, Jan. 1967; also *Stanford Electronic Laboratories Tech. Rept. 6103–10, SEL-65-011*, Stanford, Calif., March 1965.

[8] E. A. Patrick and J. C. Hancock, Nonsupervised Sequential Classification and Recognition of Patterns, *IEEE Trans. Information Theory*, Vol. IT-12, No. 3, pp. 362–372, July 1966.

[9] J. C. Hancock and E. A. Patrick, Interactive Computation of Aposteriori Probability for M-ary Nonsupervised Adaptation, *IEEE Trans. Information Theory*, Vol. IT-12, No. 4, pp. 483–484, Oct. 1966.

[10] E. A. Patrick, On A Class of Unsupervised Estimation Problems, *IEEE Trans. Information Theory*, Vol. IT-14, No. 3, pp. 407–415, May 1968.

[11] G. G. Hilborn, Jr., and D. G. Lainiotis, Optimal Unsupervised Learning Multicategory Dependent Hypothesis Pattern Recognition, *IEEE Trans. Information Theory*, Vol. IT-14, No. 3, pp. 468–470, May 1968.

[12] E. A. Patrick and J. P. Costello, On Unsupervised Estimation Algorithms, *IEEE Trans. Information Theory*, Vol. IT-16, No. 5, pp. 556–569, Sept. 1970.

[13] E. A. Patrick, Learning Probability Spaces for Classification and Recognition of Patterns With or Without Supervision, Ph.D. Thesis, Purdue University, Lafayette, Ind., Nov. 1965.

[14] E. A. Patrick and J. C. Hancock, The Nonsupervised Learning of Probability Spaces and Recognition of Patterns, *IEEE Intern. Convention Record*, Part II, 1965.

[15] H. Teicher, On the Mixture of Distributions, *Ann. Math. Statistics*, Vol. 31, No. 1, pp. 55–73, March 1961.

[16] H. Teicher, Identifiability of Finite Mixtures, *Ann. Math. Statistics*, Vol. 34, No. 4, pp. 1265–1269, Dec. 1963.

[17] H. Teicher, Identifiability of Mixtures, *Ann. Math. Statistics*, Vol. 32, No. 1, pp. 244–248, March 1961.

[18] N. Barndorff, Identifiability of Mixtures of Exponential Families, *J. Math. Anal. Appl.*, Vol. 12, pp. 115–121, 1965.

[19] S. Yakowitz and John Spragins, A Characterization Theorem on the Identifiability of Finite Mixtures, presented at the 1966 International Communications Conference, June 1966; later in *Ann. Math. Statistics*, Vol. 39, No. 1, pp. 209–214, Feb. 1968.

[20] H. Teicher, Identifiability of Mixtures of Product Measures, *Ann. Math. Statistics*, Vol. 38, No. 4, pp. 1300–1302, Aug. 1967.

[21] D. B. Cooper and P. W. Cooper, Nonsupervised Adaptive Signal Detection and Pattern Recognition, *Information and Control*, Vol. 7, No. 3, pp. 416–444, 1964.

[22] D. B. Cooper, On the Existence of Nonsupervised Adaptive Signal Detectors; and Dector Estimation Using Stochastic Approximation Methods, Ph.D. Dissertation, Columbia University, New York, April 1966.

[23] P. W. Cooper, Some Topics on Nonsupervised Adaptive Detection for Multivariate Normal Distributions, *Computer and Information Sciences*, Vol. II, Academic Press, Inc., New York, 1967.

[24] E. A. Patrick, Asymptotic Distribution of Maximum Likelihood Estimators for a Nonsupervised Adaptive Receiver, *IEEE Intern. Communication Conference Record*, Philadelphia, June 1966.

[25] J. H. Wolfe, NORMIX: Computational Methods for Estimating the Parameters of Multivariate Normal Mixtures of Distributions, *Activity, Research Memorandum SRM68-6, U. S. Naval Personnel Research*, San Diego, Calif., Aug. 1967.

[26] D. J. Sakrison, Stochastic Approximation, a Recursive Method for Solving Regression Problems, *Advances in Communication Systems*, Vol. 2, pp. 51–106, A. V. Balakrishnan, ed., Academic Press, Inc., New York, 1966.

[27] J. Kiefer and J. Wolfowitz, Consistency of the Maximum Likelihood Estimator in the Presence of Infinitely Many Unknown Parameters, *Ann. Math. Statistics*, Vol. 27, pp. 884–906, 1956.

[28] L. LeCam, *On Some Asymptotic Properties of Maximum Likelihood Estimates and Related Bayes Estimates* (University of California Publications in Statistics, Vol. 1), University of California Press, Berkeley, Calif., 1953, pp. 277–300.

[29] A. Wald, Note on the Consistency of the Maximum Likelihood Estimate, *Ann. Math. Statistics*, Vol. 20, pp. 595–601, 1949.

[30] L. LeCam, On The Asymptotic Theory of Estimation and Testing Hypotheses, *Proceedings of the Third Berkeley Symposium on Mathematical Statistics and Probability*, University of California Press, Berkeley, Calif., 1955.

[31] J. MacQueen, Some Methods for Classification and Analysis of Multivariate Observations, *Proceedings of the Fifth Berkeley Symposium on Mathematical Statistics and Probability*, Vol. 2, University of California Press, Berkeley, Calif., 1967.

[32] H. J. Scudder, Probability of Error of Some Adaptive Pattern-Recognition Machines, *IEEE Trans. Information Theory*, Vol. IT-11, No. 3, pp. 363–371, July, 1965.

[33] E. A. Patrick and J. P. Costello, Asymptotic Probability of Error Using Two Decision Directed Estimators for Two Unknown Mean Vectors, *IEEE Trans. Information Theory*, Vol. IT-14, No. 1, pp. 160–162, Jan. 1968.

[34] W. D. Gregg and J. C. Hancock, An Optimum Decision Directed Scheme for Gaussian Mixtures, *IEEE Trans. Information Theory*, Vol. IT-14, No. 3, pp. 451–461, May 1968.

[35] E. A. Patrick, J. P. Costello, and F. C. Monds, Decision Directed Estimation of a Two Class Decision Boundary, *IEEE Trans. Computers*, Vol. C-19, No. 3, pp. 197–205, March 1970.

[36] K. Abend, Compound Decision Procedures for Pattern Recognition, *Proc. Natl. Electronics Conf.*, Vol. 22, pp. 770–780, 1966.

[37] J. R. Van Ryzin, The Compound Decision Problem with the $m \times n$ Finite Loss Matrix, *Ann. Math. Statistics*, Vol. 37, No. 2, pp. 412–424, April 1966.

[38] J. R. Van Ryzin, The Sequential Compound Decision Problem with $m \times n$ Finite Loss Matrix, *Ann. Math. Statistics*, Vol. 37, No. 4, pp. 954–975, Aug. 1966.

[39] N. Alens, Compound Bayes Learning Without a Teacher, *Stanford University Tech. Rept. 6151–2*, Stanford, Calif., Aug. 1967.

[40] E. Samuel, Convergence of the Losses of Certain Decision Rules for the Sequential Compound Decision Problem, *Ann. Math. Statistics*, Vol. 35, No. 4, pp. 1606–1621, 1964.

[41] E. Samuel, Asymptotic Solution of the Sequential Compound Decision Problem, *Ann. Math. Statistics*, Vol. 34, No. 3, pp. 1079–1094, Sept. 1963.

[42] J. R. Van Ryzin, Asymptotic Solutions to Compound Decision Problems, *Ph.D. Thesis*, Dept. of Statistics, Michigan State Univ., 1964.

[43] H. Robbins, The Empirical Bayes Approach to Statistical Decision Problems, *Ann. Math. Statistics*, Vol. 35, No. 1, pp. 1–20, March 1964.

[44] W. R. Blischke, Moment Estimators for the Parameters of Two Binomial Distributions, *Ann. Math. Statistics*, Vol. 33, No. 1, pp. 444–454, June 1962.

[45] E. A. Patrick and G. Carayannopoulos, Codes for Unsupervised Estimation of Source and Binary Channel Probabilities, *Information and Control*, Vol. 14, No. 4, pp. 358–375, April 1970.

[46] T. L. Stewart and E. A. Patrick, Design and Performance of Adaptive Receivers with Unknown Synchronization and Unknown Signals, *IEEE Intern. Communications Conf. Record*, Philadelphia, June 1966.

[47] S. C. Fralick, G. L. Slenkorick, and D. L. Wilson, Design and Performance of an Adaptive Receiver for Signals of Unknown Frequency, *IEEE Intern. Communications Conf. Record*, Philadelphia, June 1966.

[48] J. D. Spragins, Learning Without a Teacher, *IEEE Trans. Information Theory*, Vol. IT-12, No. 2, pp. 223–230, April 1966.

[49] E. A. Patrick, Concepts of an Estimation System, Adaptive System, and a Network of Adaptive Estimation Systems, *IEEE Trans. System Science and Cybernetics*, Vol. SSC-5, No. 1, pp. 79–85, Jan. 1969.

[50] K. S. Fu, *Sequential Methods in Pattern Recognition and Machine Learning*, Academic Press Inc., New York, 1968.

[51] L. Kanal, ed., *Pattern Recognition*, Thompson Book Co., Washington, D.C., 1968.

[52] S. Watanabe, ed., *Methodologies of Pattern Recognition*, Academic Press, Inc., New York, 1969.

[53] J. T. Tou, ed., *Computers and Information Sciences*, Vol. II, Academic Press, Inc., New York, 1967, pp. 57–89.

[54] A. Rosenfeld, Picture Processing by Computer, *Computing Surveys*, Vol. 1, No. 3, pp. 146–174, Sept. 1969.

[55] G. Nagy and G. L. Shelton, Jr., Self-Corrective Character Recognition System, *IEEE Trans. Information Theory*, Vol. IT-12, No. 2, pp. 215–222, April 1966.

[56] S. Kullback, *Information Theory and Statistics*, John Wiley & Sons, Inc., New York, 1959.

[57] M. Loeve, *Probability Theory*, 3rd ed., Van Nostrand Reinhold, New York, 1963.

[58] W. Rudin, *Real and Complex Analysis*, McGraw-Hill Book Company, Inc., New York, 1966.

[59] E. L. Lehmann, *Testing Statistical Hypotheses*, John Wiley & Sons, Inc., New York, 1959, pp. 12–23.

[60] E. A. Patrick and L. Liporace, Unsupervised Estimation of Parametric Mixtures, *Purdue University School of Electrical Engineering Tech. Rept. EE 70-31*, Lafayette, Ind., Aug. 1970.

[61] H. Robbins and S. Monroe, A Stochastic Approximation Method, *Ann. Math. Statistics*, Vol. 22, No. 3, pp. 400–407, Sept. 1951.

[62] J. Kiefer and J. Wolfowitz, Stochastic Estimation of the Maximum of a Regression Function, *Ann. Math. Statistics*, Vol. 23, pp. 462–466, Sept. 1952.

[63] J. Blum, Multidimensional Stochastic Approximation Methods, *Ann. Math. Statistics*, Vol. 25, No. 4, pp. 734–744, Dec. 1954.

[64] A. Dvoretzky, On Stochastic Approximation, *Proceedings of the Third Berkeley Symposium on Mathematical Statistics and Probability*, Vol. 1, University of California Press, Berkeley, Calif., 1956, pp. 39–55.

[65] D. Wilde, *Optimum Seeking Methods*, Prentice-Hall, Inc., Englewood Cliffs, N.J., 1964, pp. 159–192.

[66] H. Kesten, Accelerated Stochastic Approximation, *Ann. Math. Statistics*, Vol. 29, No. 1, pp. 41–58, 1958.

[67] D. Wilde, *Optimum Seeking Methods*, Prentice-Hall, Inc., Englewood Cliffs, N.J., 1964.

[68] H. Robbins, Mixtures of Distributions, *Ann. Math. Statistics*, Vol. 19, No. 3, pp. 360–369, Sept. 1948.

[69] S. Yakowitz, A Consistent Estimator for the Identification of Finite Mixtures, *Ann. Math. Statistics*, Vol. 40, No. 5, pp. 1728–1735, 1969.

[70] E. A. Patrick and J. P. Costello, Unsupervised Estimation and Processing of Unknown Signals, *Purdue University School of Electrical Engineering Tech. Rept. EE 69–18*, Lafayette, Ind., June 1969.

[71] J. Ball, Isodata: Data Analysis in the Social Sciences: What About the Details, *Proceedings of the Fall Joint Computer Conference*, pp. 533–559, 1965.

[72] E. A. Patrick, D. R. Anderson, and F. K. Bechtel, Mapping Multidimensional Space to One-Dimension for Computer Output Display, *IEEE Trans. Computers*, Vol. C-17, No. 10, pp. 949–953, Oct. 1968.

[73] R. N. Shepard and J. O. Carroll, Parametric Representation of Nonlinear Data Structures, *Multivariate Analysis*, P. R. Krishnaiah, ed., Academic Press, Inc., New York, pp. 561–592, June, 1966.

[74] R. A. Jarvis, Adaptive Global Search in a Time-Variant Environment Using a Probabilistic Automaton with Pattern Recognition Supervision, *IEEE Trans. System Science and Cybernetics*, Vol. SSC-6, No. 3, pp. 209–217, July 1970.

[75] K. S. Miller, *Multidimensional Gaussian Distributions*, John Wiley & Sons, Inc., New York, 1964.

[76] G. A. Butler, A Vector Field Approach to Cluster Analysis, *Pattern Recognition*, Vol. 1, No. 4, pp. 291–299, July 1969.

[77] C. Abraham, Evaluation of Clusters on the Basis of Random Graph Theory, *IBM Research Memo.*, IBM Corp., Yorktown Heights, N.Y., Nov. 1962.

[78] B. G. Batchelor and B. R. Wilkins, Method for Location of Clusters of Patterns to Initialize a Learning Machine, *Electronics Letters*, Vol. 5, No. 20, pp. 481–483, Oct. 2, 1969.

[79] G. Nagy, State of the Art in Pattern Recognition, *Proc. IEEE*, Vol. 56, No. 5, pp. 836–860, May 1967.

[80] E. A. Patrick and F. P. Fischer, II, Cluster Mapping with Experimental Computer Graphics, *IEEE Trans. Computers*, Vol. C-18, No. 11, pp. 987–991, Nov. 1969.

[81] P. W. Cooper, The Hyperplane in Pattern Recognition, *Cybernetica (Namur)*, Vol. 5, No. 4, pp. 215–238, 1962.

[82] E. A. Patrick, G. L. Carayannopoulos, and J. P. Costello, Five Results on Unsupervised Learning Systems, *Purdue University School of Electrical Engineering Tech. Rept. EE 66–21*, Lafayette, Ind., Dec. 1966.

[83] L. A. Zadeh, Fuzzy Sets, *Information and Control*, Vol. 8, No. 3, pp. 338–353, 1965.

[84] T. Kaminuma, T. Takebowa, and S. Watanabe, Reduction of Clustering Problems to Pattern Recognition, *Pattern Recognition* Vol. 1, No. 3, pp. 195–205, 1969.

[85] R. M. Haralick and G. L. Kelley, Pattern Recognition with Measurement Space and Spatial Clustering for Multiple Images, *Proc. IEEE*, Vol. 57, No. 4, pp. 654–665, 1969.

[86] E. H. Ruspini, A New Approach to Clustering, *Information and Control*, Vol. 15, No. 1, pp. 22–32, 1969.

[87] G. A. Butler, Clustering Using A Computer Output Display, Abstract of Pittsburgh 1970 Pattern Recognition Workshop, *IEEE Trans. Systems Man and Cybernetics*, Vol. SMC-1, No. 3, Oct. 1971.

[88] C. A. Caceres and A. E. Ribli, *Diagnostic Computers*, Charles C Thompson, Publisher, Springfield Ill., 1969.

[89] L. B. Lusted, Introduction to Medical Decision Making, Charles C Thompson, Publisher, Springfield Ill., 1968.

Problems

[1] Show that

$$\left(\sum_{k=1}^{r} u_k\right)^s = \sum_{\alpha_1=0}^{s} \sum_{\alpha_2=0}^{\alpha_1} \cdots \sum_{\alpha_{r-1}=0}^{\alpha_{r-2}} \binom{s}{\alpha_1}\binom{\alpha_1}{\alpha_2} \cdots \binom{\alpha_{r-2}}{\alpha_{r-1}} u_1^{\alpha_1} u_2^{\alpha_2} \cdots u_{r-1}^{\alpha_{r-1}} u_r^{s-\alpha_1-\alpha_2\cdots\alpha_{r-1}}.$$

[2] The notation $A \bmod(B)$ means $A - [A/B]B$, where $[A/B]$ is the largest integer $\leq A/B$. Verify the following tables for $B = 3$ and $B = 2$, respectively.

<table>
<tr><td colspan="2" align="center">B = 3</td><td colspan="2" align="center">B = 2</td></tr>
<tr><td align="center">A</td><td align="center">A mod(B)</td><td align="center">A</td><td align="center">A mod(B)</td></tr>
<tr><td align="center">0</td><td align="center">0</td><td align="center">0</td><td align="center">0</td></tr>
<tr><td align="center">1</td><td align="center">1</td><td align="center">1</td><td align="center">1</td></tr>
<tr><td align="center">2</td><td align="center">2</td><td align="center">2</td><td align="center">0</td></tr>
<tr><td align="center">3</td><td align="center">0</td><td align="center">3</td><td align="center">1</td></tr>
<tr><td align="center">4</td><td align="center">1</td><td align="center">4</td><td align="center">0</td></tr>
<tr><td align="center">5</td><td align="center">2</td><td align="center">5</td><td align="center">1</td></tr>
</table>

[3] Critically compare the following clustering procedures:
(a) Chain map.
(b) Maximum distance procedure.
(c) Method in Section 5-4.8.
(d) Cluster map (gravity technique).
(e) Continuity map.
(f) Decision directed.
(g) Method of Kaminuma, Takebowa, and Watanabe [84].
(h) Clustering using a priori supplied similarity functions.
(i) Similarity by sharing of near neighbors.

[4] Concerning the proof of Theorem 1, show that

$$E\left[\left|\sum_{j=1}^{n} [\ln h(\mathbf{x}_j \mid \mathbf{b}^k) - \ln h(\mathbf{x}_j \mid \mathbf{b}^*) + d^k]\right|^2\right]$$

$$\leq n^{s/2}\, \frac{s + 2^{s-1} - 1}{s/2!} \sum_{i=0}^{s} \binom{s}{i}(d^k)^{s-i} E[|\ln h(\mathbf{x} \mid \mathbf{b}^k) - \ln h(\mathbf{x} \mid \mathbf{b}^*)|^i].$$

[5] This problem concerns the proof of Theorem 2. With reference to the sketch here, show that the theorem follows for $4\delta = \min\{\eta(\mathbf{b}'') - \eta(\mathbf{b}^r)\}$, where the minimum is over all $b'' \in \mathscr{I}_{(\epsilon/2)}$ and $\mathbf{b}^r \in \mathscr{B}' - \mathscr{I}_{(\epsilon)}$.

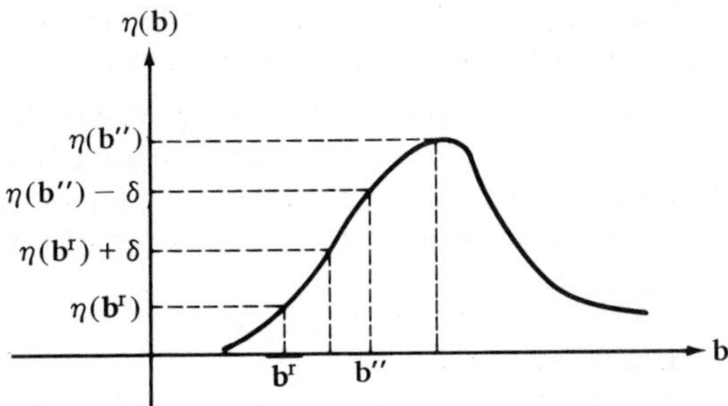

[6] Let there be a finite-size parameter set $\mathscr{B}^V$ as in Section 5-3.4. Verify that the average norm-square error of the Bayes estimator is

$$\sigma^2 = \sum_{j \neq m} \sum_{i \neq m} (\mathbf{b}_i - \mathbf{b}_m)^t (\mathbf{b}_j - \mathbf{b}_m) E[p'(\mathbf{b}_i \,|\, \dot{\mathbf{x}}_n) p'(\mathbf{b}_j \,|\, \dot{\mathbf{x}}_n)],$$

where $\mathbf{b}_m$ is the solution maximizing $\eta(\mathbf{b})$ and $p'(\mathbf{b}_i \,|\, \dot{\mathbf{x}}_n)$ is the discrete, a posteriori density of $\mathbf{b}_i$.

[7] The variance of the Bayes estimator for $\mathbf{b}^m$, given a discrete parameter space, is bounded as

$$\sigma^2(n) < \sum_{j \neq m} \sum_{i \neq m} (\mathbf{b}^i - \mathbf{b}^m)^t (\mathbf{b}^j - \mathbf{b}^m) \exp(-n2\delta_i),$$

where

$$\delta_i = \tfrac{1}{3}[\eta(\mathbf{b}^m) - \eta(\mathbf{b}^i)].$$

Note that the variance can increase as the number of points V in $\mathscr{B}^V$ increases. Does this suggest that estimation uncertainty increases as the number of alternatives increases? Discuss why this suggests that certain pattern-recognition problems may be unsolvable for a fixed number of training samples n when there is limited a priori knowledge.

[8] Carry out the evaluation of the integral (25) of Section 5-4.6, to show

$$c_{ij} = \int N(\mathbf{x} \,|\, \mathbf{m}_i, \mathbf{\Sigma}_i) N(\mathbf{x} \,|\, \mathbf{m}_j, \mathbf{\Sigma}_j) \, d\mathbf{x}$$

$$= (2\pi)^{-L/2} \,|\mathbf{\Sigma}_i|^{-1/2} \,|\mathbf{\Sigma}_j|^{-1/2} \,|\mathbf{\Sigma}_i^{-1} + \mathbf{\Sigma}_j^{-1}|^{-1/2}$$

$$\times \exp\{-\tfrac{1}{2}[(\mathbf{m}_i - \mathbf{m})^t \mathbf{\Sigma}_i^{-1}(\mathbf{m}_i - \mathbf{m}) + (\mathbf{m}_j - \mathbf{m})^t \mathbf{\Sigma}_j^{-1}(\mathbf{m}_j - \mathbf{m})]\},$$

where

$$\mathbf{m} = (\mathbf{\Sigma}_i^{-1} + \mathbf{\Sigma}_j^{-1})^{-1}(\mathbf{\Sigma}_i^{-1}\mathbf{m}_i + \mathbf{\Sigma}_j^{-1}\mathbf{m}_j).$$

[9] From Section 5-4.6, a high signal-to-noise ratio approximation leads to a simplified regression function,

$$\Gamma(\mathbf{b}) = \sum_{i=1}^{M} \frac{1}{n} \sum_{s=1}^{n} \exp\left[-\frac{1}{2} \sum_{s=1}^{n} \frac{(x_{s_r} - m_{i_r})^2}{(\sigma_{i_r})^2}\right].$$

Suggest how $\Gamma(\mathbf{b})$ can be used to construct a "chain map" type of procedure for displaying hyperspace clusters in two dimensions.

[10] Let $\mathbf{x}_1, \mathbf{x}_2, \ldots, \mathbf{x}_n$ be parameter conditionally independent and identically distributed from the mixture $h(\mathbf{x} \mid \mathbf{b})$. Then the Bayes estimator for $\mathbf{b}^*$ can be constructed at stage n. Compare the Bayes, quasi-Bayes, stochastic approximation, and stochastic hill-climbing estimators for $\mathbf{b}^*$ with respect to each of the following properties:

(a) Is it iterative in that the samples $\mathbf{x}_1, \mathbf{x}_2, \ldots, \mathbf{x}_n$ need not be retained for use in updating at stage $\mathbf{x}_{n+1}$?

(b) When used in iterative form starting with sample $\mathbf{x}_1$ and processing up to $\mathbf{x}_n$ once, compare the performance of these estimators.

(c) What estimator would require the least storage, neglecting storage of the samples $\mathbf{x}_1, \mathbf{x}_2, \ldots, \mathbf{x}_n$?

(d) What estimators are impractical for a continuous parameter space?

(e) What estimator is likely to have poorest performance?

CHAPTER 6

Dimensionality Reduction: Feature Selection and Feature Extraction

6-1 Introduction

One of the classical problems in pattern recognition and communications is to reduce the dimensionality of the measurement vector $\mathbf{x}$ from L dimensions to l dimensions, $l < L$. Early work in discriminant analysis and pattern recognition had the objective of designing a filter to map the L-dimensional vector $\mathbf{x}$ to the lower-dimensional space so that decision making could take place in the lower-dimensional space. One advantage of this concept of dimensionality reduction is that classification in the lower-dimensional space is faster and less complex; and the filter can be designed once (off line or during a research phase). Clearly this can be a desirable thing to do. A simple example of this kind of dimensionality reduction is where l of the components of $\mathbf{x}$ are selected; this is referred to as *feature selection*, with the components the features. Because early emphasis was on this feature-selection concept, another very important consideration was frequently overlooked; *that consideration is to reduce dimensionality as a consequence of introducing a problem model or problem knowledge.* If a relationship is known to exist between the components of two specific dimensions, then loosely speaking that relationship provides for *samples of the component in one dimension to assist in estimating the probability density function of parameters characterizing the other dimension.* Rather than having two sets of parameters characterizing the respective dimensions, it may be possible to eliminate one set of parameters; i.e., the relationship provides for eliminating "nuisance" parameters.

It is well accepted as a practical matter that a waveform, picture, or vector arising from the pattern should be preprocessed. For example, as discussed in Chapter 1, a waveform is infinite-dimensional if viewed as in the vector space $\mathscr{E}_\infty$. It is desirable to use basis functions appropriately chosen for the problem to map the waveforms in $\mathscr{E}_\infty$ to a vector $\mathbf{x}$ in $\mathscr{E}_L$ with L as small as possible. Because of the great variety of possible preprocessing procedures, this is currently more of an art than a mathematical discipline. Of course, knowledge of properties of basis functions, such as discussed in Chapter 1, is useful for practicing this art. It is easy for the artistic nature of the preprocessing procedure to obscure the basic mathematical statistical reasons why classification performance can be improved by preprocessing.

Suppose we ask if a dimensionality-reducing operation can be estimated using training samples? The answer is yes, but it may be advisable to also utilize problem knowledge. In the spirit of Bayes, the number of training samples required to estimate the dimensionality-reducing operation with a given degree of uncertainty can be reduced by utilizing an a priori fuzzy assumption for the operation.

6-2 Feature Extraction Versus Feature Selection

Feature extraction is the reduction of a set of measurements containing a relatively large amount of data but a smaller amount of useful information to a set containing a relatively small amount of data (features). To obtain this complexity reduction, a priori structure usually must be available. A frequently used but often unsuccessful method of feature extraction from waveforms is where an analog/digital converter extracts a finite number of time samples from a continuous waveform $f(t)$. Other elementary examples include the use of exponential basis functions and trigonometric basis functions (see Chapter 1).

There is the intuitive feeling that the more known about a waveform a priori, the smaller is the size of the set of basis functions required to represent the waveform. In the example of the analog/digital converter, the number of required time samples is proportional to the waveform bandwidth if this bandwidth is considered a priori knowledge. Using this relatively limited a priori knowledge, the number of time samples may be prohibitively large† for subsequent decision making. On the other hand, if it is known a priori, for

---

†Prohibitively large, both from the standpoint of being cumbersome and the standpoint of degraded performance due to the absence of relationships among measurements.

example, that the waveform is a linear combination of three sinusoids, then the waveform is represented by the three corresponding Fourier coefficients.

A priori knowledge, such as was used in the sinusoidal-basis-function example above, cannot be estimated using a finite number of samples; it can be obtained through using knowledge from the field of problem knowledge (an adaptive procedure requiring a reference)† or with an infinite number of training samples. It has not been found possible to place man's field of knowledge about a problem area into a computer. Therefore man is now our best source of models which provide relationships among measurements $x_1, x_2, \ldots, x_L$ to produce features $y_1, y_2, \ldots, y_l, l \leq L$.

A Priori Knowledge for Feature Extraction

Essentially there are two ways to obtain a priori knowledge for feature extraction. One is an *ad hoc, approach* where features are extracted based on human judgment. The other is based on the construction of features, possibly nonlinear functions of the original measurements, by studying the acoustics, boundary structure, antenna structure, biological model, medical knowledge, etc., of the problem. In Sections 6-2 through 6-11 the dimensionality-reduction procedures do not provide for utilizing problem knowledge but rather are based on *estimating significant directions* in the measurement space for representing the pattern samples. Beginning with Section 6-11 a framework is developed for inserting pragmatic type of problem knowledge into the dimensionality-reduction process. Such nonlinear relationships are discussed in Sections 6-12, 6-13, and 6-14. This approach is developed further in Chapter 7.

Suppose that $\mathscr{F}_i$ is a family of basis functions and $\bar{\mathscr{F}} = \{\mathscr{F}_i\}$ is the set of families under consideration a problem, containing $\mathscr{F}_1, \mathscr{F}_2, \ldots, \mathscr{F}_M$. Let f be a given function which is to be represented or approximated by a subset of the basis functions in the family $\mathscr{F}_i$. The criterion for selecting the family $\mathscr{F}_i$ will be that the resulting basis set be of *minimal size* for a given "approximation error." We ask the question: Can an $\mathscr{F}_i$, best in the above sense, be found without trying each $\mathscr{F}_i$ one by one and observing the approximation error? It is possible but not sufficiently pragmatic to merit formal study. An analytical technique can be used to generate the desired $\mathscr{F}_i$ by minimizing approximation error or it must be done by an experiment where each $\mathscr{F}_i$ is tried, one by one.

Whether the above problem of selecting $\mathscr{F}_i$ is approached analytically or experimentally, the degree of success will depend on how well the set of families $\bar{\mathscr{F}}$ characterize the problem under consideration. That is, the families $\mathscr{F}_i \subset \bar{\mathscr{F}}$ should have been generated by studying the problem.

---

†See Section 6-3, for example, where it is shown how a priori knowledge can be traded for samples.

One concept of stochastic dimensionality reduction is to select the "best" family of basis functions spanning an l-dimensional space $\mathcal{V}_l$ given a family spanning an L-dimensional space $\mathcal{V}_L$, where $\mathcal{V}_l$ may be a subspace of $\mathcal{V}_L$. The subspace picked should be "best" in the sense that it provides reduced dimensionality or complexity while maintaining a "high" performance index. Usually, two or more classes are considered at the same time. The performance index, for example, can be a measure of properties which characterize differences between the classes as well as within each class.

Classical Feature Extraction Using an A/D Converter

Nearly everyone is familiar with analog/digital conversion, where a sequence of functions $f_s(t)$, $s = 1, 2, \ldots, n$, are converted to the computer's binary language. Suppose that $f_s(t)$ is converted to an L-dimensional vector

$$\mathbf{x}_s = [f_s(t_1), f_s(t_2), \ldots, f_s(t_L)] \triangleq [x_1, x_2, \ldots, x_L], \tag{1}$$

where the components in $\mathbf{x}_s$ are samples of the function $f_s(t)$. Feature extraction thus is accomplished using a sampling device that corresponds to approximating $f_s(t)$ using $\{\sin(\cdot)/(\cdot)\}$ basis functions according to the sampling theorem [1]; the time increments $(t_{i+1} - t_i)$ for "good" approximation are inversely proportional to the bandwidth of $f_s(t)$. In practice, L resulting through application of the sampling theorem can be very large compared with other methods of feature extraction; and we conclude from this that *bandwidth may not constitute much a priori knowledge.*

The L-dimensional vectors $\mathbf{x}_s$, $s = 1, 2, \ldots, n$, can be placed in computer storage either for subsequent simple retrieval or to be used as a training set for supervised (Chapter 4) or unsupervised (Chapter 5) training.

Since we are about to discuss procedures for *stochastic dimensionality reduction*, it is appropriate to summarize possible approaches to dimensionality reduction before embarking on discussion of specific approaches. This philosophy will be revisited beginning in Section 6-12, where the framework for pragmatic dimensionality reduction is developed which provides for reducing dimensionality utilizing both problem knowledge and training samples (stochastic).

Measurement vectors $\mathbf{x}_1, \mathbf{x}_2, \ldots, \mathbf{x}_n$ are to be processed where the vectors consist of $\mathbf{x}_1^i, \mathbf{x}_2^i, \ldots, \mathbf{x}_{n_i}^i$, $i = 1, 2, \ldots, M$, from M respective classes. The following ideas suggest procedures that may be useful in the decision-making process:

1. Consider a mixture of measurement vectors $\mathbf{x}_1, \mathbf{x}_2, \ldots, \mathbf{x}_n$ and a transformation of $\mathbf{x} \in \mathcal{V}_L$ to $\mathbf{y} \in \mathcal{V}_l$ to obtain $\mathbf{y}_1, \mathbf{y}_2, \ldots, \mathbf{y}_n$, which *minimize an average square error between $\mathbf{y}_i$ and $\mathbf{x}_i$, $i = 1, 2, \ldots, n$.*
2. If $n \ll L$, it may be that few, if any, measurement vectors will occur

at a later time which are very different from the initial n vectors. In this case the n vectors can be used as a spanning set, and thus dimensionality is n rather than L. A procedure for obtaining a basis from this spanning set is the *Gram–Schmidt procedure* discussed in Section 6-5.

3. In Section 6-6, a procedure called *transposed vectors* is discussed for finding components of **x** which are stochastically similar; when such components are found there is no need to retain more than one of them. To reduce nuisance, it may be better to eliminate this redundancy using problem knowledge rather than relying completely on training samples.

4. A *transformation of measurement vectors* $\mathbf{x}_1, \mathbf{x}_2, \ldots, \mathbf{x}_n$ to l-dimensional vectors $\mathbf{y}_1, \mathbf{y}_2, \ldots, \mathbf{y}_n$ is developed in Section 6-7 *for maximizing the scatter* of the latter vectors. This concept is more useful for providing insight than as an operational procedure for dimensionality reduction.

5. In Section 6-8 a transformation is developed for two classes such that in the transformed space a *distance between the two classes of vectors is maximized.*

6. In Section 6-9 a transformation is developed for *minimizing the distance among vectors for a single class.* It is more useful for insight than as an operational procedure for dimensionality reduction.

7. An approach, called *nonparametric feature selection,* is presented in Section 6-10. It differs from the previous approaches in that the previous approaches require that the class densities be unimodel.

None of the above stochastic approaches alone provides an adequate answer to why dimensionality reduction is part of the decision-making process. There are problems where one or more of them may be useful, but they do not provide for inserting problem knowledge and then updating problem knowledge. They just are not pragmatic by themselves. Nevertheless, they deserve presentation prior to Sections 6-11 and 6-12, where framework for a pragmatic approach is developed. The reader will be able to find references containing modifications and extensions of these procedures.

6-3 Six Principles of Dimensionality Reduction

In this section six principles of *dimensionality reduction* are defined. These principles are presented to indicate what it is about dimensionality reduction that can improve performance or reduce complexity. The reader may wish to examine how the seven procedures outlined in the previous section comply with these principles. *The first principle* is that measurement vectors $\mathbf{x}_s^i$, $s =$

1, 2, ..., n_i, are used to estimate a parameter vector $\mathbf{b}_i$ characterizing $f(\mathbf{x}\,|\,\omega_i)$, $i = 1, 2, \ldots, M$. The number of independent scalars in $\mathbf{b}_i$ is the *dimensionality of the parameter space of ith class-conditional density function.* A priori knowledge specifies a constraint on the densities $f(\mathbf{x}\,|\,\omega_i)$, $i = 1, 2, \ldots, M$. When this constraint is imposed, the components of $\mathbf{b}_i$ are no longer independent. Hence, they may be replaced by a smaller independent set denoted vector $\mathbf{b}_i'$. It is better to estimate $\mathbf{b}_i'$ than to estimate $\mathbf{b}_i$ because, for example, it may be possible to average estimates in $\mathbf{b}_i$ to form estimates in $\mathbf{b}_i'$, resulting in the latter having lower variance. This concept is shown in Figure 6.1. A priori knowledge relating $f(\mathbf{x}\,|\,\omega_i)$ and $f(\mathbf{x}\,|\,\omega_j)$, $i \neq j$, may also be

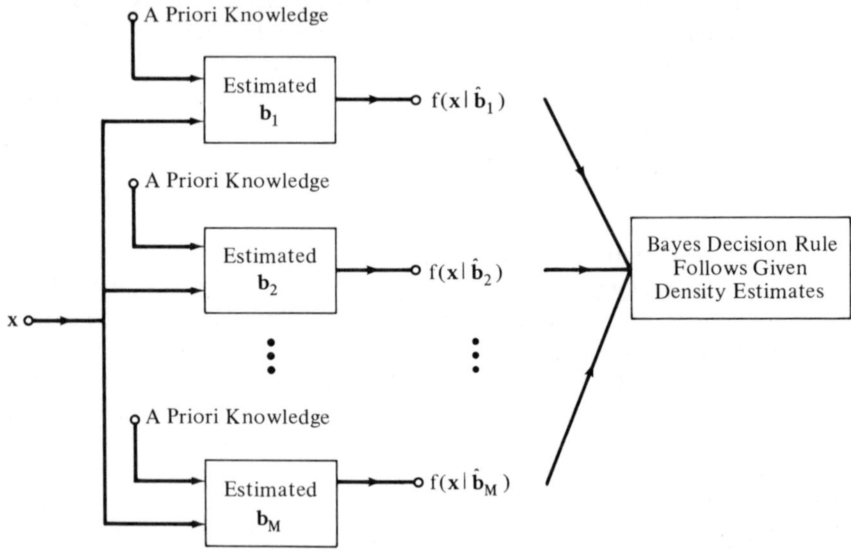

Fig. 6.1 Class conditional dimensionality reduction

available. For example, it may be known that both probability densities have the same covariance matrix $\boldsymbol{\Sigma}$, allowing samples from both classes to be used to estimate $\boldsymbol{\Sigma}$. Effectively there are then twice as many samples and lower uncertainty. This example may seem trivial, but it is easy for one to forget about such simple ideas.

A second principle, shown illustrated in Figure 6.2, is where a subspace of $\mathscr{V}_L$ is sought on which to map the mixture of measurement vectors. Then these vectors $\mathbf{y}$ in the subspace, $\mathscr{V}_l$, are used to train a decision rule. The underlying idea here is that we do not require complete knowledge of $f(\mathbf{x}\,|\,\omega_i)$, $i = 1, 2, \ldots, M$, but expect that knowledge of $f(\mathbf{y}\,|\,\omega_i)$ will suffice, where $\mathbf{y}$ is a projection of $\mathbf{x}$ into a l-dimensional subspace ($l < L$). Since $l < L$, it is easier to estimate the parameters characterizing $f(\mathbf{y}\,|\,\omega_i)$ than $f(\mathbf{x}\,|\,\omega_i)$ as shown

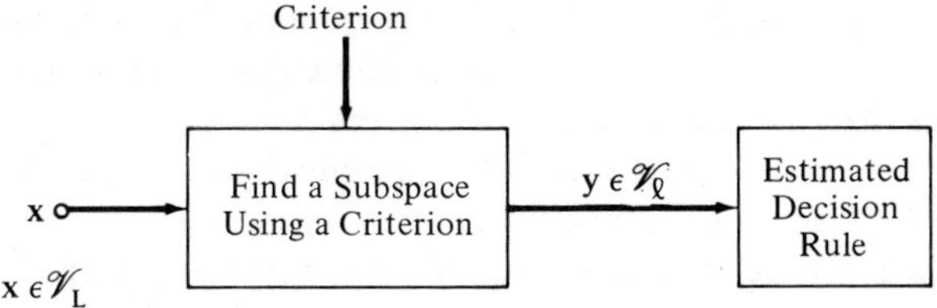

Fig. 6.2 Mixture dimensionality reduction using a criterion

in Figure 6.3. The choice of subspace will depend upon a criterion such as approximation error or maximizing experimental separability of the class-conditional probability densities. Of course, the parameters characterizing the transformation must be estimated using the criterion.

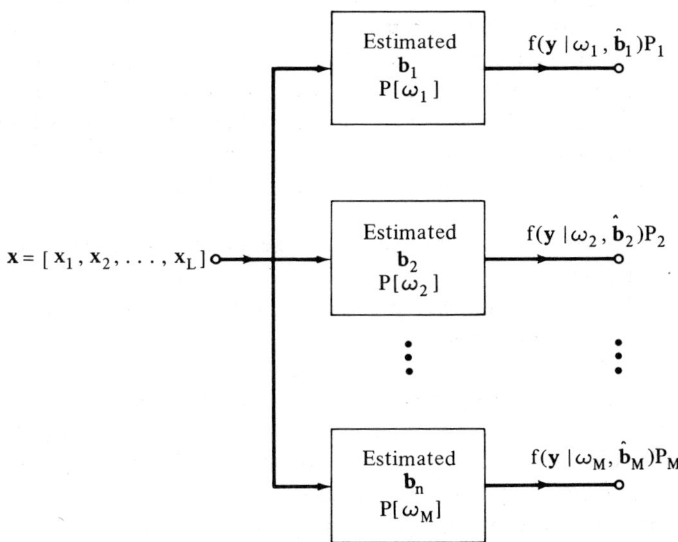

Fig. 6.3 Dimensionality reduction utilizing a subspace

The two principles presented so far concern reducing the number of parameters characterizing the class-conditional probability density functions. As an alternative, *a third principle* is that the decision boundary can be estimated directly. If it is known a priori that the decision boundary has a certain parametric form with few parameters, it may be possible to estimate these parameters. An example of this is the estimation of the mean of the mixture of measurement vectors in the one-dimensional two-class Gaussian decision problem.

If the form of the decision boundary is unknown, in theory it can be approximated by segments of linear hyperplanes. To adequately do this, however, may require introduction of parameters characterizing each segment, making the total number of parameters quite large.

A fourth principle is typical of the "diagnosis–treatment" cycle in computer-assisted medical diagnosis. Let the measurement vector be $\dot{\mathbf{x}}_r = [\mathbf{x}_1, \mathbf{x}_2, \ldots, \mathbf{x}_r]$, where $\mathbf{x}_s$ is a vector of measurements after the sth test. If $\mathbf{x}_s$ is from $f(\mathbf{x}_s \,|\, \omega_{is})$, $i = 1, 2, \ldots, M$, then the density of $\dot{\mathbf{x}}_r$ can be characterized by $f(\dot{\mathbf{x}}_r \,|\, \pi)$, where the sequence $\pi = [\omega_{1s}, \omega_{2s}, \ldots, \omega_{rs}]$. Each sequence π may be thought of as a disease complex and $\dot{\mathbf{x}}_r$ as a symptom complex. The number of different sequences equals $(M)^r$ (which is large), but it may be reduced using problem knowledge to eliminate certain of the symptom-complex $\dot{\mathbf{x}}_r \longrightarrow$ disease-complex π relationships. The probabilities of sequences π provide transition probabilities for schedule planning. Also, by examination, certain sequences π can be eliminated. Sequence probabilities can be utilized in making decisions at any stage to determine whether the diagnosis is complete or additional tests are to be made with corresponding diagnosis and possibly a prescription of additional tests. Estimation of densities $f(\mathbf{x}_r \,|\, \pi_j)$, $j = 1, 2, \ldots, (M)^r$, is a difficult problem; approximations used to condition the density of one subset on properties of another subset seem desirable. This leads us to using techniques in Chapters 4 and 5, for obtaining $f(\mathbf{y} \,|\, \pi_r)$ for those sequences considered important.

1. Find regions of $\mathscr{V}_{rL}$ where only one sequence has nonzero probability measure.
2. In other regions extract properties or features that lead to distinguishing among sequences.

A fifth principle is that measurements may be mixed: some discrete and some continuous. Discrete measurements may delineate regions in the measurement space while a class-conditional probability density function of the continuous measurements is constructed in these regions. Also a discrete measurement implies that the probability density must be significantly changing from one discrete point to the next. Otherwise a discrete measurement is not justified.

A sixth principle is that features may be viewed as nonlinear relationships among measurements. These relationships act to establish equivalent regions in the measurement space.

You always will be able to retreat to safe ground by remembering that the ultimate goal is to estimate the class conditional probability densities in the measurement space.

The reader will find [2, 3, 4, 5, 7, 8] worthwhile supplementary reading.

6-4 Feature Selection with Minimum Average Square Error

Let $\boldsymbol{\varphi}_1, \boldsymbol{\varphi}_2, \ldots, \boldsymbol{\varphi}_L$ be L-dimensional orthonormal basis vectors† in $\mathscr{V}_L$ (to be determined) and form the linear combination

$$\sum_{\xi=1}^{l} c_{s\xi}\boldsymbol{\varphi}_\xi, \qquad l < L, s = 1, 2, \ldots, l, \tag{1}$$

which is to approximate the measurement vectors $\{\mathbf{x}_s\}_{s=1}^{n}$. A well-known approximation problem is that of using (1) to approximate $\mathbf{x}_s$ on the average, i.e., against the statistics of $\mathbf{x}$. To obtain the solution define a distance e_s between (1) and $\mathbf{x}_s$ as follows:

$$e_s = \frac{\left\| \mathbf{x}_s - \sum_{\xi=1}^{l} c_{s\xi}\boldsymbol{\varphi}_\xi \right\|^2}{\|\mathbf{x}_s\|^2}. \tag{2}$$

The average distance over the set of data vectors is

$$\bar{e} = (1/n) \sum_{s=1}^{n} e_s. \tag{3}$$

Define

$$\boldsymbol{\Phi} = [\boldsymbol{\varphi}_1, \boldsymbol{\varphi}_2, \ldots, \boldsymbol{\varphi}_l]. \tag{4}$$

The problem then is to minimize $\bar{e}$ over all admissible $\boldsymbol{\Phi}$:

$$\min_{\boldsymbol{\Phi}} \sum_{s=1}^{n} \frac{\left(\mathbf{x}_s - \sum_{\xi=1}^{l} c_{s\xi}\boldsymbol{\varphi}_\xi, \ \mathbf{x}_s - \sum_{\xi=1}^{l} c_{s\xi}\boldsymbol{\varphi}_\xi \right)}{\|\mathbf{x}_s\|^2}$$

$$= \min_{\boldsymbol{\Phi}} \sum_{s=1}^{n} \frac{(\mathbf{x}_s, \mathbf{x}_s) - \sum_{\xi=1}^{l} (\mathbf{x}_s, \boldsymbol{\varphi}_\xi)^2}{\|\mathbf{x}_s\|^2}, \tag{5a}$$

where

$$c_{s\xi} = (\mathbf{x}_s, \boldsymbol{\varphi}_s). \tag{5b}$$

Equation (5a) is equivalent to

$$\max_{\boldsymbol{\Phi}} \sum_{\xi=1}^{l} \sum_{s=1}^{n} \frac{(\mathbf{x}_s, \boldsymbol{\varphi}_s)^2}{\|\mathbf{x}_s\|^2} = \max_{\boldsymbol{\Phi}} \sum_{\xi=1}^{l} \left[\sum_{i=1}^{L} \sum_{j=1}^{L} \sum_{s=1}^{n} \frac{x_{si} x_{sj} \varphi_{\xi i} \varphi_{\xi j}}{\|\mathbf{x}_s\|^2} \right]. \tag{6}$$

†$\boldsymbol{\varphi}_\xi = \sum_{j=1}^{L} \varphi_{\xi j}\mathbf{e}_j$, where $\varphi_{\xi j}$ is a constant for all ξ and j, and $\mathbf{e}_j$ is an L-tuple.

Then the maximization in (6) can be achieved by maximizing each term in the brackets with respect to $\boldsymbol{\varphi}_\xi$, $\xi = 1, 2, \ldots, l$, because each of these terms is ≥ 0. Thus seek†

$$\max_{\boldsymbol{\varphi}} \left[\sum_{i=1}^{L} \sum_{j=1}^{L} \hat{\rho}_{ij} \varphi_{\xi i} \varphi_{\xi j} \right], \tag{7}$$

where

$$\hat{\rho}_{ij} = \sum_{s=1}^{n} \frac{x_{si} x_{sj}}{\| \mathbf{x}_s \|^2}. \tag{8}$$

Next (7) can be conveniently written

$$\max_{\boldsymbol{\varphi}_\xi} (\mathbf{P}\boldsymbol{\varphi}_\xi, \boldsymbol{\varphi}_\xi); \| \boldsymbol{\varphi}_\xi \| = 1, \qquad \boldsymbol{\varphi}_\xi \perp \boldsymbol{\varphi}_1 \perp \boldsymbol{\varphi}_2 \perp \cdots \perp \boldsymbol{\varphi}_{\xi-1}, \tag{9}$$

where $\hat{\mathbf{P}}$ is a matrix transformation defined by

$$\hat{\mathbf{P}}\boldsymbol{\varphi}_\xi = \left[\sum_{j=1}^{L} \hat{\rho}_{1j} \varphi_{\xi j}, \sum_{j=1}^{L} \hat{\rho}_{2j} \varphi_{\xi j}, \ldots, \sum_{j=1}^{L} \hat{\rho}_{Lj} \varphi_{\xi j} \right]. \tag{10}$$

Because $\hat{\mathbf{P}}$ is self-adjoint, it can be shown (see Problem 2) that $\boldsymbol{\varphi}_\xi$ satisfying (9) is the eigenvector corresponding to the largest eigenvalue λ_ξ, where

$$\lambda_\xi \boldsymbol{\varphi}_\xi = \left[\sum_{j=1}^{L} \hat{\rho}_{1j} \varphi_{\xi j}, \sum_{j=1}^{L} \hat{\rho}_{2j} \varphi_{\xi j}, \ldots, \sum_{j=1}^{L} \hat{\rho}_{Lj} \varphi_{\xi j} \right]. \tag{11}$$

The vector $\boldsymbol{\varphi}$ corresponding to the second largest eigenvalue produces the second maximum and so forth. Select the l eigenvectors corresponding to the l largest eigenvalues (of (11)) to obtain a basis set $\boldsymbol{\varphi}_1, \boldsymbol{\varphi}_2, \ldots, \boldsymbol{\varphi}_l$ achieving minimum $\bar{e}$ (5) over the set of all possible basis functions.

If the rank of $\mathbf{P}$ is $l' < l$, then only l' eigenvalues are nonzero. The maximum in (9) corresponding to a zero eigenvalue is zero. Thus, the use of dimensions $l' + 1, l' + 2, \ldots, l$ does not reduce $\bar{e}$ in (3) or (5). Similarly, if $\lambda_{l'+1} \ll \lambda_{l'}$, the reduction in $\bar{e}$ by using $l' + 1$ dimensions will be small, so that it will not be worthwhile using more than l' dimensions.

The rank of $\mathbf{P}$ is less than or equal to n, the number of samples. Therefore, if $n < L$, dimensionality reduction may be applied to produce $l'' \leq n < L$ dimensional vectors. If l'' is not much less than $n \ll L$, the utility of this dimensionality reduction is questionable. A situation where $l'' \cong n$ suggests that future samples $\mathbf{x}_{n+1}, \mathbf{x}_{n+2}, \ldots$, may produce significant error $\bar{e}$ unless

---

†ρ_{ij} is an estimate of a *correlation* coefficient in a covariance matrix Σ obtained by averaging over the n data vectors $\mathbf{x}_1, \mathbf{x}_2, \ldots, \mathbf{x}_n$.

dimensionality l'' is increased. When l'' no longer increases as n increases, this is a good indication that a spanning set has been achieved.

The new features obtained for the measurement vector $\mathbf{x}_s$ are c_{s1}, c_{s2}, ..., c_{sl}; thus $\mathbf{x}_s \rightarrow \mathbf{y}_s$,

$$\mathbf{y} = [c_{s1}, c_{s2}, \ldots, c_{sl}]. \tag{12}$$

A block diagram of the dimensionality-reduction procedure suggested by (8) and (12) is shown in Figure 6.4.

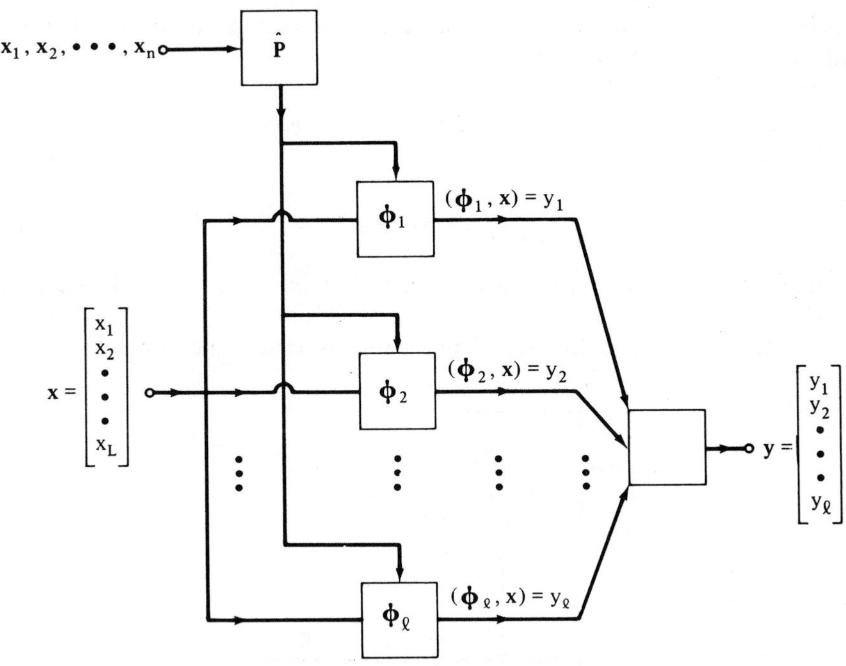

Fig. 6.4 Dimensionality reduction where $\phi_1, \phi_2, \ldots, \phi_l$ are l eigenvectors of the estimated normalized correlation matrix $\hat{\mathbf{P}}$ corresponding to l largest eigenvalues.

6-5 Applying Gram–Schmidt to Measurement Vectors

Consider again the sequences of measurement vectors $\mathbf{x}_s$, $s = 1, 2, \ldots, n$. An orthonormal spanning set for this set of n vectors can be obtained by the Gram–Schmidt process,

$$\psi_1 = \frac{\mathbf{x}_1}{\|\mathbf{x}_1\|}$$

$$\psi_2 = \frac{\mathbf{x}_2 - (\mathbf{x}_2, \psi_1)\psi_1}{\|\mathbf{x}_2 - (\mathbf{x}_2, \psi_1)\psi_1\|}$$

$$\vdots$$

$$\psi_{n'} = \frac{\mathbf{x}_{n'} - \displaystyle\sum_{s=1}^{n'-1} (\mathbf{x}_s, \psi_s)\psi_s}{\left\|\mathbf{x}_{n'} - \displaystyle\sum_{s=1}^{n'-1} (\mathbf{x}_s, \psi_s)\psi_s\right\|}, \qquad n' \leq n, \tag{1}$$

where n' is the number of linearly independent vectors resulting. Then the data vector $\mathbf{x}_s$ is represented as

$$\mathbf{x}_s = \sum_{\xi=1}^{n'} c_{s\xi}\psi_\xi, \qquad n' \leq n, \tag{2}$$

where

$$c_{s\xi} = (\mathbf{x}_s, \psi_\xi). \tag{3}$$

Thus, each vector $\mathbf{x}_s$ is equivalent to a vector $[c_{s1}, c_{s2}, \ldots, c_{sn'}]$, where $n' \leq n$.

One objection to the above procedure is that a measurement vector

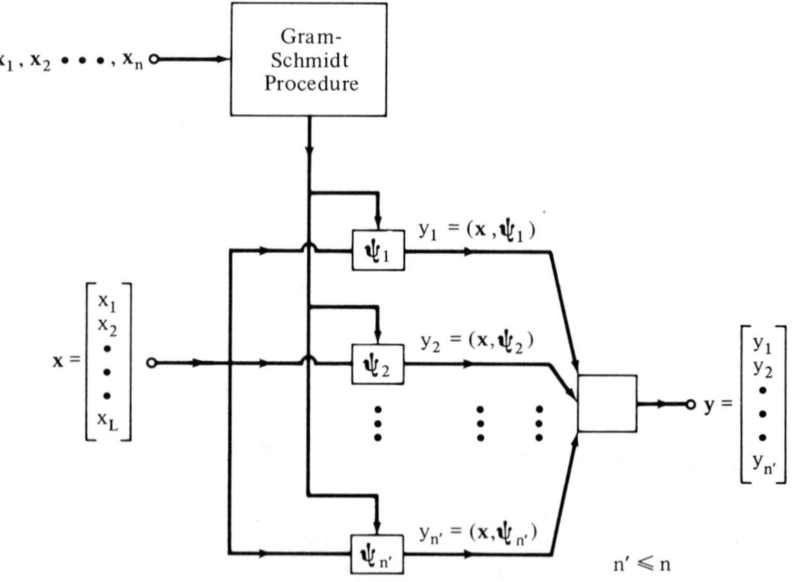

Fig. 6.5 Dimensionality reduction where $\psi_1, \psi_2, \ldots, \psi_n$, are obtained from $\mathbf{x}_1, \mathbf{x}_2, \ldots, \mathbf{x}_n$ using Gram–Schmidt.

$\mathbf{x}_{n+1}$ may not lie in the space spanned by $\mathbf{\psi}_1, \ldots, \mathbf{\psi}_n$. Provision can be made for this possibility by computing

$$\mathbf{x}_{n+1} - \sum_{s=1}^{n} (\mathbf{x}_{n+1}, \mathbf{\psi}_s)\mathbf{\psi}_s. \tag{4}$$

If this is not the zero vector, then, properly normalized, it is set equal to $\mathbf{\psi}_{n+1}$ and the size of the spanning set is increased by 1. Of course, there is the possibility that it will be necessary to add a basis function to the spanning set every time a new data vector is processed. This possibility has high probability when $n' \cong n$ and low probability when $n' \ll n$.

Using the Gram–Schmidt procedure to find an orthonormal basis set appears easier than calculating eigenvectors. Both procedures result in a basis spanning a subspace; however, the eigenvector approach provides an ordering of the basis vectors (eigenvectors) according to energy (eigenvalues), making it possible to reduce dimensionality to l'', achieving a specified error $\bar{e}$. An illustration of the Gram–Schmidt procedure is shown in Figure 6.5.

6-6 Transposed Vectors

Place the n measurement vectors as columns in a matrix:

$$\begin{bmatrix} \mathbf{v}_1^t \\ \mathbf{v}_2^t \\ \cdot \\ \cdot \\ \cdot \\ \mathbf{v}_L^t \end{bmatrix} = \begin{bmatrix} x_{11}, x_{21}, \ldots, x_{n1} \\ x_{12}, x_{22}, \ldots, x_{n2} \\ \cdot \quad \cdot \quad\quad \cdot \\ \cdot \quad \cdot \quad\quad \cdot \\ \cdot \quad \cdot \quad\quad \cdot \\ x_{1L}, x_{2L}, \ldots, x_{nL} \end{bmatrix}. \tag{1}$$

Then if $\mathbf{v}_i = \mathbf{v}_j$, $i \neq j$, it is not necessary to retain both the ith and the jth measurements in $\mathbf{x}$; rather, condense the two measurements into one. This *suggests applying a clustering procedure*† to the *transposed vectors* $\mathbf{v}_1^t$, $\mathbf{v}_2^t$, $\ldots, \mathbf{v}_L^t$ to locate such similar components. If the clustering procedure determines that $d(\mathbf{v}_i, \mathbf{v}_j) \cong 0$ for an appropriate distance measure d and $i \neq j$, then measurements i and j are accepted as equivalent. It is desirable to establish equivalent measurements, utilizing problem knowledge, rather than relying completely on training samples.

The procedure presented in this section is applied to the mixture of n vector samples from M classes. For example, shown in Figure 6.6 with $M = 3$, the eigenvector corresponding to largest eigenvalue λ, would be $\mathbf{\phi}_1 =$

†From Chapter 5.

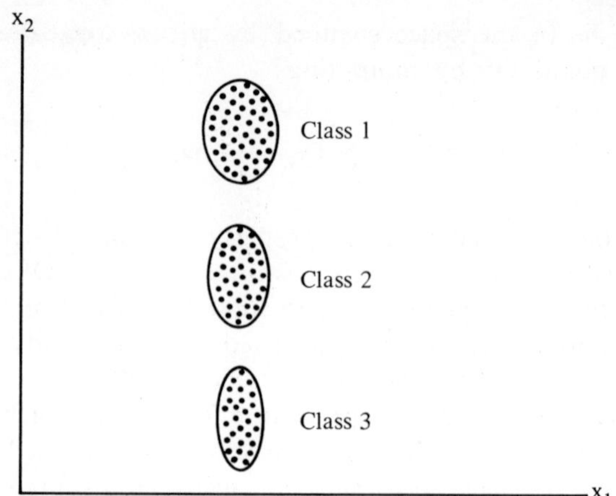

Fig. 6.6 Three class example where $e_2 = [0, 1]$ would be the significant direction of pooled samples.

$e_2 = [0, 1]$. Thus, $(x, \varphi_1) = x_2$ would be a single feature for classifying these three classes of samples with zero error. On the other hand, the two classes shown in Figure 6.7 also would have $\varphi_1 = e_1 = [0, 1]$ as the significant direc-

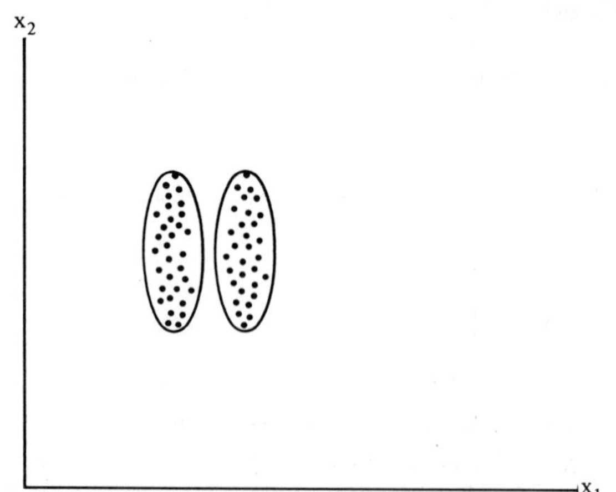

Fig. 6.7 Two class example where significant direction for pooled samples is $e_2 = [0, 1]$

tion, and the feature $(x, \varphi_1) = x_2$ would result in high classification error, but the classes in Figure 6.7 are not overlapping such that it should be possible to design a classifier with zero error.

To avoid such difficulties researchers have been concerned with dimensionality-reducing transformations from $\mathcal{V}_L$ to $\mathcal{V}_l$ which strive to maximize "interclass distance" while minimizing each "intraclass distance." This approach alleviates much of the problem, but it is difficult to extend the method beyond the two-category case ($M = 2$), and it has associated implementation complexities. More promising approaches seek to locate the clusters for each category and construct a feature vector with components corresponding to properties of these clusters. The reason that they may be more practical is because a clustering approach to unsupervised estimation may be more practical than most parameter-search procedures (concluded from Chapter 5).

6-7 Scatter Matrices

Let $\mathbf{x}_1, \mathbf{x}_2, \ldots, \mathbf{x}_n$ be n L-dimensional measurement vectors from the density $h(\mathbf{x})$ which may be a mixture density of class-conditional densities $f(\mathbf{x}|\omega_i)$, $i = 1, 2, \ldots, M$. Define the sample mean of the measurement vectors

$$\hat{\mathbf{m}} \triangleq \frac{1}{n} \sum_{s=1}^{n} \mathbf{x}_s \tag{1}$$

and the *sample covariance matrix*

$$\hat{\boldsymbol{\Sigma}} \triangleq \frac{1}{n-1} [\hat{\sigma}_{ij}], \tag{2}$$

where

$$\hat{\sigma}_{ij} = \sum_{s=1}^{n} (x_{si} - \hat{m}_i)(x_{sj} - \hat{m}_j), \qquad i, j = 1, 2, \ldots, L. \tag{3}$$

The matrix $[\hat{\sigma}_{ij}]$ is called the *scatter matrix about the measurement vector sample mean*. If $\mathbf{m} = E[\mathbf{x}]$, then $\mathbf{V} = [\hat{v}_{ij}]$, where

$$\hat{v}_{ij} = \hat{v}_{ji} \triangleq \sum_{s=1}^{n} (x_{si} - m_i)(x_{sj} - m_j) \tag{4}$$

is the scatter about the mean (true mean); then

$$E[|\mathbf{V}|] = L! \binom{n}{L} |\boldsymbol{\Sigma}|, \tag{5}$$

where $\boldsymbol{\Sigma}$ is the covariance matrix of distribution.

Theorem   If $\mathbf{x}_1, \mathbf{x}_2, \ldots, \mathbf{x}_n$, $L \leq n$, is a sample from $N(\mathbf{x}|\mathbf{m}, \boldsymbol{\Sigma})$, then the elements $\hat{v}_{ij}$ of $\hat{\mathbf{V}}$ have the Wishart distribution:

$$g(\{\hat{v}_{ij}\}) = \frac{|\sigma_{ij}|^{n/2} |\hat{v}_{ij}|^{(n-L-1)/2} \exp[-\frac{1}{2} \sum_{i=1}^{L} \sum_{j=1}^{L} \sigma_{ij}\hat{v}_{ij}]}{(2)^{Ln/2}(\pi)^{L(L-1)/4}\Gamma(n/2)\Gamma(n-1/2)\cdots\Gamma(n-L+1/2)}$$

in the $\frac{1}{2}L(L+1)$-dimensional region for which $\{\hat{v}_{ij}\}$ is positive definite and 0 otherwise. Because the Wishart distribution is characterized by L, n, and $\boldsymbol{\Sigma} = [\sigma_{ij}]$, it is convenient to denote the distribution by $W(\hat{\mathbf{V}}|\boldsymbol{\Sigma}, L, n)$.

Theorem The elements of $\hat{\boldsymbol{\Sigma}}$ and $\hat{\mathbf{m}}$ are independent sets of random variables having distributions $W(\hat{\boldsymbol{\Sigma}}|\boldsymbol{\Sigma}, L, n-1)$ and $N(\hat{\mathbf{m}}|\mathbf{m}, \boldsymbol{\Sigma}|n)$, respectively.

The above two theorems are useful in deriving the Bayes estimators for $\boldsymbol{\Sigma}$ and $\mathbf{m}$ and studying reproducing densities. The results of such studies are not very profound, essentially stating that the covariance matrix is estimated by a current sample covariance matrix weighted with an a priori "sample" covariance matrix, and similarly for the mean vector. These theorems are useful for studying performance based on n samples.

Transformation Maximizing Scatter

In Section 6-4 a procedure for transforming measurement vectors $\mathbf{x}_1$, $\mathbf{x}_2$, ..., $\mathbf{x}_n$ into feature vectors $\mathbf{y}_1$, $\mathbf{y}_2$, ..., $\mathbf{y}_n$, respectively, was developed to minimize average error, where $\mathbf{y} \in \mathscr{V}_l$ and $\mathbf{x} \in \mathscr{V}_L$, $l \leq L$. The procedure illustrated in Figure 6.4 has similarities with an approach where vectors $\mathbf{x}$ are transformed to vectors $\mathbf{y}$ so as to maximize the "scatter" of the new vectors (against an appropriate constraint). The latter approach is summarized in a following theorem. Let the transformed vectors be defined $\mathbf{y}_s = [y_{s1}, y_{s2}, \ldots, y_{sl}]$, where

$$y_{sp} = \sum_{i=1}^{L} c_{pi} x_{si}, \qquad p = 1, 2, \ldots, l, \tag{6}$$

$$\sum_{i=1}^{L} c_{pi}^2 = 1, \qquad p = 1, 2, \ldots, l. \tag{7}$$

Let $\hat{\boldsymbol{\Sigma}}' = [\hat{\sigma}'_{ij}]$ be the sample covariance matrix of $\mathbf{y}_s$, $s = 1, 2, \ldots, n$. The scatter is defined as $|\hat{\boldsymbol{\Sigma}}'|$. Then

Theorem Suppose $\mathbf{x}_1$, $\mathbf{x}_2$, ..., $\mathbf{x}_n$ is a set of measurement vectors of size $n > L$ from an L-dimensional distribution whose covariance matrix is positive definite, and $\hat{\boldsymbol{\Sigma}}'$ is positive definite with probability 1. The vectors $\mathbf{c}_p = [c_{p1}, c_{p2}, \ldots, c_{pL}]$, $p = 1, 2, \ldots, l$, which maximize the scatter $|\hat{\boldsymbol{\Sigma}}'|$ are solutions of

$$\hat{\boldsymbol{\Sigma}}' \mathbf{c}_p = \lambda_p \mathbf{c}_p, \qquad p = 1, 2, \ldots, l, \tag{8}$$

where $\lambda_1 > \lambda_2 > \cdots > \lambda_l$ are the largest eigenvalues of $\hat{\boldsymbol{\Sigma}}'$. These vectors

$\mathbf{c}_1, \ldots, \mathbf{c}_l$ are orthogonal and

$$\max |\hat{\boldsymbol{\Sigma}}'| = \prod_{\xi=1}^{l} \lambda_\xi. \tag{9}$$

The procedure suggested by (5) and (7) is illustrated by Figure 6.8.

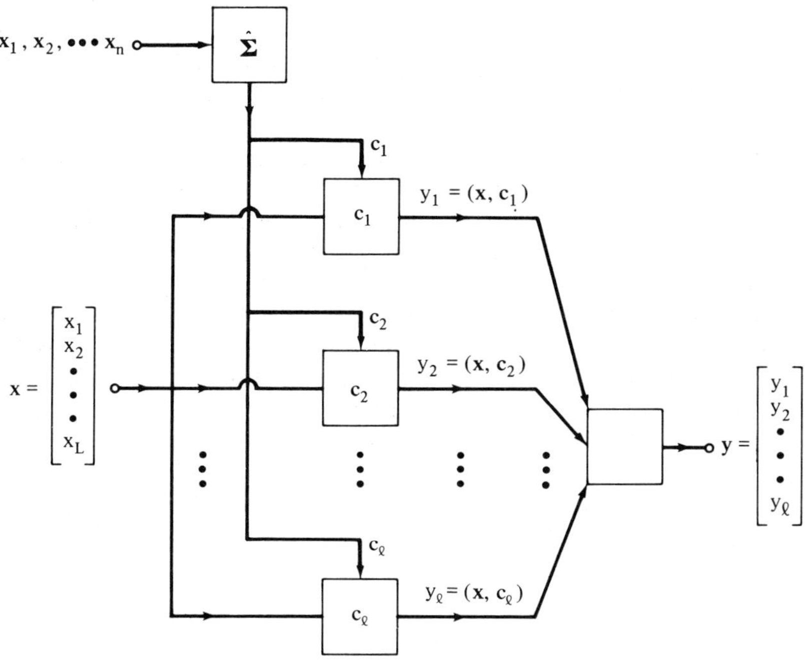

Fig. 6.8 Transformation of vectors $\mathbf{x} \in \mathscr{V}_L$ to vectors $\mathbf{y} \in \mathscr{V}_l$, which maximizes the "scatter" (determinant of the sample covariance matrix) of samples $\mathbf{y}$.

Discussion

The procedure presented in this section is an intraclass procedure since it processes a single set of training samples. Difficulties in applying this procedure to dimensionality reduction for use in pattern recognition are as follows:

1. Provisions for considering properties among classes have not been developed.
2. Features $y_1, y_2, \ldots, y_l$ obtained processing a set of measurement vectors for one class cannot be used in general for another class.

6-8 Maximizing Interclass Distance (Two Classes)

The approaches presented thus far do not directly process the class samples individually but process mixture samples.† Suppose n samples are from a mixture $h(\mathbf{x}) = \sum_{i=1}^{M} f(\mathbf{x}\,|\,\omega_i)P_i$; the following definitions are appropriate:

> *Intraclass features:* The measurement vectors from a single category ω_i are considered when generating a transformed space $\mathcal{V}_i$. Features are the components of the measurement vectors that have been transformed to $\mathcal{V}_i$ (also appropriately called within-class features).
>
> *Interclass features:* Sets of measurement vectors from two or more classes are individually considered at the same time when generating these features, which are used to differentiate among the classes.

Restrict attention to two classes ($M = 2$) with respective sets of measurement vectors $\mathbf{x}_1^i, \mathbf{x}_2^i, \ldots, \mathbf{x}_{n_i}^i$ (where $n_i > L$), $i = 1, 2$. Denote by $\mathbf{\Sigma}_i = \{\sigma_{kj}^i\}$ and $\mathbf{m}_i$ the covariance matrix and mean vector for class i, and by $\mathbf{\Sigma} = \{\sigma_{kj}\}$ and $\mathbf{m}$ that for the mixture of measurement vectors (all $n_1 + n_2$ samples pooled together).

Let the following matrices be defined:

Within scatter matrix:‡

$$\hat{\mathbf{\Sigma}}^W \triangleq \hat{\mathbf{\Sigma}}_1 + \hat{\mathbf{\Sigma}}_2. \tag{1a}$$

Between scatter matrix:

$$\hat{\mathbf{\Sigma}}^B \triangleq \hat{\mathbf{\Sigma}} - \hat{\mathbf{\Sigma}}^W. \tag{1b}$$

Now the measurement vectors from the respective classes are transformed from $\mathcal{V}_L$ to $\mathcal{V}_I$ using

$$y_s^i = \sum_{k=1}^{L} c_k x_{sk}^i, \qquad s = 1, 2, \ldots, n_i,\, i = 1, 2. \tag{2}$$

Denote by $\hat{\mu}_1$ and $\hat{\mu}_2$ the sample means of the two transformed sets of samples and by $\hat{\mu}$ the sample mean of the mixture of transformed samples. *Note that the transformation (2) takes a vector $\mathbf{x}_s^i$ to a scalar y_s^i.* Define:

---

†Techniques can be developed which apply these procedures individually to each class's training samples. But then there are "mismatched" transformed spaces for the respective classes.

‡$\hat{\mathbf{\Sigma}}^W$ is the sum of sample covariance matrices and thus is an average "scatter."

$$s_W = \sum_{i=1}^{2} \sum_{s=1}^{n_i} (y_s^i - \hat{\mu}_i)^2, \tag{3a}$$

$$s_B = \sum_{i=1}^{2} (\hat{\mu}_i - \hat{\mu}). \tag{3b}$$

Now, the objective of the approach being presented is to determine $[c_1, c_2, \ldots, c_L] = \mathbf{c}$, which maximizes s_B for a fixed s_W. This is equivalent to minimizing $s_W/(s_W + s_B)$.

Theorem   Let $\hat{\boldsymbol{\Sigma}}^W$ and $\hat{\boldsymbol{\Sigma}}^B$ be within and between scatters defined in (1) with $n_i > L$ and $\hat{\boldsymbol{\Sigma}}^W$ positive definite with probability 1. With s_W and s_B defined by (3), $\mathbf{c}$ maximizing

$$q = \frac{s_W}{s_W + s_B} \tag{4}$$

with s_W fixed is the solution of [5]

$$\hat{\boldsymbol{\Sigma}}^B \mathbf{c} = \lambda \boldsymbol{\Sigma}^W \mathbf{c}, \tag{5}$$

or

$$[(\hat{\boldsymbol{\Sigma}}^W)^{-1} \hat{\boldsymbol{\Sigma}}^B] \mathbf{c} = \lambda \mathbf{c}. \tag{6}$$

From (5), the conclusion is that $\mathbf{c}$ is the eigenvector of the matrix $[(\hat{\boldsymbol{\Sigma}}^W)^{-1} \hat{\boldsymbol{\Sigma}}^B]$ corresponding to eigenvalue λ. The procedure suggested by (2) and (6) is illustrated in Figure 6.9.

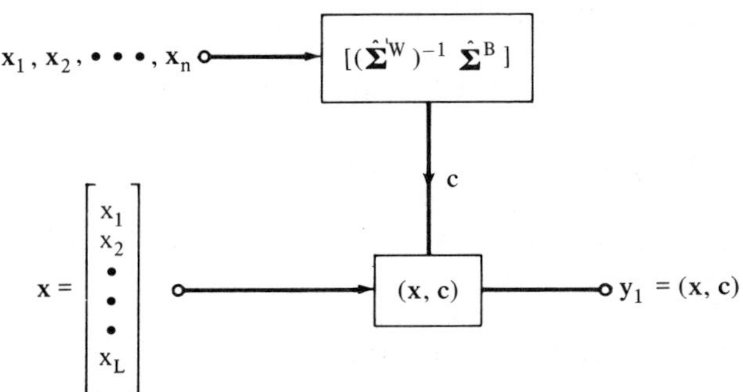

Fig. 6.9 Transformation of vectors $\mathbf{x} \in \mathcal{V}_L$ to a single feature $y \in \mathcal{V}_1$ which minimizes $q = s_W/(s_W + s_B)$

Example   Suppose $\boldsymbol{\Sigma}_i$ is diagonal with elements $(\sigma_k^i)^2$, $k = 1, 2, \ldots, L$. Then from (6), find the eigenvector $\mathbf{c}$ of the diagonal matrix with entries

$$\frac{(\hat{\sigma}_k)^2 - [(\hat{\sigma}_k^1)^2 + (\hat{\sigma}_k^2)^2]}{(\hat{\sigma}_k^1)^2 + (\hat{\sigma}_k^2)^2}, \qquad k = 1, 2, \ldots, L,$$

corresponding to the largest eigenvalue. This is a trivial situation because the largest eigenvalue is the largest entry in the matrix.

6-9 Minimizing Intraclass Distance

In this section a procedure is developed for transforming n classified measurement vectors in $\mathscr{V}_L$ into feature vectors in $\mathscr{V}_l$ such that an appropriately defined intraclass distance is minimized in $\mathscr{V}_l$, $l \leq L$. The use of such a procedure for dimensionality reduction is generally questionable until it is incorporated with other procedures. The results, however, provide worthwhile insight into the dimensionality-reduction problem.

Let $\mathbf{y} \in \mathscr{V}_l$ be transformed from the vector $\mathbf{z}$ using the transformation

$$\mathbf{y} = \mathbf{DAz}, \tag{1}$$

where $\mathbf{z} = \mathbf{x}/\|\mathbf{x}\|$ and $\mathbf{A}$ is an $l \times L$ matrix transformation which *projects* $\mathbf{x} \in \mathscr{V}_L$ to a vector in $\mathscr{V}_l$; $\mathbf{D}$ is an $l \times l$ diagonal matrix which contracts the resulting vector to produce $\mathbf{y} \in \mathscr{V}_l$.

Define the expected distance of samples $\mathbf{x}$ from a point $\boldsymbol{\mu} = E[\mathbf{z}]$ as

$$d \triangleq E[|\mathbf{z} - \boldsymbol{\mu}|^2] = \operatorname{tr} \boldsymbol{\Sigma}, \tag{2}$$

where $\boldsymbol{\Sigma}$ is the covariance matrix of samples $\mathbf{z}$. In the transformed space, the distance as a function $\mathbf{A}$, $\mathbf{D}$, $d'(\mathbf{A}; \mathbf{D})$, is

$$d'(\mathbf{A}, \mathbf{D}) = \operatorname{tr}[\mathbf{DDA\Sigma A}^t], \tag{3}$$

where the following derivation has been utilized:

$$E[(\mathbf{DAz})(\mathbf{DAz})^t] = E[\mathbf{DAzz}^t(\mathbf{DA})^t] = \mathbf{DA\Sigma A}^t\mathbf{D}^t = \mathbf{DDA\Sigma A}^t,$$

with the last following because $\mathbf{D}$ is diagonal.

It will be required that the contraction part of the transformation, $\mathbf{D}$, is subject to a constant volume constraint†; i.e., $|\mathbf{D}| = 1$.

Assuming that the projection map $\mathbf{A}$ is known, the contraction map $\mathbf{D}$ subject to the constant-volume constraint is as follows:

Theorem The distance $d'(\mathbf{A}, \mathbf{D})$ is minimum for $\mathbf{A}$ known and $|\mathbf{D}| = 1$ if the diagonal contraction matrix $\mathbf{D}$ in its inverse form, is

---

†This eliminates the trivial solution where $\mathbf{D}^{-1} = \mathbf{0}$.

$$
\mathbf{D}^{-1} = \frac{1}{\left[\prod_{k=1}^{l} (\alpha_k)\right]^{1/2l}}
\begin{bmatrix}
\alpha_1^{1/2} & 0 & \cdot & \cdot & \cdot & 0 \\
0 & \alpha_2^{1/2} & \cdot & \cdot & \cdot & 0 \\
\cdot & & & & & \\
\cdot & & & & & \\
\cdot & & & & & \\
\cdot & \cdot & \cdot & \cdot & \cdot & \alpha_l^{1/2}
\end{bmatrix},
\tag{4}
$$

where α_k, $k = 1, 2, \ldots, l$, are the l smallest eigenvalues of the covariance matrix $\boldsymbol{\Sigma}$. Furthermore, the minimum intraset distance in $\mathcal{V}_l$ is

$$
d'(\mathbf{A}; \mathbf{D}) = l\left(\prod_{k=1}^{l} \alpha_k\right)^{1/l},
\tag{5}
$$

if $\mathbf{A}$ has rows $\mathbf{a}_1, \mathbf{a}_2, \ldots, \mathbf{a}_l$ which are the eigenvectors of $\boldsymbol{\Sigma}$ corresponding to the l smallest eigenvalues. Equation (5) follows since

$$
\mathbf{DD} = \left[\prod_{k=1}^{l} (\alpha_k)\right]^{1/l}
\begin{bmatrix}
\alpha_1^{-1} & & & \\
& \alpha_2^{-1} & & \\
& & \cdot & \\
& & & \cdot \\
& & & & \cdot \\
& & & & & \alpha_l^{-1}
\end{bmatrix},
$$

while

$$
\mathbf{A\Sigma A} =
\begin{bmatrix}
\alpha_1 & & & \\
& \alpha_2 & & \\
& & \cdot & \\
& & & \cdot \\
& & & & \cdot \\
& & & & & \alpha_l
\end{bmatrix}
$$

because the columns of $\mathbf{A}$ are eigenvectors of $\boldsymbol{\Sigma}$.

Theorem If $\mathbf{z}$ is from $N(\mathbf{z}\,|\,\mathbf{m}, \boldsymbol{\Sigma})$ and $\mathbf{y} = \mathbf{Az}$, then the $l \times L$ matrix transformation $\mathbf{A}$ which minimizes the *entropy function*

$$
H = -\int [\ln h(\mathbf{y})]h(\mathbf{y})\,d\mathbf{y}
\tag{6}
$$

is that for which the rows $\mathbf{a}_1, \mathbf{a}_2, \ldots, \mathbf{a}_l$ of $\mathbf{A}$ are the l eigenvectors associated with the l smallest eigenvalues of $\boldsymbol{\Sigma}$.

The procedure suggested by (1), (3), (4), and (5) is illustrated in Figure 6.10.

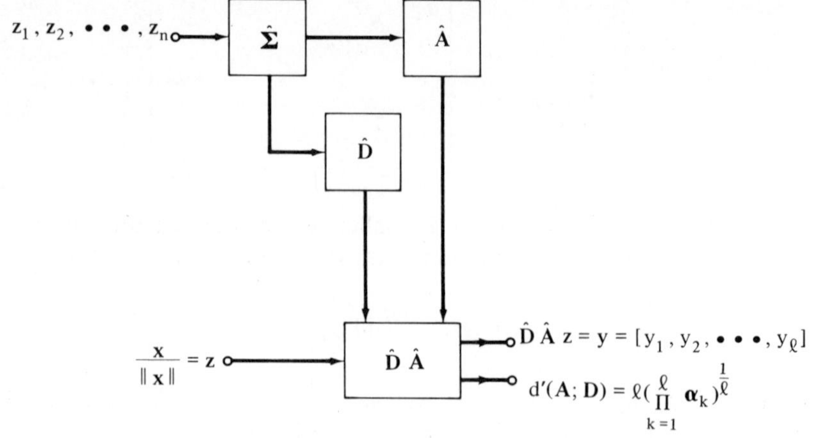

Fig. 6.10 Transformation of normalized vectors $\mathbf{z} \in \mathcal{V}_L$ to vectors $\mathbf{y} \in \mathcal{V}_l$ such that a distance $d'(\mathbf{A}, \mathbf{D})$ for samples in $\mathcal{V}_l$ is minimized.

6-10 Patrick–Fischer Nonparametric Feature Selection

6-10.1 Introduction

In this section a procedure developed by Patrick and Fischer [14] is presented. It is assumed that $M = 2$ and two sets of measurement vectors are mapped from $\mathcal{V}_L$ to $\mathcal{V}_l$; these two groups in $\mathcal{V}_L$ are denoted

$$S_i = \{\mathbf{x}_1^i, \mathbf{x}_2^i, \ldots, \mathbf{x}_{n_i}^i\}, \qquad i = 1, 2, \tag{1}$$

which are from densities $f(\mathbf{x} \mid \omega_i)$, $i = 1, 2$, respectively. Of particular importance is that $f(\mathbf{x} \mid \omega_i)$ *can be a mixture, for example multimodal, in contrast with the procedures presented in previous sections* of this chapter. Many parametric probability density functions (p.d.f's) cannot be adequately described by their covariance matrix and mean vector alone.†

Sebestyen [8] considered a nonparametric approach, where directions in $\mathcal{V}_L$ are found which essentially maximize a global interclass distance while keeping global intraclass distances constant. In the current section the Patrick–Fischer nonparametric-feature-selection procedure utilizes a local interclass structure. The best subspace $\mathcal{M} = \mathcal{V}_l$ is found in the measurement space $\mathcal{X} = \mathcal{V}_L$ such that the distances between the components of S_1

---

†It is not difficult to exhibit radically different p.d.f.'s with the same covariance matrix [9].

and S_2 in $\mathcal{M}$ are a maximum. This distance criterion is used instead of Bayes risk because of the difficulty arising in evaluating the latter. Appropriately estimated p.d.f.'s $\hat{f}(\mathbf{x}\,|\,\omega_i)$, $i = 1,\, 2$, are used in conjunction with a distance criterion between estimated functions. This distance on $\mathcal{M}$ is a relatively simple mathematical function of the mapping $\mathbf{A}$; this mapping can be selected to maximize the induced distance.

6-10.2 Distance Measure d(A)

Projection Maps

Suppose that $\mathcal{M} = \mathcal{V}_i$ is a vector subspace in $\mathcal{X} = \mathcal{V}_L$. Then $\mathcal{M}$ is uniquely defined as follows: If $\mathbf{x} \in \mathcal{X}$, then $\mathbf{x} = \mathbf{x}' + \mathbf{x}''$, $\mathbf{x}' \cdot \mathbf{x}'' = 0$, $\mathbf{x}' \in \mathcal{M}$, and $\mathbf{x}'' \in \mathcal{M}^\perp$. Hence, $\mathbf{x}'$ is the "projection" of $\mathbf{x}$ onto $\mathcal{M}$.

Let $\{\mathbf{e}_1, \mathbf{e}_2, \ldots, \mathbf{e}_L\}$ be an orthonormal basis of $\mathcal{X} = \mathcal{V}_L$ and $\{\mathbf{v}_1, \mathbf{v}_2, \ldots, \mathbf{v}_l\}$ a particular orthonormal basis of $\mathcal{M}$, where $\mathbf{v}_i \in \mathcal{V}_L$. With respect to these two sets of basis vectors there is a unique linear transformation $\mathbf{A}$ from $\mathcal{X}$ to $\mathcal{M}$ such that $\mathbf{y} = \mathbf{A}\mathbf{x}$ (i.e., $\mathbf{y} = \mathbf{x}'$ in the above notation),

$$
\mathbf{A} = \begin{bmatrix} a_{11} & a_{12} & \cdots & a_{1L} \\ a_{21} & a_{22}. & & \\ \cdot & & \cdot & \\ \cdot & & & \cdot \\ \cdot & & & \cdot \\ a_{l1} & \cdots & \cdots & a_{lL} \end{bmatrix} \triangleq \begin{bmatrix} \mathbf{v}_1^t \\ \mathbf{v}_2^t \\ \cdot \\ \cdot \\ \cdot \\ \mathbf{v}_l^t \end{bmatrix}. \tag{2}
$$

Distance Measure

Let a data vector $\mathbf{x}_s^i \in \mathcal{V}_L$ be transformed to $\mathbf{A}\mathbf{x}_s^i \in \mathcal{V}_i$ and define a distance measure

$$
d^2(\mathbf{A}) \triangleq \sum_{r=1}^{n_1} \sum_{s=1}^{n_1} c_{rs}^{1,1} + \sum_{r=1}^{n_2} \sum_{s=1}^{n_2} c_{rs}^{2,2} - 2 \sum_{r=1}^{n_1} \sum_{s=1}^{n_2} c_{rs}^{1,2}, \tag{3a}
$$

where

$$
c_{rs}^{j,k} = \frac{P_j P_k}{n_j n_k} \left(\frac{1}{\sqrt{2\pi}\,\sigma} \right)^l \exp\left(-\frac{1}{4\sigma^2} |\mathbf{A}(\mathbf{x}_r^j - \mathbf{x}_s^k)|^2 \right), \qquad \mathbf{A}\mathbf{x}_r^j \in \mathcal{M}. \tag{3b}
$$

The terms $c_{rs}^{j,k}$ can be interpreted as a non-Euclidean distance between $\mathbf{x}_r^j$ and $\mathbf{x}_s^k$. For example, $c_{rs}^{j,k}$ increases as $|\mathbf{x}_r^j - \mathbf{x}_r^k|$ decreases. If $j = k$, the distance is an *intraclass* distance; if $j \neq k$, it is an *interclass* distance. The objective is to solve for $\mathbf{A}$ maximizing $d(\mathbf{A})$.

An illustration of a comparison between Euclidean distance measure and $d(\mathbf{A})$ is shown in Figure 6.11 as a function of Euclidean distance, for

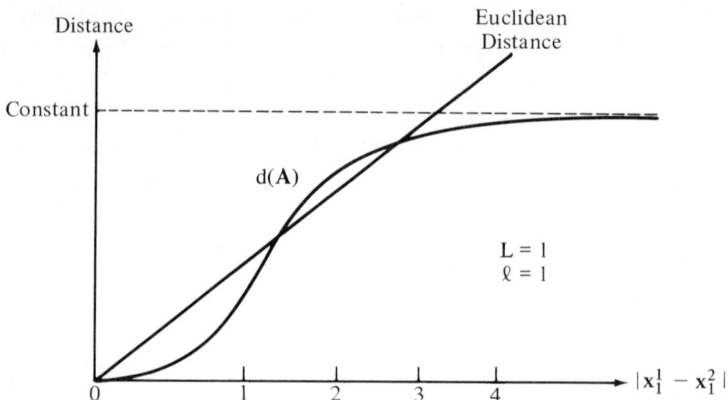

Fig. 6.11 Comparison of Euclidean distance measure with $d(\mathbf{A})$

$L = 1$, $l = 1$, $S_1 = x_1^1$, $S_2 = x_1^2$. Pairs of samples far apart in $\mathcal{M}$ have little contribution.

6-10.3 *Maximizing d(A) by Method of Steepest Ascent*

The matrix $\mathbf{A}$ is in the $(l \times L)$-dimensional space $\mathcal{T}$ of linear transformation, but it is also in a special set $\mathcal{P}$ of projection maps. Denote a basis for $\mathcal{T}$ by the set $\mathbf{u}_{ij}$, $1 \leq i \leq l$, $1 \leq j \leq L$; the matrix representation $\mathbf{A}$ consists of coefficients associated with the above basis vectors of $\mathcal{F}$. Then $\mathbf{A} \in \mathcal{P}$ iff the row vectors $\boldsymbol{\varphi}_i$ of $\mathbf{A}$ are an orthonormal set spanning $\mathcal{M}$.

The function $d(\mathbf{A})$ defined by (3a) and (3b) is defined for $\mathbf{A}$ a projection map since $\mathbf{A}x_r^j \in \mathcal{M}$. Suppose $\mathbf{A}_m$ is the projection map obtained after the mth stage in the method of steepest ascent. The gradient $\nabla d(\mathbf{A})$ is found at $\mathbf{A} = \mathbf{A}_m$. $\nabla d(\mathbf{A}_m)$ also is an element of $\mathcal{T}$ in which to increment $\mathbf{A}_m$ to achieve maximum increase in $d(\mathbf{A})$. The subsidiary conditions that $\mathbf{A}$ remain a projection map are evaluated in the second subsection; the gradient is evaluated in the following subsection.

Gradient

Consider $\nabla d(\mathbf{A})$, where

$$d(\mathbf{A}) = \left[\sum_{j=1}^{2} \sum_{k=1}^{2} \sum_{r=1}^{n_1} \sum_{s=1}^{n_2} \mu_{jk} \left(\frac{1}{\sqrt{2\pi}\,\sigma} \right)^l \frac{P_j P_k}{n_j n_k} \exp\left(-\frac{1}{4\sigma^2} |\mathbf{A}(x_r^j - x_s^k)|^2 \right) \right]^{1/2},$$

$$(4)$$

and

$$\mu_{jk} = \begin{cases} 1, & j = k, \\ -1, & j \neq k. \end{cases}$$

Then

$$\nabla d(\mathbf{A}) = \frac{1}{2d(\mathbf{A})} \sum_{j=1}^{2} \sum_{k=1}^{2} \sum_{r=1}^{n_1} \sum_{s=1}^{n_2} \mu_{jk} \left(\frac{1}{\sqrt{2\pi}\,\sigma}\right)^l \frac{P_j P_k}{n_j n_k}$$

$$\times \nabla \left[\exp\left(-\frac{1}{4\sigma^2} |\mathbf{A}(\mathbf{x}_r^j - \mathbf{x}_s^k)|^2\right) \right]. \tag{5}$$

Now, letting $\boldsymbol{\delta}_{rs}^{jk} = \mathbf{x}_r^j - \mathbf{x}_s^k$, then

$$\nabla \left[\exp\left(-\frac{1}{4\sigma^2} |\mathbf{A}\boldsymbol{\delta}_{rs}^{jk}|^2\right) \right] = \exp\left(-\frac{1}{4\sigma^2} |\mathbf{A}\boldsymbol{\delta}_{rs}^{jk}|^2\right)\left(-\frac{1}{4\sigma^2}\right)\nabla[|\mathbf{A}\boldsymbol{\delta}_{rs}^{jk}|^2]. \tag{6}$$

But

$$\boldsymbol{\delta}_{rs}^{jk} = [\delta_{rs_1}^{jk}, \delta_{rs_2}^{jk}, \ldots, \delta_{rsL}^{jk}]; \tag{7}$$

thus

$$|\mathbf{A}\boldsymbol{\delta}_{rs}^{jk}|^2 = (\mathbf{A}\boldsymbol{\delta}_{rs}^{jk})^t(\mathbf{A}\boldsymbol{\delta}_{rs}^{jk})$$

$$= \sum_{\xi=1}^{l} \left(\sum_{\eta=1}^{L} a_{\xi\eta}\delta_{rs_\eta}^{jk}\right)^2 \tag{8}$$

since

$$\nabla d(A) = \frac{\partial d(\mathbf{A})}{\partial A_{11}}\mathbf{u}_{11} + \cdots + \frac{\partial d(\mathbf{A})}{\partial A_{lL}}\mathbf{u}_{lL}.$$

Thus, it follows that

$$\nabla[|\mathbf{A}\boldsymbol{\delta}_{rs}^{jk}|^2] = \sum_{\xi=1}^{l} \left[2\left(\sum_{\eta=1}^{L} a_{\xi\eta}\delta_{rs_\eta}^{jk}\right)\delta_{rs_\eta}^{jk}\right]\mathbf{u}_{\xi\eta}. \tag{9}$$

Inserting (9) in (6) and then the result in (5) gives

$$\nabla d(\mathbf{A}) = -\frac{1}{8\sigma^2\, d(\mathbf{A})} \sum_{j=1}^{2} \sum_{k=1}^{2} \sum_{r=1}^{n_1} \sum_{s=1}^{n_2} \left[\mu_{rt}\left(\frac{1}{\sqrt{2\pi}\,\sigma}\right)^l \frac{P_j P_k}{n_j n_k}\right.$$

$$\times \exp\left(-\frac{1}{4\sigma^2} |\mathbf{A}\boldsymbol{\delta}_{rs}^{jk}|^2\right) \sum_{\xi=1}^{l} \left[2\left(\sum_{\eta=1}^{L} a_{\xi\eta}\delta_{rs_\eta}^{jk}\right)\delta_{rs_\eta}^{jk}\right]\mathbf{u}_{\xi\eta}. \tag{10}$$

Let

$$(\lambda_{rs}^{jk})_{\xi\eta} \triangleq (\mathbf{a}_\xi, \boldsymbol{\delta}_{rs}^{jk})\delta_{rs_\eta}^{jk}; \tag{11}$$

then

$$\nabla(d(\mathbf{A})) = c(\mathbf{A}) \sum_{\xi=1}^{l} \sum_{\eta=1}^{L} \left[\sum_{j=1}^{2} \sum_{k=1}^{2} \sum_{r=1}^{n_1} \sum_{s=1}^{n_2} \mu_{jk}(\lambda_{rs}^{jk})_{\xi\eta}\right]\mathbf{u}_{\xi\eta}, \tag{12}$$

where $c(\mathbf{A})$ is a constant depending on $\mathbf{A}$ but independent of the matrix elements. Recall that $\mu_{rt} = 1$ for $j = k$ and -1 for $j \neq k$.

Theorem The normalized gradient $\mathbf{V}(d(\mathbf{A}))$ in direction $u_{\xi\eta}$ is $[\sum_{j=1}^{2} \sum_{k=1}^{2} \sum_{r=1}^{n_1} \sum_{s=1}^{n_2} (\lambda_{rs}^{jk})_{\xi\eta}]$; this is the relative amount that element $a_{\xi\eta}$ of $\mathbf{A}$ is incremented in the method of steepest ascent. $(\lambda_{rs}^{jk})_{\xi\eta}$ is the contribution to the increment by the pair of samples $\mathbf{x}_r^j$ and $\mathbf{x}_s^k$. Note that $(\lambda_{rs}^{jk})_{\xi\eta}$ according to (11), is the projection of the ξth row vector $\mathbf{a}_\xi$ of $\mathbf{A}$ onto $\boldsymbol{\delta}_{rs}^{jk} = \mathbf{x}_s^j - \mathbf{x}_x^k$.

It is convenient to write (12) as

$$\mathbf{V}(d(\mathbf{A})) = c(\mathbf{A}) \sum_{\xi=1}^{l} \sum_{\eta=1}^{L} (\Delta_{\xi\eta})\mathbf{u}_{\xi\eta} \tag{13}$$

and define a matrix of increments

$$\boldsymbol{\Delta} \triangleq \{\Delta_{\xi\eta}\} \triangleq \sum_{j=1}^{2} \sum_{k=1}^{2} \sum_{r=1}^{n_1} \sum_{s=1}^{n_2} \boldsymbol{\Delta}_{rs}^{jk}. \tag{14}$$

Example Assume that $L = 3$, $l = 2$, $\mathbf{x}_1^1 = \{[1, 0, 0]\}$, $\mathbf{x}_1^2 = \{[0, 1, 0]\}$, $n_1 = n_2 = 1$, and

$$\mathbf{A}_m = \begin{bmatrix} 1 & 0 & 0 \\ 0 & 0 & 1 \end{bmatrix}.$$

Hence $\mathbf{v}_1 = (1, 0, 0)$, $\mathbf{v}_2 = (0, 0, 1)$, and $\mathcal{M}_m$ is the $\mathbf{e}_1$, $\mathbf{e}_3$ plane as illustrated in Figure 6.12. Using $\boldsymbol{\delta}_{rs}^{jk} = \mathbf{x}_r^j - \mathbf{x}_s^k$,

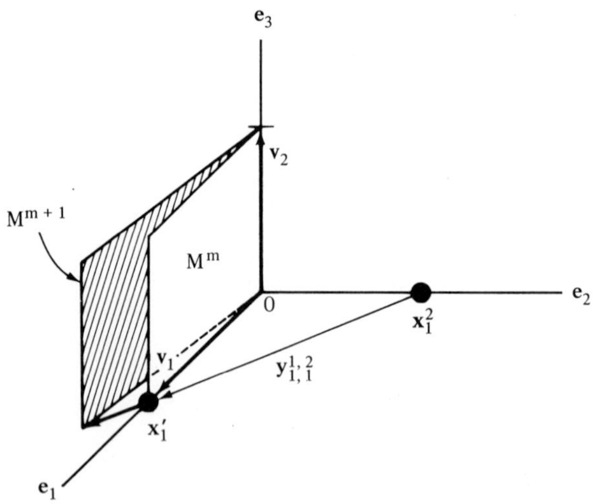

Fig. 6.12 Geometric illustration of gradient of $\mathbf{A}$

$$\boldsymbol{\delta}_{11}^{11} = \begin{bmatrix} 0 \\ 0 \\ 0 \end{bmatrix}, \qquad \boldsymbol{\delta}_{11}^{22} = \begin{bmatrix} 0 \\ 0 \\ 0 \end{bmatrix}, \qquad \boldsymbol{\delta}_{11}^{12} = \begin{bmatrix} 1 \\ -1 \\ 0 \end{bmatrix},$$

and

$$\boldsymbol{\Delta}_{11}^{11} = \boldsymbol{\Delta}_{11}^{22} = \mathbf{0},$$

$$\boldsymbol{\Delta}_{11}^{12} = \begin{bmatrix} 1 & -1 & 0 \\ 0 & 0 & 0 \end{bmatrix},$$

and it follows that

$$\nabla(d(\mathbf{A})) = c(\mathbf{A}) \begin{bmatrix} 1 & -1 & 0 \\ 0 & 0 & 0 \end{bmatrix}.$$

Thus, given $\mathbf{A}_m$, the direction $\nabla d(\mathbf{A})$ is found which maximizes the slope of $d(\mathbf{A})$ at $\mathbf{A} = \mathbf{A}_m$.

An illustration of this nonparametric feature-selection procedure is presented in Figure 6.13.

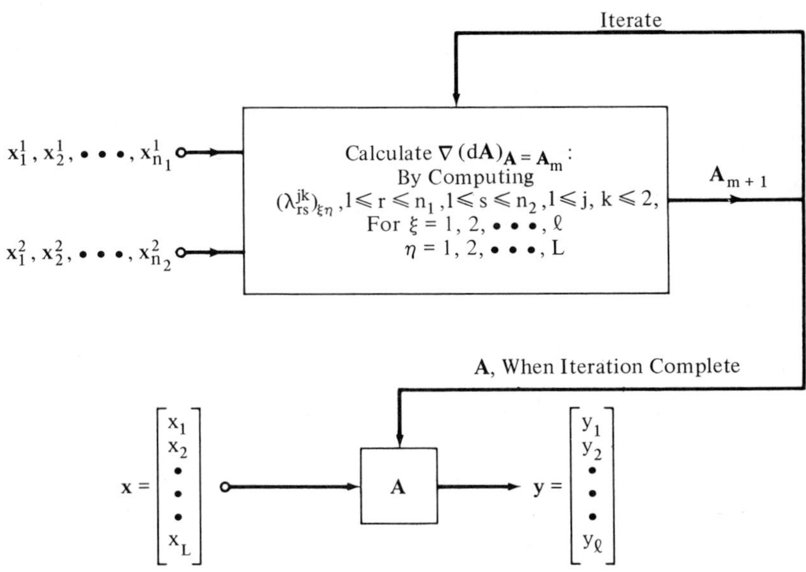

Fig. 6.13 Illustration of nonparametric feature selection

Projection-Map Constraint

The constraint $\nabla d(\mathbf{A})$ such that $\mathbf{A}$ remain a projection map is evaluated now; it is shown that $\nabla d(\mathbf{A})$ must have row vectors that are orthogonal to every row vector of $\mathbf{A}$ at each stage of the hill-climbing process.

Let $\mathbf{A}_{m+1}$ be the incremented map such that

$$\mathbf{A}_{m+1} = \mathbf{A}_m + \epsilon \nabla d(\mathbf{A}), \tag{15}$$

where ϵ is a small positive real number. Then

$$\mathbf{A}_{m+1} = \begin{bmatrix} a_{11} + \epsilon g_{11}, \ldots, a_{1L} + \epsilon g_{1L} \\ \cdot \\ \cdot \\ \cdot \\ a_{l1} + \epsilon g_{l1}, \ldots, a_{lL} + \epsilon g_{lL} \end{bmatrix}.$$

For $\mathbf{A}_{m+1}$ to be a projection map, it is necessary and sufficient that

$$(\mathbf{v}_i^{m+1}, \mathbf{v}_i^{m+1}) = 1, \qquad 1 \leq i \leq l,$$
$$(\mathbf{v}_i^{m+1}, \mathbf{v}_k^{m+1}) = 0, \qquad i \neq k, 1 \leq i \leq l.$$

The first constraint above implies that

$$\sum_{j=1}^{L} (a_{ij} + \epsilon g_{ij})^2 = \sum_{j=1}^{L} (a_{ij})^2 + 2\epsilon \sum_{j=1}^{L} a_{ij}g_{ij} + \epsilon^2 \sum_{j=1}^{L} g_{ij} = 1, \qquad 1 \leq i \leq l.$$

Presuming that $\mathbf{A}_m$ is a projection map, the first term equals 1. For arbitrarily small ϵ, the last term may be neglected, resulting in

$$\sum_{j=1}^{L} a_{ij}g_{kj} = 0, \qquad 1 \leq i \leq l.$$

Letting $\mathbf{w}_i^t$ be the ith-row vector of $\nabla d(\mathbf{A})$, this implies that

$$(\mathbf{w}_i, \mathbf{v}_i) = 0, \qquad 1 \leq i \leq l. \tag{16a}$$

The second constraint implies that

$$\sum_{j=1}^{L} (a_{ij} + \epsilon g_{ij})(a_{kj} + \epsilon g_{kj}) = 0, \qquad 1 \leq i \neq k \leq l;$$

thus

$$\sum_{j=1}^{L} a_{ij}g_{ij} + \epsilon \sum_{j=1}^{L} (a_{ij}g_{kj} + a_{kj}g_{ij}) + \epsilon^2 \sum_{j=1}^{L} g_{ij}g_{kj} = 0.$$

Since $\mathbf{A}_m$ is a projection map, the first term is 0. For small enough ϵ, the last term may be neglected. Thus,

$$\sum_{j=1}^{L} (a_{ij}g_{kj} + a_{kj}g_{ij}) = 0$$

or

$$(\mathbf{v}_i, \mathbf{w}_k) + (\mathbf{v}_k, \mathbf{w}_i) = 0, \qquad 1 \leq i \neq k \leq l.$$

Thus, either $(\mathbf{v}_i, \mathbf{w}_k) = 0$ or $(\mathbf{v}_i, \mathbf{w}_k) + (\mathbf{v}_k, \mathbf{w}_i) = 0$, $1 \leq i \neq k \leq l$. It is easy to see that the latter allows rotation in the plane spanned by $\mathbf{v}_i$ and $\mathbf{v}_k$, while the former does not. However, rotation of the basis vectors results in the same subspace $\mathcal{M}$. Because we wish to determine $\mathcal{M}$ irrespective of the particular basis spanning $\mathcal{M}$, we consider the more restrictive case,

$$(\mathbf{v}_i, \mathbf{w}_k) = 0, \qquad 1 \leq i \neq k \leq l. \tag{16b}$$

Combining (16a) and (16b) results in

$$(\mathbf{v}_i, \mathbf{w}_i) = 0, \qquad 1 \leq i, k \leq l. \tag{17}$$

The set of all vectors in $\mathcal{T}$ with row vectors $\mathbf{v}_i$, which satisfy (17), forms a linear vector subspace $\mathcal{T}'$ in $\mathcal{T}$ which is tangent to the hypersurface $\mathcal{P}$ at $\mathbf{A}_{m+1}$. Hence, the direction in which to increment $\mathbf{A}$ such that $\mathbf{A}$ remains a projection map is $\nabla d(\mathbf{A})_{\mathcal{T}'}$, the component of $\nabla d(\mathbf{A})$ in $\mathcal{T}'$,

$$\mathbf{w}'_i = \mathbf{w}_i - \sum_{j=1}^{l} (\mathbf{w}_i, \mathbf{v}_j)\mathbf{v}_j, \qquad 1 \leq j \leq l, \tag{18}$$

where $(\mathbf{w}'_i)^t$ is the ith row of $\nabla d(\mathbf{A})$. Then $\mathbf{A}_{m+1}$ is obtained by incrementing:

$$\mathbf{A}_{m+1} = \mathbf{A}_m + \epsilon \nabla d(\mathbf{A}_m)_{\mathcal{T}'}. \tag{19}$$

6-10.4 *Integral-Square-Distance Criterion*

The previously defined distance criterion naturally arises when the class densities are approximated by potential functions. That is, let $\hat{f}(\mathbf{x}\,|\,\omega_i)$ be represented by the weighting-function (potential-function) technique introduced in Section 4-3.1:

$$\hat{f}(\mathbf{x}\,|\,\omega_1) \triangleq \frac{1}{[h(n_i)]^L} \frac{1}{n_i} \sum_{s=1}^{n_i} K(\mathbf{Ax}, \mathbf{Ax}_s^i), \tag{20}$$

where $K(\cdot)$ is a weighting function and $h(n_i)$ is a positive-valued function of n_i tending to zero as n_i increases. If $K(\cdot)$ and $h(n_i)$ have several practical properties easily met, then $\hat{f}(\mathbf{x}\,|\,\omega_i) \xrightarrow{\text{w.p.1}} f(\mathbf{x}\,|\,\omega_i)$.

Separation between the images of the two groups S_1 and S_2 on $\mathcal{M}$ can be established by defining the distance between the two induced estimated distributions on $\mathcal{M}$; one distance measure is

$$d(w, z) \triangleq \left[\int [w(\mathbf{x}) - z(\mathbf{x})]^2 \, d\mathbf{x} \right]^{1/2} \tag{21}$$

for two functions $w(\cdot)$ and $z(\cdot)$. Desirable properties of this distance measure are

1. It is a metric on the space of square-integrable functions and generates a natural inner product.
2. If $w = z$, $d(w, z) = 0$.
3. If the induced value of $\int w(\mathbf{x})z(\mathbf{x}) \, d\mathbf{x}$ decreases, the induced distance $d(w, z)$ increases; the former is a measure of *separability*.
4. If the induced value of $d(w, z)$ increases because either $\|w(\mathbf{x})\|^2$ or $\|z(\mathbf{x})\|^2$ increases, this is not undesirable.

Let $K(\mathbf{Ax} \mid \mathcal{M})$ denote the induced image of $K(\mathbf{x})$ on $\mathcal{M}$, and, similarly, let $\hat{f}(\mathbf{Ax} \mid \omega_i, \mathcal{M})$ denote the induced estimated density of $f(\mathbf{x} \mid \omega_i)$ on $\mathcal{M}$, with both functions nonzero only for $\mathbf{Ax} \in \mathcal{M}$. Then

$$\hat{f}(\mathbf{Ax} \mid \omega_i, \mathcal{M}) = \frac{1}{n_i} \sum_{s=1}^{n_i} \frac{1}{h(n_i)^l} K(\mathbf{Ax}, \mathbf{Ax}_s^i \mid \mathcal{M}), \; \mathbf{Ax} \in \mathcal{M}. \tag{22}$$

Denote the distance between the two groups S_1 and S_2 as $d(S_1, S_2 \mid \mathcal{M})$,

$$d(S_1, S_2 \mid \mathcal{M}) = d(\mathbf{A}) \triangleq d(P_1 \hat{f}(\mathbf{Ax} \mid \omega_1, \mathcal{M}), P_2 \hat{f}(\mathbf{Ax} \mid \omega_2, \mathcal{M})), \tag{23}$$

which is a function of $\mathbf{A}$ and the weighting function $K(\cdot)$ for $\mathbf{Ax} \in \mathcal{M}$. From (22) and (23),

$$d(\mathbf{A}) = \left[\int_{\mathbf{Ax} \in \mathcal{M}} \left[\frac{P_1}{n_1} \sum_{r=1}^{n_1} \frac{1}{h(n_1)^l} K(\mathbf{Ax}, \mathbf{Ax}_r^1 \mid \mathcal{M}) - \frac{P_2}{n_2} \sum_{s=1}^{n_2} \frac{1}{h(n_2)} \right.\right.$$
$$\left.\left. \times \; K(\mathbf{Ax}, \mathbf{Ax}_s^2 \mid \mathcal{M}) \right]^2 d\mathbf{x} \right]^{1/2}. \tag{24}$$

Expanding the integral,

$$d(\mathbf{A}) = \left[\int_{\mathbf{Ax} \in \mathcal{M}} \sum_{j=1}^{2} \sum_{k=1}^{2} \sum_{r=1}^{n_1} \sum_{s=1}^{n_2} \xi_{jk} \frac{P_j P_k}{n_r n_s} \left[\frac{1}{h(n_j) h(n_k)} \right]^l \right.$$
$$\left. \times \; K(\mathbf{Ax}, \mathbf{Ax}_r^j \mid \mathcal{M}) \cdot K(\mathbf{Ax}, \mathbf{Ax}_s^k \mid \mathcal{M}) \, d\mathbf{x} \right]^{1/2}, \tag{25}$$

where

$$\xi_{jk} = \begin{cases} 1, & j = k, \\ -1, & j \neq k. \end{cases} \tag{26}$$

Equation (25) condenses into the following form (used in the previous sections):

$$d(\mathbf{A}) = \left(\sum_{r=1}^{n_1} \sum_{s=1}^{n_2} c_{rs}^{11} + \sum_{r=1}^{n_1} \sum_{s=1}^{n_2} c_{rs}^{22} - 2 \sum_{r=1}^{n_2} \sum_{s=1}^{n_2} c_{rs}^{12} \right)^{1/2}, \tag{27}$$

where

$$c_{rs}^{jk} \triangleq \frac{P_j P_k}{n_r n_s} \left[\frac{1}{h(n_r)h(n_s)} \right]^l$$

$$\times \int_{\mathbf{Ax}\in\mathcal{M}} K(\mathbf{Ax}, \mathbf{Ax}_r^j \mid \mathcal{M}) \cdot K(\mathbf{Ax}, \mathbf{Ax}_s^k \mid \mathcal{M}) \, d\mathbf{x}. \tag{28}$$

The coefficient c_{rs}^{jk} can be interpreted as a non-Euclidean measure of proximity between $\mathbf{x}_r^j$ and $\mathbf{x}_s^k$. For example, if $K(\cdot \mid \mathcal{M})$ is a Gaussian function, c_{rs}^{jk} increases as $|\mathbf{x}_r^j - \mathbf{x}_s^k|$ decreases. If $j = k$, the distance is an intraclass distance; if $j \neq k$, it is an interclass distance. The best $\mathcal{M}$ for a given K is defined to be the one maximizing $d(\mathbf{A})$; the corresponding projection map $\mathbf{A}$ is the linear transformation from $\mathcal{X} = \mathcal{V}_L$ to $\mathcal{M} = \mathcal{V}_i$ which maximizes $d(\mathbf{A})$.

If

$$K(\mathbf{Ax}, \mathbf{Ax}_r^j \mid \mathcal{M}) = \left(\frac{1}{\sqrt{2\pi}\,\sigma} \right)^l \exp\left(-\frac{1}{2\sigma^2} \| \mathbf{Ax} - \mathbf{Ax}_r^j \|^2 \right), \tag{29}$$

then

$$c_{rs}^{jk} = \frac{P_j P_k}{n_r n_s} \left(\frac{1}{\sqrt{2\pi}\,\sigma} \right)^l \exp\left(-\frac{1}{4\sigma^2} \| \mathbf{Ax}_r^j - \mathbf{Ax}_s^k \|^2 \right), \tag{30}$$

and we observe that c_{rs}^{jk} increases as $\| \mathbf{x}_r^j - \mathbf{x}_s^k \|$ decreases.

6-10.5 *Average-Square-Error Distance Criterion*

The integral square-error criterion (21) can append errors to increase the value of $d(w, z)$ in regions of the observation space where samples never occur. Meisel [15] suggested an average-square-error criterion,

$$q^2(\mathbf{A}) = \frac{P_1}{n_1} \sum_{r=1}^{n_1} [P_1 f(\mathbf{Ax}_r^1 \mid \omega_1, \mathcal{M}) - P_2 f(\mathbf{Ax}_r^1 \mid \omega_2, \mathcal{M})]^2$$

$$+ \frac{P_2}{n_2} \sum_{s=1}^{n_2} [P_2 f(\mathbf{Ax}_s^2 \mid \omega_1, \mathcal{M}) - P_2 f(\mathbf{Ax}_s^2 \mid \omega_2, \mathcal{M})]^2. \tag{31}$$

Equation (27) still holds, with

$$c_{rs}^{jk} = \frac{P_1}{n_1} \sum_{k=1}^{n_1} K(\mathbf{Ax}_k^1, \mathbf{Ax}_r^j) \cdot K(\mathbf{Ax}_k^1, \mathbf{Ax}_s^k)$$

$$+ \frac{P_2}{n_2} \sum_{k=1}^{n_2} K(\mathbf{Ax}_k^2, \mathbf{Ax}_r^j) \cdot K(\mathbf{Ax}_k^2, \mathbf{Ax}_s^k). \tag{32}$$

Define a criterion $q^2(\mathbf{A})$ to be the sum of all pairwise mean-square errors:

$$q^2(\mathbf{A}) = \sum_{u=1}^{M} \sum_{v=1}^{M} \frac{P_u}{n_u} \sum_{r_u=1}^{n_u} [P_u f(\mathbf{A}\mathbf{x}_{r_u}^u | \omega_u, \mathscr{M}) - P_v f(\mathbf{A}\mathbf{x}_{r_u}^u | \omega_v, \mathscr{M})]^2; \quad (33)$$

then seek $\mathbf{A}$ such that $q^2(\mathbf{A})$ is maximized. The reader may be interested in ways to implement and modify this multiclass criteria.

6-11 A Bayes Framework for Dimensionality Reduction

Estimation of a p.d.f. $h(\mathbf{x} | \mathbf{b})$ when the dimensionality of L is large is a very important problem. It is well known that large dimensionality L can be a nuisance. It is important to reduce the nuisance of large L by introducing problem knowledge which provides relationships among the components of $\mathbf{x}$. With these relationships, the number of parameters in $\mathbf{b}$ required for estimating $h(\mathbf{x})$ may be considerably reduced.

In this section it is shown how a Bayes framework is used to handle the problem where several components of $\mathbf{x}$ can depend on other components of $\mathbf{x}$, using conditional density functions. A procedure using estimation in one subspace followed by conditional estimation in another subspace is suggested. This Bayes framework was presented by Patrick [19] in 1969.

Suppose that an L-dimensional measurement vector $\mathbf{x}_s$ for pattern s is partitioned to contain k subsets of component, i.e.,

$$[\mathbf{x}_{s1}, \mathbf{x}_{s2}, \ldots, \mathbf{x}_{sk}], \quad (1)$$

where $\mathbf{x}_{s1}, \mathbf{x}_{s2}, \ldots, \mathbf{x}_{sk}$ each contain L/k components. Each vector $\mathbf{x}_{s\xi}$ is in a space $\mathscr{V}_{L/K}$ of dimensionality L/K.

Let Ω be the decision space containing the categories from which the pattern vectors $\mathbf{x}_s$, $s = 1, 2, \ldots, n$, arise. Let Ω_ξ be the decision space if $\mathbf{x}_{s\xi}$ is the measurement vector, $\xi = 1, 2, \ldots, k$.

Let $\omega_{i\xi}$ denote the event that a vector in the ξth partition is from category i. Then

$$\Omega_\xi = \{\omega_{i\xi}\}_{i=1}^{M}, \quad (2)$$

where it is assumed that there are M points† in decision space Ω_ξ.

---

†It is possible that any of the spaces Ω_ξ could have fewer than M points; for example, suppose two of the categories have vectors $\mathbf{x}_{s\xi}$ which are zero vectors for that ξth subset.

The ξth subset decision gives the category ω_i which caused $\mathbf{x}_{s\xi}$ for the sth sample. In general there is, of course, dependence between local regions, and taking this dependence into account increases system complexity. Simplifying assumptions about this dependence, if possible, are desirable. If it is assumed that there is, for instance, a scalar "output" from the decision for one subset, this "output" can be used as an "input" using another subset.

Let $h(\mathbf{x}_s | \mathbf{b})$ be the L-dimensional density of the vector $\mathbf{x}_s$, given the parameter vector point $\mathbf{b}$. Then, using rules for conditional probability,

$$h(\mathbf{x}_s | \mathbf{b}) = h(\mathbf{x}_{s1} | \mathbf{b})h(\mathbf{x}_{s2} | \mathbf{x}_{s1}, \mathbf{b})$$

$$\cdots h(\mathbf{x}_{sk} | \mathbf{x}_{s1}, \ldots, \mathbf{x}_{s,k-1}, \mathbf{b}). \tag{3}$$

Events $(\mathbf{x}_\xi, \omega_{i\xi})$, $i = 1, 2, \ldots, M$, are mutually exclusive and exhaustive for each $\xi = 1, 2, \ldots, k$; therefore, each of the densities on the right-hand side of (3) can be written as mixture densities, and (3) can be rewritten as follows:

$$h(\mathbf{x}_s | \mathbf{b}) = \sum_{i=1}^{M} h(\mathbf{x}_{s1} | \mathbf{b}, \omega_{i1})P(\omega_{i1}) \sum_{i=1}^{M} h(\mathbf{x}_{s2} | \mathbf{x}_{s1}, \mathbf{b}, \omega_{i2})P(\omega_{i2})$$

$$\cdots \sum_{i=1}^{M} h(\mathbf{x}_{sk} | \mathbf{x}_{s1}, \ldots, \mathbf{x}_{s,k-1}, \mathbf{b}_{ik}, \omega_{ik})P(\omega_{ik}). \tag{4}$$

Conditioning on Decisions

One approach to simplifying (4) (an approximation) is to replace the conditioning of a density function for one subset on measurements for another subset with the decision made with the latter on a measurement vector. That is, rewrite (4) as

$$h(\mathbf{x}_s | \mathbf{b}) = \sum_{i=1}^{M} h(\mathbf{x}_{s1} | \mathbf{b}_{i1}, \omega_{i1})P(\omega_{i1}) \sum_{i=1}^{M} h(\mathbf{x}_{s2} | d(\mathbf{x}_{s1}), \mathbf{b}_{i2}, \omega_{i2})P(\omega_{i2})$$

$$\cdots \sum_{i=1}^{M} h(\mathbf{x}_{sk} | d(\mathbf{x}_{s1}, \ldots, \mathbf{x}_{s,k-1}), \mathbf{b}_{ik}, \omega_{ik})P(\omega_{ik}). \tag{5}$$

Observe that there are M densities $h(\mathbf{x}_{s1} | \mathbf{b}_{i1}, \omega_{i1})$, M^2 densities $h(\mathbf{x}_{s2} | d(\mathbf{x}_{s1}), \mathbf{b}_{i2}, \omega_{i2}), \ldots, M^2$ densities $h(\mathbf{x}_{sk} | d(\mathbf{x}_{s1}, \ldots, \mathbf{x}_{s,k-1}), \mathbf{b}_{ik}, \omega_{ik})$. Thus there are $M + (k - 1) M^2$ densities which must be computed. Examples for various values of k and M are shown in the table below.

L	k	M	No. of densities
50	10	5	255
50	10	10	910
50	10	2	38

Each of the densities in the table would be five-dimensional. One procedure for evaluating (5) is as follows, assuming that n_i supervised samples are available from each category:

1. Estimate $h(\mathbf{x}_{s1} | \mathbf{b}_{i1}, \omega_{i1})$, $i = 1, 2, \ldots, M$, using the respective supervised samples. If $\mathscr{F}$ is assumed Gaussian, then $\{\mathbf{m}_{i1}, \mathbf{\Sigma}_{i1}\}_{i=1}^{M}$ can denote the parameters estimated.
2. Estimate M^2 densities $h(\mathbf{x}_{s2} | d(\mathbf{x}_{s2}), \mathbf{b}_{i2}, \omega_{i2})$, $\omega_{i2} = 1, 2, \ldots, M$; $d(\mathbf{x}_{s2}) = 1, 2, \ldots, M$. Step 2 requires reprocessing all n samples.

6-12 Pragmatic Dimensionality Reduction

Procedures for dimensionality reduction largely have been statistical in nature, as discussed in previous sections. Much motivation for these procedures was to develop a transformation from $\mathscr{V}_L$ to $\mathscr{V}_l$, with measurement vectors $\dot{\mathbf{x}}_{n_i}^i$, $i = 1, 2, \ldots, M$, used to estimate parameters of the transformation; the idea is that if such a transformation is designed once, then a measurement vector $\mathbf{x} \in \mathscr{V}_L$ can be mapped to a vector $\mathbf{y} \in \mathscr{V}_l$ where classification is accomplished with less complexity because of decreased dimensionality. The technique presented in previous sections of this chapter were developed in this spirit.

Issue can be taken with the relative significance of the above concept of dimensionality reduction maintaining that the *fundamental objective of dimensionality reduction may be to improve performance.* Furthermore, reduced complexity in $\mathscr{V}_l$ may not result because of the complexity required to implement the transformation from $\mathbf{x}$ to $\mathbf{y}$. Thus an important concept of dimensionality reduction is developed below.

M-class dimensionality reduction from $\mathscr{V}_L$ to $\mathscr{V}_l$ should seem to follow the following guidelines:

1. In general *dimensionality reduction must be considered local*; i.e., it is applied to *regions* of the observation space (measurement space) rather than globally. There may be different distance measures for these respective regions. A region for this purpose can be defined as a set of points $\mathbf{x}$ in $\mathscr{V}_L$ where the same dimensionality-reduction procedure applies for the points $\mathbf{x}$. See guideline 6.
2. Measurements denoted generically $\mathbf{x}$ are to be projected from $\mathscr{V}_L$ to $\mathscr{V}_l$ to achieve the highest "distance separations" among the M classes. If the transformation utilizes a priori knowledge relating the components or some of the components of $\mathbf{x}$, then increased "distance separations" are possible.
3. For some problems dimensionality reduction in a region may be achieved with a single linear transformation; in general we shall not be so fortunate.

4. Because relationships among measurements† (observations) may vary from one class to another, *the facility to introduce individual relationships for each class is desired.* This is one of the reasons that seeking a "nonlinear matched filter" for each class may be an acceptable view of the pattern recognition problem.

5. The *local intrinsic dimensionality* of **x** for class *i* is approximately the

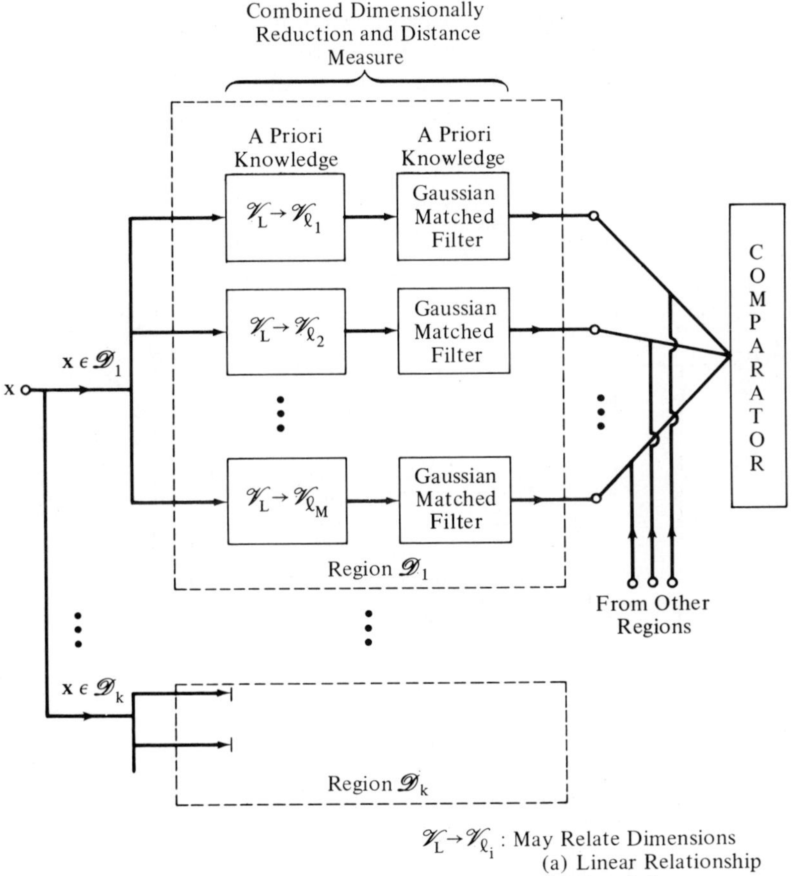

$\mathscr{V}_L \to \mathscr{V}_{\ell_i}$: May Relate Dimensions
    (a) Linear Relationship
    (b) Correlation
    (c) Equating a Dimension
       to a Constant
    (d) Generally, Imposing
       an Ellipse

Fig. 6.14 Combined dimensionality reduction and distance measure in *K* regions of measurement space

†Components of the measurement vector **x**.

rank of the covariance matrix $\boldsymbol{\Sigma}_i$ of class i in the local region concerned. This is the smallest local dimensionality that can be used for class i without loss of information. There are exceptions to this definition.

6. *Nonlinear relationships* among the components of $\mathbf{x}$ may provide for *eliminating some local regions*, because such relationships provide interregion relationships. See guideline 1.

7. When L is large, *it may be desirable to process subsets* of the L dimensions. Because there may be correlations among properties of these subsets, these correlations must be considered.

8. Eventually, a decision rule utilizing distance measures $d_i(\mathbf{x})$, $i = 1, 2, \ldots, M$, and a comparator will be involved as a final stage.

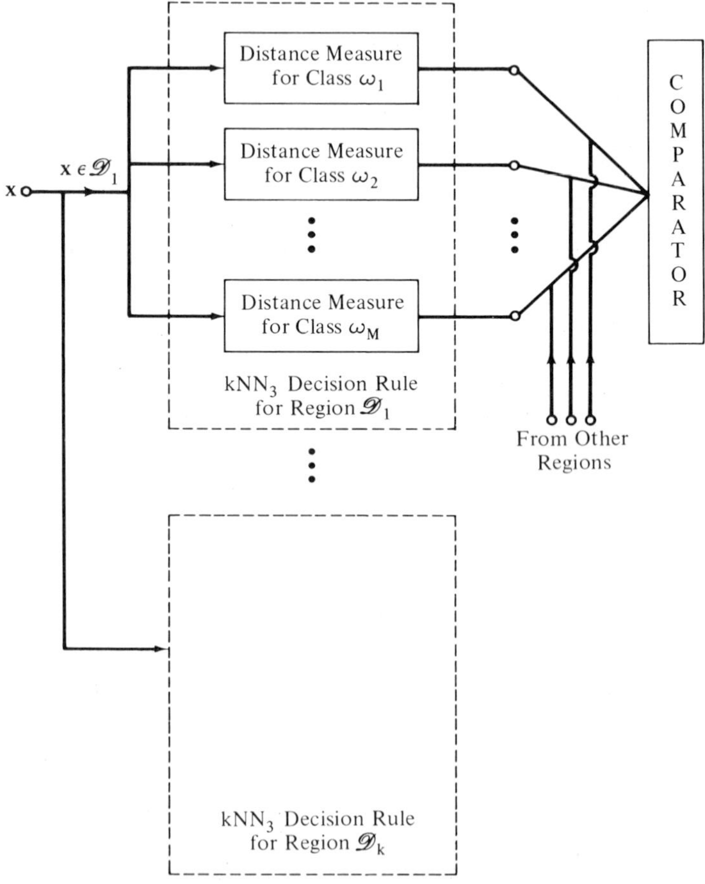

Fig. 6.15 Procedure similar to that in Fig. 6.14 utilizing kNN$_3$ decision rules in local regions.

A system utilizing local regions (1), relationships among $x_1, x_2, \ldots, x_L$ for each class (4), (6), and the final stage (8) is shown in Figure 6.14. The map $\mathscr{V}_L \longrightarrow \mathscr{V}_{l_i}$ suggested in (4) and (6) is provided from a priori problem knowledge and updated utilizing training samples. Essentially all this has inserted a local distance measure for each class at each point $\mathbf{x}$ in the region. Decision making can be viewed as according to the $k\mathrm{NN}_3$ decision rule of Chapter 4 where the above procedures (1)–(8) have been used to construct local distance measures for each class. This series of operations (1)–(8) are applied for each class in the region $\mathscr{I}_k$ concerned, and for all regions. The reader will find that these ideas are used in designing the interactive system presented in Chapter 7.

A system quite similar to that in Figure 6.14 is shown in Figure 6.15.

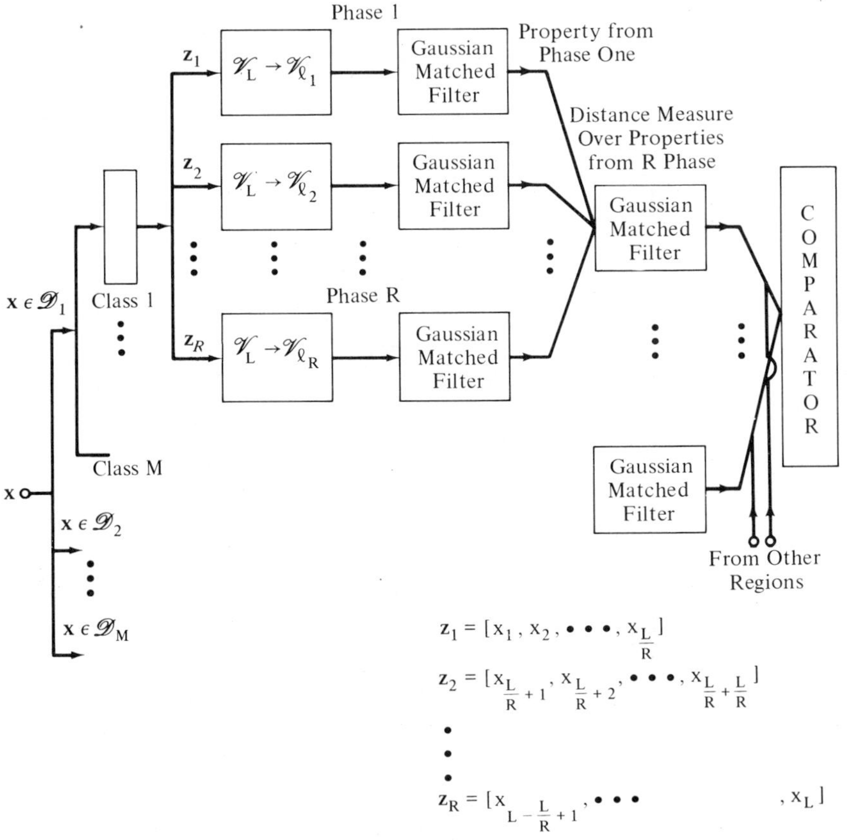

Fig. 6.16 System in Fig. 6.14 extended to allow processing subsets $\mathbf{z}_1, \mathbf{z}_2, \ldots, \mathbf{z}_R$ of $\mathbf{x}$ with subsequent recombination.

The latter system shows the use of $k\mathrm{NN}_3$ decision rules in place of the local region operation described above.

The system shown in Figure 6.16 provides the multiphasic concept by processing subsets $z_1, z_2, \ldots, z_R$ of x, extracting properties from these subsets, and subsequently introducing correlation to obtain the overall distance measure.

Another possible system, which can easily be interrupted under the Bayes framework, is to make decisions for each of the subsets $z_1, z_2, \ldots, z_R$. Then a combiner, for example using a majority-rule strategy, makes the final decision (see Figure 6.17).

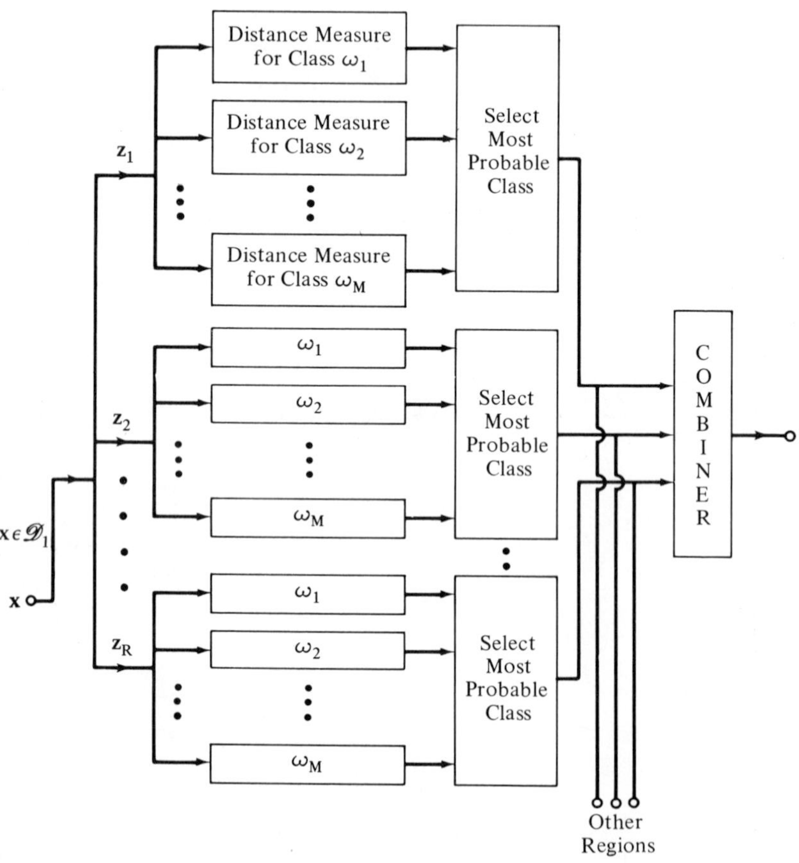

Fig. 6.17 Modification of system shown in Fig. 6.16; Decisions are made on subset z/j and then a combiner decides given the R decisions for x in the region concerned.

6-13 Nonlinear Relationships for Reducing Dimensionality

6-13.1 A Priori Knowledge versus Estimation

In the previous section guidelines for dimensionality reduction are suggested which provide for inserting problem knowledge (for each class) in regions of the measurement space. This knowledge relates the measurements in the measurement space and provides for improved performance given a fixed number of training vectors. For example, if all the means and covariances $\mathbf{m}_{ij}$ and $\mathbf{\Sigma}_{ij}$ are known when $f(\mathbf{x}\,|\,i)$ is a mixture of multivariate Gaussian densities, the Bayes rule can be applied; otherwise these parameters can be estimated. This is an alternative: These parameters can be supplied interactively by a professional who uses his experience to essentially build a model in the computer.

6-13.2 A Priori Supplied Nonlinear Functions

If an expert is to supply a priori knowledge, he should be able to do that using concepts convenient to him. For example, an internist may not have medical knowledge in terms of a covariance matrix of measurements consisting of signs, symptoms, laboratory tests, etc. On the other hand, he may know that in a particular situation one blood measurement is elevated while another blood measurement is down. If the values of the respective measurements are x_1 and x_2, then the ratio $y_1 = x_2/x_1$ would reflect this "up–down" concept. The ratio x_2/x_1 is a nonlinear mapping of the measurements x_1 and x_2. The physician may think in terms of a threshold $x_2/x_1 = a$ for separating categories; if he does, interdisciplinary communication problems make it difficult to convert this a priori knowledge to entries in a covariance matrix, until now one of the natural languages of decision theory.†
A two-category example involving this nonlinear relationship, called *ratio*, is shown in Figure 6.18. By using the feature $y_1 = x_2/x_1$ the two categories can be correctly classified as follows (assuming a known):

$$y_1 = \frac{x_2}{x_1} > a: \qquad \text{decide category 1,}$$

†Another illustrative example involves the diagnosis of acute viral hepatitis versus obstructive jaundice. Using two measurements consisting of the amount of bilirubin in the blood and the time of onset of jaundice, the acute viral hepatitis has a high amount of bilirubin in the blood with jaundice onset several days after acute symptoms appear (moderate temperature and abdominal pain). Obstructive jaundice has moderate bilirubin in the blood with early jaundice. This kind of a priori problem knowledge is discovered by man through clinical medicine, autopsy, and, of course, medical books. The computer does not have such a field of knowledge; therefore man must be able to express this field of knowledge to the computer.

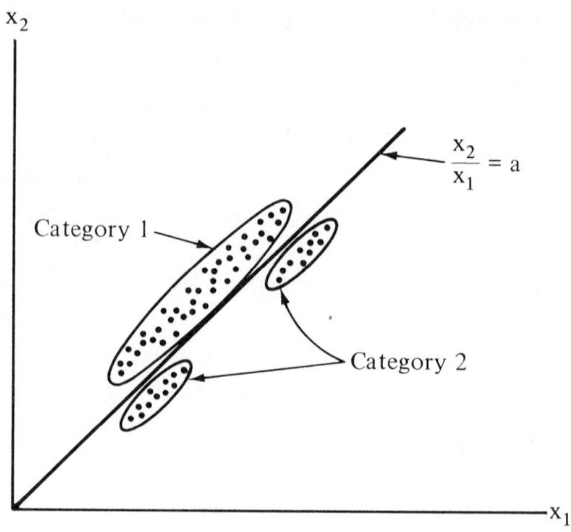

Fig. 6.18 Example of nonlinear mapping "ratio"

$$y_1 = \frac{x_2}{x_1} < a: \qquad \text{decide category 2}$$

Of course it is necessary that a be available—say supplied by the professional. An alternative is to use the mapped samples to estimate a, utilizing any a priori value of a.

A slight modification of the nonlinear mapping, ratio, is a nonlinear mapping, *translated ratio*, shown in Figure 6.19.

Another nonlinear relationship for producing a feature is called *distance from origin* and illustrated in Figure 6.20.

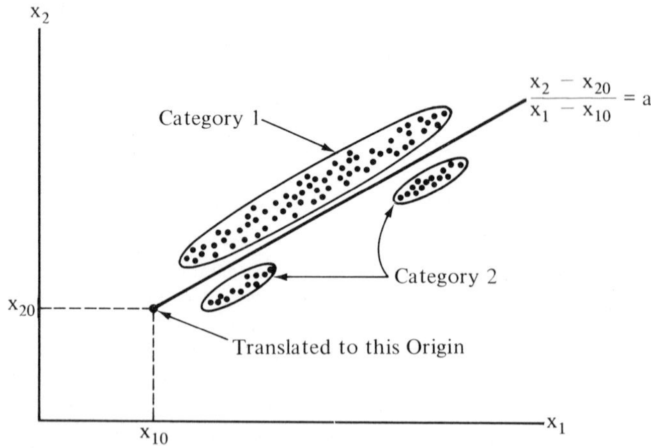

Fig. 6.19 Example of nonlinear mapping "translated ratio"

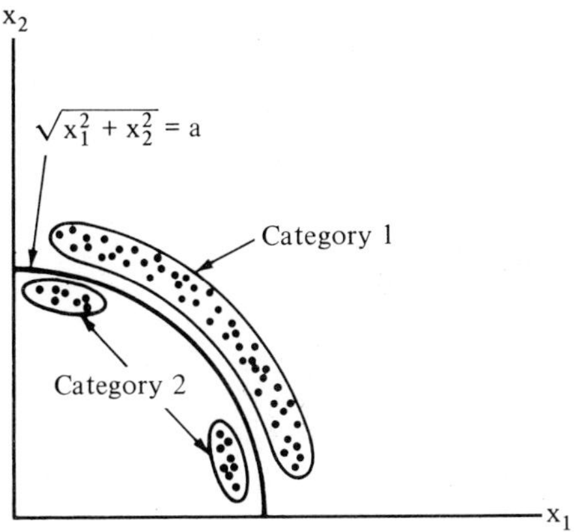

Fig. 6.20 Illustration of "distance"

Distance from Origin

The new feature is $\sqrt{x_1^2 + x_2^2} = y_2$. Correct classification is achieved by the following:

$$y_1 = \sqrt{x_1^2 + x_2^2} > a: \quad \text{decide category 1,}$$

$$y_1 = \sqrt{x_1^2 + x_2^2} < a: \quad \text{decide category 2.}$$

The nonlinear relationships ratio and distance can be used to define a piecewise decision boundary as shown in Figure 6.21.

In the example shown in Figure 6.21 there are six categories. Given five parameters a_1, a_2, a_3, b_1, b_2 and two features y_1, y_2, the six categories are separated as follows:

$$\begin{aligned}
&\text{decide category 1:} && b_1 < y_2 < \infty, \\
&\text{decide category 2:} && a_2 < y_1 < \infty, 0 < y_2 < b_1, \\
&\text{decide category 3:} && a_1 < y_1 < a_2, 0 < y_2 < b_1, \\
&\text{decide category 4:} && 0 < y_1 < a_1, 0 < y_2 < b_2, \\
&\text{decide category 5:} && a_3 < y_1 < a_1, b_2 < y_2 < \infty, \\
&\text{decide category 6:} && 0 < y_1 < a_3, b_2 < y_2 < \infty.
\end{aligned}$$

Hyperbola

Another nonlinear relationship called "hyperbola" is

$$y_1 = x_1 \cdot x_2$$

and is illustrated in Figure 6.22.

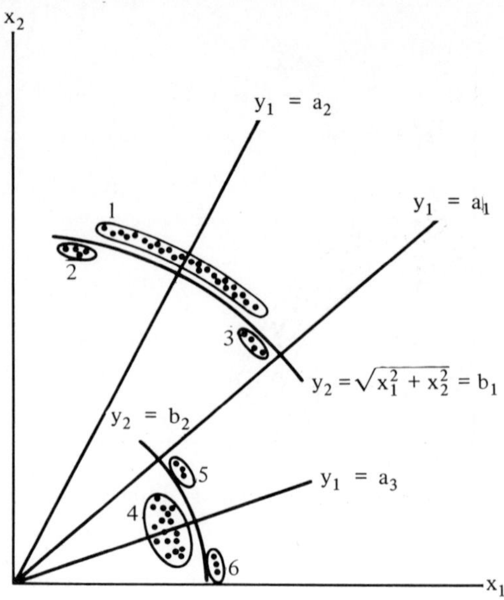

Fig. 6.21 Piecewise nonlinear decision boundary utilizing nonlinear relationships "ratio" and "distance"

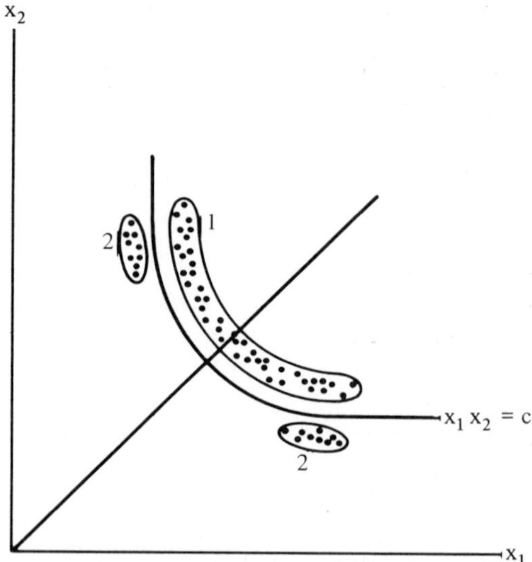

Fig. 6.22 Nonlinear map "hyperbola"

A locus of points $\mathbf{x}$ such that $(\mathbf{x} - \mathbf{m})'\mathbf{\Sigma}^{-1}(\mathbf{x} - \mathbf{m}) = $ constant describes a hyper-ellipsoid. For different values of the constant, different hyper-ellipsoids are described. Thus a hyper-ellipsoid provides a relationship among the components in $\mathbf{x}$ and provides a method of feature extraction. Consider

$$y_1 = (\mathbf{x} - \mathbf{m})'\mathbf{\Sigma}^{-1}(\mathbf{x} - \mathbf{m})$$

or

$$y_1 = \exp[-(\mathbf{x} - \mathbf{m})'\mathbf{\Sigma}^{-1}(\mathbf{x} - \mathbf{m})].$$

Then an equivalence set of points is defined by $y_1 = $ constant or $y_1 > $ constant or $a < y_1 < b$, etc.

A three-dimensional example ($L = 3$) is illustrated via two of its subspaces in Figure 6.23.

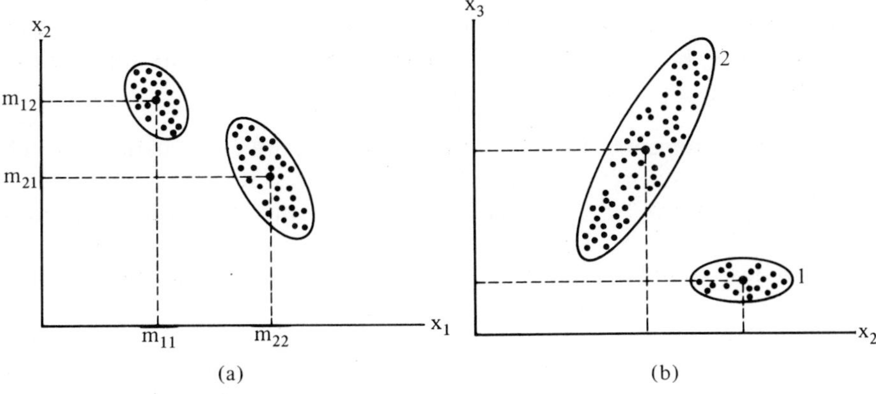

Fig. 6.23(a) Subspace spanned by x_1, x_2 **(b)** Subspace spanned by x_2, x_3

6-13.3 Examples: Nonlinear Functions Arising in Biomedicine

Biological Cells

An illustration of how problem knowledge leads to nonlinear relationships which provide a priori knowledge and reduce dimensionality is provided by a problem in classifying biological cells. These results, from Belson, Dudley, and Ledley [16], involve neurons with consideration only of the nucleus and perikaryon. Measurements extracted by the authors were

$$a = \text{area,}$$
$$r_1 = \text{maximum perpendicular radii (left),}$$
$$r_2 = \text{maximum perpendicular radii (right),}$$
$$d = \text{length of maximum diameter,}$$
$$e = \text{eccentricity,}$$

for both the cell as a whole and the nucleus, both represented as ellipsoids of revolution. The authors used the following nonlinear relationships among the above five measurements:

$$y_1 = \text{``roundness''} = \frac{r_1 + r_2}{d}, \text{ sum, ratio,}$$

$$y_2 = \text{``rectangularity''} = \frac{(r_1 + r_2)d}{a}, \text{ sum, ratio, product,}$$

$$y_3 = \text{``skewness''} = \frac{e}{d}, \text{ ratio.}$$

Medical Diagnosis

Introduction† A flow diagram for computer-assisted diagnosis suggested by Ledley [17] is shown in Figure 6.24. The following definitions apply to this flow diagram:

Measurements: Data about the state of health of the patient, including signs and laboratory test results.

Symptom profile: Combination of symptoms not necessarily fully known.

Disease complex: Combination of diseases that the patient may have at the same time.

$$\text{disease} \triangleq d_i, \qquad i = 1, 2, \ldots, M,$$
$$\text{measurements} \triangleq x_j, \qquad j = 1, 2, \ldots, L.$$

Medical Knowledge In general a set of L measurements $x_1, x_2, \ldots, x_L$ and a set of M diseases $d_1, d_2, \ldots, d_M$ will be under consideration. The disease–measurement relationships that constitute medical knowledge can be expressed as a function of the diseases under consideration. Deterministic relationships among measurements and diseases, one type of medical knowledge, can be used to eliminate measurement sequences from the measurement-sequence space. To illustrate, consider two diseases, d_1 and d_2, and two

---

†Like other researchers, Ledley [17] indicates that symptoms can be dependent on each other. Yet there appear to be almost no multidimensional statistics available for respective classes.

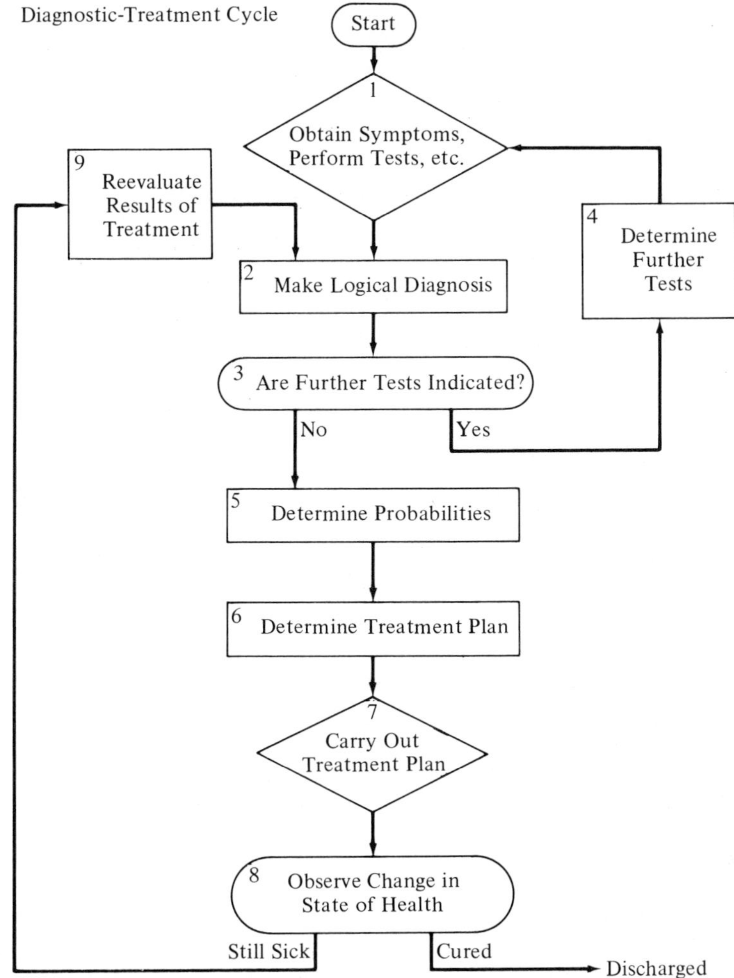

Fig. 6.24 Flow diagram of methods developed

measurements, x_1 and x_2. Suppose that in a diagnostic textbook, the following statements† were made concerning relationships among d_1, d_2, x_1, and x_2:

If a patient has disease 2, he must have
measurement 1: $\qquad\qquad\qquad\qquad\qquad d_2 \longrightarrow x_1$

If a patient has disease 1 and not disease 2,
he must have measurement 2: $\qquad\qquad\qquad d_1 \cdot \bar{d}_2 \longrightarrow x_2$

†Notation $a \cdot b$ means a and b, $a + b$ means a or b, $\bar{a}$ means not a.

If a patient has disease 2 and not disease 1, he cannot have measurement 2: $\qquad \bar{d}_1 \cdot d_2 \longrightarrow \bar{x}_2$

If a patient has either or both of the measurements, he must have either or both of the diseases: $\qquad x_1 + x_2 \longrightarrow d_1 + d_2$

Since the medical knowledge indicates all these relations hold,

$$\text{medical knowledge} = [(d_2 \longrightarrow x_1) \cdot (d_1 \cdot \bar{d}_2 \longrightarrow x_2) \cdot (\bar{d}_1 \cdot d_2 \longrightarrow \bar{x}_2)$$
$$\cdot \, (x_1 + x_2 \longrightarrow d_1 + d_2)]. \tag{1}$$

If a particular patient presents

$$G = \bar{x}_1, x_2, \tag{2}$$

then

$$F = d_1 \cdot \bar{d}_2. \tag{3}$$

Ledley formulates the medical-diagnosis problem of determining diseases d as: Given medical knowledge K, a patient presenting measurements $\mathbf{x}$ has disease d:

$$K \longrightarrow (\mathbf{x} \longrightarrow d). \tag{4}$$

An expression of the form (4) is about as good as any other to show how problem knowledge K is the base on which the relationship $\mathbf{x} \longrightarrow d$ is constructed. Assuming that (4) is unique, the inverse relationship

$$K \longrightarrow (d \longrightarrow \mathbf{x}) \tag{5}$$

exists, indicating that if diseases d are cured, the patient's measurements will be normal.

A set of relationships among all L measurements and M diseases is not practical, since there are 2^{L+M} deterministic relationships assuming x_i a binary feature and $d_i = 0$ or 1 corresponding to the disease being present or not; *fortunately medical knowledge K can be used to eliminate some of the conceivable symptom–disease complex combinations.* In the example above, $d_2 \longrightarrow x_1$ means that if a patient has d_2, then he must have x_1; hence $d_2 \cdot \bar{x}_1$ is an impossible event. Thus,

$$x_1 = 0, \qquad x_2 = 0,$$
$$d_1 = 0, \qquad d_2 = 1,$$

is impossible.

Computer-assisted medical diagnosis and treatment requires computation of class-conditional densities, $p(\mathbf{x}|\mathbf{d}_j)$, and a priori class probabilities, $p(\mathbf{d}_j)$. Of course, if performance using deterministic relationships in the example above are acceptable, then these probabilities are straightforward. On the other hand, if the measurement vector $\mathbf{x}$ is random, even given one specific class $\mathbf{d}_k$, then the multidimensional density of $\mathbf{x}$ is required—it must be estimated.

6-14 Utilizing A Priori Knowledge to Map to Space with Euclidean Metric

One of the fundamental problems in a pragmatic approach to pattern recognition is how to utilize a priori problem knowledge in obtaining a solution to the decision-making problem. Our guideline is the Bayes decision rule, which requires only that the class-conditional densities $f(\mathbf{x}|i)$ and the class probabilities $P_i, i = 1, 2, \ldots, M$, be available for the M classes. The problem is how to utilize the a priori problem knowledge along with training samples from the respective classes in estimating the respective $f(\mathbf{x}|i)$ with minimum uncertainty.

Some possible relationships among the components of a measurement vector $\mathbf{x}$ were considered in Section 6-13. It is desirable to be able to adapt these relationships to specific *regions* of the measurement space, because this provides a piecewise distance measure in the measurement space. The resulting piecewise, nonlinear distance measure might be viewed as an approximation to some general nonlinear distance measure.

The premise for using nonlinear relationships is to map the measurement vectors $\mathbf{x}_1^i, \mathbf{x}_2^i, \ldots, \mathbf{x}_{n_i}^i$ for class i to a space where the samples form a spherical, uniform class-conditional density. The parameters characterizing the nonlinear relationships can be updated with training samples. A provision can be made for changing the nonlinear relationships used in the respective regions to form the nonlinear distance measure by interactive intervention. Note that the class-conditional probability densities still are being estimated; for example, suppose that samples are in the following ring and it is known that the probability density is uniform within the ring.

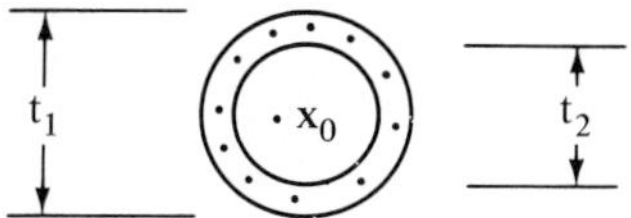

All samples in the region

$$\mathbf{x}: t_1 \leq |\mathbf{x} - \mathbf{x}_0| \leq t_2$$

can be mapped into a region on the real line $[t_1, t_2]$. Probability density at any point in the wedge is obtained by estimating the density on the real line which will have lower variance because of the use of equivalent samples.

Operations

The components $x_1, x_2, \ldots, x_L$ of a measurement vector $\mathbf{x}$ are used with operations to produce features $y_1, y_2, \ldots, y_l$. An operation can describe a region in the measurement space or constitute a nonlinear relationship among $x_1, x_2, \ldots, x_L$ to produce a feature.

Region The operation selects a region in $\mathscr{V}_L$, the measurement space, in which to extract properties from any measurement vector in that region. When unsupervised, clustering may be useful for finding regions. A supervised example is one in which the regions are selected by an operator interactively.

Correlation Inserter A nonlinear or linear function of selected measurements which reflects a priori problem knowledge is constructed. Possible relationships include

ratio
sum
weighted sum
blanking (knowledge that a measurement is insignificant for a particular class)
ellipsoid
ring
product

step function: $u_0(t - t_0) = \begin{cases} 0, & t < t_0, \\ 1, & t \geq t_0 \end{cases}$

ramp function: $u_1(t - t_0) = \int_0^t u_0(t - t_0)\, dt$

parabolic function: $u_2(t - t_0) = \int_0^t u_1(t - t_0)\, dt$

intercept: point on one of the measurement axes where a linear fit to a cluster intercepts that axis

Sequence Features

1. Lack of consistency in a sequence.
2. $x_1 \in \mathscr{A}$ and $x_2 \in \mathscr{B}$ and $x_3 \in \mathscr{C}$ and $x_4 \in \mathscr{D}$: for example, multiple objects in range or in bearing given sonar echos.
3. If $x_1 \in \mathscr{A}$, $x_2 \in \mathscr{B}$, $x_3 \in \mathscr{C}$, $x_4 \in \mathscr{D}$, let $y_1 = \sum_{i=11}^{14} x_i$: for example, x_{11} may be the reflectivity associated with object 1, x_{12} the reflectivity associated with object 2, etc.

4. Estimated signal-to-noise ratio.

A table of nonlinear relationships is presented in Chapter 7 where a procedure for utilizing region-forming operations along with nonlinear relationships is presented.

It may be expedient to select subgroups of $x_1, x_2, \ldots, x_k$ and then apply operations of region and correlation inserter to the individual subsets. Operations that simply select measurements within a subset or form two subsets are defined below.

Within Subset   This operation selects measurements from within a specific subset of measurements. Then operations region and correlation inserter are applied.

Between Subset   This operation selects measurements from two or more specific subsets.

Limit Inserter —The "limit inserter" can simply be a procedure which says that points in a certain region of the measurement space have the same probability density; an example is the ring inserter previously illustrated. There are several special considerations:

1. Relative frequency in a region constructed by the limit inserter is an estimate of class-conditional probability density and is directly used in the Bayes decision rule.
2. The actual value of the feature resulting from the correlation inserter is important; for example, the feature can be regarded as a component in the observation vector **x**. The new features obtained using the above operations should have statistics more nearly spherical with relatively small correlation among these features. The remaining correlation may be removed by reapplying operations region, correlation inserter, and limit inserter to the last feature vector. Then, finally, a $k\mathrm{NN}_3$ decision rule with Euclidean distance measure would be expected to perform well.

Layered Concept

Thus **x** is converted to a set of features **y** where the above operations have been applied. This conversion can be applied over and over in layers until (hopefully) uncorrelated features result so that the Euclidean metric can be used. Any stage at which the feature vector **x** for a class is deemed Euclidean, the feature-extraction procedure terminates and the classification stage can be activated. Classification is achieved by measuring the class-conditional density in the final feature space.

This procedure consists of several operations implementing the following concepts:

1. Equivalence of covariance matrix of one region with that of another region.
2. Constructing one nonlinear function to encompass the piecewise nonlinear functions.
3. Implement concept of finding nonlinear relationships for a number of large regions† (may lose less information this way than by an alternative way). Then the subregions of a region might be separated by simpler functions.
4. Repeat the process, extracting properties from respective subsets of dimensions, which gives correlations among these subsets. This gives rise to a layered concept.

Examples

Several of the examples of the types of problems that may arise in computer-assisted medical diagnosis are illustrated in Figure 6.25. For the multiclass, two-dimensional problems illustrated in Figure 6.25, adequate features are those which reflect a priori knowledge that for an abnormal class, measurements differ from measurements for a normal class in Euclidean distance and then in ratio. Denoting the measurements $[x_1, x_2] = \mathbf{x}$ with $E[\mathbf{x}\,|\,\text{normal}] \triangleq [\mathbf{x}_{1_0}, \mathbf{x}_{2_0}]$, then the features, denoted y_2 and y_2, are

$$y_1 = \sqrt{(x_2 - x_{2_0})^2 + (x_1 - x_{1_0})^2},$$
$$y_2 = \frac{x_2 - x_{2_0}}{x_1 - x_{1_0}}.$$

Now, suppose we know that the normal class is $y_1 \leq t$. This a priori knowledge possibly can be inserted either by constructing new features as functions of the features y_1 and y_2 or by using weights on y_1 and y_2. Choosing the former approach:

> announce normal $y_1 \leq t$,
> announce abnormal $y_1 > t$,
> abnormal subclass depends on y_2.

Note that there is correlation between y_1 and y_2 which is class dependent. This correlation, in words, is to the effect that for the normal class, y_1 is

†Straightens out the space.

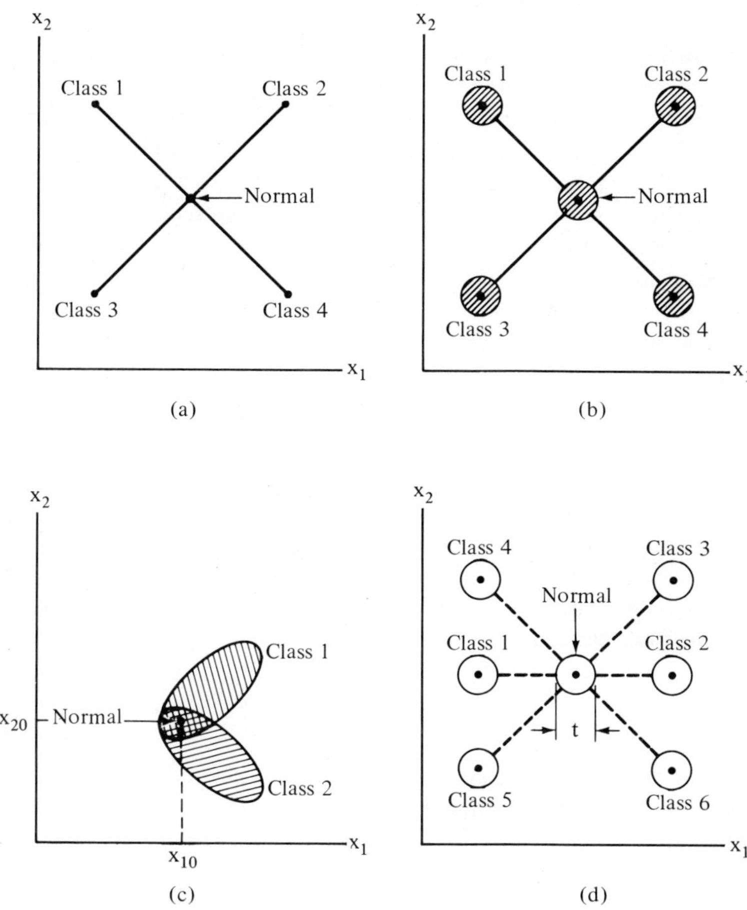

Fig. 6.25 (a) Illustration of four abnormal classes and the single normal class **(b)** Illustration before except with fuzzy classes **(c)** Two class version of above **(d)** Illustration of where a measurement (x_2) does not change for class 1, class 2, and normal.

small, but for the abnormal classes, y_1 is large and then y_2 is a significant feature. It is difficult to see how $y = [y_1, y_2]$ could be assumed a Gaussian random vector for the respective classes because of difficulty of expressing this correlation in a covariance matrix. The above examples can easily be extended to L dimensions.

Even if the final feature space remains high-dimensional but the statistics for individual classes are spherical in this space, a relatively simple classification procedure can be selected from Chapter 4.

The operations of limit inserter and correlation inserter help specify the probability density structure for respective classes and provide nonlinear correlation information which seems very difficult to insert using parametric-density-function structure. There is, however, another aspect of this correlation structure and that is that, say, measurements x_1 and x_2 may vary in a fuzzy, deterministic way as x_3 varies. Then an equivalence region can be constructed corresponding to the locus of points x_1, x_2, and x_3, and all points in this equivalence region can be said to have the same class-conditional density which is the accumulation of the densities at the respective points— thus, a new operation: *accumulate density on equivalent regions.*

As an example, consider as a rule the function

$$f(\mathbf{x}) = \frac{P}{(2\pi)^{1/2}\,|\mathbf{\Sigma}|^{1/2}}\,\exp[-\tfrac{1}{2}(\mathbf{x}-\mathbf{m})\mathbf{\Sigma}^{-1}(\mathbf{x}-\mathbf{m})],$$

which describes the locus of points $\mathbf{x}$ such as $f(\mathbf{x}) = $ constant and specifies that the same density, $f(\mathbf{x})$, is attached to all points on a locus. If $f(\mathbf{x})$ is being estimated using samples $\mathbf{x}_1, \mathbf{x}_2, \ldots, \mathbf{x}_n$, then an enhanced density estimate is obtained by averaging the density estimate at each point. For example, if the locus is discretized $\mathbf{x}^1, \mathbf{x}^2, \ldots, \mathbf{x}^R$ and

$$(f(\mathbf{x}^j))_n = \frac{k_j}{n\Phi(\mathbf{x}^j, \mathbf{x}_n)},$$

where k_j is the number of samples associated with the region about $\mathbf{x}^j$ with volume $\Phi(\mathbf{x}^j, \mathbf{x}_n)$, then an enhanced estimate is

$$(f(\mathbf{x}))_n \triangleq \frac{1}{R}\sum_{j=1}^{R}(f(\mathbf{x}^j))_n, \qquad \mathbf{x} \text{ any } \mathbf{x}^j, j = 1, 2, \ldots, R.$$

An extension of the above concept is that there can be very complex clusters in measurement space. Clusters for two different classes of data can be interwoven as, for example, interwoven hyper-coil springs shown in Figure 6.26. Points along each coil are part of an equivalence region, and class-conditional density at any point along a coil can be enhanced by forming an appropriate average of estimated densities at points along the coil.

There may be a need to define locuses such as hyper-spirals, hyper-oscillations, hyper-saws, hyper-battle-axes, hyper-drapples, etc. *Without the knowledge that respective classes have possible data points along complex locuses, the data points for different classes will "look"† close together and it will not be possible to separate points from different classes.*

---

†The look will be with a Euclidean distance measure in the absence of other knowledge.

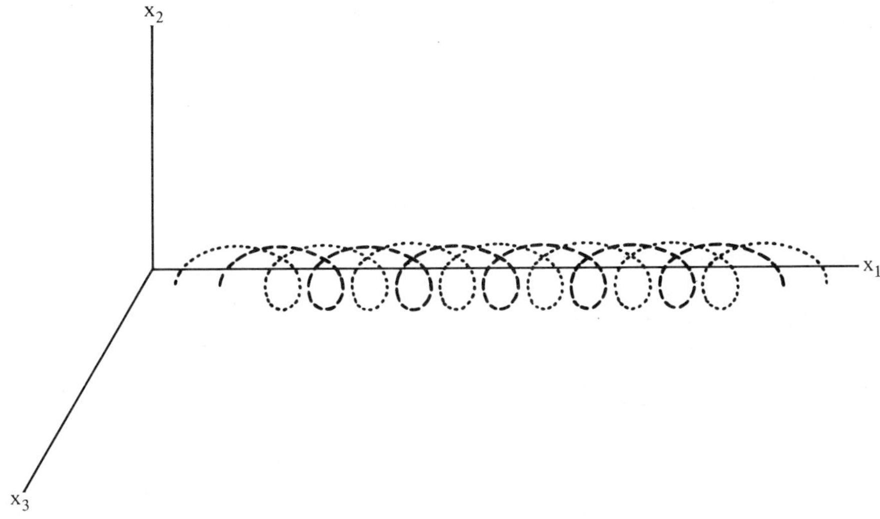

Fig. 6.26 Two coil, spring-like clusters which are interwoven

*Justifying Nonlinear Relationships Because of Nuisance
and Complexity*

Occasionally in research it is desirable to justify an approach. A justification for using nonlinear functions to obtain features rather than working in the measurement space is seen by considering the covariance matrix Σ needed to characterize a Gaussian density. There are L^2 parameters in a $L \times L$ covariance matrix but only L variances and L means. This suggests that if nonlinear relationships result in a diagonalized feature space, there will be fewer parameters to estimate.

For example, in the new space it should be easier to estimate $\mathbf{b}^*$ using a criterion $1/n \sum_{s=1}^{n} \ln h(\mathbf{x}_s | \mathbf{b})$, assuming the parameter space is identifiable.

Mathematics of Feature Extraction

Define a space $\mathscr{S}$ with points $\mathbf{x} \in \mathscr{X}$ over a field F with the operations

$$\mathbf{x} + \mathbf{y} \in \mathscr{S},$$

$$a\mathbf{x} \in \mathscr{S},$$

$$\frac{x_i}{x_j} \in \mathscr{S},$$

$$x_i x_j \in \mathscr{S},$$

$$\sum_{i=1}^{L} x_i^2 \in \mathscr{S}.$$

Thus,

$$x_i - x_{i_0} \in \mathscr{S},$$

$$\frac{x_i - x_{i_0}}{x_j - x_{j_0}} \in \mathscr{S},$$

$$1 + x_i + x_i^2 + x_i^3 + \cdots \in \mathscr{S}, \qquad \text{i.e., the space of polynomials.}$$

A linear or nonlinear transformation of a vector $\mathbf{x} \in \mathscr{S}$ to a vector $\mathbf{y} \in \mathscr{M}$, $\mathscr{M} \in \mathscr{S}$, is of interest. For example, when is the uncertainty associated with estimating parameters characterizing the metric $d(\mathbf{y}_1, \mathbf{y}_2)$ less than uncertainty associated with estimating the metric $d(\mathbf{x}_1, \mathbf{x}_2)$? Results discussed through Section 6-10 use intraclass distance (or interclass distance when the vectors are in two different classes) as the criterion rather than the more desirable criterion of the uncertainty in estimating parameters characterizing the metric which is based on problem knowledge. *Results showing that particular nonlinear relationships result in reduced estimation uncertainty leading to greater estimated distance between classes (with increased confidence) would have considerable value.* A measure of the probability of error resulting through using the transformations would be valuable.

An objective of feature extraction is to be able to compute $p(\mathbf{y}\,|\,i)$. The vector $\mathbf{y}$ is in a subspace (not the usual subspace of a vector space) where there is less variation among pattern samples. *The real merit of nonlinear feature extraction appears to be for those problems where successive use of nonlinear relationships leads to a relatively simple way of estimating respective class-conditional density functions. Also, a priori knowledge can be introduced in a relatively simple way.*

As a further example, consider the two-class problem shown in Figure 6.27a; possible features are

$$y_1^2 = \left| \frac{x_2 - m_2^2}{x_1 - m_1^2} \right|,$$

$$y_1^1 = \left| \frac{x_2 - m_2^1}{x_1 - m_1^1} \right|,$$

where y_1^1 is the first new feature for class 1 and y_1^2 the first new feature for class 2. Now, these features vary greatly (y_1^i does not represent a very stable property of class i), and this is a disadvantage. On the other hand, the single feature

$$y_1 = \frac{x_2}{x_1}$$

can be used as a feature, as shown in Figure 6.27b, for either class, and

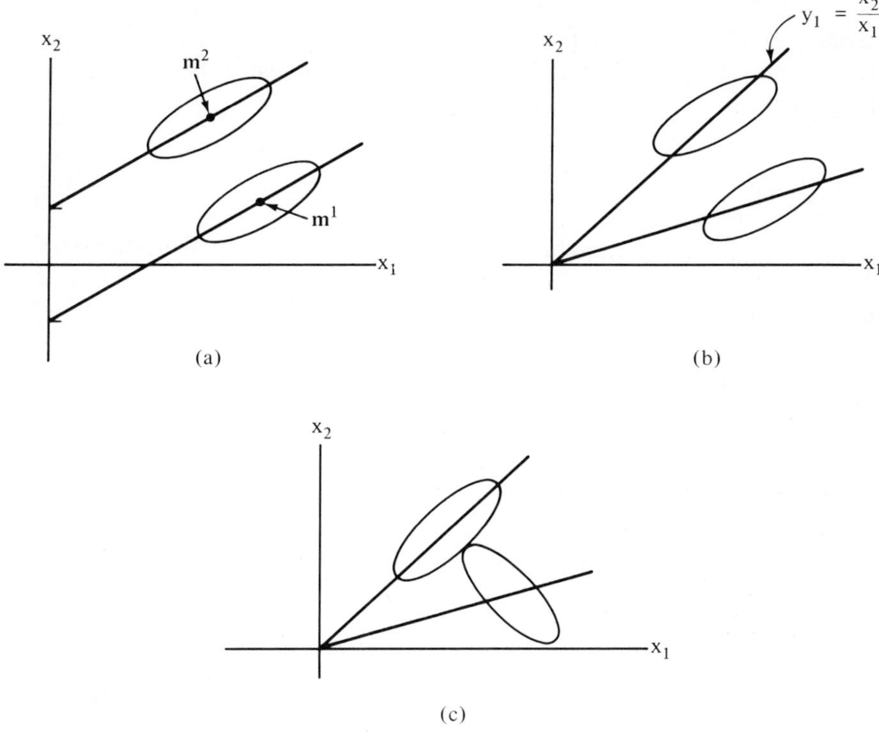
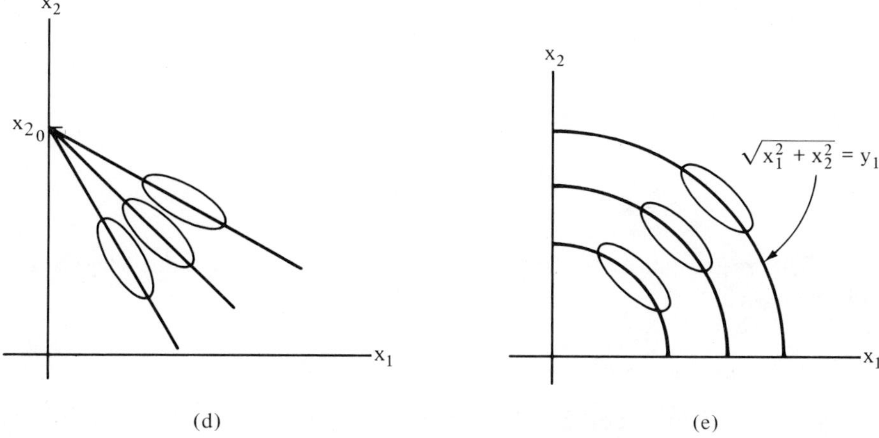

Fig. 6.27 Example using nonlinear feature extraction

465

significant differences in this feature indicate different classes. This same
feature may even be acceptable for the problem shown in Figure 6.27c. The
translated ratio feature,

$$y_1 = \frac{x_2 - x_{2_0}}{x_1},$$

requiring estimation of the parameter x_{2_0}, can be used for the problem shown
in Figure 6.27d, although the feature, distance, also could be used as shown
in Figure 6.27e.

Layered Feature Extraction

Is it possible to apply transformation to features **y** to produce new features
z such that **z** is of decreased dimensionality, decreased overlap among class-
conditional densities, resulting in a single nonlinear transformation from
x to **z**? It may not be possible or desirable to accomplish this for all problems;
examples of such a procedure are shown in Figure 6.28.

Two Ratios

Suppose that $L = 3$, $\mathbf{x} = [\mathbf{x}_1, \mathbf{x}_2, \mathbf{x}_3]$, $M = 2$, and that a subspace density
projection is as shown in Figure 6.28a. The ratio x_2/x_1 is suggested from a
two-dimensional subspace. Then, suppose that density projections onto
x_2, x_2/x_1 subspace are as shown. The feature,

$$y_1 = \frac{x_3}{x_2/x_1}$$

then contains the a priori knowledge

class 1: suggested by large values of y_1,
class 2: suggested by small values of y_1.

The reader should try to reconstruct three-dimensional classes for
this example.

Ratio and Scaled Ratio

Considering Figure 28b, the ratio x_2/x_1 is suggested from the two-dimensional projection onto x_1 and x_2. Then, if the two-class densities project
onto x_3, x_2/x_1, as shown, a suggested feature is

$$y_1 = \frac{x_3 - x_{3_0}}{x_2/x_1},$$

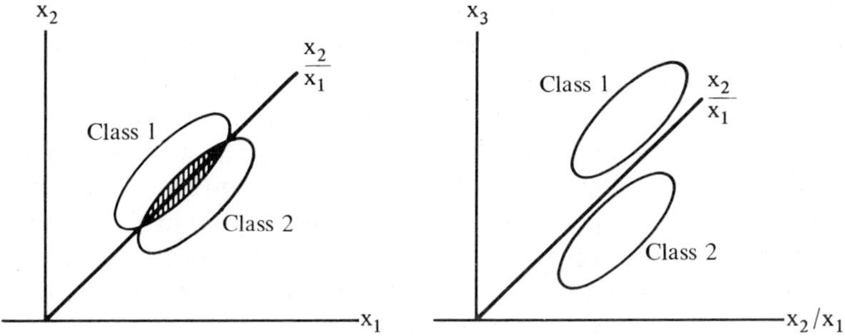

(a) Three-dimensional, two-class example

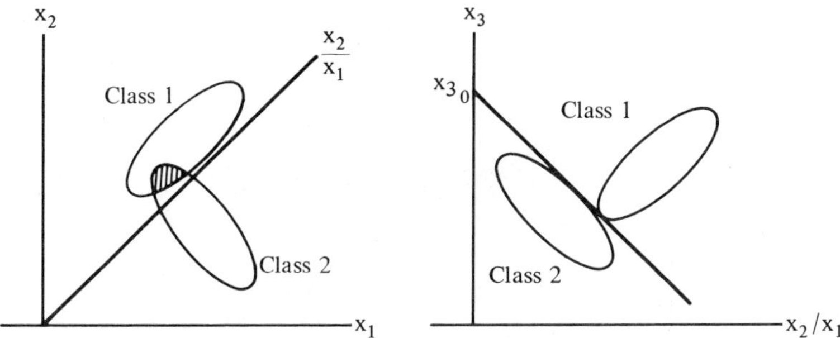

(b) Three-dimensional, two-class example

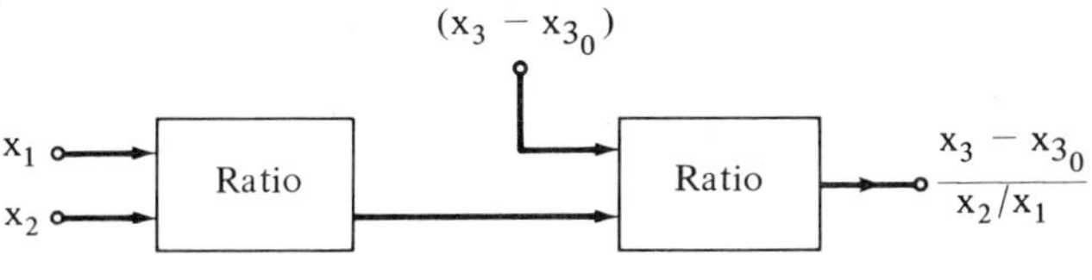

(c) Block diagram of Fig. 6.28b

Fig. 6.28

which contains a priori knowledge:

$$\text{class 1: suggested by large values of } y_1,$$
$$\text{class 2: suggested by small values of } y_1.$$

Block Diagram

For the above example, the block diagram shown in Figure 6.28c is instructive. Letting $\boxed{\text{ratio}}$ signify the ratio operation, we see how y_1 results from two ratio operations in sequence.

Suppose that $\mathbf{x}_1, \mathbf{x}_2, \ldots, \mathbf{x}_n$ are measurements at n different times. A property or feature of such a sequence, illustrated in Figure 6.29a for two classes, is the regression line of the sequence. For example, the intercepts $x_{2_0}^2$ and $x_{2_0}^1$ are values of a feature y_1 which distinguishes the classes as time increases. This could well be an illustration of a treatment-diagnosis cycle or successive echos in sonar. This property or feature illustrated in Figure 6.29a fails when, for example, a sequence of patterns from one class may be as shown in Figure 6.29b. For this class, a feature could be "lack of consistency" or "consistency on two out of three successive patterns."

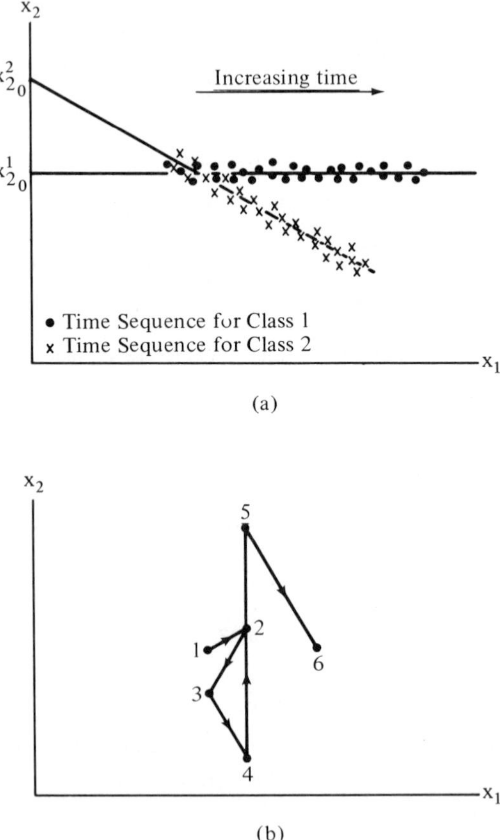

(a)

(b)

Fig. 6.29 Illustration of two classes of two-dimensional pattern samples
(a) From a time sequence
(b) Not from a time sequence

Suppose we form

$$\frac{\dfrac{1}{n-1}\displaystyle\sum_{s=1}^{v}\left\|\left(\mathbf{x}_s-\frac{1}{n}\sum_{s=1}^{n}\mathbf{x}_s\right)\left(\mathbf{x}_s-\frac{1}{n}\sum_{s=1}^{n}\mathbf{x}_s\right)^{t}\right\|}{\dfrac{1}{n-1}\displaystyle\sum_{s=v+1}^{2v}\left\|\left(\mathbf{x}_s-\frac{1}{n}\sum_{s=1}^{n}\mathbf{x}_s\right)\left(\mathbf{x}_s-\frac{1}{n}\sum_{s=1}^{n}\mathbf{x}_s\right)^{t}\right\|},$$

which is the ratio of the norm of matrix of variances of the first v samples to the norm of the vector of variances of the second v samples. If the first v samples correspond to reflection from a submarine and the second v samples correspond to reverberation, this feature corresponds to an estimated signal-to-noise ratio.

Introducing Correlation Using Conditional Density Functions

Suppose the resulting feature vector for, say, a two-class problem contains features $\mathbf{y}_i$ *especially designed for class i and features* $\mathbf{y}_j$ *especially designed for class j utilizing problem knowledge*†:

$$\mathbf{y} = [\mathbf{y}_i, \mathbf{y}_j].$$

We might suspect that features $\mathbf{y}_j$ are a nuisance for estimating the class-conditional density for class i but yet should be used in the decision-making process. The class-conditional probability densities of $\mathbf{y}$ are

$$f(\mathbf{y}\,|\,i) = f(\mathbf{y}_i, \mathbf{y}_j\,|\,i) = f(\mathbf{y}_i\,|\,i, \mathbf{y}_j)f(\mathbf{y}_j\,|\,i),$$

$$f(\mathbf{y}\,|\,j) = f(\mathbf{y}_i, \mathbf{y}_j\,|\,j) = f(\mathbf{y}_j\,|\,j, \mathbf{y}_i)f(\mathbf{y}_i\,|\,j).$$

Let $d(\mathbf{y}_i) = i$ mean that the decision rule using feature vector $\mathbf{y}_i$ decides class i. Then the Bayes framework for dimensionality reduction presented in Section 6-11 suggests that the following *approximations may apply* for some problems:

$$f(\mathbf{y}\,|\,i) \cong \begin{cases} f(\mathbf{y}_i\,|\,i, d(\mathbf{y}_j) = i), & d(\mathbf{y}_j) = i, \\ f(\mathbf{y}_i\,|\,i, d(\mathbf{y}_j) = j), & d(\mathbf{y}_j) = j, \end{cases}$$

$$f(\mathbf{y}\,|\,j) \cong \begin{cases} f(\mathbf{y}_j\,|\,j, d(\mathbf{y}_i) = j), & d(\mathbf{y}_i) = j, \\ f(\mathbf{y}_j\,|\,j, d(\mathbf{y}_i) = i), & d(\mathbf{y}_i) = i. \end{cases}$$

Thus, the feature vector $\mathbf{y}_j$ *contributes in a relatively simple way to detecting class i after the approximation.*

†In medicine, for example, properties which differentiate among classes may not be known because the classes may not be known. Thus one can approach the problem by *designing features for each class suspected using one's field of knowledge.*

The feature vector $\mathbf{y}_j$ designed for class j may be considered an auxiliary feature vector for class i. In the classification process both feature vector $\mathbf{y}_i$ and feature vector $\mathbf{y}_j$ are constructed or extracted from the pattern to be classified (since the class of the pattern is unknown). *If, for example, feature vector $\mathbf{y}_j$ very strongly suggests that the pattern is NOT from class j, then this is information to use along with $\mathbf{y}_i$ in determining the probability that the pattern IS from class i.*

A flow diagram illustrating the above theory is shown in Figure 6.30. For each class, a set of nonlinear relationships are applied to the measurements to construct the vector of features for that class. Then, for class i, the ith class-conditional density of $\mathbf{y}_i$ is computed conditioned on all possible decisions made by the other class-conditional computers. The pattern then is classified from class a if $P_a f(\mathbf{y}_a \,|\, a, d_{i_1}, d_{i_2}, d_{i_3}, \ldots, d_{i_{a-1}}, d_{i_{a+1}}, d_{i_M})$ is the largest of these probabilities.

Discussion

The use of nonlinear relationships as just discussed provides a way to construct a problem model interactively. For a particular problem, however, it may be most desirable for the researcher to construct this model without computer assistance. The merit of computer assisted construction of models for pattern recognition remains to be evaluated.

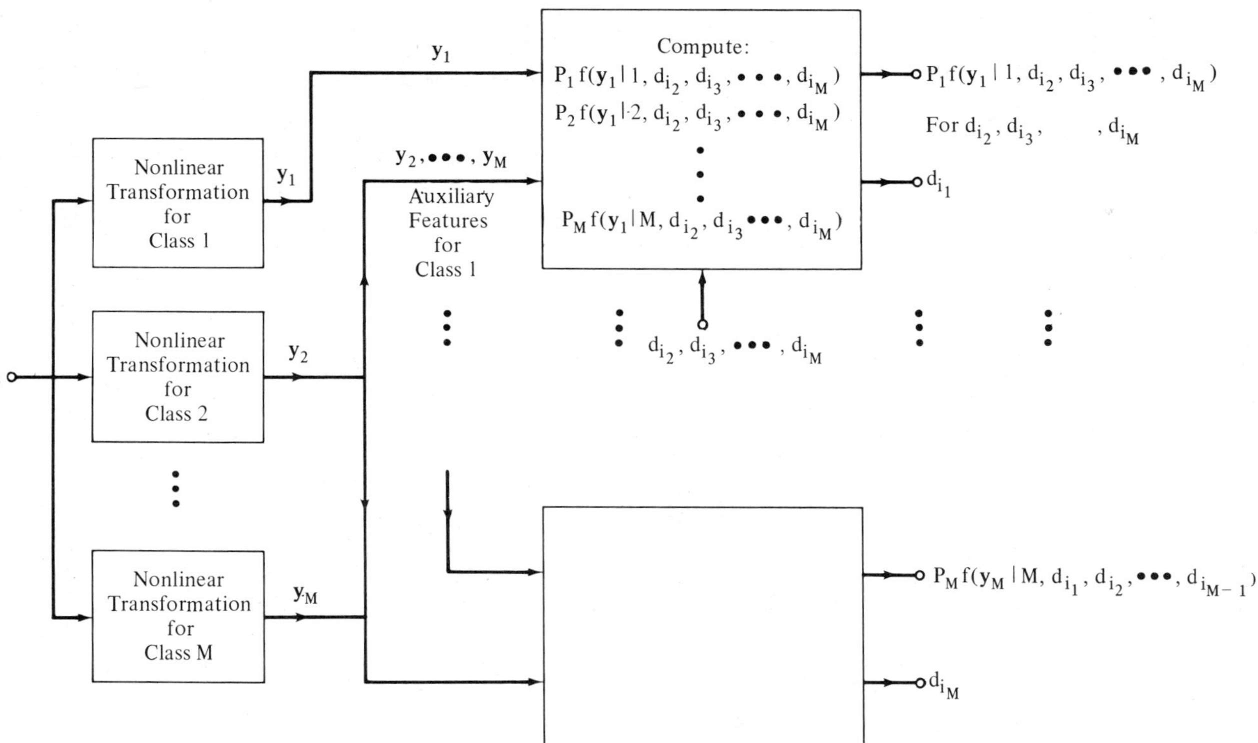

Fig. 6.30 Features extracted using nonlinear relationships followed by computing class conditional densities.

Suggested Reading for Chapter 6

[1] M. Schwartz, *Information Transmission, Modulation, and Noise*, McGraw-Hill Book Company, Inc., New York, 1959.

[2] J. Indritz, *Methods in Analysis*, The Macmillan Company, New York, 1963.

[3] C. L. Lawrence, Characteristic Properties of the Segmented Rational Minmax Approximation Problem, *Numer. Math.*, Vol. 6, pp. 293–301, Nov. 1964.

[4] G. Meinardus, *Approximation of Functions: Theory and Numerical Methods* (Springer Tracts in Natural Philosophy, Vol. 13), Springer-Verlag, New York, 1967.

[5] S. S. Wilks, *Mathematical Statistics*, John Wiley & Sons, Inc., New York, 1963, Chap. 18.

[6] I. O. Spragins, Reproducing Distributions for Machine Learning, *Stanford Electronics Laboratories Tech. Rept. 6103–7*, Stanford, Calif., Nov. 1963.

[7] J. T. Tou and P. R. Hedyon, Some Approaches to Optimum Feature Extraction, *Computer and Information Sciences*, Vol. II, J. T. Tou, ed., Academic Press, Inc., New York, 1967, pp. 57–89.

[8] G. S. Sebestyen, *Decision-Making Processes in Pattern Recognition*, The Macmillan Company, New York, 1962.

[9] G. H. Ball, Data Analysis in the Social Sciences: What About the Details?, *Proceedings of the Fall Joint Computer Conference* (AFIPS Proc. Vol. 27, pt. 1), Spartan Books, New York, 1965, pp. 533–559.

[10] E. Parzen, On Estimation of a Probability Density Function and Mode, *Ann. Math. Statistics*, Vol. 33, pp. 1065–1076, Sept. 1962.

[11] V. K. Murthy, Nonparametric Estimation of Multivariate Densities with Applications, presented at the International Symposium on Multivariate Analysis, Wright-Patterson Air Force Base, Ohio, June 1965.

[12] K. S. Miller, *Multidimensional Gaussian Distribution*, John Wiley & Sons, Inc., New York, 1964, p. 24.

[13] L. A. Zadeh, Fuzzy Sets, *Information and Control*, Vol. 8, pp. 338–353, June 1965.

[14] E. A. Patrick and F. P. Fischer, Non-Parametric Feature Selection, *IEEE Trans. Information Theory*, Vol. IT-15, No. 5, pp. 577–584, Sept. 1969.

[15] W. S. Meisel, On Nonparametric Feature Selection, *IEEE Trans. Information Theory*, pp. 105–106, Jan. 1971.

[16] M. Belson, W. W. Dudley, Jr., and R. S. Ledley, Automatic Computer Measurements of Neurons, *Pattern Recognition*, Vol. 2, Pergamon Press, Oxford, 1968, pp. 119–128.

[17] R. S. Ledley, Practical Problems in the Use of Computer in Medical Diagnosis, Special Issue on Technology and Health Services, *Proc. IEEE*, Vol. 57, No. 11, pp. 1900–1918, Nov. 1969.

[18] N. I. Noiseeva and V. V. Usov, Some Medical and Mathematical Aspects of Computer Diagnosis, *Proc. IEEE*, Vol. 57, No. 11, pp. 1919–1925, Nov. 1969.

[19] E. A. Patrick, Concepts of an Estimation System, Adaptive Systems, and a Network of Adaptive Estimation Systems, *IEEE Trans. Systems Science and Cybernetics*, Vol. SSC-5, No. 1, pp. 79–85, Jan. 1969.

Problems

[1] Suppose $\mathbf{x}_1, \mathbf{x}_2, \ldots, \mathbf{x}_n$ are n vectors from $h(\mathbf{x})$ and it is not known if $h(\mathbf{x})$ is a mixture (more than one category) or if $h(\mathbf{x})$ is a single-category density function.

(a) Show that an average square error,

$$\bar{e} = \sum_{s=1}^{n} e_s,$$

approximation for the data vectors could lead to a single feature (one-dimensional observation vectors) which would separate the three categories shown:

(b) Show that this approach would fail to obtain a single feature, when there are four classes as shown, resulting in zero experimental error even though the classes have disjoint support (are nonoverlapping):

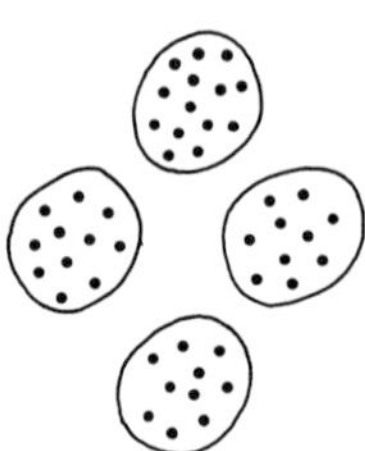

[2] Why, in Section 6-4, does the procedure involve finding eigenvectors of a matrix of normalized correlation coefficients $\hat{\rho}_{iv}$ rather than of a covariance matrix? Your answer should not merely summarize the mathematical derivation.

(a) If $\mathbf{x}$ is $N(\mathbf{x}|\mathbf{m}, \mathbf{I})$, show that $\mathbf{y} = \mathbf{A}\mathbf{x}$ is $N(\mathbf{y}|\mathbf{Am}, \mathbf{I})$ if $\mathbf{A}^t = \mathbf{A}^{-1}$. If $\mathbf{A}^t = \mathbf{A}^{-1}$, $\mathbf{A}$ is called an orthogonal matrix.

(b) Let $\mathbf{A}$ be an $L \times L$ matrix whose columns $\mathbf{a}_1, \mathbf{a}_2, \ldots, \mathbf{a}_L$ are orthonormal. Show that $\mathbf{A}^t\mathbf{A} = \mathbf{I}$ and thus $\mathbf{A}^t = \mathbf{A}^{-1}$.

(c) Suppose that $\mathbf{A}$ is an $L \times l$ matrix whose columns $\mathbf{a}_1, \mathbf{a}_2, \ldots, \mathbf{a}_l$ are orthonormal. Show that $\mathbf{A}^t\mathbf{A}$ is an $l \times l$ identity matrix; thus, $\mathbf{A}^{-1} = \mathbf{A}^t$.

[3] Assume that $h(\mathbf{x}|\mathbf{b}^*) = \sum_{i=1}^{M} f(\mathbf{x}|\mathbf{b}_i^*, i)P_i^*$ and that samples $\mathbf{x}_1, \mathbf{x}_2, \ldots, \mathbf{x}_n$ from $h(\mathbf{x})$ are available.

(a) Give a consistent estimator for $E[\mathbf{x}]$; give a consistent estimator for $E[\ln h(\mathbf{x}|\mathbf{b})]$.

(b) Suggest a consistent estimator for $\mathbf{b}^*$ given the unsupervised samples $\mathbf{x}_1, \mathbf{x}_2, \ldots, \mathbf{x}_n$.

(c) Suppose that $f(\mathbf{x}|\boldsymbol{\alpha}_j)$, $j = 1, 2, \ldots, N$, are all the possible densities $\in \mathscr{F}$ and that they are "nonoverlapping." Complete the following N blocks to provide consistent estimators for $P_1, P_2, \ldots, P_N$.

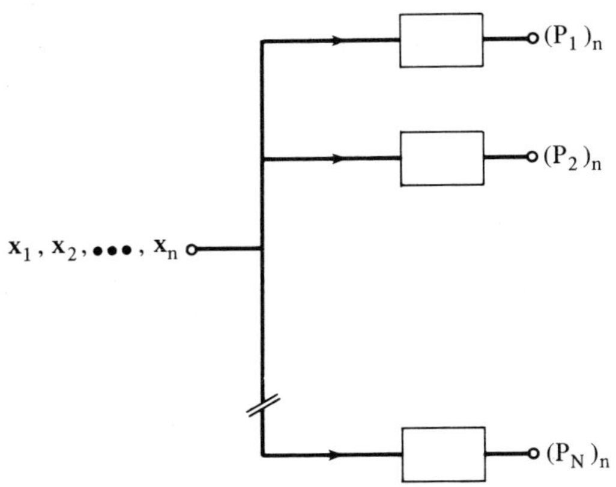

How is M determined?

(d) Show that this is multiclass dimensionality reduction (feature selection) from $\mathscr{V}_\infty$ to $\mathscr{V}_1$ with a single feature for each class.

[4] The following questions are concerned with dimensionality reduction from $\mathscr{V}_L$ to $\mathscr{V}_l$ (feature selection): $L \geq l$.

(a) If $\mathbf{x}$, an L-dimensional vector, is approximated by $\hat{\mathbf{x}} = \sum_{i=1}^{l} c_i \boldsymbol{\varphi}_i$, $l \leq L$, $\boldsymbol{\varphi}_i \in \mathscr{V}_L$, $i = 1, 2, \ldots, l$, the new features c_i are given by ___________________________ if the optimality criteria used is________

____

(b) Suppose data vectors $\mathbf{x}_1, \mathbf{x}_2, \ldots, \mathbf{x}_n$ are provided and the transposed matrix formed; how can a clustering procedure be used to eliminate redundant components (features) in $\mathbf{x}$?

(c) For the same situation as in (b), how can a clustering procedure be used to eliminate redundant components (features) in $\mathbf{x}$ for *subgroups* of the training vectors?

[5] A block diagram of a procedure for feature selection is as follows:

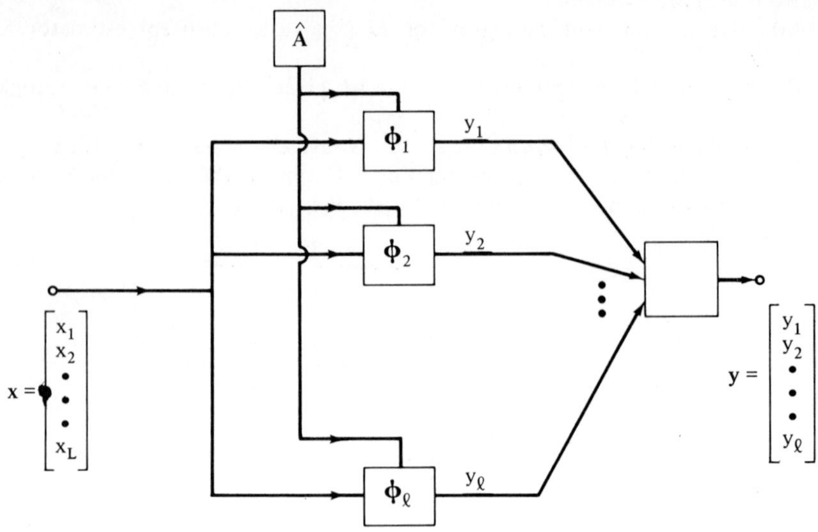

The vectors $\boldsymbol{\varphi}_1, \boldsymbol{\varphi}_2, \ldots, \boldsymbol{\varphi}_l$, $l \leq L$, are chosen so that

$$\bar{e} = \sum_{s=1}^{n} e_s$$

is minimized. Answer the following questions:
(a) What is an appropriate e_s, where e_s is an error criterion?
(b) How are the elements of the matrix $\hat{\mathbf{A}}$ estimated using $\mathbf{x}_1, \mathbf{x}_2, \ldots, \mathbf{x}_n$?
(c) How are $\boldsymbol{\varphi}_1, \boldsymbol{\varphi}_2, \ldots, \boldsymbol{\varphi}_l$ determined from $\hat{\mathbf{A}}$?
(d) How is y_i determined?

[6] Give precise definitions for the following:
(a) *Nuisance parameters* involved in parameter estimation and how they are involved in dimensionality reduction.
(b) *Supervised samples* $\mathbf{x}_1^i, \mathbf{x}_2^i, \ldots, \mathbf{x}_{n_i}^i$, $i = 1, 2, \ldots, M$.
(c) *Unsupervised samples* $\mathbf{x}_1, \mathbf{x}_2, \ldots, \mathbf{x}_n$.
(d) *Covariance matrix* and *correlation matrix*.
(e) Equipotential, arising from $d(\mathbf{x}, \mathbf{m}) = N(\mathbf{x}|\mathbf{m}, \boldsymbol{\Sigma})$.
(f) Matrix of *transposed vectors* given data vectors $\mathbf{x}_1, \mathbf{x}_2, \ldots, \mathbf{x}_n$.
(g) *Consistent estimator*.

[7] Show that (5a) is equivalent to (6) in Section 6-4.

[8] Using the method of Lagrange multipliers show that

$$\max_{\Phi_\xi} \sum_{i=1}^{L} \sum_{j=1}^{L} \hat{\rho}_{ij}\varphi_{\xi i}\varphi_{\xi j}$$

with constraint

$$\sum_{k=1}^{L} \varphi_{\xi K}^2 = 1$$

is achieved if

$$\sum_{j=1}^{L} \hat{\rho}_{ij}\varphi_{\xi j} = \lambda_\xi \varphi_{\xi j},$$

where λ_ξ (an eigenvalue) is the Lagrange multiplier.

CHAPTER 7

Pattern Recognition Through Statistical Verification of A Priori Problem Knowledge

7-1 Introduction

In this last chapter the experience gained and techniques developed are combined to show how a priori problem knowledge and training samples are jointly used to determine a decision rule $d(\mathbf{x})$. The problem solution begins with a researcher having some knowledge about each of M classes. This knowledge is in the form of relationships among the measurements $x_1, x_2, \ldots, x_L$ for each suspected class. There may not be M classes but M is a value chosen at the beginning. We know from Chapter 5 that M classes can be identified if $\mathscr{F}$ is identifiable and $n \longrightarrow \infty$. For finite n, M can be determined along with corresponding classes only insofar as the results make sense. The chance of sample groupings making sense for finite n will improve as the a priori knowledge the researcher has about the M classes increases. *If the data* $\mathbf{x}_1, \mathbf{x}_2, \ldots, \mathbf{x}_n$ *does not match the a priori knowledge, then man using his field of knowledge must modify the a priori knowledge being used by the computer.* The vehicle with which man can introduce his knowledge into the computer is via the relationships among the measurements $x_1, x_2, \ldots, x_L$ for each suspected class.

Thus given a model for a class, results in Chapter 4 on supervised estimation indicate how to update parameters characterizing the probability

478

density in that model if there are supervised samples. If the samples are unsupervised, then we are back to the situation discussed in the above paragraph where one can cautiously apply techniques from Chapter 5 on unsupervised estimation. Again, when measurement vectors are unsupervised, parameters characterizing class models (agreed on a priori) can be updated (Bayes, Bayes suggested decision directed, decision directed, chain map, etc.) *and new classes might be suggested by samples not well matched to the a priori defined classes (updated versions).*

The correctness of class descriptions after processing n samples will depend on how well these descriptions make sense to the expert with his relatively vast field of problem knowledge. If man could determine that the models he has supplied the computer are not consistent with the data, then he should be able to modify his models in the computer. The following sections describe how man's field of knowledge can be used to provide relationships among $x_1, x_2, \ldots, x_L$ for each class and how this directly helps to determine the class-conditional probability density functions. It is also shown how this a priori problem knowledge can be updated using samples $\mathbf{x}_1, \mathbf{x}_2, \ldots, \mathbf{x}_n$ and how the knowledge can be adapted by man.

7-2 Notation

At the outset a measurement space consistent with previous chapters and a relationship space are introduced. It is difficult to find examples of research by statisticians and information theorists concerned with pattern recognition which provides for using a priori problem knowledge in pattern recognition. This is because a statistical approach to decision making uses samples in the measurement space to estimate class-conditional probability densities and a priori class probabilities. *Use of such training samples in the measurement space is only one of two important ways to facilitate the decision-making process. The other is to use relationships supplied by man where he uses his field of knowledge about the problem.*

To be precise, let $\mathscr{X}$ denote the measurement space which is an L-dimensional vector space containing $\mathbf{x} = [x_1, x_2, \ldots, x_L]$ which is a measurement vector with L components. There exist M classes $i = 1, 2, \ldots, M$, corresponding class-conditional densities $f(\mathbf{x}|i)$, and a priori class probabilities P_i, $i = 1, 2, \ldots, M$.

Given $f(\mathbf{x}|i)$ and P_i, $i = 1, 2, \ldots, M$, along with loss functions L_{ji}, a minimum risk decision rule $d(\mathbf{x})$ is

$$d(\mathbf{x}) = a, \sum_{i=1}^{M} L_{ai} f(\mathbf{x}|i) P_i = \min_{k=1, 2, \ldots, M} \left\{ \sum_{i=1}^{M} L_{ki} f(\mathbf{x}|i) P_i \right\}, \qquad (1)$$

which is a mapping from the measurement space $\mathscr{X}$ to the decision space.

If $M, f(\mathbf{x}|i)$, and P_i are possibly unknown, their true values will as in previous chapters be denoted $M^*, f^*(\mathbf{x}|i), P_i^*$. Estimation of these parameters using training samples $\mathbf{x}_1, \mathbf{x}_2, \ldots, \mathbf{x}_n$, each sample in the measurement space, has been extensively studied [1, 2, 3, 4, 5] as detailed in previous chapters. The decision space usually is larger than the class space, the latter of size M^*. Determining the number of classes M^* representative of the samples $\mathbf{x}_1, \mathbf{x}_2, \ldots, \mathbf{x}_n$, for n finite (small), appears after very careful study in the previous chapters (especially Chapter 5) to be a dilemma. If one approaches the problem by asking how many classes are present in samples $\mathbf{x}_1, \mathbf{x}_2, \ldots, \mathbf{x}_n$, the answer is that there could be $1, 2, \ldots$, or n, or more, because a determination of the number of classes in finite size data depends on the a priori knowledge available about the classes. Furthermore, determination of a decision rule depends on the a priori knowledge available.

A priori problem knowledge provides information about some of the $f(\mathbf{x}|i)$, and possibly some of the P_i, before any training samples are taken. This a priori knowledge is in the form of relationships among the components $x_1, x_2, \ldots, x_L$ in the measurement vector $\mathbf{x}$ for a particular class. Thus it is appropriate to define a relationship space $\mathcal{R}$. Relationships can provide ranges for values of x_i, indicate correlations between x_i and x_j, $i \neq j$, and more generally state equivalence among "regions" in the measurement space. Relationships are supplied by man hopefully as a result of his vast field of knowledge about a problem. Examples can be cited where at least a nearly infinite number n of training samples would be required to learn a relationship to provide acceptable estimation of $f(\mathbf{x}|i)$.

It is probably safe to say that most successful applications of pattern recognition have involved use of relationships to construct the $f(\mathbf{x}|i)$ and P_i used in decision making. On the other hand the scientific method has for a long time suggested verifying accuracy of a priori supplied models by trying the models on samples. This suggests an approach based on finding how well a set of a priori supplied relationships fit samples. This is consistent with the Bayes philosophy of calculating an a posteriori value for how well a specific "structure" or model fits the data. Then, for example, a minimum variance estimate of the true structure is a conditional (a posteriori) average over all the structures.

This is a good place to summarize: It is suggested that an approach be developed where sets of relationships (such as those introduced in Chapter 6) provide a priori knowledge about functions $f(\mathbf{x}|i)$. *Next, training samples $\mathbf{x}_1, \mathbf{x}_2, \ldots, \mathbf{x}_n$ are used to give a posteriori probabilities for these sets of relationships; i.e., presumably one set of relationships will match the data (be a posteriori more probable†) better than the other sets of relationships.*

Evaluation of a posteriori probabilities for the respective sets of rela-

†This is precisely the Bayes framework.

tionships is an estimation procedure while suggesting new sets of relationships is an adaptive procedure [6]. Man is better at suggesting new sets of relationships than is a computer, and is likely to remain so for many, many years. Other theoretical studies of a priori knowledge in the form of a priori probability density include [8, 9, 10].

There may be opposition from some researchers who feel that analyzing how well samples match various sets of relationships, or that study of sets of relationships for specific problems is not good theoretical research. An answer to any such opposition is that there is a strong need for such analysis and study because high-quality scientific work can be communicated in terms of these relationships and their analysis for particular samples.

A set of relationships $\mathscr{R}$ provides information about how components $x_1, x_2, \ldots, x_L$ are related for each class. Additional information can be used to indicate probability density at points in the measurement space $\mathscr{X}$ delimited by the relationships in $\mathscr{R}$. *Together, the relationships in $\mathscr{R}$ and assignment of probability density is a structure in $\mathscr{S}$.*

Letting $\mathscr{R}_i$ and $\mathscr{S}_i$ be sets of relationships and structures, respectively, for class i, a particular structure in $\mathscr{S}_i$ is characterized by a parameter point $\mathbf{b}_i$ in the parameter space $\mathscr{B}_i$. Parameter points $\mathbf{b}_1, \mathbf{b}_2, \ldots, \mathbf{b}_M$ together with mixing parameters $P_1, P_2, \ldots, P_M$ constitute the parameter point $\mathbf{b}$ in the parameter space $\mathscr{B}$.

Let $\hat{f}(\mathbf{x} \,|\, i, S_i, \mathbf{b}_i(S_i))$ denote an estimate of $f(\mathbf{x} \,|\, i)$ using structure S_i with parameter $\mathbf{b}_i(S_i)$ characterizing structure S_i. There are several properties of $\hat{f}(\mathbf{x} \,|\, i)$ which have relevance in establishing an approach aimed at minimizing risk as opposed to a hypothesis-testing approach. A justification of the minimum risk approach is as follows: If p_{12} is the probability of deciding class 1 when class 2 is true (type 1 error) and p_{21} is the probability of deciding class 2 when class 1 is true (type 2 error), then

1. p_{12} cannot be calculated without knowledge of $f(\mathbf{x} \,|\, 2)$; p_{21} cannot be calculated without knowledge of $f(\mathbf{x} \,|\, 1)$. Because usually one is concerned with both p_{12} and p_{21}, these probabilities must be "traded-off" as in the minimum risk approach.
2. Thus from 1 even if one is "only interested" in recognizing class 1, he must be interested in class 2 properties in order not to falsely recognize class 1.

The above discussion provides insight into the selection of the measurements $x_1, x_2, \ldots, x_L$. Loosely speaking, a measurement is added if its use can improve performance. More nearly precisely, a measurement should be selected using models for all classes concerned so as to provide for better class separation.

7-3 Relevant Properties of $\hat{f}(\mathbf{x}|i)$

The loosest possible constraint on $\hat{f}(\mathbf{x}|i)$ is that it be a functional such that

1. $\hat{f}(\mathbf{x}|i) \geq 0, \ \forall \ \mathbf{x} \in \mathcal{X}$,
2. $\int_{\mathcal{X}} \hat{f}(\mathbf{x}|i) \, d\mathbf{x} = 1$.

Next it is pointed out that

3. For large n, there is no difficulty in obtaining estimates $\hat{f}(\mathbf{x}|i)$ which are arbitrarily close to $f(\mathbf{x}|i)$ [7] as discussed in Chapter 4.
4. The number of degrees of freedom allowed in specifying $\hat{f}(\mathbf{x}|i)$ depends upon what is known about the relationship of probability density at one point to probability density at another point.

A natural feeling about a structure S_i is that the more known about it a priori, then the fewer are the degrees of freedom which must be "tied down" by training samples. The number of degrees of freedom is defined as the number of components in $\mathbf{b}_i$. It will be shown that small sample size performance in conditional decision making is related to the degrees of freedom (number of components in $\mathbf{b}_i$) rather than the dimensionality L of $\mathcal{X}$ (number of components in $\mathbf{x}$).

Next, should an S_i^* be determined and $\mathbf{b}_i^*(S_i^*)$ estimated from training samples such that

$$\hat{f}(\mathbf{x}|i, S_i^*, \mathbf{b}_i^*) = f(\mathbf{x}|i), \ \forall \ \mathbf{x} \, ?$$

An answer is that it may be unnecessary to seek such unique S_i^*, $\mathbf{b}_i^*(S_i^*)$ in order to achieve maximum conditional performance. Thus

5. It may not be necessary to search for S_i^* and $\mathbf{b}_i^*(S_i^*)$ in order to maximize small sample size performance.

Examples of Structures

As an example of a very structured situation, consider where it is known that $f(\mathbf{x}|i) = 0$ if $\mathbf{x} \neq \mathbf{x}_1$ and $\mathbf{x} \neq \mathbf{x}_2$. That is,

$$f(\mathbf{x}|i) = p(\mathbf{x}_1|i)\delta(\mathbf{x} - \mathbf{x}_1) + (1 - p(\mathbf{x}_1|i))\delta(\mathbf{x} - \mathbf{x}_2),$$

with there being only one degree of freedom. An estimator for $f(\mathbf{x}|i)$ is

$$\hat{f}(\mathbf{x}|i) = \frac{n_1^i}{n_1^i + n_2^i}\delta(\mathbf{x} - \mathbf{x}_1) + \frac{n_2^i}{n_1^i + n_2^i}\delta(\mathbf{x} - \mathbf{x}_2),$$

where n_1^i = number of samples in class i's training set at $\mathbf{x}_1$ and n_2^i = number of samples in class i's training set at $\mathbf{x}_2$.

As a second example, suppose it is known that all components x_1, x_2, $\ldots$, x_L of $\mathbf{x}$ from $f(\mathbf{x}|i)$ are statistically independent and identically distributed from $N(\mu, 1)$. A very good way to estimate $f(\mathbf{x}|i)$ is to form the statistic

$$\hat{\mu} = \frac{1}{n_i L} \sum_{s=1}^{n_i} \sum_{j=1}^{L} x_{sj}^i$$

and substitute it into the Gaussian functional,

$$\hat{f}(\mathbf{x}|i) = \frac{1}{(2\pi)^{L/2}} \exp\left(-\tfrac{1}{2} \sum_{j=1}^{L} (x_j - \hat{\mu})^2\right).$$

In this example $\hat{\mu}$ converges faster as dimensionality L increases. This shows that if relationships are available to reduce the number of degrees of freedom, then increasing dimensionality L can help performance rather than hinder performance.

A third example is a situation where very little is known about $f(\mathbf{x}|i)$: All that is known is that $f(\mathbf{x}|i)$ is symmetrical about the origin. Thus, $f(\mathbf{x}_1|i) = f(\mathbf{x}_2|i)$ if $\|\mathbf{x}_1\| = \|\mathbf{x}_2\|$. An estimator for $f(\mathbf{x}|i)$ is

$$\hat{f}(\mathbf{x}|i) = \frac{\text{mass in } \mathscr{I}(\mathbf{x})}{\text{volume of } \mathscr{I}(\mathbf{x})},$$

where $\mathscr{I}(x)$ is a neighborhood of $\mathbf{x}$.

These examples illustrate the important property that [6] relationships aid small sample size estimation rather than result from the estimation.

7-4 Framework for Introducing Structure

A framework for introducing structure is the so called "fixed-bin" model where $\mathscr{X}$ is partitioned into R^L bins. The bin probabilities $\{p_j^i\}_{j=1}^{R^L}$ characterizing the multinomial probability density approximation to $f(\mathbf{x}|i)$ can be estimated by

$$(p_j^i)_{n_i} = \frac{n_{ij}}{n_i},$$

where n_{ij} is the number of class i training samples in the jth bin. Mean square error between the estimate and the underlying bin probability for the jth bin is

$$e^2 = \sum_{j=1}^{R^L} e_j^2 = \frac{1}{R^L} \sum_{j=1}^{R^L} [(p_j^i)_{n_i} - p_j^i]^2.$$

The number of class i samples required to give $e_j^2 < \delta$, $\delta > 0$, with confidence $c < 1$ can be calculated:

$$p([(p_j^i)_{n_i} - p_j^i]^2 < \delta) > c.$$

In many cases, this n_i is "too large." Then it becomes necessary to use samples in the kth bin to estimate p_j^i along with samples in the jth bin. For example, suppose it is known that $p_j^i = p_k^i$, $j \neq k$; then letting

$$(p_j^i)_{n_i} = \frac{1}{2}\frac{n_{ij}}{n_i} + \frac{1}{2}\frac{n_{ik}}{n_i}$$

reduces the variance of $(p_j^i)_{n_i}$ to that obtained with $2n_i$ samples as opposed to only n_i samples.

This "fixed-bin model" consisting of R^L "bin probabilities" will be used as the framework for introducing structure S_i. The definition of structure is a set of relationships among $\{p_j^i\}$, $j = 1, 2, \ldots, R^L$, for each class $i = 1, 2, \ldots, M$. Obviously, it is not possible to consider all possible relationships as R^L becomes large. A pragmatic solution to this problem is to consider relationships which are a function of $\mathbf{x}$ and set up an equivalence among certain p_j^i's and thus the corresponding $\mathbf{x}$'s.

Family of Structure S

Step 1

The family of structures $S \in \mathscr{S}$ will now be defined. First, a region $\mathscr{I}$ of the measurement space $\mathscr{X}$ is defined by a characteristic function,

$$I(\mathbf{x}) = \begin{cases} 1, & \mathbf{x} \in \mathscr{I}, \\ 0, & \mathbf{x} \notin \mathscr{I}. \end{cases}$$

Regions† $\mathscr{I}'_1, \mathscr{I}'_2, \ldots, \mathscr{I}'_{v-1}$ are supplied by a user with corresponding indicator functions $I'_1, I'_2, \ldots, I'_{v-1}$. The method of describing these regions will be presented shortly. From these $v - 1$ regions $\mathscr{I}'_1, \mathscr{I}'_2, \ldots, \mathscr{I}'_{v-1}$, orthogonal regions $\mathscr{I}_1, \mathscr{I}_2, \ldots, \mathscr{I}_v$ are constructed which have indicator functions.

$$I_1(\mathbf{x}) = I'_1(\mathbf{x})$$
$$I_2(\mathbf{x}) = I'_2(\mathbf{x}) \cap I_1^c(\mathbf{x})$$

†The idea of using operations to locate regions in the measurement space is introduced in Chapter 6.

$$I_3(\mathbf{x}) = I_3'(\mathbf{x}) \cap I_1^c(\mathbf{x}) \cap I_2^c(\mathbf{x})$$

$$\vdots$$

$$I_{v-1}(\mathbf{x}) = I_{v-1}'(\mathbf{x}) \cap I_1^c(\mathbf{x}) \cap I_2^c(\mathbf{x}) \cap I_{v-2}^c(\mathbf{x})$$

$$I_v(\mathbf{x}) = I_1(\mathbf{x}) \cap I_2^c(\mathbf{x}) \cap I_{v-1}^c(\mathbf{x})$$

More generally, the previous notation is needed for each of M classes. Thus let V_i, $\{I_{i,j}'\}_{j=1}^{V_i}$, $\{I_{ij}\}_{j=1}^{V_i}$, $\{\mathscr{I}_{ij}'\}_{j=1}^{V_i}$, and $\{\mathscr{I}_{ij}\}_{j=1}^{V_i}$ be defined for the ith class.

The regions $\mathscr{I}_j'$ are described using *functions including logic functions* from a table of functions $c(\mathbf{x})$ presented shortly.

It may be desirable that $I_j(\mathbf{x})$ be characterized by parameters which are determined by samples. These parameters are determined in such a way as to "fit" $I_j(\mathbf{x})$ to the data; thus a criteria in terms of fit is implied. For example, a possibility is

$$I_j(\mathbf{x}) = \begin{cases} 1: x_1 > \hat{\mu} \\ 0 \text{ otherwise,} \end{cases}$$

where $\hat{\mu}$ is the sample mean.

Step 2

There exists a probability density function $f(\mathbf{x}\,|\,i)$, $\mathbf{x} \in \mathscr{I}_{ij}$, and $\mathbf{x}$ is an L-dimensional vector. Although this approach will not be taken, it is possible that $I_{ij}(\mathbf{x})$ and a probability density function defined on this region is sufficient for decision making for some problems. However, ordinarily it may not have been convenient for the user to express all his a priori knowledge about $f(\mathbf{x}\,|\,i)$ in terms of $\{\mathscr{I}_{ij}\}_{j=1}^{V_i}$. Rather, he may have additional knowledge suggesting forming the *feature vector*

$$\mathbf{g}^i(\mathbf{x}) = [g_1^i(\mathbf{x}), g_2^i(\mathbf{x}), \ldots, g_l^i(\mathbf{x})], \qquad \mathbf{x} \in \mathscr{I}_{ij}.$$

The functions $g_1^i(\mathbf{x})$ can reflect a priori knowledge such as correlation among measurements.† These functions are selected from a table of functions discussed shortly.

Whereas step 1 allows inserting a priori knowledge about how $\mathbf{x}$ is *limited* in the measurement space, step 2 allows inserting a priori knowledge

†An operation called correlation inserter was introduced in Chapter 6 where several examples are presented. These examples show why a function $g^i(\mathbf{x})$ in the process of feature extraction establishes an equivalence region in the measurement space. One such equivalence is what is known as correlation.

such as *correlations* among the components in $\mathbf{x}$ for class i. Step 3 will involve a correction for *scaling* the class-conditional probability density function as a result of the transformation introduced because of step 2.

A function $g(\mathbf{x})$ can be characterized by parameters which are determined from the samples. For example,

$$g(\mathbf{x}) = (\mathbf{x} - \hat{\mathbf{m}})'\Sigma^{-1}(\mathbf{x} - \hat{\mathbf{m}}),$$

where $\hat{\mathbf{m}}$ and $\hat{\Sigma}$ are the sample mean and sample covariance matrix, respectively. Essentially, as before, the function $g(\mathbf{x})$ is being used to fit structure of a priori determined form to the data.

Step 3

The probability density function $f(\mathbf{g}_i(\mathbf{x})\,|\,i)$, $\mathbf{x} \in \mathscr{I}_{ij}$, is estimated. Effectively, the functions $g_i(\mathbf{x})$ result in an equivalence among a certain number of bins in the fixed-bin model for class i. This equivalence leads to enhanced probability density estimation.

The decision rule uses the probability density functions $f(\mathbf{x}\,|\,i)$, $i = 1, 2, \ldots, M$. Therefore, with a Jacobian $J(\mathbf{x})$, the density $f(\mathbf{x}\,|\,i)$ is determined from $f(\mathbf{g}_i(\mathbf{x})\,|\,i)$ as

$$f(\mathbf{x}\,|\,i) = \frac{f(\mathbf{g}_i(\mathbf{x})\,|\,i)}{|J(\mathbf{x})|}.$$

The Jacobian can be calculated in terms of a change in volume about $\mathbf{x}$ for a given change in volume about $\mathbf{g}_i(\mathbf{x})$.

In summary, a structure S in the family $\mathscr{S}$ of structures consists of the regions $\mathscr{I}_j$, $j = 1, 2, \ldots, V$, determined by functions $c(\mathbf{x})$, the feature vector $\mathbf{g}(\mathbf{x})$, $\mathbf{x} \in \mathscr{I}_j$, and the Jacobian for the transformation. A structure S causes an equivalence among certain regions in the fixed-bin model.† There also exists a family $\mathscr{F}'$ of probability density functions $f(\mathbf{g}(\mathbf{x}))$ generated by members S of $\mathscr{S}$ and members $f(\mathbf{x})$ of $\mathscr{F}$.

At the outset the family $\mathscr{F}$ of density functions for a particular problem may be unknown, and it may not be possible ever to learn $\mathscr{F}$ for a particular problem. Rather, it may make most sense to expect the family $\mathscr{F}'$ to be some rather simple family such as multivariate Gaussian, a mixture of Gaussian, or uniform. The latter would be the result of having carefully introduced problem knowledge into the creation of S.

Another way to view S is that it is a problem model constructed within the Bayes framework. The structure or problem model S is especially suitable for an interactive computer approach in that it allows man to convey his field of knowledge to the Bayes framework.

---

†The fixed-bin model becomes less of a mathematical approximation as $R^L \longrightarrow \infty$.

There are functions which come to mind as typical for $g(\mathbf{x})$ or $c(\mathbf{x})$. These functions, mostly nonlinear, may be thought of as primitive functions for introducing a priori knowledge. Typical functions are

$a_0 + a_1 x_j + a_2 x_j^2 + \cdots + a_k x_j^k, j = 1, 2, \ldots, L$

	polynomial of a measurement x_j
$\exp(x_j), j = 1, 2, \ldots, L$	exponential
$\ln(x_j), j = 1, 2, \ldots, L$	logarithmic
x_j/x_k, any $j \neq k$	ratio
$x_j + x_k$, any $j \neq k$	arithmetic average
$x_j x_k$, any $j \neq k$	product
$\sin(x_j), \cos(x_j), \tan(x_j)$	trigonometric
$\sin^{-1}(x_j), \cos^{-1}(x_j), \tan^{-1}(x_j)$	inverse trigonometric
$\sqrt{x_j x_k}, j \neq k$	geometric average
$\sqrt{\dfrac{x_j^2 + x_k^2}{2}}$	root mean square
$\mathrm{abs}(x_j)$	absolute
$(\mathbf{x} - \mathbf{m})'\mathbf{\Sigma}^{-1}(\mathbf{x} - \mathbf{m})$	quadratic form
$\max(x_i, x_j), \min(x_i, x_j)$	maximum, minimum

The regions $I(\mathbf{x})$ are created using the functions $c_k(\mathbf{x})$ in combination with logical operations from the following table.

$c(\mathbf{x}) \gtrless a$	Inequality
$I_i'(\mathbf{x}) \cup I_j'(\mathbf{x}), i \neq j$	Or
$I_i'(\mathbf{x}) \cap I_j'(\mathbf{x}), i \neq j$	And
$I_i'^c(\mathbf{x})$	Not

7-5 Compiling

To obtain $f(\mathbf{g}_i(\mathbf{x}) \mid i)$ on the computer, it is desirable for the user to be able to insert a structure S^i for each of M classes. Then, training samples $\mathbf{x}_1^i, \mathbf{x}_2^i, \ldots, \mathbf{x}_{n_i}^i$ are transformed to $\mathbf{g}_i(\mathbf{x}_1^i), \mathbf{g}_i(\mathbf{x}_2^i), \ldots, \mathbf{g}_i(\mathbf{x}_{n_i}^i)$. Local density estimation then is possible in this transformed space.

The following is an illustration of a sequence of steps useful in compiling a program for a particular problem:

Step 1:   Insert $L, M, \{n_i\}_{i=1}^M$.

Step 2:   Store data $\{\mathbf{x}_s^i\}_{s=1}^{n_i}, i = 1, 2, \ldots, M$.

Step 3:   Are regions $\mathscr{I}_j$ the same for all classes? If not, $V_i \neq V \; \forall \; i$.

Step 4:   Supply V_i, l_i.

Step 5:   Enter $I'_{ji}, j = 1, 2, \ldots, V_i, i = 1, 2, \ldots, M$.

Step 6:   Construct $g^i_1, g^i_2, \ldots, g^i_{l_i}, i = 1, 2, \ldots, M$.
             Display $\hat{f}(g^i_j)$ during this construction.

Of course, there is a possibility that one would wish to write a subroutine consisting of nonlinear functions for a particular problem and insert this subroutine in the list of relationships.

Step 7:   Determine $\hat{f}(\mathbf{g}_i(\mathbf{x})|i), i = 1, 2, \ldots, M$, and Jacobian for each class; then classify $\mathbf{x}$.

When the number L of measurements is very large, as in medicine, the regions $\{S'_{ij}\}$ are imposed such that one set of measurements are effectively used at first; another set of the measurements is used next. Thus if after using one set of the measurements a decision indicates it is desirable to branch to another set [6] for a decision, this is possible while keeping within our framework.

7-6 Unsupervised Mode

In an unsupervised mode, estimation of $f(\mathbf{g}_i(\mathbf{x})|i)$ essentially completes the problem solution. An unsupervised mode results when it is desired to use an unclassified sample $\mathbf{x}$ to update the system. Samples can be used to update each S_i using Bayes suggested decision directed discussed in Chapter 2. If $f(\mathbf{g}_i(\mathbf{x})|i)$ is below an a priori prescribed threshold for the sample $\mathbf{x} \; \forall \; i$, there is a possibility it belongs to a new class. Another possibility is that the existing M structures should be modified to accommodate this sample.

The user may determine that existing classes make sense or do not make sense. They would not make sense, for example, if when samples from class i are treated as one class a contradiction results in terms of other knowledge possessed by the user. To be more precise with this example, suppose the L measurements consists of symptoms, signs, and laboratory test results for a patient and the objective is diagonsis. The user may find that different treatments are required to produce a "cure" for patients in a single class i. This may suggest to the user that he should use these *treatments as additional measurements*, redefine class structures, and separate the class i samples into multiple classes.

Suggested Reading for Chapter 7

[1] E. A. Patrick, On a Class of Unsupervised Estimation Problems, *IEEE Trans. Information Theory*, Vol. IT-14, pp. 407–418, May 1968.

[2] E. A. Patrick and J. P. Costello, On Unsupervised Estimation Problems, *IEEE Trans. Information Theory*, pp. 556–569, Sept. 1970.

[3] Yu-Chi Ho and Ashok K. Agrawala, On Pattern Classification Algorithms—Introduction and Survey, *Proc. IEEE*, Vol. 56, No. 12, pp. 2101–2113, Dec. 1968.

[4] G. Nagy, State of the Art in Pattern Recognition, *Proc. IEEE*, Vol. 56, No. 5, pp. 836–862, May 1968.

[5] D. O. Loftsgaarden and C. P. Quesenberry, A Nonparametric Estimate of a Multivariate Density Function, *Ann. Math. Statistics*, Vol. 36, pp. 1049–1051, 1965.

[6] E. A. Patrick, Concepts of an Estimation System, Adaptive System, and a Network of Adaptive Estimation Systems, *IEEE Trans. System Science and Cybernetics*, Vol. SSC-5, No. 1, pp. 79–85, Jan. 1969.

[7] E. A. Patrick and F. P. Fischer, Generalized k-Nearest-Neighbor Decision Rule, *J. Information and Control*, Vol. 16, No. 2, pp. 128–152, April 1970.

[8] E. Jaynes, Prior Probabilities, *IEEE Trans. System Science and Cybernetics*, Vol. 4, No. 3, pp. 227–241, Sept. 1968.

[9] L. Hartigan, Invariant Prior Distributions, *Ann. Math. Statistics*, Vol. 35, pp. 836–845, June 1964.

[10] N. S. Tzanes and J. P. Noonan, A Theory of Prior Probability, *Proceedings of the Kelly Communications Conference*, pp. 20–31, University of Missouri at Rolla, Rolla, Missouri, 1970.

Conclusion

The brief Chapter 7 was included to emphasize that in pattern recognition both a priori problem knowledge and training data can be important. Until we have computers which can contain man's field of knowledge and other powers, man will have to create the models or structures for his problems. On the other hand, the scientific method has long been used by man to verify his models. In pattern recognition, this latter process is equivalent to using training samples to update.

Man then finds pattern recognition as a modern scientific method with the upshot that computers are programmed to automatically make decisions, recall facts, and verify models. Pattern recognition does not take the process of creating problem solutions away from man.

Many aspects of feature extraction are beyond the scope of this book. For example, isolating and extracting features from objects in images is a specialty area in feature extraction. As another example, equipment used for pattern recognition is a specialty area. An understanding of the material in *Fundamentals of Pattern Recognition* is important for individuals working in such specialty areas.

Author Index

Fisz, 56
Fix and Hodges, 172, 193, 215,
        217, 219, 220
Fralick, 288, 331
Fralick, Senkorick, and Wilson, 401
Fraser, 143
Fu, 116, 401
Fu and Henrichon, 213, 277

G

Glaser, 399
Gradshtyen, 248, 249, 257
Gregg and Hancock, 383, 400

H

Hancock and Patrick, 289
Hancock and Wintz, 170
Haralick and Kelley, 407
Hart, 172, 220, 223, 227, 242, 260
Hartigan, 481
Hellman, 224, 228
Helstrom, 170, 171
Henrici, 116
Hilborn and Lainiotis, 289
Hinich, 291
Ho and Agrawala, 1, 173
Ho and Lee, 162
Hogg and Craig, 56

I

Indritz, 418

J

Jakowatz, Shuey, and White, 291
Jarvis, 356
Jaynes, 481

K

Kailath, 170

Kaminuma, Takebowa, and
        Watanabe, 373, 408
Kanal, ed., 1, 401
Kaplan, 157
Kashyap and Blaydon, 148, 216
Keehn, 97, 100, 147, 215
Kemperman, 142
Kesten, 116, 309
Kiefer and Wolfowitz, 165, 302
Koford and Groner, 270
Kullback, 165, 173

L

Lawrence, 418
LeCam, 70, 113, 303, 309, 332
Ledley, 454
Lehman, 303
Loeve, 56, 232, 252, 253, 297, 298
Loftsgaarden and Quesenberry,
        148, 219, 236, 237, 250,
        480
Lusted, 401

M

MacQueen, 340, 379, 397, 399
McShane and Botts, 188, 210
Meinardus, 418
Meisel, 441
Miller, 342
Murthy, 148

N

Nagy, 1, 173, 358, 480
Nagy and Shelton, 379, 401
Nilsson, 1, 213, 268, 275
Noiseeva, 1
Noiseeva and Usov, 473

P

Papoulis, 1, 56